Federal Food, Drug, and Cosmetic Act

The United States Federal FD&C Act

Concise Reference

Federal Food, Drug, and Cosmetic Act

The United States Federal FD&C Act

Concise Reference

Federal Food, Drug, and Cosmetic Act: The United States Federal FD&C Act Concise Reference

PharmaLogika, Inc.
PO Box 461
Willow Springs, NC 27592

www.pharmalogika.com

Author / Editor: Mindy J. Allport-Settle

Published by PharmaLogika, Inc.

Printed in the United States of America. First Printing.

ISBN 0-9830719-0-X
ISBN-13 978-0-9830719-0-7

Contents

Part II

Preface

About this Book

This book is designed to be a unified reference source for the U.S. Federal Food, Drug, and Cosmetic Act and is designed to be used both as a reference for experienced industry representatives and as a training resource for those new to the industry.

The included *Introduction to the FDA and the FD&C Act* (Chapter 2 of this book) is designed to provide a foundation for understanding the background of the FDA, its guidelines, its relationship with other countries and its relationship with manufacturers and distributors.

About this Reference Edition of the Federal Food, Drug, and Cosmetic Act (FD&C Act)

This book is a compilation of the FDA's online reference edition of the Federal Food, Drug and Cosmetic Act which is based on the publication Compilation of Selected Acts Within the Jurisdiction of the Committee on Energy and Commerce; Food, Drug, and Related Law, As Amended Through December 31, 2004, prepared for the use of the Committee on Energy and Commerce, U.S. House of Representatives, March 2005. Updates have been made in the online edition as the act was amended since that time. Notes in the text indicate when the online version was updated, rather than the date the change was enacted and are footnoted as such.

Included Documents and Features

Federal Food, Drug, and Cosmetic Act:

- *Introduction to the FDA and the FD&C Act*
- *Part I: Federal Food, Drug, and Cosmetic Act*
    - *Section Number Reference: Federal Food, Drug, and Cosmetic Act*
    - *FD&C Act Chapters I and II: Short Title and Definitions*
    - *FD&C Act Chapter III: Prohibited Acts and Penalties*
    - *FD&C Act Chapter IV: FoodFD&C Act Chapter V: Drugs and Devices*
    - *FD&C Act Chapter VI: Cosmetics*
    - *FD&C Act Chapter VII: General Authority*

- *FD&C Act Chapter VIII: Imports and Exports*
- *FD&C Act Chapter IX: MiscellaneousSignificant Amendments to the FD&C Act*

Reference Tools

- *Part II: Combined Glossary and Index*

About the Reference Tools

FDA Overview and Orientation and the Introduction to the FD&C Act

The FDA overview provides the reader with a brief history of the Food and Drug Administration (FDA) and explains not only what the Federal Food, Drug, and Cosmetic Act (FD&C Act) is, but why it exists and how it came to be. The introduction also provides a guide to the FDA's approach to regulatory management and enforcement.

Combined Glossary

The Combined Glossary includes all of the glossaries from each chapter of the FD&C Act listed alphabetically rather than by document.

When a word or term appears multiple times in the regulation and guidance documents, the word will appear multiple times in the Combined Glossary if there is a variation in the definition. Each duplicate entry is indented to highlight that it is a duplicate and the earliest reference to the entry is listed first. The source for each entry is bracketed (i.e., [21 CFR § 50]) for ease of reference. While the definitions are similar from one regulatory or guidance document to the next, they are not always identical.

Combined Index for all Regulations

The index is composed of a list of both words and terms specific to the FD&C Act.

Pharmaceutical, biotechnology, and medical device companies as well as food and cosmetic manufacturers use terminology that combines scientific and technical jargon with legal phrases and concepts.

The index provides keywords and terminology as a tool to easily locate specific references across all chapters rather than having to rely on memory or paging through each chapter individually.

Introduction to the FDA and the FD&C Act

The Food and Drug Administration (FDA)

The United States Food and Drug Administration (FDA) is responsible for protecting and promoting the nation's public health.

The programs for safety regulation vary widely by the type of product, its potential risks, and the regulatory powers granted to the agency. For example, the FDA regulates almost every facet of prescription drugs, including testing, manufacturing, labeling, advertising, marketing, efficacy and safety. FDA regulation of cosmetics, however, is focused primarily on labeling and safety. The FDA regulates most products with a set of published standards enforced by a combination of facility inspections, voluntary company reporting standards, and public and consumer watchdog activity.

The FDA frequently works in conjunction with other Federal agencies including the Department of Agriculture, Drug Enforcement Administration, Customs and Border Protection, and Consumer Product Safety Commission.

Historical Origins of Federal Food and Drug Regulation

Prior to the 20th century, there were few federal laws regulating the contents and sale of domestically produced food and pharmaceuticals before the 20th century (with one exception being the short-lived Vaccine Act of 1813). Some state laws provided varying degrees of protection against unethical sales practices, such as misrepresenting the ingredients of food products or therapeutic substances.

The history of the FDA can be traced to the latter part of the 19th century and the U.S. Department of Agriculture's Division of Chemistry (later Bureau of Chemistry). Under Harvey Washington Wiley, appointed chief chemist in 1883, the Division began conducting research into the adulteration and misbranding of food and drugs on the American market. Although they had no regulatory powers, the Division published its findings from 1887 to 1902 in a ten-part series entitled Foods and Food Adulterants. Wiley used these findings, and alliances with diverse organizations (such as state regulators, the General Federation of Women's Clubs, and national associations of physicians and pharmacists) to lobby for a new federal law to set uniform standards for food and drugs to enter into interstate commerce.

Wiley's advocacy came at a time when the public had become alert to hazards in the marketplace by journalists and became part of a general trend for increased federal regulation in matters pertinent to public safety during the Progressive Era.[1] The 1902 Biologics Control Act was put in place after diphtheria antitoxin was collected from a horse named Jim who also had tetanus, resulting in several deaths.

The 1906 Food and Drug Act and creation of the FDA

In June 1906, President Theodore Roosevelt signed into law the Food and Drug Act, also known as the "Wiley Act" after its chief advocate.[2] The Act prohibited, under penalty of seizure of goods, the interstate transport of food which had been "adulterated," with that term referring to the addition of fillers of reduced "quality or strength," coloring to conceal "damage or inferiority," formulation with additives "injurious to health," or the use of "filthy, decomposed, or putrid" substances. The act applied similar penalties to the interstate marketing of "adulterated" drugs, in which the "standard of strength, quality, or purity" of the active ingredient was not either stated clearly on the label or listed in the United States Pharmacopoeia or the National Formulary. The act also banned "misbranding" of food and drugs.[3] The responsibility for examining food and drugs for such "adulteration" or "misbranding" was given to Wiley's USDA Bureau of Chemistry.[4] Strength, quality, identity, potency, and purity (SQuIPP) are currently the key product safety standards, with only two measures added since 1906 Act.

Wiley used these new regulatory powers to pursue an aggressive campaign against the manufacturers of foods with chemical additives, but the Chemistry Bureau's authority was soon checked by judicial decisions, as well as by the creation of the Board of Food and Drug Inspection and the Referee Board of Consulting Scientific Experts as separate organizations within the USDA in 1907 and 1908 respectively. A 1911 Supreme Court decision ruled that the 1906 act did not apply to false claims of therapeutic efficacy,[5] in response to which a 1912 amendment added "false and fraudulent" claims of "curative or therapeutic effect" to the Act's definition of "misbranded." However, these powers continued to be narrowly defined by the courts, which set high standards for proof of fraudulent intent.[6] In 1927, the Bureau of Chemistry's regulatory powers were reorganized under a new USDA body, the Food, Drug, and Insecticide organization. This name was shortened to the Food and Drug Administration (FDA) three years later.[7]

---

[1] A History of the FDA at www.FDA.gov.

[2] A History of the FDA at www.FDA.gov.

[3] Text in quotation marks is the original text of the 1906 Food and Drugs Act and Amendments.

[4] A History of the FDA at www.FDA.gov.

[5] United States v. Johnson (31 S. Ct. 627 May 29, 1911, decided).

[6] A History of the FDA at www.FDA.gov.

[7] Milestones in U.S. Food and Drug Law History at www.FDA.gov.

The 1938 Food, Drug, and Cosmetic Act

By the 1930s, muckraking journalists, consumer protection organizations, and federal regulators began mounting a campaign for stronger regulatory authority by publicizing a list of injurious products which had been ruled permissible under the 1906 law, including radioactive beverages, cosmetics which caused blindness, and worthless "cures" for diabetes and tuberculosis. The resulting proposed law was unable to get through the Congress of the United States for five years, but was rapidly enacted into law following the public outcry over the 1937 Elixir Sulfanilamide tragedy, in which over 100 people died after using a drug formulated with a toxic, untested solvent. The only way that the FDA could even seize the product was due to a misbranding problem: an "Elixir" was defined as a medication dissolved in ethanol, not the diethylene glycol used in the Elixir Sulfanilamide.

President Franklin Delano Roosevelt signed the new Food, Drug, and Cosmetic Act (FD&C Act) into law on June 24, 1938. The new law significantly increased federal regulatory authority over drugs by mandating a pre-market review of the safety of all new drugs, as well as banning false therapeutic claims in drug labeling without requiring that the FDA prove fraudulent intent. The law also authorized factory inspections and expanded enforcement powers, set new regulatory standards for foods, and brought cosmetics and therapeutic devices under federal regulatory authority. This law, though extensively amended in subsequent years, remains the central foundation of FDA regulatory authority to the present day.[8]

Early FD&C Act amendments: 1938-1958

Soon after passage of the 1938 Act, the FDA began to designate certain drugs as safe for use only under the supervision of a medical professional, and the category of 'prescription-only' drugs was securely codified into law by the 1951 Durham-Humphrey Amendment.[9] While pre-market testing of drug efficacy was not authorized under the 1938 FD&C Act, subsequent amendments such as the Insulin Amendment and Penicillin Amendment did mandate potency testing for formulations of specific lifesaving pharmaceuticals.[10] The FDA began enforcing its new powers against drug manufacturers who could not substantiate the efficacy claims made for their drugs, and the United States Court of Appeals for the Ninth Circuit ruling in Alberty Food Products Co. v. United States (1950) found that drug manufacturers could not evade the "false therapeutic claims" provision of the 1938 act by simply omitting the intended use of a drug from the drug's label. These developments confirmed extensive powers for the FDA to enforce post-marketing recalls of ineffective drugs.[11] Much of the FDA's regulatory attentions in this era were directed towards abuse of amphetamines and barbiturates, but the agency also reviewed some 13,000 new drug applications between 1938 and 1962. While the science of toxicology

---

[8] A History of the FDA at www.FDA.gov.
[9] A History of the FDA at www.FDA.gov.
[10] Milestones in U.S. Food and Drug Law History at www.FDA.gov
[11] A History of the FDA at www.FDA.gov.

was in its infancy at the start of this era, rapid advances in experimental assays for food additive and drug safety testing were made during this period by FDA regulators and others.[12]

Legislation

The Food and Drugs Act of 1906 was the first of more than 200 laws that constitute one of the world's most comprehensive and effective networks of public health and consumer protections. Here are a few of the congressional milestones:

- The Federal Food, Drug, and Cosmetic Act of 1938 was passed after a legally marketed toxic elixir killed 107 people, including many children. The FD&C Act completely overhauled the public health system. Among other provisions, the law authorized the FDA to demand evidence of safety for new drugs, issue standards for food, and conduct factory inspections.
- The Kefauver-Harris Amendments of 1962, which were inspired by the thalidomide tragedy in Europe (and the FDA's vigilance that prevented the drug's marketing in the United States), strengthened the rules for drug safety and required manufacturers to prove their drugs' effectiveness.
- The Medical Device Amendments of 1976 followed a U.S. Senate finding that faulty medical devices had caused 10,000 injuries, including 731 deaths. The law applied safety and effectiveness safeguards to new devices.

Today, the FDA regulates $1 trillion worth of products a year. It ensures the safety of all food except for meat, poultry and some egg products; ensures the safety and effectiveness of all drugs, biological products (including blood, vaccines and tissues for transplantation), medical devices, and animal drugs and feed; and makes sure that cosmetics and medical and consumer products that emit radiation do no harm.

FD&C Act Chapter Summary

I. Short Title

II. Definitions

III. Prohibited Acts and Penalties

This section contains both civil law and criminal law clauses. Most violations under the act are civil, though repeated, intentional, and fraudulent violations are covered as criminal law. All violations of the FD&C Act require interstate commerce because of the commerce clause, but this is often interpreted broadly and few products other than raw produce are considered outside of the scope of the act.

---

[12] A History of the FDA at www.FDA.gov.

Notably, the FD&C Act uses strict liability due to the Dotterweich and Park[13] Supreme Court cases. It is one of a very small number of criminal statutes that does.

IV. Food

There is a distinction in food adulteration between "good and bad" those that are added and those that are naturally present. Substances that are added are held to a stricter "may render (it) injurious to health" standard, whereas substances that are naturally present need only be at a level that "does not ordinarily render it injurious to health"

V. Drugs and Devices

- 505 is the description of the drug approval process
- 510(k) is the section that allows for clearance of class II medical devices
- 515 is the description of the (class III) device approval process

VI. Cosmetics

VII. General Authority

- 704 allows inspections of regulated entities. Inspection results are reported on Form 483.

VIII. Imports and Exports

IX. Miscellaneous

Overview of Selected FD&C Act Topics

Homeopathic medications

Homeopathic preparations are regulated and protected under Sections 201(g) and 201(j), provided that such medications are formulated from substances listed in the Homeopathic Pharmacopoeia of the United States, which the Act recognizes as an official drug compendium.

Bottled water

Bottled water is regulated by FDA as a food. The Agency has published identity standards for types of water (mineral water, spring water), and regulations covering water processing and bottling, water quality and product labeling.

---

[13] United States v. Dotterweich, 320 U.S. 277 (1943) and United States v. Park, 421 U. S. 658 (1975) - US Supreme Court Cases from Justia & Oyez

Cosmetics

This Act defines cosmetics as products for "cleansing, beautifying, promoting attractiveness, or altering the appearance." In this sense the FDA can classify cosmetics without actually regulating them. This allows a manufacturer the ability to use ingredients or raw materials and market the final product without government approval.

Section 510(k) clearances and the device approval process

Section 510(k) of the Federal Food, Drug, and Cosmetic Act requires those device manufacturers who must register to notify FDA at least 90 days in advance of their intent to market a medical device (Premarket Notification, PMN, or 510(k) Notification).

Premarket Notification allows FDA to determine whether the device is equivalent to a device already placed into one of the three classification categories. Thus, "new" devices (not in commercial distribution prior to May 28, 1976) that have not been classified can be properly identified.

Any device that reaches market via a 510(k) notification must be "substantially equivalent" to a device on the market prior to May 28, 1976 (a "predicate device"). If a device being submitted is significantly different, relative to a pre-1976 device, in terms of design, material, chemical composition, energy source, manufacturing process, or intended use, the device nominally must go through a premarket approval, or PMA.

This has been implemented by splitting devices into three classes:

Class I: Devices that do not require premarket approval or clearance but must follow general controls. Dental floss is a class I device.

Class II: Devices that are cleared using the 510(k) process. Diagnostic tests, cardiac catheters, and amalgam alloys used to fill cavities are all class II devices. The "predicate device" in question is often quite different, and this process is largely used to clear devices for marketing which do not meet the criteria to be considered class III. Hearing aids are class II devices.

Class III: Devices that are approved by the Premarket Approval (PMA) process, analogous to a New Drug Application. These tend to be devices that are permanently implanted into a human body or may be necessary to sustain life. An artificial heart meets both criteria. The most commonly recognized class III device is an Automated External Defibrillator. Devices that do not meet either criterion are generally cleared as class II devices.

A device that reaches market via the 510(k) process is not considered to be "approved" by the FDA. Nevertheless, it can be marketed and sold in the United States. They are generally referred to as "cleared" or "510(k) cleared" devices.

Good Manufacturing Practices vs. Current Good Manufacturing Practices

The terms "Good Manufacturing Practices (GMPs)" and "Current Good Manufacturing Practices (CGMPs or cGMPs[14])" are often used interchangeably both in industry and by FDA inspectors.

"Good Manufacturing Practices" generally refers to the legal mandates detailed in Title 21 of the Code of Federal Regulations (21CFR). "Current Good Manufacturing Practices" refers not only to the legal requirements, but to the guidance provided by the FDA and the standards practiced in industry that are not memorialized as law.

Organizational Structure

The FDA is an agency within the United States Department of Health and Human Services responsible for protecting and promoting the nation's public health. It is organized into the following major subdivisions, each focused on a major area of regulatory responsibility:

- The Office of the Commissioner (OC)
- The Center for Drug Evaluation and Research (CDER)
- The Center for Biologics Evaluation and Research (CBER)
- The Center for Food Safety and Applied Nutrition (CFSAN)
- The Center for Devices and Radiological Health (CDRH)
- The Center for Veterinary Medicine (CVM)
- The National Center for Toxicological Research (NCTR)
- The Office of Regulatory Affairs (ORA)
- The Office of Criminal Investigations (OCI)

How does the FDA communicate with Industry?

Code of Federal Regulations[15]

The Code of Federal Regulations (CFR) is the codification of the general and permanent rules and regulations (sometimes called administrative law) published in the Federal Register by the executive departments and agencies of the Federal Government of the United States. The CFR is published by the Office of the Federal Register, an agency of the National Archives and Records Administration (NARA).

The CFR is divided into 50 titles that represent broad areas subject to Federal regulation. Title 21 is the portion of the Code of Federal Regulations that governs

[14] The lower case "c" was coined in industry to differentiate between the law, emphasized with capital letters, and the current accepted industry practice not mandated by law.
[15] Available CFR Titles on GPO Access at http://www.access.gpo.gov/nara/cfr/cfr-table-search.html#page1

food and drugs within the United States for the Food and Drug Administration (FDA), the Drug Enforcement Administration (DEA), and the Office of National Drug Control Policy (ONDCP).

It is divided into three chapters:

- Chapter I — Food and Drug Administration
- Chapter II — Drug Enforcement Administration
- Chapter III — Office of National Drug Control Policy

Guidance Documents

Guidance documents represent the Agency's current thinking on a particular subject. They do not create or confer any rights for or on any person and do not operate to bind FDA or the public. An alternative approach may be used if such approach satisfies the requirements of the applicable statute, regulations, or both. For information on a specific guidance document, please contact the originating office. Another method of obtaining guidance documents is through the Division of Drug Information.

Federal Register

The Federal Register (since March 14, 1936), abbreviated FR, or sometimes Fed. Reg.) is the official journal of the federal government of the United States that contains most routine publications and public notices of government agencies. It is a daily (except holidays) publication.

The Federal Register is compiled by the Office of the Federal Register (within the National Archives and Records Administration) and is printed by the Government Printing Office.

There are no copyright restrictions on the Federal Register as it is a work of the U.S. government. It is in the public domain.[16]

Citations from the Federal Register are [volume] FR [page number] ([date]), e.g., 65 FR 741 (2000-10-01).

Direct Communication and Letters

The FDA interacts with consumers, health professionals, and industry representatives through letters, meetings (requested by either the FDA or the industry representatives), and telephone calls.

While not all questions can be answered over the phone, the FDA prefers telephone interactions over physical meetings (when a teleconference can reasonably replace a face-to-face meeting).

---

[16] The Federal Register at the GPO, online in both text and PDF, from 1994 on.

www.FDA.gov

The FDA maintains a website at www.fda.gov that is focused on three key audiences:

- consumers
- health professionals
- industry representatives

Through collaboration with users in testing site-wide designs, FDA.gov provides online access to its guidance documents, communication with industry, consumers, and health professionals. Information is categorized by topic, with related subjects consolidated in sections on the site.

Additionally, FDA.gov provides a search engine for Title 21 of the CFR that makes finding keyword references throughout the title more accessible.

Conferences

The FDA routinely sends speakers to industry conferences where they are available to answer questions on their particular area of expertise.

False Statement to a Federal Agency

The U.S. Code of Federal Regulations (CFR) makes it a federal crime for anyone willfully and knowingly to make a false or fraudulent statement to a department or agency of the United States. The false statement must be related to a material matter, and the defendant must have acted willfully and with knowledge of the falsity. It is not necessary to show that the government agency was in fact deceived or misled. The issue of materiality is one of law for the courts. The maximum penalty is five years' imprisonment and a $10,000 fine.

A person may be guilty of a violation without proof that he or she had knowledge that the matter was within the jurisdiction of a federal agency. A businessperson may violate this law by making a false statement to another firm or person with knowledge that the information will be submitted to a government agency. Businesses must take care to avoid exaggerations in the context of any matter that may come within the jurisdiction of a federal agency.

CFR Title 21 - Food and Drugs: Parts 1 to 1499[17]

General

(1) General enforcement regulations

(2) General administrative rulings and decisions

[17] All of the 21CFR regulations can be searched online for no charge at http://www.accessdata.fda.gov/scripts/cdrh/cfdocs/cfcfr/cfrsearch.cfm

(3) Product jurisdiction

(5) Organization

(7) Enforcement policy

(10) Administrative practices and procedures

(11) Electronic records; electronic signatures

(12) Formal evidentiary public hearing

(13) Public hearing before a public board of inquiry

(14) Public hearing before a public advisory committee

(15) Public hearing before the commissioner

(16) Regulatory hearing before the food and drug administration

(17) Civil money penalties hearings

(19) Standards of conduct and conflicts of interest

(20) Public information

(21) Protection of privacy

(25) Environmental impact considerations

(26) Mutual recognition of pharmaceutical good manufacturing practice

(50) Protection of human subjects

(54) Financial disclosure by clinical investigators

(56) Institutional review boards

(58) Good laboratory practice for nonclinical laboratory studies

(60) Patent term restoration

(70) Color additives

(71) Color additive petitions

(73) Listing of color additives exempt from certification

(74) Listing of color additives subject to certification

(80) Color additive certification

(81) General specifications and general restrictions for provisional color additives for use in foods, drugs, and cosmetics

(82) Listing of certified provisionally listed colors and specifications

(83-98) [reserved]

(99) Dissemination of information on unapproved/new uses for marketed drugs, biologics, and devices

Foods

(100) General

(101) Food labeling

(102) Common or usual name for nonstandardized foods

(104) Nutritional quality guidelines for foods

(105) Foods for special dietary use

(106) Infant formula quality control procedures

(107) Infant formula

(108) Emergency permit control

(109) Unavoidable contaminants in food for human consumption and food-packaging material

(110) Current good manufacturing practice in manufacturing, packing, or holding human food

(111) Current good manufacturing practice in manufacturing, packaging, labeling, or holding operations for dietary supplements

(113) Thermally processed low-acid foods packaged in hermetically sealed containers

(114) Acidified foods

(115) Shell eggs

(119) Dietary supplements that present a significant or unreasonable risk

(120) Hazard analysis and critical control point (HACCP) systems

(123) Fish and fishery products

(129) Processing and bottling of bottled drinking water

(130) Food standards: general

(131) Milk and cream

(133) Cheeses and related cheese products

(135) Frozen desserts

(136) Bakery products

(137) Cereal flours and related products

(139) Macaroni and noodle products

(145) Canned fruits

(146) Canned fruit juices

(150) Fruit butters, jellies, preserves, and related products

(152) Fruit pies

(155) Canned vegetables

(156) Vegetable juices

(158) Frozen vegetables

(160) Eggs and egg products

(161) Fish and shellfish

(163) Cacao products

(164) Tree nut and peanut products

(165) Beverages

(166) Margarine

(168) Sweeteners and table syrups

(169) Food dressings and flavorings

(170) Food additives

(171) Food additive petitions

(172) Food additives permitted for direct addition to food for human consumption

(173) Secondary direct food additives permitted in food for human consumption

(174) Indirect food additives: general

(175) Indirect food additives: adhesives and components of coatings

(176) Indirect food additives: paper and paperboard components

(177) Indirect food additives: polymers

(178) Indirect food additives: adjuvants, production aids, and sanitizers

(179) Irradiation in the production, processing and handling of food

(180) Food additives permitted in food or in contact with food on an interim basis pending additional study

(181) Prior-sanctioned food ingredients

(182) Substances generally recognized as safe

(184) Direct food substances affirmed as generally recognized as safe

(186) Indirect food substances affirmed as generally recognized as safe

(189) Substances prohibited from use in human food

(190) Dietary supplements

(191-199) [reserved]

Drugs

(200) General

(201) Labeling

(202) Prescription drug advertising

(203) Prescription drug marketing

(205) Guidelines for state licensing of wholesale prescription drug distributors

(206) Imprinting of solid oral dosage form drug products for human use

(207) Registration of producers of drugs and listing of drugs in commercial distribution

(208) Medication guides for prescription drug products

(209) Requirement for authorized dispensers and pharmacies to distribute a side effects statement

(210) Current good manufacturing practice in manufacturing, processing, packing, or holding of drugs; general

(211) Current good manufacturing practice for finished pharmaceuticals

(216) Pharmacy compounding

(225) Current good manufacturing practice for medicated feeds

(226) Current good manufacturing practice for type A medicated articles

(250) Special requirements for specific human drugs

(290) Controlled drugs

(299) Drugs; official names and established names

New Drugs and Over-the-Counter Drug Products

(300) General

(310) New drugs

(312) Investigational new drug application

(314) Applications for FDA approval to market a new drug

(315) Diagnostic radiopharmaceuticals

(316) Orphan drugs

(320) Bioavailability and bioequivalence requirements

(328) Over-the-counter drug products intended for oral ingestion that contain alcohol

(330) Over-the-counter (OTC) human drugs which are generally recognized as safe and effective and not misbranded

(331) Antacid products for over-the-counter (OTC) human use

(332) Antiflatulent products for over-the-counter human use

(333) Topical antimicrobial drug products for over-the-counter recognized as safe and effective and not misbranded

(335) Antidiarrheal drug products for over-the-counter human use

(336) Antiemetic drug products for over-the-counter human use

(338) Nighttime sleep-aid drug products for over-the-counter human use

(340) Stimulant drug products for over-the-counter human use

(341) Cold, cough, allergy, bronchodilator, and antiasthmatic drug products for over-the-counter human use

(343) Internal analgesic, antipyretic, and antirheumatic drug products for over-the-counter human use

(344) Topical OTIC drug products for over-the-counter human use

(346) Anorectal drug products for over-the-counter human use

(347) Skin protectant drug products for over-the-counter human use

(348) External analgesic drug products for over-the-counter human use

(349) Ophthalmic drug products for over-the-counter human use

(350) Antiperspirant drug products for over-the-counter human use

(352) Sunscreen drug products for over-the-counter human use [stayed indefinitely]

(355) Anticaries drug products for over-the-counter human use

(357) Miscellaneous internal drug products for over-the-counter human use

(358) Miscellaneous external drug products for over-the-counter human use

(361) Prescription drugs for human use generally recognized as safe and effective and not misbranded: drugs used in research

(369) Interpretative statements re warnings on drugs and devices for over-the-counter sale

(370-499) [reserved]

Veterinary Products

(500) General

(501) Animal food labeling

(502) Common or usual names for nonstandardized animal foods

(509) Unavoidable contaminants in animal food and food-packaging material

(510) New animal drugs

(511) New animal drugs for investigational use

(514) New animal drug applications

(515) Medicated feed mill license

(516) New animal drugs for minor use and minor species

(520) Oral dosage form new animal drugs

(522) Implantation or injectable dosage form new animal drugs

(524) Ophthalmic and topical dosage form new animal drugs

(526) Intramammary dosage forms

(529) Certain other dosage form new animal drugs

(530) Extralabel drug use in animals

(556) Tolerances for residues of new animal drugs in food

(558) New animal drugs for use in animal feeds

(564) [reserved]

(570) Food additives

(571) Food additive petitions

(573) Food additives permitted in feed and drinking water of animals

(579) Irradiation in the production, processing, and handling of animal feed and pet food

(582) Substances generally recognized as safe

(584) Food substances affirmed as generally recognized as safe in feed and drinking water of animals

(589) Substances prohibited from use in animal food or feed

(590-599) [reserved]

Biologics

(600) Biological products: general

(601) Licensing

(606) Current good manufacturing practice for blood and blood components

(607) Establishment registration and product listing for manufacturers of human blood and blood products

(610) General biological products standards

(630) General requirements for blood, blood components, and blood components, and blood derivatives

(640) Additional standards for human blood and blood products

(660) Additional standards for diagnostic substances for laboratory tests

(680) Additional standards for miscellaneous products

Cosmetics

(700) General

(701) Cosmetic labeling

(710) Voluntary registration of cosmetic product establishments

(720) Voluntary filing of cosmetic product ingredient composition statements

(740) Cosmetic product warning statements

(741-799) [reserved]

Medical Devices

(800) General

(801) Labeling

(803) Medical device reporting

(806) Medical devices; reports of corrections and removals

(807) Establishment registration and device listing for manufacturers and initial importers of devices

(808) Exemptions from federal preemption of state and local medical device requirements

(809) In vitro diagnostic products for human use

(810) Medical device recall authority

(812) Investigational device exemptions

(813) [reserved]

(814) Premarket approval of medical devices

(820) Quality system regulation

(821) Medical device tracking requirements

(822) Postmarket surveillance

(860) Medical device classification procedures

(861) Procedures for performance standards development

(862) Clinical chemistry and clinical toxicology devices

(864) Hematology and pathology devices

(866) Immunology and microbiology devices

(868) Anesthesiology devices

(870) Cardiovascular devices

(872) Dental devices

(874) Ear, nose, and throat devices

(876) Gastroenterology-urology devices

(878) General and plastic surgery devices

(880) General hospital and personal use devices

(882) Neurological devices

(884) Obstetrical and gynecological devices

(886) Ophthalmic devices

(888) Orthopedic devices

(890) Physical medicine devices

(892) Radiology devices

(895) Banned devices

(898) Performance standard for electrode lead wires and patient cables

Mammography

(900) Mammography

Radiological Health

(1000) General

(1002) Records and reports

(1003) Notification of defects or failure to comply

(1004) Repurchase, repairs, or replacement of electronic products

(1005) Importation of electronic products

(1010) Performance standards for electronic products: general

(1020) Performance standards for ionizing radiation emitting products

(1030) Performance standards for microwave and radio frequency emitting products

(1040) Performance standards for light-emitting products

(1050) Performance standards for sonic, infrasonic, and ultrasonic radiation-emitting products

Regulations under Certain Other Acts

(1210) Regulations under the federal import milk act

(1230) Regulations under the federal caustic poison act

(1240) Control of communicable diseases

(1250) Interstate conveyance sanitation

(1251-1269) [reserved]

(1270) Human tissue intended for transplantation

(1271) Human cells, tissues, and cellular and tissue-based products

(1272-1299) [reserved]

Controlled Substances

(1300) Definitions

(1301) Registration of manufacturers, distributors, and dispensers of controlled substances

(1302) Labeling and packaging requirements for controlled substances

(1303) Quotas

(1304) Records and reports of registrants

(1305) Orders for schedule I and II controlled substances

(1306) Prescriptions

(1307) Miscellaneous

(1308) Schedules of controlled substances

(1309) Registration of manufacturers, distributors, importers and exporters of List I chemicals

(1310) Records and reports of listed chemicals and certain machines

(1311) Digital certificates

(1312) Importation and exportation of controlled substances

(1313) Importation and exportation of list I and list II chemicals

(1314) Retail sale of scheduled listed chemical products

(1315) Importation and production quotas for ephedrine, pseudoephedrine, and phenylpropanolamine

(1316) Administrative functions, practices, and procedures

Office of National Drug Control Policy

(1400) [reserved]

(1401) Public availability of information

(1402) Mandatory declassification review

(1403) Uniform administrative requirements for grants and cooperative agreements to state and local governments

(1404) Governmentwide debarment and suspension (nonprocurement)

(1405) Governmentwide requirements for drug-free workplace (financial assistance)

(1406-1499) [reserved]

Part I

Federal Food, Drug, and Cosmetic Act

Section Number Reference: Federal Food, Drug, and Cosmetic Act

- Chapter I: Short Title
- Chapter II: Definitions
- Chapter III: Prohibited Acts and Penalties
- Chapter IV: Food
- Chapter V: Drugs and Devices
- Chapter VI: Cosmetics
- Chapter VII: General Authority
- Chapter VIII: Imports and Exports
- Chapter IX: Miscellaneous

Cross-reference of Section Numbers: FD&C Act and United States Code

Section Title	**FD&C Act Number**	**U.S. Code Section Number (21 U.S.C)**
Chapter I (U.S.C. Subchapter I)--		
Short Title	1	301
Chapter II (U.S.C. Subchapter II)--		
Definitions	201	321
Chapter III (U.S.C. Subchapter III)--Prohibited Acts and Penalties		
Prohibited Acts	301	331
Injunction Proceedings	302	332
Penalties	303	333
Seizure	304	334

Section Title	FD&C Act Number	U.S. Code Section Number (21 U.S.C)
Hearing Before Report of Criminal Violation	305	335
Debarment, Temporary Denial of Approval, and Suspension	306	335a
Civil Penalties	307	335b
Authority to Withdraw Approval of Abbreviated Drug Applications	308	335c
Report of Minor Violations	309	336
Proceedings in Name of United States; Provision as to Subpoenas	310	337
Chapter IV (U.S.C. Subchapter IV)--Food		
Definitions and Standards for Food	401	341
Adulterated Food	402	342
Misbranded Food	403	343
Enacted without a section heading.	403A	343--1
Dietary Supplement Labeling Exemptions	403B	343--2
Disclosure	403C	343--3
Emergency Permit Control	404	344
Regulations Making Exemptions	405	345
Tolerances for Poisonous Ingredients in Food	406	346
Oleomargarine or Margarine	407	347
Tolerances and Exemptions for Pesticide Chemical Residues	408	346a
Food Additives	409	348
Bottled Drinking Water Standards	410	349
Vitamins and Minerals	411	350
Requirements for Infant Formulas	412	350a
New Dietary Ingredients	413	350b
Maintenance and Inspection of Records	414	350c
Registration of Food Facilities	415	350d
Sanitary transportation practices	416	350e
Reportable food registry	417	350f

Section Title	FD&C Act Number	U.S. Code Section Number (21 U.S.C)
Chapter V (U.S.C. Subchapter V)--Drugs and Devices Subchapter A (U.S.C. Part A)-- Drugs and Devices		
Adulterated Drugs and Devices	501	351
Misbranded Drugs and Devices	502	352
Exemptions and Consideration for Certain Drugs, Devices, and Biological Products	503	353
Pharmacy Compounding	503A	353a
Veterinary Feed Directive Drugs	504	354
New Drugs	505	355
Risk Evaluation and Mitigation Strategies	505-1	355-1
Pediatric Studies of Drugs	505A	355a
Research Into Pediatric Uses for Drugs and Biological Products	505B	355c
Internal committee for review of pediatric plans, assessments, deferrals, and waivers	505C	355d
Pharmaceutical security	505D	355e
Fast Track Products	506	356
Manufacturing Changes	506A	356a
Reports of Postmarketing Studies	506B	356b
Discontinuance of a Life Saving Product	506C	356c
Repealed	507	357
Authority to Designate Official Names	508	358
Nonapplicability to Cosmetics	509	359
Registration of Producers of Drugs and Devices	510	360
Clinical trial guidance for antibiotic drugs	511	360a
New Animal Drugs	512	360b
Classification of Devices Intended for Human Use	513	360c
Performance Standards	514	360d
Premarket Approval	515	360e
Pediatric uses of devices	515A	3.60E+01
Banned Devices	516	360f

Section Title	FD&C Act Number	U.S. Code Section Number (21 U.S.C)
Judicial Review	517	360g
Notification and Other Remedies	518	360h
Records and Reports on Devices	519	360i
General Provisions Respecting Control of Devices Intended for Human Use	520	360j
State and Local Requirements Respecting Devices	521	360k
Postmarket Surveillance	522	360l
Accredited Persons	523	360m
Subchapter B (U.S.C. Part B)--Drugs for Rare Diseases or Conditions		
Priority review to encourage treatments for tropical diseases	524	360n
Recommendations for Investigations of Drugs for Rare Diseases and Conditions	525	360aa
Designation of Drugs for Rare Diseases or Conditions	526	360bb
Protection for Drugs for Rare Diseases or Conditions	527	360cc
Open Protocols for Investigations of Drugs for Rare Diseases or Conditions	528	360dd
Subchapter C (U.S.C. Part C)—Electronic Product Radiation Control		
Definitions	531	360hh
Electronic Product Radiation Control Program	532	360ii
Studies by the Secretary	533	360jj
Performance Standards for Electronic Products	534	360kk
Notification of Defects In, and Repair or Replacement Of, Electronic Products	535	360ll
Imports	536	360mm
Inspection and Reports	537	360nn
Prohibited Acts	538	360oo
Enforcement	539	360pp
Repealed	540	360qq

Section Title	FD&C Act Number	U.S. Code Section Number (21 U.S.C)
Federal-State Cooperation	541	360rr
Effect on State Standards	542	360ss
Subchapter D (U.S.C. Part D)—Dissemination of Treatment Information		
Requirements for Dissemination of Treatment Information on Drugs or Devices	551	360aaa
Information Authorized to be Disseminated	552	360aaa-1
Establishment of List of Articles and Publications Disseminated and List of Providers That Received Articles and Reference Publications	553	360aaa-2
Requirement Regarding Submission of Supplemental Application for New Use; Exemption from Requirement	554	360aaa-3
Corrective Actions; Cessation of Dissemination	555	360aaa-4
Definitions	556	360aaa-5
Rules of Construction	557	360aaa-6
Subchapter E (U.S.C. Part E)—General Provisions Relating to Drugs and Devices		
Expanded Access to Unapproved Therapies and Diagnostics	561	360bbb
Dispute Resolution	562	360bbb-1
Classification of Products	563	360bbb-2
Authorization for Medical Products for Use in Emergencies	564	360bbb-3
Technical assistance	565	360bbb-4
Critical Path Public-Private Partnerships	566	360bbb-5
Risk Communication	567	360bbb-6
Subchapter F (U.S.C. Part F)—New Animal Drugs for Minor Use and Minor Species		
Conditional Approval of New Animal Drugs for Minor Use and Minor Species	571	360ccc
Index of Legally Marketed Unapproved New Animal Drugs for Minor Species	572	360ccc-1

Section Title	FD&C Act Number	U.S. Code Section Number (21 U.S.C)
Designated New Animal Drugs for Minor Use or Minor Species	573	360ccc-2
Chapter VI (U.S.C. Subchapter VI)—Cosmetics		
Adulterated Cosmetics	601	361
Misbranded Cosmetics	602	362
Regulations Making Exemptions	603	363
Chapter VII (U.S.C. Subchapter VII)—General Authority **Subchapter A (U.S.C. Part A)—General Administrative Provisions**		
Regulations and Hearings	701	371
Examinations and Investigations	702	372
Records of Interstate Shipment	703	373
Factory Inspection	704	374
Publicity	705	375
Seafood Inspection	706	376
Advertising of Certain Foods	707	378
Confidential Information	708	379
Presumption	709	379a
Consolidated Administrative and Laboratory Facility	710	379b
Automation of Food and Drug Administration	711	379d
Conflicts of interest	712	379d-1
Policy on the review and clearance of scientific articles published by FDA employees	713	379d-2
Subchapter B (U.S.C. Part B)—Colors		
Listing and Certification of Color Additives for Foods, Drugs, and Cosmetics	721	379e
Subchapter C (U.S.C. Part C)—Fees **Part 1 (U.S.C. Subpart 1)—Freedom of Information Fees**		

Section Title	**FD&C Act Number**	**U.S. Code Section Number (21 U.S.C)**
Recovery and Retention of Fees for Freedom of Information Requests	731	379f
Part 2 (U.S.C. Subpart 2)—Fees Relating to Drugs		
Definitions	735	379g
Authority to Assess and Use Drug Fees	736	379h
Fees relating to advisory review of prescription-drug television advertising	736a	379h-1
Reauthorization; reporting requirements	736b	79h-2
Part 3 (U.S.C. Subpart 3)—Fees Relating to Devices		
Definitions	737	379i
Authority to Assess and Use Device Fees	738	379j
Reauthorization; reporting requirements	738a	379j-1
Part 4 (U.S.C. Subpart 4)—Fees Relating to Animal Drugs		
Definitions	739	379j-11
Authority to Assess and Use Animal Drug Fees	740	379j-12
Subchapter D (Part D)—Information and Education		
Information System	741	379k
Education	742	379l
Subchapter E (U.S.C. Part E)—Environmental Impact Review		
Environmental Impact	746	379o
Subchapter F (U.S.C. Part F)—National Uniformity for Nonprescription Drugs and Preemption for Labeling or Packaging of Cosmetics		
National Uniformity for Nonprescription Drugs	751	379r
Preemption for Labeling or Packaging of Cosmetics	752	379s
Subchapter G (U.S.C. Part G)—Safety Reports		
Safety Report Disclaimers	756	379v
Subchapter H—Serious Adverse Event Reports		

Section Title	FD&C Act Number	U.S. Code Section Number (21 U.S.C)
Serious adverse event reporting for nonprescription drugs	760	379aa
Serious adverse event reporting for dietary supplements	761	379aa-1
Subchapter I—Reagan-Udall Foundation for the Food and Drug Administration		
Establishment and functions of the Foundation	770	379dd
Location of Foundation	771	379dd-1
Activities of the Food and Drug Administration	772	379dd-2
Chapter VIII (U.S.C. Subchapter VIII)—Imports and Exports		
Imports and Exports	801	381
Exports of Certain Unapproved Products	802	382
Office of International Relations	803	383
Importation of Prescription Drugs	804	384
Chapter IX (U.S.C. Subchapter IX)—Miscellaneous		
Separability Clause	901	391
Effective Date and Repeals	902	392
Food and Drug Administration	903	393
Scientific Review Groups	904	394
Loan Repayment Program	905	395
Practice of Medicine	906	396
Contracts for Expert Review	907	396
Notices to States Regarding Imported Food	908	398
Grants to States for Inspections	909	399
Office of the Chief Scientist	910	399a

FD&C Act Chapters I and II: Short Title and Definitions

FD&C Act Chapter I — Short Title

Section 1 . [21 U.S.C. 301] [Ŧ]

This Act may be cited as the Federal Food, Drug, and Cosmetic Act.

Chapter II — Definitions

Sec. 201. [21 U.S.C. 321][1]

SEC. 201. [21 U.S.C. 321] Definitions; generally

For the purposes of this Act— [2]

(a)(1) The term "***State***", except as used in the last sentence of section 702(a), means any State or Territory of the United States , the District of Columbia , and the Commonwealth of Puerto Rico .

(2) The term "***Territory***" means any Territory or possession of the United States , including the District of Columbia , and excluding the Commonwealth of Puerto Rico and the Canal Zone.

Ŧ Available on the FDA website at: http://www.fda.gov/RegulatoryInformation/Legislation/FederalFoodDrugandCosmeticActFDCAct/FDCActChaptersIandIIShortTitleandDefinitions/ucm086297.htm

1 The following additional definitions applicable to this Act are provided for in other Acts:
Butter. The Act of March 4, 1923 (21 U.S.C. 321a), defines butter as "the food product usually known as butter, and which is made exclusively from milk or cream, or both, with or without common salt, and with or without additional coloring matter, and containing not less than 80 per centum by weight of milk fat, all tolerances having been allowed for."
Package. The Act of July 24, 1919 (21 U.S.C. 321b), states "The word 'package' shall include and shall be construed to include wrapped meats inclosed in papers or other materials as prepared by the manufacturers thereof for sale."
Nonfat Dry Milk, Milk. The Act of July 2, 1956 (21 U.S.C. 321c), defines nonfat dry milk as "the product resulting from the removal of fat and water from milk, and contains the lactose, milk proteins, and milk minerals in the same relative proportions as in the fresh milk from which made. It contains not over 5 per centum by weight of moisture. The fat content is not over 11/2 per centum by weight unless otherwise indicated.", and defines milk to mean sweet milk of cows.

2 See footnote for section 403(h)(3) regarding the stylistic use of a list consisting of "(a)", "(b)", etc.

(b) The term "***interstate commerce***" means (1) commerce between any State or Territory and any place outside thereof, and (2) commerce within the District of Columbia or within any other Territory not organized with a legislative body.

(c) The term "***Department***" means the Department of Health and Human Services.

(d) The term "***Secretary***" means the Secretary of Health and Human Services.

(e) The term "***person***" includes individual, partnership, corporation, and association.

(f) [1] The term "***food***" means (1) articles used for food or drink for man or other animals, (2) chewing gum, and (3) articles used for components of any such article.

(g)(1) The term "***drug***" means (A) articles recognized in the official United States Pharmacopoeia, official Homoeopathic Pharmacopoeia of the United States, or official National Formulary, or any supplement to any of them; and (B) articles intended for use in the diagnosis, cure, mitigation, treatment, or prevention of disease in man or other animals; and (C) articles (other than food) intended to affect the structure or any function of the body of man or other animals; and (D) articles intended for use as a component of any article specified in clause (A), (B), or (C). A food or dietary supplement for which a claim, subject to sections 403(r)(1)(B) and 403(r)(3) or sections 403(r)(1)(B) and 403(r)(5)(D), is made in accordance with the requirements of section 403(r) is not a drug solely because the label or the labeling contains such a claim. A food, dietary ingredient, or dietary supplement for which a truthful and not misleading statement is made in accordance with section 403(r)(6) is not a drug under clause (C) solely because the label or the labeling contains such a statement.

(2) The term "***counterfeit drug***" means a drug which, or the container or labeling of which, without authorization, bears the trademark, trade name, or other identifying mark, imprint, or device, or any likeness thereof, of a drug manufacturer, processor, packer, or distributor other than the person or persons who in fact manufactured, processed, packed, or distributed such drug and which thereby falsely purports or is represented to be the product of, or to have been packed or distributed by, such other drug manufacturer, processor, packer, or distributor.

(h) The term "***device***" (except when used in paragraph (n) of this section and in sections 301(i), 403(f), 502(c), and 602(c)) means an instrument, apparatus, implement, machine, contrivance, implant, in vitro reagent, or other similar or related article, including any component, part, or accessory, which is--

(1) recognized in the official National Formulary, or the United States Pharmacopeia, or any supplement to them,

(2) intended for use in the diagnosis of disease or other conditions, or in the cure, mitigation, treatment, or prevention of disease, in man or other animals, or

(3) intended to affect the structure or any function of the body of man or other animals, and which does not achieve its primary intended purposes through chemical action within or on the body of man or other animals and which is not dependent upon being metabolized for the achievement of its primary intended purposes.

(i) The term "***cosmetic***" means (1) articles intended to be rubbed, poured, sprinkled, or sprayed on, introduced into, or otherwise applied to the human body or any part thereof for cleansing, beautifying, promoting attractiveness, or altering the appearance, and (2) articles intended for use as a component of any such articles; except that such term shall not include soap.

(j) The term "***official compendium***" means the official United States Pharmacopoeia, official Homoeopathic Pharmacopoeia of the United States, official National Formulary, or any supplement to any of them.

(k) The term "***label***" means a display of written, printed, or graphic matter upon the immediate container of any article; and a requirement made by or under authority of this Act that any word, statement, or other information appear on the label shall not be considered to be complied with unless such word, statement, or other information also appears on the outside container or wrapper, if any there be, of the retail package of such article, or is easily legible through the outside container or wrapper.

(l) The term "***immediate container***" does not include package liners.

(m) The term "***labeling***" means all labels and other written, printed, or graphic matters (1) upon any article or any of its containers or wrappers, or (2) accompanying such article.

(n) If an article is alleged to be misbranded because the labeling or advertising is misleading, then in determining whether the labeling or advertising is misleading there shall be taken into account (among other things) not only representations made or suggested by statement, word, design, device, or any combination thereof, but also the extent to which the labeling or advertising fails to reveal facts material in the light of such representations or material with respect to consequences which may result from the use of the article to which the labeling or advertising relates under the conditions of use prescribed in the labeling or advertising thereof or under such conditions of use as are customary or usual.

(o) The representation of a drug, in its labeling, as an antiseptic shall be considered to be a representation that it is a germicide, except in the case of a drug purporting to be, or represented as, an antiseptic for inhibitory use as a wet dressing, ointment, dusting powder, or such other use as involves prolonged contact with the body.

(p) The term "***new drug***" means— [3]

(1) Any drug (except a new animal drug or an animal feed bearing or containing a new animal drug) the composition of which is such that such drug is not generally recognized, among experts qualified by scientific training and experience to evaluate the safety and effectiveness of drugs, as safe and effective for use under the condition prescribed, recommended, or suggested in the labeling thereof, except that such a drug not so recognized shall not be deemed to be a "new drug" if at any time prior to the enactment of this Act [enacted June 25, 1938] it was subject to the Food and Drugs Act of June 30, 1906, as amended, and if at such time its labeling contained the same representations concerning the conditions of its use; or

(2) Any drug (except a new animal drug or an animal feed bearing or containing a new animal drug) the composition of which is such that such drug, as a result of investigations to determine its safety and effectiveness for use under such conditions, has become so recognized, but which has not, otherwise than in such investigations, been used to a material extent or for a material time under such conditions.

(q)(1)(A) Except as provided in clause (B), the term "pesticide chemical" means any substance that is a pesticide within the meaning of the Federal Insecticide, Fungicide, and Rodenticide Act, including all active and inert ingredients of such pesticide. Notwithstanding any other provision of law, the term "pesticide" within such meaning includes ethylene oxide and propylene oxide when such substances are applied on food.

(B) In the case of the use, with respect to food, of a substance described in clause (A) to prevent, destroy, repel, or mitigate microorganisms (including bacteria, viruses, fungi, protozoa, algae, and slime), the following applies for purposes of clause (A):

(i) The definition in such clause for the term "pesticide chemical" does not include the substance if the substance is applied for such use on food, or the substance is included for such use in water that comes into contact with the food, in the preparing, packing, or holding of the food for commercial purposes. The substance is not excluded under this subclause from such definition if the substance is ethylene oxide or propylene oxide, and is applied for such use on

[3] The amendments made to this Act by the Drug Amendments of 1962 included amendments establishing the requirement that new drugs be effective. Section 107(c) of such Public Law concerned the applicability of the amendments, and is included in the appendix to this compilation.

food. The substance is not so excluded if the substance is applied for such use on a raw agricultural commodity, or the substance is included for such use in water that comes into contact with the commodity, as follows:

(I) The substance is applied in the field.

(II) The substance is applied at a treatment facility where raw agricultural commodities are the only food treated, and the treatment is in a manner that does not change the status of the food as a raw agricultural commodity (including treatment through washing, waxing, fumigating, and packing such commodities in such manner).

(III) The substance is applied during the transportation of such commodity between the field and such a treatment facility.

(ii) The definition in such clause for the term "pesticide chemical" does not include the substance if the substance is a food contact substance as defined in section 409(h)(6), and any of the following circumstances exist: The substance is included for such use in an object that has a food contact surface but is not intended to have an ongoing effect on any portion of the object; the substance is included for such use in an object that has a food contact surface and is intended to have an ongoing effect on a portion of the object but not on the food contact surface; or the substance is included for such use in or is applied for such use on food packaging (without regard to whether the substance is intended to have an ongoing effect on any portion of the packaging). The food contact substance is not excluded under this subclause from such definition if any of the following circumstances exist: The substance is applied for such use on a semipermanent or permanent food contact surface (other than being applied on food packaging); or the substance is included for such use in an object that has a semipermanent or permanent food contact surface (other than being included in food packaging) and the substance is intended to have an ongoing effect on the food contact surface.

With respect to the definition of the term "***pesticide***" that is applicable to the Federal Insecticide, Fungicide, and Rodenticide Act, this clause does not exclude any substance from such definition.

(2) The term "***pesticide chemical residue***" means a residue in or on raw agricultural commodity or processed food of—

(A) a pesticide chemical; or

(B) any other added substance that is present on or in the commodity or food primarily as a result of the metabolism or other degradation of a pesticide chemical.

(3) Notwithstanding subparagraphs (1) and (2), the Administrator may by regulation except a substance from the definition of "pesticide chemical" or "pesticide chemical residue" if—

(A) its occurrence as a residue on or in a raw agricultural commodity or processed food is attributable primarily to natural causes or to human activities not involving the use of any substances for a pesticidal purpose in the production, storage, processing, or transportation of any raw agricultural commodity or processed food; and

(B) the Administrator, after consultation with the Secretary, determines that the substance more appropriately should be regulated under one or more provisions of this Act other than sections 402(a)(2)(B) and 408.

(r) The term "***raw agricultural commodity***" means any food in its raw or natural state, including all fruits that are washed, colored, or otherwise treated in their unpeeled natural form prior to marketing.

(s) The term "***food additive***" means any substance the intended use of which results or may reasonably be expected to result, directly or indirectly, in its becoming a component or otherwise affecting the characteristics of any food (including any substance intended for use in producing, manufacturing, packing, processing, preparing, treating, packaging, transporting, or holding food; and including any source of radiation intended for any such use), if such substance is not generally recognized, among experts qualified by scientific training and experience to evaluate its safety, as having been adequately shown through scientific procedures (or, in the case of a substance used in food prior to January 1, 1958, through either scientific procedures or experience based on common use in food) to be safe under the conditions of its intended use; except that such term does not include—

(1) a pesticide chemical residue in or on a raw agricultural commodity or processed food; or

(2) a pesticide chemical; or

(3) a color additive; or

(4) any substance used in accordance with a sanction or approval granted prior to the enactment of this paragraph[4] pursuant to this Act [enacted Sept. 6, 1958], the Poultry Products Inspection Act (21 U.S.C. 451 and the following) or the Meat Inspection Act of March 4, 1907 (34 Stat. 1260), as amended and extended (21 U.S.C. 71 and the following);

[4] Paragraph (s) was added by Public Law 85–929, which was enacted September 6, 1958.

(5) a new animal drug; or

(6) an ingredient described in paragraph (ff) in, or intended for use in, a dietary supplement.

(t)(1) The term "***color additive***" means a material which—

(A) is a dye, pigment, or other substance made by a process of synthesis or similar artifice, or extracted, isolated, or otherwise derived, with or without intermediate or final change of identity, from a vegetable, animal, mineral, or other source, and

(B) when added or applied to a food, drug, or cosmetic, or to the human body or any part thereof, is capable (alone or through reaction with other substance) of imparting color thereto; except that such term does not include any material which the Secretary, by regulation, determines is used (or intended to be used) solely for a purpose or purposes other than coloring.

(2) The term "***color***" includes black, white, and intermediate grays.

(3) Nothing in subparagraph (1) of this paragraph shall be construed to apply to any pesticide chemical, soil or plant nutrient, or other agricultural chemical solely because of its effect in aiding, retarding, or otherwise affecting, directly or indirectly, the growth or other natural physiological processes of produce of the soil and thereby affecting its color, whether before or after harvest.

(u) The term "***safe***," as used in paragraph (s) of this section and in sections 409, 512, 571, and 721, has reference to the health of man or animal.

(v) The term "***new animal drug***" means any drug intended for use for animals other than man, including any drug intended for use in animal feed but not including such animal feed—

(1) the composition of which is such that such drug is not generally recognized, among experts qualified by scientific training and experience to evaluate the safety and effectiveness of animal drugs, as safe and effective for use under the conditions prescribed, recommended, or suggested in the labeling thereof; except that such a drug not so recognized shall not be deemed to be a "new animal drug" if at any time prior to June 25, 1938, it was subject to the Food and Drug Act of June 30, 1906, as amended, and if at such time its labeling contained the same representations concerning the conditions of its use; or

(2) the composition of which is such that such drug, as a result of investigations to determine its safety and effectiveness for use under such conditions, has become so recognized but which has not, otherwise than in such investigations, been used to a material extent or for a material time under such conditions.

Provided that [5] any drug intended for minor use or use in a minor species that is not the subject of a final regulation published by the Secretary through notice and comment rulemaking finding that the criteria of paragraphs (1) and (2) have not been met (or that the exception to the criterion in paragraph (1) has been met) is a new animal drug.

(w) The term "***animal feed***", as used in paragraph (w) [(v)][6] of this section, in section 512, and in provisions of this Act referring to such paragraph or section, means an article which is intended for use for food for animals other than man and which is intended for use as a substantial source of nutrients in the diet of the animal, and is not limited to a mixture intended to be the sole ration of the animal.

(x) The term "***informal hearing***" means a hearing which is not subject to section 554, 556, or 557 of title 5 of the United States Code and which provides for the following:

(1) The presiding officer in the hearing shall be designated by the Secretary from officers and employees of the Department who have not participated in any action of the Secretary which is the subject of the hearing and who are not directly responsible to an officer or employee of the Department who has participated in any such action.

(2) Each party to the hearing shall have the right at all times to be advised and accompanied by an attorney.

(3) Before the hearing, each party to the hearing shall be given reasonable notice of the matters to be considered at the hearing, including a comprehensive statement of the basis for the action taken or proposed by the Secretary which is the subject of the hearing and a general summary of the information which will be presented by the Secretary at the hearing in support of such action.

(4) At the hearing the parties to the hearing shall have the right to hear a full and complete statement of the action of the Secretary which is the subject of the

---

[5] The proviso appears so as to reflect the probable intent of the Congress. See section 102(b)(5)(B) of Public Law 108–282, which in amending section 201(v) above referred to "paragraph (2)" of the section. The reference probably should have been to "subparagraph (2)". (See footnote for section 403(h)(3) regarding the stylistic use of a list consisting of "(a)", "(b)", etc.)

With respect to the placement of the proviso, section 102(b)(5)(B) of such Public Law provided for placement "after" paragraph (2) (not at the end of paragraph (2)), yet did not indicate separate indentation. The proviso has been placed after and below subparagraph (2), with separate indentation, to indicate the probable intent of the Congress, although such placement of matter that is not a complete sentence calls for striking the period at the end of subparagraph (2) and inserting a semicolon, which section 102(b)(5)(B) of such Public Law did not do. (Compare with matter after and below section 201(t)(1)(B), for example.)

[6] So in law. Probably should be paragraph "(v)".

hearing together with the information and reasons supporting such action, to conduct reasonable questioning, and to present any oral or written information relevant to such action.

(5) The presiding officer in such hearing shall prepare a written report of the hearing to which shall be attached all written material presented at the hearing. The participants in the hearing shall be given the opportunity to review and correct or supplement the presiding officer's report of the hearing.

(6) The Secretary may require the hearing to be transcribed. A party to the hearing shall have the right to have the hearing transcribed at his expense. Any transcription of a hearing shall be included in the presiding officer's report of the hearing.

(y) The term "***saccharin***" includes calcium saccharin, sodium saccharin, and ammonium saccharin.

(z) The term "***infant formula***" means a food which purports to be or is represented for special dietary use solely as a food for infants by reason of its simulation of human milk or its suitability as a complete or partial substitute for human milk.

(aa) The term "***abbreviated drug application***" means an application submitted under section 505(j) for the approval of a drug that relies on the approved application of another drug with the same active ingredient to establish safety and efficacy, and—

(1) in the case of section 306, includes a supplement to such an application for a different or additional use of the drug but does not include a supplement to such an application for other than a different or additional use of the drug, and

(2) in the case of sections 307 and 308, includes any supplement to such an application.

(bb) The term "***knowingly***" or "knew" means that a person, with respect to information—

(1) has actual knowledge of the information, or

(2) acts in deliberate ignorance or reckless disregard of the truth or falsity of the information.

(cc) For purposes of section 306, the term "***high managerial agent***"—

(1) means—

(A) an officer or director of a corporation or an association,

(B) a partner of a partnership, or

(C) any employee or other agent of a corporation, association, or partnership, having duties such that the conduct of such officer, director, partner, employee, or agent may fairly be assumed to represent the policy of the corporation, association, or partnership, and

(2) includes persons having management responsibility for—

(A) submissions to the Food and Drug Administration regarding the development or approval of any drug product, any drug product,

(B) production, quality assurance, or quality control of any drug product, or

(C) research and development of any drug product.

(dd) For purposes of sections 306 and 307, the term "***drug product***" means a drug subject to regulation under section 505, 512, or 802 of this Act or under section 351 of the Public Health Service Act.

(ee) The term "***Commissioner***" means the Commissioner of Food and Drugs.

(ff) The term "***dietary supplement***"—

(1) means a product (other than tobacco) intended to supplement the diet that bears or contains one or more of the following dietary ingredients:

(A) a vitamin;

(B) a mineral;

(C) an herb or other botanical;

(D) an amino acid;

(E) a dietary substance for use by man to supplement the diet by increasing the total dietary intake; or

(F) a concentrate, metabolite, constituent, extract, or combination of any ingredient described in clause (A), (B), (C), (D), or (E);

(2) means a product that—

(A)(i) is intended for ingestion in a form described in section 411(c)(1)(B)(i); or

(ii) complies with section 411(c)(1)(B)(ii);

(B) is not represented for use as a conventional food or as a sole item of a meal or the diet; and

(C) is labeled as a dietary supplement; and

(3) does—

(A) include an article that is approved as a new drug under section 505 or licensed as a biologic under section 351 of the Public Health Service Act (42 U.S.C. 262) and was, prior to such approval, certification, or license, marketed as a dietary supplement or as a food unless the Secretary has issued a regulation, after notice and comment, finding that the article, when used as or in a dietary supplement under the conditions of use and dosages set forth in the labeling for such dietary supplement, is unlawful under section 402(f); and

(B) not include—

(i) an article that is approved as a new drug under section 505, certified as an antibiotic under section 507 [7], or licensed as a biologic under section 351 of the Public Health Service Act (42 U.S.C. 262), or

(ii) an article authorized for investigation as a new drug, antibiotic, or biological for which substantial clinical investigations have been instituted and for which the existence of such investigations has been made public, which was not before such approval, certification, licensing, or authorization marketed as a dietary supplement or as a food unless the Secretary, in the Secretary's discretion, has issued a regulation, after notice and comment, finding that the article would be lawful under this Act.

Except for purposes of section 201(g), a dietary supplement shall be deemed to be a food within the meaning of this Act.

(gg) The term "***processed food***" means any food other than a raw agricultural commodity and includes any raw agricultural commodity that has been subject to processing, such as canning, cooking, freezing, dehydration, or milling.

(hh) The term "***Administrator***" means the Administrator of the United States Environmental Protection Agency.

(ii) The term "***compounded positron emission tomography drug***"—

(1) means a drug that—

(A) exhibits spontaneous disintegration of unstable nuclei by the emission of positrons and is used for the purpose of providing dual photon positron emission tomographic diagnostic images; and

(B) has been compounded by or on the order of a practitioner who is licensed by a State to compound or order compounding for a drug described in subparagraph (A), and is compounded in accordance with

[7] So in law. Section 507 was repealed by section 125(b)(1) of Public Law 105–115 (111 Stat. 2325).

that State's law, for a patient or for research, teaching, or quality control; and

(2) includes any nonradioactive reagent, reagent kit, ingredient, nuclide generator, accelerator, target material, electronic synthesizer, or other apparatus or computer program to be used in the preparation of such a drug.

(jj) The term "***antibiotic drug***" means any drug (except drugs for use in animals other than humans) composed wholly or partly of any kind of penicillin, streptomycin, chlortetracycline, chloramphenicol, bacitracin, or any other drug intended for human use containing any quantity of any chemical substance which is produced by a micro-organism and which has the capacity to inhibit or destroy micro-organisms in dilute solution (including a chemically synthesized equivalent of any such substance) or any derivative thereof.

(kk) The term "***priority supplement***" means [8] a drug application referred to in section 101(4) of the Food and Drug Administration Modernization Act of 1997 (111 Stat. 2298).

(ll)(1) The term "***single-use device***" means a device that is intended for one use, or on a single patient during a single procedure.

(2)(A) The term "***reprocessed***", with respect to a single-use device, means an original device that has previously been used on a patient and has been subjected to additional processing and manufacturing for the purpose of an additional single use on a patient. The subsequent processing and manufacture of a reprocessed single-use device shall result in a device that is reprocessed within the meaning of this definition.

(B) A single-use device that meets the definition under clause (A) shall be considered a reprocessed device without regard to any description of the device used by the manufacturer of the device or other persons, including a description that uses the term "recycled" rather than the term "reprocessed".

(3) The term "***original device***" means a new, unused single-use device.

(mm)(1) The term "***critical reprocessed single-use device***" means a reprocessed single-use device that is intended to contact normally sterile tissue or body spaces during use.

(2) The term "***semi-critical reprocessed single-use device***" means a reprocessed single-use device that is intended to contact intact mucous membranes and not penetrate normally sterile areas of the body.

[8] Indentation is so in law. See section 5(b)(1) of Public Law 107–109 (115 Stat. 1413).

(nn) The term "***major species***" means cattle, horses, swine, chickens, turkeys, dogs, and cats, except that the Secretary may add species to this definition by regulation.

(oo) The term "***minor species***" means animals other than humans that are not major species.

(pp) The term "***minor use***" means the intended use of a drug in a major species for an indication that occurs infrequently and in only a small number of animals or in limited geographical areas and in only a small number of animals annually.

(qq) The term "***major food allergen***" means any of the following:

(1) Milk, egg, fish (e.g., bass, flounder, or cod), Crustacean shellfish (e.g., crab, lobster, or shrimp), tree nuts (e.g., almonds, pecans, or walnuts), wheat, peanuts, and soybeans.

(2) A food ingredient that contains protein derived from a food specified in paragraph [9] (1), except the following:

(A) Any highly refined oil derived from a food specified in paragraph (1) and any ingredient derived from such highly refined oil.

(B) A food ingredient that is exempt under paragraph (6) or (7) of section 403(w).

[9] So in law. See section 203(c)(1) of Public Law 108–282. Probably should be "subparagraph". See footnote for section 403(h)(3).

FD&C Act Chapter III: Prohibited Acts and Penalties

Sections in Chapter III

SEC. 301. [21 USC §331] Prohibited acts

Note: revisions were posted to this section in February 2008.

The following acts and the causing thereof are hereby prohibited: [1]

(a) The introduction or delivery for introduction into interstate commerce of any food, drug, device, or cosmetic that is adulterated or misbranded.

(b) The adulteration or misbranding of any food, drug, device, or cosmetic in interstate commerce.

---

[1] See footnote for section 403(h)(3) regarding the stylistic use of a list consisting of "(a)", "(b)", etc.

(c) The receipt in interstate commerce of any food, drug, device, or cosmetic that is adulterated or misbranded, and the delivery or proffered delivery thereof for pay or otherwise.

(d) The introduction or delivery for introduction into interstate commerce of any article in violation of section 404, 505 or 564.

(e) The refusal to permit access to or copying of any record as required by section 412, 414, 416, 417(g), 504, 564, 703, 704(a), 760, or 761; or the failure to establish or maintain any record, or make any report, required under section 412, 414(b), 416, 417, 504, 505(i) or (k), 512(a)(4)(C), 512 (j), (l) or (m), 572(i),[2] 515(f), 519, 564, 760, or 761 or the refusal to permit access to or verification or copying of any such required record.

(f) The refusal to permit entry or inspection as authorized by section 704.

(g) The manufacture, within any Territory of any food, drug, device, or cosmetic that is adulterated or misbranded.

(h) The giving of a guaranty or undertaking referred to in section 303(c)(2), which guaranty or undertaking is false, except by a person who relied upon a guaranty or undertaking to the same effect signed by, containing the name and address of, the person residing in the United States from whom he received in good faith the food, drug, device, or cosmetic; or the giving of a guaranty or undertaking referred to in section 303(c)(3), which guaranty or undertaking is false.

(i) (1) Forging, counterfeiting, simulating, or falsely representing, or without proper authority using any mark, stamp, tag, label, or other identification device authorized or required by regulations promulgated under the provisions of section 404 or 721.

(2) Making, selling, disposing of, or keeping in possession, control, or custody, or concealing any punch, die, plate, stone, or other thing designed to print, imprint, or reproduce the trademark, trade name, or other identifying mark, imprint, or device of another or any likeness of any of the foregoing upon any drug or container or labeling thereof so as to render such drug a counterfeit drug.

(3) The doing of any act which causes a drug to be a counterfeit drug, or the sale or dispensing, or the holding for sale or dispensing, of a counterfeit drug.

(j) The using by any person to his own advantage or revealing, other than to the Secretary or officers or employees of the Department, or to the courts when relevant in any judicial proceeding under this Act, any information acquired under

[2] The period is so in law. See section 102(b)(5)(C) of Public Law 108-282

authority of section 404, 409, 412, 414, 505, 510, 512, 513, 514, 515, 516, 518, 519, 520, 571, 572, 573, [3] 704, 708, or 721 concerning any method or process which as a trade secret is entitled to protection; or the violating of section 408(i)(2) or any regulation issued under that section.[4] This paragraph does not authorize the withholding of information from either House of Congress or from, to the extent of matter within its jurisdiction, any committee or subcommittee of such committee or any joint committee of Congress or any subcommittee of such joint committee.

(k) The alteration, mutilation, destruction, obliteration, or removal of the whole or any part of the labeling of, or the doing of any other act with respect to, a food, drug, device, or cosmetic, if such act is done while such article is held for sale (whether or not the first sale) after shipment in interstate commerce and results in such article being adulterated or misbranded.

(l) [Deleted] [5]

(m) The sale or offering for sale of colored oleomargarine or colored margarine, or the possession or serving of colored oleomargarine or colored margarine in violation of sections 407(b) or 407(c).

(n) The using, in labeling, advertising or other sales promotion of any reference to any report or analysis furnished in compliance with section 704.

(o) In the case of a prescription drug distributed or offered for sale in interstate commerce, the failure of the manufacturer, packer, or distributor thereof to maintain for transmittal, or to transmit, to any practitioner licensed by applicable State law to administer such drug who makes written request for information as to such drug, true and correct copies of all printed matter which is required to be included in any package in which that drug is distributed or sold, or such other printed matter as is approved by the Secretary. Nothing in this paragraph shall be construed to exempt any person from any labeling requirement imposed by or under other provisions of this Act .

(p) The failure to register in accordance with section 510, the failure to provide any information required by section 510(j) or 510(k), 21 USC § 360(j) or (k)] or the failure to provide a notice required by section 510(j)(2).

(q)(1) The failure or refusal to (A) comply with any requirement prescribed under section 518 or 520(g), (B) furnish any notification or other material or information

[3] The period is so in law. See section 102f(b)(5)(D) of Public Law 108-282.
[4] So in law. See the amendment made by section 403 of Public Law 104–170 (110 Stat. 1514).
[5] Paragraph (l) was struck by section 421 of Public Law 105–115 (111 Stat. 2380).

required by or under section 519 or 520(g), or (C) comply with a requirement under section 522.

(2) With respect to any device, the submission of any report that is required by or under this Act that is false or misleading in any material respect.

(r) The movement of a device in violation of an order under section 304(g) or the removal or alteration of any mark or label required by the order to identify the device as detained.

(s) The failure to provide the notice required by section 412(c) or 412(e), the failure to make the reports required by section 412(f)(1)(B), the failure to retain the records required by section 412(b)(4), or the failure to meet the requirements prescribed under section 412(f)(3).

(t) The importation of a drug in violation of section 801(d)(1) , the sale, purchase, or trade of a drug or drug sample or the offer to sell, purchase, or trade a drug or drug sample in violation of section 503(c), the sale, purchase, or trade of a coupon, the offer to sell, purchase, or trade such a coupon, or the counterfeiting of such a coupon in violation of section 503(c)(2), the distribution of a drug sample in violation of section 503(d) or the failure to otherwise comply with the requirements of section 503(d), or the distribution of drugs in violation of section 503(e) or the failure to otherwise comply with the requirements of section 503(e).

(u) The failure to comply with any requirements of the provisions of, or any regulations or orders of the Secretary, under section 512(a)(4)(A), 512(a)(4)(D), or 512(a)(5).

(v) The introduction or delivery for introduction into interstate commerce of a dietary supplement that is unsafe under section 413.

(w) The making of a knowingly false statement in any statement, certificate of analysis, record, or report required or requested under section 801(d)(3); the failure to submit a certificate of analysis as required under such section; the failure to maintain records or to submit records or reports as required by such section; the release into interstate commerce of any article or portion thereof imported into the United States under such section or any finished product made from such article or portion, except for export in accordance with section 801(e) or 802, or with section 351(h) of the Public Health Service Act [42 USC § 262(h)]; or the failure to so export or to destroy such an article or portions thereof, or such a finished product.

(x) The falsification of a declaration of conformity submitted under section 514(c) or the failure or refusal to provide data or information requested by the Secretary under paragraph (3) of such section.

(y) In the case of a drug, device, or food –

(1) the submission of a report or recommendation by a person accredited under section 523 that is false or misleading in any material respect;

(2) the disclosure by a person accredited under section 523 of confidential commercial information or any trade secret without the express written consent of the person who submitted such information or secret to such person; or

(3) the receipt by a person accredited under section 523 of a bribe in any form or the doing of any corrupt act by such person associated with a responsibility delegated to such person under this Act.

(z) [Terminated] [6]

(aa) The importation of a prescription drug in violation of section 804, the falsification of any record required to be maintained or provided to the Secretary under section, or any other violation of regulations under such section.

(bb) The transfer of an article of food in violation of an order under section 304(h), or the removal or alteration of any mark or label required by the order to identify the article as detained.

(cc) The importing or offering for import into the United States of an article of food by, with the assistance of, or at the direction of, a person debarred under section 306(b)(3).

(dd) The failure to register in accordance with section 415.

(ee) The importing or offering for import into the United States of an article of food in violation of the requirements under section 801(m).

(ff) The importing or offering for import into the United States of a drug or device with respect to which there is a failure to comply with a request of the Secretary to submit to the Secretary a statement under section 801(o).

(gg) The knowing failure to comply with paragraph (7)(E) of section 704(g); the knowing inclusion by a person accredited under paragraph (2) of such section of

[6] Paragraph (z) was added by subsection (b) of section 401(b) of Public Law 105–115 (111 Stat. 2364). Subsection (e) of such section provides as follows:

(e) SUNSET.—The amendments made by this section cease to be effective September 30, 2006, or 7 years after the date on which the Secretary promulgates the regulations described in subsection (c), whichever is later.

false information in an inspection report under paragraph (7)(A) of such section; or the knowing failure of such a person to include material facts in such a report.

(hh) The failure by a shipper, carrier by motor vehicle or rail vehicle, receiver, or any other person engaged in the transportation of food to comply with the sanitary transportation practices prescribed by the Secretary under section 416.

(ii) The falsification of a report of a serious adverse event submitted to a responsible person (as defined under section 760 or 761) or the falsification of a serious adverse event report (as defined under section 760 or 761) submitted to the Secretary.

(jj) (1) The failure to submit the certification required by section 402(j)(5)(B) of the Public Health Service Act [42 USC § 282(j)(5)(B)], or knowingly submitting a false certification under such section.

(2) The failure to submit clinical trial information required under subsection (j) of section 402 of the Public Health Service Act [42 USC § 282].

(3) The submission of clinical trial information under subsection (j) of section 402 of the Public Health Service Act [42 USC § 282] that is false or misleading in any particular under paragraph (5)(D) of such subsection (j).

(kk) [Note: This subsection takes effect 180 days after enactment of Act Sept. 27, 2007, P.L. 110-85, as provided by § 909(a) of such Act, which appears as a note to this section.] The dissemination of a television advertisement without complying with section 503B [21 USC § 353b].

(ll) The introduction or delivery for introduction into interstate commerce of any food to which has been added a drug approved under section 505 [21 USC § 355], a biological product licensed under section 351 of the Public Health Service Act [42 USC § 262], or a drug or a biological product for which substantial clinical investigations have been instituted and for which the existence of such investigations has been made public, unless--

(1) such drug or such biological product was marketed in food before any approval of the drug under section 505 [21 USC § 355], before licensure of the biological product under such section 351 [42 USC § 262], and before any substantial clinical investigations involving the drug or the biological product have been instituted;

(2) the Secretary, in the Secretary's discretion, has issued a regulation, after notice and comment, approving the use of such drug or such biological product in the food;

(3) the use of the drug or the biological product in the food is to enhance the safety of the food to which the drug or the biological product is added or

applied and not to have independent biological or therapeutic effects on humans, and the use is in conformity with--

(A) a regulation issued under section 409 [21 USC § 348] prescribing conditions of safe use in food;

(B) a regulation listing or affirming conditions under which the use of the drug or the biological product in food is generally recognized as safe;

(C) the conditions of use identified in a notification to the Secretary of a claim of exemption from the premarket approval requirements for food additives based on the notifier's determination that the use of the drug or the biological product in food is generally recognized as safe, provided that the Secretary has not questioned the general recognition of safety determination in a letter to the notifier;

(D) a food contact substance notification that is effective under section 409(h) [21 USC § 348(h)]; or

(E) such drug or biological product had been marketed for smoking cessation prior to the date of the enactment of the Food and Drug Administration Amendments Act of 2007 [enacted Sept. 27, 2007]; or

(4) the drug is a new animal drug whose use is not unsafe under section 512 [21 USC § 360b].

(mm) The failure to submit a report or provide a notification required under section 417(d) [21 USC § 350f(d)].

(nn) The falsification of a report or notification required under section 417(d) [21 USC § 350f(d)].

SEC. 302. [21 USC §332] Injunction proceedings

(a) The district courts of the United States and the United States courts of the Territories shall have jurisdiction, for cause shown [7] to restrain violations of section 301, except paragraphs (h), (i), and (j).

(b) In case of violation of an injunction or restraining order issued under this section, which also constitutes a violation of this Act, trial shall be by the court, or, upon demand of the accused, by a jury.

SEC. 303. [21 USC §333] Penalties

Note: revisions were posted to this section in February 2008.

[Note: See prospective amendment note below.]

[7] So in law. Probably should be followed by a comma.

(a) Violation of 21 USC § 331; second violation; intent to defraud or mislead.

(1) Any person who violates a provision of section 301 shall be imprisoned for not more than one year or fined not more than $1,000, or both.

(2) Notwithstanding the provisions of paragraph (1) of this section, if any person commits such a violation after a conviction of him under this section has become final, or commits such a violation with the intent to defraud or mislead, such person shall be imprisoned for not more than three years or fined not more than $10,000 or both.

(b) Prescription drug market violations

(1) Notwithstanding subsection (a), any person who violates section 301(t) by—

(A) knowingly importing a drug in violation of section 801(d)(1),

(B) knowingly selling, purchasing, or trading a drug or drug sample or knowingly offering to sell, purchase, or trade a drug or drug sample, in violation of section 503(c)(1),

(C) knowingly selling, purchasing, or trading a coupon, knowingly offering to sell, purchase, or trade such a coupon, or knowingly counterfeiting such a coupon, in violation of section 503(c)(2), or

(D) knowingly distributing drugs in violation of section 503(e)(2)(A),

shall be imprisoned for not more than 10 years or fined not more than $250,000, or both.

(2) Any manufacturer or distributor who distributes drug samples by means other than the mail or common carrier whose representative, during the course of the representative's employment or association with that manufacturer or distributor, violated section 301(t) because of a violation of section 503(c)(1) or violated any State law prohibiting the sale, purchase, or trade of a drug sample subject to section 503(b) or the offer to sell, purchase, or trade such a drug sample shall, upon conviction of the representative for such violation, be subject to the following civil penalties:

(A) A civil penalty of not more than $50,000 for each of the first two such violations resulting in a conviction of any representative of the manufacturer or distributor in any 10-year period.

(B) A civil penalty of not more than $1,000,000 for each violation resulting in a conviction of any representative after the second conviction in any 10-year period.

For the purposes of this paragraph, multiple convictions of one or more persons arising out of the same event or transaction, or a related series of events or transactions, shall be considered as one violation.

(3) Any manufacturer or distributor who violates section 301(t) because of a failure to make a report required by section 503(d)(3)(E) shall be subject to a civil penalty of not more than $100,000.

(4)(A) If a manufacturer or distributor or any representative of such manufacturer or distributor provides information leading to the institution of a criminal proceeding against, and conviction of, any representative of that manufacturer or distributor for a violation of section 301(t) because of a sale, purchase, or trade or offer to purchase, sell, or trade a drug sample in violation of section 503(c)(1) or for a violation of State law prohibiting the sale, purchase, or trade or offer to sell, purchase, or trade a drug sample, the conviction of such representative shall not be considered as a violation for purposes of paragraph (2).

(B) If, in an action brought under paragraph (2) against a manufacturer or distributor relating to the conviction of a representative of such manufacturer or distributor for the sale, purchase, or trade of a drug or the offer to sell, purchase, or trade a drug, it is shown, by clear and convincing evidence—

(i) that the manufacturer or distributor conducted, before the institution of a criminal proceeding against such representative for the violation which resulted in such conviction, an investigation of events or transactions which would have led to the reporting of information leading to the institution of a criminal proceeding against, and conviction of, such representative for such purchase, sale, or trade or offer to purchase, sell, or trade, or

(ii) that, except in the case of the conviction of a representative employed in a supervisory function, despite diligent implementation by the manufacturer or distributor of an independent audit and security system designed to detect such a violation, the manufacturer or distributor could not reasonably have been expected to have detected such violation, the conviction of such representative shall not be considered as a conviction for purposes of paragraph (2).

(5) If a person provides information leading to the institution of a criminal proceeding against, and conviction of, a person for a violation of section 301(t) because of the sale, purchase, or trade of a drug sample or the offer to sell, purchase, or trade a drug sample in violation of section 503(c)(1), such person shall be entitled to one-half of the criminal fine imposed and collected for such violation but not more than $125,000.

(6) Notwithstanding subsection (a), any person who is a manufacturer or importer of a prescription drug under section 804(b) and knowingly fails to comply with a requirement of section 804(e) that is applicable to such manufacturer or importer, respectively, shall be imprisoned for not more than 10 years or fined not more than $250,000, or both.

(c) Exceptions in certain cases of good faith, etc. No person shall be subject to the penalties of subsection (a)(1) of this section, (1) for having received in interstate commerce any article and delivered it or proffered delivery of it, if such delivery or proffer was made in good faith, unless he refuses to furnish on request of an officer or employee duly designated by the Secretary the name and address of the person from whom he purchased or received such article and copies of all documents, if any there be, pertaining to the delivery of the article to him; or (2) for having violated section 301(a) or (d), if he establishes a guaranty or undertaking signed by, and containing the name and address of, the person residing in the United States from whom he received in good faith the article, to the effect, in case of an alleged violation of section 301(a), that such article is not adulterated or misbranded, within the meaning of this Act, designating this Act, or to the effect, in case of an alleged violation of section 301(d), that such article is not an article which may not, under the provisions of section 404 or 505, be introduced into interstate commerce; or (3) for having violated section 301(a), where the violation exists because the article is adulterated by reason of containing a color additive not from a batch certified in accordance with regulations promulgated by the Secretary under this Act, if such person establishes a guaranty or undertaking signed by, and containing the name and address of, the manufacturer of the color additive, to the effect that such color additive was from a batch certified in accordance with the applicable regulations promulgated by the Secretary under this Act; or (4) for having violated section 301 (b), (c), or (k) by failure to comply with section 502(f) in respect to an article received in interstate commerce to which neither section 503(a) nor section 503(b)(1) is applicable, if the delivery or proffered delivery was made in good faith and the labeling at the time thereof contained the same directions for use and warning statements as were contained in the labeling at the time of such receipt of such article; or (5) for having violated section 301(i)(2) if such person acted in good faith and had no reason to believe that use of the punch, die, plate, stone, or other thing involved would result in a drug being a counterfeit drug, or for having violated section 301(i)(3) if the person doing the act or causing it to be done acted in good faith and had no reason to believe that the drug was a counterfeit drug.

(d) Exceptions involving misbranded food. No person shall be subject to the penalties of subsection (a)(1) of this section for a violation of section 301 involving misbranded food if the violation exists solely because the food is misbranded under section 403(a)(2) because of its advertising.

(e) Prohibited distribution of human growth hormone.

(1) Except as provided in paragraph (2), whoever knowingly distributes, or possesses with intent to distribute, human growth hormone for any use in humans other than the treatment of a disease or other recognized medical condition, where such use has been authorized by the Secretary of Health and Human Services under section 505 and pursuant to the order of a

physician, is guilty of an offense punishable by not more than 5 years in prison, such fines as are authorized by title 18, United States Code, or both.

(2) Whoever commits any offense set forth in paragraph (1) and such offense involves an individual under 18 years of age is punishable by not more than 10 years imprisonment, such fines as are authorized by title 18, United States Code, or both.

(3) Any conviction for a violation of paragraphs (1) and (2) of this subsection shall be considered a felony violation of the Controlled Substances Act for the purposes of forfeiture under section 413 of such Act.

(4) As used in this subsection the term "human growth hormone" means somatrem, somatropin, or an analogue of either of them.

(5) The Drug Enforcement Administration is authorized to investigate offenses punishable by this subsection.

(f) Violations related to devices.

(1)(A) 8 Except as provided in subparagraph (B), any person who violates a requirement of this Act which relates to devices shall be liable to the United States for a civil penalty in an amount not to exceed $15,000 for each such violation, and not to exceed $1,000,000 for all such violations adjudicated in a single proceeding. For purposes of the preceding sentence, a person accredited under paragraph (2) of section 704(g) who is substantially not in compliance with the standards of accreditation under such section, or who poses a threat to public health or fails to act in a manner that is consistent with the purposes of such section, shall be considered to have violated a requirement of this Act that relates to devices.

(B) Subparagraph (A) shall not apply—

(i) to any person who violates the requirements of section 519(a) or 520(f) unless such violation constitutes (I) a significant or knowing departure from such requirements, or (II) a risk to public health,

(ii) to any person who commits minor violations of section 519(e) or 519(g) (only with respect to correction reports) if such person demonstrates substantial compliance with such section, or

(iii) to violations of section 501(a)(2)(A) which involve one or more devices which are not defective.

(2)(A) Any person who introduces into interstate commerce or delivers for introduction into interstate commerce an article of food that is adulterated within the meaning of section 402(a)(2)(B) shall be subject to a civil money penalty of not more than $50,000 in the case of an individual and $250,000 in the case of any other person for such introduction or delivery, not to exceed $500,000 for all such violations adjudicated in a single proceeding.

(B) This paragraph shall not apply to any person who grew the article of food that is adulterated. If the Secretary assesses a civil penalty against any person under this paragraph, the Secretary may not use the criminal authorities under this section to sanction such person for the introduction or delivery for introduction into interstate commerce of the article of food that is adulterated. If the Secretary assesses a civil penalty against any person under this paragraph, the Secretary may not use the seizure authorities of section 304 or the injunction authorities of section 302 with respect to the article of food that is adulterated.

(C) In a hearing to assess a civil penalty under this paragraph, the presiding officer shall have the same authority with regard to compelling testimony or production of documents as a presiding officer has under section 408(g)(2)(B). The third sentence of paragraph (5)(A) shall not apply to any investigation under this paragraph.

(3)(A) Any person who violates section 301(jj) [21 USC § 331(jj)] shall be subject to a civil monetary penalty of not more than $ 10,000 for all violations adjudicated in a single proceeding.

(B) If a violation of section 301(jj) [21 USC § 331(jj)] is not corrected within the 30-day period following notification under section 402(j)(5)(C)(ii) [21 USC § 342(j)(5)(C)(ii)], the person shall, in addition to any penalty under subparagraph (A), be subject to a civil monetary penalty of not more than $ 10,000 for each day of the violation after such period until the violation is corrected.

(4) [Note: This paragraph takes effect 180 days after enactment of Act Sept. 27, 2007, P.L. 110-85, as provided by § 909(a) of such Act, which appears as 21 USC § 331 note.]

(A) Any responsible person (as such term is used in section 505-1 [21 USC § 355-1]) that violates a requirement of section 505(o), 505(p), or 505-1 [21 USC § 355(o), 355(p), or 355-1] shall be subject to a civil monetary penalty of--

(i) not more than $ 250,000 per violation, and not to exceed $ 1,000,000 for all such violations adjudicated in a single proceeding; or

(ii) in the case of a violation that continues after the Secretary provides written notice to the responsible person, the responsible person shall be subject to a civil monetary penalty of $ 250,000 for the first 30-day period (or any portion thereof) that the responsible person continues to be in violation, and such amount shall double for every 30-day period thereafter that the violation continues, not to exceed $ 1,000,000 for any 30-day period, and not to exceed $ 10,000,000 for all such violations adjudicated in a single proceeding.

(B) In determining the amount of a civil penalty under subparagraph (A)(ii), the Secretary shall take into consideration whether the responsible person is making efforts toward correcting the violation of the requirement of section 505(o), 505(p), or 505-1 [21 USC § 355(o), 355(p), or 355-1] for which the responsible person is subject to such civil penalty.

(5) (A) A civil penalty under paragraph (1), (2), or (3) shall be assessed by the Secretary by an order made on the record after opportunity for a hearing provided in accordance with this subparagraph and section 554 of title 5, United States Code. Before issuing such an order, the Secretary shall give written notice to the person to be assessed a civil penalty under such order of the Secretary's proposal to issue such order and provide such person an opportunity for a hearing on the order. In the course of any investigation, the Secretary may issue subpoenas requiring the attendance and testimony of witnesses and the production of evidence that relates to the matter under investigation.

(B) In determining the amount of a civil penalty, the Secretary shall take into account the nature, circumstances, extent, and gravity of the violation or violations and, with respect to the violator, ability to pay, effect on ability to continue to do business, any history of prior such violations, the degree of culpability, and such other matters as justice may require.

(C) The Secretary may compromise, modify, or remit, with or without conditions, any civil penalty which may be assessed under paragraph (1), (2), or (3). The amount of such penalty, when finally determined, or the amount agreed upon in compromise, may be deducted from any sums owing by the United States to the person charged.

(6) Any person who requested, in accordance with paragraph (5)(A), a hearing respecting the assessment of a civil penalty and who is aggrieved by an order assessing a civil penalty may file a petition for judicial review of such order with the United States Court of Appeals for the District of Columbia Circuit or for any other circuit in which such person resides or transacts business. Such a petition may only be filed within the 60-day period beginning on the date the order making such assessment was issued.

(7) If any person fails to pay an assessment of a civil penalty—

(A) after the order making the assessment becomes final, and if such person does not file a petition for judicial review of the order in accordance with paragraph (6), or

(B) after a court in an action brought under paragraph (6) has entered a final judgment in favor of the Secretary, the Attorney General shall recover the amount assessed (plus interest at currently prevailing rates from the date of the expiration of the 60-day period referred to in paragraph (6) or the date of such final judgment, as the case may be) in an action brought in any appropriate district court of the United States. In such an action, the validity, amount, and appropriateness of such penalty shall not be subject to review.

(g) [Note: This subsection takes effect 180 days after enactment of Act Sept. 27, 2007, P.L. 110-85, as provided by § 909(a) of such Act, which appears as 21 USC § 331 note.]

(1) With respect to a person who is a holder of an approved application under section 505 [21 USC § 355] for a drug subject to section 503(b) [21 USC § 353(b)] or under section 351 of the Public Health Service Act [42 USC § 262], any such person who disseminates or causes another party to disseminate a direct-to-consumer advertisement that is false or misleading shall be liable to the United States for a civil penalty in an amount not to exceed $ 250,000 for the first such violation in any 3-year period, and not to exceed $ 500,000 for each subsequent violation in any 3-year period. No other civil monetary penalties in this Act (including the civil penalty in section 303(f)(4) [subsec. (f)(4) of this section]) shall apply to a violation regarding direct-to-consumer advertising. For purposes of this paragraph: (A) Repeated dissemination of the same or similar advertisement prior to the receipt of the written notice referred to in paragraph (2) for such advertisements shall be considered one violation. (B) On and after the date of the receipt of such a notice, all violations under this paragraph occurring in a single day shall be considered one violation. With respect to advertisements that appear in magazines or other publications that are published less frequently than daily, each issue date (whether weekly or monthly) shall be treated as a single day for the purpose of calculating the number of violations under this paragraph.

(2) A civil penalty under paragraph (1) shall be assessed by the Secretary by an order made on the record after providing written notice to the person to be assessed a civil penalty and an opportunity for a hearing in accordance with this paragraph and section 554 of title 5, United States Code. If upon receipt of the written notice, the person to be assessed a civil penalty objects and requests a hearing, then in the course of any investigation related to such hearing, the Secretary may issue subpoenas requiring the attendance and testimony of witnesses and the production of evidence that relates to the matter under investigation, including information pertaining to the factors described in paragraph (3).

(3) The Secretary, in determining the amount of the civil penalty under paragraph (1), shall take into account the nature, circumstances, extent, and gravity of the violation or violations, including the following factors:

(A) Whether the person submitted the advertisement or a similar advertisement for review under section 736A [21 USC § 379h-1].

(B) Whether the person submitted the advertisement for review if required under section 503B [21 USC § 353b].

(C) Whether, after submission of the advertisement as described in subparagraph (A) or (B), the person disseminated or caused another party to disseminate the advertisement before the end of the 45-day comment period.

(D) Whether the person incorporated any comments made by the Secretary with regard to the advertisement into the advertisement prior to its dissemination.

(E) Whether the person ceased distribution of the advertisement upon receipt of the written notice referred to in paragraph (2) for such advertisement.

(F) Whether the person had the advertisement reviewed by qualified medical, regulatory, and legal reviewers prior to its dissemination.

(G) Whether the violations were material.

(H) Whether the person who created the advertisement or caused the advertisement to be created acted in good faith.

(I) Whether the person who created the advertisement or caused the advertisement to be created has been assessed a civil penalty under this provision within the previous 1-year period.

(J) The scope and extent of any voluntary, subsequent remedial action by the person.

(K) Such other matters, as justice may require.

(4) (A) Subject to subparagraph (B), no person shall be required to pay a civil penalty under paragraph (1) if the person submitted the advertisement to the Secretary and disseminated or caused another party to disseminate such advertisement after incorporating each comment received from the Secretary.

(B) The Secretary may retract or modify any prior comments the Secretary has provided to an advertisement submitted to the Secretary based on new information or changed circumstances, so long as the Secretary provides written notice to the person of the new views of the Secretary on the advertisement and provides a reasonable time for modification or correction of the advertisement prior to seeking any civil penalty under paragraph (1).

(5) The Secretary may compromise, modify, or remit, with or without conditions, any civil penalty which may be assessed under paragraph (1). The amount of such penalty, when finally determined, or the amount charged upon in compromise, may be deducted from any sums owed by the United States to the person charged.

(6) Any person who requested, in accordance with paragraph (2), a hearing with respect to the assessment of a civil penalty and who is aggrieved by an order assessing a civil penalty, may file a petition for de novo judicial review of such order with the United States Court of Appeals for the District of Columbia Circuit or for any other circuit in which such person resides or transacts business. Such a petition may only be filed within the 60-day period beginning on the date the order making such assessments was issued.

(7) If any person fails to pay an assessment of a civil penalty under paragraph (1)--

(A) after the order making the assessment becomes final, and if such person does not file a petition for judicial review of the order in accordance with paragraph (6), or

(B) after a court in an action brought under paragraph (6) has entered a final judgment in favor of the Secretary, the Attorney General of the United States shall recover the amount assessed (plus interest at currently prevailing rates from the date of the expiration of the 60-day period referred to in paragraph (6) or the date of such final judgment, as the case may be) in an action brought in any appropriate district court of the United States. In such an action, the validity, amount, and appropriateness of such penalty shall not be subject to review.

SEC. 304. [21 USC §334] Seizure

(a) Grounds and jurisdiction.

(1) Any article of food, drug, or cosmetic that is adulterated or misbranded when introduced into or while in interstate commerce or while held for sale (whether or not the first sale) after shipment in interstate commerce, or which may not, under the provisions of section 301(ll), 404 or 505, be introduced into interstate commerce, shall be liable to be proceeded against while in interstate commerce, or at any time thereafter, on libel of information and condemned in any district court of the United States or United States court of a Territory within the jurisdiction of which the article is found. No libel for condemnation shall be instituted under this Act, for any alleged misbranding if there is pending in any court a libel for condemnation proceeding under this Act based upon the same alleged misbranding, and not more than one such proceeding shall be instituted if no such proceeding is so pending, except that such limitations shall not apply (A) when such misbranding has been the basis of a prior judgment in favor of the United States, in a criminal, injunction, or libel for condemnation proceeding under this Act, or (B) when the Secretary has probable cause to believe from facts found, without hearing, by him or any officer or employee of the Department that the misbranded article is dangerous to health, or that the labeling of the misbranded article is fraudulent, or would be in a material

respect misleading to the injury or damage of the purchaser or consumer. In any case where the number of libel for condemnation proceedings is limited as above provided the proceeding pending or instituted shall, on application of the claimant, seasonably made, be removed for trial to any district agreed upon by stipulation between the parties, or, in case of failure to so stipulate within a reasonable time, the claimant may apply to the court of the district in which the seizure has been made, and such court (after giving the United States attorney for such district reasonable notice and opportunity to be heard) shall by order, unless good cause to the contrary is shown, specify a district of reasonable proximity to the claimant's principal place of business, to which the case shall be removed for trial.

(2) The following shall be liable to be proceeded against at any time on libel of information and condemned in any district court of the United States or United States court of a Territory within the jurisdiction of which they are found: (A) Any drug that is a counterfeit drug, (B) Any container of a counterfeit drug, (C) Any punch, die, plate, stone, labeling, container, or other thing used or designed for use in making a counterfeit drug or drugs, and (D) Any adulterated or misbranded device.

(3)(A) Except as provided in subparagraph (B), no libel for condemnation may be instituted under paragraph (1) or (2) against any food which -

(i) is misbranded under section 403(a)(2) because of its advertising, and

(ii) is being held for sale to the ultimate consumer in an establishment other than an establishment owned or operated by a manufacturer, packer, or distributor of the food.

(B) A libel for condemnation may be instituted under paragraph (1) or (2) against a food described in subparagraph (A) if –

(i)(I) the food's advertising which resulted in the food being misbranded under section 403(a)(2) was disseminated in the establishment in which the food is being held for sale to the ultimate consumer,

(II) such advertising was disseminated by, or under the direction of, the owner or operator of such establishment, or

(III) all or part of the cost of such advertising was paid by such owner or operator; and

(ii) the owner or operator of such establishment used such advertising in the establishment to promote the sale of the food.

(b) Procedure; multiplicity of pending proceedings. The article, equipment, or other thing proceeded against shall be liable to seizure by process pursuant to the libel, and the procedure in cases under this section shall conform, as nearly as may be, to the procedure in admiralty; except that on demand of either party any issue of fact joined in any such case shall be tried by jury. When libel for condemnation

Chapter III

proceedings under this section, involving the same claimant and the same issues of adulteration or misbranding, are pending in two or more jurisdictions, such pending proceedings, upon application of the claimant seasonably made to the court of one such jurisdiction, shall be consolidated for trial by order of such court, and tried in (1) any district selected by the claimant where one of such proceedings is pending; or (2) a district agreed upon by stipulation between the parties. If no order for consolidation is so made within a reasonable time, the claimant may apply to the court of one such jurisdiction, and such court (after giving the United States attorney for such district reasonable notice and opportunity to be heard) shall by order, unless good cause to the contrary is shown, specify a district of reasonable proximity to the claimant's principal place of business, in which all such pending proceedings shall be consolidated for trial and tried. Such order of consolidation shall not apply so as to require the removal of any case the date for trial of which has been fixed. The court granting such order shall give prompt notification thereof to the other courts having jurisdiction of the cases covered thereby.

(c) Availability of samples of seized goods prior to trial. The court at any time after seizure up to a reasonable time before trial shall by order allow any party to a condemnation proceeding, his attorney or agent, to obtain a representative sample of the article seized and a true copy of the analysis, if any, on which the proceeding is based and the identifying marks or numbers, if any, of the packages from which the samples analyzed were obtained.

(d) Disposition of goods after decree of condemnation; claims for remission or mitigation of forfeitures.

(1) Any food, drug, device, or cosmetic condemned under this section shall, after entry of the decree, be disposed of by destruction or sale as the court may, in accordance with the provisions of this section, direct and the proceeds thereof, if sold, less the legal costs and charges, shall be paid into the Treasury of the United States; but such article shall not be sold under such decree contrary to the provisions of this Act or the laws of the jurisdiction in which sold. After entry of the decree and upon the payment of the costs of such proceedings and the execution of a good and sufficient bond conditioned that such article shall not be sold or disposed of contrary to the provisions of this Act or the laws of any State or Territory in which sold, the court may by order direct that such article be delivered to the owner thereof to be destroyed or brought into compliance with the provisions of this Act, under the supervision of an officer or employee duly designated by the Secretary, and the expenses of such supervision shall be paid by the person obtaining release of the article under bond. If the article was imported into the United States and the person seeking its release establishes (A) that the adulteration, misbranding, or violation did not occur after the article was imported, and (B) that he had no cause for believing that it was adulterated,

misbranded, or in violation before it was released from customs custody, the court may permit the article to be delivered to the owner for exportation in lieu of destruction upon a showing by the owner that all of the conditions of section 801(e) can and will be met. The provisions of this sentence shall not apply where condemnation is based upon violation of section 402(a)(1), (2), or (6), section 501(a)(3), section 502(j), or section 601(a) or (d). Where such exportation is made to the original foreign supplier, then subparagraphs (A) and (B) of section 801(e) and the preceding sentence shall not be applicable; and in all cases of exportation the bond shall be conditioned that the article shall not be sold or disposed of until the applicable conditions of section 801(e) have been met. Any person seeking to export an imported article pursuant to any of the provisions of this subsection shall establish that the article was intended for export at the time the article entered commerce. Any article condemned by reason of its being an article which may not, under section 404 or 505, be introduced into interest to commerce, shall be disposed of by destruction.

(2) The provisions of paragraph (1) of this subsection shall, to the extent deemed appropriate by the court, apply to any equipment or other thing which is not otherwise within the scope of such paragraph and which is referred to in paragraph (2) of subsection (a).

(3) Whenever in any proceeding under this section, involving paragraph (2) of subsection (a), the condemnation of any equipment or thing (other than a drug) is decreed, the court shall allow the claim of any claimant, to the extent of such claimant's interest, for remission or mitigation of such forfeiture if such claimant proves to the satisfaction of the court (i) that he has not committed or caused to be committed any prohibited act referred to in such paragraph (2) and has no interest in any drug referred to therein, (ii) that he has an interest in such equipment or other thing as owner or lienor or otherwise, acquired by him in good faith, and (iii) that he at no time had any knowledge or reason to believe that such equipment or other thing was being or would be used in, or to facilitate, the violation of laws of the United States relating to counterfeit drugs.

(e) Costs. When a decree of condemnation is entered against the article, court costs and fees, and storage and other proper expenses, shall be awarded against the person, if any, intervening as claimant of the article.

(f) Removal of case for trial. In the case of removal for trial of any case as provided by subsection (a) or (b)--

(1) The clerk of the court from which removal is made shall promptly transmit to the court in which the case is to be tried all records in the case necessary in order that such court may exercise jurisdiction.

(2) The court to which such case was removed shall have the powers and be subject to the duties, for purposes of such case, which the court from which removal was made would have had, or to which such court would have been subject, if such case had not been removed.

(g) Administrative restraint; detention orders.

(1) If during an inspection conducted under section 704 of a facility or a vehicle, a device which the officer or employee making the inspection has reason to believe is adulterated or misbranded is found in such facility or vehicle, such officer or employee may order the device detained (in accordance with regulations prescribed by the Secretary) for a reasonable period which may not exceed twenty days unless the Secretary determines that a period of detention greater than twenty days is required to institute an action under subsection (a) or section 302, in which case he may authorize a detention period of not to exceed thirty days. Regulations of the Secretary prescribed under this paragraph shall require that before a device may be ordered detained under this paragraph the Secretary or an officer or employee designated by the Secretary approve such order. A detention order under this paragraph may require the labeling or marking of a device during the period of its detention for the purpose of identifying the device as detained. Any person who would be entitled to claim a device if it were seized under subsection (a) may appeal to the Secretary a detention of such device under this paragraph. Within five days of the date an appeal of a detention is filed with the Secretary, the Secretary shall after affording opportunity for an informal hearing by order confirm the detention or revoke it.

(2)(A) Except as authorized by subparagraph (B), a device subject to a detention order issued under paragraph (1) shall not be moved by any person from the place at which it is ordered detained until--

(i) released by the Secretary, or

(ii) the expiration of the detention period applicable to such order, whichever occurs first.

(B) A device subject to a detention order under paragraph (1) may be moved –

(i) in accordance with regulations prescribed by the Secretary, and

(ii) if not in final form for shipment, at the discretion of the manufacturer of the device for the purpose of completing the work required to put it in such form.

(h) Administrative detention of foods.

(1) Detention authority.

(A) In general. An officer or qualified employee of the Food and Drug Administration may order the detention, in accordance with this subsection, of any article of food that is found during an inspection, examination, or investigation under this Act conducted by such officer or qualified employee, if the officer or qualified employee has credible evidence or information indicating that such article presents a threat of serious adverse health consequences or death to humans or animals.

(B) Secretary's approval.--An article of food may be ordered detained under subparagraph (A) only if the Secretary or an official designated by the Secretary approves the order. An official may not be so designated unless the official is the director of the district under this Act in which the article involved is located, or is an official senior to such director.

(2) Period of detention. An article of food may be detained under paragraph (1) for a reasonable period, not to exceed 20 days, unless a greater period, not to exceed 30 days, is necessary, to enable the Secretary to institute an action under subsection (a) or section 302. The Secretary shall by regulation provide for procedures for instituting such action on an expedited basis with respect to perishable foods.

(3) Security of detained article. An order under paragraph (1) with respect to an article of food may require that such article be labeled or marked as detained, and shall require that the article be removed to a secure facility, as appropriate. An article subject to such an order shall not be transferred by any person from the place at which the article is ordered detained, or from the place to which the article is so removed, as the case may be, until released by the Secretary or until the expiration of the detention period applicable under such order, whichever occurs first. This subsection may not be construed as authorizing the delivery of the article pursuant to the execution of a bond while the article is subject to the order, and section 801(b) does not authorize the delivery of the article pursuant to the execution of a bond while the article is subject to the order.

(4) Appeal of detention order.

(A) In general. With respect to an article of food ordered detained under paragraph (1), any person who would be entitled to be a claimant for such article if the article were seized under subsection (a) may appeal the order to the Secretary. Within five days after such an appeal is filed, the Secretary, after providing opportunity for an informal hearing, shall confirm or terminate the order involved, and such confirmation by the Secretary shall be considered a final agency action for purposes of section 702 of title 5, United States Code. If during such five-day period the Secretary fails to provide such an opportunity, or to confirm or terminate such order, the order is deemed to be terminated.

(B) Effect of instituting court action. The process under subparagraph (A) for the appeal of an order under paragraph (1) terminates if the Secretary institutes an action under subsection (a) or section 302 regarding the article of food involved.

SEC. 305. [21 USC §335] Hearing Before Report of Criminal Violation

Before any violation of this Act is reported by the Secretary to any United States attorney for institution of a criminal proceeding, the person against whom such proceeding is contemplated shall be given appropriate notice and an opportunity to present his views, either orally or in writing, with regard to such contemplated proceeding.

SEC. 306. [21 USC §335a] Debarment, Temporary Denial of Approval, and Suspension

(a) MANDATORY DEBARMENT; CERTAIN DRUG APPLICATIONS. –

(1) CORPORATIONS, PARTNERSHIPS, AND ASSOCIATIONS. -- If the Secretary finds that a person other than an individual has been convicted, after the date of enactment of this section, of a felony under Federal law for conduct relating to the development or approval, including the process for development or approval, of any abbreviated drug application, the Secretary shall debar such person from submitting, or assisting in the submission of, any such application.

(2) INDIVIDUALS. -- If the Secretary finds that an individual has been convicted of a felony under Federal law for conduct –

(A) relating to the development or approval, including the process for development or approval, of any drug product, or

(B) otherwise relating to the regulation of any drug product under this Act, the Secretary shall debar such individual from providing services in any capacity to a person that has an approved or pending drug product application.

(b) Permissive Debarment; Certain Drug Applications; Food Imports.—

(1) IN GENERAL. -- The Secretary, on the Secretary's own initiative or in response to a petition, may, in accordance with paragraph (2), debar –

(A) a person other than an individual from submitting or assisting in the submission of any abbreviated drug application, or

(B) an individual from providing services in any capacity to a person that has an approved or pending drug product application. , or

(C) a person from importing an article of food or offering such an article for import into the United States.

(2) PERSONS SUBJECT TO Permissive debarment; certain drug applications. -- The following persons are subject to debarment under subparagraph (A) or (B) of paragraph (1):

(A) CORPORATIONS, PARTNERSHIPS, AND ASSOCIATIONS. -- Any person other than an individual that the Secretary finds has been convicted –

(i) for conduct that –

(I) relates to the development or approval, including the process for the development or approval, of any abbreviated drug application; and

(II) is a felony under Federal law (if the person was convicted before the date of enactment of this section), a misdemeanor under Federal law, or a felony under State law, or

(ii) of a conspiracy to commit, or aiding or abetting, a criminal offense described in clause (i) or a felony described in subsection (a)(1),

if the Secretary finds that the type of conduct which served as the basis for such conviction undermines the process for the regulation of drugs.

(B) INDIVIDUALS. –

(i) Any individual whom the Secretary finds has been convicted of –

(I) a misdemeanor under Federal law or a felony under State law for conduct relating to the development or approval, including the process for development or approval, of any drug product or otherwise relating to the regulation of drug products under this Act, or

(II) a conspiracy to commit, or aiding or abetting, such criminal offense or a felony described in subsection (a)(2),

if the Secretary finds that the type of conduct which served as the basis for such conviction undermines the process for the regulation of drugs.

(ii) Any individual whom the Secretary finds has been convicted of –

(I) a felony which is not described in subsection (a)(2) or clause (i) of this subparagraph and which involves bribery, payment of illegal gratuities, fraud, perjury, false statement, racketeering, blackmail, extortion, falsification or destruction of records, or interference with, obstruction of an investigation into, or prosecution of, any criminal offense, or

(II) a conspiracy to commit, or aiding or abetting, such felony,

If the Secretary finds, on the basis of the conviction of such individual and other information, that such individual has demonstrated a pattern of conduct sufficient to find that there is reason to believe that such individual may violate requirements under this Act relating to drug products.

(iii) Any individual whom the Secretary finds materially participated in acts that were the basis for a conviction for an offense described in subsection (a) or in clause (i) or (ii) for which a conviction was obtained, if the Secretary finds, on the basis of such participation and other information, that such individual has demonstrated a pattern of conduct sufficient to find that there is reason to believe that such individual may violate requirements under this Act relating to drug products.

(iv) Any high managerial agent whom the Secretary finds –

(I) worked for, or worked as a consultant for, the same person as another individual during the period in which such other individual took actions for which a felony conviction was obtained and which resulted in the debarment under subsection (a)(2), or clause (i), of such other individual,

(II) had actual knowledge of the actions described in subclause (I) of such other individual, or took action to avoid such actual knowledge, or failed to take action for the purpose of avoiding such actual knowledge,

(III) knew that the actions described in subclause (I) were violative of law, and

(IV) did not report such actions, or did not cause such actions to be reported, to an officer, employee, or agent of the Department or to an appropriate law enforcement officer, or failed to take other appropriate action that would have ensured that the process for the regulation of drugs was not undermined, within a reasonable time after such agent first knew of such actions,

if the Secretary finds that the type of conduct which served as the basis for such other individual's conviction undermines the process for the regulation of drugs.

(3) Persons subject to permissive debarment; food importation.--A person is subject to debarment under paragraph (1)(C) if--

(A) the person has been convicted of a felony for conduct relating to the importation into the United States of any food; or

(B) the person has engaged in a pattern of importing or offering for import adulterated food that presents a threat of serious adverse health consequences or death to humans or animals.

(4) STAY OF CERTAIN ORDERS. An order of the Secretary under clause (iii) or (iv) of paragraph (2)(B) shall not take effect until 30 days after the order has been issued.

(c) DEBARMENT PERIODS AND CONSIDERATIONS. --

(1) EFFECT OF DEBARMENT. -- The Secretary -

(A) shall not accept or review (other than in connection with an audit under this section) any abbreviated drug application submitted by or with the assistance of a person debarred under subsection (a)(1) or (b)(2)(A) during the period such person is debarred,

(B) shall, during the period of a debarment under subsection (a)(2) or (b)(2)(B), debar an individual from providing services in any capacity to a person that has an approved or pending drug product application and shall not accept or review (other than in connection with an audit under this section) an abbreviated drug application from such individual, and

(C) shall, if the Secretary makes the finding described in paragraph (6) or (7) of section 307(a), assess a civil penalty in accordance with section 307.

(2) DEBARMENT PERIODS. --

(A) IN GENERAL. -- The Secretary shall debar a person under subsection (a) or (b) for the following periods:

(i) The period of debarment of a person (other than an individual) under subsection (a)(1) shall not be less than 1 year or more than 10 years, but if an act leading to a subsequent debarment under subsection (a) occurs within 10 years after such person has been debarred under subsection (a)(1), the period of debarment shall be permanent.

(ii) The debarment of an individual under subsection (a)(2) shall be permanent.

(iii) The period of debarment of any person under paragraph (2) or (3) of subsection (b) shall not be more than 5 years. The Secretary may determine whether debarment periods shall run concurrently or consecutively in the case of a person debarred for multiple offenses.

(B) NOTIFICATION. -- Upon a conviction for an offense described in subsection (a) or (b) or upon execution of an agreement with the United States to plead guilty to such an offense, the person involved may notify the Secretary that the person acquiesces to debarment and such person's debarment shall commence upon such notification.

(3) CONSIDERATIONS. -- In determining the appropriateness and the period of a debarment of a person under subsection (b) and any period of

Chapter III

debarment beyond the minimum specified in subparagraph (A)(i) of paragraph (2), the Secretary shall consider where applicable -

(A) the nature and seriousness of any offense involved,

(B) the nature and extent of management participation in any offense involved, whether corporate policies and practices encouraged the offense, including whether inadequate institutional controls contributed to the offense,

(C) the nature and extent of voluntary steps to mitigate the impact on the public of any offense involved, including the recall or the discontinuation of the distribution of suspect drugs, full cooperation with any investigations (including the extent of disclosure to appropriate authorities of all wrongdoing), the relinquishing of profits on drug approvals fraudulently obtained, and any other actions taken to substantially limit potential or actual adverse effects on the public health,

(D) whether the extent to which changes in ownership, management, or operations have corrected the causes of any offense involved and provide reasonable assurances that the offense will not occur in the future,

(E) whether the person to be debarred is able to present adequate evidence that current production of drugs subject to abbreviated drug applications and all pending abbreviated drug applications are free of fraud or material false statements, and

(F) prior convictions under this Act or under other Acts involving matters within the jurisdiction of the Food and Drug Administration.

(d) TERMINATION OF DEBARMENT. --

(1) APPLICATION. -- Any person that is debarred under subsection (a) (other than a person permanently debarred) or any person that is debarred under subsection (b) of this section may apply to the Secretary for termination of the debarment under this subsection. Any information submitted to the Secretary under this paragraph does not constitute an amendment or supplement to pending or approved abbreviated drug applications.

(2) DEADLINE. -- The Secretary shall grant or deny any application respecting a debarment which is submitted under paragraph (1) within 180 days of the date the application is submitted.

(3) ACTION BY THE SECRETARY. –

(A) CORPORATIONS. --

(i) CONVICTION REVERSAL. -- If the conviction which served as the basis for the debarment of a person under subsection (a)(1) (b) or paragraph (2)(A) or (3) of subsection is reversed, the Secretary shall withdraw the order of debarment.

(ii) APPLICATION. -- Upon application submitted under paragraph (1), the Secretary shall terminate the debarment of a person if the Secretary finds that –

(I) changes in ownership, management, or operations have fully corrected the causes of the offense involved and provide reasonable assurances that the offense will not occur in the future, and

(II) in applicable cases, sufficient audits, conducted by the Food and Drug Administration or by independent experts acceptable to the Food and Drug Administration, demonstrate that pending applications and the development of drugs being tested before the submission of an application are free of fraud or material false statements.

In the case of persons debarred under subsection (a)(1), such termination shall take effect no earlier than the expiration of one year from the date of the debarment.

(B) INDIVIDUALS. –

(i) CONVICTION REVERSAL. -- If the conviction which served as the basis for the debarment of an individual under subsection (a)(2) or clause (i), (ii), (iii), or (iv) of subsection (b)(2)(B) or subsection (b)(3) is reversed, the Secretary shall withdraw the order of debarment.

(ii) APPLICATION. -- Upon application submitted under paragraph (1), the Secretary shall terminate the debarment of an individual who has been debarred under subsection (b)(2)(B) or subsection (b)(3) if such termination serves the interests of justice and adequately protects the integrity of the drug approval process or the food importation process, as the case may be.

(4) SPECIAL TERMINATION. –

(A) APPLICATION. -- Any person that is debarred under subsection (a)(1) (other than a person permanently debarred under subsection (c)(2)(A)(i)) or any individual who is debarred under subsection (a)(2) may apply to the Secretary for special termination of debarment under this subsection. Any information submitted to the Secretary under this subparagraph does not constitute an amendment or supplement to pending or approved abbreviated drug applications.

(B) CORPORATIONS. -- Upon an application submitted under subparagraph (A), the Secretary may take the action described in subparagraph (D) if the Secretary, after an informal hearing, finds that –

Chapter III

(i) the person making the application under subparagraph (A) has demonstrated that the felony conviction which was the basis for such person's debarment involved the commission of an offense which was not authorized, requested, commanded, performed, or recklessly tolerated by the board of directors or by a high managerial agent acting on behalf of the person within the scope of the board's or agent's office or employment,

(ii) all individuals who were involved in the commission of the offense or who knew or should have known of the offense have been removed from employment involving the development or approval of any drug subject to sections [8] 505,

(iii) the person fully cooperated with all investigations and promptly disclosed all wrongdoing to the appropriate authorities, and

(iv) the person acted to mitigate any impact on the public of any offense involved, including the recall, or the discontinuation of the distribution, of any drug with respect to which the Secretary requested a recall or discontinuation of distribution due to concerns about the safety or efficacy of the drug.

(C) INDIVIDUALS. -- Upon an application submitted under subparagraph (A), the Secretary may take the action described in subparagraph (D) if the Secretary, after an informal hearing, finds that such individual has provided substantial assistance in the investigations or prosecutions of offenses which are described in subsection (a) or (b) or which relate to any matter under the jurisdiction of the Food and Drug Administration.

(D) SECRETARIAL ACTION -- The action referred to in subparagraphs (B) and (C) is –

(i) in the case of a person other than an individual –

(I) terminating the debarment immediately, or

(II) limiting the period of debarment to less than one year, and

(ii) in the case of an individual, limiting the period of debarment to less than permanent but to no less than 1 year, whichever best serves the interest of justice and protects the integrity of the drug approval process.

(e) PUBLICATION AND LIST OF DEBARRED PERSONS. -- The Secretary shall publish in the Federal Register the name of any person debarred under subsection (a) or (b), the effective date of the debarment, and the period of the debarment. The Secretary shall also maintain and make available to the public a list, updated

[8] So in law. See section 125(b)(2)(C) of Public Law 105-115 (111 Stat. 2325). Probably should be "section".

no less often than quarterly, of such persons, of the effective dates and minimum periods of such debarments, and of the termination of debarments.

(f) TEMPORARY DENIAL OF APPROVAL. --

(1) IN GENERAL. -- The Secretary, on the Secretary's own initiative or in response to a petition, may, in accordance with paragraph (3), refuse by order, for the period prescribed by paragraph (2), to approve any abbreviated drug application submitted by any person –

(A) if such person is under an active Federal criminal investigation in connection with an action described in subparagraph (B),

(B) if the Secretary finds that such person –

(i) has bribed or attempted to bribe, has paid or attempted to pay an illegal gratuity, or has induced or attempted to induce another person to bribe or pay an illegal gratuity to any officer, employee, or agent of the Department of Health and Human Services or to any other Federal, State, or local official in connection with any abbreviated drug application, or has conspired to commit, or aided or abetted, such actions, or

(ii) has knowingly made or caused to be made a pattern or practice of false statements or misrepresentations with respect to material facts relating to any abbreviated drug application, or the production of any drug subject to an abbreviated drug application, to any officer, employee, or agent of the Department of Health and Human Services, or has conspired to commit, or aided or abetted, such actions, and

(C) if a significant question has been raised regarding –

(i) the integrity of the approval process with respect to such abbreviated drug application, or

(ii) the reliability of data in or concerning such person's abbreviated drug application.

Such an order may be modified or terminated at any time.

(2) APPLICABLE PERIOD. --

(A) IN GENERAL. -- Except as provided in subparagraph (B), a denial of approval of an application of a person under paragraph (1) shall be in effect for a period determined by the Secretary but not to exceed 18 months beginning on the date the Secretary finds that the conditions described in subparagraphs (A), (B), and (C) of paragraph (1) exist. The Secretary shall terminate such denial -

(i) if the investigation with respect to which the finding was made does not result in a criminal charge against such person, if criminal charges have been brought and the charges have been dismissed, or if a judgment of acquittal has been entered, or

(ii) if the Secretary determines that such finding was in error.

(B) EXTENSION. -- If, at the end of the period described in subparagraph (A), the Secretary determines that a person has been criminally charged for an action described in subparagraph (B) of paragraph (1), the Secretary may extend the period of denial of approval of an application for a period not to exceed 18 months. The Secretary shall terminate such extension if the charges have been dismissed, if a judgment of acquittal has been entered, or if the Secretary determines that the finding described in subparagraph (A) was in error.

(3) INFORMAL HEARING. -- Within 10 days of the date an order is issued under paragraph (1), the Secretary shall provide such person with an opportunity for an informal hearing, to be held within such 10 days, on the decision of the Secretary to refuse approval of an abbreviated drug application. Within 60 days of the date on which such hearing is held, the Secretary shall notify the person given such hearing whether the Secretary's refusal of approval will be continued, terminated, or otherwise modified. Such notification shall be final agency action.

(g) SUSPENSION AUTHORITY. --

(1) IN GENERAL. -- If -

(A) the Secretary finds -

(i) that a person has engaged in conduct described in subparagraph (B) of subsection (f)(1) in connection with 2 or more drugs under abbreviated drug applications, or

(ii) that a person has engaged in flagrant and repeated, material violations of good manufacturing practice or good laboratory practice in connection with the development, manufacturing, or distribution of one or more drugs approved under an abbreviated drug application during a 2-year period, and -

(I) such violations may undermine the safety and efficacy of such drugs, and

(II) the causes of such violations have not been corrected within a reasonable period of time following notice of such violations by the Secretary, and

(B) such person is under an active investigation by a Federal authority in connection with a civil or criminal action involving conduct described in subparagraph (A), the Secretary shall issue an order suspending the distribution of all drugs the development or approval of which was related to such conduct described in subparagraph (A) or suspending the distribution of all drugs approved under abbreviated drug applications of such person if the Secretary finds that such conduct may have affected the development or approval of a significant number of drugs which the Secretary is unable to identify. The Secretary shall exclude a drug from such order if the Secretary determines that such conduct was not likely to have influenced the safety or efficacy of such drug.

(2) PUBLIC HEALTH WAIVER. -- The Secretary shall, on the Secretary's own initiative or in response to a petition, waive the suspension under paragraph (1) (involving an action described in paragraph (1)(A)(i)) with respect to any drug if the Secretary finds that such waiver is necessary to protect the public health because sufficient quantities of the drug would not otherwise be available. The Secretary shall act on any petition seeking action under this paragraph within 180 days of the date the petition is submitted to the Secretary.

(h) TERMINATION OF SUSPENSION. -- The Secretary shall withdraw an order of suspension of the distribution of a drug under subsection (g) if the person with respect to whom the order was issued demonstrates in a petition to the Secretary -

(1)(A) on the basis of an audit by the Food and Drug Administration or by experts acceptable to the Food and Drug Administration, or on the basis of other information, that the development, approval, manufacturing, and distribution of such drug is in substantial compliance with the applicable requirements of this Act, and

(B) changes in ownership, management, or operations –

(i) fully remedy the patterns or practices with respect to which the order was issued, and

(ii) provide reasonable assurances that such actions will not occur in the future, or

(2) the initial determination was in error.

The Secretary shall act on a submission of a petition under this subsection within 180 days of the date of its submission and the Secretary may consider the petition concurrently with the suspension proceeding. Any information submitted to the Secretary under this subsection does not constitute an amendment or supplement to a pending or approved abbreviated drug application.

(i) PROCEDURE. -- The Secretary may not take any action under subsection (a), (b), (c), (d)(3), (g), or (h) with respect to any person unless the Secretary has issued an order for such action made on the record after opportunity for an agency hearing on disputed issues of material fact. In the course of any investigation or hearing under this subsection, the Secretary may administer oaths and affirmations, examine witnesses, receive evidence, and issue subpoenas requiring the attendance and testimony of witnesses and the production of evidence that relates to the matter under investigation.

(j) JUDICAL REVIEW

(1) IN GENERAL. -- Except as provided in paragraph (2), any person that is the subject of an adverse decision under subsection (a), (b), (c), (d), (f), (g), or (h) may obtain a review of such decision by the United States Court of Appeals for the District of Columbia or for the circuit in which the person resides, by filing in such court (within 60 days following the date the person is notified of the Secretary's decision) a petition requesting that the decision be modified or set aside.

(2) EXCEPTION. -- Any person that is the subject of an adverse decision under clause (iii) or (iv) of subsection (b)(2)(B) may obtain a review of such decision by the United States District Court for the District of Columbia or a district court of the United States for the district in which the person resides, by filing in such court (within 30 days following the date the person is notified of the Secretary's decision) a complaint requesting that the decision be modified or set aside. In such an action, the court shall determine the matter de novo.

(k) CERTIFICATION. -- Any application for approval of a drug product shall include -

(1) a certification that the applicant did not and will not use in any capacity the services of any person debarred under subsection (a) or (b), in connection with such application, and

(2) if such application is an abbreviated drug application, a list of all convictions, described in subsections (a) and (b) which occurred within the previous 5 years, of the applicant and affiliated persons responsible for the development or submission of such application.

(l) APPLICABILITY. --

(1) CONVICTION. -- For purposes of this section, a person is considered to have been convicted of a criminal offense -

(A) when a judgment of conviction has been entered against the person by a Federal or State court, regardless of whether there is an appeal pending,

(B) when a plea of guilty or nolo contendere by the person has been accepted by a Federal or State court, or

(C) when the person has entered into participation in a first offender, deferred adjudication, or other similar arrangement or program where judgment of conviction has been withheld.

(2) EFFECTIVE DATES. -- Subsection (a), subparagraph (A) of subsection (b)(2), and subsection (b)(3)(A) clauses (i) and (ii) of subsection (b)(2)(B) shall not apply to a conviction which occurred more than 5 years before the initiation of an agency action proposed to be taken under subsection (a) or (b). Clauses (iii) and (iv) of subsection (b)(2)(B) , subsection (b)(3)(B) and subsections (f) and (g) shall not apply to an act or action which occurred more than 5 years before the initiation of an agency action proposed to be taken under subsection (b), (f), or (g). Clause (iv) of subsection (b)(2)(B) shall not apply to an action which occurred before June 1, 1992 . Subsection (k) shall not apply to applications submitted to the Secretary before June 1, 1992.

(m) Devices; Mandatory Debarment Regarding Third-Party Inspections and Reviews.—

(1) In general.--If the Secretary finds that a person has been convicted of a felony under section 301(gg), the Secretary shall debar such person from being accredited under section 523(b) or 704(g)(2) and from carrying out activities under an agreement described in section 803(b).

(2) Debarment period.--The Secretary shall debar a person under paragraph (1) for the following periods:

(A) The period of debarment of a person (other than an individual) shall not be less than 1 year or more than 10 years, but if an act leading to a subsequent debarment under such paragraph occurs within 10 years after such person has been debarred under such paragraph, the period of debarment shall be permanent.

(B) The debarment of an individual shall be permanent.

(3) Termination of debarment; judicial review; other matters.--Subsections (c)(3), (d), (e), (i), (j), and (l)(1) apply with respect to a person (other than an individual) or an individual who is debarred under paragraph (1) to the same extent and in the same manner as such subsections apply with respect to a person who is debarred under subsection (a)(1), or an individual who is debarred under subsection (a)(2), respectively.

SEC. 307. [21 USC §335b] Civil Penalties

(a) IN GENERAL.—Any person that the Secretary finds—

(1) knowingly made or caused to be made, to any officer, employee, or agent of the Department of Health and Human Services, a false statement or

misrepresentation of a material fact in connection with an abbreviated drug application,

(2) bribed or attempted to bribe or paid or attempted to pay an illegal gratuity to any officer, employee, or agent of the Department of Health and Human Services in connection with an abbreviated drug application,

(3) destroyed, altered, removed, or secreted, or procured the destruction, alteration, removal, or secretion of, any material document or other material evidence which was the property of or in the possession of the Department of Health and Human Services for the purpose of interfering with that Department's discharge of its responsibilities in connection with an abbreviated drug application,

(4) knowingly failed to disclose, to an officer or employee of the Department of Health and Human Services, a material fact which such person had an obligation to disclose relating to any drug subject to an abbreviated drug application,

(5) knowingly obstructed an investigation of the Department of Health and Human Services into any drug subject to an abbreviated drug application,

(6) is a person that has an approved or pending drug product application and has knowingly—

(A) employed or retained as a consultant or contractor, or

(B) otherwise used in any capacity the services of, a person who was debarred under section 306, or

(7) is an individual debarred under section 306 and, during the period of debarment, provided services in any capacity to a person that had an approved or pending drug product application, shall be liable to the United States for a civil penalty for each such violation in an amount not to exceed $250,000 in the case of an individual and $1,000,000 in the case of any other person.

(b) PROCEDURE.—

(1) IN GENERAL.—

(A) ACTION BY THE SECRETARY.—A civil penalty under subsection (a) shall be assessed by the Secretary on a person by an order made on the record after an opportunity for an agency hearing on disputed issues of material fact and the amount of the penalty. In the course of any investigation or hearing under this subparagraph, the Secretary may administer oaths and affirmations, examine witnesses, receive evidence, and issue subpoenas requiring the attendance and testimony of witnesses and the production of evidence that relates to the matter under investigation.

(B) ACTION BY THE ATTORNEY GENERAL.—In lieu of a proceeding under subparagraph (A), the Attorney General may, upon request of the Secretary, institute a civil action to recover a civil money penalty in the amount and for any of the acts set forth in subsection (a). Such an action may be instituted separately from or in connection with any other claim, civil or criminal, initiated by the Attorney General under this Act.

(2) AMOUNT.—In determining the amount of a civil penalty under paragraph (1), the Secretary or the court shall take into account the nature, circumstances, extent, and gravity of the act subject to penalty, the person's ability to pay, the effect on the person's ability to continue to do business, any history of prior, similar acts, and such other matters as justice may require.

(3) LIMITATION ON ACTIONS.—No action may be initiated under this section—

(A) with respect to any act described in subsection (a) that occurred before the date of the enactment of this section, or

(B) more than 6 years after the date when facts material to the act are known or reasonably should have been known by the Secretary but in no event more than 10 years after the date the act took place.

(c) JUDICIAL REVIEW.—Any person that is the subject of an adverse decision under subsection (b)(1)(A) may obtain a review of such decision by the United States Court of Appeals for the District of Columbia or for the circuit in which the person resides, by filing in such court (within 60 days following the date the person is notified of the Secretary's decision) a petition requesting that the decision be modified or set aside.

(d) RECOVERY OF PENALTIES.—The Attorney General may recover any civil penalty (plus interest at the currently prevailing rates from the date the penalty became final) assessed under subsection (b)(1)(A) in an action brought in the name of the United States . The amount of such penalty may be deducted, when the penalty has become final, from any sums then or later owing by the United States to the person against whom the penalty has been assessed. In an action brought under this subsection, the validity, amount, and appropriateness of the penalty shall not be subject to judicial review.

(e) INFORMANTS.—The Secretary may award to any individual (other than an officer or employee of the Federal Government or a person who materially participated in any conduct described in subsection (a)) who provides information leading to the imposition of a civil penalty under this section an amount not to exceed—

(1) $250,000, or

(2) one-half of the penalty so imposed and collected, whichever is less. The decision of the Secretary on such award shall not be reviewable.

SEC. 308. [21 USC §335c] Authority to Withdraw Approval of Abbreviated Drug Applications

(a) IN GENERAL.—The Secretary—

(1) shall withdraw approval of an abbreviated drug application if the Secretary finds that the approval was obtained, expedited, or otherwise facilitated through bribery, payment of an illegal gratuity, or fraud or material false statement, and

(2) may withdraw approval of an abbreviated drug application if the Secretary finds that the applicant has repeatedly demonstrated a lack of ability to produce the drug for which the application was submitted in accordance with the formulations or manufacturing practice set forth in the abbreviated drug application and has introduced, or attempted to introduce, such adulterated or misbranded drug into commerce.

(b) PROCEDURE.—The Secretary may not take any action under subsection (a) with respect to any person unless the Secretary has issued an order for such action made on the record after opportunity for an agency hearing on disputed issues of material fact. In the course of any investigation or hearing under this subsection, the Secretary may administer oaths and affirmations, examine witnesses, receive evidence, and issue subpoenas requiring the attendance and testimony of witnesses and the production of evidence that relates to the matter under investigation.

(c) APPLICABILITY.—Subsection (a) shall apply with respect to offenses or acts regardless of when such offenses or acts occurred.

(d) JUDICIAL REVIEW.—Any person that is the subject of an adverse decision under subsection (a) may obtain a review of such decision by the United States Court of Appeals for the District of Columbia or for the circuit in which the person resides, by filing in such court (within 60 days following the date the person is notified of the Secretary's decision) a petition requesting that the decision be modified or set aside.

SEC. 309. [21 USC §336] Report of Minor Violations

Nothing in this Act shall be construed as requiring the Secretary to report for prosecution, or for the institution of libel or injunction proceedings, minor violations of this Act whenever he believes that the public interest will be adequately served by a suitable written notice or warning.

SEC. 310. [21 USC §337] Proceedings in Name of United States; Provision As To Subpoenas

(a) Except as provided in subsection (b), all such proceedings for the enforcement, or to restrain violations, of this Act shall be by and in the name of the United States . Subpoenas for witnesses who are required to attend a court of the United States , in any district, may run into any other district in any proceeding under this section.

(b)(1) A State may bring in its own name and within its jurisdiction proceedings for the civil enforcement, or to restrain violations, of section 401, 403(b), 403(c), 403(d), 403(e), 403(f), 403(g), 403(h), 403(i), 403(k), 403(q), or 403(r) if the food that is the subject of the proceedings is located in the State.

(2) No proceeding may be commenced by a State under paragraph (1)—

(A) before 30 days after the State has given notice to the Secretary that the State intends to bring such proceeding,

(B) before 90 days after the State has given notice to the Secretary of such intent if the Secretary has, within such 30 days, commenced an informal or formal enforcement action pertaining to the food which would be the subject of such proceeding, or

(C) if the Secretary is diligently prosecuting a proceeding in court pertaining to such food, has settled such proceeding, or has settled the informal or formal enforcement action pertaining to such food.

In any court proceeding described in subparagraph (C), a State may intervene as a matter of right.

FD&C Act Chapter IV: Food

Sections in Chapter IV

- Sec. 401. [21 USC §341] Definitions and Standards for Food
- Sec. 402. [21 USC §342] Adulterated Food
- Sec. 403. [21 USC §343] Misbranded Food
- Sec. 403A. [21 USC §343–1]
- Sec. 403B. [21 USC §343–2] Dietary Supplement Labeling Exemptions.
- Sec. 403C. [21 USC §343–3] Disclosure.
- Sec. 404. [21 USC §344] Emergency Permit Control
- Sec. 405. [21 USC §345] Regulations Making Exemptions
- Sec. 406. [21 USC §346] Tolerances for Poisonous Ingredients in Food
- Sec. 407. [21 USC §347] Oleomargarine or Margarine
- Sec. 408. [21 USC §346a] Tolerances and Exemptions for Pesticide Chemical Residues
- Sec. 409. [21 USC §348] Unsafe Food Additives
- Sec. 410. [21 USC §349] Bottled Drinking Water Standards
- Sec. 411. [21 USC §350] Vitamins and Minerals
- Sec. 412. [21 USC §350a] Requirements for Infant Formulas
- Sec. 413. [21 USC §350b] New Dietary Ingredients
- Sec. 414. [21 USC §350c] Maintenance and Inspection of Records
- Sec. 415. [21 USC §350d] Registration of Food Facilities
- Sec. 416. [21 USC §350e] Sanitary Transportation Practices
- Sec. 417. [21 USC 350f] Reportable food registry.

Sec. 401. [21 USC §341] Definitions and Standards for Food

Whenever in the judgment of the Secretary such action will promote honesty and fair dealing in the interest of consumers, he shall promulgate regulations fixing and establishing for any food, under its common or usual name so far as practicable, a reasonable definition and standard of identity, a reasonable standard of quality, or reasonable standards of fill of container. No definition and standard of identity and no standard of quality shall be established for fresh or dried fruits, fresh or dried vegetables, or butter, except that definitions and standards of identity may be established for avocados, cantaloupes, citrus fruits, and melons. In prescribing any standard of fill of container, the Secretary shall give due consideration to the natural shrinkage in storage and in transit of fresh natural food and to need for the necessary packing and protective material. In the prescribing of any standard of quality for any canned fruit or canned vegetable, consideration shall be given and due allowance made for the differing characteristics of the several varieties of such fruit or vegetable. In prescribing a definition and standard of identity for any food or class of food in which optional ingredients are permitted, the Secretary shall, for the purpose of promoting honesty and fair dealing in the interest of consumers, designate the optional ingredients which shall be named on the label. Any definition and standard of identity prescribed by the Secretary for avocados, cantaloupes, citrus fruits, or melons shall relate only to maturity and to the effects of freezing.

Sec. 402. [21 USC §342] Adulterated Food

Note: revisions were posted to this section in December 2007.

A food shall be deemed to be adulterated— [1]

(a) Poisonous, insanitary, or deleterious ingredients.

(1) If it bears or contains any poisonous or deleterious substance which may render it injurious to health; but in case the substance is not an added substance such food shall not be considered adulterated under this clause if the quantity of such substance in such food does not ordinarily render it injurious to health; [or] [2] (2)(A) [3] if it bears or contains any added poisonous or added deleterious substance (other than a substance that is a pesticide chemical residue in or on a raw agricultural commodity or processed food, a

[1] See footnote for section 403(h)(3) regarding the stylistic use of a list consisting of "(a)", "(b)", etc.

[2] So in law. See section 3(i)(1) of Public Law 103–80. Probably should be "or".

[3] Subparagraph (2) appears so as to reflect the probable intent of the Congress. Section 404 of Public Law 104–170 (110 Stat. 1514) had amendatory instructions whose probable intended effect was to strike the existing subparagraph (2) and to insert a substitute subparagraph (2). These included instructions to strike "(2)(A) if it bears'" and all that follows through "(3) if it consists", but "(3) If it consists" was the language that actually appeared. (Previously, section 3(i) of Public Law 103–80 (107 Stat. 776) had amended subparagraph (3) by striking "if it" and inserting "If it".)

food additive, a color additive, or a new animal drug) that is unsafe within the meaning of section 406; or (B) if it bears or contains a pesticide chemical residue that is unsafe within the meaning of section 408(a); or (C) if it is or if it bears or contains (i) any food additive that is unsafe within the meaning of section 409; or (ii) a new animal drug (or conversion product thereof) that is unsafe within the meaning of section 512; or (3) if it consists in whole or in part of any filthy, putrid, or decomposed substance, or if it is otherwise unfit for food; or (4) if it has been prepared, packed, or held under insanitary conditions whereby it may have become contaminated with filth, or whereby it may have been rendered injurious to health; or (5) if it is, in whole or in part, the product of a diseased animal or of an animal which has died otherwise than by slaughter; or (6) if its container is composed, in whole or in part, of any poisonous or deleterious substance which may render the contents injurious to health; or (7) if it has been intentionally subjected to radiation, unless the use of the radiation was in conformity with a regulation or exemption in effect pursuant to section 409.

(b) Absence, substitution, or addition of constituents.

(1) If any valuable constituent has been in whole or in part omitted or abstracted therefrom; or (2) if any substance has been substituted wholly or in part therefore; or (3) if damage or inferiority has been concealed in any manner; or (4) if any substance has been added thereto or mixed or packed therewith so as to increase its bulk or weight, or reduce its quality or strength, or make it appear better or of greater value than it is.

(c) Color additives. If it is, or it bears or contains, a color additive which is unsafe within the meaning of section 721(a).

(d) Confectionery containing alcohol or nonnutritive substance. If it is confectionery, and—

(1) has partially or completely imbedded therein any nonnutritive object, except that this subparagraph shall not apply in the case of any nonnutritive object if, in the judgment of the Secretary as provided by regulations, such object is of practical functional value to the confectionery product and would not render the product injurious or hazardous to health;

(2) bears or contains any alcohol other than alcohol not in excess of one-half of 1 per centum by volume derived solely from the use of flavoring extracts, except that this clause shall not apply to confectionery which is introduced or delivered for introduction into, or received or held for sale in, interstate commerce if the sale of such confectionery is permitted under the laws of the State in which such confectionery is intended to be offered for sale; or

(3) bears or contains any nonnutritive substance, except that this subparagraph shall not apply to a safe nonnutritive substance which is in or on

confectionery by reason of its use for some practical functional purpose in the manufacture, packaging, or storage of such confectionery if the use of the substance does not promote deception of the consumer or otherwise result in adulteration or misbranding in violation of any provision of this Act, except that the Secretary may, for the purpose of avoiding or resolving uncertainty as to the application of this subparagraph, issue regulations allowing or prohibiting the use of particular nonnutritive substances.

(e) Oleomargarine containing filthy, putrid, etc., matter. If it is oleomargarine or margarine or butter and any of the raw material used therein consisted in whole or in part of any filthy, putrid, or decomposed substance, or such oleomargarine or margarine or butter is otherwise unfit for food.

(f) Dietary supplement or ingredient: safety.

(1) If it is a dietary supplement or contains a dietary ingredient that—

(A) presents a significant or unreasonable risk of illness or injury under—

(i) conditions of use recommended or suggested in labeling, or

(ii) if no conditions of use are suggested or recommended in the labeling, under ordinary conditions of use;

(B) is a new dietary ingredient for which there is inadequate information to provide reasonable assurance that such ingredient does not present a significant or unreasonable risk of illness or injury;

(C) the Secretary declares to pose an imminent hazard to public health or safety, except that the authority to make such declaration shall not be delegated and the Secretary shall promptly after such a declaration initiate a proceeding in accordance with sections 554 and 556 of title 5, United States Code, to affirm or withdraw the declaration; or

(D) is or contains a dietary ingredient that renders it adulterated under paragraph (a)(1) under the conditions of use recommended or suggested in the labeling of such dietary supplement.

In any proceeding under this subparagraph, the United States shall bear the burden of proof on each element to show that a dietary supplement is adulterated. The court shall decide any issue under this paragraph on a de novo basis.

(2) Before the Secretary may report to a United States attorney a violation of paragraph [4] (1)(A) for a civil proceeding, the person against whom such proceeding would be initiated shall be given appropriate notice and the opportunity to present views, orally and in writing, at least 10 days before such notice, with regard to such proceeding.

---

[4] So in law. Probably should be "subparagraph".

(g) Dietary supplement: manufacturing practices.

(1) If it is a dietary supplement and it has been prepared, packed, or held under conditions that do not meet current good manufacturing practice regulations, including regulations requiring, when necessary, expiration date labeling, issued by the Secretary under subparagraph (2).

(2) The Secretary may by regulation prescribe good manufacturing practices for dietary supplements. Such regulations shall be modeled after current good manufacturing practice regulations for food and may not impose standards for which there is no current and generally available analytical methodology. No standard of current good manufacturing practice may be imposed unless such standard is included in a regulation promulgated after notice and opportunity for comment in accordance with chapter 5 of title 5, United States Code.

(h) Reoffer of food previously denied admission. If it is an article of food imported or offered for import into the United States and the article of food has previously been refused admission under section 801(a), unless the person reoffering the article affirmatively establishes, at the expense of the owner or consignee of the article, that the article complies with the applicable requirements of this Act, as determined by the Secretary.

(i) Unsanitary transport. If it is transported or offered for transport by a shipper, carrier by motor vehicle or rail vehicle, receiver, or any other person engaged in the transportation of food under conditions that are not in compliance with regulations promulgated under section 416.

Sec. 403. [21 USC §343] Misbranded Food

A food shall be deemed to be misbranded—[5]

(a) False or misleading label. If (1) its labeling is false or misleading in any particular, or (2) in the case of a food to which section 411 applies, its advertising is false or misleading in a material respect or its labeling is in violation of section 411(b)(2).

(b) Offer for sale under another name. If it is offered for sale under the name of another food.

(c) Imitation of another food. If it is an imitation of another food, unless its label bears, in type of uniform size and prominence, the word "imitation" and, immediately thereafter, the name of the food imitated.

(d) Misleading container. If its container is so made, formed, or filled as to be misleading.

[5] See footnote for paragraph (h)(3) regarding the stylistic use of a list consisting of "(a)", "(b)", etc.

(e) Package form. If in package form unless it bears a label containing (1) the name and place of business of the manufacturer, packer, or distributor; and (2) an accurate statement of the quantity of the contents in terms of weight, measure, or numerical count, except that under clause (2) of this paragraph reasonable variations shall be permitted, and exemptions as to small packages shall be established, by regulations prescribed by the Secretary.

(f) Prominence of information on label. If any word, statement, or other information required by or under authority of this Act to appear on the label or labeling is not prominently placed thereon with such conspicuousness (as compared with other words, statements, designs, or devices, in the labeling) and in such terms as to render it likely to be read and understood by the ordinary individual under customary conditions of purchase and use.

(g) Representation as to definition and standard of identity. If it purports to be or is represented as a food for which a definition and standard of identity has been prescribed by regulations as provided by section 401, unless (1) it conforms to such definition and standard, and (2) its label bears the name of the food specified in the definition and standard, and, insofar as may be required by such regulations, the common names of optional ingredients (other than spices, flavoring, and coloring) present in such food.

(h) Representation as to standards of quality and fill of container. If it purports to be or is represented as—

(1) a food for which a standard of quality has been prescribed by regulations as provided by section 401, and its quality falls below such standard, unless its label bears, in such manner and form as such regulations specify, a statement that it falls below such standard;

(2) a food for which a standard or standards of fill of container have been prescribed by regulations as provided by section 401, and it falls below the standard of fill of container applicable thereto, unless its label bears, in such manner and form as such regulations specify, a statement that it falls below such standard; or

(3) a food that is pasteurized unless—

(A) such food has been subjected to a safe process or treatment that is prescribed as pasteurization for such food in a regulation promulgated under this Act;

(B)(i) such food has been subjected to a safe process or treatment that—

(I) is reasonably certain to achieve destruction or elimination in the food of the most resistant microorganisms of public health significance that are likely to occur in the food;

(II) is at least as protective of the public health as a process or treatment described in subparagraph (A);

(III) is effective for a period that is at least as long as the shelf life of the food when stored under normal and moderate abuse conditions; and

(IV) is the subject of a notification to the Secretary, including effectiveness data regarding the process or treatment; and

(ii) at least 120 days have passed after the date of receipt of such notification by the Secretary without the Secretary making a determination that the process or treatment involved has not been shown to meet the requirements of subclauses (I) through (III) of clause (i) [6].

For purposes of paragraph (3) [6], a determination by the Secretary that a process or treatment has not been shown to meet the requirements of subclauses (I) through (III) of subparagraph (B)(i) [6] shall constitute final agency action under such subclauses.

(i) Label where no representation as to definition and standard of quality. Unless its label bears (1) the common or usual name of the food, if any there be, and (2) in case it is fabricated from two or more ingredients, the common or usual name of each such ingredient and if the food purports to be a beverage containing vegetable or fruit juice, a statement with appropriate prominence on the information panel of the total percentage of such fruit or vegetable juice contained in the food; except that spices, flavorings, and colors not required to be certified under section 721(c) [7] unless sold as spices, flavorings, or such colors, may be designated as spices, flavorings, and colorings without naming each. To the extent that compliance with the requirements of clause (2) of this paragraph is impracticable, or results in deception or unfair competition, exemptions shall be established by regulations promulgated by the Secretary.

(j) Representation for special dietary use. If it purports to be or is represented for special dietary uses, unless its label bears such information concerning its vitamin, mineral, and other dietary properties as the Secretary determines to be, and by regulations prescribes as, necessary in order fully to inform purchasers as to its value for such uses.

---

[6] References are so in law. See section 10808(b)(3) of Public Law 107–171 (116 Stat. 530). In order to be consistent with other cross-references within section 403 above, each reference in section 403(h)(3) to a paragraph, subparagraph, clause, or subclause should be a reference to a subparagraph, clause, subclause, or item, respectively. See, for example, cross-references in paragraph (q) (relating to nutrition information) and paragraph (r) (relating to nutrient levels and health claims).

[7] So in law. Probably should be followed by a comma.

(k) Artificial flavoring, artificial coloring, or chemical preservatives. If it bears or contains any artificial flavoring, artificial coloring, or chemical preservative, unless it bears labeling stating that fact, except that to the extent that compliance with the requirements of this paragraph is impracticable, exemptions shall be established by regulations promulgated by the Secretary. The provisions of this paragraph and paragraphs (g) and (i) with respect to artificial coloring shall not apply in the case of butter, cheese, or ice cream. The provisions of this paragraph with respect to chemical preservatives shall not apply to a pesticide chemical when used in or on a raw agricultural commodity which is the produce of the soil.

(l) Pesticide chemicals on raw agricultural commodities. If it is a raw agricultural commodity which is the produce of the soil, bearing or containing a pesticide chemical applied after harvest, unless the shipping container of such commodity bears labeling which declares the presence of such chemical in or on such commodity and the common or usual name and the function of such chemical, except that no such declaration shall be required while such commodity, having been removed from the shipping container, is being held or displayed for sale at retail out of such container in accordance with the custom of the trade.

(m) Color additives. If it is a color additive, unless its packaging and labeling are in conformity with such packaging and labeling requirements, applicable to such color additive, as may be contained in regulations issued under section 721.

(n) Packaging or labeling of drugs in violation of regulations. If its packaging or labeling is in violation of an applicable regulation issued pursuant to section 3 or 4 of the Poison Prevention Packaging Act of 1970.

(o) [Repealed] [8]

(p) [Deleted] [8]

(q) Nutrition information.

(1) Except as provided in subparagraphs (3), (4), and (5), if it is a food intended for human consumption and is offered for sale, unless its label or labeling bears nutrition information that provides—

(A)(i) the serving size which is an amount customarily consumed and which is expressed in a common household measure that is appropriate to the food, or (ii) if the use of the food is not typically expressed in a serving size, the common household unit of measure that expresses the serving size of the food,

[8] Paragraph (o) was repealed by Public Law 106–554 (114 Stat. 2763A–73). Paragraph (p) was struck by Public Law 104–124 (110 Stat. 882).

(B) the number of servings or other units of measure per container,

(C) the total number of calories—

(i) derived from any source, and

(ii) derived from the total fat,

in each serving size or other unit of measure of the food,

(D) the amount of the following nutrients: Total fat, saturated fat, cholesterol, sodium, total carbohydrates, complex carbohydrates, sugars, dietary fiber, and total protein contained in each serving size or other unit of measure,

(E) any vitamin, mineral, or other nutrient required to be placed on the label and labeling of food under this Act before October 1, 1990 , if the Secretary determines that such information will assist consumers in maintaining healthy dietary practices.

The Secretary may by regulation require any information required to be placed on the label or labeling by this subparagraph or subparagraph (2)(A) to be highlighted on the label or labeling by larger type, bold type, or contrasting color if the Secretary determines that such highlighting will assist consumers in maintaining healthy dietary practices.

(2)(A) If the Secretary determines that a nutrient other than a nutrient required by subparagraph (1)(C), (1)(D), or (1)(E) should be included in the label or labeling of food subject to subparagraph (1) for purposes of providing information regarding the nutritional value of such food that will assist consumers in maintaining healthy dietary practices, the Secretary may by regulation require that information relating to such additional nutrient be included in the label or labeling of such food.

(B) If the Secretary determines that the information relating to a nutrient required by subparagraph (1)(C), (1)(D), or (1)(E) or clause (A) of this subparagraph to be included in the label or labeling of food is not necessary to assist consumers in maintaining healthy dietary practices, the Secretary may by regulation remove information relating to such nutrient from such requirement.

(3) For food that is received in bulk containers at a retail establishment, the Secretary may, by regulation, provide that the nutrition information required by subparagraphs (1) and (2) be displayed at the location in the retail establishment at which the food is offered for sale.

(4)(A) The Secretary shall provide for furnishing the nutrition information required by subparagraphs (1) and (2) with respect to raw agricultural commodities and raw fish by issuing voluntary nutrition guidelines, as provided by clause (B) or by issuing regulations that are mandatory as provided by clause (D).

(B)(i) Upon the expiration of 12 months after the date of the enactment of the Nutrition Labeling and Education Act of 1990 [enacted Nov. 8, 1990] [9], the Secretary, after providing an opportunity for comment, shall issue guidelines for food retailers offering raw agricultural commodities or raw fish to provide nutrition information specified in subparagraphs (1) and (2). Such guidelines shall take into account the actions taken by food retailers during such 12-month period to provide to consumers nutrition information on raw agricultural commodities and raw fish. Such guidelines shall only apply—

(I) in the case of raw agricultural commodities, to the 20 varieties of vegetables most frequently consumed during a year and the 20 varieties of fruit most frequently consumed during a year, and

(II) to the 20 varieties of raw fish most frequently consumed during a year.

The vegetables, fruits, and raw fish to which such guidelines apply shall be determined by the Secretary by regulation and the Secretary may apply such guidelines regionally.

(ii) Upon the expiration of 12 months after the date of the enactment of the Nutrition Labeling and Education Act of 1990 [enacted Nov. 8, 1990] 5, the Secretary shall issue a final regulation defining the circumstances that constitute substantial compliance by food retailers with the guidelines issued under subclause (i). The regulation shall provide that there is not substantial compliance if a significant number of retailers have failed to comply with the guidelines. The size of the retailers and the portion of the market served by retailers in compliance with the guidelines shall be considered in determining whether the substantial-compliance standard has been met.

(C)(i) Upon the expiration of 30 months after the date of the enactment of the Nutrition Labeling and Education Act of 1990 [enacted Nov. 8, 1990] 5 , the Secretary shall issue a report on actions taken by food retailers to provide consumers with nutrition information for raw agricultural commodities and raw fish under the guidelines issued under clause (A). Such report shall include a determination of whether there is substantial compliance with the guidelines.

[9] Public Law 101–535, which was enacted November 8, 1990.

(ii) If the Secretary finds that there is substantial compliance with the guidelines, the Secretary shall issue a report and make a determination of the type required in subclause (i) every two years.

(D)(i) If the Secretary determines that there is not substantial compliance with the guidelines issued under clause (A), the Secretary shall at the time such determination is made issue proposed regulations requiring that any person who offers raw agricultural commodities or raw fish to consumers provide, in a manner prescribed by regulations, the nutrition information required by subparagraphs (1) and (2). The Secretary shall issue final regulations imposing such requirements 6 months after issuing the proposed regulations. The final regulations shall become effective 6 months after the date of their promulgation.

(ii) Regulations issued under subclause (i) may require that the nutrition information required by subparagraphs (1) and (2) be provided for more than 20 varieties of vegetables, 20 varieties of fruit, and 20 varieties of fish most frequently consumed during a year if the Secretary finds that a larger number of such products are frequently consumed. Such regulations shall permit such information to be provided in a single location in each area in which raw agricultural commodities and raw fish are offered for sale. Such regulations may provide that information shall be expressed as an average or range per serving of the same type of raw agricultural commodity or raw fish. The Secretary shall develop and make available to the persons who offer such food to consumers the information required by subparagraphs (1) and (2).

(iii) Regulations issued under subclause (i) shall permit the required information to be provided in each area of an establishment in which raw agricultural commodities and raw Fish are offered for sale. The regulations shall permit food retailers to display the required information by supplying copies of the information provided by the Secretary, by making the information available in brochure, notebook or leaflet form, or by posting a sign disclosing the information. Such regulations shall also permit presentation of the required information to be supplemented by a video, live demonstration, or other media which the Secretary approves.

(E) For purposes of this subparagraph, the term "fish" includes freshwater or marine fin fish, crustaceans, and mollusks, including shellfish, amphibians, and other forms of aquatic animal life.

(F) No person who offers raw agricultural commodities or raw fish to consumers may be prosecuted for minor violations of this subparagraph if there has been substantial compliance with the requirements of this paragraph.

(5)(A) Subparagraphs (1), (2), (3), and (4) shall not apply to food—

(i) which is served in restaurants or other establishments in which food is served for immediate human consumption or which is sold for sale or use in such establishments,

(ii) which is processed and prepared primarily in a retail establishment, which is ready for human consumption, which is of the type described in subclause (i), and which is offered for sale to consumers but not for immediate human consumption in such establishment and which is not offered for sale outside such establishment,

(iii) which is an infant formula subject to section 412,

(iv) which is a medical food as defined in section 5(b) of the Orphan Drug Act (21 USC 360ee(b)), or

(v) which is described in section 405(2).

(B) Subparagraphs (1) and (2) shall not apply to the label of a food if the Secretary determines by regulations that compliance with such subparagraphs is impracticable because the package of such food is too small to comply with the requirements of such subparagraphs and if the label of such food does not contain any nutrition information.

(C) If a food contains insignificant amounts, as determined by the Secretary, of all the nutrients required by subparagraphs (1) and (2) to be listed in the label or labeling of food, the requirements of such subparagraphs shall not apply to such food if the label, labeling, or advertising of such food does not make any claim with respect to the nutritional value of such food. If a food contains insignificant amounts, as determined by the Secretary, of more than one-half the nutrients required by subparagraphs (1) and (2) to be in the label or labeling of the food, the Secretary shall require the amounts of such nutrients to be stated in a simplified form prescribed by the Secretary.

(D) If a person offers food for sale and has annual gross sales made or business done in sales to consumers which is not more than $500,000 or has annual gross sales made or business done in sales of food to consumers which is not more than $50,000, the requirements of subparagraphs (1), (2), (3), and (4) shall not apply with respect to food sold by such person to consumers unless the label or labeling of food offered by such person provides nutrition information or makes a nutrition claim.

(E)(i) During the 12-month period for which an exemption from subparagraphs (1) and (2) is claimed pursuant to this subclause, the requirements of such subparagraphs shall not apply to any food product if—

(I) the labeling for such product does not provide nutrition information or make a claim subject to paragraph (r),

(II) the person who claims for such product an exemption from such subparagraphs employed fewer than an average of 100 full-time equivalent employees,

(III) such person provided the notice described in subclause (iii), and

(IV) in the case of a food product which was sold in the 12-month period preceding the period for which an exemption was claimed, fewer than 100,000 units of such product were sold in the United States during such preceding period, or in the case of a food product which was not sold in the 12-month period preceding the period for which such exemption is claimed, fewer than 100,000 units of such product are reasonably anticipated to be sold in the United States during the period for which such exemption is claimed.

(ii) During the 12-month period after the applicable date referred to in this sentence, the requirements of subparagraphs (1) and (2) shall not apply to any food product which was first introduced into interstate commerce before May 8, 1994, if the labeling for such product does not provide nutrition information or make a claim subject to paragraph (r), if such person provided the notice described in subclause (iii), and if—

(I) during the 12-month period preceding May 8, 1994, the person who claims for such product an exemption from such subparagraphs employed fewer than an average of 300 full-time equivalent employees and fewer than 600,000 units of such product were sold in the United States,

(II) during the 12-month period preceding May 8, 1995, the person who claims for such product an exemption from such subparagraphs employed fewer than an average of 300 full-time equivalent employees and fewer than 400,000 units of such product were sold in the United States, or

(III) during the 12-month period preceding May 8, 1996 , the person who claims for such product an exemption from such subparagraphs employed fewer than an average of 200 full-time equivalent employees and fewer than 200,000 units of such product were sold in the United States .

(iii) The notice referred to in subclauses (i) and (ii) shall be given to the Secretary prior to the beginning of the period during which the exemption under subclause (i) or (ii) is to be in effect, shall state that the person claiming such exemption for a food product has complied with the applicable requirements of subclause (i) or (ii), and shall—

(I) state the average number of full-time equivalent employees such person employed during the 12 months preceding the date such person claims such exemption,

(II) state the approximate number of units the person claiming the exemption sold in the United States ,

(III) if the exemption is claimed for a food product which was sold in the 12-month period preceding the period for which the exemption was claimed, state the approximate number of units of such product which were sold in the United States during such preceding period, and, if the exemption is claimed for a food product which was not sold in such preceding period, state the number of units of such product which such person reasonably anticipates will be sold in the United States during the period for which the exemption was claimed, and

(IV) contain such information as the Secretary may require to verify the information required by the preceding provisions of this subclause if the Secretary has questioned the validity of such information.

If a person is not an importer, has fewer than 10 full-time equivalent employees, and sells fewer than 10,000 units of any food product in any year, such person is not required to file a notice for such product under this subclause for such year.

(iv) In the case of a person who claimed an exemption under subclause (i) or (ii), if, during the period of such exemption, the number of full-time equivalent employees of such person exceeds the number in such subclause or if the number of food products sold in the United States exceeds the number in such subclause, such exemption shall extend to the expiration of 18 months after the date the number of full-time equivalent employees or food products sold exceeded the applicable number.

(v) For any food product first introduced into interstate commerce after May 8, 2002 , the Secretary may by regulation lower the employee or units of food products requirement of subclause (i) if the Secretary determines that the cost of compliance with such lower requirement will not place an undue burden on persons subject to such lower requirement.

(vi) For purposes of subclauses (i), (ii), (iii), (iv), and (v)—

(I) the term "unit" means the packaging or, if there is no packaging, the form in which a food product is offered for sale to consumers,

(II) the term "food product" means food in any sized package which is manufactured by a single manufacturer or which bears the same brand name, which bears the same statement of identity, and which has similar preparation methods, and

(III) the term "person" in the case of a corporation includes all domestic and foreign affiliates of the corporation.

(F) A dietary supplement product (including a food to which section 411 applies) shall comply with the requirements of subparagraphs (1) and (2) in a manner which is appropriate for the product and which is specified in regulations of the Secretary which shall provide that—

(i) nutrition information shall first list those dietary ingredients that are present in the product in a significant amount and for which a recommendation for daily consumption has been established by the Secretary, except that a dietary ingredient shall not be required to be listed if it is not present in a significant amount, and shall list any other dietary ingredient present and identified as having no such recommendation;

(ii) the listing of dietary ingredients shall include the quantity of each such ingredient (or of a proprietary blend of such ingredients) per serving;

(iii) the listing of dietary ingredients may include the source of a dietary ingredient; and

(iv) the nutrition information shall immediately precede the ingredient information required under subclause (i), except that no ingredient identified pursuant to subclause (i) shall be required to be identified a second time.

(G) Subparagraphs (1), (2), (3), and (4) shall not apply to food which is sold by a food distributor if the food distributor principally sells food to restaurants or other establishments in which food is served for immediate human consumption and does not manufacture, process, or repackage the food it sells.

(r) Nutrition levels and health-related claims.

(1) Except as provided in clauses (A) through (C) of subparagraph (5), if it is a food intended for human consumption which is offered for sale and for which a claim is made in the label or labeling of the food which expressly or by implication—

(A) characterizes the level of any nutrient which is of the type required by paragraph (q)(1) or (q)(2) to be in the label or labeling of the food unless the claim is made in accordance with subparagraph (2), or

(B) characterizes the relationship of any nutrient which is of the type required by paragraph (q)(1) or (q)(2) to be in the label or labeling of the food to a disease or a health-related condition unless the claim is made in accordance with subparagraph (3) or (5)(D).

A statement of the type required by paragraph (q) that appears as part of the nutrition information required or permitted by such paragraph is not a claim which is subject to this paragraph and a claim subject to clause (A) is not subject to clause (B).

(2)(A) Except as provided in subparagraphs (4)(A)(ii) and (4)(A)(iii) and clauses (A) through (C) of subparagraph (5), a claim described in subparagraph (1)(A)—

(i) may be made only if the characterization of the level made in the claim uses terms which are defined in regulations of the Secretary,

(ii) may not state the absence of a nutrient unless—

(I) the nutrient is usually present in the food or in a food which substitutes for the food as defined by the Secretary by regulation, or

(II) the Secretary by regulation permits such a statement on the basis of a finding that such a statement would assist consumers in maintaining healthy dietary practices and the statement discloses that the nutrient is not usually present in the food,

(iii) may not be made with respect to the level of cholesterol in the food if the food contains, as determined by the Secretary by regulation, fat or saturated fat in an amount which increases to persons in the general population the risk of disease or a health related condition which is diet related unless—

(I) the Secretary finds by regulation that the level of cholesterol is substantially less than the level usually present in the food or in a food which substitutes for the food and which has a significant market share, or the Secretary by regulation permits a statement regarding the absence of cholesterol on the basis of a finding that cholesterol is not usually present in the food and that such a statement would assist consumers in maintaining healthy dietary practices and the regulation requires that the statement disclose that cholesterol is not usually present in the food, and

(II) the label or labeling of the food discloses the level of such fat or saturated fat in immediate proximity to such claim and with appropriate prominence which shall be no less than one-half the size of the claim with respect to the level of cholesterol,

(iv) may not be made with respect to the level of saturated fat in the food if the food contains cholesterol unless the label or labeling of the food discloses the level of cholesterol in the food in immediate proximity to such claim and with appropriate prominence which shall be no less than one-half the size of the claim with respect to the level of saturated fat,

(v) may not state that a food is high in dietary fiber unless the food is low in total fat as defined by the Secretary or the label or labeling discloses the level of total fat in the food in immediate proximity to such statement and with appropriate prominence which shall be no less than one-half the size of the claim with respect to the level of dietary fiber, and

(vi) may not be made if the Secretary by regulation prohibits the claim because the claim is misleading in light of the level of another nutrient in the food.

(B) If a claim described in subparagraph (1)(A) is made with respect to a nutrient in a food and the Secretary makes a determination that the food contains a nutrient at a level that increases to persons in the general population the risk of a disease or health-related condition that is diet related, the label or labeling of such food shall contain, prominently and in immediate proximity to such claim, the following statement: "See nutrition information for ---- content." The blank shall identify the nutrient associated with the increased disease or health-related condition risk. In making the determination described in this clause, the Secretary shall take into account the significance of the food in the total daily diet.

(C) Subparagraph (2)(A) does not apply to a claim described in subparagraph (1)(A) and contained in the label or labeling of a food if such claim is contained in the brand name of such food and such brand name was in use on such food before October 25, 1989, unless the brand name contains a term defined by the Secretary under subparagraph (2)(A)(i). Such a claim is subject to paragraph (a).

(D) Subparagraph (2) does not apply to a claim described in subparagraph (1)(A) which uses the term "diet" and is contained in the label or labeling of a soft drink if (i) such claim is contained in the brand name of such soft drink, (ii) such brand name was in use on such soft drink before October 25, 1989, and (iii) the use of the term "diet" was in conformity with section 105.66 of title 21 of the Code of Federal Regulations. Such a claim is subject to paragraph (a).

(E) Subclauses (i) through (v) of subparagraph (2)(A) do not apply to a statement in the label or labeling of food which describes the percentage of vitamins and minerals in the food in relation to the amount of such vitamins and minerals recommended for daily consumption by the Secretary.

(F) Subclause (i) clause (A) does not apply to a statement in the labeling of a dietary supplement that characterizes the percentage level of a dietary ingredient for which the Secretary has not established a reference daily intake, daily recommended value, or other recommendation for daily consumption.

(G) A claim of the type described in subparagraph (1)(A) for a nutrient, for which the Secretary has not promulgated a regulation under clause (A)(i), shall be authorized and may be made with respect to a food if—

(i) a scientific body of the United States Government with official responsibility for public health protection or research directly relating to human nutrition (such as the National Institutes of Health or the Centers for Disease Control and Prevention) or the National Academy of Sciences or any of its subdivisions has published an authoritative statement, which is currently in effect, which identifies the nutrient level to which the claim refers;

(ii) a person has submitted to the Secretary, at least 120 days (during which the Secretary may notify any person who is making a claim as authorized by clause (C) that such person has not submitted all the information required by such clause) before the first introduction into interstate commerce of the food with a label containing the claim, (I) a notice of the claim, which shall include the exact words used in the claim and shall include a concise description of the basis upon which such person relied for determining that the requirements of subclause (i) have been satisfied, (II) a copy of the statement referred to in subclause (i) upon which such person relied in making the claim, and (III) a balanced representation of the scientific literature relating to the nutrient level to which the claim refers;

(iii) the claim and the food for which the claim is made are in compliance with clauses (A) and (B), and are otherwise in compliance with paragraph (a) and section 201(n); and

(iv) the claim is stated in a manner so that the claim is an accurate representation of the authoritative statement referred to in subclause (i) and so that the claim enables the public to comprehend the information provided in the claim and to understand the relative significance of such information in the context of a total daily diet.

For purposes of this clause, a statement shall be regarded as an authoritative statement of a scientific body described in subclause (i) only if the statement is published by the scientific body and shall not include a statement of an employee of the scientific body made in the individual capacity of the employee.

(H) A claim submitted under the requirements of clause (G) may be made until—

(i) such time as the Secretary issues a regulation—

(I) prohibiting or modifying the claim and the regulation has become effective, or

(II) finding that the requirements of clause (G) have not been met, including finding that the petitioner had not submitted all the information required by such clause; or

(ii) a district court of the United States in an enforcement proceeding under chapter III has determined that the requirements of clause (G) have not been met.

(3)(A) Except as provided in subparagraph (5), a claim described in subparagraph (1)(B) may only be made—

(i) if the claim meets the requirements of the regulations of the Secretary promulgated under clause (B), and

(ii) if the food for which the claim is made does not contain, as determined by the Secretary by regulation, any nutrient in an amount which increases to persons in the general population the risk of a disease or health-related condition which is diet related, taking into account the significance of the food in the total daily diet, except that the Secretary may by regulation permit such a claim based on a finding that such a claim would assist consumers in maintaining healthy dietary practices and based on a requirement that the label contain a disclosure of the type required by subparagraph (2)(B).

(B)(i) The Secretary shall promulgate regulations authorizing claims of the type described in subparagraph (1)(B) only if the Secretary determines, based on the totality of publicly available scientific evidence (including evidence from well-designed studies conducted in a manner which is consistent with generally recognized scientific procedures and principles), that there is significant scientific agreement, among experts qualified by scientific training and experience to evaluate such claims, that the claim is supported by such evidence.

(ii) A regulation described in subclause (i) shall describe—

(I) the relationship between a nutrient of the type required in the label or labeling of food by paragraph (q)(1) or (q)(2) and a disease or health-related condition, and

(II) the significance of each such nutrient in affecting such disease or health-related condition.

(iii) A regulation described in subclause (i) shall require such claim to be stated in a manner so that the claim is an accurate representation of the matters set out in subclause (ii) and so that the claim enables the public to comprehend the information provided in the claim and to understand the relative significance of such information in the context of a total daily diet.

(C) Notwithstanding the provisions of clauses (A)(i) and (B), a claim of the type described in subparagraph (1)(B) which is not authorized by the Secretary in a regulation promulgated in accordance with clause (B) shall be authorized and may be made with respect to a food if—

(i) a scientific body of the United States Government with official responsibility for public health protection or research directly relating to human nutrition (such as the National Institutes of Health or the Centers for Disease Control and Prevention) or the National Academy of Sciences or any of its subdivisions has published an authoritative statement, which is currently in effect, about the relationship between a nutrient and a disease or health-related condition to which the claim refers;

(ii) a person has submitted to the Secretary, at least 120 days (during which the Secretary may notify any person who is making a claim as authorized by clause (C) that such person has not submitted all the information required by such clause) before the first introduction into interstate commerce of the food with a label containing the claim, (I) a notice of the claim, which shall include the exact words used in the claim and shall include a concise description of the basis upon which such person relied for determining that the requirements of subclause (i) have been satisfied, (II) a copy of the statement referred to in subclause (i) upon which such person relied in making the claim, and (III) a balanced representation of the scientific literature relating to the relationship between a nutrient and a disease or health-related condition to which the claim refers;

(iii) the claim and the food for which the claim is made are in compliance with clause (A)(ii) and are otherwise in compliance with paragraph (a) and section 201(n); and

(iv) the claim is stated in a manner so that the claim is an accurate representation of the authoritative statement referred to in subclause (i) and so that the claim enables the public to comprehend the information provided in the claim and to understand the relative significance of such information in the context of a total daily diet.

For purposes of this clause, a statement shall be regarded as an authoritative statement of a scientific body described in subclause (i) only if the statement is published by the scientific body and shall not include a statement of an employee of the scientific body made in the individual capacity of the employee.

(D) A claim submitted under the requirements of clause (C) may be made until—

(i) such time as the Secretary issues a regulation under the standard in clause (B)(i)—

(I) prohibiting or modifying the claim and the regulation has become effective, or

(II) finding that the requirements of clause (C) have not been met, including finding that the petitioner has not submitted all the information required by such clause; or

(ii) a district court of the United States in an enforcement proceeding under chapter III has determined that the requirements of clause (C) have not been met.

(4)(A)(i) Any person may petition the Secretary to issue a regulation under subparagraph (2)(A)(i) or (3)(B) relating to a claim described in subparagraph (1)(A) or (1)(B). Not later than 100 days after the petition is received by the Secretary, the Secretary shall issue a final decision denying the petition or file the petition for further action by the Secretary. If the Secretary does not act within such 100 days, the petition shall be deemed to be denied unless an extension is mutually agreed upon by the Secretary and the petitioner. If the Secretary denies the petition or the petition is deemed to be denied, the petition shall not be made available to the public. If the Secretary files the petition, the Secretary shall deny the petition or issue a proposed regulation to take the action requested in the petition not later than 90 days after the date of such decision. If the Secretary does not act within such 90 days, the petition shall be deemed to be denied unless an extension is mutually agreed upon by the Secretary and the petitioner. If the Secretary issues a proposed regulation, the rulemaking shall be completed within 540 days of the date the petition is received by the Secretary. If the Secretary does not issue a regulation within such 540 days, the Secretary shall provide the Committee on Commerce of the House of Representatives and the Committee on Labor and Human Resources of the Senate the reasons action on the regulation did not occur within such 540 days.

(ii) Any person may petition the Secretary for permission to use in a claim described in subparagraph (1)(A) terms that are consistent with the terms defined by the Secretary under subparagraph

(2)(A)(i). Within 90 days of the submission of such a petition, the Secretary shall issue a final decision denying the petition or granting such permission.

(iii) Any person may petition the Secretary for permission to use an implied claim described in subparagraph (1)(A) in a brand name. After publishing notice of an opportunity to comment on the petition in the Federal Register and making the petition available to the public, the Secretary shall grant the petition if the Secretary finds that such claim is not misleading and is consistent with terms defined by the Secretary under subparagraph (2)(A)(i). The Secretary shall grant or deny the petition within 100 days of the date it is submitted to the Secretary and the petition shall be considered granted if the Secretary does not act on it within such 100 days.

(B) A petition under clause (A)(i) respecting a claim described in subparagraph (1)(A) or (1)(B) shall include an explanation of the reasons why the claim meets the requirements of this paragraph and a summary of the scientific data which supports such reasons.

(C) If a petition for a regulation under subparagraph (3)(B) relies on a report from an authoritative scientific body of the United States, the Secretary shall consider such report and shall justify any decision rejecting the conclusions of such report.

(5)(A) This paragraph does not apply to infant formulas subject to section 412(h) and medical foods as defined in section 5(b) of the Orphan Drug Act.

(B) Subclauses (iii) through (v) of subparagraph (2)(A) and subparagraph (2)(B) do not apply to food which is served in restaurants or other establishments in which food is served for immediate human consumption or which is sold for sale or use in such establishments.

(C) A subparagraph (1)(A) claim made with respect to a food which claim is required by a standard of identity issued under section 401 shall not be subject to subparagraph (2)(A)(i) or (2)(B).

(D) A subparagraph (1)(B) claim made with respect to a dietary supplement of vitamins, minerals, herbs, or other similar nutritional substances shall not be subject to subparagraph (3) but shall be subject to a procedure and standard, respecting the validity of such claim, established by regulation of the Secretary.

(6) For purposes of paragraph (r)(1)(B), a statement for a dietary supplement may be made if—

(A) the statement claims a benefit related to a classical nutrient deficiency disease and discloses the prevalence of such disease in the United States, describes the role of a nutrient or dietary ingredient intended to affect the structure or function in humans, characterizes the documented mechanism by which a nutrient or dietary ingredient acts to maintain such structure or function, or describes general well-being from consumption of a nutrient or dietary ingredient,

(B) the manufacturer of the dietary supplement has substantiation that such statement is truthful and not misleading, and

(C) the statement contains, prominently displayed and in boldface type, the following: "This statement has not been evaluated by the Food and Drug Administration. This product is not intended to diagnose, treat, cure, or prevent any disease.".

A statement under this subparagraph may not claim to diagnose, mitigate, treat, cure, or prevent a specific disease or class of diseases. If the manufacturer of a dietary supplement proposes to make a statement described in the first sentence of this subparagraph in the labeling of the dietary supplement, the manufacturer shall notify the Secretary no later than 30 days after the first marketing of the dietary supplement with such statement that such a statement is being made.

(7) The Secretary may make proposed regulations issued under this paragraph effective upon publication pending consideration of public comment and publication of a final regulation if the Secretary determines that such action is necessary—

(A) to enable the Secretary to review and act promptly on petitions the Secretary determines provide for information necessary to—

(i) enable consumers to develop and maintain healthy dietary practices;

(ii) enable consumers to be informed promptly and effectively of important new knowledge regarding nutritional and health benefits of food; or

(iii) ensure that scientifically sound nutritional and health information is provided to consumers as soon as possible; or

(B) to enable the Secretary to act promptly to ban or modify a claim under this paragraph.

Such proposed regulations shall be deemed final agency action for purposes of judicial review.

(s) Dietary supplements.

If—

(1) it is a dietary supplement; and

(2)(A) the label or labeling of the supplement fails to list—

(i) the name of each ingredient of the supplement that is described in section 201(ff); and

(ii)(I) the quantity of each such ingredient; or

(II) with respect to a proprietary blend of such ingredients, the total quantity of all ingredients in the blend;

(B) the label or labeling of the dietary supplement fails to identify the product by using the term "dietary supplement", which term may be modified with the name of such an ingredient;

(C) the supplement contains an ingredient described in section 201(ff)(1)(C), and the label or labeling of the supplement fails to identify any part of the plant from which the ingredient is derived;

(D) the supplement—

(i) is covered by the specifications of an official compendium;

(ii) is represented as conforming to the specifications of an official compendium; and

(iii) fails to so conform; or

(E) the supplement—

(i) is not covered by the specifications of an official compendium; and

(ii)(I) fails to have the identity and strength that the supplement is represented to have; or

(II) fails to meet the quality (including tablet or capsule disintegration), purity, or compositional specifications, based on validated assay or other appropriate methods, that the supplement is represented to meet.

A dietary supplement shall not be deemed misbranded solely because its label or labeling contains directions or conditions of use or warnings.

(t) Catfish. [10] If it purports to be or is represented as catfish, unless it is fish classified within the family Ictaluridae.

---

[10] 1 Section 403(t) was added by subsection (a)(2) of section 10806 of Public Law 107–171 (116 Stat. 526). Subsection (a)(1) of such section 10806 provides as follows:
(1) IN GENERAL.—Notwithstanding any other provision of law, for purposes of the FederalFood, Drug, and Cosmetic Act (21 USC 301 et seq.)—
(A) the term "catfish" may only be considered to be a common or usual name (or part thereof) for fish classified within the family Ictaluridae; and
(B) only labeling or advertising for fish classified within that family may include the term "catfish"

(u) Ginseng. [11] If it purports to be or is represented as ginseng, unless it is an herb or herbal ingredient derived from a plant classified within the genus Panax.

(v) Failure to label; health threat. If--

(1) it fails to bear a label required by the Secretary under section 801(n)(1) (relating to food refused admission into the United States);

(2) the Secretary finds that the food presents a threat of serious adverse health consequences or death to humans or animals; and

(3) upon or after notifying the owner or consignee involved that the label is required under section 801, the Secretary informs the owner or consignee that the food presents such a threat.

(w) Major food allergen labeling requirements.

(1) [12, 13, 14, 15] If it is not a raw agricultural commodity and it is, or it contains an ingredient that bears or contains, a major food allergen, unless either—

(A) the word 'Contains', followed by the name of the food source from which the major food allergen is derived, is printed immediately after or is adjacent to the list of ingredients (in a type size no smaller than the

---

[11] Section 403(u) was added by subsection (b)(2) of section 10806 of Public Law 107–171 (116 Stat. 527). Subsection (b)(1) of such section 10806 provides as follows:
(1) IN GENERAL.—Notwithstanding any other provision of law, for purposes of the Federal Food, Drug, and Cosmetic Act (21 USC 301 et seq.)—
(A) the term "ginseng" may only be considered to be a common or usual name (or part thereof) for any herb or herbal ingredient derived from a plant classified within the genus Panax; and
(B) only labeling or advertising for herbs or herbal ingredients classified within that genus may include the term "ginseng".

[12] Paragraphs (w) and (x) were added by section 203(a) of Public Law 108–282. Section 203(d) provides as follows:
(d) EFFECTIVE DATE.—The amendments made by this section shall apply to any food that is labeled on or after January 1, 2006.

[13] Section 203(b) of Public Law 108–282 provides as follows:
(b) EFFECT ON OTHER AUTHORITY.—The amendments made by this section that require a label or labeling for major food allergens do not alter the authority of the Secretary of Health and Human Services under the Federal Food, Drug, and Cosmetic Act (21 USC 301 et seq.) to require a label or labeling for other food allergens.

[14] Several provisions of paragraph (w) contain cross-references to other provisions of the paragraph, and also references to other provisions of this section (section 403). The references to subsections, paragraphs, and subparagraphs probably should be references to paragraphs, subparagraphs, and clauses, respectively. See footnote for paragraph (h)(3).

[15] Public Law 108–282 contains several sections concerning food allergens that do not make amendments to this Act (the Federal Food, Drug, and Cosmetic Act). Section 204 concerns a report to congressional committees; section 205 concerns inspections; section 206 concerns gluten labeling; section 207 concerns improvements in the collection and publication of data; section 208 concerns research; section 209 concerns the Food Code; and section 210 concerns recommendations regarding responding to food-related allergic responses.

type size used in the list of ingredients) required under subsections (g) and (i); or

(B) the common or usual name of the major food allergen in the list of ingredients required under subsections (g) and (i) is followed in parentheses by the name of the food source from which the major food allergen is derived, except that the name of the food source is not required when—

(i) the common or usual name of the ingredient uses the name of the food source from which the major food allergen is derived; or

(ii) the name of the food source from which the major food allergen is derived appears elsewhere in the ingredient list, unless the name of the food source that appears elsewhere in the ingredient list appears as part of the name of a food ingredient that is not a major food allergen under section 201(qq)(2)(A) or (B).

(2) As used in this subsection, the term 'name of the food source from which the major food allergen is derived' means the name described in section 201(qq)(1); provided that in the case of a tree nut, fish, or Crustacean shellfish, the term 'name of the food source from which the major food allergen is derived' means the name of the specific type of nut or species of fish or Crustacean shellfish.

(3) The information required under this subsection may appear in labeling in lieu of appearing on the label only if the Secretary finds that such other labeling is sufficient to protect the public health. A finding by the Secretary under this paragraph (including any change in an earlier finding under this paragraph) is effective upon publication in the Federal Register as a notice.

(4) Notwithstanding subsection (g), (i), or (k), or any other law, a flavoring, coloring, or incidental additive that is, or that bears or contains, a major food allergen shall be subject to the labeling requirements of this subsection.

(5) The Secretary may by regulation modify the requirements of subparagraph (A) or (B) of paragraph (1), or eliminate either the requirement of subparagraph (A) or the requirements of subparagraph (B) of paragraph (1), if the Secretary determines that the modification or elimination of the requirement of subparagraph (A) or the requirements of subparagraph (B) is necessary to protect the public health.

(6)(A) Any person may petition the Secretary to exempt a food ingredient described in section 201(qq)(2) from the allergen labeling requirements of this subsection.

(B) The Secretary shall approve or deny such petition within 180 days of receipt of the petition or the petition shall be deemed denied, unless an extension of time is mutually agreed upon by the Secretary and the petitioner.

(C) The burden shall be on the petitioner to provide scientific evidence (including the analytical method used to produce the evidence) that demonstrates that such food ingredient, as derived by the method specified in the petition, does not cause an allergic response that poses a risk to human health.

(D) A determination regarding a petition under this paragraph shall constitute final agency action.

(E) The Secretary shall promptly post to a public site all petitions received under this paragraph within 14 days of receipt and the Secretary shall promptly post the Secretary's response to each.

(7)(A) A person need not file a petition under paragraph (6) to exempt a food ingredient described in section 201(qq)(2) from the allergen labeling requirements of this subsection, if the person files with the Secretary a notification containing—

(i) scientific evidence (including the analytical method used) that demonstrates that the food ingredient (as derived by the method specified in the notification, where applicable) does not contain allergenic protein; or

(ii) a determination by the Secretary that the ingredient does not cause an allergic response that poses a risk to human health under a premarket approval or notification program under section 409.

(B) The food ingredient may be introduced or delivered for introduction into interstate commerce as a food ingredient that is not a major food allergen 90 days after the date of receipt of the notification by the Secretary, unless the Secretary determines within the 90-day period that the notification does not meet the requirements of this paragraph, or there is insufficient scientific evidence to determine that the food ingredient does not contain allergenic protein or does not cause an allergenic response that poses a risk to human health.

(C) The Secretary shall promptly post to a public site all notifications received under this subparagraph within 14 days of receipt and promptly post any objections thereto by the Secretary.

(x) Nonmajor food allergen labeling requirements. [16] Notwithstanding subsection (g), (i), or (k), [17] or any other law, a spice, flavoring, coloring, or incidental additive that is, or that bears or contains, a food allergen (other than a major food allergen), as determined by the Secretary by regulation, shall be disclosed in a manner specified by the Secretary by regulation.

[16] See footnote 1 to paragraph (w) regarding an effective date, and see footnote 2 to such paragraph regarding the authority of the Secretary of Health and Human Services.

[17] So in law. Probably should be "paragraph (g), (i), or (k)". See footnote 3 for paragraph (w).

Chapter IV

(y) **[Caution: This subsection is effective and applicable to any dietary supplement labeled on or after the date that is 1 year after enactment, pursuant to § 3(d)(1), (2) of Act Dec. 22, 2006, P.L. 109–462].** If it is a dietary supplement that is marketed in the United States, unless the label of such dietary supplement includes a domestic address or domestic phone number through which the responsible person (as described in section 761) may receive a report of a serious adverse event with such dietary supplement.

Sec. 403A. [21 USC §343–1]

(a) [18] Except as provided in subsection (b), no State or political subdivision of a State may directly or indirectly establish under any authority or continue in effect as to any food in interstate commerce—

(1) any requirement for a food which is the subject of a standard of identity established under section 401 that is not identical to such standard of identity or that is not identical to the requirement of section 403(g), except that this paragraph does not apply to a standard of identity of a State or political subdivision of a State for maple syrup that is of the type required by sections 401 and 403(g),

(2) any requirement for the labeling of food of the type required by section 403(c), 403(e), or 403(i)(2) 403(i)(2), 403(w), or 403(x) that is not identical to the requirement of such section, except that this paragraph does not apply to a requirement of a State or political subdivision of a State that is of the type required by section 403(c) and that is applicable to maple syrup,

(3) any requirement for the labeling of food of the type required by section 403(b), 403(d), 403(f), 403(h), 403(i)(1), or 403(k) that is not identical to the requirement of such section, except that this paragraph does not apply to a requirement of a State or political subdivision of a State that is of the type required by section 403(h)(1) and that is applicable to maple syrup,

(4) any requirement for nutrition labeling of food that is not identical to the requirement of section 403(q), except a requirement for nutrition labeling of food which is exempt under subclause (i) or (ii) of section 403(q)(5)(A), or

(5) any requirement respecting any claim of the type described in section 403(r)(1) made in the label or labeling of foodthat is not identical to the requirement of section 403(r), except a requirement respecting a claim made in the label or labeling of food which is exempt under section 403(r)(5)(B).

Paragraph (3) shall take effect in accordance with section 6(b) of the Nutrition Labeling and Education Act of 1990.

---

[18] Section 403A was enacted without a section heading. See section 6(a) of Public Law 101– 535 (104 Stat. 2362).

(b) Upon petition of a State or a political subdivision of a State, the Secretary may exempt from subsection (a), under such conditions as may be prescribed by regulation, any State or local requirement that—

(1) would not cause any food to be in violation of any applicable requirement under Federal law,

(2) would not unduly burden interstate commerce, and

(3) is designed to address a particular need for information which need is not met by the requirements of the sections referred to in subsection (a).

Sec. 403B. [21 USC §343–2] Dietary Supplement Labeling Exemptions.

(a) IN GENERAL.—A publication, including an article, a chapter in a book, or an official abstract of a peer-reviewed scientific publication that appears in an article and was prepared by the author or the editors of the publication, which is reprinted in its entirety, shall not be defined as labeling when used in connection with the sale of a dietary supplement to consumers when it—

(1) is not false or misleading;

(2) does not promote a particular manufacturer or brand of a dietary supplement;

(3) is displayed or presented, or is displayed or presented with other such items on the same subject matter, so as to present a balanced view of the available scientific information on a dietary supplement;

(4) if displayed in an establishment, is physically separate from the dietary supplements; and

(5) does not have appended to it any information by sticker or any other method.

(b) APPLICATION.—Subsection (a) shall not apply to or restrict a retailer or wholesaler of dietary supplements in any way whatsoever in the sale of books or other publications as a part of the business of such retailer or wholesaler.

(c) BURDEN OF PROOF.—In any proceeding brought under subsection (a), the burden of proof shall be on the United States to establish that an article or other such matter is false or misleading.

Sec. 403C. [21 USC §343–3] Disclosure.

(a) No provision of section 201(n), 403(a), or 409 shall be construed to require on the label or labeling of a food a separate radiation disclosure statement that is more prominent than the declaration of ingredients required by section 403(i)(2).

(b) In this section, the term "radiation disclosure statement" means a written statement that discloses that a food has been intentionally subject to radiation.

Sec. 404. [21 USC §344] Emergency Permit Control

(a) Whenever the Secretary finds after investigation that the distribution in interstate commerce of any class of food may, by reason of contamination with micro-organisms during the manufacture, processing, or packing thereof in any locality, be injurious to health, and that such injurious nature cannot be adequately determined after such articles have entered interstate commerce, he then, and in such case only, shall promulgate regulations providing for the issuance, to manufacturers, processors, or packers of such class of food in such locality of permits to which shall be attached such conditions governing the manufacture, processing, or packaging of such class of food, for such temporary period of time, as may be necessary to protect the public health; and after the effective date of such regulations, and during such temporary period, no person shall introduce or deliver for introduction into interstate commerce any such food manufactured, processed, or packed by any such manufacturer, processor, or packer unless such manufacturer, processor, or packer holds a permit issued by the Secretary as provided by such regulations.

(b) The Secretary is authorized to suspend immediately upon notice any permit issued under authority of this section if it is found that any of the conditions of the permit have been violated. The holder of a permit so suspended shall be privileged at any time to apply for the reinstatement of such permit, and the Secretary shall, immediately after prompt hearing and an inspection of the establishment, reinstate such permit if it is found that adequate measures have been taken to comply with and maintain the conditions of the permit, as originally issued or as amended.

(c) Any officer or employee duly designated by the Secretary shall have access to any factory or establishment, the operator of which holds a permit from the Secretary, for the purpose of ascertaining whether or not the conditions of the permit are being complied with, and denial of access for such inspection shall be ground for suspension of the permit until such access is freely given by the operator.

Sec. 405. [21 USC §345] Regulations Making Exemptions

The Secretary shall promulgate regulations exempting from any labeling requirement of this Act (1) small open containers of fresh fruits and fresh vegetables and (2) food which is in accordance with the practice of the trade, to be processed, labeled, or repacked in substantial quantities at establishments other than those where originally processed or packed, or condition that such food is not adulterated or misbranded under the provisions of this Act upon removal from such processing, labeling, or repacking establishment. This section does not apply to the labeling requirements of sections 403(q) and 403(r).

Sec. 406. [21 USC §346] Tolerances for Poisonous Ingredients in Food

[19] Any poisonous or deleterious substance added to any food, except where such substance is required in the production thereof or cannot be avoided by good manufacturing practice shall be deemed to be unsafe for purposes of the application of clause 2)(A) of section 402(a); but when such substance is so required or cannot be so avoided, the Secretary shall promulgate regulations limiting the quantity therein or thereon to such extent as he finds necessary for the protection of public health, and any quantity exceeding the limits so fixed shall also be deemed to be unsafe for purposes of the application of clause (2)(A) of section 402(a). While such a regulation is in effect limiting the quantity of any such substance in the case of any food, such food shall not, by reason of bearing or containing any added amount of such substance, be considered to be adulterated within the meaning of clause (1) of section 402(a). In determining the quantity of such added substance to be tolerated in or on different articles of food the Secretary shall take into account the extent to which the use of such substance is required or cannot be avoided in the production of each such article, and the other ways in which the consumer may be affected by the same or other poisonous or deleterious substances.

Sec. 407. [21 USC §347] Oleomargarine or Margarine

(a) [20] Colored oleomargarine or colored margarine which is sold in the same State or Territory in which it is produced shall be subject in the same manner and to the

Chapter IV

---

[19] See the revolving fund provision in the appendix.

[20] Section 4 of Public Law 81–459 (64 Stat. 20) amended section 15 of the Federal Trade Commission Act (15 USC 55) by adding the following subsection:
"(f) For the purposes of this section and section 407 of the Federal Food, Drug, and Cosmetic Act, as amended, the term 'oleomargarine' or 'margarine' includes—
"(1) all substances, mixtures, and compounds known as oleomargarine or margarine;
"(2) all substances, mixtures, and compounds which have a consistence similar to that of butter and which contain any edible oils or fats other than milk fat if made in imitation or semblance of butter."
In repealing section 2301 of the Internal Revenue Code (relating to the tax on oleomargarine) Public Law 81–459 declared, in part: "The Congress hereby finds and declares that the sale, or the serving in public eating places, of colored oleomargarine or colored margarine without clear identification as such or which is otherwise adulterated or misbranded within the meaning of the Federal Food, Drug, and Cosmetic Act depresses the market in interstate commerce for butter and for oleomargarine or margarine clearly identified and neither adulterated nor misbranded, and constitutes a burden on interstate commerce in such articles. Such burden exists, irrespective of whether such oleomargarine or margarine originates from an interstate source or from the State in which it is sold."
Section 6 of such Public Law states that "nothing in this Act shall be construed as authorizing the possession, sale, or serving of colored oleomargarine or colored margarine in any State or Territory in contravention of the laws of such State or Territory."

same extent to the provisions of this Act as if it had been introduced in interstate commerce.

(b) No person shall sell, or offer for sale, colored oleomargarine or colored margarine unless—

(1) such oleomargarine or margarine is packaged,

(2) the net weight of the contents of any package sold in a retail establishment is one pound or less,

(3) there appears on the label of the package (A) the word "oleomargarine" or "margarine" in type or lettering at least as large as any other type or lettering on such label, and (B) a full and accurate statement of all the ingredients contained in such oleomargarine, or margarine, and

(4) each part of the contents of the package is contained in a wrapper which bears the word "oleomargarine" or "margarine" in type or lettering not smaller than 20-point type.

The requirements of this subsection shall be in addition to and not in lieu of any of the other requirements of this Act.

(c) No person shall possess in a form ready for serving colored oleomargarine or colored margarine at a public eating place unless a notice that oleomargarine or margarine is served is displayed prominently and conspicuously in such place and in such manner as to render it likely to be read and understood by the ordinary individual being served in such eating place or is printed or is otherwise set forth on the menu in type or lettering not smaller than that normally used to designate the serving of other food items. No person shall serve colored oleomargarine or colored margarine at a public eating place, whether or not any charge is made therefore, unless (1) each separate serving bears or is accompanied by labeling identifying it as oleomargarine or margarine, or (2) each separate serving thereof is triangular in shape.

(d) Colored oleomargarine or colored margarine when served with meals at a public eating place shall at the time of such service be exempt from the labeling requirements of section 403 (except (a) and 403 (f)) [21] if it complies with the requirements of subsection (b) of this section.

(e) For the purpose of this section colored oleomargarine or colored margarine is oleomargarine or margarine having a tint or shade containing more than one and six-tenths degrees of yellow, or of yellow and red collectively, but with an excess of yellow over red, measured in terms of Lovibond tintometer scale or its equivalent.

[21] So in law. Probably should be "(except paragraphs (a) and (f))".

Sec. 408. [21 USC §346a] Tolerances and Exemptions for Pesticide Chemical Residues

(a) REQUIREMENT FOR TOLERANCE OR EXEMPTION.—

(1) GENERAL RULE.—Except as provided in paragraph (2) or (3), any pesticide chemical residue in or on a food shall be deemed unsafe for the purpose of section 402(a)(2)(B) unless—

(A) a tolerance for such pesticide chemical residue in or on such food is in effect under this section and the quantity of the residue is within the limits of the tolerance; or

(B) an exemption from the requirement of a tolerance is in effect under this section for the pesticide chemical residue.

For the purposes of this section, the term "food", when used as a noun without modification, shall mean a raw agricultural commodity or processed food.

(2) PROCESSED FOOD.—Notwithstanding paragraph (1)—

(A) if a tolerance is in effect under this section for a pesticide chemical residue in or on a raw agricultural commodity, a pesticide chemical residue that is present in or on a processed food because the food is made from that raw agricultural commodity shall not be considered unsafe within the meaning of section 402(a)(2)(B) despite the lack of a tolerance for the pesticide chemical residue in or on the processed food if the pesticide chemical has been used in or on the raw agricultural commodity in conformity with a tolerance under this section, such residue in or on the raw agricultural commodity has been removed to the extent possible in good manufacturing practice, and the concentration of the pesticide chemical residue in the processed food is not greater than the tolerance prescribed for the pesticide chemical residue in the raw agricultural commodity; or

(B) if an exemption for the requirement for a tolerance is in effect under this section for a pesticide chemical residue in or on a raw agricultural commodity, a pesticide chemical residue that is present in or on a processed food because the food is made from that raw agricultural commodity shall not be considered unsafe within the meaning of section 402(a)(2)(B).

(3) RESIDUES OF DEGRADATION PRODUCTS.—If a pesticide chemical residue is present in or on a food because it is a metabolite or other degradation product of a precursor substance that itself is a pesticide chemical or pesticide chemical residue, such a residue shall not be considered to be unsafe within the meaning of section 402(a)(2)(B) despite the lack of a

Chapter IV

tolerance or exemption from the need for a tolerance for such residue in or on such food if—

(A) the Administrator has not determined that the degradation product is likely to pose any potential health risk from dietary exposure that is of a different type than, or of a greater significance than, any risk posed by dietary exposure to the precursor substance;

(B) either—

(i) a tolerance is in effect under this section for residues of the precursor substance in or on the food, and the combined level of residues of the degradation product and the precursor substance in or on the food is at or below the stoichiometrically equivalent level that would be permitted by the tolerance if the residue consisted only of the precursor substance rather than the degradation product; or

(ii) an exemption from the need for a tolerance is in effect under this section for residues of the precursor substance in or on the food; and

(C) the tolerance or exemption for residues of the precursor substance does not state that it applies only to particular named substances and does not state that it does not apply to residues of the degradation product.

(4) EFFECT OF TOLERANCE OR EXEMPTION.—While a tolerance or exemption from the requirement for a tolerance is in effect under this section for a pesticide chemical residue with respect to any food, the food shall not by reason of bearing or containing any amount of such a residue be considered to be adulterated within the meaning of section 402(a)(1).

(b) AUTHORITY AND STANDARD FOR TOLERANCE.—

(1) AUTHORITY.—The Administrator may issue regulations establishing, modifying, or revoking a tolerance for a pesticide chemical residue in or on a food—

(A) in response to a petition filed under subsection (d); or

(B) on the Administrator's own initiative under subsection (e).

As used in this section, the term "modify" shall not mean expanding the tolerance to cover additional foods.

(2) STANDARD.—

(A) GENERAL RULE.—

(i) STANDARD.—The Administrator may establish or leave in effect a tolerance for a pesticide chemical residue in or on a food only if the Administrator determines that the tolerance is safe. The Administrator shall modify or revoke a tolerance if the Administrator determines it is not safe.

(ii) DETERMINATION OF SAFETY.—As used in this section, the term "safe", with respect to a tolerance for a pesticide chemical residue, means that the Administrator has determined that there is a reasonable certainty that no harm will result from aggregate exposure to the pesticide chemical residue, including all anticipated dietary exposures and all other exposures for which there is reliable information.

(iii) RULE OF CONSTRUCTION.—With respect to a tolerance, a pesticide chemical residue meeting the standard under clause (i) is not an eligible pesticide chemical residue for purposes of subparagraph (B).

(B) TOLERANCES FOR ELIGIBLE PESTICIDE CHEMICAL RESIDUES.—

(i) DEFINITION.—As used in this subparagraph, the term "eligible pesticide chemical residue" means a pesticide chemical residue as to which—

(I) the Administrator is not able to identify a level of exposure to the residue at which the residue will not cause or contribute to a known or anticipated harm to human health (referred to in this section as a "non-threshold effect");

(II) the lifetime risk of experiencing the non-threshold effect is appropriately assessed by quantitative risk assessment; and

(III) with regard to any known or anticipated harm to human health for which the Administrator is able to identify a level at which the residue will not cause such harm (referred to in this section as a "threshold effect"), the Administrator determines that the level of aggregate exposure is safe.

(ii) DETERMINATION OF TOLERANCE.—Notwithstanding subparagraph (A)(i), a tolerance for an eligible pesticide chemical residue may be left in effect or modified under this subparagraph if—

(I) at least one of the conditions described in clause (iii) is met; and

(II) both of the conditions described in clause (iv) are met.

Chapter IV

(iii) CONDITIONS REGARDING USE.—For purposes of clause (ii), the conditions described in this clause with respect to a tolerance for an eligible pesticide chemical residue are the following:

(I) Use of the pesticide chemical that produces the residue protects consumers from adverse effects on health that would pose a greater risk than the dietary risk from the residue.

(II) Use of the pesticide chemical that produces the residue is necessary to avoid a significant disruption in domestic production of an adequate, wholesome, and economical food supply.

(iv) CONDITIONS REGARDING RISK.—For purposes of clause (ii), the conditions described in this clause with respect to a tolerance for an eligible pesticide chemical residue are the following:

(I) The yearly risk associated with the nonthreshold effect from aggregate exposure to the residue does not exceed 10 times the yearly risk that would be allowed under subparagraph (A) for such effect.

(II) The tolerance is limited so as to ensure that the risk over a lifetime associated with the nonthreshold effect from aggregate exposure to the residue is not greater than twice the lifetime risk that would be allowed under subparagraph (A) for such effect.

(v) REVIEW.—Five years after the date on which the Administrator makes a determination to leave in effect or modify a tolerance under this subparagraph, and thereafter as the Administrator deems appropriate, the Administrator shall determine, after notice and opportunity for comment, whether it has been demonstrated to the Administrator that a condition described in clause (iii)(I) or clause (iii)(II) continues to exist with respect to the tolerance and that the yearly and lifetime risks from aggregate exposure to such residue continue to comply with the limits specified in clause (iv). If the Administrator determines by such date that such demonstration has not been made, the Administrator shall, not later than 180 days after the date of such determination, issue a regulation under subsection (e)(1) to modify or revoke the tolerance.

(vi) INFANTS AND CHILDREN.—Any tolerance under this subparagraph shall meet the requirements of subparagraph (C).

(C) EXPOSURE OF INFANTS AND CHILDREN.—In establishing, modifying, leaving in effect, or revoking a tolerance or exemption for a pesticide chemical residue, the Administrator—

(i) shall assess the risk of the pesticide chemical residue based on—

(I) available information about consumption patterns among infants and children that are likely to result in disproportionately high consumption of foods containing or bearing such residue among infants and children in comparison to the general population;

(II) available information concerning the special susceptibility of infants and children to the pesticide chemical residues, including neurological differences between infants and children and adults, and effects of in utero exposure to pesticide chemicals; and

(III) available information concerning the cumulative effects on infants and children of such residues and other substances that have a common mechanism of toxicity; and

(ii) shall—

(I) ensure that there is a reasonable certainty that no harm will result to infants and children from aggregate exposure to the pesticide chemical residue; and

(II) publish a specific determination regarding the safety of the pesticide chemical residue for infants and children.

The Secretary of Health and Human Services and the Secretary of Agriculture, in consultation with the Administrator, shall conduct surveys to document dietary exposure to pesticides among infants and children. In the case of threshold effects, for purposes of clause (ii)(I) an additional tenfold margin of safety for the pesticide chemical residue and other sources of exposure shall be applied for infants and children to take into account potential pre- and postnatal toxicity and completeness of the data with respect to exposure and toxicity to infants and children. Notwithstanding such requirement for an additional margin of safety, the Administrator may use a different margin of safety for the pesticide chemical residue only if, on the basis of reliable data, such margin will be safe for infants and children.

(D) FACTORS.—In establishing, modifying, leaving in effect, or revoking a tolerance or exemption for a pesticide chemical residue, the Administrator shall consider, among other relevant factors—

(i) the validity, completeness, and reliability of the available data from studies of the pesticide chemical and pesticide chemical residue;

(ii) the nature of any toxic effect shown to be caused by the pesticide chemical or pesticide chemical residue in such studies;

(iii) available information concerning the relationship of the results of such studies to human risk;

(iv) available information concerning the dietary consumption patterns of consumers (and major identifiable subgroups of consumers);

(v) available information concerning the cumulative effects of such residues and other substances that have a common mechanism of toxicity;

(vi) available information concerning the aggregate exposure levels of consumers (and major identifiable subgroups of consumers) to the pesticide chemical residue and to other related substances, including dietary exposure under the tolerance and all other tolerances in effect for the pesticide chemical residue, and exposure from other non-occupational sources;

(vii) available information concerning the variability of the sensitivities of major identifiable subgroups of consumers;

(viii) such information as the Administrator may require on whether the pesticide chemical may have an effect in humans that is similar to an effect produced by a naturally occurring estrogen or other endocrine effects; and

(ix) safety factors which in the opinion of experts qualified by scientific training and experience to evaluate the safety of food additives are generally recognized as appropriate for the use of animal experimentation data.

(E) DATA AND INFORMATION REGARDING ANTICIPATED AND ACTUAL RESIDUE LEVELS.—

(i) AUTHORITY.—In establishing, modifying, leaving in effect, or revoking a tolerance for a pesticide chemical residue, the Administrator may consider available data and information on the anticipated residue levels of the pesticide chemical in or on food and the actual residue levels of the pesticide chemical that have been measured in food, including residue data collected by the Food and Drug Administration.

(ii) REQUIREMENT.—If the Administrator relies on anticipated or actual residue levels in establishing, modifying, or leaving in effect a tolerance, the Administrator shall pursuant to subsection (f)(1) require that data be provided five years after the date on which the tolerance is established, modified, or left in effect, and thereafter as the Administrator deems appropriate, demonstrating that such residue levels are not above the levels so relied on. If such data are not so provided, or if the data do not demonstrate that the residue levels are not above the levels so relied on, the Administrator shall, not later than 180 days after the date on which the data were required to be provided, issue a regulation under subsection (e)(1), or an order under subsection (f)(2), as appropriate, to modify or revoke the tolerance.

(F) PERCENT OF FOOD ACTUALLY TREATED.—In establishing, modifying, leaving in effect, or revoking a tolerance for a pesticide chemical residue, the Administrator may, when assessing chronic dietary risk, consider available data and information on the percent of food actually treated with the pesticide chemical (including aggregate pesticide use data collected by the Department of Agriculture) only if the Administrator—

(i) finds that the data are reliable and provide a valid basis to show what percentage of the food derived from such crop is likely to contain such pesticide chemical residue;

(ii) finds that the exposure estimate does not understate exposure for any significant subpopulation group;

(iii) finds that, if data are available on pesticide use and consumption of food in a particular area, the population in such area is not dietarily exposed to residues above those estimated by the Administrator; and

(iv) provides for the periodic reevaluation of the estimate of anticipated dietary exposure.

(3) DETECTION METHODS.—

(A) GENERAL RULE.—A tolerance for a pesticide chemical residue in or on a food shall not be established or modified by the Administrator unless the Administrator determines, after consultation with the Secretary, that there is a practical method for detecting and measuring the levels of the pesticide chemical residue in or on the food.

(B) DETECTION LIMIT.—A tolerance for a pesticide chemical residue in or on a food shall not be established at or modified to a level lower than the limit of detection of the method for detecting and measuring the pesticide chemical residue specified by the Administrator under subparagraph (A).

(4) INTERNATIONAL STANDARDS.—In establishing a tolerance for a pesticide chemical residue in or on a food, the Administrator shall determine whether a maximum residue level for the pesticide chemical has been established by the Codex Alimentarius Commission. If a Codex maximum residue level has been established for the pesticide chemical and the Administrator does not propose to adopt the Codex level, the Administrator shall publish for public comment a notice explaining the reasons for departing from the Codex level.

(c) AUTHORITY AND STANDARD FOR EXEMPTIONS.—

(1) AUTHORITY.—The Administrator may issue a regulation establishing, modifying, or revoking an exemption from the requirement for a tolerance for a pesticide chemical residue in or on food—

(A) in response to a petition filed under subsection (d); or

(B) on the Administrator's initiative under subsection (e).

(2) STANDARD.—

(A) GENERAL RULE.—

(i) STANDARD.—The Administrator may establish or leave in effect an exemption from the requirement for a tolerance for a pesticide chemical residue in or on food only if the Administrator determines that the exemption is safe. The Administrator shall modify or revoke an exemption if the Administrator determines it is not safe.

(ii) DETERMINATION OF SAFETY.—The term "safe", with respect to an exemption for a pesticide chemical residue, means that the Administrator has determined that there is a reasonable certainty that no harm will result from aggregate exposure to the pesticide chemical residue, including all anticipated dietary exposures and all other exposures for which there is reliable information.

(B) FACTORS.—In making a determination under this paragraph, the Administrator shall take into account, among other relevant considerations, the considerations set forth in subparagraphs (C) and (D) of subsection (b)(2).

(3) LIMITATION.— An exemption from the requirement for a tolerance for a pesticide chemical residue in or on food shall not be established or modified by the Administrator unless the Administrator determines, after consultation with the Secretary—

(A) that there is a practical method for detecting and measuring the levels of such pesticide chemical residue in or on food; or

(B) that there is no need for such a method, and states the reasons for such determination in issuing the regulation establishing or modifying the exemption.

(d) PETITION FOR TOLERANCE OR EXEMPTION.—

(1) PETITIONS AND PETITIONERS.— Any person may file with the Administrator a petition proposing the issuance of a regulation—

(A) establishing, modifying, or revoking a tolerance for a pesticide chemical residue in or on a food; or

(B) establishing, modifying, or revoking an exemption from the requirement of a tolerance for such a residue.

(2) PETITION CONTENTS.—

(A) ESTABLISHMENT.—A petition under paragraph (1) to establish a tolerance or exemption for a pesticide chemical residue shall be supported by such data and information as are specified in regulations issued by the Administrator, including—

(i)(I) an informative summary of the petition and of the data, information, and arguments submitted or cited in support of the petition; and

(II) a statement that the petitioner agrees that such summary or any information it contains may be published as a part of the notice of filing of the petition to be published under this subsection and as part of a proposed or final regulation issued under this section;

(ii) the name, chemical identity, and composition of the pesticide chemical residue and of the pesticide chemical that produces the residue;

(iii) data showing the recommended amount, frequency, method, and time of application of that pesticide chemical; (iv) full reports of tests and investigations made with respect to the safety of the pesticide chemical, including full information as to the methods and controls used in conducting those tests and investigations;

(v) full reports of tests and investigations made with respect to the nature and amount of the pesticide chemical residue that is likely to remain in or on the food, including a description of the analytical methods used;

(vi) a practical method for detecting and measuring the levels of the pesticide chemical residue in or on the food, or for exemptions, a statement why such a method is not needed;

(vii) a proposed tolerance for the pesticide chemical residue, if a tolerance is proposed;

(viii) if the petition relates to a tolerance for a processed food, reports of investigations conducted using the processing method(s) used to produce that food;

(ix) such information as the Administrator may require to make the determination under subsection (b)(2)(C);

(x) such information as the Administrator may require on whether the pesticide chemical may have an effect in humans that is similar to an effect produced by a naturally occurring estrogen or other endocrine effects;

(xi) information regarding exposure to the pesticide chemical residue due to any tolerance or exemption already granted for such residue;

(xii) practical methods for removing any amount of the residue that would exceed any proposed tolerance; and

(xiii) such other data and information as the Administrator requires by regulation to support the petition.

If information or data required by this subparagraph is available to the Administrator, the person submitting the petition may cite the availability of the information or data in lieu of submitting it. The Administrator may require a petition to be accompanied by samples of the pesticide chemical with respect to which the petition is filed.

(B) MODIFICATION OR REVOCATION.— The Administrator may by regulation establish the requirements for information and data to support a petition to modify or revoke a tolerance or to modify or revoke an exemption from the requirement for a tolerance.

(3) NOTICE.—A notice of the filing of a petition that the Administrator determines has met the requirements of paragraph (2) shall be published by the Administrator within 30 days after such determination. The notice shall announce the availability of a description of the analytical methods available to the Administrator for the detection and measurement of the pesticide chemical residue with respect to which the petition is filed or shall set forth the petitioner's statement of why such a method is not needed. The notice shall include the summary required by paragraph (2)(A)(i)(I).

(4) ACTIONS BY THE ADMINISTRATOR.—

(A) IN GENERAL.—The Administrator shall, after giving due consideration to a petition filed under paragraph (1) and any other information available to the Administrator—

(i) issue a final regulation (which may vary from that sought by the petition) establishing, modifying, or revoking a tolerance for the pesticide chemical residue or an exemption of the pesticide chemical residue from the requirement of a tolerance (which final regulation shall be issued without further notice and without further period for public comment);

(ii) issue a proposed regulation under subsection (e), and thereafter issue a final regulation under such subsection; or

(iii) issue an order denying the petition.

(B) PRIORITIES.—The Administrator shall give priority to petitions for the establishment or modification of a tolerance or exemption for a pesticide chemical residue that appears to pose a significantly lower risk to human health from dietary exposure than pesticide chemical residues that have tolerances in effect for the same or similar uses.

(C) EXPEDITED REVIEW OF CERTAIN PETITIONS.—

(i) DATE CERTAIN FOR REVIEW.—If a person files a complete petition with the Administrator proposing the issuance of a regulation establishing a tolerance or exemption for a pesticide chemical residue that presents a lower risk to human health than a pesticide chemical residue for which a tolerance has been left in effect or modified under subsection (b)(2)(B), the Administrator shall complete action on such petition under this paragraph within 1 year.

(ii) REQUIRED DETERMINATIONS.—If the Administrator issues a final regulation establishing a tolerance or exemption for a safer pesticide chemical residue under clause (i), the Administrator shall, not later than 180 days after the date on which the regulation is issued, determine whether a condition described in subclause (I) or (II) of subsection (b)(2)(B)(iii) continues to exist with respect to a tolerance that has been left in effect or modified under subsection (b)(2)(B). If such condition does not continue to exist, the Administrator shall, not later than 180 days after the date on which the determination under the preceding sentence is made, issue a regulation under subsection (e)(1) to modify or revoke the tolerance.

(e) ACTION ON ADMINISTRATOR'S OWN INITIATIVE.—

(1) GENERAL RULE.—The Administrator may issue a regulation—

(A) establishing, modifying, suspending under subsection (l)(3), or revoking a tolerance for a pesticide chemical or a pesticide chemical residue;

(B) establishing, modifying, suspending under subsection (l)(3), or revoking an exemption of a pesticide chemical residue from the requirement of a tolerance; or

(C) establishing general procedures and requirements to implement this section.

(2) NOTICE.—Before issuing a final regulation under paragraph (1), the Administrator shall issue a notice of proposed rulemaking and provide a period of not less than 60 days for public comment on the proposed regulation, except that a shorter period for comment may be provided if the Administrator for good cause finds that it would be in the public interest to do so and states the reasons for the finding in the notice of proposed rulemaking.

(f) SPECIAL DATA REQUIREMENTS.—

(1) REQUIRING SUBMISSION OF ADDITIONAL DATA.—If the Administrator determines that additional data or information are reasonably required to support the continuation of a tolerance or exemption that is in effect under this section for a pesticide chemical residue on a food, the Administrator shall—

(A) issue a notice requiring the person holding the pesticide registrations associated with such tolerance or exemption to submit the data or information under section 3(c)(2)(B) of the Federal Insecticide, Fungicide, and Rodenticide Act;

(B) issue a rule requiring that testing be conducted on a substance or mixture under section 4 of the Toxic Substances Control Act; or

(C) publish in the Federal Register, after first providing notice and an opportunity for comment of not less than 60 days' duration, an order—

(i) requiring the submission to the Administrator by one or more interested persons of a notice identifying the person or persons who will submit the required data and information;

(ii) describing the type of data and information required to be submitted to the Administrator and stating why the data and information could not be obtained under the authority of section 3(c)(2)(B) of the Federal Insecticide, Fungicide, and Rodenticide Act or section 4 of the Toxic Substances Control Act;

(iii) describing the reports of the Administrator required to be prepared during and after the collection of the data and information;

(iv) requiring the submission to the Administrator of the data, information, and reports referred to in clauses (ii) and (iii); and

(v) establishing dates by which the submissions described in clauses (i) and (iv) must be made.

The Administrator may under subparagraph (C) revise any such order to correct an error. The Administrator may under this paragraph require data or information pertaining to whether the pesticide chemical may have an effect in humans that is similar to an effect produced by a naturally occurring estrogen or other endocrine effects.

(2) NONCOMPLIANCE.—If a submission required by a notice issued in accordance with paragraph (1)(A), a rule issued under paragraph (1)(B), or an order issued under paragraph (1)(C) is not made by the time specified in such notice, rule, or order, the Administrator may by order published in the Federal Register modify or revoke the tolerance or exemption in question. In any review of such an order under subsection (g)(2), the only material issue shall be whether a submission required under paragraph (1) was not made by the time specified.

(g) EFFECTIVE DATE, OBJECTIONS, HEARINGS, AND ADMINISTRATIVE REVIEW.—

(1) EFFECTIVE DATE.—A regulation or order issued under subsection (d)(4), (e)(1), or (f)(2) shall take effect upon publication unless the regulation or order specifies otherwise. The Administrator may stay the effectiveness of the regulation or order if, after issuance of such regulation or order, objections are filed with respect to such regulation or order pursuant to paragraph (2).

(2) FURTHER PROCEEDINGS.—

(A) OBJECTIONS.—Within 60 days after a regulation or order is issued under subsection (d)(4), (e)(1)(A), (e)(1)(B), (f)(2), (n)(3), or (n)(5)(C), any person may file objections thereto with the Administrator, specifying with particularity the provisions of the regulation or order deemed objectionable and stating reasonable grounds therefor. If the regulation or order was issued in response to a petition under subsection (d)(1), a copy of each objection filed by a person other than the petitioner shall be served by the Administrator on the petitioner.

(B) HEARING.—An objection may include a request for a public evidentiary hearing upon the objection. The Administrator shall, upon the initiative of the Administrator or upon the request of an interested person and after due notice, hold a public evidentiary hearing if and to the extent the Administrator determines that such a public hearing is necessary to receive factual evidence relevant to material issues of fact raised by the objections. The presiding officer in such a hearing may authorize a party to obtain discovery from other persons and may upon a showing of good cause made by a party issue a subpoena to compel testimony or production of documents from any person. The presiding officer shall be governed by the Federal Rules of Civil Procedure in making any order for the protection of the witness or the content of documents produced and shall order the payment of reasonable fees and expenses as a condition to requiring testimony of the witness. On contest, such a subpoena may be enforced by a Federal district court.

(C) FINAL DECISION.—As soon as practicable after receiving the arguments of the parties, the Administrator shall issue an order stating the action taken upon each such objection and setting forth any revision to the regulation or prior order that the Administrator has found to be warranted. If a hearing was held under subparagraph (B), such order and any revision to the regulation or prior order shall, with respect to questions of fact at issue in the hearing, be based only on substantial evidence of record at such hearing, and shall set forth in detail the findings of facts and the conclusions of law or policy upon which the order or regulation is based.

(h) JUDICIAL REVIEW.—

(1) PETITION.—In a case of actual controversy as to the validity of any regulation issued under subsection (e)(1)(C), or any order issued under subsection (f)(1)(C) or (g)(2)(C), or any regulation that is the subject of such an order, any person who will be adversely affected by such order or regulation may obtain judicial review by filing in the United States Court of Appeals for the circuit wherein that person resides or has its principal place of business, or in the United States Court of Appeals for the District of Columbia Circuit, within 60 days after publication of such order or regulation, a petition praying that the order or regulation be set aside in whole or in part.

(2) RECORD AND JURISDICTION.—A copy of the petition under paragraph (1) shall be forthwith transmitted by the clerk of the court to the Administrator, or any officer designated by the Administrator for that purpose, and thereupon the Administrator shall file in the court the record of the proceedings on which the Administrator based the order or regulation, as provided in section 2112 of title 28, United States Code. Upon the filing of such a petition, the court shall have exclusive jurisdiction to affirm or set aside the order or regulation complained of in whole or in part. As to orders issued following a public evidentiary hearing, the findings of the Administrator with respect to questions of fact shall be sustained only if supported by substantial evidence when considered on the record as a whole.

(3) ADDITIONAL EVIDENCE.—If a party applies to the court for leave to adduce additional evidence and shows to the satisfaction of the court that the additional evidence is material and that there were reasonable grounds for the failure to adduce the evidence in the proceeding before the Administrator, the court may order that the additional evidence (and evidence in rebuttal thereof) shall be taken before the Administrator in the manner and upon the terms and conditions the court deems proper. The Administrator may modify prior findings as to the facts by reason of the additional evidence so taken and may modify the order or regulation accordingly. The Administrator shall file with the court any such modified finding, order, or regulation.

(4) FINAL JUDGMENT; SUPREME COURT REVIEW.—The judgment of the court affirming or setting aside, in whole or in part, any regulation or any order and any regulation which is the subject of such an order shall be final, subject to review by the Supreme Court of the United States as provided in section 1254 of title 28 of the United States Code. The commencement of proceedings under this subsection shall not, unless specifically ordered by the court to the contrary, operate as a stay of a regulation or order.

(5) APPLICATION.—Any issue as to which review is or was obtainable under this subsection shall not be the subject of judicial review under any other provision of law.

(i) CONFIDENTIALITY AND USE OF DATA.—

(1) GENERAL RULE.—Data and information that are or have been submitted to the Administrator under this section or section 409 in support of a tolerance or an exemption from a tolerance shall be entitled to confidential treatment for reasons of business confidentiality and to exclusive use and data compensation to the same extent provided by sections 3 and 10 of the Federal Insecticide, Fungicide, and Rodenticide Act.

(2) EXCEPTIONS.—

(A) IN GENERAL.—Data and information that are entitled to confidential treatment under paragraph (1) may be disclosed, under such security requirements as the Administrator may provide by regulation, to—

(i) employees of the United States authorized by the Administrator to examine such data and information in the carrying out of their official duties under this Act or other Federal statutes intended to protect the public health; or

(ii) contractors with the United States authorized by the Administrator to examine such data and information in the carrying out of contracts under this Act or such statutes.

(B) CONGRESS.—This subsection does not authorize the withholding of data or information from either House of Congress or from, to the extent of matter within its jurisdiction, any committee or subcommittee of such committee or any joint committee of Congress or any subcommittee of such joint committee.

(3) SUMMARIES.—Notwithstanding any provision of this subsection or other law, the Administrator may publish the informative summary required by subsection (d)(2)(A)(i) and may, in issuing a proposed or final regulation or order under this section, publish an informative summary of the data relating to the regulation or order.

(j) STATUS OF PREVIOUSLY ISSUED REGULATIONS.—

(1) REGULATIONS UNDER SECTION 406.—Regulations affecting pesticide chemical residues in or on raw agricultural commodities promulgated, in accordance with section 701(e), under the authority of section 406(a) upon the basis of public hearings instituted before January 1, 1953, shall be deemed to be regulations issued under this section and shall be subject to modification or revocation under subsections (d) and (e), and shall be subject to review under subsection (q).

(2) REGULATIONS UNDER SECTION 409.—Regulations that established tolerances for substances that are pesticide chemical residues in or on processed food, or that otherwise stated the conditions under which such

Chapter IV

pesticide chemicals could be safely used, and that were issued under section 409 on or before the date of the enactment of this paragraph, shall be deemed to be regulations issued under this section and shall be subject to modification or revocation under subsection (d) or (e), and shall be subject to review under subsection (q).

(3) REGULATIONS UNDER SECTION 408.—Regulations that established tolerances or exemptions under this section that were issued on or before the date of the enactment of this paragraph shall remain in effect unless modified or revoked under subsection (d) or (e), and shall be subject to review under subsection (q).

(4) CERTAIN SUBSTANCES.—With respect to a substance that is not included in the definition of the term 'pesticide chemical' under section 201(q)(1) but was so included on the day before the date of the enactment of the Antimicrobial Regulation Technical Corrections Act of 1998, the following applies as of such date of enactment:

(A) Notwithstanding paragraph (2), any regulation applying to the use of the substance that was in effect on the day before such date, and was on such day deemed in such paragraph to have been issued under this section, shall be considered to have been issued under section 409.

(B) Notwithstanding paragraph (3), any regulation applying to the use of the substance that was in effect on such day and was issued under this section (including any such regulation issued before the date of the enactment of the Food Quality Protection Act of 1996) is deemed to have been issued under section 409.

(k) TRANSITIONAL PROVISION.—If, on the day before the date of the enactment of this subsection, a substance that is a pesticide chemical was, with respect to a particular pesticidal use of the substance and any resulting pesticide chemical residue in or on a particular food—

(1) regarded by the Administrator or the Secretary as generally recognized as safe for use within the meaning of the provisions of subsection (a) or section 201(s) as then in effect; or

(2) regarded by the Secretary as a substance described by section 201(s)(4); such a pesticide chemical residue shall be regarded as exempt from the requirement for a tolerance, as of the date of enactment of this subsection. The Administrator shall by regulation indicate which substances are described by this subsection. Any exemption under this subsection may be modified or revoked as if it had been issued under subsection (c).

(l) HARMONIZATION WITH ACTION UNDER OTHER LAWS.—

(1) COORDINATION WITH FIFRA.—To the extent practicable and consistent with the review deadlines in subsection (q), in issuing a final rule

under this subsection that suspends or revokes a tolerance or exemption for a pesticide chemical residue in or on food, the Administrator shall coordinate such action with any related necessary action under the Federal Insecticide, Fungicide, and Rodenticide Act.

(2) REVOCATION OF TOLERANCE OR EXEMPTION FOLLOWING CANCELLATION OF ASSOCIATED REGISTRATIONS.—If the Administrator, acting under the Federal Insecticide, Fungicide, and Rodenticide Act, cancels the registration of each pesticide that contains a particular pesticide chemical and that is labeled for use on a particular food, or requires that the registration of each such pesticide be modified to prohibit its use in connection with the production, storage, or transportation of such food, due in whole or in part to dietary risks to humans posed by residues of that pesticide chemical on that food, the Administrator shall revoke any tolerance or exemption that allows the presence of the pesticide chemical, or any pesticide chemical residue that results from its use, in or on that food. Subsection (e) shall apply to actions taken under this paragraph. A revocation under this paragraph shall become effective not later than 180 days after—

(A) the date by which each such cancellation of a registration has become effective; or

(B) the date on which the use of the canceled pesticide becomes unlawful under the terms of the cancellation, whichever is later.

(3) SUSPENSION OF TOLERANCE OR EXEMPTION FOLLOWING SUSPENSION OF ASSOCIATED REGISTRATIONS.—

(A) SUSPENSION.—If the Administrator, acting under the Federal Insecticide, Fungicide, and Rodenticide Act, suspends the use of each registered pesticide that contains a particular pesticide chemical and that is labeled for use on a particular food, due in whole or in part to dietary risks to humans posed by residues of that pesticide chemical on that food, the Administrator shall suspend any tolerance or exemption that allows the presence of the pesticide chemical, or any pesticide chemical residue that results from its use, in or on that food. Subsection (e) shall apply to actions taken under this paragraph. A suspension under this paragraph shall become effective not later than 60 days after the date by which each such suspension of use has become effective.

(B) EFFECT OF SUSPENSION.—The suspension of a tolerance or exemption under subparagraph (A) shall be effective as long as the use of each associated registration of a pesticide is suspended under the Federal Insecticide, Fungicide, and Rodenticide Act. While a suspension of a tolerance or exemption is effective the tolerance or exemption shall not be considered to be in effect. If the suspension of use of the pesticide under that Act is terminated, leaving the registration of the pesticide for such use in effect under that Act, the Administrator shall rescind any associated suspension of tolerance or exemption.

(4) TOLERANCES FOR UNAVOIDABLE RESIDUES.—In connection with action taken under paragraph (2) or (3), or with respect to pesticides whose registrations were suspended or canceled prior to the date of the enactment of this paragraph under the Federal Insecticide, Fungicide, and Rodenticide Act, if the Administrator determines that a residue of the canceled or suspended pesticide chemical will unavoidably persist in the environment and thereby be present in or on a food, the Administrator may establish a tolerance for the pesticide chemical residue. In establishing such a tolerance, the Administrator shall take into account both the factors set forth in subsection (b)(2) and the unavoidability of the residue. Subsection (e) shall apply to the establishment of such tolerance. The Administrator shall review any such tolerance periodically and modify it as necessary so that it allows no greater level of the pesticide chemical residue than is unavoidable.

(5) PESTICIDE RESIDUES RESULTING FROM LAWFUL APPLICATION OF PESTICIDE.—Notwithstanding any other provision of this Act, if a tolerance or exemption for a pesticide chemical residue in or on a food has been revoked, suspended, or modified under this section, an article of that food shall not be deemed unsafe solely because of the presence of such pesticide chemical residue in or on such food if it is shown to the satisfaction of the Secretary that—

(A) the residue is present as the result of an application or use of a pesticide at a time and in a manner that was lawful under the Federal Insecticide, Fungicide, and Rodenticide Act; and

(B) the residue does not exceed a level that was authorized at the time of that application or use to be present on the food under a tolerance, exemption, food additive regulation, or other sanction then in effect under this Act; unless, in the case of any tolerance or exemption revoked, suspended, or modified under this subsection or subsection (d) or (e), the Administrator has issued a determination that consumption of the legally treated food during the period of its likely availability in commerce will pose an unreasonable dietary risk.

(6) TOLERANCE FOR USE OF PESTICIDES UNDER AN EMERGENCY EXEMPTION.—If the Administrator grants an exemption under section 18 of the Federal Insecticide, Fungicide, and Rodenticide Act (7 USC 136p) for a pesticide chemical, the Administrator shall establish a tolerance or exemption from the requirement for a tolerance for the pesticide chemical residue. Such a tolerance or exemption from a tolerance shall have an expiration date. The Administrator may establish such a tolerance or exemption without providing notice or a period for comment on the tolerance or exemption. The Administrator shall promulgate regulations within 365 days after the date of the enactment of this paragraph governing

the establishment of tolerances and exemptions under this paragraph. Such regulations shall be consistent with the safety standard under subsections (b)(2) and (c)(2) and with section 18 of the Federal Insecticide, Fungicide, and Rodenticide Act.

(m) [22] FEES.—

(1) AMOUNT.—The Administrator shall by regulation require the payment of such fees as will in the aggregate, in the judgment of the Administrator, be sufficient over a reasonable term to provide, equip, and maintain an adequate service for the performance of the Administrator's functions under this section. Under the regulations, the performance of the Administrator's services or other functions under this section, including—

(A) the acceptance for filing of a petition submitted under subsection (d);

(B) establishing, modifying, leaving in effect, or revoking a tolerance or establishing, modifying, leaving in effect, or revoking an exemption from the requirement for a tolerance under this section;

(C) the acceptance for filing of objections under subsection (g); or

(D) the certification and filing in court of a transcript of the proceedings and the record under subsection (h); may be conditioned upon the payment of such fees. The regulations may further provide for waiver or refund of fees in whole or in part when in the judgment of the Administrator such a waiver or refund is equitable and not contrary to the purposes of this subsection.

(2) DEPOSIT.—All fees collected under paragraph (1) shall be deposited in the Reregistration and Expedited Processing Fund created by section 4(k) of the Federal Insecticide, Fungicide, and Rodenticide Act. Such fees shall be available to the Administrator, without fiscal year limitation, for the performance of the Administrator's services or functions as specified in paragraph (1).

(n) NATIONAL UNIFORMITY OF TOLERANCES.—

(1) QUALIFYING PESTICIDE CHEMICAL RESIDUE.—For purposes of this subsection, the term "qualifying pesticide chemical residue" means a pesticide chemical residue resulting from the use, in production, processing, or storage of a food, of a pesticide chemical that is an active ingredient and that—

[22] Section 501(d)(2) of division G of Public Law 108–199 (118 Stat. 422) provides as follows:
(2) TOLERANCE FEES.—Notwithstanding section 408(m)(1) of the Federal Food, Drug, and Cosmetic Act (21 USC 346a(m)(1)), during the period beginning on October 1, 2003, and ending on September 30, 2008, the Administrator of the Environmental Protection Agency shall not collect any tolerance fees under that section.

Chapter IV

(A) was first approved for such use in a registration of a pesticide issued under section 3(c)(5) of the Federal Insecticide, Fungicide, and Rodenticide Act on or after April 25, 1985, on the basis of data determined by the Administrator to meet all applicable requirements for data prescribed by regulations in effect under that Act on April 25, 1985; or

(B) was approved for such use in a reregistration eligibility determination issued under section 4(g) of that Act on or after the date of enactment of this subsection.

(2) QUALIFYING FEDERAL DETERMINATION.—For purposes of this subsection, the term "qualifying Federal determination" means a tolerance or exemption from the requirement for a tolerance for a qualifying pesticide chemical residue that—

(A) is issued under this section after the date of the enactment of this subsection and determined by the Administrator to meet the standard under subsection (b)(2)(A) (in the case of a tolerance) or (c)(2) (in the case of an exemption); or

(B)(i) pursuant to subsection (j) is remaining in effect or is deemed to have been issued under this section, or is regarded under subsection (k) as exempt from the requirement for a tolerance; and

(ii) is determined by the Administrator to meet the standard under subsection (b)(2)(A) (in the case of a tolerance) or (c)(2) (in the case of an exemption).

(3) LIMITATION.—The Administrator may make the determination described in paragraph (2)(B)(ii) only by issuing a rule in accordance with the procedure set forth in subsection (d) or (e) and only if the Administrator issues a proposed rule and allows a period of not less than 30 days for comment on the proposed rule. Any such rule shall be reviewable in accordance with subsections (g) and (h).

(4) STATE AUTHORITY.—Except as provided in paragraphs (5), (6), and (8) no State or political subdivision may establish or enforce any regulatory limit on a qualifying pesticide chemical residue in or on any food if a qualifying Federal determination applies to the presence of such pesticide chemical residue in or on such food, unless such State regulatory limit is identical to such qualifying Federal determination. A State or political subdivision shall be deemed to establish or enforce a regulatory limit on a pesticide chemical residue in or on a food if it purports to prohibit or penalize the production, processing, shipping, or other handling of a food because it contains a pesticide residue (in excess of a prescribed limit).

(5) PETITION PROCEDURE.—

(A) IN GENERAL.—Any State may petition the Administrator for authorization to establish in such State a regulatory limit on a qualifying pesticide chemical residue in or on any food that is not identical to the qualifying Federal determination applicable to such qualifying pesticide chemical residue.

(B) PETITION REQUIREMENTS.—Any petition under subparagraph (A) shall—

(i) satisfy any requirements prescribed, by rule, by the Administrator; and

(ii) be supported by scientific data about the pesticide chemical residue that is the subject of the petition or about chemically related pesticide chemical residues, data on the consumption within such State of food bearing the pesticide chemical residue, and data on exposure of humans within such State to the pesticide chemical residue.

(C) AUTHORIZATION.—The Administrator may, by order, grant the authorization described in subparagraph (A) if the Administrator determines that the proposed State regulatory limit—

(i) is justified by compelling local conditions; and

(ii) would not cause any food to be a violation of Federal law.

(D) TREATMENT.—In lieu of any action authorized under subparagraph (C), the Administrator may treat a petition under this paragraph as a petition under subsection (d) to modify or revoke a tolerance or an exemption. If the Administrator determines to treat a petition under this paragraph as a petition under subsection (d), the Administrator shall thereafter act on the petition pursuant to subsection (d).

(E) REVIEW.—Any order of the Administrator granting or denying the authorization described in subparagraph (A) shall be subject to review in the manner described in subsections (g) and (h).

(6) URGENT PETITION PROCEDURE.—Any State petition to the Administrator pursuant to paragraph (5) that demonstrates that consumption of a food containing such pesticide residue level during the period of the food's likely availability in the State will pose a significant public health threat from acute exposure shall be considered an urgent petition. If an order by the Administrator to grant or deny the requested authorization in an urgent petition is not made within 30 days of receipt of the petition, the petitioning State may establish and enforce a temporary regulatory limit on a qualifying pesticide chemical residue in or on the food. The temporary regulatory limit shall be validated or terminated by the Administrator's final order on the petition.

(7) RESIDUES FROM LAWFUL APPLICATION.—No State or political subdivision may enforce any regulatory limit on the level of a pesticide chemical residue that may appear in or on any food if, at the time of the application of the pesticide that resulted in such residue, the sale of such food with such residue level was lawful under this section and under the law of such State, unless the State demonstrates that consumption of the food containing such pesticide residue level during the period of the food's likely availability in the State will pose an unreasonable dietary risk to the health of persons within such State.

(8) SAVINGS.—Nothing in this Act preempts the authority of any State or political subdivision to require that a food containing a pesticide chemical residue bear or be the subject of a warning or other statement relating to the presence of the pesticide chemical residue in or on such food.

(o) CONSUMER RIGHT TO KNOW.—Not later than 2 years after the date of the enactment of the Food Quality Protection Act of 1996, and annually thereafter, the Administrator shall, in consultation with the Secretary of Agriculture and the Secretary of Health and Human Services, publish in a format understandable to a lay person, and distribute to large retail grocers for public display (in a manner determined by the grocer), the following information, at a minimum:

(1) A discussion of the risks and benefits of pesticide chemical residues in or on food purchased by consumers.

(2) A listing of actions taken under subparagraph (B) of subsection (b)(2) that may result in pesticide chemical residues in or on food that present a yearly or lifetime risk above the risk allowed under subparagraph (A) of such subsection, and the food on which the pesticide chemicals producing the residues are used.

(3) Recommendations to consumers for reducing dietary exposure to pesticide chemical residues in a manner consistent with maintaining a healthy diet, including a list of food that may reasonably substitute for food listed under paragraph (2).

Nothing [23] in this subsection shall prevent retail grocers from providing additional information.

(p) ESTROGENIC SUBSTANCES SCREENING PROGRAM.—

(1) DEVELOPMENT.—Not later than 2 years after the date of enactment of this section, the Administrator shall in consultation with the Secretary of Health and Human Services develop a screening program, using appropriate validated test systems and other scientifically relevant information, to determine whether certain substances may have an effect in humans that is

[23] Indentation is so in law. Beginning of sentence probably should be moved to left.

similar to an effect produced by a naturally occurring estrogen, or such other endocrine effect as the Administrator may designate.

(2) IMPLEMENTATION.—Not later than 3 years after the date of enactment of this section, after obtaining public comment and review of the screening program described in paragraph (1) by the scientific advisory panel established under section 25(d) of the Federal Insecticide, Fungicide, and Rodenticide Act or the science advisory board established by section 8 of the Environmental Research, Development, and Demonstration [24] Act of 1978 (42 USC 4365), the Administrator shall implement the program.

(3) SUBSTANCES.—In carrying out the screening program described in paragraph (1), the Administrator—

(A) shall provide for the testing of all pesticide chemicals; and

(B) may provide for the testing of any other substance that may have an effect that is cumulative to an effect of a pesticide chemical if the Administrator determines that a substantial population may be exposed to such substance.

(4) EXEMPTION.—Notwithstanding paragraph (3), the Administrator may, by order, exempt from the requirements of this section a biologic substance or other substance if the Administrator determines that the substance is anticipated not to produce any effect in humans similar to an effect produced by a naturally occurring estrogen.

(5) COLLECTION OF INFORMATION.—

(A) IN GENERAL.—The Administrator shall issue an order to a registrant of a substance for which testing is required under this subsection, or to a person who manufactures or imports a substance for which testing is required under this subsection, to conduct testing in accordance with the screening program described in paragraph (1), and submit information obtained from the testing to the Administrator, within a reasonable time period that the Administrator determines is sufficient for the generation of the information.

(B) PROCEDURES.—To the extent practicable the Administrator shall minimize duplicative testing of the same substance for the same endocrine effect, develop, as appropriate, procedures for fair and equitable sharing of test costs, and develop, as necessary, procedures for handling of confidential business information.

(C) FAILURE OF REGISTRANTS TO SUBMIT INFORMATION.—

(i) SUSPENSION.— If a registrant of a substance referred to in paragraph (3)(A) fails to comply with an order under subparagraph

[24] So in law. The word "Authorization" probably should appear after "Demonstration".

(A) of this paragraph, the Administrator shall issue a notice of intent to suspend the sale or distribution of the substance by the registrant. Any suspension proposed under this paragraph shall become final at the end of the 30-day period beginning on the date that the registrant receives the notice of intent to suspend, unless during that period a person adversely affected by the notice requests a hearing or the Administrator determines that the registrant has complied fully with this paragraph.

(ii) HEARING.— If a person requests a hearing under clause (i), the hearing shall be conducted in accordance with section 554 of title 5, United States Code. The only matter for resolution at the hearing shall be whether the registrant has failed to comply with an order under subparagraph (A) of this paragraph. A decision by the Administrator after completion of a hearing shall be considered to be a final agency action.

(iii) TERMINATION OF SUSPENSIONS.—The Administrator shall terminate a suspension under this subparagraph issued with respect to a registrant if the Administrator determines that the registrant has complied fully with this paragraph.

(D) NONCOMPLIANCE BY OTHER PERSONS.—Any person (other than a registrant) who fails to comply with an order under subparagraph (A) shall be liable for the same penalties and sanctions as are provided under section 16 of the Toxic Substances Control Act (15 USC 2601 and following) in the case of a violation referred to in that section. Such penalties and sanctions shall be assessed and imposed in the same manner as provided in such section 16.

(6) AGENCY ACTION.—In the case of any substance that is found, as a result of testing and evaluation under this section, to have an endocrine effect on humans, the Administrator shall, as appropriate, take action under such statutory authority as is available to the Administrator, including consideration under other sections of this Act, as is necessary to ensure the protection of public health.

(7) REPORT TO CONGRESS.—Not later than 4 years after the date of enactment of this section, the Administrator shall prepare and submit to Congress a report containing—

(A) the findings of the Administrator resulting from the screening program described in paragraph (1);

(B) recommendations for further testing needed to evaluate the impact on human health of the substances tested under the screening program; and

(C) recommendations for any further actions (including any action described in paragraph (6)) that the Administrator determines are appropriate based on the findings.

(q) SCHEDULE FOR REVIEW.—

(1) IN GENERAL.—The Administrator shall review tolerances and exemptions for pesticide chemical residues in effect on the day before the date of the enactment of the Food Quality Protection Act of 1996, as expeditiously as practicable, assuring that—

(A) 33 percent of such tolerances and exemptions are reviewed within 3 years of the date of enactment of such Act;

(B) 66 percent of such tolerances and exemptions are reviewed within 6 years of the date of enactment of such Act; and

(C) 100 percent of such tolerances and exemptions are reviewed within 10 years of the date of enactment of such Act.

In conducting a review of a tolerance or exemption, the Administrator shall determine whether the tolerance or exemption meets the requirements of subsections [25] (b)(2) or (c)(2) and shall, by the deadline for the review of the tolerance or exemption, issue a regulation under subsection (d)(4) or (e)(1) to modify or revoke the tolerance or exemption if the tolerance or exemption does not meet such requirements.

(2) PRIORITIES.—In determining priorities for reviewing tolerances and exemptions under paragraph (1), the Administrator shall give priority to the review of the tolerances or exemptions that appear to pose the greatest risk to public health.

(3) PUBLICATION OF SCHEDULE.—Not later than 12 months after the date of the enactment of the Food Quality Protection Act of 1996, the Administrator shall publish a schedule for review of tolerances and exemptions established prior to the date of the enactment of the Food Quality Protection Act of 1996. The determination of priorities for the review of tolerances and exemptions pursuant to this subsection is not a rulemaking and shall not be subject to judicial review, except that failure to take final action pursuant to the schedule established by this paragraph shall be subject to judicial review.

(r) TEMPORARY TOLERANCE OR EXEMPTION.—The Administrator may, upon the request of any person who has obtained an experimental permit for a pesticide chemical under the Federal Insecticide, Fungicide, and Rodenticide Act or upon the Administrator's own initiative, establish a temporary tolerance or exemption for the pesticide chemical residue for the uses covered by the permit.

[25] So in law. Probably should be "subsection".

Chapter IV

Subsections (b)(2), (c)(2), (d), and (e) shall apply to actions taken under this subsection.

(s) SAVINGS CLAUSE.—Nothing in this section shall be construed to amend or modify the provisions of the Toxic Substances Control Act or the Federal Insecticide, Fungicide, and Rodenticide Act.

Sec. 409. [21 USC §348] Unsafe Food Additives

(a) A food additive shall, with respect to any particular use or intended use of such additives, be deemed to be unsafe for the purposes of the application of clause (2)(C) of section 402(a), unless—

(1) it and its use or intended use conform to the terms of an exemption which is in effect pursuant to subsection (j) of this section;

(2) there is in effect, and it and its use or intended use are in conformity with, a regulation issued under this section prescribing the conditions under which such additive may be safely used; or

(3) in the case of a food additive as defined in this Act that is a food contact substance, there is—

(A) in effect, and such substance and the use of such substance are in conformity with, a regulation issued under this section prescribing the conditions under which such additive may be safely used; or

(B) a notification submitted under subsection (h) that is effective.

While such a regulation relating to a food additive, or such a notification under subsection (h)(1) relating to a food additive that is a food contact substance, is in effect, and has not been revoked pursuant to subsection (i), a food shall not, by reason of bearing or containing such a food additive in accordance with the regulation or notification, be considered adulterated under section 402(a)(1).

(b) Petition to establish safety

(1) Any person may, with respect to any intended use of a food additive, file with the Secretary a petition proposing the issuance of a regulation prescribing the conditions under which such additive may be safely used.

(2) Such petition shall, in addition to any explanatory or supporting data, contain—

(A) the name and all pertinent information concerning such food additive, including, where available, its chemical identity and composition;

(B) a statement of the conditions of the proposed use of such additive, including all directions, recommendations, and suggestions proposed for the use of such additive, and including specimens of its proposed labeling;

(C) all relevant data bearing on the physical or other technical effect such additive is intended to produce, and the quantity of such additive required to produce such effect;

(D) a description of practicable methods for determining the quantity of such additive in or on food, and any substance formed in or on food, because of its use; and

(E) full reports of investigations made with respect to the safety for use of such additive, including full information as to the methods and controls used in conducting such investigations.

(3) Upon request of the Secretary, the petitioner shall furnish (or, if the petitioner is not the manufacturer of such additive, the petitioner shall have the manufacturer of such additive furnish, without disclosure to the petitioner), a full description of the methods used in, and the facilities and controls used for, the production of such additive.

(4) Upon request of the Secretary, the petitioner shall furnish samples of the food additive involved, or articles used as components thereof, and of the food in or on which the additive is proposed to be used.

(5) Notice of the regulation proposed by the petitioner shall be published in general terms by the Secretary within thirty days after filing.

(c) Action on the petition.

(1) The Secretary shall—

(A) by order establish a regulation (whether or not in accord with that proposed by the petitioner) prescribing, with respect to one or more proposed uses of the food additive involved, the conditions under which such additive may be safely used (including, but not limited to, specifications as to the particular food or classes of food in or on which such additive may be used, the maximum quantity which may be used or permitted to remain in or on such food, the manner in which such additive may be added to or used in or on such food, and any directions or other labeling or packaging requirements for such additive deemed necessary by him to assure the safety of such use), and shall notify the petitioner of such order and the reasons for such action; or

(B) by order deny the petition, and shall notify the petitioner of such order and of the reasons for such action.

(2) The order required by paragraph (1) (A) or (B) of this subsection shall be issued within ninety days after the date of filing of the petition, except that the Secretary may (prior to such ninetieth day), by written notice to the

petitioner, extend such ninety day period to such time (not more than one hundred and eighty days after the date of filing of the petition) as the Secretary deems necessary to enable him to study and investigate the petition.

(3) No such regulation shall issue if a fair evaluation of the data before the Secretary—

(A) fails to establish that the proposed use of the food additive, under the conditions of use to be specified in the regulation, will be safe: Provided, That no additive shall be deemed to be safe if it is found to induce cancer when ingested by man or animal, or if it is found, after tests which are appropriate for the evaluation of the safety of food additives, to induce cancer in man or animal, except that this proviso shall not apply with respect to the use of a substance as an ingredient of feed for animals which are raised for food production, if the Secretary finds (i) that, under the conditions of use and feeding specified in proposed labeling and reasonably certain to be followed in practice, such additive will not adversely affect the animals for which such feed is intended, and (ii) that no residue of the additive will be found (by methods of examination prescribed or approved by the Secretary by regulations, which regulations shall not be subject to subsections (f) and (g)) in any edible portion of such animal after slaughter or in any food yielded by or derived from the living animal; or

(B) shows that the proposed use of the additive would promote deception of the consumer in violation of this Act or would otherwise result in adulteration or in misbranding of food within the meaning of this Act.

(4) If, in the judgment of the Secretary, based upon a fair evaluation of the data before him, a tolerance limitation is required in order to assure that the proposed use of an additive will be safe, the Secretary—

(A) shall not fix such tolerance limitation at a level higher than he finds to be reasonably required to accomplish the physical or other technical effect for which such additive is intended; and

(B) shall not establish a regulation for such proposed use if he finds upon a fair evaluation of the data before him that such data do not establish that such use would accomplish the intended physical or other technical effect.

(5) In determining, for the purposes of this section, whether a proposed use of a food additive is safe, the Secretary shall consider among other relevant factors—

(A) the probable consumption of the additive and of any substance formed in or on food because of the use of the additive;

(B) the cumulative effect of such additive in the diet of man or animals, taking into account any chemically or pharmacologically related substance or substances in such diet; and

(C) safety factors which in the opinion of experts qualified by scientific training and experience to evaluate the safety of food additives are generally recognized as appropriate for the use of animal experimentation data.

(d) Regulation issued on Secretary's initiative. The Secretary may at any time, upon his own initiative, propose the issuance of a regulation prescribing, with respect to any particular use of a food additive, the conditions under which such additive may be safely used, and the reasons therefor. After the thirtieth day following publication of such a proposal, the Secretary may by order establish a regulation based upon the proposal.

(e) Publication and Effective Date of Orders. Any order, including any regulation established by such order, issued under subsection (c) or (d) of this section, shall be published and shall be effective upon publication, but the Secretary may stay such effectiveness if, after issuance of such order, a hearing is sought with respect to such order pursuant to subsection (f).

(f) Objections and Public Hearing.

(1) Within thirty days after publication of an order made pursuant to subsection (c) or (d) of this section, any person adversely affected by such an order may file objections thereto with the Secretary, specifying with particularity the provisions of the order deemed objectionable, stating reasonable grounds therefor, and requesting a public hearing upon such objections. The Secretary shall, after due notice, as promptly as possible hold such public hearing for the purpose of receiving evidence relevant and material to the issues raised by such objections. As soon as practicable after completion of the hearing, the Secretary shall by order act upon such objections and make such order public.

(2) Such order shall be based upon a fair evaluation of the entire record at such hearing, and shall include a statement setting forth in detail the findings and conclusions upon which the order is based.

(3) The Secretary shall specify in the order the date on which it shall take effect, except that it shall not be made to take effect prior to the ninetieth day after its publication, unless the Secretary finds that emergency conditions exist necessitating an earlier effective date, in which event the Secretary shall specify in the order his findings as to such conditions.

(g) Judicial Review

(1) In a case of actual controversy as to the validity of any order issued under subsection (f), including any order thereunder with respect to amendment or repeal of a regulation issued under this section, any person who will be adversely affected by such order may obtain judicial review by filing in the United States Court of Appeals for the circuit wherein such person resides or has his principal place of business, or in the United States Court of Appeals for the District of Columbia Circuit, within sixty days after the entry of such order, a petition praying that the order be set aside in whole or in part.

(2) A copy of such petition shall be forthwith transmitted by the clerk of the court to the Secretary, or any officer designated by him for that purpose, and thereupon the Secretary shall file in the court the record of the proceedings on which he based his order, as provided in section 2112 of title 28, United States Code. Upon the filing of such petition the court shall have jurisdiction, which upon the filing of the record with it shall be exclusive, to affirm or set aside the order complained of in whole or in part. Until the filing of the record the Secretary may modify or set aside his order. The findings of the Secretary with respect to questions of fact shall be sustained if based upon a fair evaluation of the entire record at such hearing.

(3) The court, on such judicial review, shall not sustain the order of the Secretary if he failed to comply with any requirement imposed on him by subsection (f)(2) of this section.

(4) If application is made to the court for leave to adduce additional evidence, the court may order such additional evidence to be taken before the Secretary and to be adduced upon the hearing in such manner and upon such terms and conditions as to the court may seem proper, if such evidence is material and there were reasonable grounds for failure to adduce such evidence in the proceedings below. The Secretary may modify his findings as to the facts and order by reason of the additional evidence so taken, and shall file with the court such modified findings and order.

(5) The judgment of the court affirming or setting aside, in whole or in part, any order under this section shall be final, subject to review by the Supreme Court of the United States upon certiorari or certification as provided in section 1254 of title 28 of the United States Code. The commencement of proceedings under this section shall not, unless specifically ordered by the court to the contrary, operate as a stay of an order.

(h) Notification Relating to a Food Contact Substance

(1) Subject to such regulations as may be promulgated under paragraph (3), a manufacturer or supplier of a food contact substance may, at least 120 days prior to the introduction or delivery for introduction into interstate commerce of the food contact substance, notify the Secretary of the identity and intended use of the food contact substance, and of the determination of the manufacturer or supplier that the intended use of such food contact

substance is safe under the standard described in subsection (c)(3)(A). The notification shall contain the information that forms the basis of the determination and all information required to be submitted by regulations promulgated by the Secretary.

(2)(A) A notification submitted under paragraph (1) shall become effective 120 days after the date of receipt by the Secretary and the food contact substance may be introduced or delivered for introduction into interstate commerce, unless the Secretary makes a determination within the 120-day period that, based on the data and information before the Secretary, such use of the food contact substance has not been shown to be safe under the standard described in subsection (c)(3)(A), and informs the manufacturer or supplier of such determination.

(B) A decision by the Secretary to object to a notification shall constitute final agency action subject to judicial review.

(C) In this paragraph, the term "food contact substance" means the substance that is the subject of a notification submitted under paragraph (1), and does not include a similar or identical substance manufactured or prepared by a person other than the manufacturer identified in the notification.

(3)(A) The process in this subsection shall be utilized for authorizing the marketing of a food contact substance except where the Secretary determines that submission and review of a petition under subsection (b) is necessary to provide adequate assurance of safety, or where the Secretary and any manufacturer or supplier agree that such manufacturer or supplier may submit a petition under subsection (b).

(B) The Secretary is authorized to promulgate regulations to identify the circumstances in which a petition shall be filed under subsection (b), and shall consider criteria such as the probable consumption of such food contact substance and potential toxicity of the food contact substance in determining the circumstances in which a petition shall be filed under subsection (b).

(4) The Secretary shall keep confidential any information provided in a notification under paragraph (1) for 120 days after receipt by the Secretary of the notification. After the expiration of such 120 days, the information shall be available to any interested party except for any matter in the notification that is a trade secret or confidential commercial information.

(5)(A)(i) Except as provided in clause (ii), the notification program established under this subsection shall not operate in any fiscal year unless—

(I) an appropriation equal to or exceeding the applicable amount under clause (iv) is made for such fiscal year for carrying out such program in such fiscal year; and

Chapter IV

(II) the Secretary certifies that the amount appropriated for such fiscal year for the Center for Food Safety and Applied Nutrition of the Food and Drug Administration (exclusive of the appropriation referred to in subclause (I)) equals or exceeds the amount appropriated for the Center for fiscal year 1997, excluding any amount appropriated for new programs.

(ii) The Secretary shall, not later than April 1, 1999, begin accepting and reviewing notifications submitted under the notification program established under this subsection if—

(I) an appropriation equal to or exceeding the applicable amount under clause (iii) is made for the last six months of fiscal year 1999 for carrying out such program during such period; and

(II) the Secretary certifies that the amount appropriated for such period for the Center for Food Safety and Applied Nutrition of the Food and Drug Administration (exclusive of the appropriation referred to in subclause (I)) equals or exceeds an amount equivalent to one-half the amount appropriated for the Center for fiscal year 1997, excluding any amount appropriated for new programs.

(iii) For the last six months of fiscal year 1999, the applicable amount under this clause is $1,500,000, or the amount specified in the budget request of the President for the six-month period involved for carrying out the notification program in fiscal year 1999, whichever is less.

(iv) For fiscal year 2000 and subsequent fiscal years, the applicable amount under this clause is $3,000,000, or the amount specified in the budget request of the President for the fiscal year involved for carrying out the notification program under this subsection, whichever is less.

(B) For purposes of carrying out the notification program under this subsection, there are authorized to be appropriated such sums as may be necessary for each of the fiscal years 1999 through fiscal year 2003, except that such authorization of appropriations is not effective for a fiscal year for any amount that is less than the applicable amount under clause (iii) or (iv) of subparagraph (A), whichever is applicable.

(C) Not later than April 1 of fiscal year 1998 and February 1 of each subsequent fiscal year, the Secretary shall submit a report to the Committees on Appropriations of the House of Representatives and the Senate, the Committee on Commerce of the House of Representatives, and the Committee on Labor and Human Resources of the Senate that provides an estimate of the Secretary of the costs of carrying out the notification program established under this subsection for the next fiscal year.

(6) In this section, the term "food contact substance" means any substance intended for use as a component of materials used in manufacturing, packing, packaging, transporting, or holding food if such use is not intended to have any technical effect in such food.

(i) Amendment or Repeal of Regulations. The Secretary shall by regulation prescribe the procedure by which regulations under the foregoing provisions of this section may be amended or repealed, and such procedure shall conform to the procedure provided in this section for the promulgation of such regulations. The Secretary shall by regulation prescribe the procedure by which the Secretary may deem a notification under subsection (h) to no longer be effective.

(j) Exemptions for Investigational Use. Without regard to subsections (b) to (i), inclusive, of this section, the Secretary shall by regulation provide for exempting from the requirements of this section any food additive, and any food bearing or containing such additive, intended solely for investigational use by qualified experts when in his opinion such exemption is consistent with the public health.

Sec. 410. [21 USC §349] Bottled Drinking Water Standards

(a) Except as provided in subsection (b), whenever the Administrator of the Environmental Protection Agency prescribes interim or revised national primary drinking water regulations under section 1412 of the Public Health Service Act, the Secretary shall consult with the Administrator and within 180 days after the promulgation of such drinking water regulations either promulgate amendments to regulations under this chapter applicable to bottled drinking water or publish in the Federal Register his reasons for not making such amendments.

(b)(1) Not later than 180 days before the effective date of a national primary drinking water regulation promulgated by the Administrator of the Environmental Protection Agency for a contaminant under section 1412 of the Safe Drinking Water Act (42 USC 300g–1), the Secretary shall promulgate a standard of quality regulation under this subsection for that contaminant in bottled water or make a finding that such a regulation is not necessary to protect the public health because the contaminant is contained in water in public water systems (as defined under section 1401(4) of such Act (42 USC 300f(4))) but not in water used for bottled drinking water. The effective date for any such standard of quality regulation shall be the same as the effective date for such national primary drinking water regulation, except for any standard of quality of regulation promulgated by the Secretary before the date of enactment of the Safe Drinking Water Act Amendments of 1996 for which (as of such date of enactment) an effective date had not been established. In the case of a standard of quality regulation to which such exception applies, the Secretary shall promulgate monitoring requirements for the contaminants covered by the regulation not later than 2 years after such date of enactment.

(2) A regulation issued by the Secretary as provided in this subsection shall include any monitoring requirements that the Secretary determines appropriate for bottled water.

(3) A regulation issued by the Secretary as provided in this subsection shall require the following:

(A) In the case of contaminants for which a maximum contaminant level is established in a national primary drinking water regulation under section 1412 of the Safe Drinking Water Act (42 USC 300g–1), the regulation under this subsection shall establish a maximum contaminant level for the contaminant in bottled water which is no less stringent than the maximum contaminant level provided in the national primary drinking water regulation.

(B) In the case of contaminants for which a treatment technique is established in a national primary drinking water regulation under section 1412 of the Safe Drinking Water Act (42 USC 300g–1), the regulation under this subsection shall require that bottled water be subject to requirements no less protective of the public health than those applicable to water provided by public water systems using the treatment technique required by the national primary drinking water regulation.

(4)(A) If the Secretary does not promulgate a regulation under this subsection within the period described in paragraph (1), the national primary drinking water regulation referred to in paragraph (1) shall be considered, as of the date on which the Secretary is required to establish a regulation under paragraph (1), as the regulation applicable under this subsection to bottled water.

(B) In the case of a national primary drinking water regulation that pursuant to subparagraph (A) is considered to be a standard of quality regulation, the Secretary shall, not later than the applicable date referred to in such subparagraph, publish in the Federal Register a notice—

(i) specifying the contents of such regulation, including monitoring requirements; and

(ii) providing that for purposes of this paragraph the effective date for such regulation is the same as the effective date for the regulation for purposes of the Safe Drinking Water Act (or, if the exception under paragraph (1) applies to the regulation, that the effective date for the regulation is not later than 2 years and 180 days after the date of enactment of the Safe Drinking Water Act Amendments of 1996).

Sec. 411. [21 USC §350] Vitamins and Minerals

(a)(1) Except as provided in paragraph (2)—

(A) the Secretary may not establish, under section 201(n), 401, or 403, maximum limits on the potency of any synthetic or natural vitamin or mineral within a food to which this section applies;

(B) the Secretary may not classify any natural or synthetic vitamin or mineral (or combination thereof) as a drug solely because it exceeds the level of potency which the Secretary determines is nutritionally rational or useful;

(C) the Secretary may not limit, under section 201(n), 401, or 403, the combination or number of any synthetic or natural—

(i) vitamin,

(ii) mineral, or

(iii) other ingredient of food,

within a food to which this section applies.

(2) Paragraph (1) shall not apply in the case of a vitamin, mineral, other ingredient of food, or food, which is represented for use by individuals in the treatment or management of specific diseases or disorders, by children, or by pregnant or lactating women. For purposes of this subparagraph 1 , the term "children" means individuals who are under the age of twelve years.

(b)(1) A food to which this section applies shall not be deemed under section 403 to be misbranded solely because its label bears, in accordance with section 403(i)(2), all the ingredients in the food or its advertising contains references to ingredients in the food which are not vitamins or minerals.

(2) The labeling for any food to which this section applies may not list its ingredients which are not dietary supplement ingredients described in section 201(ff) (i) except as a part of a list of all the ingredients of such food, and (ii) unless such ingredients are listed in accordance with applicable regulations under section 403. To the extent that compliance with clause (i) of this subparagraph is impracticable or results in deception or unfair competition, exemptions shall be established by regulations promulgated by the Secretary.

(c)(1) For purposes of this section, the term "food to which this section applies" means a food for humans which is a food for special dietary use—

(A) which is or contains any natural or synthetic vitamin or mineral, and

(B) which—

(i) is intended for ingestion in tablet, capsule, powder, softgel, gelcap, or liquid form, or

(ii) if not intended for ingestion in such a form, is not represented as conventional food and is not represented for use as a sole item of a meal or of the diet.

(2) For purposes of paragraph (1)(B)(i), a food shall be considered as intended for ingestion in liquid form only if it is formulated in a fluid carrier and it is intended for ingestion in daily quantities measured in drops or similar small units of measure.

(3) For purposes of paragraph (1) and of section 403 (j) insofar as that section is applicable to food to which this section applies, the term "special dietary use" as applied to food used by man means a particular use for which a food purports or is represented to be used, including but not limited to the following:

(A) Supplying a special dietary need that exists by reason of a physical, physiological, pathological, or other condition, including but not limited to the condition of disease, convalescence, pregnancy, lactation, infancy, allergic hypersensitivity to food, underweight, overweight, or the need to control the intake of sodium.

(B) Supplying a vitamin, mineral, or other ingredient for use by man to supplement his diet by increasing the total dietary intake.

(C) Supplying a special dietary need by reason of being a food for use as the sole item of the diet.

Sec. 412. [21 USC §350a] Requirements for Infant Formulas

(a) An infant formula, including an infant formula powder, shall be deemed to be adulterated if—

(1) such infant formula does not provide nutrients as required by subsection (i),

(2) such infant formula does not meet the quality factor requirements prescribed by the Secretary under subsection (b)(1), or

(3) the processing of such infant formula is not in compliance with the good manufacturing practices and the quality control procedures prescribed by the Secretary under subsection (b)(2).

(b)(1) The Secretary shall by regulation establish requirements for quality factors for infant formulas to the extent possible consistent with current scientific knowledge, including quality factor requirements for the nutrients required by subsection (i).

(2)(A) The Secretary shall by regulation establish good manufacturing practices for infant formulas, including quality control procedures that the Secretary determines are necessary to assure that an infant formula provides nutrients in accordance with this subsection and subsection (i) and is manufactured in a manner designed to prevent adulteration of the infant formula.

(B) The good manufacturing practices and quality control procedures prescribed by the Secretary under subparagraph (A) shall include requirements for—

(i) the testing, in accordance with paragraph (3) and by the manufacturer of an infant formula or an agent of such manufacturer, of each batch of infant formula for each nutrient required by subsection (i) before the distribution of such batch,

(ii) regularly scheduled testing, by the manufacturer of an infant formula or an agent of such manufacturer, of samples of infant formulas during the shelf life of such formulas to ensure that such formulas are in compliance with this section,

(iii) in-process controls including, where necessary, testing required by good manufacturing practices designed to prevent adulteration of each batch of infant formula, and

(iv) the conduct by the manufacturer of an infant formula or an agent of such manufacturer of regularly scheduled audits to determine that such manufacturer has complied with the regulations prescribed under subparagraph (A).

In prescribing requirements for audits under clause (iv), the Secretary shall provide that such audits be conducted by appropriately trained individuals who do not have any direct responsibility for the manufacture or production of infant formula.

(3)(A) At the final product stage, each batch of infant formula shall be tested for vitamin A, vitamin B1, vitamin C, and vitamin E to ensure that such infant formula is in compliance with the requirements of this subsection and subsection (i) relating to such vitamins.

(B) Each nutrient premix used in the manufacture of an infant formula shall be tested for each relied upon nutrient required by subsection (i) which is contained in such premix to ensure that such premix is in compliance with its specifications or certifications by a premix supplier.

(C) During the manufacturing process or at the final product stage and before distribution of an infant formula, an infant formula shall be tested for all nutrients required to be included in such formula by subsection (i) for which testing has not been conducted pursuant to subparagraph (A) or (B). Testing under this subparagraph shall be conducted to—

(i) ensure that each batch of such infant formula is in compliance with the requirements of subsection (i) relating to such nutrients, and

(ii) confirm that nutrients contained in any nutrient premix used in such infant formula are present in each batch of such infant formula in the proper concentration.

(D) If the Secretary adds a nutrient to the list of nutrients in the table in subsection (i), the Secretary shall by regulation require that the manufacturer of an infant formula test each batch of such formula for such new nutrient in accordance with subparagraph (A), (B), or (C).

(E) For purposes of this paragraph, the term "final product stage" means the point in the manufacturing process, before distribution of an infant formula, at which an infant formula is homogenous and is not subject to further degradation.

(4)(A) The Secretary shall by regulation establish requirements respecting the retention of records. Such requirements shall provide for—

(i) the retention of all records necessary to demonstrate compliance with the good manufacturing practices and quality control procedures prescribed by the Secretary under paragraph (2), including records containing the results of all testing required under paragraph (2)(B),

(ii) the retention of all certifications or guarantees of analysis by premix suppliers,

(iii) the retention by a premix supplier of all records necessary to confirm the accuracy of all premix certifications and guarantees of analysis,

(iv) the retention of—

(I) all records pertaining to the microbiological quality and purity of raw materials used in infant formula powder and in finished infant formula, and

(II) all records pertaining to food packaging materials which show that such materials do not cause an infant formula to be adulterated within the meaning of section 402(a)(2)(C),

(v) the retention of all records of the results of regularly scheduled audits conducted pursuant to the requirements prescribed by the Secretary under paragraph (2)(B)(iv), and

(vi) the retention of all complaints and the maintenance of files with respect to, and the review of, complaints concerning infant formulas which may reveal the possible existence of a hazard to health.

(B)(i) Records required under subparagraph (A) with respect to an infant formula shall be retained for at least one year after the expiration of the shelf life of such infant formula. Except as provided in clause (ii), such records shall be made available to the Secretary for review and duplication upon request of the Secretary.

(ii) A manufacturer need only provide written assurances to the Secretary that the regularly scheduled audits required by paragraph (2)(B)(iv) are being conducted by the manufacturer, and need not make available to the Secretary the actual written reports of such audits.

(c)(1) No person shall introduce or deliver for introduction into interstate commerce any new infant formula unless—

(A) such person has, before introducing such new infant formula, or delivering such new infant formula for introduction, into interstate commerce, registered with the Secretary the name of such person, the place of business of such person, and all establishments at which such person intends to manufacture such new infant formula, and

(B) such person has at least 90 days before marketing such new infant formula, made the submission to the Secretary required by subsection (c)(1).

(2) For purposes of paragraph (1), the term "new infant formula" includes—

(A) an infant formula manufactured by a person which has not previously manufactured an infant formula, and

(B) an infant formula manufactured by a person which has previously manufactured infant formula and in which there is a major change, in processing or formulation, from a current or any previous formulation produced by such manufacturer.

For purposes of this paragraph, the term "major change" has the meaning given to such term in section 106.30(c)(2) of title 21, Code of Federal Regulations (as in effect on August 1, 1986), and guidelines issued thereunder.

(d)(1) A person shall, with respect to any infant formula subject to subsection (c), make a submission to the Secretary which shall include—

(A) the quantitative formulation of the infant formula,

(B) a description of any reformulation of the formula or change in processing of the infant formula,

(C) assurances that the infant formula will not be marketed unless it meets the requirements of subsections (b)(1) and (i), as demonstrated by the testing required under subsection (b)(3), and

(D) assurances that the processing of the infant formula complies with subsection (b)(2).

(2) After the first production of an infant formula subject to subsection (c), and before the introduction into interstate commerce of such formula, the manufacturer of such formula shall submit to the Secretary, in such form as may be prescribed by the Secretary, a written verification which summarizes test results and records demonstrating that such formula complies with the requirements of subsections (b)(1), (b)(2)(A), (b)(2)(B)(i), (b)(2)(B)(iii), (b)(3)(A), (b)(3)(C), and (i).

(3) If the manufacturer of an infant formula for commercial or charitable distribution for human consumption determines that a change in the formulation of the formula or a change in the processing of the formula may affect whether the formula is adulterated under subsection (a), the manufacturer shall, before the first processing of such formula, make the submission to the Secretary required by paragraph (1).

(e)(1) If the manufacturer of an infant formula has knowledge which reasonably supports the conclusion that an infant formula which has been processed by the manufacturer and which has left an establishment subject to the control of the manufacturer—

(A) may not provide the nutrients required by subsection (i), or

(B) may be otherwise adulterated or misbranded, the manufacturer shall promptly notify the Secretary of such knowledge. If the Secretary determines that the infant formula presents a risk to human health, the manufacturer shall immediately take all actions necessary to recall shipments of such infant formula from all wholesale and retail establishments, consistent with recall regulations and guidelines issued by the Secretary.

(2) For purposes of paragraph (1), the term "knowledge" as applied to a manufacturer means (A) the actual knowledge that the manufacturer had, or (B) the knowledge which a reasonable person would have had under like circumstances or which would have been obtained upon the exercise of due care.

(f)(1) If a recall of infant formula is begun by a manufacturer, the recall shall be carried out in accordance with such requirements as the Secretary shall prescribe under paragraph (2) and—

(A) the Secretary shall, not later than the 15th day after the beginning of such recall and at least once every 15 days thereafter until the recall is terminated, review the actions taken under the recall to determine whether the recall meets the requirements prescribed under paragraph (2), and

(B) the manufacturer shall, not later than the 14th day after the beginning of such recall and at least once every 14 days thereafter until the recall is terminated, report to the Secretary the actions taken to implement the recall.

(2) The Secretary shall by regulation prescribe the scope and extent of recalls of infant formulas necessary and appropriate for the degree of risks to human health presented by the formula subject to the recall.

(3) The Secretary shall by regulation require each manufacturer of an infant formula who begins a recall of such formula because of a risk to human health to request each retail establishment at which such formula is sold or available for sale to post at the point of purchase of such formula a notice of such recall at such establishment for such time that the Secretary determines necessary to inform the public of such recall.

(g)(1) Each manufacturer of an infant formula shall make and retain such records respecting the distribution of the infant formula through any establishment owned or operated by such manufacturer as may be necessary to effect and monitor recalls of the formula. Such records shall be retained for at least one year after the expiration of the shelf life of the infant formula.

(2) To the extent that the Secretary determines that records are not being made or maintained in accordance with paragraph (1), the Secretary may by regulation prescribe the records required to be made under paragraph (1) and requirements respecting the retention of such records under such paragraph. Such regulations shall take effect on such date as the Secretary prescribes but not sooner than the 180th day after the date such regulations are promulgated. Such regulations shall apply only with respect to distributions of infant formulas made after such effective date.

(h)(1) Any infant formula which is represented and labeled for use by an infant—

(A) who has an inborn error of metabolism or a low birth weight, or

(B) who otherwise has an unusual medical or dietary problem,

is exempt from the requirements of subsections (a), (b), and (c). The manufacturer of an infant formula exempt under this paragraph shall, in the case of the exempt formula, be required to provide the notice required by subsection (e)(1) only with respect to adulteration or misbranding described in subsection (e)(1)(B) and to comply with the regulations prescribed by the Secretary under paragraph (2).

(2) The Secretary may by regulation establish terms and conditions for the exemption of an infant formula from the requirements of subsections (a), (b), and (c). An exemption of an infant formula under paragraph (1) may be withdrawn by the Secretary if such formula is not in compliance with applicable terms and conditions prescribed under this paragraph.

(i)(1) An infant formula shall contain nutrients in accordance with the table set out in this subsection or, if revised by the Secretary under paragraph (2), as so revised.

(2) The Secretary may by regulation—

(A) revise the list of nutrients in the table in this subsection, and

(B) revise the required level for any nutrient required by the table.

NUTRIENTS

Nutrient	Minimum [26]	Maximum [26]
Protein (gm)	1.8 [27]	4.5.
Fat:		
gm	3.3	6.0.
percent cal	30.0	54.0.
Essential fatty acids (linoleate):		
percent cal	2.7	
mg	300.0	
Vitamins:		
A (IU)	250.0 (75 µg) [28]	750.0 (225 µg) [28]
D (IU)	40.0	100.0.
K (µg)	4.0	
E (IU)	0.7 (with 0.7 IU/gm linoleic acid).	
C (ascorbic acid) (mg)	8.0	
B1 (thiamine) (µg)	40.0	
B2 (riboflavin) (µg)	60.0	
B6 (pyridoxine) (µg)	35.0 (with 15 µg/gm of protein in formula).	

[26] Stated per 100 kilocalories.
[27] The source of protein shall be at least nutritionally equivalent to casein.
[28] Retinol equivalents.

Nutrient	Minimum [26]	Maximum [26]
B12 (µg)	0.15	
Niacin (µg)	250.0	
Folic acid (µg)	4.0	
Pantothenic acid (µg)	300.0	
Biotin (µg)	1.5 [29]	
Choline (mg)	7.0 [29]	
Inositol (mg)	4.0 [29]	
Minerals:		
Calcium (mg)	50.0 [30]	
Phosphorus (mg)	25.0 [30]	
Magnesium (mg)	6.0	
Iron (mg)	0.15	
Iodine (µg)	5.0	
Zinc (mg)	0.5	
Copper (µg)	60.0	
Manganese (µg)	5.0	
Sodium (mg)	20.0	60.0.
Potassium (mg)	80.0	200.0.
Chloride (mg)	55.0	150.0.

Sec. 413. [21 USC §350b] New Dietary Ingredients

(a) IN GENERAL.—A dietary supplement which contains a new dietary ingredient shall be deemed adulterated under section 402(f) unless it meets one of the following requirements:

[29] Required to be included in this amount only in formulas which are not milk-based.

[30] Calcium to phosphorus ratio must be no less than 1.1 nor more than 2.0.

(1) The dietary supplement contains only dietary ingredients which have been present in the food supply as an article used for food in a form in which the food has not been chemically altered.

(2) There is a history of use or other evidence of safety establishing that the dietary ingredient when used under the conditions recommended or suggested in the labeling of the dietary supplement will reasonably be expected to be safe and, at least 75 days before being introduced or delivered for introduction into interstate commerce, the manufacturer or distributor of the dietary ingredient or dietary supplement provides the Secretary with information, including any citation to published articles, which is the basis on which the manufacturer or distributor has concluded that a dietary supplement containing such dietary ingredient will reasonably be expected to be safe.

The Secretary shall keep confidential any information provided under paragraph (2) for 90 days following its receipt. After the expiration of such 90 days, the Secretary shall place such information on public display, except matters in the information which are trade secrets or otherwise confidential, commercial information.

(b) PETITION.—Any person may file with the Secretary a petition proposing the issuance of an order prescribing the conditions under which a new dietary ingredient under its intended conditions of use will reasonably be expected to be safe. The Secretary shall make a decision on such petition within 180 days of the date the petition is filed with the Secretary. For purposes of chapter 7 of title 5, United States Code, the decision of the Secretary shall be considered final agency action.

(c) DEFINITION.—For purposes of this section, the term "new dietary ingredient" means a dietary ingredient that was not marketed in the United States before October 15, 1994 and does not include any dietary ingredient which was marketed in the United States before October 15, 1994.

Sec. 414. [21 USC §350c] Maintenance and Inspection of Records

(a) RECORDS INSPECTION. — If the Secretary has a reasonable belief that an article of food is adulterated and presents a threat of serious adverse health consequences or death to humans or animals, each person (excluding farms and restaurants) who manufactures, processes, packs, distributes, receives, holds, or imports such article shall, at the request of an officer or employee duly designated by the Secretary, permit such officer or employee, upon presentation of appropriate credentials and a written notice to such person, at reasonable times and within reasonable limits and in a reasonable manner, to have access to and copy all records relating to such article that are needed to assist the Secretary in determining whether the food is adulterated and presents a threat of serious adverse health consequences or death to humans or animals. The requirement under the preceding sentence applies to all records relating to the manufacture, processing, packing, distribution, receipt, holding, or importation of such article maintained by or on behalf of such person in any format (including paper and electronic formats) and at any location.

(b) REGULATIONS CONCERNING RECORDKEEPING.—The Secretary, in consultation and coordination, as appropriate, with other Federal departments and agencies with responsibilities for regulating food safety, may by regulation establish requirements regarding the establishment and maintenance, for not longer than two years, of records by persons (excluding farms and restaurants) who manufacture, process, pack, transport, distribute, receive, hold, or import food, which records are needed by the Secretary for inspection to allow the Secretary to identify the immediate previous sources and the immediate subsequent recipients of food, including its packaging, in order to address credible threats of serious adverse health consequences or death to humans or animals. The Secretary shall take into account the size of a business in promulgating regulations under this section.

(c) Protection of Sensitive Information.—The Secretary shall take appropriate measures to ensure that there are in effect effective procedures to prevent the unauthorized disclosure of any trade secret or confidential information that is obtained by the Secretary pursuant to this section.

(d) Limitations.—This section shall not be construed--

(1) to limit the authority of the Secretary to inspect records or to require establishment and maintenance of records under any other provision of this Act;

(2) to authorize the Secretary to impose any requirements with respect to a food to the extent that it is within the exclusive jurisdiction of the Secretary of Agriculture pursuant to the Federal Meat Inspection Act (21 USC 601 et seq.), the Poultry Products Inspection Act (21 USC 451 et seq.), or the Egg Products Inspection Act (21 USC 1031 et seq.);

(3) to have any legal effect on section 552 of title 5, United States Code, or section 1905 of title 18, United States Code; or

(4) to extend to recipes for food, financial data, pricing data, personnel data, research data, or sales data (other than shipment data regarding sales).

Sec. 415. [21 USC §350d] Registration of Food Facilities

(a) Registration.—

(1) Regulations.— In general.--The Secretary shall by regulation require that any facility engaged in manufacturing, processing, packing, or holding food for consumption in the United States be registered with the Secretary. To be registered--

(A) for a domestic facility, the owner, operator, or agent in charge of the facility shall submit a registration to the Secretary; and

(B) for a foreign facility, the owner, operator, or agent in charge of the facility shall submit a registration to the Secretary and shall include with the registration the name of the United States agent for the facility.

(2) Registration.—An entity (referred to in this section as the 'registrant') shall submit a registration under paragraph (1) to the Secretary containing information necessary to notify the Secretary of the name and address of each facility at which, and all trade names under which, the registrant conducts business and, when determined necessary by the Secretary through guidance, the general food category (as identified under section 170.3 of title 21, Code of Federal Regulations) of any food manufactured, processed, packed, or held at such facility. The registrant shall notify the Secretary in a timely manner of changes to such information.

(3) Notification.—Upon receipt of a completed registration described in paragraph (1), the Secretary shall notify the registrant of the receipt of such registration and assign a registration number to each registered facility.

(4) Records.—The Secretary shall compile and maintain an up-to-date list of facilities that are registered under this section. Such list and any registration documents submitted pursuant to this subsection shall not be subject to disclosure under section 552 of title 5, United States Code. Information derived from such list or registration documents shall not be subject to disclosure under section 552 of title 5, United States Code, to the extent that it discloses the identity or location of a specific registered person.

(b) Facility.—For purposes of this section:

(1) The term `facility' includes any factory, warehouse, or establishment (including a factory, warehouse, or establishment of an importer) that manufactures, processes, packs, or holds food. Such term does not include farms; restaurants; other retail food establishments; nonprofit food establishments in which food is prepared for or served directly to the consumer; or fishing vessels (except such vessels engaged in processing as defined in section 123.3(k) of title 21, Code of Federal Regulations).

(2) The term `domestic facility' means a facility located in any of the States or Territories.

(3)(A) The term `foreign facility' means a facility that manufacturers, processes, packs, or holds food, but only if food from such facility is exported to the United States without further processing or packaging outside the United States.

(B) A food may not be considered to have undergone further processing or packaging for purposes of subparagraph (A) solely on the basis that labeling was added or that any similar activity of a de minimis nature was carried out with respect to the food.

(c) Rule of Construction.—Nothing in this section shall be construed to authorize the Secretary to require an application, review, or licensing process.

Sec. 416. [21 USC §350e] Sanitary Transportation Practices

Note: this section was posted in September 2007.

(a) Definitions. In this section:

(1) Bulk vehicle. The term "***bulk vehicle***" includes a tank truck, hopper truck, rail tank car, hopper car, cargo tank, portable tank, freight container, or hopper bin, and any other vehicle in which food is shipped in bulk, with the food coming into direct contact with the vehicle.

(2) Transportation. The term "***transportation***" means any movement in commerce by motor vehicle or rail vehicle.

(b) Regulations. The Secretary shall by regulation require shippers, carriers by motor vehicle or rail vehicle, receivers, and other persons engaged in the transportation of food to use sanitary transportation practices prescribed by the Secretary to ensure that food is not transported under conditions that may render the food adulterated.

(c) Contents. The regulations under subsection (b) shall--

(1) prescribe such practices as the Secretary determines to be appropriate relating to--

(A) sanitation;

(B) packaging, isolation, and other protective measures;

(C) limitations on the use of vehicles;

(D) information to be disclosed--

(i) to a carrier by a person arranging for the transport of food; and

(ii) to a manufacturer or other person that--

(I) arranges for the transportation of food by a carrier; or

(II) furnishes a tank vehicle or bulk vehicle for the transportation of food; and

(E) recordkeeping; and

(2) include--

(A) a list of nonfood products that the Secretary determines may, if shipped in a bulk vehicle, render adulterated food that is subsequently transported in the same vehicle; and

(B) a list of nonfood products that the Secretary determines may, if shipped in a motor vehicle or rail vehicle (other than a tank vehicle or bulk vehicle), render adulterated food that is simultaneously or subsequently transported in the same vehicle.

(d) Waivers.

(1) In general. The Secretary may waive any requirement under this section, with respect to any class of persons, vehicles, food, or nonfood products, if the Secretary determines that the waiver--

(A) will not result in the transportation of food under conditions that would be unsafe for human or animal health; and

(B) will not be contrary to the public interest.

(2) Publication. The Secretary shall publish in the Federal Register any waiver and the reasons for the waiver.

(e) Preemption.

(1) In general. A requirement of a State or political subdivision of a State that concerns the transportation of food is preempted if--

(A) complying with a requirement of the State or political subdivision and a requirement of this section, or a regulation prescribed under this section, is not possible; or

(B) the requirement of the State or political subdivision as applied or enforced is an obstacle to accomplishing and carrying out this section or a regulation prescribed under this section.

(2) Applicability. This subsection applies to transportation that occurs on or after the effective date of the regulations promulgated under subsection (b).

(f) Assistance of other agencies. The Secretary of Transportation, the Secretary of Agriculture, the Administrator of the Environmental Protection Agency, and the heads of other Federal agencies, as appropriate, shall provide assistance on request, to the extent resources are available, to the Secretary for the purposes of carrying out this section.

Sec. 417. [21 USC 350f] Reportable food registry.

Note: This section was posted in February 2008.

(a) Definitions. In this section:

(1) Responsible party. The term "***responsible party***", with respect to an article of food, means a person that submits the registration under section 415(a) [21 USC § 350d(a)] for a food facility that is required to register under section 415(a) [21 USC § 350d(a)], at which such article of food is manufactured, processed, packed, or held.

(2) Reportable food. The term "***reportable food***" means an article of food (other than infant formula) for which there is a reasonable probability that the use of, or exposure to, such article of food will cause serious adverse health consequences or death to humans or animals.

(b) Establishment.

(1) In general. Not later than 1 year after the date of the enactment of this section [enacted Sept. 27, 2007], the Secretary shall establish within the Food and Drug Administration a Reportable Food Registry to which instances of reportable food may be submitted by the Food and Drug Administration after receipt of reports under subsection (d), via an electronic portal, from--

(A) Federal, State, and local public health officials; or

(B) responsible parties.

(2) Review by Secretary. The Secretary shall promptly review and assess the information submitted under paragraph (1) for the purposes of identifying reportable food, submitting entries to the Reportable Food Registry, acting under subsection (c), and exercising other existing food safety authorities under this Act to protect the public health.

(c) Issuance of an alert by the Secretary.

(1) In general. The Secretary shall issue, or cause to be issued, an alert or a notification with respect to a reportable food using information from the Reportable Food Registry as the Secretary deems necessary to protect the public health.

(2) Effect. Paragraph (1) shall not affect the authority of the Secretary to issue an alert or a notification under any other provision of this Act [21 USC §§ 301 et seq.].

(d) Reporting and notification.

(1) In general. Except as provided in paragraph (2), as soon as practicable, but in no case later than 24 hours after a responsible party determines that an article of food is a reportable food, the responsible party shall--

(A) submit a report to the Food and Drug Administration through the electronic portal established under subsection (b) that includes the data elements described in subsection (e) (except the elements described in paragraphs (8), (9), and (10) of such subsection); and

(B) investigate the cause of the adulteration if the adulteration of the article of food may have originated with the responsible party.

(2) No report required. A responsible party is not required to submit a report under paragraph (1) if--

(A) the adulteration originated with the responsible party;

(B) the responsible party detected the adulteration prior to any transfer to another person of such article of food; and

(C) the responsible party--

(i) corrected such adulteration; or

(ii) destroyed or caused the destruction of such article of food.

(3) Reports by public health officials. A Federal, State, or local public health official may submit a report about a reportable food to the Food and Drug Administration through the electronic portal established under subsection (b) that includes the data elements described in subsection (e) that the official is able to provide.

(4) Report number. The Secretary shall ensure that, upon submission of a report under paragraph (1) or (3), a unique number is issued through the electronic portal established under subsection (b) to the person submitting such report, by which the Secretary is able to link reports about the reportable food submitted and amended under this subsection and identify the supply chain for such reportable food.

(5) Review. The Secretary shall promptly review a report submitted under paragraph (1) or (3).

(6) Response to report submitted by a responsible party. After consultation with the responsible party that submitted a report under paragraph (1), the Secretary may require such responsible party to perform, as soon as practicable, but in no case later than a time specified by the Secretary, 1 or more of the following:

(A) Amend the report submitted by the responsible party under paragraph (1) to include the data element described in subsection (e)(9).

(B) Provide a notification--

(i) to the immediate previous source of the article of food, if the Secretary deems necessary;

(ii) to the immediate subsequent recipient of the article of food, if the Secretary deems necessary; and

(iii) that includes--

(I) the data elements described in subsection (e) that the Secretary deems necessary;

(II) the actions described under paragraph (7) that the recipient of the notification shall perform, as required by the Secretary; and

(III) any other information that the Secretary may require.

(7) Subsequent reports and notifications. Except as provided in paragraph (8), the Secretary may require a responsible party to perform, as soon as practicable, but in no case later than a time specified by the Secretary, after the responsible party receives a notification under subparagraph (C) or paragraph (6)(B), 1 or more of the following:

(A) Submit a report to the Food and Drug Administration through the electronic portal established under subsection (b) that includes those data elements described in subsection (e) and other information that the Secretary deems necessary.

(B) Investigate the cause of the adulteration if the adulteration of the article of food may have originated with the responsible party.

(C) Provide a notification--

(i) to the immediate previous source of the article of food, if the Secretary deems necessary;

(ii) to the immediate subsequent recipient of the article of food, if the Secretary deems necessary; and

(iii) that includes--

(I) the data elements described in subsection (e) that the Secretary deems necessary;

(II) the actions described under this paragraph that the recipient of the notification shall perform, as required by the Secretary; and

(III) any other information that the Secretary may require.

(8) Amended report. If a responsible party receives a notification under paragraph (6)(B) or paragraph (7)(C) with respect to an article of food after the responsible party has submitted a report to the Food and Drug Administration under paragraph (1) with respect to such article of food--

(A) the responsible party is not required to submit an additional report or make a notification under paragraph (7); and

(B) the responsible party shall amend the report submitted by the responsible party under paragraph (1) to include the data elements described in paragraph (9), and, with respect to both such notification and such report, paragraph (11) of subsection (e).

(e) Data elements. The data elements described in this subsection are the following:

(1) The registration numbers of the responsible party under section 415(a)(3) [21 USC § 350d(a)(3)].

(2) The date on which an article of food was determined to be a reportable food.

(3) A description of the article of food including the quantity or amount.

(4) The extent and nature of the adulteration.

(5) If the adulteration of the article of food may have originated with the responsible party, the results of the investigation required under paragraph (1)(B) or (7)(B) of subsection (d), as applicable and when known.

(6) The disposition of the article of food, when known.

(7) Product information typically found on packaging including product codes, use-by dates, and names of manufacturers, packers, or distributors sufficient to identify the article of food.

(8) Contact information for the responsible party.

(9) The contact information for parties directly linked in the supply chain and notified under paragraph (6)(B) or (7)(C) of subsection (d), as applicable.

(10) The information required by the Secretary to be included in a notification provided by the responsible party involved under paragraph (6)(B) or (7)(C) of subsection (d) or required in a report under subsection (d)(7)(A).

(11) The unique number described in subsection (d)(4).

(f) Coordination of Federal, State, and local efforts.

(1) Department of Agriculture. In implementing this section, the Secretary shall--

(A) share information and coordinate regulatory efforts with the Department of Agriculture; and

(B) if the Secretary receives a report submitted about a food within the jurisdiction of the Department of Agriculture, promptly provide such report to the Department of Agriculture.

(2) States and localities. In implementing this section, the Secretary shall work with the State and local public health officials to share information and coordinate regulatory efforts, in order to--

(A) help to ensure coverage of the safety of the food supply chain, including those food establishments regulated by the States and localities that are not required to register under section 415 [21 USC § 350d]; and

(B) reduce duplicative regulatory efforts.

(g) Maintenance and inspection of records. The responsible party shall maintain records related to each report received, notification made, and report submitted to the Food and Drug Administration under this section for 2 years. A responsible party shall, at the request of the Secretary, permit inspection of such records as provided for section 414 [21 USC § 350c].

(h) Request for information. Except as provided by section 415(a)(4) [21 USC § 350d(a)(4)], section 552 of title 5, United States Code, shall apply to any request for information regarding a record in the Reportable Food Registry.

(i) Safety report. A report or notification under subsection (d) shall be considered to be a safety report under section 756 [21 USC § 379v] and may be accompanied by a statement, which shall be part of any report released for public disclosure, that denies that the report or the notification constitutes an admission that the product involved caused or contributed to a death, serious injury, or serious illness.

(j) Admission. A report or notification under this section shall not be considered an admission that the article of food involved is adulterated or caused or contributed to a death, serious injury, or serious illness.

(k) Homeland Security notification. If, after receiving a report under subsection (d), the Secretary believes such food may have been deliberately adulterated, the Secretary shall immediately notify the Secretary of Homeland Security. The Secretary shall make relevant information from the Reportable Food Registry available to the Secretary of Homeland Security.

FD&C Act Chapter V: Drugs and Devices

Sections in Chapter V

Subchapter A — Drugs and Devices

- SEC. 501. [21 USC §351] Adulterated Drugs and Devices
- SEC. 502. [21 USC §352] Misbranded Drugs and Devices
- SEC. 503. [21 USC §353] Exemptions and Consideration for Certain Drugs, Devices, and Biological Products
- SEC. 503A. [21 USC §353a] Pharmacy Compounding
- SEC. 503B. [21 USC §353b] Prereview of Television Advertisements
- SEC. 504. [21 USC §354] Veterinary Feed Directive Drugs
- SEC. 505. [21 USC §355] New Drugs
- SEC. 505-1. [21 USC §355-1] Risk Evaluation and Mitigation Strategies
- SEC. 505A. [21 USC §355a] Pediatric Studies of Drugs
- SEC. 505B. [21 USC §355c] Research Into Pediatric Uses for Drugs and Biological Products
- SEC. 505C. [21 USC §355d] Internal Committee for Review of Pediatric Plans, Assessments, Deferrals, and Waivers
- SEC. 505D. [21 USC §355d] Pharmaceutical Security
- SEC. 506. [21 USC §356] Fast Track Products
- SEC. 506A. [21 USC §356a] Manufacturing Changes
- SEC. 506B. [21 USC §356b] Reports of Postmarketing Studies
- SEC. 506C. [21 USC §356c] Discontinuance of a Lifesaving Product
- SEC. 508. [21 USC §358] Authority to Designate Official Names
- SEC. 509. [21 USC §359] Nonapplicability to Cosmetics
- SEC. 510. [21 USC §360] Registration of Producers of Drugs and Devices

- SEC. 511. [21 USC §360a] Clinical Trial Guidance for Antibiotic Drugs
- SEC. 512. [21 USC §360b] New Animal Drugs
- SEC. 513. [21 USC §360c] Classification of Devices Intended for Human Use; Device Classes
- SEC. 514. [21 USC §360d] Performance Standards; Provisions of Standards
- SEC. 515. [21 USC §360e] Premarket Approval; General Requirement
- SEC. 515A. [21 USC §360e-1] Pediatric Uses of Devices
- SEC. 516. [21 USC §360f] Banned Devices; General Rule
- SEC. 517. [21 USC §360g] Judicial Review; Application of Section
- SEC. 518. [21 USC §360h] Notification and Other Remedies; Notification
- SEC. 519. [21 USC §360i] Records and Reports on Devices; General Rule
- SEC. 520. [21 USC §360j] General Provisions Respecting Control of Devices Intended for Human Use; General Rule
- SEC. 521. [21 USC §360k] State and Local Requirements Respecting Devices; General Rule
- SEC. 522. [21 USC §360l] Postmarket Surveillance
- SEC. 523. [21 USC §360m] Accredited Persons

Subchapter B — Drugs for Rare Diseases and Conditions

- SEC. 524. [21 USC §360n] Priority Review to Encourage Treatments for Tropical Diseases
- SEC. 525. [21 USC §360aa] Recommendations for Investigations of Drugs for Rare Diseases or Conditions
- SEC. 526. [21 USC §360bb] Designation of Drugs for Rare Disesases or Conditions
- SEC. 527. [21 USC §360cc] Protection for Drugs for Rare Diseases or Conditions
- SEC. 528. [21 USC §360dd] Open Protocols for Investigations of Drugs for Rare Diseases or Conditions

Subchapter C — Electronic Product Radiation Control

- SEC. 531. [21 USC §360hh] Definitions
- SEC. 532. [21 USC §360ii] Electronic Product Radiation Control Program
- SEC. 533. [21 USC §360jj] Studies by the Secretary

- SEC. 534. [21 USC §360kk] Performance Standards for Electronic Products
- SEC. 535. [21 USC §360ll] Notification of Defects in, and Repair or Replacement of, Electronic Products
- SEC. 536. [21 USC §360mm] Imports
- SEC. 537. [21 USC §360nn] Inspection and Reports
- SEC. 538. [21 USC §360oo] Prohibited Acts
- SEC. 539. [21 USC §360pp] Enforcement
- SEC. 541. [21 USC §360rr] Federal-State Cooperation
- SEC. 542. [21 USC §360ss] Effect on State Standards

Subchapter D — Dissemination of Treatment Information

- SEC. 551. [21 USC §360aaa] Requirements for Dissemination of Treatment Information on Drugs or Devices
- SEC. 552. [21 USC §360aaa–1] Information Authorized To Be Disseminated
- SEC. 553. [21 USC §360aaa–2] Establishment of List of Articles and Publications Disseminated and List of Providers That Received Articles and Reference Publications
- SEC. 554. [21 USC §360aaa–3] Requirement Regarding Submission of Supplemental Application for New Use; Exemption From Requirement
- SEC. 555. [21 USC §360aaa–4] Corrective Actions; Cessation of Dissemination
- SEC. 556. [21 USC §360aaa–5] Definitions
- SEC. 557. [21 USC §360aaa–6] Rules of Construction

Subchapter E — General Provisions Relating To Drugs And Devices

- SEC. 561. [21 USC §360bbb] Expanded Access to Unapproved Therapies and Diagnostics
- SEC. 562. [21 USC §360bbb–1] Dispute Resolution
- SEC. 563. [21 USC §360bbb–2] Classification of Products
- SEC. 564. [21 USC §360bbb–3] Authorization fo Medical Products for Use in Emergencies
- SEC. 565. [21 USC §360bbb–4] Technical Assistance
- SEC. 566. [21 USC §360bbb–5] Critical Path Public-Private Partnerships
- SEC. 567. [21 USC §360bbb–6] Risk communication

Subchapter F — New Animal Drugs for Minor Use and Minor Species

Subchapter A — Drugs and Devices

SEC. 501. [21 USC §351] Adulterated Drugs and Devices

A drug or device shall be deemed to be adulterated— [1]

(a)(1) If it consists in whole or in part of any filthy, putrid, or decomposed substance; or (2)(A) if it has been prepared, packed, or held under insanitary conditions whereby it may have been contaminated with filth, or whereby it may have been rendered injurious to health; or (B) if it is a drug and the methods used in, or the facilities or controls used for, its manufacture, processing, packing, or holding do not conform to or are not operated or administered in conformity with current good manufacturing practice to assure that such drug meets the requirements of this Act as to safety and has the identity and strength, and meets the quality and purity characteristics, which it purports or is represented to possess; or (C) if it is a compounded positron emission tomography drug and the methods used in, or the facilities and controls used for, its compounding, processing, packing, or holding do not conform to or are not operated or administered in conformity with the positron emission tomography compounding standards and the official monographs of the United States Pharmacopoeia to assure that such drug meets the requirements of this Act as to safety and has the identity and strength, and meets the quality and purity characteristics, that it purports or is represented to possess; or (3) if its container is composed, in whole or in part, of any poisonous or deleterious substance which may render the contents injurious to health; or (4) if (A) it bears or contains, for purposes of coloring only, a color additive which is unsafe within the meaning of section 721(a), or (B) it is a color additive the intended use of which in or on drugs or devices is for purposes of coloring only and is unsafe within the meaning of section 721(a); or (5) if it is a new animal drug which is unsafe within the meaning of section 512; or (6) if it is an animal feed bearing or containing a new animal drug, and such animal feed is unsafe within the meaning of section 512.

---

[1] See footnote for section 403(h)(3) regarding the stylistic use of a list consisting of "(a)", "(b)", etc.

(b) If it purports to be or is represented as a drug the name of which is recognized in an official compendium, and its strength differs from, or its quality or purity falls below, the standards set forth in such compendium. Such determination as to strength, quality, or purity shall be made in accordance with the tests or methods of assay set forth in such compendium, except that whenever tests or methods of assay have not been prescribed in such compendium, or such tests or methods of assay as are prescribed are, in the judgment of the Secretary, insufficient for the making of such determination, the Secretary shall bring such fact to the attention of the appropriate body charged with the revision of such compendium, and if such body fails within a reasonable time to prescribe tests or methods of assay which, in the judgment of the Secretary, are sufficient for purposes of this paragraph, then the Secretary shall promulgate regulations prescribing appropriate tests or methods of assay in accordance with which such determination as to strength, quality, or purity shall be made. No drug defined in an official compendium shall be deemed to be adulterated under this paragraph because it differs from the standard of strength, quality, or purity therefor set forth in such compendium, if its difference in strength, quality, or purity from such standards is plainly stated on its label. Whenever a drug is recognized in both the United States Pharmacopeia and the Homeopathic Pharmacopeia of the United States it shall be subject to the requirements of the United States Pharmacopeia unless it is labeled and offered for sale as a homeopathic drug, in which case it shall be subject to the provisions of the Homeopathic Pharmacopeia of the United States and not to those of the United States Pharmacopeia.

(c) If it is not subject to the provisions of paragraph (b) of this section and its strength differs from, or its purity or quality falls below, that which it purports or is represented to possess.

(d) If it is a drug and any substance has been (1) mixed or packed therewith so as to reduce its quality or strength or (2) substituted wholly or in part therefor.

(e)(1) If it is, or purports to be or is represented as, a device which is subject to a performance standard established under section 514, unless such device is in all respects in conformity with such standard.

(2) If it is declared to be, purports to be, or is represented as, a device that is in conformity with any standard recognized under section 514(c) unless such device is in all respects in conformity with such standard.

(f)(1) If it is a class III device—

(A)(i) which is required by a regulation promulgated under subsection (b) of section 515 to have an approval under such section of an application for premarket approval and which is not exempt from section 515 under section 520(g), and (ii)(I) for which an application for premarket approval or a notice of completion of a product development protocol was not filed with the Secretary within the ninety-day period beginning on the date of the promulgation of such regulation, or

(II) for which such an application was filed and approval of the application has been denied, suspended, or withdrawn, or such a notice was filed and has been declared not completed or the approval of the device under the protocol has been withdrawn;

(B)(i) which was classified under section 513(f) into class III, which under section 515(a) is required to have in effect an approved application for premarket approval, and which is not exempt from section 515 under section 520(g), and

(ii) which has an application which has been suspended or is otherwise not in effect; or

(C) which was classified under section 520(l) into class III, which under such section is required to have in effect an approved application under section 515, and which has an application which has been suspended or is otherwise not in effect.

(2)(A) In the case of a device classified under section 513(f) into class III and intended solely for investigational use, paragraph (1)(B) shall not apply with respect to such device during the period ending on the ninetieth day after the date of the promulgation of the regulations prescribing the procedures and conditions required by section 520(g)(2).

(B) In the case of a device subject to a regulation promulgated under subsection (b) of section 515, paragraph [2] (1) shall not apply with respect to such device during the period ending—

(i) on the last day of the thirtieth calendar month beginning after the month in which the classification of the device in class III became effective under section 513, or

(ii) on the ninetieth day after the date of the promulgation of such regulation, whichever occurs later.

(g) If it is a banned device.

(h) If it is a device and the methods used in, or the facilities or controls used for, its manufacture, packing, storage, or installation are not in conformity with applicable requirements under section 520(f)(1) or an applicable condition prescribed by an order under section 520(f)(2).

---

[2] So in law. Probably should be "subparagraph".

(i) If it is a device for which an exemption has been granted under section 520(g) for investigational use and the person who was granted such exemption or any investigator who uses such device under such exemption fails to comply with a requirement prescribed by or under such section.

SEC. 502. [21 USC §352] Misbranded Drugs and Devices

Note: revisions were posted to this section in February 2008.

[Note: See prospective amendment notes below.]

A drug or device shall be deemed to be misbranded-- [3]

(a) False or misleading label. If its labeling is false or misleading in any particular. Health care economic information provided to a formulary committee, or other similar entity, in the course of the committee or the entity carrying out its responsibilities for the selection of drugs for managed care or other similar organizations, shall not be considered to be false or misleading under this paragraph if the health care economic information directly relates to an indication approved under section 505 or under section 351(a) of the Public Health Service Act [42 USC § 262(a)] for such drug and is based on competent and reliable scientific evidence. The requirements set forth in section 505(a) or in section 351(a) of the Public Health Service Act shall not apply to health care economic information provided to such a committee or entity in accordance with this paragraph. Information that is relevant to the substantiation of the health care economic information presented pursuant to this paragraph shall be made available to the Secretary upon request. In this paragraph, the term "health care economic information" means any analysis that identifies, measures, or compares the economic consequences, including the costs of the represented health outcomes, of the use of a drug to the use of another drug, to another health care intervention, or to no intervention.

(b) Package form; Contents of label. If in package form unless it bears a label containing (1) the name and place of business of the manufacturer, packer, or distributor; and (2) an accurate statement of the quantity of the contents in terms of weight, measure, or numerical count: Provided, That under clause (2) of this paragraph reasonable variations shall be permitted, and exemptions as to small packages shall be established, by regulations prescribed by the Secretary.

(c) Prominence of information on label. If any word, statement, or other information required by or under authority of this Act to appear on the label or labeling is not prominently placed thereon with such conspicuousness (as compared with other words, statements, designs, or devices, in the labeling) and in such terms as to

[3] See footnote for section 403(h)(3) regarding the stylistic use of a list consisting of "(a)", "(b)", etc.

render it likely to be read and understood by the ordinary individual under customary conditions of purchase and use.

(d) [Repealed] [4]

(e) Designation of drugs or devices by established names.

(1)(A) If it is a drug, unless its label bears, to the exclusion of any other nonproprietary name (except the applicable systematic chemical name or the chemical formula)

(i) the established name (as defined in subparagraph (3)) of the drug, if there is such a name;

(ii) the established name and quantity or, if determined to be appropriate by the Secretary, the proportion of each active ingredient, including the quantity, kind, and proportion of any alcohol, and also including whether active or not the established name and quantity or if determined to be appropriate by the Secretary, the proportion of any bromides, ether, chloroform, acetanilide, acetophenetidin, amidopyrine, antipyrine, atropine, hyoscine, hyoscyamine, arsenic, digitalis, digitalis glucosides, mercury, ouabain, strophanthin, strychnine, thyroid, or any derivative or preparation of any such substances, contained therein, except that the requirement for stating the quantity of the active ingredients, other than the quantity of those specifically named in this subclause, shall not apply to nonprescription drugs not intended for human use; and

(iii) the established name of each inactive ingredient listed in alphabetical order on the outside container of the retail package and, if determined to be appropriate by the Secretary, on the immediate container, as prescribed in regulation promulgated by the Secretary, except that nothing in this subclause shall be deemed to require that any trade secret be divulged, and except that the requirements of this subclause with respect to alphabetical order shall apply only to nonprescription drugs that are not also cosmetics and that this subclause shall not apply to nonprescription drugs not intended for human use.

(B) For any prescription drug the established name of such drug or ingredient, as the case may be, on such label (and on any labeling on which a name for such drug or ingredient is used) shall be printed prominently and in type at least half as large as that used thereon for any proprietary name or designation for such drug or ingredient, except that

[4] Paragraph (d) was struck by section 126(6) of Public Law 105-115 (111 Stat.2327).

to the extent that compliance with the requirements of subclause (ii) or (iii) of clause (A) or this clause is impracticable, exemptions shall be established by regulations promulgated by the Secretary.

(2) If it is a device and it has an established name, unless its label bears, to the exclusion of any other nonproprietary name, its established name (as defined in subparagraph (4)) prominently printed in type at least half as large as that used thereon for any proprietary name or designation for such device, except that to the extent compliance with the requirements of this subparagraph is impracticable, exemptions shall be established by regulations promulgated by the Secretary.

(3) As used in subparagraph (1), the term "established name," with respect to a drug or ingredient thereof, means (A) the applicable official name designated pursuant to section 508, or (B) if there is no such name and such drug, or such ingredient, is an article recognized in an official compendium, then the official title thereof in such compendium, or (C) if neither clause (A) nor clause (B) of this subparagraph applies, then the common or usual name, if any, of such drug or of such ingredient, except that where clause (B) of this subparagraph applies to an article recognized in the United States Pharmacopeia and in the Homoeopathic Pharmacopoeia under different official titles, the official title used in the United States Pharmacopeia shall apply unless it is labeled and offered for sale as a homoeopathic drug, in which case the official title used in the Homoeopathic Pharmacopoeia shall apply.

(4) As used in subparagraph (2), the term "established name" with respect to a device means (A) the applicable official name of the device designated pursuant to section 508, (B) if there is no such name and such device is an article recognized in an official compendium, then the official title thereof in such compendium, or (C) if neither clause (A) nor clause (B) of this subparagraph applies, then any common or usual name of such device.

(f) Directions for use and warnings on label. Unless its labeling bears (1) adequate directions for use; and (2) such adequate warnings against use in those pathological conditions or by children where its use may be dangerous to health, or against unsafe dosage or methods or duration of administration or application, in such manner and form, as are necessary for the protection of users, except that where any requirement of clause (1) of this paragraph, as applied to any drug or device, is not necessary for the protection of the public health, the Secretary shall promulgate regulations exempting such drug or device from such requirement. Required labeling for prescription devices intended for use in health care facilities or by a health care professional and required labeling for in vitro diagnostic devices intended for use by health care professionals or in blood establishments may be made available solely by electronic means, provided that the labeling complies with all applicable requirements of law, and that the manufacturer affords such users the opportunity to request the labeling in paper form, and after such request, promptly provides the requested information without additional cost.

(g) Representations as recognized drug; packing and labeling; inconsistent requirements for designation of drug. If it purports to be a drug the name of which is recognized in an official compendium, unless it is packaged and labeled as prescribed therein. The method of packing may be modified with the consent of the Secretary. Whenever a drug is recognized in both the United States Pharmacopoeia and the Homoeopathic Pharmacopoeia of the United States, it shall be subject to the requirements of the United States Pharmacopoeia with respect to packaging and labeling unless it is labeled and offered for sale as a homoeopathic drug, in which case it shall be subject to the provisions of the Homoeopathic Pharmacopoeia of the United States, and not to those of the United States Pharmacopoeia, except that in the event of inconsistency between the requirements of this paragraph and those of paragraph (e) as to the name by which the drug or its ingredients shall be designated, the requirements of paragraph (e) shall prevail.

(h) Deteriorative drugs; packing and labeling. If it has been found by the Secretary to be a drug liable to deterioration, unless it is packaged in such form and manner, and its label bears a statement of such precautions, as the Secretary shall by regulations require as necessary for the protection of the public health. No such regulation shall be established for any drug recognized in an official compendium until the Secretary shall have informed the appropriate body charged with the revision of such compendium of the need for such packaging or labeling requirements and such body shall have failed within a reasonable time to prescribe such requirements.

(i) Drug; misleading container; imitation; offer for sale under another name. (1) If it is a drug and its container is so made, formed, or filled as to be misleading; or (2) if it is an imitation of another drug; or (3) if it is offered for sale under the name of another drug.

(j) Health-endangering when used as prescribed. If it is dangerous to health when used in the dosage or manner or with the frequency or duration prescribed, recommended, or suggested in the labeling thereof.

(k), (l) [Repealed] [5]

(m) Color additives; packing and labeling. If it is a color additive the intended use of which is for the purpose of coloring only, unless its packaging and labeling are in

[5] Paragraph (k) was struck by section 125(a)(2)(B) of Public Law 105–115 (111 Stat. 2325). Paragraph (l) was struck by section 125(b)(2)(D) of such Public Law.

conformity with such packaging and labeling requirements applicable to such color additive, as may be contained in regulations issued under section 721.

(n) Prescription drug advertisements: established name; quantitative formula; side effects, contraindications, and effectiveness; prior approval; false advertising; labeling; construction of the Convention on Psychotropic Substances. In the case of any prescription drug distributed or offered for sale in any State, unless the manufacturer, packer, or distributor thereof includes in all advertisements and other descriptive printed matter issued or caused to be issued by the manufacturer, packer, or distributor with respect to that drug a true statement of (1) the established name as defined in section 502(e) [6] [subsec. (e) of this section], printed prominently and in type at least half as large as that used for any trade or brand name thereof, (2) the formula showing quantitatively each ingredient of such drug to the extent required for labels under section 502(e) [subsec. (e) of this section] [8], and (3) such other information in brief summary relating to side effects, contraindications, and effectiveness as shall be required in regulations which shall be issued by the Secretary in accordance with the procedure specified in section 701(e) of this Act, except that (A) except in extraordinary circumstances, no regulation issued under this paragraph shall require prior approval by the Secretary of the content of any advertisement, and (B) no advertisement of a prescription drug, published after the effective date of regulations issued under this paragraph applicable to advertisements of prescription drugs, shall, with respect to the matters specified in this paragraph or covered by such regulations, be subject to the provisions of sections 12 through 17 of the Federal Trade Commission Act, as amended [15 USC 52-57]. This paragraph (n) [7] shall not be applicable to any printed matter which the Secretary determines to be labeling as defined in section 201(m) of this Act. Nothing in the Convention on Psychotropic Substances, signed at Vienna, Austria, on February 21, 1971, shall be construed to prevent drug price communications to consumers.[8]

(o) Drugs or devices from nonregistered establishments. If it was manufactured, prepared, propagated, compounded, or processed in an establishment in any State not duly registered under section 510, if it was not included in a list required by section 510(j), if a notice or other information respecting it was not provided as required by such section or section 510(k), or if it does not bear such symbols from the uniform system for identification of devices prescribed under section 510(e) as the Secretary by regulation requires.

---

[6] 2 So in law. Probably should be "paragraph (e)".
[7] So in law. Probably should be "This paragraph".
[8] Sentence was added by title I of Public Law 95–633. Section 112 of such Public Law provided as follows: "This title shall take effect on the date the Convention on Psychotropic Substances, signed at Vienna, Austria on February 21, 1971, enters into force in respect to the United States.". The Convention entered into force in respect to the United States on July 15, 1980.

(p) Packaging or labeling of drugs in violation of regulations. If it is a drug and its packaging or labeling is in violation of an applicable regulation issued pursuant to section 3 or 4 of the Poison Prevention Packaging Act of 1970 [15 USCS § 1472 or 1473].

(q) Restricted devices using false or misleading advertising or used in violation of regulations. In the case of any restricted device distributed or offered for sale in any State, if (1) its advertising is false or misleading in any particular, or (2) it is sold, distributed, or used in violation of regulations prescribed under section 520(e).

(r) Restricted devices not carrying requisite accompanying statements in advertisements and other descriptive printed matter. In the case of any restricted device distributed or offered for sale in any State, unless the manufacturer, packer, or distributor thereof includes in all advertisements and other descriptive printed matter issued or caused to be issued by the manufacturer, packer, or distributor with respect to that device (1) a true statement of the device's established name as defined in section 502(e), printed prominently and in type at least half as large as that used for any trade or brand name thereof, and (2) a brief statement of the intended uses of the device and relevant warnings, precautions, side effects, and contraindications and, in the case of specific devices made subject to a finding by the Secretary after notice and opportunity for comment that such action is necessary to protect the public health, a full description of the components of such device or the formula showing quantitatively each ingredient of such device to the extent required in regulations which shall be issued by the Secretary after an opportunity for a hearing. Except in extraordinary circumstances, no regulation issued under this paragraph shall require prior approval by the Secretary of the content of any advertisement and no advertisement of a restricted device, published after the effective date of this paragraph shall, with respect to the matters specified in this paragraph or covered by regulations issued hereunder, be subject to the provisions of sections 12 through 15 of the Federal Trade Commission Act [15 USC 52-55]. This paragraph shall not be applicable to any printed matter which the Secretary determines to be labeling as defined in section 201(m).

(s) Devices subject to performance standards not bearing requisite labeling. If it is a device subject to a performance standard established under section 514, unless it bears such labeling as may be prescribed in such performance standard.

(t) Devices for which there has been a failure or refusal to give required notification or to furnish required material or information. If it is a device and there was a failure or refusal (1) to comply with any requirement prescribed under section 518 respecting the device, (2) to furnish any material or information required by or under section 519 respecting the device, or (3) to comply with a requirement under section 522.

(u) [9] Identification of manufacturer.

(1) Subject to paragraph (2), if it is a reprocessed single-use device, unless it, or an attachment thereto, prominently and conspicuously bears the name of the manufacturer of the reprocessed device, a generally recognized abbreviation of such name, or a unique and generally recognized symbol identifying such manufacturer.

(2) If the original device or an attachment thereto does not prominently and conspicuously bear the name of the manufacturer of the original device, a generally recognized abbreviation of such name, or a unique and generally recognized symbol identifying such manufacturer, a reprocessed device may satisfy the requirements of paragraph (1) through the use of a detachable label on the packaging that identifies the manufacturer and is intended to be affixed to the medical record of a patient.

(v) [10] Reprocessed single-use device. If it is a reprocessed single-use device, unless all labeling of the device prominently and conspicuously bears the statement "Reprocessed device for single use. Reprocessed by ------." The name of the manufacturer of the reprocessed device shall be placed in the space identifying the person responsible for reprocessing.

(w) New animal drugs. If it is a new animal drug—

(1) that is conditionally approved under section 571 and its labeling does not conform with the approved application or section 571(f), or that is not conditionally approved under section 571 and its label bears the statement set forth in section 571(f)(1)(A); or

(2) that is indexed under section 572 and its labeling does not conform with the index listing under section 572(e) or 572(h), or that has not been indexed under section 572 and its label bears the statement set forth in section 572(h).

(x) If it is a nonprescription drug (as defined in section 760) that is marketed in the United States, unless the label of such drug includes a domestic address or domestic phone number through which the responsible person (as described in

Chapter V

[9] Paragraph (u) was added by section 301(a) of Public Law 107–250 (116 Stat. 1616), which was enacted October 26, 2002. Subsection (b) of such section (as amended by section 2(c)(1) of Public Law 108–214; 118 Stat. 575) provides as follows:
(b) EFFECTIVE DATE.—The amendment made by subsection (a) takes effect 36 months after the date of the enactment of this Act, and only applies to devices introduced or delivered for introduction into interstate commerce after such effective date.

[10] Paragraph (v) was added by section 302(a)(1) of Public Law 107–250 (116 Stat. 1616), which was enacted October 26, 2002. Paragraph (2) of such subsection provides as follows:
(2) EFFECTIVE DATE.—The amendment made by paragraph (1) takes effect 15 months after the date of the enactment of this Act, and only applies to devices introduced or delivered for introduction into interstate commerce after such effective date.

section 760) may receive a report of a serious adverse event (as defined in section 760) with such drug.

(y) **[Note: This subsection takes effect 180 days after enactment of Act Sept. 27, 2007, P.L. 110-85, as provided by § 909(a) of such Act, which appears as 21 USC § 331 note.]** If it is a drug subject to an approved risk evaluation and mitigation strategy pursuant to section 505(p) and the responsible person (as such term is used in section 505-1 fails to comply with a requirement of such strategy provided for under subsection (d), (e), or (f) of section 505-1.

(z) **[Note: This subsection takes effect 180 days after enactment of Act Sept. 27, 2007, P.L. 110-85, as provided by § 909(a) of such Act, which appears as 21 USC § 331 note.]** If it is a drug, and the responsible person (as such term is used in section 505(o)) is in violation of a requirement established under paragraph (3) (relating to postmarket studies and clinical trials) or paragraph (4) (relating to labeling) of section 505(o) with respect to such drug.

SEC. 503. [21 USC §353] Exemptions and Consideration for Certain Drugs, Devices, and Biological Products

(a) The Secretary is hereby directed to promulgate regulations exempting from any labeling or packaging requirement of this Act drugs and devices which are, in accordance with the practice of the trade, to be processed, labeled, or repacked in substantial quantities at establishments other than those where originally processed or packed, on condition that such drugs and devices are not adulterated or misbranded, under the provisions of this Act upon removal from such processing, labeling, or repacking establishment.

(b)(1) A drug intended for use by man which—

(A) because of its toxicity or other potentiality for harmful effect, or the method of its use, or the collateral measures necessary to its use, is not safe for use except under the supervision of a practitioner licensed by law to administer such drug; or

(B) is limited by an approved application under section 505 to use under the professional supervision of a practitioner licensed by law to administer such drug; shall be dispensed only (i) upon a written prescription of a practitioner licensed by law to administer such drug, or (ii) upon an oral prescription of such practitioner which is reduced promptly to writing and filed by the pharmacist, or (iii) by refilling any such written or oral prescription if such refilling is authorized by the prescriber either in the original prescription or by oral order which is reduced promptly to writing and filed by the pharmacist. The act of dispensing a drug contrary to the provisions of this paragraph shall be deemed to be an act which results in the drug being misbranded while held for sale.

(2) Any drug dispensed by filling or refilling a written or oral prescription of a practitioner licensed by law to administer such drug shall be exempt from the requirements of section 502, except paragraphs (a), (i) (2) and (3), (k), and (l), and the packaging requirements of paragraphs (g), (h), and (p), if the drug bears a label containing the name and address of the dispenser, the serial number and date of the prescription or of its filling, the name of the prescriber, and, if stated in the prescription, the name of the patient, and the directions for use and cautionary statements, if any, contained in such prescription. This exemption shall not apply to any drug dispensed in the course of the conduct of a business of dispensing drugs pursuant to diagnosis by mail, or to a drug dispensed in violation of paragraph (1) of this subsection.

(3) The Secretary may by regulation remove drugs subject to section 505 from the requirements of paragraph (1) of this subsection when such requirements are not necessary for the protection of the public health.

(4)(A) A drug that is subject to paragraph (1) shall be deemed to be misbranded if at any time prior to dispensing the label of the drug fails to bear, at a minimum, the symbol "Rx only".

(B) A drug to which paragraph (1) does not apply shall be deemed to be misbranded if at any time prior to dispensing the label of the drug bears the symbol described in subparagraph (A).

(5) Nothing in this subsection shall be construed to relieve any person from any requirement prescribed by or under authority of law with respect to drugs now included or which may hereafter be included within the classifications stated in section 3220 of the Internal Revenue Code (26 USC 3220), or to marihuana as defined in section 3238(b) of the Internal Revenue Code (26 USC 3238(b)).

(c)(1) No person may sell, purchase, or trade or offer to sell, purchase, or trade any drug sample. For purposes of this paragraph and subsection (d), the term "drug sample" means a unit of a drug, subject to subsection (b), which is not intended to be sold and is intended to promote the sale of the drug. Nothing in this paragraph shall subject an officer or executive of a drug manufacturer or distributor to criminal liability solely because of a sale, purchase, trade, or offer to sell, purchase, or trade in violation of this paragraph by other employees of the manufacturer or distributor.

(2) No person may sell, purchase, or trade, offer to sell, purchase, or trade, or counterfeit any coupon. For purposes of this paragraph, the term "coupon" means a form which may be redeemed, at no cost or at a reduced cost, for a drug which is prescribed in accordance with subsection (b).

(3)(A) No person may sell, purchase, or trade, or offer to sell, purchase, or trade, any drug—

(i) which is subject to subsection (b), and

(ii)(I) which was purchased by a public or private hospital or other health care entity, or

(II) which was donated or supplied at a reduced price to a charitable organization described in section 501(c)(3) of the Internal Revenue Code of 1954.

(B) Subparagraph (A) does not apply to—

(i) the purchase or other acquisition by a hospital or other health care entity which is a member of a group purchasing organization of a drug for its own use from the group purchasing organization or from other hospitals or health care entities which are members of such organization,

(ii) the sale, purchase, or trade of a drug or an offer to sell, purchase, or trade a drug by an organization described in subparagraph (A)(ii)(II) to a nonprofit affiliate of the organization to the extent otherwise permitted by law,

(iii) a sale, purchase, or trade of a drug or an offer to sell, purchase, or trade a drug among hospitals or other health care entities which are under common control,

(iv) a sale, purchase, or trade of a drug or an offer to sell, purchase, or trade a drug for emergency medical reasons, or

(v) a sale, purchase, or trade of a drug, an offer to sell, purchase, or trade a drug, or the dispensing of a drug pursuant to a prescription executed in accordance with subsection (b). For purposes of this paragraph, the term "entity" does not include a wholesale distributor of drugs or a retail pharmacy licensed under State law and the term "emergency medical reasons" includes transfers of a drug between health care entities or from a health care entity to a retail pharmacy undertaken to alleviate temporary shortages of the drug arising from delays in or interruptions of regular distribution schedules.

(d)(1) Except as provided in paragraphs (2) and (3), no person may distribute any drug sample. For purposes of this subsection, the term "distribute" does not include the providing of a drug sample to a patient by a—

(A) practitioner licensed to prescribe such drug,

(B) health care professional acting at the direction and under the supervision of such a practitioner, or

(C) pharmacy of a hospital or of another health care entity that is acting at the direction of such a practitioner and that received such sample pursuant to paragraph (2) or (3).

(2)(A) The manufacturer or authorized distributor of record of a drug subject to subsection (b) may, in accordance with this paragraph, distribute drug samples by mail or common carrier to practitioners licensed to prescribe such drugs or, at the request of a licensed practitioner, to pharmacies of hospitals or other health care entities. Such a distribution of drug samples may only be made—

(i) in response to a written request for drug samples made on a form which meets the requirements of subparagraph (B), and

(ii) under a system which requires the recipient of the drug sample to execute a written receipt for the drug sample upon its delivery and the return of the receipt to the manufacturer or authorized distributor of record.

(B) A written request for a drug sample required by subparagraph (A)(i) shall contain—

(i) the name, address, professional designation, and signature of the practitioner making the request,

(ii) the identity of the drug sample requested and the quantity requested,

(iii) the name of the manufacturer of the drug sample requested, and

(iv) the date of the request.

(C) Each drug manufacturer or authorized distributor of record which makes distributions by mail or common carrier under this paragraph shall maintain, for a period of 3 years, the request forms submitted for such distributions and the receipts submitted for such distributions and shall maintain a record of distributions of drug samples which identifies the drugs distributed and the recipients of the distributions. Forms, receipts, and records required to be maintained under this subparagraph shall be made available by the drug manufacturer or authorized distributor of record to Federal and State officials engaged in the regulation of drugs and in the enforcement of laws applicable to drugs.

(3) The manufacturer or authorized distributor of record of a drug subject to subsection (b) may, by means other than mail or common carrier, distribute drug samples only if the manufacturer or authorized distributor of record makes the distributions in accordance with subparagraph (A) and carries out the activities described in subparagraphs (B) through (F) as follows:

(A) Drug samples may only be distributed—

(i) to practitioners licensed to prescribe such drugs if they make a written request for the drug samples, or

(ii) at the written request of such a licensed practitioner, to pharmacies of hospitals or other health care entities. A written request for drug samples shall be made on a form which contains the practitioner's name, address, and professional designation, the identity of the drug sample requested, the quantity of drug samples requested, the name of the manufacturer or authorized distributor of record of the drug sample, the date of the request and signature of the practitioner making the request.

(B) Drug manufacturers or authorized distributors of record shall store drug samples under conditions that will maintain their stability, integrity, and effectiveness and will assure that the drug samples will be free of contamination, deterioration, and adulteration.

(C) Drug manufacturers or authorized distributors of record shall conduct, at least annually, a complete and accurate inventory of all drug samples in the possession of representatives of the manufacturer or authorized distributor of record. Drug manufacturers or authorized distributors of record shall maintain lists of the names and address of each of their representatives who distribute drug samples and of the sites where drug samples are stored. Drug manufacturers or authorized distributors of record shall maintain records for at least 3 years of all drug samples distributed, destroyed, or returned to the manufacturer or authorized distributor of record, of all inventories maintained under this subparagraph, of all thefts or significant losses of drug samples, and of all requests made under subparagraph (A) for drug samples. Records and lists maintained under this subparagraph shall be made available by the drug manufacturer or authorized distributor of record to the Secretary upon request.

(D) Drug manufacturers or authorized distributors of record shall notify the Secretary of any significant loss of drug samples and any known theft of drug samples.

(E) Drug manufacturers or authorized distributors of record shall report to the Secretary any conviction of their representatives for violations of subsection (c)(1) or a State law because of the sale, purchase, or trade of a drug sample or the offer to sell, purchase, or trade a drug sample.

(F) Drug manufacturers or authorized distributors of record shall provide to the Secretary the name and telephone number of the individual responsible for responding to a request for information respecting drug samples.

(e)(1)(A) Each person who is engaged in the wholesale distribution of a drug subject to subsection (b) and who is not the manufacturer or an authorized distributor of record of such drug shall, before each wholesale distribution of such drug (including each distribution to an authorized distributor of record or to a retail pharmacy), provide to the person who receives the drug a statement (in such form and containing such information as the Secretary may require) identifying each prior sale, purchase, or trade of such drug (including the date of the transaction and the names and addresses of all parties to the transaction).

(B) Each manufacturer of a drug subject to subsection (b) shall maintain at its corporate offices a current list of the authorized distributors of record of such drug.

(2)(A) No person may engage in the wholesale distribution in interstate commerce of drugs subject to subsection (b) in a State unless such person is licensed by the State in accordance with the guidelines issued under subparagraph (B).

(B) The Secretary shall by regulation issue guidelines establishing minimum standards, terms, and conditions for the licensing of persons to make wholesale distributions in interstate commerce of drugs subject to subsection (b). Such guidelines shall prescribe requirements for the storage and handling of such drugs and for the establishment and maintenance of records of the distributions of such drugs.

(3) For the purposes of this subsection and subsection (d)—

(A) the term "authorized distributors of record" means those distributors with whom a manufacturer has established an ongoing relationship to distribute such manufacturer's products, and

(B) the term "wholesale distribution" means distribution of drugs subject to subsection (b) to other than the consumer or patient but does not include intracompany sales and does not include distributions of drugs described in subsection (c)(3)(B).

(f)(1)(A) A drug intended for use by animals other than man, other than a veterinary feed directive drug intended for use in animal feed or an animal feed bearing or containing a veterinary feed directive drug, which—

(i) because of its toxicity or other potentiality for harmful effect, or the method of its use, or the collateral measures necessary for its use, is not safe for animal use except under the professional supervision of a licensed veterinarian, or

(ii) is limited by an approved application under subsection (b) of section 512, a conditionally-approved application under section 571, or an index listing under section 572 to use under the professional supervision of a licensed veterinarian, shall be dispensed only by or upon the lawful written or oral order of a licensed veterinarian in the course of the veterinarian's professional practice.

(B) For purposes of subparagraph (A), an order is lawful if the order—

(i) is a prescription or other order authorized by law,

(ii) is, if an oral order, promptly reduced to writing by the person lawfully filling the order, and filed by that person, and

(iii) is refilled only if authorized in the original order or in a subsequent oral order promptly reduced to writing by the person lawfully filling the order, and filed by that person.

(C) The act of dispensing a drug contrary to the provisions of this paragraph shall be deemed to be an act which results in the drug being misbranded while held for sale.

(2) Any drug when dispensed in accordance with paragraph (1) of this subsection—

(A) Shall be exempt from the requirements of section 502, except subsections (a), (g), (h), (i)(2), (i)(3), and (p) of such section, and

(B) shall be exempt from the packaging requirements of subsections (g), (h), and (p) of such section, if—

(i) when dispensed by a licensed veterinarian, the drug bears a label containing the name and address of the practitioner and any directions for use and cautionary statements specified by the practitioner, or

(ii) when dispensed by filling the lawful order of a licensed veterinarian, the drug bears a label containing the name and address of the dispenser, the serial number and date of the order or of its filing, the name of the licensed veterinarian, and the directions for use and cautionary statements, if any, contained in such order.

The preceding sentence shall not apply to any drug dispensed in the course of the conduct of a business of dispensing drugs pursuant to diagnosis by mail.

(3) The Secretary may by regulation exempt drugs for animals other than man subject to section 512, 571, or 572 from the requirements of paragraph (1) when such requirements are not necessary for the protection of the public health.

(4) A drug which is subject to paragraph (1) shall be deemed to be misbranded if at any time prior to dispensing its label fails to bear the statement "Caution: Federal law restricts this drug to use by or on the order of a licensed veterinarian.". A drug to which paragraph (1) does not apply shall be deemed to be misbranded if at any time prior to dispensing its label bears the statement specified in the preceding sentence.

(g)(1) The Secretary shall in accordance with this subsection assign an agency center to regulate products that constitute a combination of a drug, device, or biological product. The Secretary shall determine the primary mode of action of the combination product. If the Secretary determines that the primary mode of action is that of—

(A) a drug (other than a biological product), the agency center charged with premarket review of drugs shall have primary jurisdiction,

(B) a device, the agency center charged with premarket review of devices shall have primary jurisdiction, or

(C) a biological product, the agency center charged with premarket review of biological products shall have primary jurisdiction.

(2) Nothing in this subsection shall prevent the Secretary from using any agency resources of the Food and Drug Administration necessary to ensure adequate review of the safety, effectiveness, or substantial equivalence of an article.

(3) The Secretary shall promulgate regulations to implement market clearance procedures in accordance with paragraphs (1) and (2) not later than 1 year after the date of enactment of this subsection.[11]

(4)(A) Not later than 60 days after the date of the enactment of this paragraph [12], the Secretary shall establish within the Office of the Commissioner of Food and Drugs an office to ensure the prompt assignment of combination products to agency centers, the timely and effective premarket review of such products, and consistent and appropriate postmarket regulation of like products subject to the same statutory requirements to the extent permitted by law. Additionally, the office shall, in determining whether a product is to be designated a combination product, consult with the component within the Office of the Commissioner of Food and Drugs that is responsible for such determinations. Such office (referred to in this paragraph as the 'Office') shall have appropriate scientific and medical expertise, and shall be headed by a director.

(B) In carrying out this subsection, the Office shall, for each combination product, promptly assign an agency center with primary jurisdiction in accordance with paragraph (1) for the premarket review of such product.

(C)(i) In carrying out this subsection, the Office shall ensure timely and effective premarket reviews by overseeing the timeliness of and coordinating reviews involving more than one agency center.

Chapter V

[11] The subsection was added by section 16(a)(2) of Public Law 101–692, which was enacted November 28, 1990. The subsection was added as subsection (f), and was redesignated as subsection (g) by section 2(d)(4) of Public Law 102–108.

[12] Paragraph (4) was added by section 204(3) of Public Law 107–250 (116 Stat. 1611), which was enacted October 26, 2002.

(ii) In order to ensure the timeliness of the premarket review of a combination product, the agency center with primary jurisdiction for the product, and the consulting agency center, shall be responsible to the Office with respect to the timeliness of the premarket review.

(D) In carrying out this subsection, the Office shall ensure the consistency and appropriateness of postmarket regulation of like products subject to the same statutory requirements to the extent permitted by law.

(E)(i) Any dispute regarding the timeliness of the premarket review of a combination product may be presented to the Office for resolution, unless the dispute is clearly premature.

(ii) During the review process, any dispute regarding the substance of the premarket review may be presented to the Commissioner of Food and Drugs after first being considered by the agency center with primary jurisdiction of the premarket review, under the scientific dispute resolution procedures for such center. The Commissioner of Food and Drugs shall consult with the Director of the Office in resolving the substantive dispute.

(F) The Secretary, acting through the Office, shall review each agreement, guidance, or practice of the Secretary that is specific to the assignment of combination products to agency centers and shall determine whether the agreement, guidance, or practice is consistent with the requirements of this subsection. In carrying out such review, the Secretary shall consult with stakeholders and the directors of the agency centers. <> After such consultation, the Secretary shall determine whether to continue in effect, modify, revise, or eliminate such agreement, guidance, or practice, and shall publish in the Federal Register a notice of the availability of such modified or revised agreement, guidance or practice. Nothing in this paragraph shall be construed as preventing the Secretary from following each agreement, guidance, or practice until continued, modified, revised, or eliminated.

(G) Not later than one year after the date of the enactment of this paragraph and annually thereafter, the Secretary shall report to the appropriate committees of Congress on the activities and impact of the Office. The report shall include provisions--

(i) describing the numbers and types of combination products under review and the timeliness in days of such assignments, reviews, and dispute resolutions;

(ii) identifying the number of premarket reviews of such products that involved a consulting agency center; and

(iii) describing improvements in the consistency of postmarket regulation of combination products.

(H) Nothing in this paragraph shall be construed to limit the regulatory authority of any agency center.

(5) As used in this subsection:

(A) The term '***agency center***' means a center or alternative organizational component of the Food and Drug Administration.

(B) The term "***biological product***" has the meaning given the term in section 351(i) of the Public Health Service Act (42 USC 262(i)).

(C) The term "***market clearance***" includes—

(i) approval of an application under section 505, 507, 515, or 520(g),

(ii) a finding of substantial equivalence under this subchapter, and

(iii) approval of a biologics license application under subsection (a) of section 351 of the Public Health Service Act (42 USC 262).

SEC. 503A. [21 USC §353a] Pharmacy Compounding

(a) IN GENERAL.—Sections 501(a)(2)(B), 502(f)(1), and 505 shall not apply to a drug product if the drug product is compounded for an identified individual patient based on the unsolicited receipt of a valid prescription order or a notation, approved by the prescribing practitioner, on the prescription order that a compounded product is necessary for the identified patient, if the drug product meets the requirements of this section, and if the compounding—

(1) is by—

(A) a licensed pharmacist in a State licensed pharmacy or a Federal facility, or

(B) a licensed physician, on the prescription order for such individual patient made by a licensed physician or other licensed practitioner authorized by State law to prescribe drugs; or

(2)(A) is by a licensed pharmacist or licensed physician in limited quantities before the receipt of a valid prescription order for such individual patient; and

(B) is based on a history of the licensed pharmacist or licensed physician receiving valid prescription orders for the compounding of the drug product, which orders have been generated solely within an established relationship between—

(i) the licensed pharmacist or licensed physician; and

(ii)(I) such individual patient for whom the prescription order will be provided; or

(II) the physician or other licensed practitioner who will write such prescription order.

(b) COMPOUNDED DRUG.—

(1) LICENSED PHARMACIST AND LICENSED PHYSICIAN.—A drug product may be compounded under subsection (a) if the licensed pharmacist or licensed physician—

(A) compounds the drug product using bulk drug substances, as defined in regulations of the Secretary published at section 207.3(a)(4) of title 21 of the Code of Federal Regulations—

(i) that—

(I) comply with the standards of an applicable United States Pharmacopoeia or National Formulary monograph, if a monograph exists, and the United States Pharmacopoeia chapter on pharmacy compounding;

(II) if such a monograph does not exist, are drug substances that are components of drugs approved by the Secretary; or

(III) if such a monograph does not exist and the drug substance is not a component of a drug approved by the Secretary, that appear on a list developed by the Secretary through regulations issued by the Secretary under subsection (d);

(ii) that are manufactured by an establishment that is registered under section 510 (including a foreign establishment that is registered under section 510(i)); and

(iii) that are accompanied by valid certificates of analysis for each bulk drug substance;

(B) compounds the drug product using ingredients (other than bulk drug substances) that comply with the standards of an applicable United States Pharmacopoeia or National Formulary monograph, if a monograph exists, and the United States Pharmacopoeia chapter on pharmacy compounding;

(C) does not compound a drug product that appears on a list published by the Secretary in the Federal Register of drug products that have been withdrawn or removed from the market because such drug products or components of such drug products have been found to be unsafe or not effective; and

(D) does not compound regularly or in inordinate amounts (as defined by the Secretary) any drug products that are essentially copies of a commercially available drug product.

(2) DEFINITION.—For purposes of paragraph (1)(D), the term "essentially a copy of a commercially available drug product" does not include a drug product in which there is a change, made for an identified individual patient,

which produces for that patient a significant difference, as determined by the prescribing practitioner, between the compounded drug and the comparable commercially available drug product.

(3) DRUG PRODUCT.—A drug product may be compounded under subsection (a) only if—

(A) such drug product is not a drug product identified by the Secretary by regulation as a drug product that presents demonstrable difficulties for compounding that reasonably demonstrate an adverse effect on the safety or effectiveness of that drug product; and

(B) such drug product is compounded in a State—

(i) that has entered into a memorandum of understanding with the Secretary which addresses the distribution of inordinate amounts of compounded drug products interstate and provides for appropriate investigation by a State agency of complaints relating to compounded drug products distributed outside such State; or

(ii) that has not entered into the memorandum of understanding described in clause (i) and the licensed pharmacist, licensed pharmacy, or licensed physician distributes (or causes to be distributed) compounded drug products out of the State in which they are compounded in quantities that do not exceed 5 percent of the total prescription orders dispensed or distributed by such pharmacy or physician.

The Secretary shall, in consultation with the National Association of Boards of Pharmacy, develop a standard memorandum of understanding for use by the States in complying with subparagraph (B)(i).

(c) ADVERTISING AND PROMOTION.—A drug may be compounded under subsection (a) only if the pharmacy, licensed pharmacist, or licensed physician does not advertise or promote the compounding of any particular drug, class of drug, or type of drug. The pharmacy, licensed pharmacist, or licensed physician may advertise and promote the compounding service provided by the licensed pharmacist or licensed physician.

(d) REGULATIONS.—

(1) IN GENERAL.—The Secretary shall issue regulations to implement this section. Before issuing regulations to implement subsections (b)(1)(A)(i)(III), (b)(1)(C), or (b)(3)(A), the Secretary shall convene and consult an advisory committee on compounding unless the Secretary determines that the issuance of such regulations before consultation is necessary to protect the public health. The advisory committee shall include representatives from the National Association of Boards of Pharmacy, the United States

Pharmacopoeia, pharmacy, physician, and consumer organizations, and other experts selected by the Secretary.

(2) LIMITING COMPOUNDING.—The Secretary, in consultation with the United States Pharmacopoeia Convention, Incorporated, shall promulgate regulations identifying drug substances that may be used in compounding under subsection (b)(1)(A)(i)(III) for which a monograph does not exist or which are not components of drug products approved by the Secretary. The Secretary shall include in the regulation the criteria for such substances, which shall include historical use, reports in peer reviewed medical literature, or other criteria the Secretary may identify.

(e) APPLICATION.—This section shall not apply to—

(1) compounded positron emission tomography drugs as defined in section 201(ii); or

(2) radiopharmaceuticals.

(f) DEFINITION.—As used in this section, the term "***compounding***" does not include mixing, reconstituting, or other such acts that are performed in accordance with directions contained in approved labeling provided by the product's manufacturer and other manufacturer directions consistent with that labeling.

SEC. 503B. [21 USC §353b] Prereview of Television Advertisements

Note: This section was added in February 2008.

[Note: This section takes effect 180 days after enactment of Act Sept. 27, 2007, P.L. 110-85, as provided by § 909(a) of such Act, which appears as 21 USC § 331 note.]

(a) In general. The Secretary may require the submission of any television advertisement for a drug (including any script, story board, rough, or a completed video production of the television advertisement) to the Secretary for review under this section not later than 45 days before dissemination of the television advertisement.

(b) Review. In conducting a review of a television advertisement under this section, the Secretary may make recommendations with respect to information included in the label of the drug--

(1) on changes that are--

(A) necessary to protect the consumer good and well-being; or

(B) consistent with prescribing information for the product under review; and

(2) if appropriate and if information exists, on statements for inclusion in the advertisement to address the specific efficacy of the drug as it relates to specific population groups, including elderly populations, children, and racial and ethnic minorities.

(c) No authority to require changes. Except as provided by subsection (e), this section does not authorize the Secretary to make or direct changes in any material submitted pursuant to subsection (a).

(d) Elderly populations, children, racially and ethnically diverse communities. In formulating recommendations under subsection (b), the Secretary shall take into consideration the impact of the advertised drug on elderly populations, children, and racially and ethnically diverse communities.

(e) Specific disclosures.

(1) Serious risk; safety protocol. In conducting a review of a television advertisement under this section, if the Secretary determines that the advertisement would be false or misleading without a specific disclosure about a serious risk listed in the labeling of the drug involved, the Secretary may require inclusion of such disclosure in the advertisement.

(2) Date of approval. In conducting a review of a television advertisement under this section, the Secretary may require the advertisement to include, for a period not to exceed 2 years from the date of the approval of the drug under section 505 or section 351 of the Public Health Service Act [42 USC § 262], a specific disclosure of such date of approval if the Secretary determines that the advertisement would otherwise be false or misleading.

(f) Rule of construction. Nothing in this section may be construed as having any effect on requirements under section 502(n) or on the authority of the Secretary under section 314.550, 314.640, 601.45, or 601.94 of title 21, Code of Federal Regulations (or successor regulations).

SEC. 504. [21 USC §354] Veterinary Feed Directive Drugs

(a)(1) A drug intended for use in or on animal feed which is limited by an approved application filed pursuant to section 512(b), a conditionally-approved application filed pursuant to section 571, or an index listing pursuant to section 572 to use under the professional supervision of a licensed veterinarian is a veterinary feed directive drug. Any animal feed bearing or containing a veterinary feed directive drug shall be fed to animals only by or upon a lawful veterinary feed directive issued by a licensed veterinarian in the course of the veterinarian's professional practice. When labeled, distributed, held, and used in accordance with this section, a veterinary feed directive drug and any animal feed bearing or containing a veterinary feed directive drug shall be exempt from section 502(f).

(2) A veterinary feed directive is lawful if it—

(A) contains such information as the Secretary may by general regulation or by order require; and

(B) is in compliance with the conditions and indications for use of the drug set forth in the notice published pursuant to section 512(i), or the index listing pursuant to section 572(e).

(3)(A) Any persons involved in the distribution or use of animal feed bearing or containing a veterinary feed directive drug and the licensed veterinarian issuing the veterinary feed directive shall maintain a copy of the veterinary feed directive applicable to each such feed, except in the case of a person distributing such feed to another person for further distribution. Such person distributing the feed shall maintain a written acknowledgment from the person to whom the feed is shipped stating that that person shall not ship or move such feed to an animal production facility without a veterinary feed directive or ship such feed to another person for further distribution unless that person has provided the same written acknowledgment to its immediate supplier.

(B) Every person required under subparagraph (A) to maintain records, and every person in charge or custody thereof, shall, upon request of an officer or employee designated by the Secretary, permit such officer or employee at all reasonable times to have access to and copy and verify such records.

(C) Any person who distributes animal feed bearing or containing a veterinary feed directive drug shall upon first engaging in such distribution notify the Secretary of that person's name and place of business. The failure to provide such notification shall be deemed to be an act which results in the drug being misbranded.

(b) A veterinary feed directive drug and any feed bearing or containing a veterinary feed directive drug shall be deemed to be misbranded if their labeling fails to bear such cautionary statement and such other information as the Secretary may by general regulation or by order prescribe, or their advertising fails to conform to the conditions and indications for use published pursuant to section 512(i), or the index listing pursuant to section 572(e) or fails to contain the general cautionary statement prescribed by the Secretary.

(c) Neither a drug subject to this section, nor animal feed bearing or containing such a drug, shall be deemed to be a prescription article under any Federal or State law.

SEC. 505. [21 USC §355] New Drugs

Note: revisions were posted to this section in February 2008.

[Caution: See prospective amendment note below.]

(a) Necessity of effective approval of application. No person shall introduce or deliver for introduction into interstate commerce any new drug, unless an approval of an application filed pursuant to subsection (b) or (j) is effective with respect to such drug.

(b) Filing application; contents.

(1) Any person may file with the Secretary an application with respect to any drug subject to the provisions of subsection (a). Such person shall submit to the Secretary as a part of the application (A) full reports of investigations which have been made to show whether or not such drug is safe for use and whether such drug is effective in use; [13] (B) a full list of the articles used as components of such drug; (C) a full statement of the composition of such drug; (D) a full description of the methods used in, and the facilities and controls used for, the manufacture, processing, and packing of such drug; (E) such samples of such drug and of the articles used as components thereof as the Secretary may require; (F) specimens of the labeling proposed to be used for such drug and (G) any assessments required under section 505B. The applicant shall file with the application the patent number and the expiration date of any patent which claims the drug for which the applicant submitted the application or which claims a method of using such drug and with respect to which a claim of patent infringement could reasonably be asserted if a person not licensed by the owner engaged in the manufacture use, or sale of the drug. If an application is filed under this subsection for a drug and a patent which claims such drug or a method of using such drug is issued after the filing date but before approval of the application, the applicant shall amend the application to include the information required by the preceding sentence. Upon approval of the application, the Secretary shall publish information submitted under the two preceding sentences. The Secretary shall, in consultation with the Director of the National Institutes of Health and with representatives of the drug manufacturing industry, review and develop guidance, as appropriate, on the inclusion of women and minorities in clinical trials required by clause (A).

(2) An application submitted under paragraph (1) for a drug for which the investigations described in clause (A) of such paragraph and relied upon by the applicant for approval of the application were not conducted by or for the applicant and for which the applicant has not obtained a right of reference or use from the person by or for whom the investigations were conducted shall also include—

[13] The amendments made to this Act by the Drug Amendments of 1962 (Public Law 87–781) included amendments establishing the requirement that new drugs be effective. Section 107(c) of such Public Law concerned the applicability of the amendments, and is included in the appendix.

(A) a certification, in the opinion of the applicant and to the best of his knowledge, with respect to each patent which claims the drug for which such investigations were conducted or which claims a use for such drug for which the applicant is seeking approval under this subsection and for which information is required to be filed under paragraph (1) or subsection (c)—

(i) that such patent information has not been filed,

(ii) that such patent has expired,

(iii) of the date on which such patent will expire, or

(iv) that such patent is invalid or will not be infringed by the manufacture, use, or sale of the new drug for which the application is submitted; and

(B) if with respect to the drug for which investigations described in paragraph (1)(A) were conducted information was filed under paragraph (1) or subsection (c) for a method of use patent which does not claim a use for which the applicant is seeking approval under this subsection, a statement that the method of use patent does not claim such a use.

(3) Notice of opinion that patent is invalid or will not be infringed.--

(A) Agreement to give notice.--An applicant that makes a certification described in paragraph (2)(A)(iv) shall include in the application a statement that the applicant will give notice as required by this paragraph.

(B) Timing of notice.--An applicant that makes a certification described in paragraph (2)(A)(iv) shall give notice as required under this paragraph--

(i) if the certification is in the application, not later than 20 days after the date of the postmark on the notice with which the Secretary informs the applicant that the application has been filed; or

(ii) if the certification is in an amendment or supplement to the application, at the time at which the applicant submits the amendment or supplement, regardless of whether the applicant has already given notice with respect to another such certification contained in the application or in an amendment or supplement to the application.

(C) Recipients of notice.--An applicant required under this paragraph to give notice shall give notice to--

(i) each owner of the patent that is the subject of the certification (or a representative of the owner designated to receive such a notice); and

(ii) the holder of the approved application under this subsection for the drug that is claimed by the patent or a use of which is claimed by the patent (or a representative of the holder designated to receive such a notice).

(D) Contents of notice.--A notice required under this paragraph shall--

(i) state that an application that contains data from bioavailability or bioequivalence studies has been submitted under this subsection for the drug with respect to which the certification is made to obtain approval to engage in the commercial manufacture, use, or sale of the drug before the expiration of the patent referred to in the certification; and

(ii) include a detailed statement of the factual and legal basis of the opinion of the applicant that the patent is invalid or will not be infringed.

(4)(A) An applicant may not amend or supplement an application referred to in paragraph (2) to seek approval of a drug that is a different drug than the drug identified in the application as submitted to the Secretary.

(B) With respect to the drug for which such an application is submitted, nothing in this subsection or subsection (c)(3) prohibits an applicant from amending or supplementing the application to seek approval of a different strength.

(5)(A) The Secretary shall issue guidance for the individuals who review applications submitted under paragraph (1) or under section 351 of the Public Health Service Act [42 USCS § 262], which shall relate to promptness in conducting the review, technical excellence, lack of bias and conflict of interest, and knowledge of regulatory and scientific standards, and which shall apply equally to all individuals who review such applications.

(B) The Secretary shall meet with a sponsor of an investigation or an applicant for approval for a drug under this subsection or section 351 of the Public Health Service Act [42 USCS § 262] if the sponsor or applicant makes a reasonable written request for a meeting for the purpose of reaching agreement on the design and size of clinical trials intended to form the primary basis of an effectiveness claim. The sponsor or applicant shall provide information necessary for discussion and agreement on the design and size of the clinical trials. Minutes of any such meeting shall be prepared by the Secretary and made available to the sponsor or applicant upon request.

(C) Any agreement regarding the parameters of the design and size of clinical trials of a new drug under this paragraph that is reached between the Secretary and a sponsor or applicant shall be reduced to writing and made part of the administrative record by the Secretary. Such agreement shall not be changed after the testing begins, except—

(i) with the written agreement of the sponsor or applicant; or

(ii) pursuant to a decision, made in accordance with subparagraph (D) by the director of the reviewing division, that a substantial scientific issue essential to determining the safety or effectiveness of the drug has been identified after the testing has begun.

(D) A decision under subparagraph (C)(ii) by the director shall be in writing and the Secretary shall provide to the sponsor or applicant an opportunity for a meeting at which the director and the sponsor or applicant will be present and at which the director will document the scientific issue involved.

(E) The written decisions of the reviewing division shall be binding upon, and may not directly or indirectly be changed by, the field or compliance division personnel unless such field or compliance division personnel demonstrate to the reviewing division why such decision should be modified.

(F) No action by the reviewing division may be delayed because of the unavailability of information from or action by field personnel unless the reviewing division determines that a delay is necessary to assure the marketing of a safe and effective drug.

(G) For purposes of this paragraph, the reviewing division is the division responsible for the review of an application for approval of a drug under this subsection or section 351 of the Public Health Service Act (including all scientific and medical matters, chemistry, manufacturing, and controls).

(6) An application submitted under this subsection shall be accompanied by the certification required under section 402(j)(5)(B) of the Public Health Service Act [42 USC § 282(j)(5)(B)]. Such certification shall not be considered an element of such application.

(c) Period for approval of application; period for, notice, and expedition of hearing; period for issuance of order.

(1) Within one hundred and eighty days after the filing of an application under subsection (b), or such additional period as may be agreed upon by the Secretary and the applicant, the Secretary shall either—

(A) approve the application if he then finds that none of the grounds for denying approval specified in subsection (d) applies, or

(B) give the applicant notice of an opportunity for a hearing before the Secretary under subsection (d) on the question whether such application is approvable. If the applicant elects to accept the opportunity for hearing by written request within thirty days after such notice, such hearing shall commence not more than ninety days after the expiration of such thirty days unless the Secretary and the applicant otherwise agree.

Any such hearing shall thereafter be conducted on an expedited basis and the Secretary's order thereon shall be issued within ninety days after the date fixed by the Secretary for filing final briefs.

(2) If the patent information described in subsection (b) could not be filed with the submission of an application under subsection (b) because the application was filed before the patent information was required under subsection (b) or a patent was issued after the application was approved under such subsection, the holder of an approved application shall file with the Secretary, the patent number and the expiration date of any patent which claims the drug for which the application was submitted or which claims a method of using such drug and with respect to which a claim of patent infringement could reasonably be asserted if a person not licensed by the owner engaged in the manufacture, use, or sale of the drug. If the holder of an approved application could not file patent information under subsection (b) because it was not required at the time the application was approved, the holder shall file such information under this subsection not later than thirty days after the date of the enactment of this sentence [14], and if the holder of an approved application could not file patent information under subsection (b) because no patent had been issued when an application was filed or approved, the holder shall file such information under this subsection not later than thirty days after the date the patent involved is issued. Upon the submission of patent information under this subsection, the Secretary shall publish it.

(3) The approval of an application filed under subsection (b) which contains a certification required by paragraph (2) of such subsection shall be made effective on the last applicable date determined by applying the following to each certification made under subsection (b)(2)(A):

(A) If the applicant only made a certification described in clause (i) or (ii) of subsection (b)(2)(A) or in both such clauses, the approval may be made effective immediately.

(B) If the applicant made a certification described in clause (iii) of subsection (b)(2)(A), the approval may be made effective on the date certified under clause (iii).

(C) If the applicant made a certification described in clause (iv) of subsection (b)(2)(A), the approval shall be made effective immediately unless, before the expiration of 45 days after the date on which the notice described in subsection (b)(3) is received, an action is brought for infringement of the patent that is the subject of the certification and for which information was submitted to the Secretary under paragraph (2) or subsection (b)(1) before the date on which the application (excluding an amendment or supplement to the application) was submitted. If such an action is brought before the expiration of such days, the approval may be made

[14] Provision was added by title I of Public Law 98–417, which was enacted September 24, 1984.

effective upon the expiration of the thirty-month period beginning on the date of the receipt of the notice provided under subsection (b)(3) or such shorter or longer period as the court may order because either party to the action failed to reasonably cooperate in expediting the action, except that—

(i) if before the expiration of such period the district court decides that the patent is invalid or not infringed (including any substantive determination that there is no cause of action for patent infringement or invalidity), the approval shall be made effective on--

(I) the date on which the court enters judgment reflecting the decision; or

(II) the date of a settlement order or consent decree signed and entered by the court stating that the patent that is the subject of the certification is invalid or not infringed;

(ii) if before the expiration of such period the district court decides that the patent has been infringed--

(I) if the judgment of the district court is appealed, the approval shall be made effective on--

(aa) the date on which the court of appeals decides that the patent is invalid or not infringed (including any substantive determination that there is no cause of action for patent infringement or invalidity); or

(bb) the date of a settlement order or consent decree signed and entered by the court of appeals stating that the patent that is the subject of the certification is invalid or not infringed; or

(II) if the judgment of the district court is not appealed or is affirmed, the approval shall be made effective on the date specified by the district court in a court order under section 271(e)(4)(A) of title 35, United States Code;

(iii) if before the expiration of such period the court grants a preliminary injunction prohibiting the applicant from engaging in the commercial manufacture or sale of the drug until the court decides the issues of patent validity and infringement and if the court decides that such patent is invalid or not infringed, the approval shall be made effective as provided in clause (i); or

(iv) if before the expiration of such period the court grants a preliminary injunction prohibiting the applicant from engaging in the commercial manufacture or sale of the drug until the court decides the issues of patent validity and infringement and if the court decides that such patent has been infringed, the approval shall be made effective as provided in clause (ii).

In such an action, each of the parties shall reasonably cooperate in expediting the action.

(D) Civil action to obtain patent certainty.—

(i) Declaratory judgment absent infringement action.--

(I) In general.--No action may be brought under section 2201 of title 28, United States Code, by an applicant referred to in subsection (b)(2) for a declaratory judgment with respect to a patent which is the subject of the certification referred to in subparagraph (C) unless--

(aa) the 45-day period referred to in such subparagraph has expired;

(bb) neither the owner of such patent nor the holder of the approved application under subsection (b) for the drug that is claimed by the patent or a use of which is claimed by the patent brought a civil action against the applicant for infringement of the patent before the expiration of such period; and

(cc) in any case in which the notice provided under paragraph (2)(B) [15] relates to noninfringement, the notice was accompanied by a document described in subclause (III).

(II) Filing of civil action.--If the conditions described in items (aa), (bb), and as applicable, (cc) of subclause (I) have been met, the applicant referred to in such subclause may, in accordance with section 2201 of title 28, United States Code, bring a civil action under such section against the owner or holder referred to in such subclause (but not against any owner or holder that has brought such a civil action against the applicant, unless that civil action was dismissed without prejudice) for a declaratory judgment that the patent is invalid or will not be infringed by the drug for which the applicant seeks approval, except that such civil action may be brought for a declaratory judgment that the patent will not be infringed only in a case in which the condition described in subclause (I)(cc) is applicable. A civil action referred to in this subclause shall be brought in the judicial district where the defendant has its principal place of business or a regular and established place of business.

[15] So in law. See section 1101(b)(2)(D) of Public Law 108–173 (117 Stat. 2454). Probably should be "subsection (b)(3)".

(III) Offer of confidential access to application.--For purposes of subclause (I)(cc), the document described in this subclause is a document providing an offer of confidential access to the application that is in the custody of the applicant referred to in subsection (b)(2) for the purpose of determining whether an action referred to in subparagraph (C) should be brought. The document providing the offer of confidential access shall contain such restrictions as to persons entitled to access, and on the use and disposition of any information accessed, as would apply had a protective order been entered for the purpose of protecting trade secrets and other confidential business information. A request for access to an application under an offer of confidential access shall be considered acceptance of the offer of confidential access with the restrictions as to persons entitled to access, and on the use and disposition of any information accessed, contained in the offer of confidential access, and those restrictions and other terms of the offer of confidential access shall be considered terms of an enforceable contract. Any person provided an offer of confidential access shall review the application for the sole and limited purpose of evaluating possible infringement of the patent that is the subject of the certification under subsection (b)(2)(A)(iv) and for no other purpose, and may not disclose information of no relevance to any issue of patent infringement to any person other than a person provided an offer of confidential access. Further, the application may be redacted by the applicant to remove any information of no relevance to any issue of patent infringement.

(ii) Counterclaim to infringement action.—

(I) In general.--If an owner of the patent or the holder of the approved application under subsection (b) for the drug that is claimed by the patent or a use of which is claimed by the patent brings a patent infringement action against the applicant, the applicant may assert a counterclaim seeking an order requiring the holder to correct or delete the patent information submitted by the holder under subsection (b) or this subsection on the ground that the patent does not claim either--

(aa) the drug for which the application was approved; or

(bb) an approved method of using the drug.

(II) No independent cause of action.--Subclause (I) does not authorize the assertion of a claim described in subclause (I) in any civil action or proceeding other than a counterclaim described in subclause (I).

(iii) No damages.--An applicant shall not be entitled to damages in a civil action under clause (i) or a counterclaim under clause (ii).

(E)(i) If an application (other than an abbreviated new drug application) submitted under subsection (b) for a drug, no active ingredient (including any ester or salt of the active ingredient) of which has been approved in any other application under subsection (b), was approved during the period beginning January 1, 1982, and ending on the date of the enactment of this subsection [16], the Secretary may not make the approval of another application for a drug for which the investigations described in clause (A) of subsection (b)(1) and relied upon by the applicant for approval of the application were not conducted by or for the applicant and for which the applicant has not obtained a right of reference or use from the person by or for whom the investigations were conducted effective before the expiration of ten years from the date of the approval of the application previously approved under subsection (b).

(ii) If an application submitted under subsection (b) for a drug, no active ingredient (including any ester or salt of the active ingredient) of which has been approved in any other application under subsection (b), is approved after the date of the enactment of this clause [enacted Sept. 24, 1984], no application which refers to the drug for which the subsection (b) application was submitted and for which the investigations described in clause (A) of subsection (b)(1) and relied upon by the applicant for approval of the application were not conducted by or for the applicant and for which the applicant has not obtained a right of reference or use from the person by or for whom the investigations were conducted may be submitted under subsection (b) before the expiration of five years from the date of the approval of the application under subsection (b), except that such an application may be submitted under subsection (b) after the expiration of four years from the date of the approval of the subsection (b) application if it contains a certification of patent invalidity or noninfringement described in clause (iv) of subsection (b)(2)(A). The approval of such an application shall be made effective in accordance with this paragraph except that, if an action for patent infringement is commenced during the one-year period beginning forty-eight months after the date of the approval of the subsection (b) application, the thirty-month period referred to in subparagraph (C) shall be extended by such amount of time (if any) which is required for seven and one-half years to have elapsed from the date of approval of the subsection (b) application.

[16] See footnote for subsection (c)(2).

(iii) If an application submitted under subsection (b) for a drug, which includes an active ingredient (including any ester or salt of the active ingredient) that has been approved in another application approved under subsection (b), is approved after the date of the enactment of this clause [enacted Sept. 24, 1984] and if such application contains reports of new clinical investigations (other than bioavailability studies) essential to the approval of the application and conducted or sponsored by the applicant, the Secretary may not make the approval of an application submitted under subsection (b) for the conditions of approval of such drug in the approved subsection (b) application effective before the expiration of three years from the date of the approval of the application under subsection (b) if the investigations described in clause (A) of subsection (b)(1) and relied upon by the applicant for approval of the application were not conducted by or for the applicant and if the applicant has not obtained a right of reference or use from the person by or for whom the investigations were conducted.

(iv) If a supplement to an application approved under subsection (b) is approved after the date of enactment of this clause [enacted Sept. 24, 1984] and the supplement contains reports of new clinical investigations (other than bioavailabilty [bioavailability] [17] studies) essential to the approval of the supplement and conducted or sponsored by the person submitting the supplement, the Secretary may not make the approval of an application submitted under subsection (b) for a change approved in the supplement effective before the expiration of three years from the date of the approval of the supplement under subsection (b) if the investigations described in clause (A) of subsection (b)(1) and relied upon by the applicant for approval of the application were not conducted by or for the applicant and if the applicant has not obtained a right of reference or use from the person by or for whom the investigations were conducted.

(v) If an application (or supplement to an application) submitted under subsection (b) for a drug, which includes an active ingredient (including any ester or salt of the active ingredient) that has been approved in another application under subsection (b), was approved during the period beginning January 1, 1982, and ending on the date of the enactment of this clause [enacted Sept. 24, 1984], the Secretary may not make the approval of an application submitted under this subsection and for which the investigations described in clause (A) of subsection (b)(1) and relied upon by the applicant for approval of the application were not conducted by or for the

[17] So in law. Probably should be "bioavailability".

applicant and for which the applicant has not obtained a right of reference or use from the person by or for whom the investigations were conducted and which refers to the drug for which the subsection (b) application was submitted effective before the expiration of two years from the date of enactment of this clause [enacted Sept. 24, 1984].

(4) A drug manufactured in a pilot or other small facility may be used to demonstrate the safety and effectiveness of the drug and to obtain approval for the drug prior to manufacture of the drug in a larger facility, unless the Secretary makes a determination that a full scale production facility is necessary to ensure the safety or effectiveness of the drug.

(d) Grounds for refusing application; approval of application; "substantial evidence" defined. If the Secretary finds, after due notice to the applicant in accordance with subsection (c) and giving him an opportunity for a hearing, in accordance with said subsection, that (1) the investigations, reports of which are required to be submitted to the Secretary pursuant to subsection (b), do not include adequate tests by all methods reasonably applicable to show whether or not such drug is safe for use under the conditions prescribed, recommended, or suggested in the proposed labeling thereof; (2) the results of such tests show that such drug is unsafe for use under such conditions or do not show that such drug is safe for use under such conditions; (3) the methods used in, and the facilities and controls used for, the manufacture, processing, and packing of such drug are inadequate to preserve its identity, strength, quality, and purity; (4) upon the basis of the information submitted to him as part of the application, or upon the basis of any other information before him with respect to such drug, he has insufficient information to determine whether such drug is safe for use under such conditions; or (5) evaluated on the basis of the information submitted to him as part of the application and any other information before him with respect to such drug, there is a lack of substantial evidence that the drug will have the effect it purports or is represented to have under the conditions of use prescribed, recommended, or suggested in the proposed labeling thereof; or (6) the application failed to contain the patent information prescribed by subsection (b); or (7) based on a fair evaluation of all material facts, such labeling is false or misleading in any particular; he shall issue an order refusing to approve the application. If, after such notice and opportunity for hearing, the Secretary finds that clauses (1) through (6) do not apply, he shall issue an order approving the application. As used in this subsection and subsection (e), the term "substantial evidence" means evidence consisting of adequate and well-controlled investigations, including clinical investigations, by experts qualified by scientific training and experience to evaluate the effectiveness of the drug involved, on the basis of which it could fairly and responsibly be concluded by such experts that the drug will have the effect it purports or is represented to have under the conditions of use prescribed, recommended, or suggested in the labeling or proposed labeling thereof. If the Secretary determines, based on relevant science, that data from one adequate and well-controlled clinical investigation and confirmatory evidence (obtained prior to or after such investigation) are sufficient to establish effectiveness, the Secretary may consider such data and evidence to constitute substantial evidence for purposes of the preceding sentence.

(e) Withdrawal of approval; grounds; immediate suspension upon finding imminent hazard to public health. The Secretary shall, after due notice and opportunity for hearing to the applicant, withdraw approval of an application with respect to any drug under this section if the Secretary finds (1) that clinical or other experience, tests, or other scientific data show that such drug is unsafe for use under the conditions of use upon the basis of which the application was approved; (2) that new evidence of clinical experience, not contained in such application or not available to the Secretary until after such application was approved, or tests by new methods, or tests by methods not deemed reasonably applicable when such application was approved, evaluated together with the evidence available to the Secretary when the application was approved, shows that such drug is not shown to be safe for use under the conditions of use upon the basis of which the application was approved; or (3) on the basis of new information before him with respect to such drug, evaluated together with the evidence available to him when the application was approved, that there is a lack of substantial evidence that the drug will have the effect it purports or is represented to have under the conditions of use prescribed, recommended, or suggested in the labeling thereof; or (4) the patent information prescribed by subsection (c) was not filed within thirty days after the receipt of written notice from the Secretary specifying the failure to file such information; or (5) that the application contains any untrue statement of a material fact: Provided, That if the Secretary (or in his absence the officer acting as Secretary) finds that there is an imminent hazard to the public health, he may suspend the approval of such application immediately, and give the applicant prompt notice of his action and afford the applicant the opportunity for an expedited hearing under this subsection; but the authority conferred by this proviso to suspend the approval of an application shall not be delegated. The Secretary may also, after due notice and opportunity for hearing to the applicant, withdraw the approval of an application submitted under subsection (b) or (j) with respect to any drug under this section if the Secretary finds (1) that the applicant has failed to establish a system for maintaining required records, or has repeatedly or deliberately failed to maintain such records or to make required reports, in accordance with a regulation or order under subsection (k) or to comply with the notice requirements of section 510(k)(2), or the applicant has refused to permit access to, or copying or verification of, such records as required by paragraph (2) of such subsection; or (2) that on the basis of new information before him, evaluated together with the evidence before him when the application was approved, the methods used in, or the facilities and controls used for, the manufacture, processing, and packing of such drug are inadequate to assure and preserve its identity, strength, quality, and purity and were not made adequate within a reasonable time after receipt of written notice from the Secretary specifying the matter complained of; or (3) that on the basis of new information before him, evaluated together with the evidence before him when the application was approved, the labeling of such drug, based on a fair evaluation of all material facts, is false or misleading in any particular and was not corrected within a reasonable time after receipt of written notice from the Secretary specifying the matter complained of. Any order under this subsection shall state the findings upon which it is based.

(f) Revocation of order refusing, withdrawing or suspending approval of application. Whenever the Secretary finds that the facts so require, he shall revoke any previous order under subsection (d) or (e) refusing, withdrawing, or suspending approval of an application and shall approve such application or reinstate such approval, as may be appropriate.

(g) Service of orders. Orders of the Secretary issued under this section shall be served (1) in person by any officer or employee of the department designated by the Secretary or (2) by mailing the order by registered mail or by certified mail addressed to the applicant or respondent at his last-known address in the records of the Secretary.

(h) Appeal from order. An appeal may be taken by the applicant from an order of the Secretary refusing or withdrawing approval of an application under this section. Such appeal shall be taken by filing in the United States court of appeals for the circuit wherein such applicant resides or has his principal place of business, or in the United States Court of Appeals for the District of Columbia Circuit, within sixty days after the entry of such order, a written petition praying that the order of the Secretary be set aside. A copy of such petition shall be forthwith transmitted by the clerk of the court to the Secretary, or any officer designated by him for that purpose, and thereupon the Secretary shall certify and file in the court the record upon which the order complained of was entered, as provided in section 2112 of title 28, United States Code. Upon the filing of such petition such court shall have exclusive jurisdiction to affirm or set aside such order, except that until the filing of the record the Secretary may modify or set aside his order. No objection to the order of the Secretary shall be considered by the court unless such objection shall have been urged before the Secretary or unless there were reasonable grounds for failure so to do. The finding of the Secretary as to the facts, if supported by substantial evidence, shall be conclusive. If any person shall apply to the court for leave to adduce additional evidence, and shall show to the satisfaction of the court that such additional evidence is material and that there were reasonable grounds for failure to adduce such evidence in the proceeding before the Secretary, the court may order such additional evidence to be taken before the Secretary and to be adduced upon the hearing in such manner and upon such terms and conditions as to the court may seem proper. The Secretary may modify his findings as to the facts by reason of the additional evidence so taken, and he shall file with the court such modified findings which, if supported by substantial evidence, shall be conclusive, and his recommendation, if any, for the setting aside of the original order. The judgment of the court affirming or setting aside any such order of the Secretary shall be final, subject to review by the Supreme Court of the United States upon certiorari or certification as provided in section 1254 of title 28 of the United States Code. The commencement of proceedings under this subsection shall not, unless specifically ordered by the court to the contrary, operate as a stay of the Secretary's order.

(i) Exemptions of drugs for research; discretionary and mandatory conditions; direct reports to Secretary.

(1) The Secretary shall promulgate regulations for exempting from the operation of the foregoing subsections of this section drugs intended solely for investigational use by experts qualified by scientific training and experience to investigate the safety and effectiveness of drugs. Such regulations may, within the discretion of the Secretary, among other conditions relating to the protection of the public health, provide for conditioning such exemption upon—

(A) the submission to the Secretary, before any clinical testing of a new drug is undertaken, of reports, by the manufacturer or the sponsor of the investigation of such drug, of preclinical tests (including tests on animals) of such drug adequate to justify the proposed clinical testing;

(B) the manufacturer or the sponsor of the investigation of a new drug proposed to be distributed to investigators for clinical testing obtaining a signed agreement from each of such investigators that patients to whom the drug is administered will be under his personal supervision, or under the supervision of investigators responsible to him, and that he will not supply such drug to any other investigator, or to clinics, for administration to human beings;

(C) the establishment and maintenance of such records, and the making of such reports to the Secretary, by the manufacturer or the sponsor of the investigation of such drug, of data (including but not limited to analytical reports by investigators) obtained as the result of such investigational use of such drug, as the Secretary finds will enable him to evaluate the safety and effectiveness of such drug in the event of the filing of an application pursuant to subsection (b) ; and

(D) [18] the submission to the Secretary by the manufacturer or the sponsor of the investigation of a new drug of a statement of intent regarding whether the manufacturer or sponsor has plans for assessing pediatric safety and efficacy.

[18] Indentation is so in law. See section 15(c) of Public Law 107–109 (115 Stat. 1420).

(2) Subject to paragraph (3), a clinical investigation of a new drug may begin 30 days after the Secretary has received from the manufacturer or sponsor of the investigation a submission containing such information about the drug and the clinical investigation, including—

(A) information on design of the investigation and adequate reports of basic information, certified by the applicant to be accurate reports, necessary to assess the safety of the drug for use in clinical investigation; and

(B) adequate information on the chemistry and manufacturing of the drug, controls available for the drug, and primary data tabulations from animal or human studies.

(3)(A) At any time, the Secretary may prohibit the sponsor of an investigation from conducting the investigation (referred to in this paragraph as a "clinical hold") if the Secretary makes a determination described in subparagraph (B). The Secretary shall specify the basis for the clinical hold, including the specific information available to the Secretary which served as the basis for such clinical hold, and confirm such determination in writing.

(B) For purposes of subparagraph (A), a determination described in this subparagraph with respect to a clinical hold is that—

(i) the drug involved represents an unreasonable risk to the safety of the persons who are the subjects of the clinical investigation, taking into account the qualifications of the clinical investigators, information about the drug, the design of the clinical investigation, the condition for which the drug is to be investigated, and the health status of the subjects involved; or

(ii) the clinical hold should be issued for such other reasons as the Secretary may by regulation establish (including reasons established by regulation before the date of the enactment of the Food and Drug Administration Modernization Act of 1997 [enacted Nov. 21, 1997]).

(C) Any written request to the Secretary from the sponsor of an investigation that a clinical hold be removed shall receive a decision, in writing and specifying the reasons therefor, within 30 days after receipt of such request. Any such request shall include sufficient information to support the removal of such clinical hold.

(4) Regulations under paragraph (1) shall provide that such exemption shall be conditioned upon the manufacturer, or the sponsor of the investigation, requiring that experts using such drugs for investigational purposes certify to such manufacturer or sponsor that they will inform any human beings to whom such drugs, or any controls used in connection therewith, are being administered, or their representatives, that such drugs are being used for investigational purposes and will obtain the consent of such human beings or

their representatives, except where it is not feasible or it is contrary to the best interests of such human beings. Nothing in this subsection shall be construed to require any clinical investigator to submit directly to the Secretary reports on the investigational use of drugs. The Secretary shall update such regulations to require inclusion in the informed consent documents and process a statement that clinical trial information for such clinical investigation has been or will be submitted for inclusion in the registry data bank pursuant to subsection (j) of section 402 of the Public Health Service Act [42 USC § 282].

(j) Abbreviated new drug applications.

(1) Any person may file with the Secretary an abbreviated application for the approval of a new drug.

(2)(A) An abbreviated application for a new drug shall contain—

(i) information to show that the conditions of use prescribed, recommended, or suggested in the labeling proposed for the new drug have been previously approved for a drug listed under paragraph (7) (hereinafter in this subsection referred to as a "listed drug");

(ii)(I) if the listed drug referred to in clause (i) has only one active ingredient, information to show that the active ingredient of the new drug is the same as that of the listed drug;

(II) if the listed drug referred to in clause (i) has more than one active ingredient, information to show that the active ingredients of the new drug are the same as those of the listed drug, or

(III) if the listed drug referred to in clause (i) has more than one active ingredient and if one of the active ingredients of the new drug is different and the application is filed pursuant to the approval of a petition filed under subparagraph (C), information to show that the other active ingredients of the new drug are the same as the active ingredients of the listed drug, information to show that the different active ingredient is an active ingredient of a listed drug or of a drug which does not meet the requirements of section 201(p), and such other information respecting the different active ingredient with respect to which the petition was filed as the Secretary may require;

(iii) information to show that the route of administration, the dosage form, and the strength of the new drug are the same as those of the listed drug referred to in clause (i), or, if the route of administration, the dosage form, or the strength of the new drug is different and the application is filed pursuant to the approval of a petition filed under subparagraph (C), such information respecting the route of administration, dosage form, or strength with respect to which the petition was filed as the Secretary may require;

(iv) information to show that the new drug is bioequivalent to the listed drug referred to in clause (i), except that if the application is filed pursuant to the approval of a petition filed under subparagraph (C), information to show that the active ingredients of the new drug are of the same pharmacological or therapeutic class as those of the listed drug referred to in clause (i) and the new drug can be expected to have the same therapeutic effect as the listed drug when administered to patients for a condition of use referred to in clause (i);

(v) information to show that the labeling proposed for the new drug is the same as the labeling approved for the listed drug referred to in clause (i) except for changes required because of differences approved under a petition filed under subparagraph (C) or because the new drug and the listed drug are produced or distributed by different manufacturers;

(vi) the items specified in clauses (B) through (F) of subsection (b)(1);

(vii) a certification, in the opinion of the applicant and to the best of his knowledge, with respect to each patent which claims the listed drug referred to in clause (i) or which claims a use for such listed drug for which the applicant is seeking approval under this subsection and for which information is required to be filed under subsection (b) or (c)—

(I) that such patent information has not been filed,

(II) that such patent has expired,

(III) of the date on which such patent will expire, or

(IV) that such patent is invalid or will not be infringed by the manufacture, , use, or sale of the new drug for which the application is submitted; and

(viii) if with respect to the listed drug referred to in clause (i) information was filed under subsection (b) or (c) for a method of use patent which does not claim a use for which the applicant is seeking approval under this subsection, a statement that the method of use patent does not claim such a use.

The Secretary may not require that an abbreviated application contain information in addition to that required by clauses (i) through (viii).

(B) Notice of opinion that patent is invalid or will not be infringed.—

(i) Agreement to give notice.--An applicant that makes a certification described in subparagraph (A)(vii)(IV) shall include in the application a statement that the applicant will give notice as required by this subparagraph.

(ii) Timing of notice.--An applicant that makes a certification described in subparagraph (A)(vii)(IV) shall give notice as required under this subparagraph—

(I) if the certification is in the application, not later than 20 days after the date of the postmark on the notice with which the Secretary informs the applicant that the application has been filed; or

(II) if the certification is in an amendment or supplement to the application, at the time at which the applicant submits the amendment or supplement, regardless of whether the applicant has already given notice with respect to another such certification contained in the application or in an amendment or supplement to the application.

(iii) Recipients of notice.--An applicant required under this subparagraph to give notice shall give notice to--

(I) each owner of the patent that is the subject of the certification (or a representative of the owner designated to receive such a notice); and

(II) the holder of the approved application under subsection (b) for the drug that is claimed by the patent or a use of which is claimed by the patent (or a representative of the holder designated to receive such a notice).

(iv) Contents of notice.--A notice required under this subparagraph shall--

(I) state that an application that contains data from bioavailability or bioequivalence studies has been submitted under this subsection for the drug with respect to which the certification is made to obtain approval to engage in the commercial manufacture, use, or sale of the drug before the expiration of the patent referred to in the certification; and

(II) include a detailed statement of the factual and legal basis of the opinion of the applicant that the patent is invalid or will not be infringed.

(C) If a person wants to submit an abbreviated application for a new drug which has a different active ingredient or whose route of administration, dosage form, or strength differ from that of a listed drug, such person shall submit a petition to the Secretary seeking permission to file such an application. The Secretary shall approve or disapprove a petition submitted under this subparagraph within ninety days of the date the petition is submitted. The Secretary shall approve such a petition unless the Secretary finds—

(i) that investigations must be conducted to show the safety and effectiveness of the drug or of any of its active ingredients, the route of administration, the dosage form, or strength which differ from the listed drug; or

(ii) that any drug with a different active ingredient may not be adequately evaluated for approval as safe and effective on the basis of the information required to be submitted in an abbreviated application.

(D)(i) An applicant may not amend or supplement an application to seek approval of a drug referring to a different listed drug from the listed drug identified in the application as submitted to the Secretary.

(ii) With respect to the drug for which an application is submitted, nothing in this subsection prohibits an applicant from amending or supplementing the application to seek approval of a different strength.

(iii) Within 60 days after the date of the enactment of the Medicare Prescription Drug, Improvement, and Modernization Act of 2003 [enacted Dec. 8, 2003], [19] the Secretary shall issue guidance defining the term "listed drug" for purposes of this subparagraph.

(3)(A) The Secretary shall issue guidance for the individuals who review applications submitted under paragraph (1), which shall relate to promptness in conducting the review, technical excellence, lack of bias and conflict of interest, and knowledge of regulatory and scientific standards, and which shall apply equally to all individuals who review such applications.

(B) The Secretary shall meet with a sponsor of an investigation or an applicant for approval for a drug under this subsection if the sponsor or applicant makes a reasonable written request for a meeting for the purpose of reaching agreement on the design and size of bioavailability and bioequivalence studies needed for approval of such application. The sponsor or applicant shall provide information necessary for discussion and agreement on the design and size of such studies. Minutes of any such meeting shall be prepared by the Secretary and made available to the sponsor or applicant.

[19] Public Law 108–173, enacted December 8, 2003.

(C) Any agreement regarding the parameters of design and size of bioavailability and bioequivalence studies of a drug under this paragraph that is reached between the Secretary and a sponsor or applicant shall be reduced to writing and made part of the administrative record by the Secretary. Such agreement shall not be changed after the testing begins, except—

(i) with the written agreement of the sponsor or applicant; or

(ii) pursuant to a decision, made in accordance with subparagraph (D) by the director of the reviewing division, that a substantial scientific issue essential to determining the safety or effectiveness of the drug has been identified after the testing has begun.

(D) A decision under subparagraph (C)(ii) by the director shall be in writing and the Secretary shall provide to the sponsor or applicant an opportunity for a meeting at which the director and the sponsor or applicant will be present and at which the director will document the scientific issue involved.

(E) The written decisions of the reviewing division shall be binding upon, and may not directly or indirectly be changed by, the field or compliance office personnel unless such field or compliance office personnel demonstrate to the reviewing division why such decision should be modified.

(F) No action by the reviewing division may be delayed because of the unavailability of information from or action by field personnel unless the reviewing division determines that a delay is necessary to assure the marketing of a safe and effective drug.

(G) For purposes of this paragraph, the reviewing division is the division responsible for the review of an application for approval of a drug under this subsection (including scientific matters, chemistry, manufacturing, and controls).

(4) Subject to paragraph (5), the Secretary shall approve an application for a drug unless the Secretary finds—

(A) the methods used in, or the facilities and controls used for, the manufacture, processing, and packing of the drug are inadequate to assure and preserve its identity, strength, quality, and purity;

(B) information submitted with the application is insufficient to show that each of the proposed conditions of use have been previously approved for the listed drug referred to in the application;

(C)(i) if the listed drug has only one active ingredient, information submitted with the application is insufficient to show that the active ingredient is the same as that of the listed drug;

(ii) if the listed drug has more than one active ingredient, information submitted with the application is insufficient to show that the active ingredients are the same as the active ingredients of the listed drug, or

(iii) if the listed drug has more than one active ingredient and if the application is for a drug which has an active ingredient different from the listed drug, information submitted with the application is insufficient to show—

(I) that the other active ingredients are the same as the active ingredients of the listed drug, or

(II) that the different active ingredient is an active ingredient of a listed drug or a drug which does not meet the requirements of section 201(p). or no petition to file an application for the drug with the different ingredient was approved under paragraph (2)(C);

(D)(i) if the application is for a drug whose route of administration, dosage form, or strength of the drug is the same as the route of administration, dosage form, or strength of the listed drug referred to in the application, information submitted in the application is insufficient to show that the route of administration, dosage form, or strength is the same as that of the listed drug, or

(ii) if the application is for a drug whose route of administration, dosage form, or strength of the drug is different from that of the listed drug referred to in the application, no petition to file an application for the drug with the different route of administration, dosage form, or strength was approved under paragraph (2)(C);

(E) if the application was filed pursuant to the approval of a petition under paragraph (2)(C), the application did not contain the information required by the Secretary respecting the active ingredient, route of administration, dosage form, or strength which is not the same;

(F) information submitted in the application is insufficient to show that the drug is bioequivalent to the listed drug referred to in the application or, if the application was filed pursuant to a petition approved under paragraph (2)(C), information submitted in the application is insufficient to show that the active ingredients of the new drug are of the same pharmacological or therapeutic class as those of the listed drug referred to in paragraph (2)(A)(i) and that the new drug can be expected to have the same therapeutic effect as the listed drug when administered to patients for a condition of use referred to in such paragraph;

(G) information submitted in the application is insufficient to show that the labeling proposed for the drug is the same as the labeling approved for the listed drug referred to in the application except for changes required because of differences approved under a petition filed under paragraph (2)(C) or because the drug and the listed drug are produced or distributed by different manufacturers;

(H) information submitted in the application or any other information available to the Secretary shows that (i) the inactive ingredients of the drug are unsafe for use under the conditions prescribed, recommended, or suggested in the labeling proposed for the drug, or (ii) the composition of the drug is unsafe under such conditions because of the type or quantity of inactive ingredients included or the manner in which the inactive ingredients are included;

(I) the approval under subsection (c) of the listed drug referred to in the application under this subsection has been withdrawn or suspended for grounds described in the first sentence of subsection (e), the Secretary has published a notice of opportunity for hearing to withdraw approval of the listed drug under subsection (c) for grounds described in the first sentence of subsection (e), the approval under this subsection of the listed drug referred to in the application under this subsection has been withdrawn or suspended under paragraph (6), or the Secretary has determined that the listed drug has been withdrawn from sale for safety or effectiveness reasons;

(J) the application does not meet any other requirement of paragraph (2)(A); or

(K) the application contains an untrue statement of material fact.

(5)(A) Within one hundred and eighty days of the initial receipt of an application under paragraph (2) or within such additional period as may be agreed upon by the Secretary and the applicant, the Secretary shall approve or disapprove the application.

(B) The approval of an application submitted under paragraph (2) shall be made effective on the last applicable date determined by applying the following to each certification made under paragraph (2)(A)(vii):

(i) If the applicant only made a certification described in subclause (I) or (II) of paragraph (2)(A)(vii) or in both such subclauses, the approval may be made effective immediately.

(ii) If the applicant made a certification described in subclause (III) of paragraph (2)(A)(vii), the approval may be made effective on the date certified under subclause (III).

(iii) If the applicant made a certification described in subclause (IV) of paragraph (2)(A)(vii), the approval shall be made effective immediately unless, before the expiration of 45 days after the date on which the notice described in paragraph (2)(B) is received, an action is brought for infringement of the patent that is the subject of the certification and for which information was submitted to the Secretary under subsection (b)(1) or (c)(2) before the date on which the application (excluding an amendment or supplement to the application), which the Secretary later determines to be substantially complete, was submitted. If such an action is brought before the expiration of such days, the approval shall be made effective upon the expiration of the thirty-month period beginning on the date of the receipt of the notice provided under paragraph (2)(B)(i) or such shorter or longer period as the court may order because either party to the action failed to reasonably cooperate in expediting the action, except that—

(I) if before the expiration of such period the district court decides that the patent is invalid or not infringed (including any substantive determination that there is no cause of action for patent infringement or invalidity), the approval shall be made effective on--

(aa) the date on which the court enters judgment reflecting the decision; or

(bb) the date of a settlement order or consent decree signed and entered by the court stating that the patent that is the subject of the certification is invalid or not infringed;

(II) if before the expiration of such period the district court decides that the patent has been infringed--

(aa) if the judgment of the district court is appealed, the approval shall be made effective on--

(AA) the date on which the court of appeals decides that the patent is invalid or not infringed (including any substantive determination that there is no cause of action for patent infringement or invalidity); or

(BB) the date of a settlement order or consent decree signed and entered by the court of appeals stating that the patent that is the subject of the certification is invalid or not infringed; or

(bb) if the judgment of the district court is not appealed or is affirmed, the approval shall be made effective on the date specified by the district court in a court order under section 271(e)(4)(A) of title 35, United States Code;

(III) if before the expiration of such period the court grants a preliminary injunction prohibiting the applicant from engaging in the commercial manufacture or sale of the drug until the court decides the issues of patent validity and infringement and if the court decides that such patent is invalid or not infringed, the approval shall be made effective as provided in subclause (I); or

(IV) if before the expiration of such period the court grants a preliminary injunction prohibiting the applicant from engaging in the commercial manufacture or sale of the drug until the court decides the issues of patent validity and infringement and if the court decides that such patent has been infringed, the approval shall be made effective as provided in subclause (II).

In such an action, each of the parties shall reasonably cooperate in expediting the action.

(iv) 180-day exclusivity period.

(I) Effectiveness of application. Subject to subparagraph (D), if the application contains a certification described in paragraph (2)(A)(vii)(IV) and is for a drug for which a first applicant has submitted an application containing such a certification, the application shall be made effective on the date that is 180 days after the date of the first commercial marketing of the drug (including the commercial marketing of the listed drug) by any first applicant.

(II) Definitions. In this paragraph:

(aa) 180-day exclusivity period. The term "***180-day exclusivity period***" means the 180-day period ending on the day before the date on which an application submitted by an applicant other than a first applicant could become effective under this clause.

(bb) First applicant. As used in this subsection, the term "***first applicant***" means an applicant that, on the first day on which a substantially complete application containing a certification described in paragraph (2)(A)(vii)(IV) is submitted for approval of a drug, submits a substantially complete application that contains and lawfully maintains a certification described in paragraph (2)(A)(vii)(IV) for the drug.

(cc) Substantially complete application. As used in this subsection, the term "***substantially complete application***" means an application under this subsection that on its face is sufficiently complete to permit a substantive review and contains all the information required by paragraph (2)(A).

(dd) Tentative approval.

(AA) In general. The term "***tentative approval***" means notification to an applicant by the Secretary that an application under this subsection meets the requirements of paragraph (2)(A), but cannot receive effective approval because the application does not meet the requirements of this subparagraph, there is a period of exclusivity for the listed drug under subparagraph (F) or section 505A, or there is a 7-year period of exclusivity for the listed drug under section 527.

(BB) Limitation. A drug that is granted tentative approval by the Secretary is not an approved drug and shall not have an effective approval until the Secretary issues an approval after any necessary additional review of the application.

(C) Civil action to obtain patent certainty.

(i) Declaratory judgment absent infringement action.

(I) In general. No action may be brought under section 2201 of title 28, United States Code, by an applicant under paragraph (2) for a declaratory judgment with respect to a patent which is the subject of the certification referred to in subparagraph (B)(iii) unless--

(aa) the 45-day period referred to in such subparagraph has expired;

(bb) neither the owner of such patent nor the holder of the approved application under subsection (b) for the drug that is claimed by the patent or a use of which is claimed by the patent brought a civil action against the applicant for infringement of the patent before the expiration of such period; and

(cc) in any case in which the notice provided under paragraph (2)(B) relates to noninfringement, the notice was accompanied by a document described in subclause (III).

(II) Filing of civil action. If the conditions described in items (aa), (bb), and as applicable, (cc) of subclause (I) have been met, the applicant referred to in such subclause may, in accordance with section 2201 of title 28, United States Code, bring a civil action under such section against the owner or holder referred to in such subclause (but not against any owner or holder that has brought such a civil action against the applicant, unless that civil action was dismissed without prejudice) for a declaratory judgment that the patent is invalid or will not be infringed by the drug for which the applicant seeks approval, except that such civil action may be brought for a declaratory judgment that the patent will not be infringed only in a case in which the condition described in subclause (I)(cc) is applicable. A civil action referred to in this subclause shall be brought in the judicial district where the defendant has its principal place of business or a regular and established place of business.

(III) Offer of confidential access to application. For purposes of subclause (I)(cc), the document described in this subclause is a document providing an offer of confidential access to the application that is in the custody of the applicant under paragraph (2) for the purpose of determining whether an action referred to in subparagraph (B)(iii) should be brought. The document providing the offer of confidential access shall contain such restrictions as to persons entitled to access, and on the use and disposition of any information accessed, as would apply had a protective order been entered for the purpose of protecting trade secrets and other confidential business information. A request for access to an application under an offer of confidential access shall be considered acceptance of the offer of confidential access with the restrictions as to persons entitled to access, and on the use and disposition of any information accessed, contained in the offer of confidential access, and those restrictions and other terms of the offer of confidential access shall be considered terms of an enforceable contract. Any person provided an offer of confidential access shall review the application for the sole and limited purpose of evaluating possible infringement of the patent that is the subject of the certification under paragraph (2)(A)(vii)(IV) and for no other purpose, and may not disclose information of no relevance to any issue of patent infringement to any person other than a person provided an offer of confidential access. Further, the application may be redacted by the applicant to remove any information of no relevance to any issue of patent infringement.

(ii) Counterclaim to infringement action.

(I) In general. If an owner of the patent or the holder of the approved application under subsection (b) for the drug that is claimed by the patent or a use of which is claimed by the patent brings a patent infringement action against the applicant, the applicant may assert a counterclaim seeking an order requiring the holder to correct or delete the patent information submitted by the holder under subsection (b) or (c) on the ground that the patent does not claim either--

(aa) the drug for which the application was approved; or

(bb) an approved method of using the drug.

(II) No independent cause of action. Subclause (I) does not authorize the assertion of a claim described in subclause (I) in any civil action or proceeding other than a counterclaim described in subclause (I).

(iii) No damages. An applicant shall not be entitled to damages in a civil action under clause (i) or a counterclaim under clause (ii).

(D) Forfeiture of 180-day exclusivity period.

(i) Definition of forfeiture event. In this subparagraph, the term "forfeiture event," with respect to an application under this subsection, means the occurrence of any of the following:

(I) Failure to market. The first applicant fails to market the drug by the later of--

(aa) the earlier of the date that is--

(AA) 75 days after the date on which the approval of the application of the first applicant is made effective under subparagraph (B)(iii); or

(BB) 30 months after the date of submission of the application of the first applicant; or

(bb) with respect to the first applicant or any other applicant (which other applicant has received tentative approval), the date that is 75 days after the date as of which, as to each of the patents with respect to which the first applicant submitted and lawfully maintained a certification qualifying the first applicant for the 180-day exclusivity period under subparagraph (B)(iv), at least 1 of the following has occurred:

(AA) In an infringement action brought against that applicant with respect to the patent or in a declaratory judgment action brought by that applicant with respect to the patent, a court enters a final decision from which no appeal (other than a petition to the Supreme Court for a writ of certiorari) has been or can be taken that the patent is invalid or not infringed.

(BB) In an infringement action or a declaratory judgment action described in subitem (AA), a court signs a settlement order or consent decree that enters a final judgment that includes a finding that the patent is invalid or not infringed.

(CC) The patent information submitted under subsection (b) or (c) is withdrawn by the holder of the application approved under subsection (b).

(II) Withdrawal of application. The first applicant withdraws the application or the Secretary considers the application to have been withdrawn as a result of a determination by the Secretary that the application does not meet the requirements for approval under paragraph (4).

(III) Amendment of certification. The first applicant amends or withdraws the certification for all of the patents with respect to which that applicant submitted a certification qualifying the applicant for the 180-day exclusivity period.

(IV) Failure to obtain tentative approval. The first applicant fails to obtain tentative approval of the application within 30 months after the date on which the application is filed, unless the failure is caused by a change in or a review of the requirements for approval of the application imposed after the date on which the application is filed.

(V) Agreement with another applicant, the listed drug application holder, or a patent owner. The first applicant enters into an agreement with another applicant under this subsection for the drug, the holder of the application for the listed drug, or an owner of the patent that is the subject of the certification under paragraph (2)(A)(vii)(IV), the Federal Trade Commission or the Attorney General files a complaint, and there is a final decision of the Federal Trade Commission or the court with regard to the complaint from which no appeal (other than a petition to the Supreme Court for a writ of certiorari) has been or can be taken that the agreement has violated the antitrust laws (as defined in section 1 of the Clayton Act (15 USC 12), except that the term includes section 5 of the Federal Trade Commission Act (15 USC 45) to the extent that that section applies to unfair methods of competition).

(VI) Expiration of all patents. All of the patents as to which the applicant submitted a certification qualifying it for the 180-day exclusivity period have expired.

(ii) Forfeiture. The 180-day exclusivity period described in subparagraph (B)(iv) shall be forfeited by a first applicant if a forfeiture event occurs with respect to that first applicant.

(iii) Subsequent applicant. If all first applicants forfeit the 180-day exclusivity period under clause (ii)--

(I) approval of any application containing a certification described in paragraph (2)(A)(vii)(IV) shall be made effective in accordance with subparagraph (B)(iii); and

(II) no applicant shall be eligible for a 180-day exclusivity period.

(E) If the Secretary decides to disapprove an application, the Secretary shall give the applicant notice of an opportunity for a hearing before the Secretary on the question of whether such application is approvable. If the applicant elects to accept the opportunity for hearing by written request within thirty days after such notice, such hearing shall commence not more than ninety days after the expiration of such thirty days unless the Secretary and the applicant otherwise agree. Any such hearing shall thereafter be conducted on an expedited basis and the Secretary's order thereon shall be issued within ninety days after the date fixed by the Secretary for filing final briefs.

(F)(i) If an application (other than an abbreviated new drug application) submitted under subsection (b) for a drug, no active ingredient (including any ester or salt of the active ingredient) of which has been approved in any other application under subsection (b), was approved during the period beginning January 1, 1982, and ending on the date of the enactment of this subsection [enacted Sept. 24, 1984] [20], the Secretary may not make the approval of an application submitted under this subsection which refers to the drug for which the subsection (b) application was submitted effective before the expiration of ten years from the date of the approval of the application under subsection (b).

(ii) If an application submitted under subsection (b) for a drug, no active ingredient (including any ester or salt of the active ingredient) of which has been approved in any other application under subsection (b), is approved after the date of the enactment of this subsection, no application may be submitted under this subsection which refers to the drug for which the subsection (b) application was submitted before the expiration of five years from the date of the approval of the application under subsection (b), except that such an application may be submitted under this subsection after the expiration of four years from the date of the approval of the subsection (b) application if it contains a certification of patent invalidity or noninfringement described in subclause (IV) of paragraph (2)(A)(vii). The approval of such an application shall be made effective in accordance with subparagraph (B) except that, if an action for patent infringement is commenced during the one-year

[20] This subsection was added by title I of Public Law 98–417, which was enacted September 24, 1984.

period beginning forty-eight months after the date of the approval of the subsection (b) application, the thirty-month period referred to in subparagraph (B)(iii) shall be extended by such amount of time (if any) which is required for seven and one-half years to have elapsed from the date of approval of the subsection (b) application.

(iii) If an application submitted under subsection (b) for a drug, which includes an active ingredient (including any ester or salt of the active ingredient) that has been approved in another application approved under subsection (b), is approved after the date of enactment of this subsection [20] and if such application contains reports of new clinical investigations (other than bioavailability studies) essential to the approval of the application and conducted or sponsored by the applicant, the Secretary may not make the approval of an application submitted under this subsection for the conditions of approval of such drug in the subsection (b) application effective before the expiration of three years from the date of the approval of the application under subsection (b) for such drug.

(iv) If a supplement to an application approved under subsection (b) is approved after the date of enactment of this subsection [enacted Sept. 24, 1984][20] and the supplement contains reports of new clinical investigations (other than bioavailability studies) essential to the approval of the supplement and conducted or sponsored by the person submitting the supplement, the Secretary may not make the approval of an application submitted under this subsection for a change approved in the supplement effective before the expiration of three years from the date of the approval of the supplement under subsection (b).

(v) If an application (or supplement to an application) submitted under subsection (b) for a drug, which includes an active ingredient (including any ester or salt of the active ingredient) that has been approved in another application under subsection (b), was approved during the period beginning January 1, 1982, and ending on the date of the enactment of this subsection [enacted Sept. 24, 1984] [21], the Secretary may not make the approval of an application submitted under this subsection which refers to the drug for which the subsection (b) application was submitted or which refers to a change approved in a supplement to the subsection (b) application effective before the expiration of two years from the date of enactment of this subsection [enacted Sept. 24, 1984] [21].

(6) If a drug approved under this subsection refers in its approved application to a drug the approval of which was withdrawn or suspended for grounds

[21] 1 See footnote for clause (i).

described in the first sentence of subsection (e) or was withdrawn or suspended under this paragraph or which, as determined by the Secretary, has been withdrawn from sale for safety or effectiveness reasons, the approval of the drug under this subsection shall be withdrawn or suspended—

(A) for the same period as the withdrawal or suspension under subsection (e) of this paragraph, or

(B) if the listed drug has been withdrawn from sale, for the period of withdrawal from sale or, if earlier, the period ending on the date the Secretary determines that the withdrawal from sale is not for safety or effectiveness reasons.

(7)(A)(i) Within sixty days of the date of the enactment of this subsection [enacted Sept. 24, 1984] [22], the Secretary shall publish and make available to the public—

(I) a list in alphabetical order of the official and proprietary name of each drug which has been approved for safety and effectiveness under subsection (c) before the date of the enactment of this subsection [enacted Sept. 24, 1984] ;

(II) the date of approval if the drug is approved after 1981 and the number of the application which was approved; and

(III) whether in vitro or in vivo bioequivalence studies, or both such studies, are required for applications filed under this subsection which will refer to the drug published.

(ii) Every thirty days after the publication of the first list under clause (i) the Secretary shall revise the list to include each drug which has been approved for safety and effectiveness under subsection (c) or approved under this subsection during the thirty day period.

(iii) When patent information submitted under subsection (b) or (c) respecting a drug included on the list is to be published by the Secretary, the Secretary shall, in revisions made under clause (ii), include such information for such drug.

(B) A drug approved for safety and effectiveness under subsection (c) or approved under this subsection shall, for purposes of this subsection, be considered to have been published under subparagraph (A) on the date of its approval or the date of enactment [enacted Sept. 24, 1984] [23], whichever is later.

[22] See footnote for paragraph (5)(F)(i).

[23] 1 See footnote for paragraph (5)(F)(i).

(C) If the approval of a drug was withdrawn or suspended for grounds described in the first sentence of subsection (e) or was withdrawn or suspended under paragraph (6) or if the Secretary determines that a drug has been withdrawn from sale for safety or effectiveness reasons, it may not be published in the list under subparagraph (A) or, if the withdrawal or suspension occurred after its publication in such list, it shall be immediately removed from such list—

(i) for the same period as the withdrawal or suspension under subsection (e) or paragraph (6), or

(ii) if the listed drug has been withdrawn from sale, for the period of withdrawal from sale or, if earlier, the period ending on the date the Secretary determines that the withdrawal from sale is not for safety or effectiveness reasons.

A notice of the removal shall be published in the Federal Register.

(8) [24] For purposes of this subsection:

(A)(i) The term "bioavailability" means the rate and extent to which the active ingredient or therapeutic ingredient is absorbed from a drug and becomes available at the site of drug action.

(ii) For a drug that is not intended to be absorbed into the bloodstream, the Secretary may assess bioavailability by scientifically valid measurements intended to reflect the rate and extent to which the active ingredient or therapeutic ingredient becomes available at the site of drug action.

(B) A drug shall be considered to be bioequivalent to a listed drug if—

(i) the rate and extent of absorption of the drug do not show a significant difference from the rate and extent of absorption of the listed drug when administered at the same molar dose of the therapeutic ingredient under similar experimental conditions in either a single dose or multiple doses; or

(ii) the extent of absorption of the drug does not show a significant difference from the extent of absorption of the listed drug when administered at the same molar dose of the therapeutic ingredient under similar experimental conditions in either a single dose or multiple doses and the difference from the listed drug in the rate of absorption of the drug is intentional, is reflected in its proposed

[24] Subsection (a) of section 1103 of Public Law 108–173 (117 Stat. 2460) amended subparagraph (A) of paragraph (8) to read as provided above, and also added to such paragraph subparagraph (C) (see next page). Subsection (b) of such section 1103 provides as follows: "The amendment made by subsection (a) does not alter the standards for approval of drugs under section 505(j) of the Federal Food, Drug, and Cosmetic Act (21 USC 355(j)).".

labeling, is not essential to the attainment of effective body drug concentrations on chronic use, and is considered medically insignificant for the drug.

(C) For a drug that is not intended to be absorbed into the bloodstream, the Secretary may establish alternative, scientifically valid methods to show bioequivalence if the alternative methods are expected to detect a significant difference between the drug and the listed drug in safety and therapeutic effect.

(9) The Secretary shall, with respect to each application submitted under this subsection, maintain a record of—

(A) the name of the applicant,

(B) the name of the drug covered by the application,

(C) the name of each person to whom the review of the chemistry of the application was assigned and the date of such assignment, and

(D) the name of each person to whom the bioequivalence review for such application was assigned and the date of such assignment.

The information the Secretary is required to maintain under this paragraph with respect to an application submitted under this subsection shall be made available to the public after the approval of such application.

(k) Records and reports; required information; regulations and orders; access to records.

(1) In the case of any drug for which an approval of an application filed under subsection (b) or (j) is in effect, the applicant shall establish and maintain such records, and make such reports to the Secretary, of data relating to clinical experience and other data or information, received or otherwise obtained by such applicant with respect to such drug, as the Secretary may by general regulation, or by order with respect to such application, prescribe on the basis of a finding that such records and reports are necessary in order to enable the Secretary to determine, or facilitate a determination, whether there is or may be ground for invoking subsection (e) of this section. Regulations and orders issued under this subsection and under subsection (i) shall have due regard for the professional ethics of the medical profession and the interests of patients and shall provide, where the Secretary deems it to be appropriate, for the examination, upon request, by the persons to whom such regulations or orders are applicable, of similar information received or otherwise obtained by the Secretary.

(2) Every person required under this section to maintain records, and every person in charge or custody thereof, shall, upon request of an officer or

employee designated by the Secretary, permit such officer or employee at all reasonable times to have access to and copy and verify such records.

(3) Active postmarket risk identification **[Caution: This paragraph takes effect 180 days after enactment of Act Sept. 27, 2007, P.L. 110-85, as provided by § 909(a) of such Act, which appears as 21 USC § 331 note.]**.

(A) Definition. In this paragraph, the term "data" refers to information with respect to a drug approved under this section or under section 351 of the Public Health Service Act [42 USC § 262], including claims data, patient survey data, standardized analytic files that allow for the pooling and analysis of data from disparate data environments, and any other data deemed appropriate by the Secretary.

(B) Development of postmarket risk identification and analysis methods. The Secretary shall, not later than 2 years after the date of the enactment of the Food and Drug Administration Amendments Act of 2007 [enacted Sept. 27, 2007], in collaboration with public, academic, and private entities--

(i) develop methods to obtain access to disparate data sources including the data sources specified in subparagraph (C);

(ii) develop validated methods for the establishment of a postmarket risk identification and analysis system to link and analyze safety data from multiple sources, with the goals of including, in aggregate--

(I) at least 25,000,000 patients by July 1, 2010; and

(II) at least 100,000,000 patients by July 1, 2012; and

(iii) convene a committee of experts, including individuals who are recognized in the field of protecting data privacy and security, to make recommendations to the Secretary on the development of tools and methods for the ethical and scientific uses for, and communication of, postmarketing data specified under subparagraph (C), including recommendations on the development of effective research methods for the study of drug safety questions.

(C) Establishment of the postmarket risk identification and analysis system.

(i) In general. The Secretary shall, not later than 1 year after the development of the risk identification and analysis methods under subparagraph (B), establish and maintain procedures--

(I) for risk identification and analysis based on electronic health data, in compliance with the regulations promulgated under section 264(c) of the Health Insurance Portability and Accountability Act of 1996 [42 USC § 1320d-2 note], and in a manner that does not disclose individually identifiable health information in violation of paragraph (4)(B);

(II) for the reporting (in a standardized form) of data on all serious adverse drug experiences (as defined in section 505-1(b) [21 USC § 355-1(b)]) submitted to the Secretary under paragraph (1), and those adverse events submitted by patients, providers, and drug sponsors, when appropriate;

(III) to provide for active adverse event surveillance using the following data sources, as available:

(aa) Federal health-related electronic data (such as data from the Medicare program and the health systems of the Department of Veterans Affairs);

(bb) private sector health-related electronic data (such as pharmaceutical purchase data and health insurance claims data); and

(cc) other data as the Secretary deems necessary to create a robust system to identify adverse events and potential drug safety signals;

(IV) to identify certain trends and patterns with respect to data accessed by the system;

(V) to provide regular reports to the Secretary concerning adverse event trends, adverse event patterns, incidence and prevalence of adverse events, and other information the Secretary determines appropriate, which may include data on comparative national adverse event trends; and

(VI) to enable the program to export data in a form appropriate for further aggregation, statistical analysis, and reporting.

(ii) Timeliness of reporting. The procedures established under clause (i) shall ensure that such data are accessed, analyzed, and reported in a timely, routine, and systematic manner, taking into consideration the need for data completeness, coding, cleansing, and standardized analysis and transmission.

(iii) Private sector resources. To ensure the establishment of the active postmarket risk identification and analysis system under this subsection not later than 1 year after the development of the risk identification and analysis methods under subparagraph (B), as required under clause (i), the Secretary may, on a temporary or permanent basis, implement systems or products developed by private entities.

(iv) Complementary approaches. To the extent the active postmarket risk identification and analysis system under this subsection is not sufficient to gather data and information relevant to a priority drug safety question, the Secretary shall develop, support, and participate in complementary approaches to gather and analyze such data and information, including--

(I) approaches that are complementary with respect to assessing the safety of use of a drug in domestic populations not included, or underrepresented, in the trials used to approve the drug (such as older people, people with comorbidities, pregnant women, or children); and

(II) existing approaches such as the Vaccine Adverse Event Reporting System and the Vaccine Safety Datalink or successor databases.

(v) Authority for contracts. The Secretary may enter into contracts with public and private entities to fulfill the requirements of this subparagraph.

(4) Advanced analysis of drug safety data **[Caution: This paragraph takes effect 180 days after enactment of Act Sept. 27, 2007, P.L. 110-85, as provided by § 909(a) of such Act, which appears as 21 USC § 331 note.]**.

(A) Purpose. The Secretary shall establish collaborations with public, academic, and private entities, which may include the Centers for Education and Research on Therapeutics under section 912 of the Public Health Service Act [42 USCS § 299b-1], to provide for advanced analysis of drug safety data described in paragraph (3)(C) and other information that is publicly available or is provided by the Secretary, in order to--

(i) improve the quality and efficiency of postmarket drug safety risk-benefit analysis;

(ii) provide the Secretary with routine access to outside expertise to study advanced drug safety questions; and

(iii) enhance the ability of the Secretary to make timely assessments based on drug safety data.

(B) Privacy. Such analysis shall not disclose individually identifiable health information when presenting such drug safety signals and trends or when responding to inquiries regarding such drug safety signals and trends.

(C) Public process for priority questions. At least biannually, the Secretary shall seek recommendations from the Drug Safety and Risk Management Advisory Committee (or any successor committee) and from other advisory committees, as appropriate, to the Food and Drug Administration on--

(i) priority drug safety questions; and

(ii) mechanisms for answering such questions, including through--

(I) active risk identification under paragraph (3); and

(II) when such risk identification is not sufficient, postapproval studies and clinical trials under subsection (o)(3).

(D) Procedures for the development of drug safety collaborations.

(i) In general. Not later than 180 days after the date of the establishment of the active postmarket risk identification and analysis system under this subsection, the Secretary shall establish and implement procedures under which the Secretary may routinely contract with one or more qualified entities to--

(I) classify, analyze, or aggregate data described in paragraph (3)(C) and information that is publicly available or is provided by the Secretary;

(II) allow for prompt investigation of priority drug safety questions, including--

(aa) unresolved safety questions for drugs or classes of drugs; and

(bb) for a newly-approved drugs, safety signals from clinical trials used to approve the drug and other preapproval trials; rare, serious drug side effects; and the safety of use in domestic populations not included, or underrepresented, in the trials used to approve the drug (such as older people, people with comorbidities, pregnant women, or children);

(III) perform advanced research and analysis on identified drug safety risks;

(IV) focus postapproval studies and clinical trials under subsection (o)(3) more effectively on cases for which reports under paragraph (1) and other safety signal detection is not sufficient to resolve whether there is an elevated risk of a serious adverse event associated with the use of a drug; and

(V) carry out other activities as the Secretary deems necessary to carry out the purposes of this paragraph.

(ii) Request for specific methodology. The procedures described in clause (i) shall permit the Secretary to request that a specific methodology be used by the qualified entity. The qualified entity shall work with the Secretary to finalize the methodology to be used.

(E) Use of analyses. The Secretary shall provide the analyses described in this paragraph, including the methods and results of such analyses, about a drug to the sponsor or sponsors of such drug.

(F) Qualified entities.

(i) In general. The Secretary shall enter into contracts with a sufficient number of qualified entities to develop and provide information to the Secretary in a timely manner.

(ii) Qualification. The Secretary shall enter into a contract with an entity under clause (i) only if the Secretary determines that the entity has a significant presence in the United States and has one or more of the following qualifications:

(I) The research, statistical, epidemiologic, or clinical capability and expertise to conduct and complete the activities under this paragraph, including the capability and expertise to provide the Secretary de-identified data consistent with the requirements of this subsection.

(II) An information technology infrastructure in place to support electronic data and operational standards to provide security for such data.

(III) Experience with, and expertise on, the development of drug safety and effectiveness research using electronic population data.

(IV) An understanding of drug development or risk/benefit balancing in a clinical setting.

(V) Other expertise which the Secretary deems necessary to fulfill the activities under this paragraph.

(G) Contract requirements. Each contract with a qualified entity under subparagraph (F)(i) shall contain the following requirements:

(i) Ensuring privacy. The qualified entity shall ensure that the entity will not use data under this subsection in a manner that--

(I) violates the regulations promulgated under section 264(c) of the Health Insurance Portability and Accountability Act of 1996 [42 USC § 1320d-2 note];

(II) violates sections 552 or 552a of title 5, United States Code, with regard to the privacy of individually-identifiable beneficiary health information; or

(III) discloses individually identifiable health information when presenting drug safety signals and trends or when responding to inquiries regarding drug safety signals and trends. Nothing in this clause prohibits lawful disclosure for other purposes.

(ii) Component of another organization. If a qualified entity is a component of another organization--

(I) the qualified entity shall establish appropriate security measures to maintain the confidentiality and privacy of such data; and

(II) the entity shall not make an unauthorized disclosure of such data to the other components of the organization in breach of such confidentiality and privacy requirement.

(iii) Termination or nonrenewal. If a contract with a qualified entity under this subparagraph is terminated or not renewed, the following requirements shall apply:

(I) Confidentiality and privacy protections. The entity shall continue to comply with the confidentiality and privacy requirements under this paragraph with respect to all data disclosed to the entity.

(II) Disposition of data. The entity shall return any data disclosed to such entity under this subsection to which it would not otherwise have access or, if returning the data is not practicable, destroy the data.

(H) Competitive procedures. The Secretary shall use competitive procedures (as defined in section 4(5) of the Federal Procurement Policy Act [Office of Federal Procurement Policy Act] [41 USC § 403(5)]) to enter into contracts under subparagraph (G).

(I) Review of contract in the event of a merger or acquisition. The Secretary shall review the contract with a qualified entity under this paragraph in the event of a merger or acquisition of the entity in order to ensure that the requirements under this paragraph will continue to be met.

(J) Coordination. In carrying out this paragraph, the Secretary shall provide for appropriate communications to the public, scientific, public health, and medical communities, and other key stakeholders, and to the extent practicable shall coordinate with the activities of private entities, professional associations, or other entities that may have sources of drug safety data.

(5) The Secretary shall--

(A) conduct regular, bi-weekly screening of the Adverse Event Reporting System database and post a quarterly report on the Adverse Event Reporting System Web site of any new safety information or potential signal of a serious risk identified by Adverse Event Reporting System within the last quarter;

(B) report to Congress not later than 2 year [years] after the date of the enactment of the Food and Drug Administration Amendments Act of 2007 [enacted Sept. 27, 2007] on procedures and processes of the Food and Drug Administration for addressing ongoing post market safety issues identified by the Office of Surveillance and Epidemiology and how recommendations of the Office of Surveillance and Epidemiology are handled within the agency; and

(C) on an annual basis, review the entire backlog of postmarket safety commitments to determine which commitments require revision or should be eliminated, report to the Congress on these determinations, and assign start dates and estimated completion dates for such commitments.

(l) Public disclosure of safety and effectiveness data.

(1) Safety and effectiveness data and information which has been submitted in an application under subsection (b) for a drug and which has not previously been disclosed to the public shall be made available to the public, upon request, unless extraordinary circumstances are shown—

(A) if no work is being or will be undertaken to have the application approved,

(B) if the Secretary has determined that the application is not approvable and all legal appeals have been exhausted,

(C) if approval of the application under subsection (c) is withdrawn and all legal appeals have been exhausted,

(D) if the Secretary has determined that such drug is not a new drug, or

(E) upon the effective date of the approval of the first application under subsection (j) which refers to such drug or upon the date upon which the approval of an application under subsection (j) which refers to such drug could be made effective if such an application had been submitted.

(2) Action package for approval.

(A) Action package. The Secretary shall publish the action package for approval of an application under subsection (b) or section 351 of the Public Health Service Act [42 USC § 262] on the Internet Web site of the Food and Drug Administration--

(i) not later than 30 days after the date of approval of such application for a drug no active ingredient (including any ester or salt of the active ingredient) of which has been approved in any other application under this section or section 351 of the Public Health Service Act [42 USC § 262]; and

(ii) not later than 30 days after the third request for such action package for approval received under section 552 of title 5, United States Code, for any other drug.

(B) Immediate publication of summary review. Notwithstanding subparagraph (A), the Secretary shall publish, on the Internet Web site of the Food and Drug Administration, the materials described in subparagraph (C)(iv) not later than 48 hours after the date of approval of the drug, except where such materials require redaction by the Secretary.

(C) Contents. An action package for approval of an application under subparagraph (A) shall be dated and shall include the following:

(i) Documents generated by the Food and Drug Administration related to review of the application.

(ii) Documents pertaining to the format and content of the application generated during drug development.

(iii) Labeling submitted by the applicant.

(iv) A summary review that documents conclusions from all reviewing disciplines about the drug, noting any critical issues and disagreements with the applicant and within the review team and how they were resolved, recommendations for action, and an explanation of any nonconcurrence with review conclusions.

(v) The Division Director and Office Director's decision document which includes--

(I) a brief statement of concurrence with the summary review;

(II) a separate review or addendum to the review if disagreeing with the summary review; and

(III) a separate review or addendum to the review to add further analysis.

(vi) Identification by name of each officer or employee of the Food and Drug Administration who--

(I) participated in the decision to approve the application; and

(II) consents to have his or her name included in the package.

(D) Review. A scientific review of an application is considered the work of the reviewer and shall not be altered by management or the reviewer once final.

(E) Confidential information. This paragraph does not authorize the disclosure of any trade secret, confidential commercial or financial information, or other matter listed in section 552(b) of title 5, United States Code.

(m) "**Patent**" defined. For purposes of this section, the term "patent" means a patent issued by the United States Patent and Trademark Office.

(n) Scientific advisory panels.

(1) For the purpose of providing expert scientific advice and recommendations to the Secretary regarding a clinical investigation of a drug or the approval for marketing of a drug under section 505 [this section] or section 351 of the Public Health Service Act [42 USC § 262], the Secretary shall establish panels of experts or use panels of experts established before the date of enactment of the Food and Drug Administration Modernization Act of 1997 [enacted Nov. 21, 1997], or both.

(2) The Secretary may delegate the appointment and oversight authority granted under section 904 to a director of a center or successor entity within the Food and Drug Administration.

(3) The Secretary shall make appointments to each panel established under paragraph (1) so that each panel shall consist of—

(A) members who are qualified by training and experience to evaluate the safety and effectiveness of the drugs to be referred to the panel and who, to the extent feasible, possess skill and experience in the development, manufacture, or utilization of such drugs;

(B) members with diverse expertise in such fields as clinical and administrative medicine, pharmacy, pharmacology, pharmacoeconomics, biological and physical sciences, and other related professions;

(C) a representative of consumer interests, and a representative of interests of the drug manufacturing industry not directly affected by the matter to be brought before the panel; and

(D) two or more members who are specialists or have other expertise in the particular disease or condition for which the drug under review is proposed to be indicated.

Scientific, trade, and consumer organizations shall be afforded an opportunity to nominate individuals for appointment to the panels. No individual who is in the regular full-time employ of the United States and engaged in the administration of this Act may be a voting member of any panel. The Secretary shall designate one of the members of each panel to serve as chairman thereof.

(4) The Secretary shall, as appropriate, provide education and training to each new panel member before such member participates in a panel's activities, including education regarding requirements under this Act and related regulations of the Secretary, and the administrative processes and procedures related to panel meetings.

(5) Panel members (other than officers or employees of the United States), while attending meetings or conferences of a panel or otherwise engaged in its business, shall be entitled to receive compensation for each day so engaged, including traveltime, at rates to be fixed by the Secretary, but not to exceed the daily equivalent of the rate in effect for positions classified above grade GS-15 of the General Schedule. While serving away from their homes or regular places of business, panel members may be allowed travel expenses (including per diem in lieu of subsistence) as authorized by section 5703 of title 5, United States Code, for persons in the Government service employed intermittently.

(6) The Secretary shall ensure that scientific advisory panels meet regularly and at appropriate intervals so that any matter to be reviewed by such a panel can be presented to the panel not more than 60 days after the matter is ready for such review. Meetings of the panel may be held using electronic communication to convene the meetings.

(7) Within 90 days after a scientific advisory panel makes recommendations on any matter under its review, the Food and Drug Administration official responsible for the matter shall review the conclusions and recommendations of the panel, and notify the affected persons of the final decision on the matter, or of the reasons that no such decision has been reached. Each such final decision shall be documented including the rationale for the decision.

(8) [Redesignated]

(o) Postmarket studies and clinical trials; labeling **[Caution: This subsection takes effect 180 days after enactment of Act Sept. 27, 2007, P.L. 110-85, as provided by § 909(a) of such Act, which appears as 21 USC § 331 note.]**.

(1) In general. A responsible person may not introduce or deliver for introduction into interstate commerce the new drug involved if the person is in violation of a requirement established under paragraph (3) or (4) with respect to the drug.

(2) Definitions. For purposes of this subsection:

(A) Responsible person. The term "***responsible person***" means a person who--

(i) has submitted to the Secretary a covered application that is pending; or

(ii) is the holder of an approved covered application.

(B) Covered application. The term "***covered application***" means--

(i) an application under subsection (b) for a drug that is subject to section 503(b) [21 USC § 353(b)]; and

Chapter V

(ii) an application under section 351 of the Public Health Service Act [42 USC § 262].

(C) New safety information; serious risk. The terms "***new safety information***", "***serious risk***", and "***signal of a serious risk***" have the meanings given such terms in section 505-1(b) [21 USC § 355-1(b)].

(3) Studies and clinical trials.

(A) In general. For any or all of the purposes specified in subparagraph (B), the Secretary may, subject to subparagraph (D), require a responsible person for a drug to conduct a postapproval study or studies of the drug, or a postapproval clinical trial or trials of the drug, on the basis of scientific data deemed appropriate by the Secretary, including information regarding chemically-related or pharmacologically-related drugs.

(B) Purposes of study or clinical trial. The purposes referred to in this subparagraph with respect to a postapproval study or postapproval clinical trial are the following:

(i) To assess a known serious risk related to the use of the drug involved.

(ii) To assess signals of serious risk related to the use of the drug.

(iii) To identify an unexpected serious risk when available data indicates the potential for a serious risk.

(C) Establishment of requirement after approval of covered application. The Secretary may require a postapproval study or studies or postapproval clinical trial or trials for a drug for which an approved covered application is in effect as of the date on which the Secretary seeks to establish such requirement only if the Secretary becomes aware of new safety information.

(D) Determination by Secretary.

(i) Postapproval studies. The Secretary may not require the responsible person to conduct a study under this paragraph, unless the Secretary makes a determination that the reports under subsection (k)(1) and the active postmarket risk identification and analysis system as available under subsection (k)(3) will not be sufficient to meet the purposes set forth in subparagraph (B).

(ii) Postapproval clinical trials. The Secretary may not require the responsible person to conduct a clinical trial under this paragraph, unless the Secretary makes a determination that a postapproval study or studies will not be sufficient to meet the purposes set forth in subparagraph (B).

(E) Notification; timetables; periodic reports.

(i) Notification. The Secretary shall notify the responsible person regarding a requirement under this paragraph to conduct a postapproval study or clinical trial by the target dates for communication of feedback from the review team to the responsible person regarding proposed labeling and postmarketing study commitments as set forth in the letters described in section 101(c) of the Food and Drug Administration Amendments Act of 2007 [21 USC § 379g note].

(ii) Timetable; periodic reports. For each study or clinical trial required to be conducted under this paragraph, the Secretary shall require that the responsible person submit a timetable for completion of the study or clinical trial. With respect to each study required to be conducted under this paragraph or otherwise undertaken by the responsible person to investigate a safety issue, the Secretary shall require the responsible person to periodically report to the Secretary on the status of such study including whether any difficulties in completing the study have been encountered. With respect to each clinical trial required to be conducted under this paragraph or otherwise undertaken by the responsible person to investigate a safety issue, the Secretary shall require the responsible person to periodically report to the Secretary on the status of such clinical trial including whether enrollment has begun, the number of participants enrolled, the expected completion date, whether any difficulties completing the clinical trial have been encountered, and registration information with respect to the requirements under section 402(j) of the Public Health Service Act [42 USC § 282(j)]. If the responsible person fails to comply with such timetable or violates any other requirement of this subparagraph, the responsible person shall be considered in violation of this subsection, unless the responsible person demonstrates good cause for such noncompliance or such other violation. The Secretary shall determine what constitutes good cause under the preceding sentence.

(F) Dispute resolution. The responsible person may appeal a requirement to conduct a study or clinical trial under this paragraph using dispute resolution procedures established by the Secretary in regulation and guidance.

(4) Safety labeling changes requested by Secretary.

(A) New safety information. If the Secretary becomes aware of new safety information that the Secretary believes should be included in the labeling of the drug, the Secretary shall promptly notify the responsible person or, if the same drug approved under section 505(b) [subsec. (b) of this section] is not currently marketed, the holder of an approved application under 505(j) [subsec. (j) of this section].

(B) Response to notification. Following notification pursuant to subparagraph (A), the responsible person or the holder of the approved application under section 505(j) [subsec. (j) of this section] shall within 30 days--

(i) submit a supplement proposing changes to the approved labeling to reflect the new safety information, including changes to boxed warnings, contraindications, warnings, precautions, or adverse reactions; or

(ii) notify the Secretary that the responsible person or the holder of the approved application under section 505(j) [subsec. (j) of this section] does not believe a labeling change is warranted and submit a statement detailing the reasons why such a change is not warranted.

(C) Review. Upon receipt of such supplement, the Secretary shall promptly review and act upon such supplement. If the Secretary disagrees with the proposed changes in the supplement or with the statement setting forth the reasons why no labeling change is necessary, the Secretary shall initiate discussions to reach agreement on whether the labeling for the drug should be modified to reflect the new safety information, and if so, the contents of such labeling changes.

(D) Discussions. Such discussions shall not extend for more than 30 days after the response to the notification under subparagraph (B), unless the Secretary determines an extension of such discussion period is warranted.

(E) Order. Within 15 days of the conclusion of the discussions under subparagraph (D), the Secretary may issue an order directing the responsible person or the holder of the approved application under section 505(j) [subsec. (j) of this section] to make such a labeling change as the Secretary deems appropriate to address the new safety information. Within 15 days of such an order, the responsible person or the holder of the approved application under section 505(j) [subsec. (j) of this section] shall submit a supplement containing the labeling change.

(F) Dispute resolution. Within 5 days of receiving an order under subparagraph (E), the responsible person or the holder of the approved application under section 505(j) may appeal using dispute resolution procedures established by the Secretary in regulation and guidance.

(G) Violation. If the responsible person or the holder of the approved application under section 505(j) [subsec. (j) of this section] has not submitted a supplement within 15 days of the date of such order under subparagraph (E), and there is no appeal or dispute resolution proceeding pending, the responsible person or holder shall be considered to be in violation of this subsection. If at the conclusion of any dispute resolution procedures the Secretary determines that a supplement must be submitted and such a supplement is not submitted within 15 days of the date of that determination, the responsible person or holder shall be in violation of this subsection.

(H) Public health threat. Notwithstanding subparagraphs (A) through (F), if the Secretary concludes that such a labeling change is necessary to protect the public health, the Secretary may accelerate the timelines in such subparagraphs.

(I) Rule of construction. This paragraph shall not be construed to affect the responsibility of the responsible person or the holder of the approved application under section 505(j) [subsec. (j) of this section] to maintain its label in accordance with existing requirements, including subpart B of part 201 and sections 314.70 and 601.12 of title 21, Code of Federal Regulations (or any successor regulations).

(5) Non-delegation. Determinations by the Secretary under this subsection for a drug shall be made by individuals at or above the level of individuals empowered to approve a drug (such as division directors within the Center for Drug Evaluation and Research).

(p) Risk evaluation and mitigation strategy [Caution: This subsection takes effect 180 days after enactment of Act Sept. 27, 2007, P.L. 110-85, as provided by § 909(a) of such Act, which appears as 21 USC § 331 note.].

(1) In general. A person may not introduce or deliver for introduction into interstate commerce a new drug if--

(A)(i) the application for such drug is approved under subsection (b) or (j) and is subject to section 503(b) [21 USC § 353(b)]; or

(ii) the application for such drug is approved under section 351 of the Public Health Service Act [42 USC § 262]; and

(B) a risk evaluation and mitigation strategy is required under section 505-1 [21 USC § 355-1] with respect to the drug and the person fails to maintain compliance with the requirements of the approved strategy or with other requirements under section 505-1 [21 USC § 355-1], including requirements regarding assessments of approved strategies.

(2) Certain postmarket studies. The failure to conduct a postmarket study under section 506 [21 USC § 356], subpart H of part 314, or subpart E of part 601 of title 21, Code of Federal Regulations (or any successor regulations), is deemed to be a violation of paragraph (1).

(q) Petitions and civil actions regarding approval of certain applications.

(1) In general.

(A) Determination. The Secretary shall not delay approval of a pending application submitted under subsection (b)(2) or (j) because of any request to take any form of action relating to the application, either before or during consideration of the request, unless--

(i) the request is in writing and is a petition submitted to the Secretary pursuant to section 10.30 or 10.35 of title 21, Code of Federal Regulations (or any successor regulations); and

(ii) the Secretary determines, upon reviewing the petition, that a delay is necessary to protect the public health.

(B) Notification. If the Secretary determines under subparagraph (A) that a delay is necessary with respect to an application, the Secretary shall provide to the applicant, not later than 30 days after making such determination, the following information:

(i) Notification of the fact that a determination under subparagraph (A) has been made.

(ii) If applicable, any clarification or additional data that the applicant should submit to the docket on the petition to allow the Secretary to review the petition promptly.

(iii) A brief summary of the specific substantive issues raised in the petition which form the basis of the determination.

(C) Format. The information described in subparagraph (B) shall be conveyed via either, at the discretion of the Secretary--

(i) a document; or

(ii) a meeting with the applicant involved.

(D) Public disclosure. Any information conveyed by the Secretary under subparagraph (C) shall be considered part of the application and shall be subject to the disclosure requirements applicable to information in such application.

(E) Denial based on intent to delay. If the Secretary determines that a petition or a supplement to the petition was submitted with the primary purpose of delaying the approval of an application and the petition does not on its face raise valid scientific or regulatory issues, the Secretary may deny the petition at any point based on such determination. The Secretary may issue guidance to describe the factors that will be used to determine under this subparagraph whether a petition is submitted with the primary purpose of delaying the approval of an application.

(F) Final agency action. The Secretary shall take final agency action on a petition not later than 180 days after the date on which the petition is submitted. The Secretary shall not extend such period for any reason, including--

(i) any determination made under subparagraph (A);

(ii) the submission of comments relating to the petition or supplemental information supplied by the petitioner; or

(iii) the consent of the petitioner.

(G) Extension of 30-month period. If the filing of an application resulted in first-applicant status under subsection (j)(5)(D)(i)(IV) and approval of the application was delayed because of a petition, the 30-month period under such subsection is deemed to be extended by a period of time equal to the period beginning on the date on which the Secretary received the petition and ending on the date of final agency action on the petition (inclusive of such beginning and ending dates), without regard to whether the Secretary grants, in whole or in part, or denies, in whole or in part, the petition.

(H) Certification. The Secretary shall not consider a petition for review unless the party submitting such petition does so in written form and the subject document is signed and contains the following certification: 'I certify that, to my best knowledge and belief: (a) this petition includes all information and views upon which the petition relies; (b) this petition includes representative data and/or information known to the petitioner which are unfavorable to the petition; and (c) I have taken reasonable steps to ensure that any representative data and/or information which are unfavorable to the petition were disclosed to me. I further certify that the information upon which I have based the action requested herein first became known to the party on whose behalf this petition is submitted on or about the following date: ________________. If I received or expect to receive payments, including cash and other forms of consideration, to file this information or its contents, I received or expect to receive those payments from the following persons or organizations: ________________. I verify under penalty of perjury that the foregoing is true and correct as of the date of the submission of this petition.', with the date on which such information first became known to such party and the names of such persons or organizations inserted in the first and second blank space, respectively.

(I) Verification. The Secretary shall not accept for review any supplemental information or comments on a petition unless the party submitting such information or comments does so in written form and the subject document is signed and contains the following verification: 'I certify that, to my best knowledge and belief: (a) I have not intentionally delayed submission of this document or its contents; and (b) the information upon which I have based the action requested herein first became known to me on or about _______________. If I received or expect to receive payments, including cash and other forms of consideration, to file this information or its contents, I received or expect to receive those payments from the following persons or organizations: __________. I verify under penalty of perjury that the foregoing is true and correct as of the date of the submission of this petition.', with the date on which such information first became known to the party and the names of such persons or organizations inserted in the first and second blank space, respectively.

(2) Exhaustion of administrative remedies.

(A) Final agency action within 180 days. The Secretary shall be considered to have taken final agency action on a petition if--

(i) during the 180-day period referred to in paragraph (1)(F), the Secretary makes a final decision within the meaning of section 10.45(d) of title 21, Code of Federal Regulations (or any successor regulation); or

(ii) such period expires without the Secretary having made such a final decision.

(B) Dismissal of certain civil actions. If a civil action is filed against the Secretary with respect to any issue raised in the petition before the Secretary has taken final agency action on the petition within the meaning of subparagraph (A), the court shall dismiss without prejudice the action for failure to exhaust administrative remedies.

(C) Administrative record. For purposes of judicial review related to the approval of an application for which a petition under paragraph (1) was submitted, the administrative record regarding any issue raised by the petition shall include--

(i) the petition filed under paragraph (1) and any supplements and comments thereto;

(ii) the Secretary's response to such petition, if issued; and

(iii) other information, as designated by the Secretary, related to the Secretary's determinations regarding the issues raised in such petition, as long as the information was considered by the agency no later than the date of final agency action as defined under subparagraph (2)(A), and regardless of whether the Secretary responded to the petition at or before the approval of the application at issue in the petition.

(3) Annual report on delays in approvals per petitions. The Secretary shall annually submit to the Congress a report that specifies--

(A) the number of applications that were approved during the preceding 12-month period;

(B) the number of such applications whose effective dates were delayed by petitions referred to in paragraph (1) during such period;

(C) the number of days by which such applications were so delayed; and

(D) the number of such petitions that were submitted during such period.

(4) Exceptions. This subsection does not apply to--

(A) a petition that relates solely to the timing of the approval of an application pursuant to subsection (j)(5)(B)(iv); or

(B) a petition that is made by the sponsor of an application and that seeks only to have the Secretary take or refrain from taking any form of action with respect to that application.

(5) Definitions.

(A) Application. For purposes of this subsection, the term "***application***" means an application submitted under subsection (b)(2) or (j).

(B) Petition. For purposes of this subsection, other than paragraph (1)(A)(i), the term "***petition***" means a request described in paragraph (1)(A)(i).

(r) Postmarket drug safety information for patients and providers.

(1) Establishment. Not later than 1 year after the date of the enactment of the Food and Drug Administration Amendments Act of 2007 [enacted Sept. 27, 2007], the Secretary shall improve the transparency of information about drugs and allow patients and health care providers better access to information about drugs by developing and maintaining an Internet Web site that--

(A) provides links to drug safety information listed in paragraph (2) for prescription drugs that are approved under this section or licensed under section 351 of the Public Health Service Act [42 USC § 262]; and

(B) improves communication of drug safety information to patients and providers.

(2) Internet web site. The Secretary shall carry out paragraph (1) by--

(A) developing and maintaining an accessible, consolidated Internet Web site with easily searchable drug safety information, including the information found on United States Government Internet Web sites, such as the United States National Library of Medicine's Daily Med and Medline Plus Web sites, in addition to other such Web sites maintained by the Secretary;

(B) ensuring that the information provided on the Internet Web site is comprehensive and includes, when available and appropriate--

(i) patient labeling and patient packaging inserts;

(ii) a link to a list of each drug, whether approved under this section or licensed under such section 351 [42 USC § 262], for which a Medication Guide, as provided for under part 208 of title 21, Code of Federal Regulations (or any successor regulations), is required;

(iii) a link to the registry and results data bank provided for under subsections (i) and (j) of section 402 of the Public Health Service Act [42 USC § 282];

(iv) the most recent safety information and alerts issued by the Food and Drug Administration for drugs approved by the Secretary under this section, such as product recalls, warning letters, and import alerts;

(v) publicly available information about implemented RiskMAPs and risk evaluation and mitigation strategies under subsection (o);

(vi) guidance documents and regulations related to drug safety; and

(vii) other material determined appropriate by the Secretary;

(C) providing access to summaries of the assessed and aggregated data collected from the active surveillance infrastructure under subsection (k)(3) to provide information of known and serious side-effects for drugs approved under this section or licensed under such section 351 [42 USC § 262];

(D) preparing, by 18 months after approval of a drug or after use of the drug by 10,000 individuals, whichever is later, a summary analysis of the adverse drug reaction reports received for the drug, including identification of any new risks not previously identified, potential new risks, or known risks reported in unusual number;

(E) enabling patients, providers, and drug sponsors to submit adverse event reports through the Internet Web site;

(F) providing educational materials for patients and providers about the appropriate means of disposing of expired, damaged, or unusable medications; and

(G) supporting initiatives that the Secretary determines to be useful to fulfill the purposes of the Internet Web site.

(3) Posting of drug labeling. The Secretary shall post on the Internet Web site established under paragraph (1) the approved professional labeling and any required patient labeling of a drug approved under this section or licensed under such section 351 [42 USC § 262] not later than 21 days after the date

the drug is approved or licensed, including in a supplemental application with respect to a labeling change.

(4) Private sector resources. To ensure development of the Internet Web site by the date described in paragraph (1), the Secretary may, on a temporary or permanent basis, implement systems or products developed by private entities.

(5) Authority for contracts. The Secretary may enter into contracts with public and private entities to fulfill the requirements of this subsection.

(6) Review. The Advisory Committee on Risk Communication under section 567 [21 USC § 360bbb-6] shall, on a regular basis, perform a comprehensive review and evaluation of the types of risk communication information provided on the Internet Web site established under paragraph (1) and, through other means, shall identify, clarify, and define the purposes and types of information available to facilitate the efficient flow of information to patients and providers, and shall recommend ways for the Food and Drug Administration to work with outside entities to help facilitate the dispensing of risk communication information to patients and providers.

(s) Referral to advisory committee. Prior to the approval of a drug no active ingredient (including any ester or salt of the active ingredient) of which has been approved in any other application under this section or section 351 of the Public Health Service Act [42 USC § 262], the Secretary shall--

(1) refer such drug to a Food and Drug Administration advisory committee for review at a meeting of such advisory committee; or

(2) if the Secretary does not refer such a drug to a Food and Drug Administration advisory committee prior to the approval of the drug, provide in the action letter on the application for the drug a summary of the reasons why the Secretary did not refer the drug to an advisory committee prior to approval.

(t) Database for authorized generic drugs.

(1) In general.

(A) Publication. The Commissioner shall--

(i) not later than 9 months after the date of the enactment of the Food and Drug Administration Amendments Act of 2007 [enacted Sept. 27, 2007], publish a complete list on the Internet Web site of the Food and Drug Administration of all authorized generic drugs (including drug trade name, brand company manufacturer, and the date the authorized generic drug entered the market); and

(ii) update the list quarterly to include each authorized generic drug included in an annual report submitted to the Secretary by the sponsor of a listed drug during the preceding 3-month period.

(B) Notification. The Commissioner shall notify relevant Federal agencies, including the Centers for Medicare & Medicaid Services and the Federal Trade Commission, when the Commissioner first publishes the information described in subparagraph (A) that the information has been published and that the information will be updated quarterly.

(2) Inclusion. The Commissioner shall include in the list described in paragraph (1) each authorized generic drug included in an annual report submitted to the Secretary by the sponsor of a listed drug after January 1, 1999.

(3) Authorized generic drug. In this section, the term "authorized generic drug" means a listed drug (as that term is used in subsection (j)) that--

(A) has been approved under subsection (c); and

(B) is marketed, sold, or distributed directly or indirectly to retail class of trade under a different labeling, packaging (other than repackaging as the listed drug in blister packs, unit doses, or similar packaging for use in institutions), product code, labeler code, trade name, or trade mark than the listed drug.

(u) Certain drugs containing single enantiomers.

(1) In general. For purposes of subsections (c)(3)(E)(ii) and (j)(5)(F)(ii), if an application is submitted under subsection (b) for a non-racemic drug containing as an active ingredient (including any ester or salt of the active ingredient) a single enantiomer that is contained in a racemic drug approved in another application under subsection (b), the applicant may, in the application for such non-racemic drug, elect to have the single enantiomer not be considered the same active ingredient as that contained in the approved racemic drug, if--

(A)(i) the single enantiomer has not been previously approved except in the approved racemic drug; and

(ii) the application submitted under subsection (b) for such non-racemic drug--

(I) includes full reports of new clinical investigations (other than bioavailability studies)--

(aa) necessary for the approval of the application under subsections (c) and (d); and

(bb) conducted or sponsored by the applicant; and

(II) does not rely on any investigations that are part of an application submitted under subsection (b) for approval of the approved racemic drug; and

(B) the application submitted under subsection (b) for such non-racemic drug is not submitted for approval of a condition of use--

(i) in a therapeutic category in which the approved racemic drug has been approved; or

(ii) for which any other enantiomer of the racemic drug has been approved.

(2) Limitation.

(A) No approval in certain therapeutic categories. Until the date that is 10 years after the date of approval of a non-racemic drug described in paragraph (1) and with respect to which the applicant has made the election provided for by such paragraph, the Secretary shall not approve such non-racemic drug for any condition of use in the therapeutic category in which the racemic drug has been approved.

(B) Labeling. If applicable, the labeling of a non-racemic drug described in paragraph (1) and with respect to which the applicant has made the election provided for by such paragraph shall include a statement that the non-racemic drug is not approved, and has not been shown to be safe and effective, for any condition of use of the racemic drug.

(3) Definition.

(A) In general. For purposes of this subsection, the term "therapeutic category" means a therapeutic category identified in the list developed by the United States Pharmacopeia pursuant to section 1860D-4(b)(3)(C)(ii) of the Social Security Act [42 USC § 1395w-104(b)(3)(C)(ii)] and as in effect on the date of the enactment of this subsection [enacted Sept. 27, 2007].

(B) Publication by Secretary. The Secretary shall publish the list described in subparagraph (A) and may amend such list by regulation.

(4) Availability. The election referred to in paragraph (1) may be made only in an application that is submitted to the Secretary after the date of the enactment of this subsection [enacted Sept. 27, 2007] and before October 1, 2012.

SEC. 505-1. [21 USC §355-1] Risk Evaluation and Mitigation Strategies

Note: This section was added in February 2008.

[Caution: This section takes effect 180 days after enactment of Act Sept. 27, 2007, P.L. 110-85, as provided by § 909(a) of such Act, which appears as 21 USC § 331 note.]

(a) Submission of proposed strategy.

(1) Initial approval. If the Secretary, in consultation with the office responsible for reviewing the drug and the office responsible for postapproval safety with respect to the drug, determines that a risk evaluation and mitigation strategy is necessary to ensure that the benefits of the drug outweigh the risks of the drug, and informs the person who submits such application of such determination, then such person shall submit to the Secretary as part of such application a proposed risk evaluation and mitigation strategy. In making such a determination, the Secretary shall consider the following factors:

(A) The estimated size of the population likely to use the drug involved.

(B) The seriousness of the disease or condition that is to be treated with the drug.

(C) The expected benefit of the drug with respect to such disease or condition.

(D) The expected or actual duration of treatment with the drug.

(E) The seriousness of any known or potential adverse events that may be related to the drug and the background incidence of such events in the population likely to use the drug.

(F) Whether the drug is a new molecular entity.

(2) Postapproval requirement.

(A) In general. If the Secretary has approved a covered application (including an application approved before the effective date of this section) and did not when approving the application require a risk evaluation and mitigation strategy under paragraph (1), the Secretary, in consultation with the offices described in paragraph (1), may subsequently require such a strategy for the drug involved (including when acting on a supplemental application seeking approval of a new indication for use of the drug) if the Secretary becomes aware of new safety information and makes a determination that such a strategy is necessary to ensure that the benefits of the drug outweigh the risks of the drug.

(B) Submission of proposed strategy. Not later than 120 days after the Secretary notifies the holder of an approved covered application that the Secretary has made a determination under subparagraph (A) with respect to the drug involved, or within such other reasonable time as the Secretary requires to protect the public health, the holder shall submit to the Secretary a proposed risk evaluation and mitigation strategy.

(3) Abbreviated new drug applications. The applicability of this section to an application under section 505(j) is subject to subsection (i).

(4) Non-delegation. Determinations by the Secretary under this subsection for a drug shall be made by individuals at or above the level of individuals empowered to approve a drug (such as division directors within the Center for Drug Evaluation and Research).

(b) Definitions. For purposes of this section:

(1) Adverse drug experience. The term "***adverse drug experience***" means any adverse event associated with the use of a drug in humans, whether or not considered drug related, including--

(A) an adverse event occurring in the course of the use of the drug in professional practice;

(B) an adverse event occurring from an overdose of the drug, whether accidental or intentional;

(C) an adverse event occurring from abuse of the drug;

(D) an adverse event occurring from withdrawal of the drug; and

(E) any failure of expected pharmacological action of the drug.

(2) Covered application. The term "***covered application***" means an application referred to in section 505(p)(1)(A).

(3) New safety information. The term "***new safety information***", with respect to a drug, means information derived from a clinical trial, an adverse event report, a postapproval study (including a study under section 505(o)(3)), or peer-reviewed biomedical literature; data derived from the postmarket risk identification and analysis system under section 505(k); or other scientific data deemed appropriate by the Secretary about--

(A) a serious risk or an unexpected serious risk associated with use of the drug that the Secretary has become aware of (that may be based on a new analysis of existing information) since the drug was approved, since the risk evaluation and mitigation strategy was required, or since the last assessment of the approved risk evaluation and mitigation strategy for the drug; or

(B) the effectiveness of the approved risk evaluation and mitigation strategy for the drug obtained since the last assessment of such strategy.

(4) Serious adverse drug experience. The term "***serious adverse drug experience***" is an adverse drug experience that--

(A) results in--

(i) death;

(ii) an adverse drug experience that places the patient at immediate risk of death from the adverse drug experience as it occurred (not including an adverse drug experience that might have caused death had it occurred in a more severe form);

(iii) inpatient hospitalization or prolongation of existing hospitalization;

(iv) a persistent or significant incapacity or substantial disruption of the ability to conduct normal life functions; or

(v) a congenital anomaly or birth defect; or

(B) based on appropriate medical judgment, may jeopardize the patient and may require a medical or surgical intervention to prevent an outcome described under subparagraph (A).

(5) Serious risk. The term "***serious risk***" means a risk of a serious adverse drug experience.

(6) Signal of a serious risk. The term "***signal of a serious risk***" means information related to a serious adverse drug experience associated with use of a drug and derived from--

(A) a clinical trial;

(B) adverse event reports;

(C) a postapproval study, including a study under section 505(o)(3);

(D) peer-reviewed biomedical literature;

(E) data derived from the postmarket risk identification and analysis system under section 505(k)(4); or

(F) other scientific data deemed appropriate by the Secretary.

(7) Responsible person. The term "***responsible person***" means the person submitting a covered application or the holder of the approved such application.

(8) Unexpected serious risk. The term "***unexpected serious risk***" means a serious adverse drug experience that is not listed in the labeling of a drug, or that may be symptomatically and pathophysiologically related to an adverse drug experience identified in the labeling, but differs from such adverse drug experience because of greater severity, specificity, or prevalence.

(c) Contents. A proposed risk evaluation and mitigation strategy under subsection (a) shall--

(1) include the timetable required under subsection (d); and

(2) to the extent required by the Secretary, in consultation with the office responsible for reviewing the drug and the office responsible for postapproval safety with respect to the drug, include additional elements described in subsections (e) and (f).

(d) Minimal strategy. For purposes of subsection (c)(1), the risk evaluation and mitigation strategy for a drug shall require a timetable for submission of assessments of the strategy that--

(1) includes an assessment, by the date that is 18 months after the strategy is initially approved;

(2) includes an assessment by the date that is 3 years after the strategy is initially approved;

(3) includes an assessment in the seventh year after the strategy is so approved; and

(4) subject to paragraphs (1), (2), and (3)--

(A) is at a frequency specified in the strategy;

(B) is increased or reduced in frequency as necessary as provided for in subsection (g)(4)(A); and

(C) is eliminated after the 3-year period described in paragraph (1) if the Secretary determines that serious risks of the drug have been adequately identified and assessed and are being adequately managed.

(e) Additional potential elements of strategy.

(1) In general. The Secretary, in consultation with the offices described in subsection (c)(2), may under such subsection require that the risk evaluation and mitigation strategy for a drug include 1 or more of the additional elements described in this subsection if the Secretary makes the determination required with respect to each element involved.

(2) Medication guide; patient package insert. The risk evaluation and mitigation strategy for a drug may require that, as applicable, the responsible person develop for distribution to each patient when the drug is dispensed--

(A) a Medication Guide, as provided for under part 208 of title 21, Code of Federal Regulations (or any successor regulations); and

(B) a patient package insert, if the Secretary determines that such insert may help mitigate a serious risk of the drug.

(3) Communication plan. The risk evaluation and mitigation strategy for a drug may require that the responsible person conduct a communication plan to health care providers, if, with respect to such drug, the Secretary determines

that such plan may support implementation of an element of the strategy (including under this paragraph). Such plan may include--

(A) sending letters to health care providers;

(B) disseminating information about the elements of the risk evaluation and mitigation strategy to encourage implementation by health care providers of components that apply to such health care providers, or to explain certain safety protocols (such as medical monitoring by periodic laboratory tests); or

(C) disseminating information to health care providers through professional societies about any serious risks of the drug and any protocol to assure safe use.

(f) Providing safe access for patients to drugs with known serious risks that would otherwise be unavailable.

(1) Allowing safe access to drugs with known serious risks. The Secretary, in consultation with the offices described in subsection (c)(2), may require that the risk evaluation and mitigation strategy for a drug include such elements as are necessary to assure safe use of the drug, because of its inherent toxicity or potential harmfulness, if the Secretary determines that--

(A) the drug, which has been shown to be effective, but is associated with a serious adverse drug experience, can be approved only if, or would be withdrawn unless, such elements are required as part of such strategy to mitigate a specific serious risk listed in the labeling of the drug; and

(B) for a drug initially approved without elements to assure safe use, other elements under subsections (c), (d), and (e) are not sufficient to mitigate such serious risk.

(2) Assuring access and minimizing burden. Such elements to assure safe use under paragraph (1) shall--

(A) be commensurate with the specific serious risk listed in the labeling of the drug;

(B) within 30 days of the date on which any element under paragraph (1) is imposed, be posted publicly by the Secretary with an explanation of how such elements will mitigate the observed safety risk;

(C) considering such risk, not be unduly burdensome on patient access to the drug, considering in particular--

(i) patients with serious or life-threatening diseases or conditions; and

(ii) patients who have difficulty accessing health care (such as patients in rural or medically underserved areas); and

(D) to the extent practicable, so as to minimize the burden on the health care delivery system--

(i) conform with elements to assure safe use for other drugs with similar, serious risks; and

(ii) be designed to be compatible with established distribution, procurement, and dispensing systems for drugs.

(3) Elements to assure safe use. The elements to assure safe use under paragraph (1) shall include 1 or more goals to mitigate a specific serious risk listed in the labeling of the drug and, to mitigate such risk, may require that--

(A) health care providers who prescribe the drug have particular training or experience, or are specially certified (the opportunity to obtain such training or certification with respect to the drug shall be available to any willing provider from a frontier area in a widely available training or certification method (including an on-line course or via mail) as approved by the Secretary at reasonable cost to the provider);

(B) pharmacies, practitioners, or health care settings that dispense the drug are specially certified (the opportunity to obtain such certification shall be available to any willing provider from a frontier area);

(C) the drug be dispensed to patients only in certain health care settings, such as hospitals;

(D) the drug be dispensed to patients with evidence or other documentation of safe-use conditions, such as laboratory test results;

(E) each patient using the drug be subject to certain monitoring; or

(F) each patient using the drug be enrolled in a registry.

(4) Implementation system. The elements to assure safe use under paragraph (1) that are described in subparagraphs (B), (C), and (D) of paragraph (3) may include a system through which the applicant is able to take reasonable steps to--

(A) monitor and evaluate implementation of such elements by health care providers, pharmacists, and other parties in the health care system who are responsible for implementing such elements; and

(B) work to improve implementation of such elements by such persons.

(5) Evaluation of elements to assure safe use. The Secretary, through the Drug Safety and Risk Management Advisory Committee (or successor committee) of the Food and Drug Administration, shall—

(A) seek input from patients, physicians, pharmacists, and other health care providers about how elements to assure safe use under this subsection for 1 or more drugs may be standardized so as not to be--

(i) unduly burdensome on patient access to the drug; and

(ii) to the extent practicable, minimize the burden on the health care delivery system;

(B) at least annually, evaluate, for 1 or more drugs, the elements to assure safe use of such drug to assess whether the elements--

(i) assure safe use of the drug;

(ii) are not unduly burdensome on patient access to the drug; and

(iii) to the extent practicable, minimize the burden on the health care delivery system; and

(C) considering such input and evaluations--

(i) issue or modify agency guidance about how to implement the requirements of this subsection; and

(ii) modify elements under this subsection for 1 or more drugs as appropriate.

(6) Additional mechanisms to assure access. The mechanisms under section 561 to provide for expanded access for patients with serious or life-threatening diseases or conditions may be used to provide access for patients with a serious or life-threatening disease or condition, the treatment of which is not an approved use for the drug, to a drug that is subject to elements to assure safe use under this subsection. The Secretary shall promulgate regulations for how a physician may provide the drug under the mechanisms of section 561.

(7) Waiver in public health emergencies. The Secretary may waive any requirement of this subsection during the period described in section 319(a) of the Public Health Service Act [42 USC § 247d(a)] with respect to a qualified countermeasure described under section 319F-1(a)(2) of such Act [42 USC § 247d-6a(a)(2)], to which a requirement under this subsection has been applied, if the Secretary has--

(A) declared a public health emergency under such section 319 [42 USC § 247d]; and

(B) determined that such waiver is required to mitigate the effects of, or reduce the severity of, such public health emergency.

(8) Limitation. No holder of an approved covered application shall use any element to assure safe use required by the Secretary under this subsection to block or delay approval of an application under section 505(b)(2) or (j) or to prevent application of such element under subsection (i)(1)(B) to a drug that is the subject of an abbreviated new drug application.

(g) Assessment and modification of approved strategy.

(1) Voluntary assessments. After the approval of a risk evaluation and mitigation strategy under subsection (a), the responsible person involved may, subject to paragraph (2), submit to the Secretary an assessment of, and propose a modification to, the approved strategy for the drug involved at any time.

(2) Required assessments. A responsible person shall, subject to paragraph (5), submit an assessment of, and may propose a modification to, the approved risk evaluation and mitigation strategy for a drug--

(A) when submitting a supplemental application for a new indication for use under section 505(b) or under section 351 of the Public Health Service Act [42 USC § 262], unless the drug is not subject to section 503(b) and the risk evaluation and mitigation strategy for the drug includes only the timetable under subsection (d);

(B) when required by the strategy, as provided for in such timetable under subsection (d);

(C) within a time period to be determined by the Secretary, if the Secretary, in consultation with the offices described in subsection (c)(2), determines that new safety or effectiveness information indicates that--

(i) an element under subsection (d) or (e) should be modified or included in the strategy; or

(ii) an element under subsection (f) should be modified or included in the strategy; or

(D) within 15 days when ordered by the Secretary, in consultation with the offices described in subsection (c)(2), if the Secretary determines that there may be a cause for action by the Secretary under section 505(e).

(3) Requirements for assessments. An assessment under paragraph (1) or (2) of an approved risk evaluation and mitigation strategy for a drug shall include--

(A) with respect to any goal under subsection (f), an assessment of the extent to which the elements to assure safe use are meeting the goal or whether the goal or such elements should be modified;

(B) with respect to any postapproval study required under section 505(o) or otherwise undertaken by the responsible person to investigate a safety issue, the status of such study, including whether any difficulties completing the study have been encountered; and

(C) with respect to any postapproval clinical trial required under section 505(o) or otherwise undertaken by the responsible party to investigate a safety issue, the status of such clinical trial, including whether enrollment has begun, the number of participants enrolled, the expected completion date, whether any difficulties completing the clinical trial have been encountered, and registration information with respect to requirements under subsections (i) and (j) of section 402 of the Public Health Service Act [42 USC § 282] .

(4) Modification. A modification (whether an enhancement or a reduction) to the approved risk evaluation and mitigation strategy for a drug may include the addition or modification of any element under subsection (d) or the addition, modification, or removal of any element under subsection (e) or (f), such as--

(A) modifying the timetable for assessments of the strategy as provided in subsection (d)(3), including to eliminate assessments; or

(B) adding, modifying, or removing an element to assure safe use under subsection (f).

(h) Review of proposed strategies; review of assessments of approved strategies.

(1) In general. The Secretary, in consultation with the offices described in subsection (c)(2), shall promptly review each proposed risk evaluation and mitigation strategy for a drug submitted under subsection (a) and each assessment of an approved risk evaluation and mitigation strategy for a drug submitted under subsection (g).

(2) Discussion. The Secretary, in consultation with the offices described in subsection (c)(2), shall initiate discussions with the responsible person for purposes of this subsection to determine a strategy not later than 60 days after any such assessment is submitted or, in the case of an assessment submitted under subsection (g)(2)(D), not later than 30 days after such assessment is submitted.

(3) Action.

(A) In general. Unless the dispute resolution process described under paragraph (4) or (5) applies, the Secretary, in consultation with the offices described in subsection (c)(2), shall describe any required risk evaluation and mitigation strategy for a drug, or any modification to any required strategy--

(i) as part of the action letter on the application, when a proposed strategy is submitted under subsection (a) or a modification to the strategy is proposed as part of an assessment of the strategy submitted under subsection (g)(1); or

(ii) in an order issued not later than 90 days after the date discussions of such modification begin under paragraph (2), when a modification to the strategy is proposed as part of an assessment of the strategy submitted under subsection (g)(1) or under any of subparagraphs (B) through (D) of subsection (g)(2).

(B) Inaction. An approved risk evaluation and mitigation strategy shall remain in effect until the Secretary acts, if the Secretary fails to act as provided under subparagraph (A).

(C) Public availability. Any action letter described in subparagraph (A)(i) or order described in subparagraph (A)(ii) shall be made publicly available.

(4) Dispute resolution at initial approval. If a proposed risk evaluation and mitigation strategy is submitted under subsection (a)(1) in an application for initial approval of a drug and there is a dispute about the strategy, the responsible person shall use the major dispute resolution procedures as set forth in the letters described in section 101(c) of the Food and Drug Administration Amendments Act of 2007.

(5) Dispute resolution in all other cases.

(A) Request for review.

(i) In general. Not earlier than 15 days, and not later than 35 days, after discussions under paragraph (2) have begun, the responsible person may request in writing that a dispute about the strategy be reviewed by the Drug Safety Oversight Board under subsection (j), except that the determination of the Secretary to require a risk evaluation and mitigation strategy is not subject to review under this paragraph. The preceding sentence does not prohibit review under this paragraph of the particular elements of such a strategy.

(ii) Scheduling. Upon receipt of a request under clause (i), the Secretary shall schedule the dispute involved for review under subparagraph (B) and, not later than 5 business days of scheduling the dispute for review, shall publish by posting on the Internet or otherwise a notice that the dispute will be reviewed by the Drug Safety Oversight Board.

(B) Scheduling review. If a responsible person requests review under subparagraph (A), the Secretary--

(i) shall schedule the dispute for review at 1 of the next 2 regular meetings of the Drug Safety Oversight Board, whichever meeting date is more practicable; or

(ii) may convene a special meeting of the Drug Safety Oversight Board to review the matter more promptly, including to meet an action deadline on an application (including a supplemental application).

(C) Agreement after discussion or administrative appeals.

(i) Further discussion or administrative appeals. A request for review under subparagraph (A) shall not preclude further discussions to reach agreement on the risk evaluation and mitigation strategy, and such a request shall not preclude the use of administrative appeals within the Food and Drug Administration to reach agreement on the strategy, including appeals as described in the letters described in section 101(c) of the Food and Drug Administration Amendments Act of 2007 for procedural or scientific matters involving the review of human drug applications and supplemental applications that cannot be resolved at the divisional level. At the time a review has been scheduled under subparagraph (B) and notice of such review has been posted, the responsible person shall either withdraw the request under subparagraph (A) or terminate the use of such administrative appeals.

(ii) Agreement terminates dispute resolution. At any time before a decision and order is issued under subparagraph (G) , the Secretary (in consultation with the offices described in subsection (c)(2)) and the responsible person may reach an agreement on the risk evaluation and mitigation strategy through further discussion or administrative appeals, terminating the dispute resolution process, and the Secretary shall issue an action letter or order, as appropriate, that describes the strategy.

(D) Meeting of the Board. At a meeting of the Drug Safety Oversight Board described in subparagraph (B), the Board shall--

(i) hear from both parties via written or oral presentation; and

(ii) review the dispute.

(E) Record of proceedings. The Secretary shall ensure that the proceedings of any such meeting are recorded, transcribed, and made public within 90 days of the meeting. The Secretary shall redact the transcript to protect any trade secrets and other information that is exempted from disclosure under section 552 of title 5, United States Code, or section 552a of title 5, United States Code.

(F) Recommendation of the Board. Not later than 5 days after any such meeting, the Drug Safety Oversight Board shall provide a written recommendation on resolving the dispute to the Secretary. Not later than 5 days after the Board provides such written recommendation to the Secretary, the Secretary shall make the recommendation available to the public.

(G) Action by the Secretary.

(i) Action letter. With respect to a proposal or assessment referred to in paragraph (1), the Secretary shall issue an action letter that resolves the dispute not later than the later of--

(I) the action deadline for the action letter on the application; or

(II) 7 days after receiving the recommendation of the Drug Safety Oversight Board.

(ii) Order. With respect to an assessment of an approved risk evaluation and mitigation strategy under subsection (g)(1) or under any of subparagraphs (B) through (D) of subsection (g)(2), the Secretary shall issue an order, which shall be made public, that resolves the dispute not later than 7 days after receiving the recommendation of the Drug Safety Oversight Board.

(H) Inaction. An approved risk evaluation and mitigation strategy shall remain in effect until the Secretary acts, if the Secretary fails to act as provided for under subparagraph (G).

(I) Effect on action deadline. With respect to a proposal or assessment referred to in paragraph (1), the Secretary shall be considered to have met the action deadline for the action letter on the application if the responsible person requests the dispute resolution process described in this paragraph and if the Secretary—

(i) has initiated the discussions described under paragraph (2) not less than 60 days before such action deadline; and

(ii) has complied with the timing requirements of scheduling review by the Drug Safety Oversight Board, providing a written recommendation, and issuing an action letter under subparagraphs (B), (F), and (G), respectively.

(J) Disqualification. No individual who is an employee of the Food and Drug Administration and who reviews a drug or who participated in an administrative appeal under subparagraph (C)(i) with respect to such drug may serve on the Drug Safety Oversight Board at a meeting under subparagraph (D) to review a dispute about the risk evaluation and mitigation strategy for such drug.

(K) Additional expertise. The Drug Safety Oversight Board may add members with relevant expertise from the Food and Drug Administration, including the Office of Pediatrics, the Office of Women's Health, or the Office of Rare Diseases, or from other Federal public health or health care agencies, for a meeting under subparagraph (D) of the Drug Safety Oversight Board.

(6) Use of advisory committees. The Secretary may convene a meeting of 1 or more advisory committees of the Food and Drug Administration to--

(A) review a concern about the safety of a drug or class of drugs, including before an assessment of the risk evaluation and mitigation strategy or strategies of such drug or drugs is required to be submitted under any of subparagraphs (B) through (D) of subsection (g)(2);

(B) review the risk evaluation and mitigation strategy or strategies of a drug or group of drugs; or

(C) review a dispute under paragraph (4) or (5).

(7) Process for addressing drug class effects.

(A) In general. When a concern about a serious risk of a drug may be related to the pharmacological class of the drug, the Secretary, in consultation with the offices described in subsection (c)(2), may defer assessments of the approved risk evaluation and mitigation strategies for such drugs until the Secretary has convened 1 or more public meetings to consider possible responses to such concern.

(B) Notice. If the Secretary defers an assessment under subparagraph (A), the Secretary shall--

(i) give notice of the deferral to the holder of the approved covered application not later than 5 days after the deferral;

(ii) publish the deferral in the Federal Register; and

(iii) give notice to the public of any public meetings to be convened under subparagraph (A), including a description of the deferral.

(C) Public meetings. Such public meetings may include--

(i) 1 or more meetings of the responsible person for such drugs;

(ii) 1 or more meetings of 1 or more advisory committees of the Food and Drug Administration, as provided for under paragraph (6); or

(iii) 1 or more workshops of scientific experts and other stakeholders.

(D) Action. After considering the discussions from any meetings under subparagraph (A), the Secretary may--

(i) announce in the Federal Register a planned regulatory action, including a modification to each risk evaluation and mitigation strategy, for drugs in the pharmacological class;

(ii) seek public comment about such action; and

(iii) after seeking such comment, issue an order addressing such regulatory action.

(8) International coordination. The Secretary, in consultation with the offices described in subsection (c)(2), may coordinate the timetable for submission of assessments under subsection (d), or a study or clinical trial under section 505(o)(3), with efforts to identify and assess the serious risks of such drug by the marketing authorities of other countries whose drug approval and risk management processes the Secretary deems comparable to the drug approval and risk management processes of the United States. If the Secretary takes

action to coordinate such timetable, the Secretary shall give notice to the responsible person.

(9) Effect. Use of the processes described in paragraphs (7) and (8) shall not be the sole source of delay of action on an application or a supplement to an application for a drug.

(i) Abbreviated new drug applications.

(1) In general. A drug that is the subject of an abbreviated new drug application under section 505(j) is subject to only the following elements of the risk evaluation and mitigation strategy required under subsection (a) for the applicable listed drug:

(A) A Medication Guide or patient package insert, if required under subsection (e) for the applicable listed drug.

(B) Elements to assure safe use, if required under subsection (f) for the listed drug. A drug that is the subject of an abbreviated new drug application and the listed drug shall use a single, shared system under subsection (f). The Secretary may waive the requirement under the preceding sentence for a drug that is the subject of an abbreviated new drug application, and permit the applicant to use a different, comparable aspect of the elements to assure safe use, if the Secretary determines that--

(i) the burden of creating a single, shared system outweighs the benefit of a single, system, taking into consideration the impact on health care providers, patients, the applicant for the abbreviated new drug application, and the holder of the reference drug product; or

(ii) an aspect of the elements to assure safe use for the applicable listed drug is claimed by a patent that has not expired or is a method or process that, as a trade secret, is entitled to protection, and the applicant for the abbreviated new drug application certifies that it has sought a license for use of an aspect of the elements to assure safe use for the applicable listed drug and that it was unable to obtain a license.

A certification under clause (ii) shall include a description of the efforts made by the applicant for the abbreviated new drug application to obtain a license. In a case described in clause (ii), the Secretary may seek to negotiate a voluntary agreement with the owner of the patent, method, or process for a license under which the applicant for such abbreviated new drug application may use an aspect of the elements to assure safe use, if required under subsection (f) for the applicable listed drug, that is claimed by a patent that has not expired or is a method or process that as a trade secret is entitled to protection.

(2) Action by Secretary. For an applicable listed drug for which a drug is approved under section 505(j), the Secretary--

(A) shall undertake any communication plan to health care providers required under subsection (e)(3) for the applicable listed drug; and

(B) shall inform the responsible person for the drug that is so approved if the risk evaluation and mitigation strategy for the applicable listed drug is modified.

(j) Drug Safety Oversight Board.

(1) In general. There is established a Drug Safety Oversight Board.

(2) Composition; meetings. The Drug Safety Oversight Board shall--

(A) be composed of scientists and health care practitioners appointed by the Secretary, each of whom is an employee of the Federal Government;

(B) include representatives from offices throughout the Food and Drug Administration, including the offices responsible for postapproval safety of drugs;

(C) include at least 1 representative each from the National Institutes of Health and the Department of Health and Human Services (other than the Food and Drug Administration);

(D) include such representatives as the Secretary shall designate from other appropriate agencies that wish to provide representatives; and

(E) meet at least monthly to provide oversight and advice to the Secretary on the management of important drug safety issues.

SEC. 505A. [21 USC §355a] Pediatric Studies of Drugs

(a) [25] Definitions. As used in this section, the term "***pediatric studies***" or "***studies***" means at least one clinical investigation (that, at the Secretary's discretion, may include pharmacokinetic studies) in pediatric age groups (including neonates in appropriate cases) in which a drug is anticipated to be used, and, at the discretion of the Secretary, may include preclinical studies.

(b) Market exclusivity for new drugs.

(1) In general. Except as provided in paragraph (2), if, prior to approval of an application that is submitted under section 505(b)(1), the Secretary determines that information relating to the use of a new drug in the pediatric population may produce health benefits in that population, the Secretary makes a written request for pediatric studies (which shall include a timeframe

[25] Section 16 of Public Law 107–109 (115 Stat. 1421) requires the Comptroller General of the United States, in consultation with the Secretary of Health and Human Services, to submit to Congress a report that relates to section 505A and to section 409I of the Public Health Service Act. The report is required to be submitted not later than October 1, 2006.

for completing such studies), the applicant agrees to the request, such studies are completed using appropriate formulations for each age group for which the study is requested within any such timeframe, and the reports thereof are submitted and accepted in accordance with subsection (d)(2) or accepted in accordance with subsection (d)(3)—

(A)(i)(I) the period referred to in subsection (c)(3)(E)(ii) of section 505, and in subsection (j)(5)(F)(ii) of such section, is deemed to be five years and six months rather than five years, and the references in subsections (c)(3)(E)(ii) and (j)(5)(F)(ii) of such section to four years, to forty-eight months, and to seven and one-half years are deemed to be four and one-half years, fifty-four months, and eight years, respectively; or

(II) the period referred to in clauses (iii) and (iv) of subsection (c)(3)(E) of such section, and in clauses (iii) and (iv) of subsection (j)(5)(F) of such section, is deemed to be three years and six months rather than three years; and

(ii) if the drug is designated under section 526 for a rare disease or condition, the period referred to in section 527(a) is deemed to be seven years and six months rather than seven years; and

(B)(i) if the drug is the subject of—

(I) a listed patent for which a certification has been submitted under subsection (b)(2)(A)(ii) or (j)(2)(A)(vii)(II) of section 505 and for which pediatric studies were submitted prior to the expiration of the patent (including any patent extensions); or

(II) a listed patent for which a certification has been submitted under subsections (b)(2)(A)(iii) or (j)(2)(A)(vii)(III) of section 505,

the period during which an application may not be approved under section 505(c)(3) or section 505(j)(5)(B) shall be extended by a period of six months after the date the patent expires (including any patent extensions); or

(ii) if the drug is the subject of a listed patent for which a certification has been submitted under subsection (b)(2)(A)(iv) or (j)(2)(A)(vii)(IV) of section 505, and in the patent infringement litigation resulting from the certification the court determines that the patent is valid and would be infringed, the period during which an application may not be approved under section 505(c)(3) or section 505(j)(5)(B) shall be extended by a period of six months after the date the patent expires (including any patent extensions).

(2) Exception. The Secretary shall not extend the period referred to in paragraph (1)(A) or (1)(B) if the determination made under subsection (d)(3) is made later than 9 months prior to the expiration of such period.

(c) Market exclusivity for already-marketed drugs.

(1) In general. Except as provided in paragraph (2), if the Secretary determines that information relating to the use of an approved drug in the pediatric population may produce health benefits in that population and makes a written request to the holder of an approved application under section 505(b)(1) for pediatric studies (which shall include a timeframe for completing such studies), the holder agrees to the request, such studies are completed using appropriate formulations for each age group for which the study is requested within any such timeframe, and the reports thereof are submitted and accepted in accordance with subsection (d)(3)—

(A)(i)(I) the period referred to in subsection (c)(3)(E)(ii) of section 505, and in subsection (j)(5)(F)(ii) of such section, is deemed to be five years and six months rather than five years, and the references in subsections (c)(3)(E)(ii) and (j)(5)(F)(ii) of such section to four years, to forty-eight months, and to seven and one-half years are deemed to be four and one-half years, fifty-four months, and eight years, respectively; or

(II) the period referred to in clauses (iii) and (iv) of subsection (c)(3)(D) of such section, and in clauses (iii) and (iv) of subsection (j)(5)(F) of such section, is deemed to be three years and six months rather than three years; and

(ii) if the drug is designated under section 526 for a rare disease or condition, the period referred to in section 527(a) is deemed to be seven years and six months rather than seven years; and

(B)(i) if the drug is the subject of—

(I) a listed patent for which a certification has been submitted under subsection (b)(2)(A)(ii) or (j)(2)(A)(vii)(II) of section 505 and for which pediatric studies were submitted prior to the expiration of the patent (including any patent extensions); or

(II) a listed patent for which a certification has been submitted under subsection (b)(2)(A)(iii) or (j)(2)(A)(vii)(III) of section 505,

the period during which an application may not be approved under section 505(c)(3) or section 505(j)(5)(B)(ii) shall be extended by a period of six months after the date the patent expires (including any patent extensions); or

(ii) if the drug is the subject of a listed patent for which a certification has been submitted under subsection (b)(2)(A)(iv) or (j)(2)(A)(vii)(IV) of section 505, and in the patent infringement litigation resulting from the certification the court determines that the patent is valid and would be infringed, the period during which an application may not be approved under section 505(c)(3) or section 505(j)(5)(B) shall be extended by a period of six months after the date the patent expires (including any patent extensions).

(2) Exception. The Secretary shall not extend the period referred to in paragraph (1)(A) or (1)(B) if the determination made under subsection (d)(3) is made later than 9 months prior to the expiration of such period.

(d) Conduct of pediatric studies.

(1) Request for studies.

(A) In general, the Secretary may, after consultation with the sponsor of an application for an investigational new drug under section 505(i); the sponsor of an application for a new drug under section 505(b)(1); or the holder of an approved application for a drug under section 505(b)(1), issue to the sponsor or holder a written request for the conduct of pediatric studies for such drug. In issuing such request, the Secretary shall take into account adequate representation of children of ethnic and racial minorities. Such request to conduct pediatric studies shall be in writing and shall include a timeframe for such studies and a request to the sponsor or holder to propose pediatric labeling resulting from such studies.

(B) Single written request. A single written request--

(i) may relate to more than one use of a drug; and

(ii) may include uses that are both approved and unapproved.

(2) Written request for pediatric studies.

(A) Request and response.

(i) In general. If the Secretary makes a written request for pediatric studies (including neonates, as appropriate) under subsection (b) or (c), the applicant or holder, not later than 180 days after receiving the written request, shall respond to the Secretary as to the intention of the applicant or holder to act on the request by--

(I) indicating when the pediatric studies will be initiated, if the applicant or holder agrees to the request; or

(II) indicating that the applicant or holder does not agree to the request and stating the reasons for declining the request.

(ii) Disagree with request. If, on or after the date of the enactment of the Best Pharmaceuticals for Children Act of 2007 [enacted Sept. 27, 2007], the applicant or holder does not agree to the request on the grounds that it is not possible to develop the appropriate pediatric formulation, the applicant or holder shall submit to the Secretary the reasons such pediatric formulation cannot be developed.

(B) Adverse event reports. An applicant or holder that, on or after the date of the enactment of the Best Pharmaceuticals for Children Act of 2007 [enacted Sept. 27, 2007], agrees to the request for such studies shall provide the Secretary, at the same time as the submission of the reports of such studies, with all postmarket adverse event reports regarding the drug that is the subject of such studies and are available prior to submission of such reports.

(3) Meeting the studies requirement. Not later than 180 days after the submission of the reports of the studies, the Secretary shall accept or reject such reports and so notify the sponsor or holder. The Secretary's only responsibility in accepting or rejecting the reports shall be to determine, within the 180-day period, whether the studies fairly respond to the written request, have been conducted in accordance with commonly accepted scientific principles and protocols, and have been reported in accordance with the requirements of the Secretary for filing.

(4) Effect of subsection. Nothing in this subsection alters or amends section 301(j) of this Act or section 552 of title 5 or section 1905 of title 18, United States Code.

(e) Notice of determinations on studies requirement.

(1) In general. The Secretary shall publish a notice of any determination, made on or after the date of the enactment of the Best Pharmaceuticals for Children Act of 2007 [enacted Sept. 27, 2007], that the requirements of subsection (d) have been met and that submissions and approvals under subsection (b)(2) or (j) of section 505 for a drug will be subject to the provisions of this section. Such notice shall be published not later than 30 days after the date of the Secretary's determination regarding market exclusivity and shall include a copy of the written request made under subsection (b) or (c).

(2) Identification of certain drugs. The Secretary shall publish a notice identifying any drug for which, on or after the date of the enactment of the Best Pharmaceuticals for Children Act of 2007 [enacted Sept. 27, 2007], a pediatric formulation was developed, studied, and found to be safe and effective in the pediatric population (or specified subpopulation) if the pediatric formulation for such drug is not introduced onto the market within one year after the date that the Secretary publishes the notice described in paragraph (1). Such notice identifying such drug shall be published not later than 30 days after the date of the expiration of such one year period.

(f) Internal review of written requests and pediatric studies.

(1) Internal review. The Secretary shall utilize the internal review committee established under section 505C to review all written requests issued on or after the date of the enactment of the Best Pharmaceuticals for Children Act of 2007 [enacted Sept. 27, 2007], in accordance with paragraph (2).

(2) Review of written requests. The committee referred to in paragraph (1) shall review all written requests issued pursuant to this section prior to being issued.

(3) Review of pediatric studies. The committee referred to in paragraph (1) may review studies conducted pursuant to this section to make a recommendation to the Secretary whether to accept or reject such reports under subsection (d)(3).

(4) Activity by committee. The committee referred to in paragraph (1) may operate using appropriate members of such committee and need not convene all members of the committee.

(5) Documentation of committee action. For each drug, the committee referred to in paragraph (1) shall document, for each activity described in paragraph (2) or (3), which members of the committee participated in such activity.

(6) Tracking pediatric studies and labeling changes. The Secretary, in consultation with the committee referred to in paragraph (1), shall track and make available to the public, in an easily accessible manner, including through posting on the Web site of the Food and Drug Administration--

(A) the number of studies conducted under this section and under section 409I of the Public Health Service Act [42 USC § 284m];

(B) the specific drugs and drug uses, including labeled and off-labeled indications, studied under such sections;

(C) the types of studies conducted under such sections, including trial design, the number of pediatric patients studied, and the number of centers and countries involved;

(D) the number of pediatric formulations developed and the number of pediatric formulations not developed and the reasons such formulations were not developed;

(E) the labeling changes made as a result of studies conducted under such sections;

(F) an annual summary of labeling changes made as a result of studies conducted under such sections for distribution pursuant to subsection (k)(2); and

(G) information regarding reports submitted on or after the date of the enactment of the Best Pharmaceuticals for Children Act of 2007 [enacted Sept. 27, 2007].

(g) Limitations. Notwithstanding subsection (c)(2), a drug to which the six-month period under subsection (b) or (c) has already been applied--

(1) may receive an additional six-month period under subsection (c)(1)(A)(i)(II) for a supplemental application if all other requirements under this section are satisfied, except that such drug may not receive any additional such period under subsection (c)(1)(B); and

(2) may not receive any additional such period under subsection (c)(1)(A)(ii).

(h) Relationship to pediatric research requirements. Notwithstanding any other provision of law, if any pediatric study is required by a provision of law (including a regulation) other than this section and such study meets the completeness, timeliness, and other requirements of this section, such study shall be deemed to satisfy the requirement for market exclusivity pursuant to this section.

(i) Labeling changes.

(1) Priority status for pediatric applications and supplements. Any application or supplement to an application under section 505 proposing a labeling change as a result of any pediatric study conducted pursuant to this section--

(A) shall be considered to be a priority application or supplement; and

(B) shall be subject to the performance goals established by the Commissioner for priority drugs.

(2) Dispute resolution.

(A) Request for labeling change and failure to agree. If, on or after the date of the enactment of the Best Pharmaceuticals for Children Act of 2007 [enacted Sept. 27, 2007], the Commissioner determines that the sponsor and the Commissioner have been unable to reach agreement on appropriate changes to the labeling for the drug that is the subject of the application, not later than 180 days after the date of submission of the application--

(i) the Commissioner shall request that the sponsor of the application make any labeling change that the Commissioner determines to be appropriate; and

(ii) if the sponsor of the application does not agree within 30 days after the Commissioner's request to make a labeling change requested by the Commissioner, the Commissioner shall refer the matter to the Pediatric Advisory Committee.

(B) Action by the pediatric advisory committee. Not later than 90 days after receiving a referral under subparagraph (A)(ii), the Pediatric Advisory Committee shall--

(i) review the pediatric study reports; and

(ii) make a recommendation to the Commissioner concerning appropriate labeling changes, if any.

(C) Consideration of recommendations. The Commissioner shall consider the recommendations of the Pediatric Advisory Committee and, if appropriate, not later than 30 days after receiving the recommendation, make a request to the sponsor of the application to make any labeling change that the Commissioner determines to be appropriate.

(D) Misbranding. If the sponsor of the application, within 30 days after receiving a request under subparagraph (C), does not agree to make a labeling change requested by the Commissioner, the Commissioner may deem the drug that is the subject of the application to be misbranded.

(E) No effect on authority. Nothing in this subsection limits the authority of the United States to bring an enforcement action under this Act when a drug lacks appropriate pediatric labeling. Neither course of action (the Pediatric Advisory Committee process or an enforcement action referred to in the preceding sentence) shall preclude, delay, or serve as the basis to stay the other course of action.

(j) Other labeling changes. If, on or after the date of the enactment of the Best Pharmaceuticals for Children Act of 2007 [enacted Sept. 27, 2007], the Secretary determines that a pediatric study conducted under this section does or does not demonstrate that the drug that is the subject of the study is safe and effective, including whether such study results are inconclusive, in pediatric populations or subpopulations, the Secretary shall order the labeling of such product to include information about the results of the study and a statement of the Secretary's determination.

(k) Dissemination of pediatric information.

(1) In general. Not later than 210 days after the date of submission of a report on a pediatric study under this section, the Secretary shall make available to the public the medical, statistical, and clinical pharmacology reviews of pediatric studies conducted under subsection (b) or (c).

(2) Dissemination of information regarding labeling changes. Beginning on the date of the enactment of the Best Pharmaceuticals for Children Act of 2007 [enacted Sept. 27, 2007], the Secretary shall include as a requirement of a written request that the sponsors of the studies that result in labeling changes that are reflected in the annual summary developed pursuant to subsection (f)(3)(F) distribute, at least annually (or more frequently if the Secretary determines that it would be beneficial to the public health), such information to physicians and other health care providers.

(3) Effect of subsection. Nothing in this subsection alters or amends section 301(j) of this Act or section 552 of title 5 or section 1905 of title 18, United States Code.

(l) Adverse event reporting.

(1) Reporting in year one. Beginning on the date of the enactment of the Best Pharmaceuticals for Children Act of 2007 [enacted Sept. 27, 2007], during the one-year period beginning on the date a labeling change is approved pursuant to subsection (i), the Secretary shall ensure that all adverse event reports that have been received for such drug (regardless of when such report was received) are referred to the Office of Pediatric Therapeutics established under section 6 of the Best Pharmaceuticals for Children Act (Public Law 107-109). In considering the reports, the Director of such Office shall provide for the review of the reports by the Pediatric Advisory Committee, including obtaining any recommendations of such Committee regarding whether the Secretary should take action under this Act in response to such reports.

(2) Reporting in subsequent years. Following the one-year period described in paragraph (1), the Secretary shall, as appropriate, refer to the Office of Pediatric Therapeutics all pediatric adverse event reports for a drug for which a pediatric study was conducted under this section. In considering such reports, the Director of such Office may provide for the review of such reports by the Pediatric Advisory Committee, including obtaining any recommendation of such Committee regarding whether the Secretary should take action in response to such reports.

(3) Effect. The requirements of this subsection shall supplement, not supplant, other review of such adverse event reports by the Secretary.

(m) Clarification of interaction of market exclusivity under this section and market exclusivity awarded to an applicant for approval of a drug under section 505(j) [21 USC § 355(j)]. If a 180-day period under section 505(j)(5)(B)(iv) [21 USC § 355(j)(5)(B)(iv)] overlaps with a 6-month exclusivity period under this section, so that the applicant for approval of a drug under section 505(j) [21 USC § 355(j)] entitled to the 180-day period under that section loses a portion of the 180-day period to which the applicant is entitled for the drug, the 180-day period shall be extended from--

(1) the date on which the 180-day period would have expired by the number of days of the overlap, if the 180-day period would, but for the application of this subsection, expire after the 6-month exclusivity period; or

(2) the date on which the 6-month exclusivity period expires, by the number of days of the overlap if the 180-day period would, but for the application of this subsection, expire during the six-month exclusivity period.

(n) Referral if pediatric studies not completed.

(1) In general. Beginning on the date of the enactment of the Best Pharmaceuticals for Children Act of 2007 [enacted Sept. 27, 2007], if pediatric studies of a drug have not been completed under subsection (d) and if the Secretary, through the committee established under section 505C [21 USC § 355d], determines that there is a continuing need for information relating to the use of the drug in the pediatric population (including neonates, as appropriate), the Secretary shall carry out the following:

(A) For a drug for which a listed patent has not expired, make a determination regarding whether an assessment shall be required to be submitted under section 505B(b) [21 USC § 355c(b)]. Prior to making such a determination, the Secretary may not take more than 30 days to certify whether the Foundation for the National Institutes of Health has sufficient funding at the time of such certification to initiate and fund all of the studies in the written request in their entirety within the timeframes specified within the written request. Only if the Secretary makes such certification in the affirmative, the Secretary shall refer all pediatric studies in the written request to the Foundation for the National Institutes of Health for the conduct of such studies, and such Foundation shall fund such studies. If no certification has been made at the end of the 30-day period, or if the Secretary certifies that funds are not sufficient to initiate and fund all the studies in their entirety, the Secretary shall consider whether assessments shall be required under section 505B(b) [21 USC § 355c(b)] for such drug.

(B) For a drug that has no listed patents or has 1 or more listed patents that have expired, the Secretary shall refer the drug for inclusion on the list established under section 409I of the Public Health Service Act [21 USC § 284m] for the conduct of studies.

(2) Public notice. The Secretary shall give the public notice of a decision under paragraph (1)(A) not to require an assessment under section 505B and the basis for such decision.

(3) Effect of subsection. Nothing in this subsection alters or amends section 301(j) of this Act or section 552 of title 5 or section 1905 of title 18, United States Code.

(o) Prompt approval of drugs under section 505(j) when pediatric information is added to labeling.

(1) General rule. A drug for which an application has been submitted or approved under section 505(j) shall not be considered ineligible for approval under that section or misbranded under section 502 on the basis that the labeling of the drug omits a pediatric indication or any other aspect of labeling pertaining to pediatric use when the omitted indication or other

aspect is protected by patent or by exclusivity under clause (iii) or (iv) of section 505(j)(5)(F).

(2) Labeling. Notwithstanding clauses (iii) and (iv) of section 505(j)(5)(F) , the Secretary may require that the labeling of a drug approved under section 505(j) that omits a pediatric indication or other aspect of labeling as described in paragraph (1) include--

(A) a statement that, because of marketing exclusivity for a manufacturer--

(i) the drug is not labeled for pediatric use; or

(ii) in the case of a drug for which there is an additional pediatric use not referred to in paragraph (1), the drug is not labeled for the pediatric use under paragraph (1); and

(B) a statement of any appropriate pediatric contraindications, warnings, or precautions that the Secretary considers necessary.

(3) Preservation of pediatric exclusivity and other provisions. This subsection does not affect--

(A) the availability or scope of exclusivity under this section;

(B) the availability or scope of exclusivity under section 505 for pediatric formulations;

(C) the question of the eligibility for approval of any application under section 505(j) that omits any other conditions of approval entitled to exclusivity under clause (iii) or (iv) of section 505(j)(5)(F); or

(D) except as expressly provided in paragraphs (1) and (2), the operation of section 505 .

(p) Institute of Medicine study. Not later than 3 years after the date of the enactment of the Best Pharmaceuticals for Children Act of 2007 [enacted Sept. 27, 2007], the Secretary shall enter into a contract with the Institute of Medicine to conduct a study and report to Congress regarding the written requests made and the studies conducted pursuant to this section. The Institute of Medicine may devise an appropriate mechanism to review a representative sample of requests made and studies conducted pursuant to this section in order to conduct such study. Such study shall--

(1) review such representative written requests issued by the Secretary since 1997 under subsections (b) and (c);

(2) review and assess such representative pediatric studies conducted under subsections (b) and (c) since 1997 and labeling changes made as a result of such studies;

(3) review the use of extrapolation for pediatric subpopulations, the use of alternative endpoints for pediatric populations, neonatal assessment tools, and ethical issues in pediatric clinical trials;

(4) review and assess the pediatric studies of biological products as required under subsections (a) and (b) of section 505B; and

(5) make recommendations regarding appropriate incentives for encouraging pediatric studies of biologics.

(q) Sunset. A drug may not receive any 6-month period under subsection (b) or (c) unless--

(1) on or before October 1, 2012, the Secretary makes a written request for pediatric studies of the drug;

(2) on or before October 1, 2012, an application for the drug is accepted for filing under section 505(b); and

(3) all requirements of this section are met.

SEC. 505B. [21 USC §355c] Research Into Pediatric Uses for Drugs and Biological Products

Note: This section was added in February 2008.

(a) [26] New drugs and biological products.

---

[26] Section 2 of Public Law 108–155 (117 Stat. 1936) added section 505B above. Section 4 of such Act (117 Stat. 1942) provides as follows:
SEC. 4. EFFECTIVE DATE.
(a) IN GENERAL.—Subject to subsection (b), this Act and the amendments made by this Act take effect on the date of enactment of this Act.

(b) APPLICABILITY TO NEW DRUGS AND BIOLOGICAL PRODUCTS.—
(1) IN GENERAL.—Subsection (a) of section 505B of the Federal Food, Drug, and Cosmetic Act (as added by section 2) shall apply to an application described in paragraph (1) of that subsection submitted to the Secretary of Health and Human Services on or after April 1, 1999.
(2) WAIVERS AND DEFERRALS.—
(A) WAIVER OR DEFERRAL GRANTED.—If, with respect to an application submitted to the Secretary of Health and Human Services between April 1, 1999, and the date of enactment of this Act, a waiver or deferral of pediatric assessments was granted under regulations of the Secretary then in effect, the waiver or deferral shall be a waiver or deferral under subsection (a) of section 505B of the Federal Food, Drug, and Cosmetic Act, except that any date specified in such a deferral shall be extended by the number of days that is equal to the number of days between October 17, 2002, and the date of enactment of this Act.
(B) WAIVER AND DEFERRAL NOT GRANTED.—If, with respect to an application submitted to the Secretary of Health and Human Services between April 1, 1999, and the date of enactment of this Act, neither a waiver nor deferral of pediatric assessments was granted under regulations of the Secretary then in effect, the person that submitted the application shall be required to submit assessments under subsection (a)(2) of section 505B of the Federal Food, Drug, and Cosmetic Act on the date that is the later of—

Chapter V

(1) In general. A person that submits, on or after the date of the enactment of the Pediatric Research Equity Act of 2007 [enacted Sept. 27, 2007], an application (or supplement to an application)—

(A) under section 505 for a new active ingredient, new indication, new dosage form, new dosing regimen, or new route of administration, or

(B) under section 351 of the Public Health Service Act (42 USC 262) for a new active ingredient, new indication, new dosage form, new dosing regimen, or new route of administration

shall submit with the application the assessments described in paragraph (2).

(2) Assessments.

(A) In general. The assessments referred to in paragraph (1) shall contain data, gathered using appropriate formulations for each age group for which the assessment is required, that are adequate—

(i) to assess the safety and effectiveness of the drug or the biological product for the claimed indications in all relevant pediatric subpopulations; and

(ii) to support dosing and administration for each pediatric subpopulation for which the drug or the biological product is safe and effective.

(B) Similar course of disease or similar effect of drug or biological product.

(i) In general. If the course of the disease and the effects of the drug are sufficiently similar in adults and pediatric patients, the Secretary may conclude that pediatric effectiveness can be extrapolated from adequate and well-controlled studies in adults, usually supplemented with other information obtained in pediatric patients, such as pharmacokinetic studies.

(ii) Extrapolation between age groups. A study may not be needed in each pediatric age group if data from one age group can be extrapolated to another age group.

(iii) Information on extrapolation. A brief documentation of the scientific data supporting the conclusion under clauses (i) and (ii)

(i) the date that is 1 year after the date of enactment of this Act; or
(ii) such date as the Secretary may specify under subsection (a)(3) of that section; unless the Secretary grants a waiver under subsection (a)(4) of that section.
(c) NO LIMITATION OF AUTHORITY.—Neither the lack of guidance or regulations to implement this Act or the amendments made by this Act nor the pendency of the process for issuing guidance or regulations shall limit the authority of the Secretary of Health and Human Services under, or defer any requirement under, this Act or those amendments.

shall be included in any pertinent reviews for the application under section 505 of this Act or section 351 of the Public Health Service Act (42 U.S.C. 262).

(3) Deferral.

(A) In general. On the initiative of the Secretary or at the request of the applicant, the Secretary may defer submission of some or all assessments required under paragraph (1) until a specified date after approval of the drug or issuance of the license for a biological product if—

(i) the Secretary finds that--

(I) the drug or biological product is ready for approval for use in adults before pediatric studies are complete;

(II) pediatric studies should be delayed until additional safety or effectiveness data have been collected; or

(III) there is another appropriate reason for deferral; and

(ii) the applicant submits to the Secretary—

(I) certification of the grounds for deferring the assessments;

(II) a description of the planned or ongoing studies; and

(III) evidence that the studies are being conducted or will be conducted with due diligence and at the earliest possible time.

(IV) a timeline for the completion of such studies.

(B) Annual review.

(i) In general. On an annual basis following the approval of a deferral under subparagraph (A), the applicant shall submit to the Secretary the following information:

(I) Information detailing the progress made in conducting pediatric studies.

(II) If no progress has been made in conducting such studies, evidence and documentation that such studies will be conducted with due diligence and at the earliest possible time.

(ii) Public availability. The information submitted through the annual review under clause (i) shall promptly be made available to the public in an easily accessible manner, including through the Web site of the Food and Drug Administration.

(4) Waivers.

(A) Full waiver. On the initiative of the Secretary or at the request of an applicant, the Secretary shall grant a full waiver, as appropriate, of the requirement to submit assessments for a drug or biological product under this subsection if the applicant certifies and the Secretary finds that--

(i) necessary studies are impossible or highly impracticable (because, for example, the number of patients is so small or the patients are geographically dispersed);

(ii) there is evidence strongly suggesting that the drug or biological product would be ineffective or unsafe in all pediatric age groups; or

(iii) the drug or biological product—

(I) does not represent a meaningful therapeutic benefit over existing therapies for pediatric patients; and

(II) is not likely to be used in a substantial number of pediatric patients.

(B) partial waiver. On the initiative of the Secretary or at the request of an applicant, the Secretary shall grant a partial waiver, as appropriate, of the requirement to submit assessments for a drug or biological product under this subsection with respect to a specific pediatric age group if the applicant certifies and the Secretary finds that—

(i) necessary studies are impossible or highly impracticable (because, for example, the number of patients in that age group is so small or patients in that age group are geographically dispersed);

(ii) there is evidence strongly suggesting that the drug or biological product would be ineffective or unsafe in that age group;

(iii) the drug or biological product—

(I) does not represent a meaningful therapeutic benefit over existing therapies for pediatric patients in that age group; and

(II) is not likely to be used by a substantial number of pediatric patients in that age group; or

(iv) the applicant can demonstrate that reasonable attempts to produce a pediatric formulation necessary for that age group have failed

(C) Pediatric formulation not possible. If a waiver is granted on the ground that it is not possible to develop a pediatric formulation, the waiver shall cover only the pediatric groups requiring that formulation. An applicant seeking either a full or partial waiver shall submit to the Secretary documentation detailing why a pediatric formulation cannot be developed and, if the waiver is granted, the applicant's submission shall promptly be made available to the public in an easily accessible manner, including through posting on the Web site of the Food and Drug Administration.

(D) Labeling requirement. If the Secretary grants a full or partial waiver because there is evidence that a drug or biological product would be ineffective or unsafe in pediatric populations, the information shall be included in the labeling for the drug or biological product.

(b) Marketed drugs and biological products.

(1) In general. After providing notice in the form of a letter (that, for a drug approved under section 505, references a declined written request under section 505A for a labeled indication which written request is not referred under section 505A(n)(1)(A) to the Foundation of the National Institutes of Health for the pediatric studies), the Secretary may (by order in the form of a letter) require the sponsor or holder of an approved application for a drug under section 505 or the holder of a license for a biological product under section 351 of the Public Health Service Act [42 USC 262] to submit by a specified date the assessments described in subsection (a)(2), if the Secretary finds that—

(A)(i) the drug or biological product is used for a substantial number of pediatric patients for the labeled indications; and

(ii) adequate pediatric labeling could confer a benefit on pediatric patients;

(B) there is reason to believe that the drug or biological product would represent a meaningful therapeutic benefit over existing therapies for pediatric patients for 1 or more of the claimed indications; or

(C) the absence of adequate pediatric labeling could pose a risk to pediatric patients.

(2) Waivers.

(A) Full waiver. At the request of an applicant, the Secretary shall grant a full waiver, as appropriate, of the requirement to submit assessments under this subsection if the applicant certifies and the Secretary finds that--

(i) necessary studies are impossible or highly impracticable (because, for example, the number of patients in that age group is so small or patients in that age group are geographically dispersed); or

(ii) there is evidence strongly suggesting that the drug or biological product would be ineffective or unsafe in all pediatric age groups.

(B) Partial waiver. At the request of an applicant, the Secretary shall grant a partial waiver, as appropriate, of the requirement to submit assessments under this subsection with respect to a specific pediatric age group if the applicant certifies and the Secretary finds that--

(i) necessary studies are impossible or highly impracticable (because, for example, the number of patients in that age group is so small or patients in that age group are geographically dispersed);

(ii) there is evidence strongly suggesting that the drug or biological product would be ineffective or unsafe in that age group;

(iii)(I) the drug or biological product--

(aa) does not represent a meaningful therapeutic benefit over existing therapies for pediatric patients in that age group; and

(bb) is not likely to be used in a substantial number of pediatric patients in that age group; and

(II) the absence of adequate labeling could not pose significant risks to pediatric patients; or

(iv) the applicant can demonstrate that reasonable attempts to produce a pediatric formulation necessary for that age group have failed.

(C) Pediatric formulation not possible. If a waiver is granted on the ground that it is not possible to develop a pediatric formulation, the waiver shall cover only the pediatric groups requiring that formulation. An applicant seeking either a full or partial waiver shall submit to the Secretary documentation detailing why a pediatric formulation cannot be developed and, if the waiver is granted, the applicant's submission shall promptly be made available to the public in an easily accessible manner, including through posting on the Web site of the Food and Drug Administration.

(D) Labeling requirement. If the Secretary grants a full or partial waiver because there is evidence that a drug or biological product would be ineffective or unsafe in pediatric populations, the information shall be included in the labeling for the drug or biological product.

(3) Effect of subsection. Nothing in this subsection alters or amends section 301(j) of this Act or section 552 of title 5 [5 USC § 552] or section 1905 of title 18, United States Code [18 USC § 1905].

(c) Meaningful therapeutic benefit. For the purposes of paragraph (4)(A)(iii)(I) and (4)(B)(iii)(I) of subsection (a) and paragraphs (1)(B) and (2)(B)(iii)(I)(aa) of subsection (b), a drug or biological product shall be considered to represent a meaningful therapeutic benefit over existing therapies if the Secretary determines that--

(1) if approved, the drug or biological product could represent an improvement in the treatment, diagnosis, or prevention of a disease, compared with

marketed products adequately labeled for that use in the relevant pediatric population; or

(2) the drug or biological product is in a class of products or for an indication for which there is a need for additional options.

(d) Submission of assessments. If a person fails to submit an assessment described in subsection (a)(2), or a request for approval of a pediatric formulation described in subsection (a) or (b), in accordance with applicable provisions of subsections (a) and (b)--

(1) the drug or biological product that is the subject of the assessment or request may be considered misbranded solely because of that failure and subject to relevant enforcement action (except that the drug or biological product shall not be subject to action under section 303); but

(2) the failure to submit the assessment or request shall not be the basis for a proceeding--

(A) to withdraw approval for a drug under section 505(e); or

(B) to revoke the license for a biological product under section 351 of the Public Health Service Act [42 USC § 262].

(e) Meetings. Before and during the investigational process for a new drug or biological product, the Secretary shall meet at appropriate times with the sponsor of the new drug or biological product to discuss--

(1) information that the sponsor submits on plans and timelines for pediatric studies; or

(2) any planned request by the sponsor for waiver or deferral of pediatric studies.

(f) Review of pediatric plans, assessments, deferrals, and waivers.

(1) Review. Beginning not later than 30 days after the date of the enactment of the Pediatric Research Equity Act of 2007 [enacted Sept. 27, 2007], the Secretary shall utilize the internal committee established under section 505C [21 USC § 355d] to provide consultation to reviewing divisions on all pediatric plans and assessments prior to approval of an application or supplement for which a pediatric assessment is required under this section and all deferral and waiver requests granted pursuant to this section.

(2) Activity by committee. The committee referred to in paragraph (1) may operate using appropriate members of such committee and need not convene all members of the committee.

(3) Documentation of committee action. For each drug or biological product, the committee referred to in paragraph (1) shall document, for each activity

described in paragraph (4) or (5), which members of the committee participated in such activity.

(4) Review of pediatric plans, assessments, deferrals, and waivers. Consultation on pediatric plans and assessments by the committee referred to in paragraph (1) pursuant to this section shall occur prior to approval of an application or supplement for which a pediatric assessment is required under this section. The committee shall review all requests for deferrals and waivers from the requirement to submit a pediatric assessment granted under this section and shall provide recommendations as needed to reviewing divisions, including with respect to whether such a supplement, when submitted, shall be considered for priority review.

(5) Retrospective review of pediatric assessments, deferrals, and waivers. Not later than 1 year after the date of the enactment of the Pediatric Research Equity Act of 2007 [enacted Sept. 27, 2007], the committee referred to in paragraph (1) shall conduct a retrospective review and analysis of a representative sample of assessments submitted and deferrals and waivers approved under this section since the enactment of the Pediatric Research Equity Act of 2003 [enacted Sept. 27, 2007]. Such review shall include an analysis of the quality and consistency of pediatric information in pediatric assessments and the appropriateness of waivers and deferrals granted. Based on such review, the Secretary shall issue recommendations to the review divisions for improvements and initiate guidance to industry related to the scope of pediatric studies required under this section.

(6) Tracking of assessments and labeling changes. The Secretary, in consultation with the committee referred to in paragraph (1), shall track and make available to the public in an easily accessible manner, including through posting on the Web site of the Food and Drug Administration--

(A) the number of assessments conducted under this section;

(B) the specific drugs and biological products and their uses assessed under this section;

(C) the types of assessments conducted under this section, including trial design, the number of pediatric patients studied, and the number of centers and countries involved;

(D) the total number of deferrals requested and granted under this section and, if granted, the reasons for such deferrals, the timeline for completion, and the number completed and pending by the specified date, as outlined in subsection (a)(3);

(E) the number of waivers requested and granted under this section and, if granted, the reasons for the waivers;

(F) the number of pediatric formulations developed and the number of pediatric formulations not developed and the reasons any such formulation was not developed;

(G) the labeling changes made as a result of assessments conducted under this section;

(H) an annual summary of labeling changes made as a result of assessments conducted under this section for distribution pursuant to subsection (h)(2);

(I) an annual summary of information submitted pursuant to subsection (a)(3)(B); and

(J) the number of times the committee referred to in paragraph (1) made a recommendation to the Secretary under paragraph (4) regarding priority review, the number of times the Secretary followed or did not follow such a recommendation, and, if not followed, the reasons why such a recommendation was not followed.

(g) Labeling changes.

(1) Dispute resolution.

(A) Request for labeling change and failure to agree. If, on or after the date of the enactment of the Pediatric Research Equity Act of 2007 [enacted Sept. 27, 2007], the Commissioner determines that a sponsor and the Commissioner have been unable to reach agreement on appropriate changes to the labeling for the drug that is the subject of the application or supplement, not later than 180 days after the date of the submission of the application or supplement--

(i) the Commissioner shall request that the sponsor of the application make any labeling change that the Commissioner determines to be appropriate; and

(ii) if the sponsor does not agree within 30 days after the Commissioner's request to make a labeling change requested by the Commissioner, the Commissioner shall refer the matter to the Pediatric Advisory Committee.

(B) Action by the Pediatric Advisory Committee. Not later than 90 days after receiving a referral under subparagraph (A)(ii), the Pediatric Advisory Committee shall--

(i) review the pediatric study reports; and

(ii) make a recommendation to the Commissioner concerning appropriate labeling changes, if any.

(C) Consideration of recommendations. The Commissioner shall consider the recommendations of the Pediatric Advisory Committee and, if appropriate, not later than 30 days after receiving the recommendation, make a request to the sponsor of the application or supplement to make any labeling changes that the Commissioner determines to be appropriate.

(D) Misbranding. If the sponsor of the application or supplement, within 30 days after receiving a request under subparagraph (C), does not agree to make a labeling change requested by the Commissioner, the Commissioner may deem the drug that is the subject of the application or supplement to be misbranded.

(E) No effect on authority. Nothing in this subsection limits the authority of the United States to bring an enforcement action under this Act when a drug lacks appropriate pediatric labeling. Neither course of action (the Pediatric Advisory Committee process or an enforcement action referred to in the preceding sentence) shall preclude, delay, or serve as the basis to stay the other course of action.

(2) Other labeling changes. If, on or after the date of the enactment of the Pediatric Research Equity Act of 2007 [enacted Sept. 27, 2007], the Secretary makes a determination that a pediatric assessment conducted under this section does or does not demonstrate that the drug that is the subject of such assessment is safe and effective in pediatric populations or subpopulations, including whether such assessment results are inconclusive, the Secretary shall order the label of such product to include information about the results of the assessment and a statement of the Secretary's determination.

(h) Dissemination of pediatric information.

(1) In general. Not later than 210 days after the date of submission of a pediatric assessment under this section, the Secretary shall make available to the public in an easily accessible manner the medical, statistical, and clinical pharmacology reviews of such pediatric assessments, and shall post such assessments on the Web site of the Food and Drug Administration.

(2) Dissemination of information regarding labeling changes. Beginning on the date of the enactment of the Pediatric Research Equity Act of 2007 [enacted Sept. 27, 2007], the Secretary shall require that the sponsors of the assessments that result in labeling changes that are reflected in the annual summary developed pursuant to subsection (f)(6)(H) distribute such information to physicians and other health care providers.

(3) Effect of subsection. Nothing in this subsection shall alter or amend section 301(j) of this Act [21 USC § 331(j)] or section 552 of title 5 [5 USC § 552] or section 1905 of title 18, United States Code [18 USC § 1905].

(i) Adverse event reporting.

(1) Reporting in year one. Beginning on the date of the enactment of the Pediatric Research Equity Act of 2007 [enacted Sept. 27, 2007], during the one-year period beginning on the date a labeling change is made pursuant to subsection (g), the Secretary shall ensure that all adverse event reports that have been received for such drug (regardless of when such report was received) are referred to the Office of Pediatric Therapeutics. In considering such reports, the Director of such Office shall provide for the review of such reports by the Pediatric Advisory Committee, including obtaining any recommendations of such committee regarding whether the Secretary should take action under this Act in response to such reports.

(2) Reporting in subsequent years. Following the one-year period described in paragraph (1), the Secretary shall, as appropriate, refer to the Office of Pediatric Therapeutics all pediatric adverse event reports for a drug for which a pediatric study was conducted under this section. In considering such reports, the Director of such Office may provide for the review of such reports by the Pediatric Advisory Committee, including obtaining any recommendation of such Committee regarding whether the Secretary should take action in response to such reports.

(3) Effect. The requirements of this subsection shall supplement, not supplant, other review of such adverse event reports by the Secretary.

(j) SCOPE OF AUTHORITY- Nothing in this section provides to the Secretary any authority to require a pediatric assessment of any drug or biological product, or any assessment regarding other populations or uses of a drug or biological product, other than the pediatric assessments described in this section.

(k) Orphan drugs. Unless the Secretary requires otherwise by regulation, this section does not apply to any drug for an indication for which orphan designation has been granted under section 526 [21 USC § 360bb].

(l) Institute of Medicine study.

(1) In general. Not later than three years after the date of the enactment of the Pediatric Research Equity Act of 2007 [enacted Sept. 27, 2007], the Secretary shall contract with the Institute of Medicine to conduct a study and report to Congress regarding the pediatric studies conducted pursuant to this section or precursor regulations since 1997 and labeling changes made as a result of such studies.

(2) Content of study. The study under paragraph (1) shall review and assess the use of extrapolation for pediatric subpopulations, the use of alternative endpoints for pediatric populations, neonatal assessment tools, the number and type of pediatric adverse events, and ethical issues in pediatric clinical trials.

(3) Representative sample. The Institute of Medicine may devise an appropriate mechanism to review a representative sample of studies conducted pursuant to this section from each review division within the Center for Drug Evaluation and Research in order to make the requested assessment.

(m) Integration with other pediatric studies. The authority under this section shall remain in effect so long as an application subject to this section may be accepted for filing by the Secretary on or before the date specified in section 505A(q) [21 USC § 355a(q)].

SEC. 505C. [21 USC §355d] Internal Committee for Review of Pediatric Plans, Assessments, Deferrals, and Waivers

Note: This section was added in February 2008.

The Secretary shall establish an internal committee within the Food and Drug Administration to carry out the activities as described in sections 505A(f) and 505B(f). Such internal committee shall include employees of the Food and Drug Administration, with expertise in pediatrics (including representation from the Office of Pediatric Therapeutics), biopharmacology, statistics, chemistry, legal issues, pediatric ethics, and the appropriate expertise pertaining to the pediatric product under review, such as expertise in child and adolescent psychiatry, and other individuals designated by the Secretary.

SEC. 505D. [21 USC §355d] Pharmaceutical Security

Note: This section was added in February 2008.

(a) In general. The Secretary shall develop standards and identify and validate effective technologies for the purpose of securing the drug supply chain against counterfeit, diverted, subpotent, substandard, adulterated, misbranded, or expired drugs.

(b) Standards development.

(1) In general. The Secretary shall, in consultation with the agencies specified in paragraph (4), manufacturers, distributors, pharmacies, and other supply chain stakeholders, prioritize and develop standards for the identification, validation, authentication, and tracking and tracing of prescription drugs.

(2) Standardized numeral identifier. Not later than 30 months after the date of the enactment of the Food and Drug Administration Amendments Act of 2007 [enacted Sept. 27, 2007], the Secretary shall develop a standardized numerical identifier (which, to the extent practicable, shall be harmonized with international consensus standards for such an identifier) to be applied to a prescription drug at the point of manufacturing and repackaging (in which case the numerical identifier shall be linked to the numerical identifier applied

at the point of manufacturing) at the package or pallet level, sufficient to facilitate the identification, validation, authentication, and tracking and tracing of the prescription drug.

(3) Promising technologies. The standards developed under this subsection shall address promising technologies, which may include--

(A) radio frequency identification technology;

(B) nanotechnology;

(C) encryption technologies; and

(D) other track-and-trace or authentication technologies.

(4) Interagency collaboration. In carrying out this subsection, the Secretary shall consult with Federal health and security agencies, including--

(A) the Department of Justice;

(B) the Department of Homeland Security;

(C) the Department of Commerce; and

(D) other appropriate Federal and State agencies.

(c) Inspection and enforcement.

(1) In general. The Secretary shall expand and enhance the resources and facilities of agency components of the Food and Drug Administration involved with regulatory and criminal enforcement of this Act [21 USC §§ 301 et seq.] to secure the drug supply chain against counterfeit, diverted, subpotent, substandard, adulterated, misbranded, or expired drugs including biological products and active pharmaceutical ingredients from domestic and foreign sources.

(2) Activities. The Secretary shall undertake enhanced and joint enforcement activities with other Federal and State agencies, and establish regional capacities for the validation of prescription drugs and the inspection of the prescription drug supply chain.

(d) Definition. In this section, the term "***prescription drug***" means a drug subject to section 503(b)(1) [21 USC § 353(b)(1)].

SEC. 506. [21 USC §356] Fast Track Products

(a) DESIGNATION OF DRUG AS A FAST TRACK PRODUCT.—

(1) IN GENERAL.—The Secretary shall, at the request of the sponsor of a new drug, facilitate the development and expedite the review of such drug if it is intended for the treatment of a serious or life-threatening condition and it demonstrates the potential to address unmet medical needs for such a

condition. (In this section, such a drug is referred to as a "fast track product".)

(2) REQUEST FOR DESIGNATION.—The sponsor of a new drug may request the Secretary to designate the drug as a fast track product. A request for the designation may be made concurrently with, or at any time after, submission of an application for the investigation of the drug under section 505(i) or section 351(a)(3) of the Public Health Service Act.

(3) DESIGNATION.—Within 60 calendar days after the receipt of a request under paragraph (2), the Secretary shall determine whether the drug that is the subject of the request meets the criteria described in paragraph (1). If the Secretary finds that the drug meets the criteria, the Secretary shall designate the drug as a fast track product and shall take such actions as are appropriate to expedite the development and review of the application for approval of such product.

(b) APPROVAL OF APPLICATION FOR A FAST TRACK PRODUCT.—

(1) IN GENERAL.—The Secretary may approve an application for approval of a fast track product under section 505(c) or section 351 of the Public Health Service Act upon a determination that the product has an effect on a clinical endpoint or on a surrogate endpoint that is reasonably likely to predict clinical benefit.

(2) LIMITATION.—Approval of a fast track product under this subsection may be subject to the requirements—

(A) that the sponsor conduct appropriate post-approval studies to validate the surrogate endpoint or otherwise confirm the effect on the clinical endpoint; and

(B) that the sponsor submit copies of all promotional materials related to the fast track product during the preapproval review period and, following approval and for such period thereafter as the Secretary determines to be appropriate, at least 30 days prior to dissemination of the materials.

(3) EXPEDITED WITHDRAWAL OF APPROVAL.—The Secretary may withdraw approval of a fast track product using expedited procedures (as prescribed by the Secretary in regulations which shall include an opportunity for an informal hearing) if—

(A) the sponsor fails to conduct any required post-approval study of the fast track drug with due diligence;

(B) a post-approval study of the fast track product fails to verify clinical benefit of the product;

(C) other evidence demonstrates that the fast track product is not safe or effective under the conditions of use; or

(D) the sponsor disseminates false or misleading promotional materials with respect to the product.

(c) REVIEW OF INCOMPLETE APPLICATIONS FOR APPROVAL OF A FAST TRACK PRODUCT.—

(1) IN GENERAL.—If the Secretary determines, after preliminary evaluation of clinical data submitted by the sponsor, that a fast track product may be effective, the Secretary shall evaluate for filing, and may commence review of portions of, an application for the approval of the product before the sponsor submits a complete application. The Secretary shall commence such review only if the applicant—

(A) provides a schedule for submission of information necessary to make the application complete; and

(B) pays any fee that may be required under section 736.

(2) EXCEPTION.—Any time period for review of human drug applications that has been agreed to by the Secretary and that has been set forth in goals identified in letters of the Secretary (relating to the use of fees collected under section 736 to expedite the drug development process and the review of human drug applications) shall not apply to an application submitted under paragraph (1) until the date on which the application is complete.

(d) AWARENESS EFFORTS.—The Secretary shall—

(1) develop and disseminate to physicians, patient organizations, pharmaceutical and biotechnology companies, and other appropriate persons a description of the provisions of this section applicable to fast track products; and

(2) establish a program to encourage the development of surrogate endpoints that are reasonably likely to predict clinical benefit for serious or life-threatening conditions for which there exist significant unmet medical needs.

SEC. 506A. [21 USC §356a] Manufacturing Changes

(a) IN GENERAL.—With respect to a drug for which there is in effect an approved application under section 505 or 512 or a license under section 351 of the Public Health Service Act, a change from the manufacturing process approved pursuant to such application or license may be made, and the drug as made with the change may be distributed, if—

(1) the holder of the approved application or license (referred to in this section as a "holder") has validated the effects of the change in accordance with subsection (b); and

(2)(A) in the case of a major manufacturing change, the holder has complied with the requirements of subsection (c); or

(B) in the case of a change that is not a major manufacturing change, the holder complies with the applicable requirements of subsection (d).

(b) VALIDATION OF EFFECTS OF CHANGES.—For purposes of subsection (a)(1), a drug made with a manufacturing change (whether a major manufacturing change or otherwise) may be distributed only if, before distribution of the drug as so made, the holder involved validates the effects of the change on the identity, strength, quality, purity, and potency of the drug as the identity, strength, quality, purity, and potency may relate to the safety or effectiveness of the drug.

(c) MAJOR MANUFACTURING CHANGES.—

(1) REQUIREMENT OF SUPPLEMENTAL APPLICATION.—For purposes of subsection (a)(2)(A), a drug made with a major manufacturing change may be distributed only if, before the distribution of the drug as so made, the holder involved submits to the Secretary a supplemental application for such change and the Secretary approves the application. The application shall contain such information as the Secretary determines to be appropriate, and shall include the information developed under subsection (b) by the holder in validating the effects of the change.

(2) CHANGES QUALIFYING AS MAJOR CHANGES.—For purposes of subsection (a)(2)(A), a major manufacturing change is a manufacturing change that is determined by the Secretary to have substantial potential to adversely affect the identity, strength, quality, purity, or potency of the drug as they may relate to the safety or effectiveness of a drug. Such a change includes a change that—

(A) is made in the qualitative or quantitative formulation of the drug involved or in the specifications in the approved application or license referred to in subsection (a) for the drug (unless exempted by the Secretary by regulation or guidance from the requirements of this subsection);

(B) is determined by the Secretary by regulation or guidance to require completion of an appropriate clinical study demonstrating equivalence of the drug to the drug as manufactured without the change; or

(C) is another type of change determined by the Secretary by regulation or guidance to have a substantial potential to adversely affect the safety or effectiveness of the drug.

(d) OTHER MANUFACTURING CHANGES.—

(1) IN GENERAL.—For purposes of subsection (a)(2)(B), the Secretary may regulate drugs made with manufacturing changes that are not major manufacturing changes as follows:

(A) The Secretary may in accordance with paragraph (2) authorize holders to distribute such drugs without submitting a supplemental application for such changes.

(B) The Secretary may in accordance with paragraph (3) require that, prior to the distribution of such drugs, holders submit to the Secretary supplemental applications for such changes.

(C) The Secretary may establish categories of such changes and designate categories to which subparagraph (A) applies and categories to which subparagraph (B) applies.

(2) CHANGES NOT REQUIRING SUPPLEMENTAL APPLICATION.—

(A) SUBMISSION OF REPORT.—A holder making a manufacturing change to which paragraph (1)(A) applies shall submit to the Secretary a report on the change, which shall contain such information as the Secretary determines to be appropriate, and which shall include the information developed under subsection (b) by the holder in validating the effects of the change. The report shall be submitted by such date as the Secretary may specify.

(B) AUTHORITY REGARDING ANNUAL REPORTS.—In the case of a holder that during a single year makes more than one manufacturing change to which paragraph (1)(A) applies, the Secretary may in carrying out subparagraph (A) authorize the holder to comply with such subparagraph by submitting a single report for the year that provides the information required in such subparagraph for all the changes made by the holder during the year.

(3) CHANGES REQUIRING SUPPLEMENTAL APPLICATION.—

(A) SUBMISSION OF SUPPLEMENTAL APPLICATION.—The supplemental application required under paragraph (1)(B) for a manufacturing change shall contain such information as the Secretary determines to be appropriate, which shall include the information developed under subsection (b) by the holder in validating the effects of the change.

(B) AUTHORITY FOR DISTRIBUTION.—In the case of a manufacturing change to which paragraph (1)(B) applies:

(i) The holder involved may commence distribution of the drug involved 30 days after the Secretary receives the supplemental application under such paragraph, unless the Secretary notifies the holder within such 30-day period that prior approval of the application is required before distribution may be commenced.

(ii) The Secretary may designate a category of such changes for the purpose of providing that, in the case of a change that is in such category, the holder involved may commence distribution of the drug involved upon the receipt by the Secretary of a supplemental application for the change.

(iii) If the Secretary disapproves the supplemental application, the Secretary may order the manufacturer to cease the distribution of the drugs that have been made with the manufacturing change.

SEC. 506B. [21 USC §356b] Reports of Postmarketing Studies

(a) SUBMISSION.—

(1) IN GENERAL.—A sponsor of a drug that has entered into an agreement with the Secretary to conduct a postmarketing study of a drug shall submit to the Secretary, within 1 year after the approval of such drug and annually thereafter until the study is completed or terminated, a report of the progress of the study or the reasons for the failure of the sponsor to conduct the study. The report shall be submitted in such form as is prescribed by the Secretary in regulations issued by the Secretary.

(2) AGREEMENTS PRIOR TO EFFECTIVE DATE.—Any agreement entered into between the Secretary and a sponsor of a drug, prior to the date of enactment of the Food and Drug Administration Modernization Act of 1997, to conduct a postmarketing study of a drug shall be subject to the requirements of paragraph (1). An initial report for such an agreement shall be submitted within 6 months after the date of the issuance of the regulations under paragraph (1).

(b) CONSIDERATION OF INFORMATION AS PUBLIC INFORMATION.—Any information pertaining to a report described in subsection (a) shall be considered to be public information to the extent that the information is necessary—

(1) to identify the sponsor; and

(2) to establish the status of a study described in subsection (a) and the reasons, if any, for any failure to carry out the study.

(c) STATUS OF STUDIES AND REPORTS.—The Secretary shall annually develop and publish in the Federal Register a report that provides information on the status of the postmarketing studies—

(1) that sponsors have entered into agreements to conduct; and

(2) for which reports have been submitted under subsection (a)(1).

(d) DISCLOSURE.—If a sponsor fails to complete an agreed upon study required by this section by its original or otherwise negotiated deadline, the Secretary shall publish a statement on the Internet site of the Food and Drug Administration stating that the study was not completed and, if the reasons for such failure to complete the study were not satisfactory to the Secretary, a statement that such reasons were not satisfactory to the Secretary.

(e) NOTIFICATION.—With respect to studies of the type required under section 506(b)(2)(A) or under section 314.510 or 601.41 of title 21, Code of Federal Regulations, as each of such sections was in effect on the day before the effective date 29 of this subsection, the Secretary may require that a sponsor who, for reasons not satisfactory to the Secretary, fails to complete by its deadline a study under any of such sections of such type for a drug or biological product (including such a study conducted after such effective date) notify practitioners who prescribe such drug or biological product of the failure to complete such study and the questions of clinical benefit, and, where appropriate, questions of safety, that remain unanswered as a result of the failure to complete such study. Nothing in this subsection shall be construed as altering the requirements of the types of studies required under section 506(b)(2)(A) or under section 314.510 or 601.41 of title 21, Code of Federal Regulations, as so in effect, or as prohibiting the Secretary from modifying such sections of title 21 of such Code to provide for studies in addition to those of such type..

SEC. 506C. [21 USC §356c] Discontinuance of a Lifesaving Product

(a) IN GENERAL.—A manufacturer that is the sole manufacturer of a drug—

(1) that is—

(A) life-supporting;

(B) life-sustaining; or

(C) intended for use in the prevention of a debilitating disease or condition;

(2) for which an application has been approved under section 505(b) or 505(j); and

(3) that is not a product that was originally derived from human tissue and was replaced by a recombinant product, shall notify the Secretary of a discontinuance of the manufacture of the drug at least 6 months prior to the date of the discontinuance.

(b) REDUCTION IN NOTIFICATION PERIOD.—The notification period required under subsection (a) for a manufacturer may be reduced if the manufacturer certifies to the Secretary that good cause exists for the reduction, such as a situation in which—

(1) a public health problem may result from continuation of the manufacturing for the 6-month period;

(2) a biomaterials shortage prevents the continuation of the manufacturing for the 6-month period;

(3) a liability problem may exist for the manufacturer if the manufacturing is continued for the 6-month period;

(4) continuation of the manufacturing for the 6-month period may cause substantial economic hardship for the manufacturer;

(5) the manufacturer has filed for bankruptcy under chapter 7 or 11 of title 11, United States Code; or

(6) the manufacturer can continue the distribution of the drug involved for 6 months.

(c) DISTRIBUTION.—To the maximum extent practicable, the Secretary shall distribute information on the discontinuation of the drugs described in subsection (a) to appropriate physician and patient organizations.

[Section 507 repealed by Pub. L. 105–115, November 21, 1997.]

SEC. 508. [21 USC §358] Authority to Designate Official Names

(a) [27] The Secretary may designate an official name for any drug or device if he determines that such action is necessary or desirable in the interest of usefulness and simplicity. Any official name designated under this section for any drug or device shall be the only official name of that drug or device used in any official compendium published after such name has been prescribed or for any other purpose of this Act. In no event, however, shall the Secretary establish an official name so as to infringe a valid trademark.

(b) Within a reasonable time after the effective date of this section, and at such other times as he may deem necessary, the Secretary shall cause a review to be made of the official names by which drugs are identified in the official United States Pharmacopeia, the official Homeopathic Pharmacopeia of the United States, and the official National Formulary, and all supplements thereto, and at such times as he may deem necessary shall cause a review to be made of the official names by which devices are identified in any official compendium (and all supplements thereto) to determine whether revision of any of those names is necessary or desirable in the interest of usefulness and simplicity.

(c) Whenever he determines after any such review that (1) any such official name is unduly complex or is not useful for any other reason, (2) two or more official names have been applied to a single drug or device, or to two or more drugs which are identical in chemical structure and pharmacological action and which are substantially identical in strength, quality, and purity, or to two or more

[27] Section 507 was struck by section 125(b)(1) of Public Law 105–115 (111 Stat. 2325).

devices which are substantially equivalent in design and purpose or (3) no official name has been applied to a medically useful drug or device, he shall transmit in writing to the compiler of each official compendium in which that drug or drugs or device are identified and recognized his request for the recommendation of a single official name for such drug or drugs or device which will have usefulness and simplicity. Whenever such a single official name has not been recommended within one hundred and eighty days after such request, or the Secretary determines that any name so recommended is not useful for any reason, he shall designate a single official name for such drug or drugs or device. Whenever he determines that the name so recommended is useful, he shall designate that name as the official name of such drug or drugs or device. Such designation shall be made as a regulation upon public notice and in accordance with the procedure set forth in section 553 of title 5, United States Code.

(d) After each such review, and at such other times as the Secretary may determine to be necessary or desirable, the Secretary shall cause to be compiled, published, and publicly distributed a list which shall list all revised official names of drugs or devices designated under this section and shall contain such descriptive and explanatory matter as the Secretary may determine to be required for the effective use of those names.

(e) Upon a request in writing by any compiler of any official compendium that the Secretary exercise the authority granted to him under section 508(a), he shall upon public notice and in accordance with the procedure set forth in section 553 of title 5, United States Code designate the official name of the drug or device for which the request is made.

SEC. 509. [21 USC §359] Nonapplicability to Cosmetics

This chapter, as amended by the Drug Amendments of 1962, shall not apply to any cosmetic unless such cosmetic is also a drug or device or component thereof.

SEC. 510. [21 USC §360] Registration of Producers of Drugs and Devices

Note: revisions were posted to this section in February 2008.

(a) [28] Definitions. As used in this section—

[28] The purpose of section 510 was stated in section 301 of Public Law 82–781 as follows:
"SEC. 301. The Congress hereby finds and declares that in order to make regulation of interstate commerce in drugs effective, it is necessary to provide for registration and inspection of all establishments in which drugs are manufactured, prepared, propagated, compounded, or processed; that the products of all such establishments are likely to enter the channels of interstate commerce and directly affect such commerce; and that the regulation of interstate commerce in drugs without provision for registration and inspection of establishments that may be engaged only in intrastate commerce in such drugs would discriminate against and

(1) the term "***manufacture, preparation, propagation, compounding, or processing***" shall include repackaging or otherwise changing the container, wrapper, or labeling of any drug package or device package in furtherance of the distribution of the drug or device from the original place of manufacture to the person who makes final delivery or sale to the ultimate consumer or user; and

(2) the term "***name***" shall include in the case of a partnership the name of each partner and, in the case of a corporation, the name of each corporate officer and director, and the State of incorporation.

(b) Annual registration.

(1) On or before December 31 of each year every person who owns or operates any establishment in any State engaged in the manufacture, preparation, propagation, compounding, or processing of a drug or drugs or a device or devices shall register with the Secretary his name, places of business, and all such establishments.

(2) During the period beginning on October 1 and ending on December 31 of each year, every person who owns or operates any establishment in any State engaged in the manufacture, preparation, propagation, compounding, or processing of a device or devices shall register with the Secretary his name, places of business, and all such establishments.

(c) New producers. Every person upon first engaging in the manufacture, preparation, propagation, compounding, or processing of a drug or drugs or a device or devices in any establishment which he owns or operates in any State shall immediately register with the Secretary his name, place of business, and such establishment.

(d) Additional establishments. Every person duly registered in accordance with the foregoing subsections of this section shall immediately register with the Secretary any additional establishment which he owns or operates in any State and in which he begins the manufacture, preparation, propagation, compounding, or processing of a drug or drugs or a device or devices.

(e) Registration number; uniform system for identification of devices intended for human use. The Secretary may assign a registration number to any person or any establishment registered in accordance with this section. The Secretary may also assign a listing number to each drug or class of drugs listed under subsection (j). Any number assigned pursuant to the preceding sentence shall be the same as that assigned pursuant to the National Drug Code. The Secretary may by regulation prescribe a uniform system for the identification of devices intended for human

---

depress interstate commerce in such drugs, and adversely burden, obstruct, and affect such interstate commerce."

use and may require that persons who are required to list such devices pursuant to subsection (j) shall list such devices in accordance with such system.

(f) Availability of registrations for inspection. The Secretary shall make available for inspection, to any person so requesting, any registration filed pursuant to this section; except that any list submitted pursuant to paragraph (3) of subsection (j) and the information accompanying any list or notice filed under paragraph (1) or (2) of that subsection shall be exempt from such inspection unless the Secretary finds that such an exemption would be inconsistent with protection of the public health.

(g) Exclusions from application of section. The foregoing subsections of this section shall not apply to—

(1) pharmacies which maintain establishments in conformance with any applicable local laws regulating the practice of pharmacy and medicine and which are regularly engaged in dispensing prescription drugs or devices, upon prescriptions of practitioners licensed to administer such drugs or devices to patients under the care of such practitioners in the course of their professional practice, and which do not manufacture, prepare, propagate, compound, or process drugs or devices for sale other than in the regular course of their business of dispensing or selling drugs or devices at retail;

(2) practitioners licensed by law to prescribe or administer drugs or devices and who manufacture, prepare, propagate, compound, or process drugs or devices solely for use in the course of their professional practice;

(3) persons who manufacture, prepare, propagate, compound, or process drugs or devices solely for use in research, teaching, or chemical analysis and not for sale;

(4) any distributor who acts as a wholesale distributor of devices, and who does not manufacture, repackage, process, or relabel a device; or

(5) such other classes of persons as the Secretary may by regulation exempt from the application of this section upon a finding that registration by such classes of persons in accordance with this section is not necessary for the protection of the public health.

In this subsection, the term "wholesale distributor" means any person (other than the manufacturer or the initial importer) who distributes a device from the original place of manufacture to the person who makes the final delivery or sale of the device to the ultimate consumer or user.

(h) Inspection of premises. Every establishment in any State registered with the Secretary pursuant to this section shall be subject to inspection pursuant to section 704 and every such establishment engaged in the manufacture, propagation, compounding, or processing of a drug or drugs or of a device or devices classified in class II or III shall be so inspected by one or more officers or employees duly designated by the Secretary , or by persons accredited to conduct inspections under section 704(g), at least once in the two-year period beginning with the date of registration of such establishment pursuant to this section and at least once in every successive two-year period thereafter.

(i) Registration of foreign establishments.

(1) Any establishment within any foreign country engaged in the manufacture, preparation, propagation, compounding, or processing of a drug or device that is imported or offered for import into the United States shall, through electronic means in accordance with the criteria of the Secretary--

(A) upon first engaging in any such activity, immediately register with the Secretary the name and place of business of the establishment, the name of the United States agent for the establishment, the name of each importer of such drug or device in the United States that is known to the establishment, and the name of each person who imports or offers for import such drug or device to the United States for purposes of importation, and

(B) each establishment subject to the requirements of subparagraph (A) shall thereafter--

(i) with respect to drugs, register with the Secretary on or before December 31 of each year; and

(ii) with respect to devices, register with the Secretary during the period beginning on October 1 and ending on December 31 of each year.

(2) The establishment shall also provide the information required by subsection (j).

(3) The Secretary is authorized to enter into cooperative arrangements with officials of foreign countries to ensure that adequate and effective means are available for purposes of determining, from time to time, whether drugs or devices manufactured, prepared, propagated, compounded, or processed by an establishment described in paragraph (1), if imported or offered for import into the United States, shall be refused admission on any of the grounds set forth in section 801(a).

(j) Filing of lists of drugs and devices manufactured, prepared, propagated and compounded by registrants; statements; accompanying disclosures.

(1) Every person who registers with the Secretary under subsection (b), (c), (d) or (i) shall, at the time of registration under any such subsection, file with the Secretary a list of all drugs and a list of all devices and a brief statement of the basis for believing that each device included in the list is a device rather than a drug (with each drug and device in each list listed by its established name

(as defined in section 502(e)) and by any proprietary name) which are being manufactured, prepared, propagated, compounded, or processed by him for commercial distribution and which he has not included in any list of drugs or devices filed by him with the Secretary under this paragraph or paragraph (2) before such time of registration. Such list shall be prepared in such form and manner as the Secretary may prescribe and shall be accompanied by—

(A) in the case of a drug or device contained in the applicable list and subject to section 505 or 512, or a device intended for human use contained in the applicable list with respect to which a performance standard has been established under section 514 or which is subject to section 515, a reference to the authority for the marketing of such drug or device and a copy of all labeling for such drug or device;

(B) in the case of any other drug or device contained in an applicable list—

(i) which drug is subject to section 503(b)(1), or which device is a restricted device, a copy of all labeling for such drug or device, a representative sampling of advertisements for such drug or device, and, upon request made by the Secretary for good cause, a copy of all advertisements for a particular drug product or device, or

(ii) which drug is not subject to section 503(b)(1) or which device is not a restricted device, the label and package insert for such drug or device and a representative sampling of any other labeling for such drug or device;

(C) in the case of any drug contained in an applicable list which is described in subparagraph (B), a quantitative listing of its active ingredient or ingredients, except that with respect to a particular drug product the Secretary may require the submission of a quantitative listing of all ingredients if he finds that such submission is necessary to carry out the purposes of this Act; and

(D) if the registrant filing a list has determined that a particular drug product or device contained in such list is not subject to section 505 or 512, or the particular device contained in such list is not subject to a performance standard established under section 514 or to section 515 or is not a restricted device[,] a brief statement of the basis upon which the registrant made such determination if the Secretary requests such a statement with respect to that particular drug product or device.

(2) Each person who registers with the Secretary under this section shall report to the Secretary, with regard to drugs once during the month of June of each year and once during the month of December of each year, and with regard to devices once each year during the period beginning on October 1 and ending on December 31, the following information:

(A) A list of each drug or device introduced by the registrant for commercial distribution which has not been included in any list previously filed by him with the Secretary under this subparagraph or paragraph (1) of this subsection. A list under this subparagraph shall list a drug or device by its established name (as defined in section 502(e)) and by any proprietary name it may have and shall be accompanied by the other information required by paragraph (1).

(B) If since the date the registrant last made a report under this paragraph (or if he has not made a report under this paragraph, since the effective date of this subsection [effective Feb. 1, 1973] [29]) he has discontinued the manufacture, preparation, propagation, compounding, or processing for commercial distribution of a drug or device included in a list filed by him under subparagraph (A) or paragraph (1); notice of such discontinuance, the date of such discontinuance, and the identity (each by established name (as defined in section 502(e)) and by any proprietary name) of such drug or device.

(C) If since the date the registrant reported pursuant to subparagraph (B) a notice of discontinuance he has resumed the manufacture, preparation, propagation, compounding, or processing for commercial distribution of the drug or device with respect to which such notice of discontinuance was reported; notice of such resumption, the date of such resumption, the identity of such drug or device (by established name (as defined in section 502(e)) and by any proprietary name), and the other information required by paragraph (1), unless the registrant has previously reported such resumption to the Secretary pursuant to this subparagraph.

(D) Any material change in any information previously submitted pursuant to this paragraph or paragraph (1).

(3) The Secretary may also require each registrant under this section to submit a list of each drug product which (A) the registrant is manufacturing, preparing, propagating, compounding, or processing for commercial distribution, and (B) contains a particular ingredient. The Secretary may not require the submission of such a list unless he has made a finding that the submission of such a list is necessary to carry out the purposes of this Act.

(k) Report preceding introduction of devices into interstate commerce. Each person who is required to register under this section and who proposes to begin the introduction or delivery for introduction into interstate commerce for commercial distribution of a device intended for human use shall, at least ninety days before making such introduction or delivery, report to the Secretary or person who is

---

[29] The effective date is February 1, 1973. This subsection was added by Public Law 92–387, which was enacted August 16, 1972. Section 5 of such Public Law provided that the amendments made by the Public Law "shall take effect on the first day of the sixth month beginning after the date of the enactment of this Act.".

accredited under section 523(a) (in such form and manner as the Secretary shall by regulation prescribe)—

(1) the class in which the device is classified under section 513 or if such person determines that the device is not classified under such section, a statement of that determination and the basis for such person's determination that the device is or is not so classified, and

(2) action taken by such person to comply with requirements under section 514 or 515 which are applicable to the device.

A notification submitted under this subsection that contains clinical trial data for an applicable device clinical trial (as defined in section 402(j)(1) of the Public Health Service Act [42 USC § 282(j)(1)]) shall be accompanied by the certification required under section 402(j)(5)(B) of such Act [42 USC § 282(j)(5)(B)]. Such certification shall not be considered an element of such notification.

(l) Exemption from reporting requirements. A report under subsection (k) is not required for a device intended for human use that is exempted from the requirements of this subsection under subsection (m) or is within a type that has been classified into class I under section 513. The exception established in the preceding sentence does not apply to any class I device that is intended for a use which is of substantial importance in preventing impairment of human health, or to any class I device that presents a potential unreasonable risk of illness or injury.

(m) List of exempt class II devices; determination by Secretary; publication in Federal Register.

(1) Not later than 60 days after the date of enactment of the Food and Drug Administration Modernization Act of 1997 [enacted Nov. 21, 1997], the Secretary shall publish in the Federal Register a list of each type of class II device that does not require a report under subsection (k) to provide reasonable assurance of safety and effectiveness. Each type of class II device identified by the Secretary as not requiring the report shall be exempt from the requirement to provide a report under subsection (k) as of the date of the publication of the list in the Federal Register. The Secretary shall publish such list on the Internet site of the Food and Drug Administration. The list so published shall be updated not later than 30 days after each revision of the list by the Secretary.

(2) Beginning on the date that is 1 day after the date of the publication of a list under this subsection, the Secretary may exempt a class II device from the requirement to submit a report under subsection (k), upon the Secretary's own initiative or a petition of an interested person, if the Secretary determines that such report is not necessary to assure the safety and effectiveness of the device. The Secretary shall publish in the Federal Register notice of the intent of the Secretary to exempt the device, or of the petition,

and provide a 30-day period for public comment. Within 120 days after the issuance of the notice in the Federal Register, the Secretary shall publish an order in the Federal Register that sets forth the final determination of the Secretary regarding the exemption of the device that was the subject of the notice. If the Secretary fails to respond to a petition within 180 days of receiving it, the petition shall be deemed to be granted.

(n) Review of report; time for determination by Secretary. The Secretary shall review the report required in subsection (k) and make a determination under section 513(f)(1) not later than 90 days after receiving the report.

(o) Reprocessed single-use devices.

(1) With respect to reprocessed single-use devices for which reports are required under subsection (k):

(A) The Secretary shall identify such devices or types of devices for which reports under such subsection must, in order to ensure that the device is substantially equivalent to a predicate device, include validation data, the types of which shall be specified by the Secretary, regarding cleaning and sterilization, and functional performance demonstrating that the single-use device will remain substantially equivalent to its predicate device after the maximum number of times the device is reprocessed as intended by the person submitting the premarket notification. Within six months after enactment of this subsection [enacted Oct. 26, 2002], the Secretary shall publish in the Federal Register a list of the types so identified, and shall revise the list as appropriate. Reports under subsection (k) for devices or types of devices within a type included on the list are, upon publication of the list, required to include such validation data.

(B) In the case of each report under subsection (k) that was submitted to the Secretary before the publication of the initial list under subparagraph (A), or any revision thereof, and was for a device or type of device included on such list, the person who submitted the report under subsection (k) shall submit validation data as described in subparagraph (A) to the Secretary not later than nine months after the publication of the list. During such nine-month period, the Secretary may not take any action under this Act against such device solely on the basis that the validation data for the device have not been submitted to the Secretary. After the submission of the validation data to the Secretary, the Secretary may not determine that the device is misbranded under section 502(o), or adulterated under section 501(f)(1)(B), or take action against the device under section 301(p) for failure to provide any information required by subsection (k) until (i) the review is terminated by withdrawal of the submission of the report under subsection (k); (ii) the Secretary finds the data to be acceptable and issues a letter; or (iii) the Secretary determines that the device is not substantially equivalent to a predicate device. Upon a determination that a device is not substantially equivalent to a predicate device, or if such submission is withdrawn, the device can no longer be legally marketed.

(C) In the case of a report under subsection (k) for a device identified under subparagraph (A) that is of a type for which the Secretary has not previously received a report under such subsection, the Secretary may, in advance of revising the list under subparagraph (A) to include such type, require that the report include the validation data specified in subparagraph (A).

(D) Section 502(o) applies with respect to the failure of a report under subsection (k) to include validation data required under subparagraph (A).

(2) With respect to critical or semi-critical reprocessed single-use devices that, under subsection (l) or (m), are exempt from the requirement of submitting reports under subsection (k):

(A) The Secretary shall identify such devices or types of devices for which such exemptions should be terminated in order to provide a reasonable assurance of the safety and effectiveness of the devices. <> The Secretary shall publish in the Federal Register a list of the devices or types of devices so identified, and shall revise the list as appropriate. The exemption for each device or type included on the list is terminated upon the publication of the list. For each report under subsection (k) submitted pursuant to this subparagraph the Secretary shall require the validation data described in paragraph (1)(A).

(B) For each device or type of device included on the list under subparagraph (A), a report under subsection (k) shall be submitted to the Secretary not later than 15 months after the publication of the initial list, or a revision of the list, whichever terminates the exemption for the device. During such 15-month period, the Secretary may not take any action under this Act against such device solely on the basis that such report has not been submitted to the Secretary. After the submission of the report to the Secretary the Secretary may not determine that the device is misbranded under section 502(o), or adulterated under section 501(f)(1)(B), or take action against the device under section 301(p) for failure to provide any information required by subsection (k) until (i) the review is terminated by withdrawal of the submission; (ii) the Secretary determines by order that the device is substantially equivalent to a predicate device; or (iii) the Secretary determines by order that the device is not substantially equivalent to a predicate device. Upon a determination that a device is not substantially equivalent to a predicate device, the device can no longer be legally marketed.

(C) In the case of semi-critical devices, the initial list under subparagraph (A) shall be published not later than 18 months after the effective date of this subsection. In the case of critical devices, the initial list under such subparagraph shall be published not later than six months after such effective date.

(D) Section 502(o) applies with respect to the failure to submit a report under subsection (k) that is required pursuant to subparagraph (A), including a failure of the report to include validation data required in such subparagraph.

(E) The termination under subparagraph (A) of an exemption under subsection (l) or (m) for a critical or semi-critical reprocessed single-use device does not terminate the exemption under subsection (l) or (m) for the original device.

(p) Electronic registration and listing. Registrations and listings under this section (including the submission of updated information) shall be submitted to the Secretary by electronic means unless the Secretary grants a request for waiver of such requirement because use of electronic means is not reasonable for the person requesting such waiver.

SEC. 511. [21 USC §360a] Clinical Trial Guidance for Antibiotic Drugs

Note: This section was added in February 2008.

(a) In general. Not later than 1 year after the date of the enactment of this section [enacted Sept. 27, 2007], the Secretary shall issue guidance for the conduct of clinical trials with respect to antibiotic drugs, including antimicrobials to treat acute bacterial sinusitis, acute bacterial otitis media, and acute bacterial exacerbation of chronic bronchitis. Such guidance shall indicate the appropriate models and valid surrogate markers.

(b) Review. Not later than 5 years after the date of the enactment of this section [enacted Sept. 27, 2007], the Secretary shall review and update the guidance described under subsection (a) to reflect developments in scientific and medical information and technology.

SEC. 512. [21 USC §360b] New Animal Drugs

(a)(1) [30, 31, 32]A new animal drug shall, with respect to any particular use or intended use of such drug, be deemed unsafe for purposes of section 501(a)(5) and section 402(a)(2)(C)(ii) unless—

---

[30] Section 511 was repealed by section 701(a) of Public Law 91–513.

(A) there is in effect an approval of an application filed pursuant to subsection (b) with respect to such use or intended use of such drug, and such drug, its labeling, and such use conform to such approved application;

(B) there is in effect a conditional approval of an application filed pursuant to section 571 with respect to such use or intended use of such drug, and such drug, its labeling, and such use conform to such conditionally approved application; or

(C) there is in effect an index listing pursuant to section 572 with respect to such use or intended use of such drug in a minor species, and such drug, its labeling, and such use conform to such index listing.

A new animal drug shall also be deemed unsafe for such purposes in the event of removal from the establishment of a manufacturer, packer, or distributor of such drug for use in the manufacture of animal feed in any State unless at the time of such removal such manufacturer, packer, or distributor has an unrevoked written statement from the consignee of such drug, or notice from the Secretary, to the effect that, with respect to the use of such drug in animal feed, such consignee (i) holds a license issued under subsection (m) and has in its possession current approved labeling for such drug in animal feed; or (ii) will, if the consignee is not a user of the drug, ship such drug only to a holder of a license issued under subsection (m).

(2) An animal feed bearing or containing a new animal drug shall, with respect to any particular use or intended use of such animal feed be deemed unsafe for purposes of section 501(a)(6) unless—

(A) there is in effect—

(i) an approval of an application filed pursuant to subsection (b) with respect to such drug, as used in such animal feed, and such animal feed and its labeling, distribution, holding, and use conform to such approved application;

(ii) a conditional approval of an application filed pursuant to section 571 with respect to such drug, as used in such animal feed, and such animal feed and its labeling, distribution, holding, and use conform to such conditionally approved application; or

(iii) an index listing pursuant to section 572 with respect to such drug, as used in such animal feed, and such animal feed and its labeling, distribution, holding, and use conform to such index listing; and

Chapter V

---

[31] Section 512 was added by Public Law 90–399, which was enacted July 13, 1968. Section 108 of such Public Law concerned the effective date and applicability of the amendment, and is included in the appendix to this compilation.

[32] Separate indentation of paragraph (1) is so in law. See section 102(b)(5)(I) of Public Law 108–282.

(B) such animal feed is manufactured at a site for which there is in effect a license issued pursuant to subsection (m)(1) to manufacture such animal feed.

(3) A new animal drug or an animal feed bearing or containing a new animal drug shall not be deemed unsafe for the purposes of section 501(a)(5) or (6) if such article is for investigational use and conforms to the terms of an exemption in effect with respect thereto under section 512(j).

(4)(A) Except as provided in subparagraph (B), if an approval of an application filed under subsection (b) is in effect with respect to a particular use or intended use of a new animal drug, the drug shall not be deemed unsafe for the purposes of paragraph (1) and shall be exempt from the requirements of section 502(f) with respect to a different use or intended use of the drug, other than a use in or on animal feed, if such use or intended use—

(i) is by or on the lawful written or oral order of a licensed veterinarian within the context of a veterinarian-client-patient relationship, as defined by the Secretary; and

(ii) is in compliance with regulations promulgated by the Secretary that establish the conditions for such different use or intended use.

The regulations promulgated by the Secretary under clause (ii) may prohibit particular uses of an animal drug and shall not permit such different use of an animal drug if the labeling of another animal drug that contains the same active ingredient and which is in the same dosage form and concentration provides for such different use.

(B) If the Secretary finds that there is a reasonable probability that a use of an animal drug authorized under subparagraph (A) may present a risk to the public health, the Secretary may—

(i) establish a safe level for a residue of an animal drug when it is used for such different use authorized by subparagraph (A); and

(ii) require the development of a practical, analytical method for the detection of residues of such drug above the safe level established under clause (i).

The use of an animal drug that results in residues exceeding a safe level established under clause (i) shall be considered an unsafe use of such drug under paragraph (1). Safe levels may be established under clause (i) either by regulation or order.

(C) The Secretary may by general regulation provide access to the records of veterinarians to ascertain any use or intended use authorized under subparagraph (A) that the Secretary has determined may present a risk to the public health.

(D) If the Secretary finds, after affording an opportunity for public comment, that a use of an animal drug authorized under subparagraph (A) presents a risk to the public health or that an analytical method required under subparagraph (B) has not been developed and submitted to the Secretary, the Secretary may, by order, prohibit any such use.

(5) If the approval of an application filed under section 505 is in effect, the drug under such application shall not be deemed unsafe for purposes of paragraph (1) and shall be exempt from the requirements of section 502(f) with respect to a use or intended use of the drug in animals if such use or intended use—

(A) is by or on the lawful written or oral order of a licensed veterinarian within the context of a veterinarian-client-patient relationship, as defined by the Secretary; and

(B) is in compliance with regulations promulgated by the Secretary that establish the conditions for the use or intended use of the drug in animals.

(6) For purposes of section 402(a)(2)(D), a use or intended use of a new animal drug shall not be deemed unsafe under this section if the Secretary establishes a tolerance for such drug and any edible portion of any animal imported into the United States does not contain residues exceeding such tolerance. In establishing such tolerance, the Secretary shall rely on data sufficient to demonstrate that a proposed tolerance is safe based on similar food safety criteria used by the Secretary to establish tolerances for applications for new animal drugs filed under subsection (b)(1). The Secretary may consider and rely on data submitted by the drug manufacturer, including data submitted to appropriate regulatory authorities in any country where the new animal drug is lawfully used or data available from a relevant international organization, to the extent such data are not inconsistent with the criteria used by the Secretary to establish a tolerance for applications for new animal drugs filed under subsection (b)(1). For purposes of this paragraph, "relevant international organization" means the Codex Alimenterius Commission or other international organization deemed appropriate by the Secretary. The Secretary may, under procedures specified by regulation, revoke a tolerance established under this paragraph if information demonstrates that the use of the new animal drug under actual use conditions results in food being imported into the United States with residues exceeding the tolerance or if scientific evidence shows the tolerance to be unsafe.

(b)(1) Any person may file with the Secretary an application with respect to any intended use or uses of a new animal drug. Such person shall submit to the Secretary as a part of the application (A) full reports of investigations which have been made to show whether or not such drug is safe and effective for use; (B) a full list of the articles used as components of such drug; (C) a full statement of the composition of such drug; (D) a full description of the methods used in, and the facilities and controls used for, the manufacture, processing, and packing of such drug; (E) such samples of such drug and of the articles used as components thereof, of any animal feed for use in or on which such drug is intended, and of the edible portions or products (before or after slaughter) of animals to which such drug (directly or in or on animal feed) is intended to be administered, as the Secretary may require; (F) specimens of the labeling proposed to be used for such drug, or in case such drug is intended for use in animal feed, proposed labeling appropriate for such use, and specimens of the labeling for the drug to be manufactured, packed, or distributed by the applicant; (G) a description of practicable methods for determining the quantity, if any, of such drug in or on food, and any substance formed in or on food, because of its use; and (H) the proposed tolerance or withdrawal period or other use restrictions for such drug if any tolerance or withdrawal period or other use restrictions are required in order to assure that the proposed use of such drug will be safe. The applicant shall file with the application the patent number and the expiration date of any patent which claims the new animal drug for which the applicant filed the application or which claims a method of using such drug and with respect to which a claim of patent infringement could reasonably be asserted if a person not licensed by the owner engaged in the manufacture, use, or sale of the drug. If an application is filed under this subsection for a drug and a patent which claims such drug or a method of using such drug is issued after the filing date but before approval of the application, the applicant shall amend the application to include the information required by the preceding sentence. Upon approval of the application, the Secretary shall publish information submitted under the two preceding sentences.

(2) Any person may file with the Secretary an abbreviated application for the approval of a new animal drug. An abbreviated application shall contain the information required by subsection (n).

(3) Any person intending to file an application under paragraph (1), section 571, or a request for an investigational exemption under subsection (j) shall be entitled to one or more conferences prior to such submission to reach an agreement acceptable to the Secretary establishing a submission or an investigational requirement, which may include a requirement for a field investigation. A decision establishing a submission or an investigational requirement shall bind the Secretary and the applicant or requestor unless (A) the Secretary and the applicant or requestor mutually agree to modify the requirement, or (B) the Secretary by written order determines that a substantiated scientific requirement essential to the determination of safety or effectiveness of the animal drug involved has appeared after the conference. No later than 25 calendar days after each such conference, the Secretary shall provide a written order setting forth a scientific justification specific to the animal drug and intended uses under consideration if the agreement referred to in the first sentence requires more than one field investigation as being essential to provide substantial evidence of effectiveness for the intended

uses of the drug. Nothing in this paragraph shall be construed as compelling the Secretary to require a field investigation.

(c)(1) Within one hundred and eighty days after the filing of an application pursuant to subsection (b), or such additional period as may be agreed upon by the Secretary and the applicant, the Secretary shall either (A) issue an order approving the application if he then finds that none of the grounds for denying approval specified in subsection (d) applies, or (B) give the applicant notice of an opportunity for a hearing before the Secretary under subsection (d) on the question whether such application is approvable. If the applicant elects to accept the opportunity for a hearing by written request within thirty days after such notice, such hearing shall commence not more than ninety days after the expiration of such thirty days unless the Secretary and the applicant otherwise agree. Any such hearing shall thereafter be conducted on an expedited basis and the Secretary's order thereon shall be issued within ninety days after the date fixed by the Secretary for filing final briefs.

(2)(A) Subject to subparagraph (C), the Secretary shall approve an abbreviated application for a drug unless the Secretary finds—

(i) the methods used in, or the facilities and controls used for, the manufacture, processing, and packing of the drug are inadequate to assure and preserve its identity, strength, quality, and purity;

(ii) the conditions of use prescribed, recommended, or suggested in the proposed labeling are not reasonably certain to be followed in practice or, except as provided in subparagraph (B), information submitted with the application is insufficient to show that each of the proposed conditions of use or similar limitations (whether in the labeling or published pursuant to subsection (i)) have been previously approved for the approved new animal drug referred to in the application;

(iii) information submitted with the application is insufficient to show that the active ingredients are the same as those of the approved new animal drug referred to in the application;

(iv)(I) if the application is for a drug whose active ingredients, route of administration, dosage form, strength, or use with other animal drugs in animal feed is the same as the active ingredients, route of administration, dosage form, strength, or use with other animal drugs in animal feed of the approved new animal drug referred to in the application, information submitted in the application is insufficient to show that the active ingredients, route of administration, dosage form, strength, or use with other animal drugs in animal feed is the same as that of the approved new animal drug, or

Chapter V

(II) if the application is for a drug whose active ingredients, route of administration, dosage form, strength, or use with other animal drugs in animal feed is different from that of the approved new animal drug referred to in the application, no petition to file an application for the drug with the different active ingredients, route of administration, dosage form, strength, or use with other animal drugs in animal feed was approved under subsection (n)(3);

(v) if the application was filed pursuant to the approval of a petition under subsection (n)(3), the application did not contain the information required by the Secretary respecting the active ingredients, route of administration, dosage form, strength, or use with other animal drugs in animal feed which is not the same;

(vi) information submitted in the application is insufficient to show that the drug is bioequivalent to the approved new animal drug referred to in the application, or if the application is filed under a petition approved pursuant to subsection (n)(3), information submitted in the application is insufficient to show that the active ingredients of the new animal drug are of the same pharmacological or therapeutic class as the pharmacological or therapeutic class of the approved new animal drug and that the new animal drug can be expected to have the same therapeutic effect as the approved new animal drug when used in accordance with the labeling;

(vii) information submitted in the application is insufficient to show that the labeling proposed for the drug is the same as the labeling approved for the approved new animal drug referred to in the application except for changes required because of differences approved under a petition filed under subsection (n)(3), because of a different withdrawal period, or because the drug and the approved new animal drug are produced or distributed by different manufacturers;

(viii) information submitted in the application or any other information available to the Secretary shows that (I) the inactive ingredients of the drug are unsafe for use under the conditions prescribed, recommended, or suggested in the labeling proposed for the drug, (II) the composition of the drug is unsafe under such conditions because of the type or quantity of inactive ingredients included or the manner in which the inactive ingredients are included, or (III) in the case of a drug for food producing animals, the inactive ingredients of the drug or its composition may be unsafe with respect to human food safety;

(ix) the approval under subsection (b)(1) of the approved new animal drug referred to in the application filed under subsection (b)(2) has been withdrawn or suspended for grounds described in paragraph (1) of subsection (e), the Secretary has published a notice of a hearing to withdraw approval of the approved new animal drug for such grounds, the approval under this paragraph of the new animal drug for which the application under subsection (b)(2) was filed has been withdrawn or suspended under subparagraph (G) for such grounds, or the Secretary has determined that the approved new animal drug has been withdrawn from sale for safety or effectiveness reasons;

(x) the application does not meet any other requirement of subsection (n); or

(xi) the application contains an untrue statement of material fact.

(B) If the Secretary finds that a new animal drug for which an application is submitted under subsection (b)(2) is bioequivalent to the approved new animal drug referred to in such application and that residues of the new animal drug are consistent with the tolerances established for such approved new animal drug but at a withdrawal period which is different than the withdrawal period approved for such approved new animal drug, the Secretary may establish, on the basis of information submitted, such different withdrawal period as the withdrawal period for the new animal drug for purposes of the approval of such application for such drug.

(C) Within 180 days of the initial receipt of an application under subsection (b)(2) or within such additional period as may be agreed upon by the Secretary and the applicant, the Secretary shall approve or disapprove the application.

(D) The approval of an application filed under subsection (b)(2) shall be made effective on the last applicable date determined under the following:

(i) If the applicant only made a certification described in clause (i) or (ii) of subsection (n)(1)(G) or in both such clauses, the approval may be made effective immediately.

(ii) If the applicant made a certification described in clause (iii) of subsection (n)(1)(G), the approval may be made effective on the date certified under clause (iii).

(iii) If the applicant made a certification described in clause (iv) of subsection (n)(1)(G), the approval shall be made effective immediately unless an action is brought for infringement of a patent which is the subject of the certification before the expiration of 45 days from the date the notice provided under subsection (n)(2)(B)(i) is received. If such an action is brought before the expiration of such days, the approval shall be made effective upon the expiration of the 30 month period beginning on the date of the receipt of the notice provided under subsection (n)(2)(B) or such shorter or longer period as the court may order because either party to the action failed to reasonably cooperate in expediting the action, except that if before the expiration of such period—

(I) the court decides that such patent is invalid or not infringed, the approval shall be made effective on the date of the court decision,

(II) the court decides that such patent has been infringed, the approval shall be made effective on such date as the court orders under section 271(e)(4)(A) of title 35, United States Code, or

(III) the court grants a preliminary injunction prohibiting the applicant from engaging in the commercial manufacture or sale of the drug until the court decides the issues of patent validity and infringement and if the court decides that such patent is invalid or not infringed, the approval shall be made effective on the date of such court decision.

In such an action, each of the parties shall reasonably cooperate in expediting the action. Until the expiration of 45 days from the date the notice made under subsection (n)(2)(B) is received, no action may be brought under section 2201 of title 28, United States Code, for a declaratory judgment with respect to the patent. Any action brought under section 2201 shall be brought in the judicial district where the defendant has its principal place of business or a regular and established place of business.

(iv) If the application contains a certification described in clause (iv) of subsection (n)(1)(G) and is for a drug for which a previous application has been filed under this subsection containing such a certification, the application shall be made effective not earlier than 180 days after—

(I) the date the Secretary receives notice from the applicant under the previous application of the first commercial marketing of the drug under the previous application, or

(II) the date of a decision of a court in an action described in subclause (III) [33] holding the patent which is the subject of the certification to be invalid or not infringed, whichever is earlier.

(E) If the Secretary decides to disapprove an application, the Secretary shall give the applicant notice of an opportunity for a hearing before the

[33] So in law. Probably should be "clause (iii)(III)".

Secretary on the question of whether such application is approvable. If the applicant elects to accept the opportunity for hearing by written request within 30 days after such notice, such hearing shall commence not more than 90 days after the expiration of such 30 days unless the Secretary and the applicant otherwise agree. Any such hearing shall thereafter be conducted on an expedited basis and the Secretary's order thereon shall be issued within 90 days after the date fixed by the Secretary for filing final briefs.

(F)(i) If an application submitted under subsection (b)(1) for a drug, no active ingredient (including any ester or salt of the active ingredient) of which has been approved in any other application under subsection (b)(1), is approved after the date of the enactment of this paragraph [34], no application may be submitted under subsection (b)(2) which refers to the drug for which the subsection (b)(1) application was submitted before the expiration of 5 years from the date of the approval of the application under subsection (b)(1), except that such an application may be submitted under subsection (b)(2) after the expiration of 4 years from the date of the approval of the subsection (b)(1) application if it contains a certification of patent invalidity or noninfringement described in clause (iv) of subsection (n)(1)(G). The approval of such an application shall be made effective in accordance with subparagraph (B) except that, if an action for patent infringement is commenced during the one-year period beginning 48 months after the date of the approval of the subsection (b) application, the 30 month period referred to in subparagraph (D)(iii) shall be extended by such amount of time (if any) which is required for seven and one-half years to have elapsed from the date of approval of the subsection (b) application.

(ii) If an application submitted under subsection (b)(1) for a drug, which includes an active ingredient (including any ester or salt of the active ingredient) that has been approved in another application approved under such subsection, is approved after the date of enactment of this paragraph 5 and if such application contains substantial evidence of the effectiveness of the drug involved, any studies of animal safety, or, in the case of food producing animals, human food safety studies (other than bioequivalence studies or residue depletion studies, except residue depletion studies for minor uses or minor species) required for the approval of the application and conducted or sponsored by the applicant, the Secretary may not make the approval of an application submitted under subsection (b)(2) for the conditions of approval of such drug in the subsection (b)(1) application effective before the expiration of 3 years from the

Chapter V

[34] The reference to "this paragraph" is a reference to paragraph (2) of subsection (c). Paragraph (2) was added by title I of Public Law 100–670, which was enacted November 16, 1988.

date of the approval of the application under subsection (b)(1) for such drug.

(iii) If a supplement to an application approved under subsection (b)(1) is approved after the date of enactment of this paragraph 2 and the supplement contains substantial evidence of the effectiveness of the drug involved, any studies of animal safety, or, in the case of food producing animals, human food safety studies (other than bioequivalence studies or residue depletion studies, except residue depletion studies for minor uses or minor species) [35] required for the approval of the supplement and conducted or sponsored by the person submitting the supplement, the Secretary may not make the approval of an application submitted under subsection (b)(2) for a change approved in the supplement effective before the expiration of 3 years from the date of the approval of the supplement.

(iv) An applicant under subsection (b)(1) who comes within the provisions of clause (i) of this subparagraph as a result of an application which seeks approval for a use solely in non-food producing animals, may elect, within 10 days of receiving such approval, to waive clause (i) of this subparagraph, in which event the limitation on approval of applications submitted under subsection (b)(2) set forth in clause (ii) of this subparagraph shall be applicable to the subsection (b)(1) application.

(v) If an application (including any supplement to a new animal drug application) submitted under subsection (b)(1) for a new animal drug for a food-producing animal use, which includes an active ingredient (including any ester or salt of the active ingredient) which has been the subject of a waiver under clause (iv) is approved after the date of enactment of this paragraph [36], and if the application contains substantial evidence of the effectiveness of the drug involved, any studies of animal safety, or human food safety studies (other than bioequivalence studies or residue depletion studies, except residue depletion studies for minor uses or minor species) required for the new approval of the application and conducted or sponsored by the applicant, the Secretary may not make the approval of an application (including any supplement to such application) submitted under subsection (b)(2) for the new conditions of approval of such drug in the subsection (b)(1)

---

[35] The language within parentheses appears so as to reflect the probable intent of the Congress. Section 102(b)(2) of Public Law 108–282 provides for amendments to the parenentical language, and states that "Section 512(c)(2)(F) (ii), (iii), and (v) of the Federal Food, Drug, and Cosmetic Act is amended by". The probable intent of the Congress was to provide that "Clauses (ii), (iii), and (v) of section 512(c)(2)(F) of the Federal Food, Drug, and Cosmetic Act are each amended by".

[36] The reference to "this paragraph" is a reference to paragraph (2) of subsection (c). Paragraph (2) was added by title I of Public Law 100–670, which was enacted November 16, 1988.

application effective before the expiration of five years from the date of approval of the application under subsection (b)(1) for such drug. The provisions of this paragraph shall apply only to the first approval for a food-producing animal use for the same applicant after the waiver under clause (iv).

(G) If an approved application submitted under subsection (b)(2) for a new animal drug refers to a drug the approval of which was withdrawn or suspended for grounds described in paragraph (1) or (2) of subsection (e) or was withdrawn or suspended under this subparagraph or which, as determined by the Secretary, has been withdrawn from sale for safety or effectiveness reasons, the approval of the drug under this paragraph shall be withdrawn or suspended—

(i) for the same period as the withdrawal or suspension under subsection (e) or this subparagraph, or

(ii) if the approved new animal drug has been withdrawn from sale, for the period of withdrawal from sale or, if earlier, the period ending on the date the Secretary determines that the withdrawal from sale is not for safety or effectiveness reasons.

(H) For purposes of this paragraph:

(i) The term "bioequivalence" means the rate and extent to which the active ingredient or therapeutic ingredient is absorbed from a new animal drug and becomes available at the site of drug action.

(ii) A new animal drug shall be considered to be bioequivalent to the approved new animal drug referred to in its application under subsection (n) if—

(I) the rate and extent of absorption of the drug do not show a significant difference from the rate and extent of absorption of the approved new animal drug referred to in the application when administered at the same dose of the active ingredient under similar experimental conditions in either a single dose or multiple doses;

(II) the extent of absorption of the drug does not show a significant difference from the extent of absorption of the approved new animal drug referred to in the application when administered at the same dose of the active ingredient under similar experimental conditions in either a single dose or multiple doses and the difference from the approved new animal drug in the rate of absorption of the drug is intentional, is reflected in its proposed labeling, is not essential to the attainment of effective drug concentrations in use, and is considered scientifically insignificant for the drug in attaining the intended purposes of its use and preserving human food safety; or

(III) in any case in which the Secretary determines that the measurement of the rate and extent of absorption or excretion of the new animal drug in biological fluids is inappropriate or impractical, an appropriate acute pharmacological effects test or other test of the new animal drug and, when deemed scientifically necessary, of the approved new animal drug referred to in the application in the species to be tested or in an appropriate animal model does not show a significant difference between the new animal drug and such approved new animal drug when administered at the same dose under similar experimental conditions.

If the approved new animal drug referred to in the application for a new animal drug under subsection (n) is approved for use in more than one animal species, the bioequivalency information described in subclauses (I), (II), and (III) shall be obtained for one species, or if the Secretary deems appropriate based on scientific principles, shall be obtained for more than one species. The Secretary may prescribe the dose to be used in determining bioequivalency under subclause (I), (II), or (III). To assure that the residues of the new animal drug will be consistent with the established tolerances for the approved new animal drug referred to in the application under subsection (b)(2) upon the expiration of the withdrawal period contained in the application for the new animal drug, the Secretary shall require bioequivalency data or residue depletion studies of the new animal drug or such other data or studies as the Secretary considers appropriate based on scientific principles. If the Secretary requires one or more residue studies under the preceding sentence, the Secretary may not require that the assay methodology used to determine the withdrawal period of the new animal drug be more rigorous than the methodology used to determine the withdrawal period for the approved new animal drug referred to in the application. If such studies are required and if the approved new animal drug, referred to in the application for the new animal drug for which such studies are required, is approved for use in more than one animal species, such studies shall be conducted for one species, or if the Secretary deems appropriate based on scientific principles, shall be conducted for more than one species.

(3) If the patent information described in subsection (b)(1) could not be filed with the submission of an application under subsection (b)(1) because the application was filed before the patent information was required under subsection (b)(1) or a patent was issued after the application was approved under such subsection, the holder of an approved application shall file with the Secretary the patent number and the expiration date of any patent which claims the new animal drug for which the application was filed or which claims a method of using such drug and with respect to which a claim of

patent infringement could reasonably be asserted if a person not licensed by the owner engaged in the manufacture, use, or sale of the drug. If the holder of an approved application could not file patent information under subsection (b)(1) because it was not required at the time the application was approved, the holder shall file such information under this subsection not later than 30 days after the date of the enactment of this sentence [37], and if the holder of an approved application could not file patent information under subsection (b)(1) because no patent had been issued when an application was filed or approved, the holder shall file such information under this subsection not later than 30 days after the date the patent involved is issued. Upon the submission of patent information under this subsection, the Secretary shall publish it.

(4) A drug manufactured in a pilot or other small facility may be used to demonstrate the safety and effectiveness of the drug and to obtain approval for the drug prior to manufacture of the drug in a larger facility, unless the Secretary makes a determination that a full scale production facility is necessary to ensure the safety or effectiveness of the drug.

(d)(1) If the Secretary finds, after due notice to the applicant in accordance with subsection (c) and giving him an opportunity for a hearing, in accordance with said subsection, that—

(A) the investigations, reports of which are required to be submitted to the Secretary pursuant to subsection (b), do not include adequate tests by all methods reasonably applicable to show whether or not such drug is safe for use under the conditions prescribed, recommended, or suggested in the proposed labeling thereof;

(B) the results of such tests show that such drug is unsafe for use under such conditions or do not show that such drug is safe for use under such conditions;

(C) the methods used in, and the facilities and controls used for, the manufacture, processing, and packing of such drug are inadequate to preserve its identity, strength, quality, and purity;

(D) upon the basis of the information submitted to him as part of the application, or upon the basis of any other information before him with respect to such drug, he has insufficient information to determine whether such drug is safe for use under such conditions;

(E) evaluated on the basis of the information submitted to him as part of the application and any other information before him with respect to such drug, there is a lack of substantial evidence that the drug will have the

[37] The sentence was added by title I of Public Law 100–670, which was enacted November 16, 1988.

effect it purports or is represented to have under the conditions of use prescribed, recommended, or suggested in the proposed labeling thereof;

(F) upon the basis of information submitted to the Secretary as part of the application or any other information before the Secretary with respect to such drug, any use prescribed, recommended, or suggested in labeling proposed for such drug will result in a residue of such drug in excess of a tolerance found by the Secretary to be safe for such drug;

(G) the application failed to contain the patent information prescribed by subsection (b)(1);

(H) based on a fair evaluation of all material facts, such labeling is false or misleading in any particular; or

(I) such drug induces cancer when ingested by man or animal or, after tests which are appropriate for the evaluation of the safety of such drug, induces cancer in man or animal, except that the foregoing provisions of this subparagraph shall not apply with respect to such drug if the Secretary finds that, under the conditions of use specified in proposed labeling and reasonably certain to be followed in practice (i) such drug will not adversely affect the animals for which it is intended, and (ii) no residue of such drug will be found (by methods of examination prescribed or approved by the Secretary by regulations, which regulations shall not be subject to subsections (c), (d), and (h)), in any edible portion of such animals after slaughter or in any food yielded by or derived from the living animals;

he shall issue an order refusing to approve the application. If, after such notice and opportunity for hearing, the Secretary finds that subparagraphs (A) through (I) do not apply, he shall issue an order approving the application.

(2) In determining whether such drug is safe for use under the conditions prescribed, recommended, or suggested in the proposed labeling thereof, the Secretary shall consider, among other relevant factors, (A) the probable consumption of such drug and of any substance formed in or on food because of the use of such drug, (B) the cumulative effect on man or animal of such drug, taking into account any chemically or pharmacologically related substance, (C) safety factors which in the opinion of experts, qualified by scientific training and experience to evaluate the safety of such drugs, are appropriate for the use of animal experimentation data, and (D) whether the conditions of use prescribed, recommended, or suggested in the proposed labeling are reasonably certain to be followed in practice. Any order issued under this subsection refusing to approve an application shall state the findings upon which it is based.

(3) As used in this section, the term "substantial evidence" means evidence consisting of one or more adequate and well controlled investigations, such as—

(A) a study in a target species;

(B) a study in laboratory animals;

(C) any field investigation that may be required under this section and that meets the requirements of subsection (b)(3) if a presubmission conference is requested by the applicant;

(D) a bioequivalence study; or

(E) an in vitro study; by experts qualified by scientific training and experience to evaluate the effectiveness of the drug involved, on the basis of which it could fairly and reasonably be concluded by such experts that the drug will have the effect it purports or is represented to have under the conditions of use prescribed, recommended, or suggested in the labeling or proposed labeling thereof.

(4) In a case in which an animal drug contains more than one active ingredient, or the labeling of the drug prescribes, recommends, or suggests use of the drug in combination with one or more other animal drugs, and the active ingredients or drugs intended for use in the combination have previously been separately approved pursuant to an application submitted under section 512(b)(1) [38] for particular uses and conditions of use for which they are intended for use in the combination—

(A) the Secretary shall not issue an order under paragraph (1)(A), (1)(B), or (1)(D) refusing to approve the application for such combination on human food safety grounds unless the Secretary finds that the application fails to establish that—

(i) none of the active ingredients or drugs intended for use in the combination, respectively, at the longest withdrawal time of any of the active ingredients or drugs in the combination, respectively, exceeds its established tolerance; or

(ii) none of the active ingredients or drugs in the combination interferes with the methods of analysis for another of the active ingredients or drugs in the combination, respectively;

(B) the Secretary shall not issue an order under paragraph (1)(A), (1)(B), or (1)(D) refusing to approve the application for such combination on target animal safety grounds unless the Secretary finds that—

(i)(I) there is a substantiated scientific issue, specific to one or more of the active ingredients or animal drugs in the combination, that

---

[38] 1 So in law. See section 102(b)(5)(K) of Public Law 108-282. Probably should be "subsection (b)(1)".

cannot adequately be evaluated based on information contained in the application for the combination (including any investigations, studies, or tests for which the applicant has a right of reference or use from the person by or for whom the investigations, studies, or tests were conducted); or

(II) there is a scientific issue raised by target animal observations contained in studies submitted to the Secretary as part of the application; and

(ii) based on the Secretary's evaluation of the information contained in the application with respect to the issues identified in clauses (i) (I) and (II), paragraph (1) (A), (B), or (D) apply;

(C) except in the case of a combination that contains a nontopical antibacterial ingredient or animal drug, the Secretary shall not issue an order under paragraph (1)(E) refusing to approve an application for a combination animal drug intended for use other than in animal feed or drinking water unless the Secretary finds that the application fails to demonstrate that—

(i) there is substantial evidence that any active ingredient or animal drug intended only for the same use as another active ingredient or animal drug in the combination makes a contribution to labeled effectiveness;

(ii) each active ingredient or animal drug intended for at least one use that is different from all other active ingredients or animal drugs used in the combination provides appropriate concurrent use for the intended target population; or

(iii) where based on scientific information the Secretary has reason to believe the active ingredients or animal drugs may be physically incompatible or have disparate dosing regimens, such active ingredients or animal drugs are physically compatible or do not have disparate dosing regimens; and

(D) the Secretary shall not issue an order under paragraph (1)(E) refusing to approve an application for a combination animal drug intended for use in animal feed or drinking water unless the Secretary finds that the application fails to demonstrate that—

(i) there is substantial evidence that any active ingredient or animal drug intended only for the same use as another active ingredient or animal drug in the combination makes a contribution to the labeled effectiveness;

(ii) each of the active ingredients or animal drugs intended for at least one use that is different from all other active ingredients or animal drugs used in the combination provides appropriate concurrent use for the intended target population;

(iii) where a combination contains more than one nontopical antibacterial ingredient or animal drug, there is substantial evidence that each of the nontopical antibacterial ingredients or animal drugs makes a contribution to the labeled effectiveness, except that for purposes of this clause, antibacterial ingredient or animal drug does not include the ionophore or arsenical classes of animal drugs; or

(iv) where based on scientific information the Secretary has reason to believe the active ingredients or animal drugs intended for use in drinking water may be physically incompatible, such active ingredients or animal drugs intended for use in drinking water are physically compatible.

(5) [39] In reviewing an application that proposes a change to add an intended use for a minor use or a minor species to an approved new animal drug application, the Secretary shall reevaluate only the relevant information in the approved application to determine whether the application for the minor use or minor species can be approved. A decision to approve the application for the minor use or minor species is not, implicitly or explicitly, a reaffirmation of the approval of the original application.

(e)(1) The Secretary shall, after due notice and opportunity for hearing to the applicant, issue an order withdrawing approval of an application filed pursuant to subsection (b) with respect to any new animal drug if the Secretary finds—

(A) that experience or scientific data show that such drug is unsafe for use under the conditions of use upon the basis of which the application was approved or the condition of use authorized under subsection (a)(4)(A);

(B) that new evidence not contained in such application or not available to the Secretary until after such application was approved, or tests by new methods, or tests by methods not deemed reasonably applicable when such application was approved, evaluated together with the evidence available to the Secretary when the application was approved, shows that such drug is not shown to be safe for use under the conditions of use upon the basis of which the application was approved or that subparagraph (I) of paragraph (1) of subsection (d) applies to such drug;

(C) on the basis of new information before him with respect to such drug, evaluated together with the evidence available to him when the application was approved, that there is a lack of substantial evidence that such drug will have the effect it purports or is represented to have under

[39] Identation is so in law. See section 102(b)(3) of Public Law 108-282.

the conditions of use prescribed, recommended, or suggested in the labeling thereof;

(D) the patent information prescribed by subsection (c)(3) was not filed within 30 days after the receipt of written notice from the Secretary specifying the failure to file such information;

(E) that the application contains any untrue statement of a material fact; or

(F) that the applicant has made any changes from the standpoint of safety or effectiveness beyond the variations provided for in the application unless he has supplemented the application by filing with the Secretary adequate information respecting all such changes and unless there is in effect an approval of the supplemental application. The supplemental application shall be treated in the same manner as the original application.

If the Secretary (or in his absence the officer acting as Secretary) finds that there is an imminent hazard to the health of man or of the animals for which such drug is intended, he may suspend the approval of such application immediately, and give the applicant prompt notice of his action and afford the applicant the opportunity for an expedited hearing under this subsection; but the authority conferred by this sentence to suspend the approval of an application shall not be delegated.

(2) The Secretary may also, after due notice and opportunity for hearing to the applicant, issue an order withdrawing the approval of an application with respect to any new animal drug under this section if the Secretary finds—

(A) that the applicant has failed to establish a system for maintaining required records, or has repeatedly or deliberately failed to maintain such records or to make required reports in accordance with a regulation or order under subsection (l), or the applicant has refused to permit access to, or copying or verification of, such records as required by paragraph (2) of such subsection;

(B) that on the basis of new information before him, evaluated together with the evidence before him when the application was approved, the methods used in, or the facilities and controls used for, the manufacture, processing, and packing of such drug are inadequate to assure and preserve its identity, strength, quality, and purity and were not made adequate within a reasonable time after receipt of written notice from the Secretary specifying the matter complained of; or

(C) that on the basis of new information before him, evaluated together with the evidence before him when the application was approved, the labeling of such drug, based on a fair evaluation of all material facts, is false or misleading in any particular and was not corrected within a reasonable time after receipt of written notice from the Secretary specifying the matter complained of.

(3) Any order under this subsection shall state the findings upon which it is based.

(f) Whenever the Secretary finds that the facts so require, he shall revoke any previous order under subsection (d), (e), or (m), or section 571 (c), (d), or (e) refusing, withdrawing, or suspending approval of an application and shall approve such application or reinstate such approval, as may be appropriate.

(g) Orders of the Secretary issued under this section, or section 571(other than orders issuing, amending, or repealing regulations) shall be served (1) in person by any officer or employee of the department designated by the Secretary or (2) by mailing the order by registered mail or by certified mail addressed to the applicant or respondent at his last known address in the records of the Secretary.

(h) An appeal may be taken by the applicant from an order of the Secretary refusing or withdrawing approval of an application filed under subsection (b) or (m) of this section. The provisions of subsection (h) of section 505 of this Act shall govern any such appeal.

(i) When a new animal drug application filed pursuant to subsection (b) or section 571 is approved, the Secretary shall by notice, which upon publication shall be effective as a regulation, publish in the Federal Register the name and address of the applicant and the conditions and indications of use of the new animal drug covered by such application, including any tolerance and withdrawal period or other use restrictions and, if such new animal drug is intended for use in animal feed, appropriate purposes and conditions of use (including special labeling requirements and any requirement that an animal feed bearing or containing the new animal drug be limited to use under the professional supervision of a licensed veterinarian) applicable to any animal feed for use in which such drug is approved, and such other information, upon the basis of which such application was approved, as the Secretary deems necessary to assure the safe and effective use of such drug. Upon withdrawal of approval of such new animal drug application or upon its suspension or upon failure to renew a conditional approval under section 571, the Secretary shall forthwith revoke or suspend, as the case may be, the regulation published pursuant to this subsection (i) [40] insofar as it is based on the approval of such application.

(j) To the extent consistent with the public health, the Secretary shall promulgate regulations for exempting from the operation of this section new animal drugs, and animal feeds bearing or containing new animal drugs, intended solely for investigational use by experts qualified by scientific training and experience to investigate the safety and effectiveness of animal drugs. Such regulations may, in the discretion of the Secretary, among other conditions relating to the protection of the public health, provide for conditioning such exemption upon the

[40] So in law. Probably should be "this subsection".

establishment and maintenance of such records, and the making of such reports to the Secretary, by the manufacturer or the sponsor of the investigation of such article, of data (including but not limited to analytical reports by investigators) obtained as a result of such investigational use of such article, as the Secretary finds will enable him to evaluate the safety and effectiveness of such article in the event of the filing of an application pursuant to this section. Such regulations, among other things, shall set forth the conditions (if any) upon which animals treated with such articles, and any products of such animals (before or after slaughter), may be marketed for food use.

(k) While approval of an application for a new animal drug is effective, a food shall not, by reason of bearing or containing such drug or any substance formed in or on the food because of its use in accordance with such application (including the conditions and indications of use prescribed pursuant to subsection (i)), be considered adulterated within the meaning of clause (1) of section 402(a).

(l)(1) In the case of any new animal drug for which an approval of an application filed pursuant to ubsection (b) or section 571 is in effect, the applicant shall establish and maintain such records, and make such reports to the Secretary, of data relating to experience, including experience with uses authorized under subsection (a)(4)(A), and other data or information, received or otherwise obtained by such applicant with respect to such drug, or with respect to animal feeds bearing or containing such drug, as the Secretary may by general regulation, or by order with respect to such application, prescribe on the basis of a finding that such records and reports are necessary in order to enable the Secretary to determine, or facilitate a determination, whether there is or may be ground for invoking subsection (e) or subsection (m)(4) of this section. Such regulation or order shall provide, where the Secretary deems it to be appropriate, for the examination, upon request, by the persons to whom such regulation or order is applicable, of similar information received or otherwise obtained by the Secretary.

(2) Every person required under this subsection to maintain records, and every person in charge or custody thereof, shall, upon request of an officer or employee designated by the Secretary, permit such officer or employee at all reasonable times to have access to and copy and verify such records.

(m)(1) Any person may file with the Secretary an application for a license to manufacture animal feeds bearing or containing new animal drugs. Such person shall submit to the Secretary as part of the application (A) a full statement of the business name and address of the specific facility at which the manufacturing is to take place and the facility's registration number, (B) the name and signature of the responsible individual or individuals for that facility, (C) a certification that the animal feeds bearing or containing new animal drugs are manufactured and labeled in accordance with the applicable regulations published pursuant to subsection (i) or for indexed new animal drugs in accordance with the index listing published pursuant to section 572(e)(2) and the labeling requirements set forth in section 572(h), and (D) a certification that the methods used in, and the facilities and controls used for, manufacturing, processing, packaging, and holding such animal feeds are in conformity with current good manufacturing practice as described in section 501(a)(2)(B).

(2) Within 90 days after the filing of an application pursuant to paragraph (1), or such additional period as may be agreed upon by the Secretary and the applicant, the Secretary shall (A) issue an order approving the application if the Secretary then finds that none of the grounds for denying approval specified in paragraph (3) applies, or (B) give the applicant notice of an opportunity for a hearing before the Secretary under paragraph (3) on the question whether such application is approvable. The procedure governing such a hearing shall be the procedure set forth in the last two sentences of subsection (c)(1).

(3) If the Secretary, after due notice to the applicant in accordance with paragraph (2) and giving the applicant an opportunity for a hearing in accordance with such paragraph, finds, on the basis of information submitted to the Secretary as part of the application, on the basis of a preapproval inspection, or on the basis of any other information before the Secretary—

(A) that the application is incomplete, false, or misleading in any particular;

(B) that the methods used in, and the facilities and controls used for, the manufacture, processing, and packing of such animal feed are inadequate to preserve the identity, strength, quality, and purity of the new animal drug therein; or

(C) that the facility manufactures animal feeds bearing or containing new animal drugs in a manner that does not accord with the specifications for manufacture or labels animal feeds bearing or containing new animal drugs in a manner that does not accord with the conditions or indications of use that are published pursuant to subsection (i) or an index listing pursuant to section 572(e),

the Secretary shall issue an order refusing to approve the application. If, after such notice and opportunity for hearing, the Secretary finds that subparagraphs (A) through (C) do not apply, the Secretary shall issue an order approving the application. An order under this subsection approving an application for a license to manufacture animal feeds bearing or containing new animal drugs shall permit a facility to manufacture only those animal feeds bearing or containing new animal drugs for which there are in effect regulations pursuant to subsection (i) or an index listing pursuant to section 572(e) relating to the use of such drugs in or on such animal feed.

(4)(A) The Secretary shall, after due notice and opportunity for hearing to the applicant, revoke a license to manufacture animal feeds bearing or containing new animal drugs under this subsection if the Secretary finds—

(i) that the application for such license contains any untrue statement of a material fact; or

(ii) that the applicant has made changes that would cause the application to contain any untrue statements of material fact or that would affect the safety or effectiveness of the animal feeds manufactured at the facility unless the applicant has supplemented the application by filing with the Secretary adequate information respecting all such changes and unless there is in effect an approval of the supplemental application.

If the Secretary (or in the Secretary's absence the officer acting as the Secretary) finds that there is an imminent hazard to the health of humans or of the animals for which such animal feed is intended, the Secretary may suspend the license immediately, and give the applicant prompt notice of the action and afford the applicant the opportunity for an expedited hearing under this subsection; but the authority conferred by this sentence shall not be delegated.

(B) The Secretary may also, after due notice and opportunity for hearing to the applicant, revoke a license to manufacture animal feed under this subsection if the Secretary finds—

(i) that the applicant has failed to establish a system for maintaining required records, or has repeatedly or deliberately failed to maintain such records or to make required reports in accordance with a regulation or order under paragraph (5)(A) of this subsection or section 504(a)(3)(A), or the applicant has refused to permit access to, or copying or verification of, such records as required by subparagraph (B) of such paragraph or section 504(a)(3)(B);

(ii) that on the basis of new information before the Secretary, evaluated together with the evidence before the Secretary when such license was issued, the methods used in, or the facilities and controls used for, the manufacture, processing, packing, and holding of such animal feed are inadequate to assure and preserve the identity, strength, quality, and purity of the new animal drug therein, and were not made adequate within a reasonable time after receipt of written notice from the Secretary, specifying the matter complained of;

(iii) that on the basis of new information before the Secretary, evaluated together with the evidence before the Secretary when such license was issued, the labeling of any animal feeds, based on a fair evaluation of all material facts, is false or misleading in any particular and was not corrected within a reasonable time after receipt of written notice from the Secretary specifying the matter complained of; or

(iv) that on the basis of new information before the Secretary, evaluated together with the evidence before the Secretary when such license was issued, the facility has manufactured, processed, packed, or held animal feed bearing or containing a new animal drug adulterated under section 501(a)(6) and the facility did not discontinue the manufacture, processing, packing, or holding of such animal feed within a reasonable time after receipt of written notice from the Secretary specifying the matter complained of.

(C) The Secretary may also revoke a license to manufacture animal feeds under this subsection if an applicant gives notice to the Secretary of intention to discontinue the manufacture of all animal feed covered under this subsection and waives an opportunity for a hearing on the matter.

(D) Any order under this paragraph shall state the findings upon which it is based.

(5) When a license to manufacture animal feeds bearing or containing new animal drugs has been issued—

(A) the applicant shall establish and maintain such records, and make such reports to the Secretary, or (at the option of the Secretary) to the appropriate person or persons holding an approved application filed under subsection (b), as the Secretary may by general regulation, or by order with respect to such application, prescribe on the basis of a finding that such records and reports are necessary in order to enable the Secretary to determine, or facilitate a determination, whether there is or may be ground for invoking subsection (e) or paragraph (4); and

(B) every person required under this subsection to maintain records, and every person in charge or custody thereof, shall, upon request of an officer or employee designated by the Secretary, permit such officer or employee at all reasonable times to have access to and copy and verify such records.

(6) To the extent consistent with the public health, the Secretary may promulgate regulations for exempting from the operation of this subsection facilities that manufacture, process, pack, or hold animal feeds bearing or containing new animal drugs.

(n)(1) An abbreviated application for a new animal drug shall contain—

(A)(i) except as provided in clause (ii), information to show that the conditions of use or similar limitations (whether in the labeling or published pursuant to subsection (i)) prescribed, recommended, or suggested in the labeling proposed for the new animal drug have been previously approved for a new animal drug listed under paragraph (4) (hereinafter in this subsection referred to as an "approved new animal drug"), and

(ii) information to show that the withdrawal period at which residues of the new animal drug will be consistent with the tolerances established for the approved new animal drug is the same as the withdrawal period previously established for the approved new animal drug or, if the withdrawal period is proposed to be different, information showing that the residues of the new animal drug at the proposed different withdrawal period will be consistent with the tolerances established for the approved new animal drug;

(B)(i) information to show that the active ingredients of the new animal drug are the same as those of the approved new animal drug, and

(ii) if the approved new animal drug has more than one active ingredient, and if one of the active ingredients of the new animal drug is different from one of the active ingredients of the approved new animal drug and the application is filed pursuant to the approval of a petition filed under paragraph (3)—

(I) information to show that the other active ingredients of the new animal drug are the same as the active ingredients of the approved new animal drug,

(II) information to show either that the different active ingredient is an active ingredient of another approved new animal drug or of an animal drug which does not meet the requirements of section 201(v), and

(III) such other information respecting the different active ingredients as the Secretary may require;

(C)(i) if the approved new animal drug is permitted to be used with one or more animal drugs in animal feed, information to show that the proposed uses of the new animal drug with other animal drugs in animal feed are the same as the uses of the approved new animal drug, and

(ii) if the approved new animal drug is permitted to be used with one or more other animal drugs in animal feed, and one of the other animal drugs proposed for use with the new animal drug in animal feed is different from one of the other animal drugs permitted to be used in animal feed with the approved new animal drug, and the application is filed pursuant to the approval of a petition filed under paragraph (3)—

(I) information to show either that the different animal drug proposed for use with the approved new animal drug in animal feed is an approved new animal drug permitted to be used in animal feed or does not meet the requirements of section 201(v) when used with another animal drug in animal feed,

(II) information to show that other animal drugs proposed for use with the new animal drug in animal feed are the same as the other animal drugs permitted to be used with the approved new animal drug, and

(III) such other information respecting the different animal drug or combination with respect to which the petition was filed as the Secretary may require,

(D) information to show that the route of administration, the dosage form, and the strength of the new animal drug are the same as those of the approved new animal drug or, if the route of administration, the dosage form, or the strength of the new animal drug is different and the application is filed pursuant to the approval of a petition filed under paragraph (3), such information respecting the route of administration, dosage form, or strength with respect to which the petition was filed as the Secretary may require;

(E) information to show that the new animal drug is bioequivalent to the approved new animal drug, except that if the application is filed pursuant to the approval of a petition filed under paragraph (3) for the purposes described in subparagraph (B) or (C), information to show that the active ingredients of the new animal drug are of the same pharmacological or therapeutic class as the pharmacological or therapeutic class of the approved new animal drug and that the new animal drug can be expected to have the same therapeutic effect as the approved new animal drug when used in accordance with the labeling;

(F) information to show that the labeling proposed for the new animal drug is the same as the labeling approved for the approved new animal drug except for changes required because of differences approved under a petition filed under paragraph (3), because of a different withdrawal period, or because the new animal drug and the approved new animal drug are produced or distributed by different manufacturers;

(G) the items specified in clauses (B) through (F) of subsection (b)(1);

(H) a certification, in the opinion of the applicant and to the best of his knowledge, with respect to each patent which claims the approved new animal drug or which claims a use for such approved new animal drug for which the applicant is seeking approval under this subsection and for which information is required to be filed under subsection (b)(1) or (c)(3)—

(i) that such patent information has not been filed,

(ii) that such patent has expired,

(iii) of the date on which such patent will expire, or

(iv) that such patent is invalid or will not be infringed by the manufacture, use, or sale of the new animal drug for which the application is filed; and

(I) if with respect to the approved new animal drug information was filed under subsection (b)(1) or (c)(3) for a method of use patent which does not claim a use for which the applicant is seeking approval of an application under subsection (c)(2), a statement that the method of use patent does not claim such a use.

The Secretary may not require that an abbreviated application contain information in addition to that required by subparagraphs (A) through (I).

(2)(A) An applicant who makes a certification described in paragraph (1)(G)(iv) shall include in the application a statement that the applicant will give the notice required by subparagraph (B) to—

(i) each owner of the patent which is the subject of the certification or the representative of such owner designated to receive such notice, and

(ii) the holder of the approved application under subsection (c)(1) for the drug which is claimed by the patent or a use of which is claimed by the patent or the representative of such holder designated to receive such notice.

(B) The notice referred to in subparagraph (A) shall state that an application, which contains data from bioequivalence studies, has been filed under this subsection for the drug with respect to which the certification is made to obtain approval to engage in the commercial manufacture, use, or sale of such drug before the expiration of the patent referred to in the certification. Such notice shall include a detailed statement of the factual and legal basis of the applicant's opinion that the patent is not valid or will not be infringed.

(C) If an application is amended to include a certification described in paragraph (1)(G)(iv), the notice required by subparagraph (B) shall be given when the amended application is filed.

(3) If a person wants to submit an abbreviated application for a new animal drug—

(A) whose active ingredients, route of administration, dosage form, or strength differ from that of an approved new animal drug, or

(B) whose use with other animal drugs in animal feed differs from that of an approved new animal drug, such person shall submit a petition to the

Secretary seeking permission to file such an application. The Secretary shall approve a petition for a new animal drug unless the Secretary finds that—

(C) investigations must be conducted to show the safety and effectiveness, in animals to be treated with the drug, of the active ingredients, route of administration, dosage form, strength, or use with other animal drugs in animal feed which differ from the approved new animal drug, or

(D) investigations must be conducted to show the safety for human consumption of any residues in food resulting from the proposed active ingredients, route of administration, dosage form, strength, or use with other animal drugs in animal feed for the new animal drug which is different from the active ingredients, route of administration, dosage form, strength, or use with other animal drugs in animal feed of the approved new animal drug.

The Secretary shall approve or disapprove a petition submitted under this paragraph within 90 days of the date the petition is submitted.

(4)(A)(i) Within 60 days of the date of the enactment of this subsection 1, the Secretary shall publish and make available to the public a list in alphabetical order of the official and proprietary name of each new animal drug which has been approved for safety and effectiveness before the date of the enactment of this subsection.

(ii) Every 30 days after the publication of the first list under clause (i) the Secretary shall revise the list to include each new animal drug which has been approved for safety and effectiveness under subsection (c) during the 30 day period.

(iii) When patent information submitted under subsection (b)(1) or (c)(3) respecting a new animal drug included on the list is to be published by the Secretary, the Secretary shall, in revisions made under clause (ii), include such information for such drug.

(B) A new animal drug approved for safety and effectiveness before the date of the enactment of this subsection or approved for safety and effectiveness under subsection (c) shall, for purposes of this subsection, be considered to have been published under subparagraph (A) on the date of its approval or the date of enactment, whichever is later.

(C) If the approval of a new animal drug was withdrawn or suspended under subsection (c)(2)(G) or for grounds described in subsection (e) or if the Secretary determines that a drug has been withdrawn from sale for safety or effectiveness reasons, it may not be published in the list under subparagraph (A) or, if the withdrawal or suspension occurred after its publication in such list, it shall be immediately removed from such list—

(i) for the same period as the withdrawal or suspension under subsection (c)(2)(G) or (e), or

(ii) if the listed drug has been withdrawn from sale, for the period of withdrawal from sale or, if earlier, the period ending on the date the Secretary determines that the withdrawal from sale is not for safety or effectiveness reasons.

A notice of the removal shall be published in the Federal Register.

(5) If an application contains the information required by clauses (A), (G), and (H) of subsection (b)(1) and such information—

(A) is relied on by the applicant for the approval of the application, and

(B) is not information derived either from investigations, studies, or tests conducted by or for the applicant or for which the applicant had obtained a right of reference or use from the person by or for whom the investigations, studies, or tests were conducted, such application shall be considered to be an application filed under subsection (b)(2).

(o) For purposes of this section, the term "patent" means a patent issued by the United States Patent and Trademark Office.

(p)(1) Safety and effectiveness data and information which has been submitted in an application filed under subsection (b)(1) or section 571(a) for a drug and which has not previously been disclosed to the public shall be made available to the public, upon request, unless extraordinary circumstances are shown—

(A) if no work is being or will be undertaken to have the application approved,

(B) if the Secretary has determined that the application is not approvable and all legal appeals have been exhausted,

(C) if approval of the application under subsection (c) is withdrawn and all legal appeals have been exhausted,

(D) if the Secretary has determined that such drug is not a new drug, or

(E) upon the effective date of the approval of the first application filed under subsection (b)(2) which refers to such drug or upon the date upon which the approval of an application filed under subsection (b)(2) which refers to such drug could be made effective if such an application had been filed.

(2) Any request for data and information pursuant to paragraph (1) shall include a verified statement by the person making the request that any data or information received under such paragraph shall not be disclosed by such person to any other person—

(A) for the purpose of, or as part of a plan, scheme, or device for, obtaining the right to make, use, or market, or making, using, or marketing, outside the United States, the drug identified in the application filed under subsection (b)(1) or section 571(a), and

(B) without obtaining from any person to whom the data and information are disclosed an identical verified statement, a copy of which is to be provided by such person to the Secretary, which meets the requirements of this paragraph.

SEC. 513. [21 USC §360c] Classification of Devices Intended for Human Use; Device Classes

(a) Device Classes

(1) There are established the following classes of devices intended for human use:

(A) CLASS I, GENERAL CONTROLS.—

(i) A device for which the controls authorized by or under section 501, 502, 510, 516, 518, 519, or 520 or any combination of such sections are sufficient to provide reasonable assurance of the safety and effectiveness of the device.

(ii) A device for which insufficient information exists to determine that the controls referred to in clause (i) are sufficient to provide reasonable assurance of the safety and effectiveness of the device or to establish special controls to provide such assurance, but because it—

(I) is not purported or represented to be for a use in supporting or sustaining human life or for a use which is of substantial importance in preventing impairment of human health, and

(II) does not present a potential unreasonable risk of illness or injury,

is to be regulated by the controls referred to in clause (i).

(B) CLASS II, SPECIAL CONTROLS.—A device which cannot be classified as a class I device because the general controls by themselves are insufficient to provide reasonable assurance of the safety and effectiveness of the device, and for which there is sufficient information to establish special controls to provide such assurance, including the promulgation of performance standards, postmarket surveillance, patient registries, development and dissemination of guidelines (including guidelines for the submission of clinical data in premarket notification submissions in accordance with section 510(k)), recommendations, and other appropriate actions as the Secretary deems necessary to provide such assurance. For a device that is purported or represented to be for a use in supporting or sustaining human life, the Secretary shall examine and identify the special controls, if any, that are necessary to provide adequate assurance of safety and effectiveness and describe how such controls provide such assurance.

(C) CLASS III, PREMARKET APPROVAL.—A device which because—

(i) it (I) cannot be classified as a class I device because insufficient information exists to determine that the application of general controls are sufficient to provide reasonable assurance of the safety and effectiveness of the device, and (II) cannot be classified as a class II device because insufficient information exists to determine that the special controls described in subparagraph (B) would provide reasonable assurance of its safety and effectiveness, and

(ii)(I) is purported or represented to be for a use in supporting or sustaining human life or for a use which is of substantial importance in preventing impairment of human health, or

(II) presents a potential unreasonable risk of illness or injury, is to be subject, in accordance with section 515, to Premarket approval to provide reasonable assurance of its safety and effectiveness.

If there is not sufficient information to establish a performance standard for a device to provide reasonable assurance of its safety and effectiveness, the Secretary may conduct such activities as may be necessary to develop or obtain such information.

(2) For purposes of this section and sections 514 and 515, the safety and effectiveness of a device are to be determined—

(A) with respect to the persons for whose use the device is represented or intended,

(B) with respect to the conditions of use prescribed, recommended, or suggested in the labeling of the device, and

(C) weighing any probable benefit to health from the use of the device against any probable risk of injury or illness from such use.

(3)(A) Except as authorized by subparagraph (B), the effectiveness of a device is, for purposes of this section and sections 514 and 515, to be determined, in accordance with regulations promulgated by the Secretary, on the basis of well-controlled investigations, including 1 or more clinical investigations where appropriate, by experts qualified by training and experience to evaluate the effectiveness of the device, from which investigations it can fairly and responsibly be concluded by qualified experts that the device will have the effect it purports or is represented to have under the conditions of use prescribed, recommended, or suggested in the labeling of the device.

(B) If the Secretary determines that there exists valid scientific evidence (other than evidence derived from investigations described in subparagraph (A))—

(i) which is sufficient to determine the effectiveness of a device, and

(ii) from which it can fairly and responsibly be concluded by qualified experts that the device will have the effect it purports or is represented to have under the conditions of use prescribed, recommended, or suggested in the labeling of the device, then, for purposes of this section and sections 514 and 515, the Secretary may authorize the effectiveness of the device to be determined on the basis of such evidence.

(C) In making a determination of a reasonable assurance of the effectiveness of a device for which an application under section 515 has been submitted, the Secretary shall consider whether the extent of data that otherwise would be required for approval of the application with respect to effectiveness can be reduced through reliance on postmarket controls.

(D)(i) The Secretary, upon the written request of any person intending to submit an application under section 515, shall meet with such person to determine the type of valid scientific evidence (within the meaning of subparagraphs (A) and (B)) that will be necessary to demonstrate for purposes of approval of an application the effectiveness of a device for the conditions of use proposed by such person. The written request shall include a detailed description of the device, a detailed description of the proposed conditions of use of the device, a proposed plan for determining whether there is a reasonable assurance of effectiveness, and, if available, information regarding the expected performance from the device. Within 30 days after such meeting, the Secretary shall specify in writing the type of valid scientific evidence that will provide a reasonable assurance that a device is effective under the conditions of use proposed by such person.

(ii) Any clinical data, including one or more well-controlled investigations, specified in writing by the Secretary for demonstrating a reasonable assurance of device effectiveness shall be specified as result of a determination by the Secretary that such data are necessary to establish device effectiveness. The Secretary shall consider, in consultation with the applicant, the least burdensome appropriate means of evaluating device effectiveness that would have a reasonable likelihood of resulting in approval.

(iii) The determination of the Secretary with respect to the specification of valid scientific evidence under clauses (i) and (ii) shall be binding upon the Secretary, unless such determination by the Secretary could be contrary to the public health.

(b) Classification; Classification Panels

(1) For purposes of—

(A) determining which devices intended for human use should be subject to the requirements of general controls, performance standards, or premarket approval, and

(B) providing notice to the manufacturers and importers of such devices to enable them to prepare for the application of such requirements to devices manufactured or imported by them,

the Secretary shall classify all such devices (other than devices classified by subsection (f)) into the classes established by subsection (a). For the purpose of securing recommendations with respect to the classification of devices, the Secretary shall establish panels of experts or use panels of experts established before the date of the enactment of this section, or both. Section 14 of the Federal Advisory Committee Act shall not apply to the duration of a panel established under this paragraph.

(2) The Secretary shall appoint to each panel established under paragraph (1) persons who are qualified by training and experience to evaluate the safety and effectiveness of the devices to be referred to the panel and who, to the extent feasible, possess skill in the use of, or experience in the development, manufacture, or utilization of, such devices. The Secretary shall make appointments to each panel so that each panel shall consist of members with adequately diversified expertise in such fields as clinical and administrative medicine, engineering, biological and physical sciences, and other related professions. In addition, each panel shall include as nonvoting members a representative of consumer interests and a representative of interests of the device manufacturing industry. Scientific, trade, and consumer organizations shall be afforded an opportunity to nominate individuals for appointment to the panels. No individual who is in the regular full-time employ of the United States and engaged in the administration of this Act may be a member of any panel. The Secretary shall designate one of the members of each panel to serve as chairman thereof.

(3) Panel members (other than officers or employees of the United States), while attending meetings or conferences of a panel or otherwise engaged in its business, shall be entitled to receive compensation at rates to be fixed by the Secretary, but not at rates exceeding the daily equivalent of the rate in effect for grade GS–18 of the General Schedule [41], for each day so engaged,

[41] The General Schedule under section 5332 of title 5, United States Code, no longer includes the grade GS-18. The grades are GS-1 through GS-15.

including travel time; and while so serving away from their homes or regular places of business each member may be allowed travel expenses (including per diem in lieu of subsistence) as authorized by section 5703 of title 5, United States Code, for persons in the Government service employed intermittently.

(4) The Secretary shall furnish each panel with adequate clerical and other necessary assistance.

(5) Classification panels covering each type of device shall be scheduled to meet at such times as may be appropriate for the Secretary to meet applicable statutory deadlines.

(6)(A) Any person whose device is specifically the subject of review by a classification panel shall have—

(i) the same access to data and information submitted to a classification panel (except for data and information that are not available for public disclosure under section 552 of title 5, United States Code) as the Secretary;

(ii) the opportunity to submit, for review by a classification panel, information that is based on the data or information provided in the application submitted under section 515 by the person, which information shall be submitted to the Secretary for prompt transmittal to the classification panel; and

(iii) the same opportunity as the Secretary to participate in meetings of the panel.

(B) Any meetings of a classification panel shall provide adequate time for initial presentations and for response to any differing views by persons whose devices are specifically the subject of a classification panel review, and shall encourage free and open participation by all interested persons.

(7) After receiving from a classification panel the conclusions and recommendations of the panel on a matter that the panel has reviewed, the Secretary shall review the conclusions and recommendations, shall make a final decision on the matter in accordance with section 515(d)(2), and shall notify the affected persons of the decision in writing and, if the decision differs from the conclusions and recommendations of the panel, shall include the reasons for the difference.

(8) A classification panel under this subsection shall not be subject to the annual chartering and annual report requirements of the Federal Advisory Committee Act.

(c) Classification Panel Organization and Operation

(1) The Secretary shall organize the panels according to the various fields of clinical medicine and fundamental sciences in which devices intended for human use are used. The Secretary shall refer a device to be classified under this section to an appropriate panel established or authorized to be used under subsection (b) for its review and for its recommendation respecting the classification of the device. The Secretary shall by regulation prescribe the procedure to be followed by the panels in making their reviews and recommendations. In making their reviews of devices, the panels, to the maximum extent practicable, shall provide an opportunity for interested persons to submit data and views on the classification of the devices.

(2)(A) Upon completion of a panel's review of a device referred to it under paragraph (1), the panel shall, subject to subparagraphs (B) and (C), submit to the Secretary its recommendation for the classification of the device. Any such recommendation shall (i) contain (I) a summary of the reasons for the recommendation, (II) a summary of the data upon which the recommendation is based, and (III) an identification of the risks to health (if any) presented by the device with respect to which the recommendation is made, and (ii) to the extent practicable, include a recommendation for the assignment of a priority for the application of the requirements of section 514 or 515 to a device recommended to be classified in class II or class III.

(B) A recommendation of a panel for the classification of a device in class I shall include a recommendation as to whether the device should be exempted from the requirements of section 510, 519, or 520(f).

(C) In the case of a device which has been referred under paragraph (1) to a panel, and which—

(i) is intended to be implanted in the human body or is purported or represented to be for a use in supporting or sustaining human life, and

(ii)(I) has been introduced or delivered for introduction into interstate commerce for commercial distribution before the date of enactment of this section, or

(II) is within a type of device which was so introduced or delivered before such date and is substantially equivalent to another device within that type,

such panel shall recommend to the Secretary that the device be classified in class III unless the panel determines that classification of the device in such class is not necessary to provide reasonable assurance of its safety and effectiveness. If a panel does not recommend that such a device be classified in class III, it shall in its recommendation to the Secretary for the classification of the device set forth the reasons for not recommending classification of the device in such class.

(3) The panels shall submit to the Secretary within one year of the date funds are first appropriated for the implementation of this section their recommendations respecting all devices of a type introduced or delivered for introduction into interstate commerce for commercial distribution before the date of the enactment of this section.

(d) Classification

(1) Upon receipt of a recommendation from a panel respecting a device, the Secretary shall publish in the Federal Register the panel's recommendation and a proposed regulation classifying such device and shall provide interested persons an opportunity to submit comments on such recommendation and the proposed regulation. After reviewing such comments, the Secretary shall, subject to paragraph (2), by regulation classify such device.

(2)(A) A regulation under paragraph (1) classifying a device in class I shall prescribe which, if any, of the requirements of section 510, 519 or 520(f) shall not apply to the device. A regulation which makes a requirement of section 510, 519, or 520(f) inapplicable to a device shall be accompanied by a statement of the reasons of the Secretary for making such requirement inapplicable.

(B) A device described in subsection (c)(2)(C) shall be classified in class III unless the Secretary determines that classification of the device in such class is not necessary to provide reasonable assurance of its safety and effectiveness. A proposed regulation under paragraph (1) classifying such a device in a class other than class III shall be accompanied by a full statement of the reasons of the Secretary (and supporting documentation and data) for not classifying such device in such class and an identification of the risks to health (if any) presented by such device.

(3) In the case of devices classified in class II and devices classified under this subsection in class III and described in section 515(b)(1) the Secretary may establish priorities which, in his discretion, shall be used in applying sections 514 and 515, as appropriate, to such devices.

(e) Classification Changes

(1) Based on new information respecting a device, the Secretary may, upon his own initiative or upon petition of an interested person, by regulation (A) change such device's classification, and (B) revoke, because of the change in classification, any regulation or requirement in effect under section 514 or 515 with respect to such device. In the promulgation of such a regulation respecting a device's classification, the Secretary may secure from the panel to which the device was last referred pursuant to subsection (c) a recommendation respecting the proposed change in the device's classification and shall publish in the Federal Register any recommendation submitted to the Secretary by the panel respecting such change. A regulation under this

subsection changing the classification of a device from class III to class II may provide that such classification shall not take effect until the effective date of a performance standard established under section 514 for such device.

(2) By regulation promulgated under paragraph (1), the Secretary may change the classification of a device from class III—

(A) to class II if the Secretary determines that special controls would provide reasonable assurance of the safety and effectiveness of the device and that general controls would not provide reasonable assurance of the safety and effectiveness of the device, or

(B) to class I if the Secretary determines that general controls would provide reasonable assurance of the safety and effectiveness of the device.

(f) Initial Classification and Reclassification of Certain Devices

(1) Any device intended for human use which was not introduced or delivered for introduction into interstate commerce for commercial distribution before the date of the enactment of this section is classified in class III unless—

(A) the device—

(i) is within a type of device (I) which was introduced or delivered for introduction into interstate commerce for commercial distribution before such date and which is to be classified pursuant to subsection (b), or (II) which was not so introduced or delivered before such date and has been classified in class I or II, and

(ii) is substantially equivalent to another device within such type, or

(B) the Secretary in response to a petition submitted under paragraph (3) has classified such device in class I or II.

A device classified in class III under this paragraph shall be classified in that class until the effective date of an order of the Secretary under paragraph (2) or (3) classifying the device in class I or II.

(2)(A) Any person who submits a report under section 510(k) for a type of device that has not been previously classified under this Act, and that is classified into class III under paragraph (1), may request, within 30 days after receiving written notice of such a classification, the Secretary to classify the device under the criteria set forth in subparagraphs (A) through (C) of subsection (a)(1). The person may, in the request, recommend to the Secretary a classification for the device. Any such request shall describe the device and provide detailed information and reasons for the recommended classification.

(B)(i) Not later than 60 days after the date of the submission of the request under subparagraph (A), the Secretary shall by written order classify the device involved. Such classification shall be the initial classification of the device for purposes of paragraph (1) and any device classified under this paragraph shall be a predicate device for determining substantial equivalence under paragraph (1).

(ii) A device that remains in class III under this subparagraph shall be deemed to be adulterated within the meaning of section 501(f)(1)(B) until approved under section 515 or exempted from such approval under section 520(g).

(C) Within 30 days after the issuance of an order classifying a device under this paragraph, the Secretary shall publish a notice in the Federal Register announcing such classification.

(3)(A) The Secretary may initiate the reclassification of a device classified into class III under paragraph (1) of this subsection or the manufacturer or importer of a device classified under paragraph (1) may petition the Secretary (in such form and manner as he shall prescribe) for the issuance of an order classifying the device in class I or class II. Within thirty days of the filing of such a petition, the Secretary shall notify the petitioner of any deficiencies in the petition which prevent the Secretary from making a decision on the petition.

(B)(i) Upon determining that a petition does not contain any deficiency which prevents the Secretary from making a decision on the petition, the Secretary may for good cause shown refer the petition to an appropriate panel established or authorized to be used under subsection (b). A panel to which such a petition has been referred shall not later than ninety days after the referral of the petition make a recommendation to the Secretary respecting approval or denial of the petition. Any such recommendation shall contain (I) a summary of the reasons for the recommendation, (II) a summary of the data upon which the recommendation is based, and (III) an identification of the risks to health (if any) presented by the device with respect to which the petition was filed. In the case of a petition for a device which is intended to be implanted in the human body or which is purported or represented to be for a use in supporting or sustaining human life, the panel shall recommend that the petition be denied unless the panel determines that the classification in class III of the device is not necessary to provide reasonable assurance of its safety and effectiveness. If the panel recommends that such petition be approved, it shall in its recommendation to the Secretary set forth its reasons for such recommendation.

(ii) The requirements of paragraphs (1) and (2) of subsection (c) (relating to opportunities for submission of data and views and recommendations respecting priorities and exemptions from sections 510, 519, and 520(f)) shall apply with respect to consideration by panels of petitions submitted under subparagraph (A).

(C)(i) Within ninety days from the date the Secretary receives the recommendation of a panel respecting a petition (but not later than 210 days after the filing of such petition) the Secretary shall by order deny or approve the petition. If the Secretary approves the petition, the Secretary shall order the classification of the device into class I or class II in accordance with the criteria prescribed by subsection (a)(1)(A) or (a)(1)(B). In the case of a petition for a device which is intended to be implanted in the human body or which is purported or represented to be for a use in supporting or sustaining human life, the Secretary shall deny the petition unless the Secretary determines that the classification in class III of the device is not necessary to provide reasonable assurance of its safety and effectiveness. An order approving such petition shall be accompanied by a full statement of the reasons of the Secretary (and supporting documentation and data) for approving the petition and an identification of the risks to health (if any) presented by the device to which such order applies.

(ii) The requirements of paragraphs (1) and (2)(A) of subsection (d) (relating to publication of recommendations, opportunity for submission of comments, and exemption from sections 510, 519, and 520(f)) shall apply with respect to action by the Secretary on petitions submitted under subparagraph (A).

(4) If a manufacturer reports to the Secretary under section 510(k) that a device is substantially equivalent to another device—

(A) which the Secretary has classified as a class III device under subsection (b),

(B) which was introduced or delivered for introduction into interstate commerce for commercial distribution before December 1, 1990, and

(C) for which no final regulation requiring premarket approval has been promulgated under section 515(b),

the manufacturer shall certify to the Secretary that the manufacturer has conducted a reasonable search of all information known or otherwise available to the manufacturer respecting such other device and has included in the report under section 510(k) a summary of and a citation to all adverse safety and effectiveness data respecting such other device and respecting the device for which the section 510(k) report is being made and which has not been submitted to the Secretary under section 519. The Secretary may require the manufacturer to submit the adverse safety and effectiveness data described in the report.

(5) The Secretary may not withhold a determination of the initial classification of a device under paragraph (1) because of a failure to comply with any

provision of this Act unrelated to a substantial equivalence decision, including a finding that the facility in which the device is manufactured is not in compliance with good manufacturing requirements as set forth in regulations of the Secretary under section 520(f) (other than a finding that there is a substantial likelihood that the failure to comply with such regulations will potentially present a serious risk to human health).

(g) Information. Within sixty days of the receipt of a written request of any person for information respecting the class in which a device has been classified or the requirements applicable to a device under this Act, the Secretary shall provide such person a written statement of the classification (if any) of such device and the requirements of this Act applicable to the device.

(h) Definitions. For purposes of this section and sections 501, 510, 514, 515, 516, 519, and 520—

(1) a reference to "***general controls***" is a reference to the controls authorized by or under sections 501, 502, 510, 516, 518, 519, and 520,

(2) a reference to "***class I***," "***class II***," or "***class III***" is a reference to a class of medical devices described in subparagraph (A), (B), or (C) of subsection (a)(1), and

(3) a reference to a "***panel under section 513***" is a reference to a panel established or authorized to be used under this section.

(i) Substantial Equivalence

(1)(A) For purposes of determinations of substantial equivalence under subsection (f) and section 520(l), the term "substantially equivalent" or "substantial equivalence" means, with respect to a device being compared to a predicate device, that the device has the same intended use as the predicate device and that the Secretary by order has found that the device—

(i) has the same technological characteristics as the predicate device, or

(ii)(I) has different technological characteristics and the information submitted that the device is substantially equivalent to the predicate device contains information, including appropriate clinical or scientific data if deemed necessary by the Secretary or a person accredited under section 523, that demonstrates that the device is as safe and effective as a legally marketed device, and (II) does not raise different questions of safety and effectiveness than the predicate device.

(B) For purposes of subparagraph (A), the term "different technological characteristics" means, with respect to a device being compared to a predicate device, that there is a significant change in the materials, design, energy source, or other features of the device from those of the predicate device.

(C) To facilitate reviews of reports submitted to the Secretary under section 510(k), the Secretary shall consider the extent to which reliance on postmarket controls may expedite the classification of devices under subsection (f)(1) of this section.

(D) Whenever the Secretary requests information to demonstrate that devices with differing technological characteristics are substantially equivalent, the Secretary shall only request information that is necessary to making substantial equivalence determinations. In making such request, the Secretary shall consider the least burdensome means of demonstrating substantial equivalence and request information accordingly.

(E)(i) Any determination by the Secretary of the intended use of a device shall be based upon the proposed labeling submitted in a report for the device under section 510(k). However, when determining that a device can be found substantially equivalent to a legally marketed device, the director of the organizational unit responsible for regulating devices (in this subparagraph referred to as the "Director") may require a statement in labeling that provides appropriate information regarding a use of the device not identified in the proposed labeling if, after providing an opportunity for consultation with the person who submitted such report, the Director determines and states in writing—

(I) that there is a reasonable likelihood that the device will be used for an intended use not identified in the proposed labeling for the device; and

(II) that such use could cause harm.

(ii) Such determination shall—

(I) be provided to the person who submitted the report within 10 days from the date of the notification of the Director's concerns regarding the proposed labeling;

(II) specify the limitations on the use of the device not included in the proposed labeling; and

(III) find the device substantially equivalent if the requirements of subparagraph (A) are met and if the labeling for such device conforms to the limitations specified in subclause (II).

(iii) The responsibilities of the Director under this subparagraph may not be delegated.

(iv) This subparagraph has no legal effect after the expiration of the five-year period beginning on the date of the enactment of the Food and Drug Administration Modernization Act of 1997.

(F) Not later than 270 days after the date of the enactment of the Food and Drug Administration Modernization Act of 1997, the Secretary shall issue guidance specifying the general principles that the Secretary will consider in determining when a specific intended use of a device is not reasonably included within a general use of such device for purposes of a determination of substantial equivalence under subsection (f) or section 520(l).

(2) A device may not be found to be substantially equivalent to a predicate device that has been removed from the market at the initiative of the Secretary or that has been determined to be misbranded or adulterated by a judicial order.

(3)(A) As part of a submission under section 510(k) respecting a device, the person required to file a premarket notification under such section shall provide an adequate summary of any information respecting safety and effectiveness or state that such information will be made available upon request by any person.

(B) Any summary under subparagraph (A) respecting a device shall contain detailed information regarding data concerning adverse health effects and shall be made available to the public by the Secretary within 30 days of the issuance of a determination that such device is substantially equivalent to another device.

SEC. 514. [21 USC §360d] Performance Standards; Provisions of Standards

(a) Provisions of Standards

(1) The special controls required by section 513(a)(1)(B) shall include performance standards for a class II device if the Secretary determines that a performance standard is necessary to provide reasonable assurance of the safety and effectiveness of the device. A class III device may also be considered a class II device for purposes of establishing a standard for the device under subsection (b) if the device has been reclassified as a class II device under a regulation under section 513(e) but such regulation provides that the reclassification is not to take effect until the effective date of such a standard for the device.

(2) A performance standard established under subsection (b) for a device—

(A) shall include provisions to provide reasonable assurance of its safe and effective performance;

(B) shall, where necessary to provide reasonable assurance of its safe and effective performance, include—

(i) provisions respecting the construction, components, ingredients, and properties of the device and its compatibility with power systems and connections to such systems,

(ii) provisions for the testing (on a sample basis or, if necessary, on an individual basis) of the device or, if it is determined that no other more practicable means are available to the Secretary to assure the conformity of the device to the standard, provisions for the testing (on a sample basis or, if necessary, on an individual basis) by the Secretary or by another person at the direction of the Secretary,

(iii) provisions for the measurement of the performance characteristics of the device,

(iv) provisions requiring that the results of each or of certain of the tests of the device required to be made under clause (ii) show that the device is in conformity with the portions of the standard for which the test or tests were required, and

(v) a provision requiring that the sale and distribution of the device be restricted but only to the extent that the sale and distribution of a device may be restricted under a regulation under section 520(e); and

(C) shall, where appropriate, require the use and prescribe the form and content of labeling for the proper installation, maintenance, operation, and use of the device.

(3) The Secretary shall provide for periodic evaluation of performance standards established under subsection (b) to determine if such standards should be changed to reflect new medical, scientific, or other technological data.

(4) In carrying out his duties under this subsection and subsection (b), the Secretary shall, to the maximum extent practicable—

(A) use personnel, facilities, and other technical support available in other Federal agencies,

(B) consult with other Federal agencies concerned with standard-setting and other nationally or internationally recognized standard-setting entities, and

(C) invite appropriate participation, through joint or other conferences, workshops, or other means, by informed persons representative of scientific, professional, industry, or consumer organizations who in his judgment can make a significant contribution.

(b) Establishment of a Standard

(1)(A) The Secretary shall publish in the Federal Register a notice of proposed rulemaking for the establishment, amendment, or revocation of any performance standard for a device.

(B) A notice of proposed rulemaking for the establishment or amendment of a performance standard for a device shall—

(i) set forth a finding with supporting justification that the performance standard is appropriate and necessary to provide reasonable assurance of the safety and effectiveness of the device,

(ii) set forth proposed findings with respect to the risk of illness or injury that the performance standard is intended to reduce or eliminate,

(iii) invite interested persons to submit to the Secretary, within 30 days of the publication of the notice, requests for changes in the classification of the device pursuant to section 513(e) based on new information relevant to the classification, and

(iv) invite interested persons to submit an existing performance standard for the device, including a draft or proposed performance standard, for consideration by the Secretary.

(C) A notice of proposed rulemaking for the revocation of a performance standard shall set forth a finding with supporting justification that the performance standard is no longer necessary to provide reasonable assurance of the safety and effectiveness of a device.

(D) The Secretary shall provide for a comment period of not less than 60 days.

(2) If, after publication of a notice in accordance with paragraph (1), the Secretary receives a request for a change in the classification of the device, the Secretary shall, within 60 days of the publication of the notice, after consultation with the appropriate panel under section 513, either deny the request or give notice of an intent to initiate such change under section 513(e).

(3)(A) After the expiration of the period for comment on a notice of proposed rulemaking published under paragraph (1) respecting a performance standard and after consideration of such comments and any report from an advisory committee under paragraph (5), the Secretary shall (i) promulgate a regulation establishing a performance standard and publish in the Federal Register findings on the matters referred to in paragraph (1), or (ii) publish a notice terminating the proceeding for the development of the standard together with the reasons for such termination. If a notice of termination is published, the Secretary shall (unless such notice is issued because the device is a banned device under section 516) initiate a proceeding under section 513(e) to reclassify the device subject to the proceeding terminated by such notice.

(B) A regulation establishing a performance standard shall set forth the date or dates upon which the standard shall take effect, but no such regulation may take effect before one year after the date of its publication unless (i) the Secretary determines that an earlier effective date is necessary for the protection of the public health and safety, or (ii) such standard has been established for a device which, effective upon the effective date of the standard, has been reclassified from class III to class II. Such date or dates shall be established so as to minimize, consistent with the public health and safety, economic loss to, and disruption or dislocation of, domestic and international trade.

(4)(A) The Secretary, upon his own initiative or upon petition of an interested person may by regulation, promulgated in accordance with the requirements of paragraphs (1), (2), and (3)(B) of this subsection, amend or revoke a performance standard.

(B) The Secretary may declare a proposed amendment of a performance standard to be effective on and after its publication in the Federal Register and until the effective date of any final action taken on such amendment if he determines that making it so effective is in the public interest. A proposed amendment of a performance standard made so effective under the preceding sentence may not prohibit, during the period in which it is so effective, the introduction or delivery for introduction into interstate commerce of a device which conforms to such standard without the change or changes provided by such proposed amendment.

(5)(A) The Secretary—

(i) may on his own initiative refer a proposed regulation for the establishment, amendment, or revocation of a performance standard, or

(ii) shall, upon the request of an interested person which demonstrates good cause for referral and which is made before the expiration of the period for submission of comments on such proposed regulation refer such proposed regulation, to an advisory committee of experts, established pursuant to subparagraph (B) for a report and recommendation with respect to any matter involved in the proposed regulation which requires the exercise of scientific judgment. If a proposed regulation is referred under this subparagraph to an advisory committee, the Secretary shall provide the advisory committee with the data and information on which such proposed regulation is based. The advisory committee shall, within sixty days of the referral of a proposed regulation and after independent study of the data and information furnished to it by the Secretary and other data and information before it, submit to the Secretary a report and recommendation respecting such regulation, together with all underlying data and information and a statement of the reason or basis for the recommendation. A copy of such report and recommendation shall be made public by the Secretary.

(B) The Secretary shall establish advisory committees (which may not be panels under section 513) to receive referrals under subparagraph (A). The Secretary shall appoint as members of any such advisory committee persons qualified in the subject matter to be referred to the committee and of appropriately diversified professional background, except that the Secretary may not appoint to such a committee any individual who is in the regular full-time employ of the United States and engaged in the administration of this Act. Each such committee shall include as nonvoting members a representative of consumer interests and a representative of interests of the device manufacturing industry. Members of an advisory committee who are not officers or employees of the United States, while attending conferences or meetings of their committee or otherwise serving at the request of the Secretary, shall be entitled to receive compensation at rates to be fixed by the Secretary, which rates may not exceed the daily equivalent of the rate in effect for grade GS–18 of the General Schedule [42], for each day (including travel time) they are so engaged; and while so serving away from their homes or regular places of business each member may be allowed travel expenses, including per diem in lieu of subsistence, as authorized by section 5703 of title 5 of the United States Code for persons in the Government service employed intermittently. The Secretary shall designate one of the members of each advisory committee to serve as chairman thereof. The Secretary shall furnish each advisory committee with clerical and other assistance, and shall by regulation prescribe the procedures to be followed by each such committee in acting on referrals made under subparagraph (A).

(c) Recognition of a Standard

(1)(A) In addition to establishing a performance standard under this section, the Secretary shall, by publication in the Federal Register, recognize all or part of an appropriate standard established by a nationally or internationally recognized standard development organization for which a person may submit a declaration of conformity in order to meet a premarket submission requirement or other requirement under this Act to which such standard is applicable.

(B) If a person elects to use a standard recognized by the Secretary under subparagraph (A) to meet the requirements described in such subparagraph, the person shall provide a declaration of conformity to the

[42] The General Schedule under section 5332 of title 5, United States Code, no longer includes the grade GS-18. The grades are GS-1 through GS-15.

Secretary that certifies that the device is in conformity with such standard. A person may elect to use data, or information, other than data required by a standard recognized under subparagraph (A) to meet any requirement regarding devices under this Act.

(2) The Secretary may withdraw such recognition of a standard through publication of a notice in the Federal Register if the Secretary determines that the standard is no longer appropriate for meeting a requirement regarding devices under this Act.

(3)(A) Subject to subparagraph (B), the Secretary shall accept a declaration of conformity that a device is in conformity with a standard recognized under paragraph (1) unless the Secretary finds—

(i) that the data or information submitted to support such declaration does not demonstrate that the device is in conformity with the standard identified in the declaration of conformity; or

(ii) that the standard identified in the declaration of conformity is not applicable to the particular device under review.

(B) The Secretary may request, at any time, the data or information relied on by the person to make a declaration of conformity with respect to a standard recognized under paragraph (1).

(C) A person making a declaration of conformity with respect to a standard recognized under paragraph (1) shall maintain the data and information demonstrating conformity of the device to the standard for a period of two years after the date of the classification or approval of the device by the Secretary or a period equal to the expected design life of the device, whichever is longer.

SEC. 515. [21 USC §360e] Premarket Approval; General Requirement

Note: revisions were posted to this section in February 2008.

(a) General Requirement. A class III device—

(1) which is subject to a regulation promulgated under subsection (b); or

(2) which is a class III device because of section 513(f), is required to have, unless exempt under section 520(g), an approval under this section of an application for premarket approval or, as applicable, an approval under subsection (c)(2) of a report seeking premarket approval.

(b) Regulation To Require Premarket Approval

(1) In the case of a class III device which—

(A) was introduced or delivered for introduction into interstate commerce for commercial distribution before the date of enactment of this section [enacted May 28, 1976]; or

(B) is (i) of a type so introduced or delivered, and (ii) is substantially equivalent to another device within that type;

the Secretary shall by regulation, promulgated in accordance with this subsection, require that such device have an approval under this section of an application for premarket approval.

(2)(A) A proceeding for the promulgation of a regulation under paragraph (1) respecting a device shall be initiated by the publication in the Federal Register of a notice of proposed rulemaking. Such notice shall contain—

(i) the proposed regulation;

(ii) proposed findings with respect to the degree of risk of illness or injury designed to be eliminated or reduced by requiring the device to have an approved application for premarket approval and the benefit to the public from use of the device;

(iii) opportunity for the submission of comments on the proposed regulation and the proposed findings; and

(iv) opportunity to request a change in the classification of the device based on new information relevant to the classification of the device.

(B) If, within fifteen days after publication of a notice under subparagraph (A), the Secretary receives a request for a change in the classification of a device, he shall, within sixty days of the publication of such notice and after consultation with the appropriate panel under section 513, by order published in the Federal Register, either deny the request for change in classification or give notice of his intent to initiate such a change under section 513(e).

(3) After the expiration of the period for comment on a proposed regulation and proposed findings published under paragraph (2) and after consideration of comments submitted on such proposed regulation and findings, the Secretary shall (A) promulgate such regulation and publish in the Federal Register findings on the matters referred to in paragraph (2)(A)(ii), or (B) publish a notice terminating the proceeding for the promulgation of the regulation together with the reasons for such termination. If a notice of termination is published, the Secretary shall (unless such notice is issued because the device is a banned device under section 516) initiate a proceeding under section 513(e) to reclassify the device subject to the proceeding terminated by such notice.

(4) The Secretary, upon his own initiative or upon petition of an interested person, may by regulation amend or revoke any regulation promulgated under this subsection. A regulation to amend or revoke a regulation under this subsection shall be promulgated in accordance with the requirements prescribed by this subsection for the promulgation of the regulation to be amended or revoked.

(c) Application for premarket approval

(1) Any person may file with the Secretary an application for premarket approval for a class III device. Such an application for a device shall contain—

(A) full reports of all information, published or known to or which should reasonably be known to the applicant, concerning investigations which have been made to show whether or not such device is safe and effective;

(B) a full statement of the components, ingredients, and properties and of the principle or principles of operation, of such device;

(C) a full description of the methods used in, and the facilities and controls used for, the manufacture, processing, and, when relevant, packing and installation of, such device;

(D) an identifying reference to any performance standard under section 514 which would be applicable to any aspect of such device if it were a class II device, and either adequate information to show that such aspect of such device fully meets such performance standard or adequate information to justify any deviation from such standard;

(E) such samples of such device and of components thereof as the Secretary may reasonably require, except that where the submission of such samples is impracticable or unduly burdensome, the requirement of this subparagraph may be met by the submission of complete information concerning the location of one or more such devices readily available for examination and testing;

(F) specimens of the labeling proposed to be used for such device; and

(G) the certification required under section 402(j)(5)(B) of the Public Health Service Act [42 USC § 282(j)(5)(B)] (which shall not be considered an element of such application); and

(H) such other information relevant to the subject matter of the application as the Secretary, with the concurrence of the appropriate panel under section 513, may require.

(2)(A) Any person may file with the Secretary a report seeking premarket approval for a class III device referred to in subsection (a) that is a reprocessed single-use device. Such a report shall contain the following:

(i) The device name, including both the trade or proprietary name and the common or usual name.

(ii) The establishment registration number of the owner or operator submitting the report.

(iii) Actions taken to comply with performance standards under section 514.

(iv) Proposed labels, labeling, and advertising sufficient to describe the device, its intended use, and directions for use.

(v) Full reports of all information, published or known to or which should be reasonably known to the applicant, concerning investigations which have been made to show whether or not the device is safe or effective.

(vi) A description of the device's components, ingredients, and properties.

(vii) A full description of the methods used in, and the facilities and controls used for, the reprocessing and packing of the device.

(viii) Such samples of the device that the Secretary may reasonably require.

(ix) A financial certification or disclosure statement or both, as required by part 54 of title 21, Code of Federal Regulations.

(x) A statement that the applicant believes to the best of the applicant's knowledge that all data and information submitted to the Secretary are truthful and accurate and that no material fact has been omitted in the report.

(xi) Any additional data and information, including information of the type required in paragraph (1) for an application under such paragraph, that the Secretary determines is necessary to determine whether there is reasonable assurance of safety and effectiveness for the reprocessed device.

(xii) Validation data described in section 510(o)(1)(A) that demonstrates that the reasonable assurance of the safety or effectiveness of the device will remain after the maximum number of times the device is reprocessed as intended by the person submitting such report.

(B) In the case of a class III device referred to in subsection (a) that is a reprocessed single-use device:

(i) Subparagraph (A) of this paragraph applies in lieu of paragraph (1).

(ii) Subject to clause (i), the provisions of this section apply to a report under subparagraph (A) to the same extent and in the same manner as such provisions apply to an application under paragraph (1).

(iii) Each reference in other sections of this Act to an application under this section, other than such a reference in section 737 or 738, shall be considered to be a reference to a report under subparagraph (A).

(iv) Each reference in other sections of this Act to a device for which an application under this section has been approved, or has been denied, suspended, or withdrawn, other than such a reference in section 737 or 738, shall be considered to be a reference to a device for which a report under subparagraph (A) has been approved, or has been denied, suspended, or withdrawn, respectively.

(3) Upon receipt of an application meeting the requirements set forth in paragraph (1), the Secretary—

(A) may on the Secretary's own initiative, or

(B) shall, upon the request of an applicant unless the Secretary finds that the information in the application which would be reviewed by a panel substantially duplicates information which has previously been reviewed by a panel appointed under section 513,

refer such application to the appropriate panel under section 513 for study and for submission (within such period as he may establish) of a report and recommendation respecting approval of the application, together with all underlying data and the reasons or basis for the recommendation. Where appropriate, the Secretary shall ensure that such panel includes, or consults with, one or more pediatric experts.

(4)(A) Prior to the submission of an application under this subsection, the Secretary shall accept and review any portion of the application that the applicant and the Secretary agree is complete, ready, and appropriate for review, except that such requirement does not apply, and the Secretary has discretion whether to accept and review such portion, during any period in which, under section 738(g), the Secretary does not have the authority to collect fees under section 738(a).

(B) Each portion of a submission reviewed under subparagraph (A) and found acceptable by the Secretary shall not be further reviewed after receipt of an application that satisfies the requirements of paragraph (1), unless a significant issue of safety or effectiveness provides the Secretary reason to review such accepted portion.

(C) Whenever the Secretary determines that a portion of a submission under subparagraph (A) is unacceptable, the Secretary shall, in writing, provide to the applicant a description of any deficiencies in such portion and identify the information that is required to correct these deficiencies, unless the applicant is no longer pursuing the application. Where appropriate, the Secretary shall ensure that such panel includes, or consults with, one or more pediatric experts.

(d) Action on an application for premarket approval

(1)(A) As promptly as possible, but in no event later than one hundred and eighty days after the receipt of an application under subsection (c) (except as provided in section 520(l)(3)(D)(ii) or unless, in accordance with subparagraph (B)(i), an additional period as agreed upon by the Secretary and the applicant), the Secretary, after considering the report and recommendation submitted under paragraph (2) of such subsection, shall—

(i) issue an order approving the application if he finds that none of the grounds for denying approval specified in paragraph (2) of this subsection applies; or

(ii) deny approval of the application if he finds (and sets forth the basis for such finding as part of or accompanying such denial) that one or more grounds for denial specified in paragraph (2) of this subsection apply.

In making the determination whether to approve or deny the application, the Secretary shall rely on the conditions of use included in the proposed labeling as the basis for determining whether or not there is a reasonable assurance of safety and effectiveness, if the proposed labeling is neither false nor misleading. In determining whether or not such labeling is false or misleading, the Secretary shall fairly evaluate all material facts pertinent to the proposed labeling.

(B)(i) The Secretary may not enter into an agreement to extend the period in which to take action with respect to an application submitted for a device subject to a regulation promulgated under subsection (b) unless he finds that the continued availability of the device is necessary for the public health.

(ii) An order approving an application for a device may require as a condition to such approval that the sale and distribution of the device be restricted but only to the extent that the sale and distribution of a device may be restricted under a regulation under section 520(e).

(iii) The Secretary shall accept and review statistically valid and reliable data and any other information from investigations conducted under the authority of regulations required by section 520(g) to make a determination of whether there is a reasonable assurance of safety and effectiveness of a device subject to a pending application under this section if—

(I) the data or information is derived from investigations of an earlier version of the device, the device has been modified during or after the investigations (but prior to submission of an application under subsection (c)) and such a modification of the device does not constitute a significant change in the design or in the basic principles of operation of the device that would invalidate the data or information; or

(II) the data or information relates to a device approved under this section, is available for use under this Act, and is relevant to the design and intended use of the device for which the application is pending.

(2) The Secretary shall deny approval of an application for a device if, upon the basis of the information submitted to the Secretary as part of the application and any other information before him with respect to such device, the Secretary finds that—

(A) there is a lack of a showing of reasonable assurance that such device is safe under the conditions of use prescribed, recommended, or suggested in the proposed labeling thereof;

(B) there is a lack of a showing of reasonable assurance that the device is effective under the conditions of use prescribed, recommended, or suggested in the proposed labeling thereof;

(C) the methods used in, or the facilities or controls used for, the manufacture, processing, packing, or installation of such device do not conform to the requirements of section 520(f);

(D) based on a fair evaluation of all material facts, the proposed labeling is false or misleading in any particular; or

(E) such device is not shown to conform in all respects to a performance standard in effect under section 514 compliance with which is a condition to approval of the application and there is a lack of adequate information to justify the deviation from such standard.

Any denial of an application shall, insofar as the Secretary determines to be practicable, be accompanied by a statement informing the applicant of the measures required to place such application in approvable form (which measures may include further research by the applicant in accordance with one or more protocols prescribed by the Secretary).

(3)(A)(i) The Secretary shall, upon the written request of an applicant, meet with the applicant, not later than 100 days after the receipt of an application that has been filed as complete under subsection (c), to discuss the review status of the application.

(ii) The Secretary shall, in writing and prior to the meeting, provide to the applicant a description of any deficiencies in the application that, at that point, have been identified by the Secretary based on an interim review of the entire application and identify the information that is required to correct those deficiencies.

(iii) The Secretary shall notify the applicant promptly of—

(I) any additional deficiency identified in the application, or

(II) any additional information required to achieve completion of the review and final action on the application,

that was not described as a deficiency in the written description provided by the Secretary under clause (ii).

(B) The Secretary and the applicant may, by mutual consent, establish a different schedule for a meeting required under this paragraph.

(4) An applicant whose application has been denied approval may, by petition filed on or before the thirtieth day after the date upon which he receives notice of such denial, obtain review thereof in accordance with either paragraph (1) or (2) of subsection (g), and any interested person may obtain review, in accordance with paragraph (1) or (2) of subsection (g), of an order of the Secretary approving an application.

(5) In order to provide for more effective treatment or diagnosis of life-threatening or irreversibly debilitating human diseases or conditions, the Secretary shall provide review priority for devices—

(A) representing breakthrough technologies,

(B) for which no approved alternatives exist,

(C) which offer significant advantages over existing approved alternatives, or

(D) the availability of which is in the best interest of the patients.

(6)(A)(i) A supplemental application shall be required for any change to a device subject to an approved application under this subsection that affects safety or effectiveness, unless such change is a modification in a manufacturing procedure or method of manufacturing and the holder of the approved application submits a written notice to the Secretary that describes in detail the change, summarizes the data or information supporting the change, and informs the Secretary that the change has been made under the requirements of section 520(f).

(ii) The holder of an approved application who submits a notice under clause (i) with respect to a manufacturing change of a device may distribute the device 30 days after the date on which the Secretary receives the notice, unless the Secretary within such 30-day period notifies the holder that the notice is not adequate and describes such further information or action that is required for acceptance of such change. If the Secretary notifies the holder that a supplemental application is required, the Secretary shall review the supplement within 135 days after the receipt of the supplement. The time used by the Secretary to review the notice of the manufacturing change shall be deducted from the 135-day review period if the notice meets appropriate content requirements for premarket approval supplements.

(B)(i) Subject to clause (ii), in reviewing a supplement to an approved application, for an incremental change to the design of a device that affects safety or effectiveness, the Secretary shall approve such supplement if—

(I) nonclinical data demonstrate that the design modification creates the intended additional capacity, function, or performance of the device; and

(II) clinical data from the approved application and any supplement to the approved application provide a reasonable assurance of safety and effectiveness for the changed device.

(ii) The Secretary may require, when necessary, additional clinical data to evaluate the design modification of the device to provide a reasonable assurance of safety and effectiveness.

(e) Withdrawal and temporary suspension of approval of application

(1) The Secretary shall, upon obtaining, where appropriate, advice on scientific matters from a panel or panels under section 513, and after due notice and opportunity for informal hearing to the holder of an approved application for a device, issue an order withdrawing approval of the application if the Secretary finds—

(A) that such device is unsafe or ineffective under the conditions of use prescribed, recommended, or suggested in the labeling thereof;

(B) on the basis of new information before him with respect to such device, evaluated together with the evidence available to him when the application was approved, that there is a lack of a showing of reasonable assurance that the device is safe or effective under the conditions of use prescribed, recommended, or suggested in the labeling thereof;

(C) that the application contained or was accompanied by an untrue statement of a material fact;

(D) that the applicant (i) has failed to establish a system for maintaining records, or has repeatedly or deliberately failed to maintain records or to make reports, required by an applicable regulation under section 519(a),

(ii) has refused to permit access to, or copying or verification of, such records as required by section 704, or (iii) has not complied with the requirements of section 510;

(E) on the basis of new information before him with respect to such device, evaluated together with the evidence before him when the application was approved, that the methods used in, or the facilities and controls used for, the manufacture, processing, packing, or installation of such device do not conform with the requirements of section 520(f) and were not brought into conformity with such requirements within a reasonable time after receipt of written notice from the Secretary of nonconformity;

(F) on the basis of new information before him, evaluated together with the evidence before him when the application was approved, that the labeling of such device, based on a fair evaluation of all material facts, is false or misleading in any particular and was not corrected within a reasonable time after receipt of written notice from the Secretary of such fact; or

(G) on the basis of new information before him, evaluated together with the evidence before him when the application was approved, that such device is not shown to conform in all respects to a performance standard which is in effect under section 514 compliance with which was a condition to approval of the application and that there is a lack of adequate information to justify the deviation from such standard.

(2) The holder of an application subject to an order issued under paragraph (1) withdrawing approval of the application may, by petition filed on or before the thirtieth day after the date upon which he receives notice of such withdrawal, obtain review thereof in accordance with either paragraph (1) or (2) of subsection (g).

(3) If, after providing an opportunity for an informal hearing, the Secretary determines there is reasonable probability that the continuation of distribution of a device under an approved application would cause serious, adverse health consequences or death, the Secretary shall by order temporarily suspend the approval of the application approved under this section. If the Secretary issues such an order, the Secretary shall proceed expeditiously under paragraph (1) to withdraw such application.

(f) Product development protocol

(1) In the case of a class III device which is required to have an approval of an application submitted under subsection (c), such device shall be considered as having such an approval if a notice of completion of testing conducted in accordance with a product development protocol approved under paragraph (4) has been declared completed under paragraph (6).

(2) Any person may submit to the Secretary a proposed product development protocol with respect to a device. Such a protocol shall be accompanied by data supporting it. If, within thirty days of the receipt of such a protocol, the Secretary determines that it appears to be appropriate to apply the requirements of this subsection to the device with respect to which the protocol is submitted, the Secretary—

(A) may, at the initiative of the Secretary, refer the proposed protocol to the appropriate panel under section 513 for its recommendation respecting approval of the protocol; or

(B) shall so refer such protocol upon the request of the submitter, unless the Secretary finds that the proposed protocol and accompanying data which would be reviewed by such panel substantially duplicate a product development protocol and accompanying data which have previously been reviewed by such a panel.

(3) A proposed product development protocol for a device may be approved only if—

(A) the Secretary determines that it is appropriate to apply the requirements of this subsection to the device in lieu of the requirement of approval of an application submitted under subsection (c); and

(B) the Secretary determines that the proposed protocol provides—

(i) a description of the device and the changes which may be made in the device,

(ii) a description of the preclinical trials (if any) of the device and a specification of (I) the results from such trials to be required before the commencement of clinical trials of the device, and (II) any permissible variations in preclinical trials and the results therefrom,

(iii) a description of the clinical trials (if any) of the device and a specification of (I) the results from such trials to be required before the filing of a notice of completion of the requirements of the protocol, and (II) any permissible variations in such trials and the results therefrom,

(iv) a description of the methods to be used in, and the facilities and controls to be used for, the manufacture, processing, and when relevant, packing and installation of the device,

(v) an identifying reference to any performance standard under section 514 to be applicable to any aspect of such device,

(vi) if appropriate, specimens of the labeling proposed to be used for such device,

(vii) such other information relevant to the subject matter of the protocol as the Secretary, with the concurrence of the appropriate panel or panels under section 513, may require, and

(viii) a requirement for submission of progress reports and, when completed, records of the trials conducted under the protocol which records are adequate to show compliance with the protocol.

(4) The Secretary shall approve or disapprove a proposed product development protocol submitted under paragraph (2) within one hundred and twenty days of its receipt unless an additional period is agreed upon by the Secretary and the person who submitted the protocol. Approval of a protocol or denial of approval of a protocol is final agency action subject to judicial review under chapter 7 of title 5, United States Code [5 USC §§ 701 et seq.].

(5) At any time after a product development protocol for a device has been approved pursuant to paragraph (4), the person for whom the protocol was approved may submit a notice of completion—

(A) stating

(i) his determination that the requirements of the protocol have been fulfilled and that, to the best of his knowledge, there is no reason bearing on safety or effectiveness why the notice of completion should not become effective, and

(ii) the data and other information upon which such determination was made, and

(B) setting forth the results of the trials required by the protocol and all the information required by subsection (c)(1).

(6)(A) The Secretary may, after providing the person who has an approved protocol an opportunity for an informal hearing and at any time prior to receipt of notice of completion of such protocol, issue a final order to revoke such protocol if he finds that—

(i) such person has failed substantially to comply with the requirements of the protocol,

(ii) the results of the trials obtained under the protocol differ so substantially from the results required by the protocol that further trials cannot be justified, or

(iii) the results of the trials conducted under the protocol or available new information do not demonstrate that the device tested under the protocol does not present an unreasonable risk to health and safety.

(B) After the receipt of a notice of completion of an approved protocol the Secretary shall, within the ninety-day period beginning on the date such notice is received, by order either declare the protocol completed or declare it not completed. An order declaring a protocol not completed may take effect only after the Secretary has provided the person who has the protocol opportunity for an informal hearing on the order. Such an order may be issued only if the Secretary finds—

(i) such person has failed substantially to comply with the requirements of the protocol,

(ii) the results of the trials obtained under the protocol differ substantially from the results required by the protocol, or

(iii) there is a lack of a showing of reasonable assurance of the safety and effectiveness of the device under the conditions of use prescribed, recommended, or suggested in the proposed labeling thereof.

(C) A final order issued under subparagraph (A) or (B) shall be in writing and shall contain the reasons to support the conclusions thereof.

(7) At any time after a notice of completion has become effective, the Secretary may issue an order (after due notice and opportunity for an informal hearing to the person for whom the notice is effective) revoking the approval of a device provided by a notice of completion which has become effective as provided in subparagraph (B) if he finds that any of the grounds listed in subparagraphs (A) through (G) of subsection (e)(1) of this section apply. Each reference in such subparagraphs to an application shall be considered for purposes of this paragraph as a reference to a protocol and the notice of completion of such protocol, and each reference to the time when an application was approved shall be considered for purposes of this paragraph as a reference to the time when a notice of completion took effect.

(8) A person who has an approved protocol subject to an order issued under paragraph (6)(A) revoking such protocol, a person who has an approved protocol with respect to which an order under paragraph (6)(B) was issued declaring that the protocol had not been completed, or a person subject to an order issued under paragraph

(7) revoking the approval of a device may, by petition filed on or before the thirtieth day after the date upon which he receives notice of such order, obtain review thereof in accordance with either paragraph (1) or (2) of subsection (g).

(g) Review

(1) Upon petition for review of—

(A) an order under subsection (d) approving or denying approval of an application or an order under subsection (e) withdrawing approval of an application, or

(B) an order under subsection (f)(6)(A) revoking an approved protocol, under subsection (f)(6)(B) declaring that an approved protocol has not been completed, or under subsection (f)(7) revoking the approval of a device,

the Secretary shall, unless he finds the petition to be without good cause or unless a petition for review of such order has been submitted under paragraph (2), hold a hearing, in accordance with section 554 of title 5 of the United States Code, on the order. The panel or panels which considered the application, protocol, or device subject to such order shall designate a member to appear and testify at any such hearing upon request of the Secretary, the petitioner, or the officer conducting the hearing, but this requirement does not preclude any other member of the panel or panels from appearing and testifying at any such hearing. Upon completion of such hearing and after considering the record established in such hearing, the Secretary shall issue an order either affirming the order subject to the hearing or reversing such order and, as appropriate, approving or denying approval of the application, reinstating the application's approval, approving the protocol, or placing in effect a notice of completion.

(2)(A) Upon petition for review of—

(i) an order under subsection (d) approving or denying approval of an application or an order under subsection (e) withdrawing approval of an application, or

(ii) an order under subsection (f)(6)(A) revoking an approved protocol, under subsection (f)(6)(B) declaring that an approved protocol has not been completed, or under subsection (f)(7) revoking the approval of a device,

the Secretary shall refer the application or protocol subject to the order and the basis for the order to an advisory committee of experts established pursuant to subparagraph (B) for a report and recommendation with respect to the order. The advisory committee shall, after independent study of the data and information furnished to it by the Secretary and other data and information before it, submit to the Secretary a report and recommendation, together with all underlying data and information and a statement of the reasons or basis for the recommendation. A copy of such report shall be promptly supplied by the Secretary to any person who petitioned for such referral to the advisory committee.

(B) The Secretary shall establish advisory committees (which may not be panels under section 513) to receive referrals under subparagraph (A). The Secretary shall appoint as members of any such advisory committee persons qualified in the subject matter to be referred to the committee and of appropriately diversified professional backgrounds, except that the Secretary may not appoint to such a committee any individual who is in the regular full-time employ of the United States and engaged in the administration of this Act.

Members of an advisory committee (other than officers or employees of the United States), while attending conferences or meetings of their committee or otherwise serving at the request of the Secretary, shall be entitled to receive compensation at rates to be fixed by the Secretary which rates may not exceed the daily equivalent for grade GS–18 of the General Schedule for each day (including travel time) they are so engaged; and while so serving away from their homes or regular places of business each member may be allowed travel expenses, including per diem in lieu of subsistence, as authorized by section 5703 of title 5 of the United States Code for persons in the Government service employed intermittently. The Secretary shall designate the chairman of an advisory committee from its members. The Secretary shall furnish each advisory committee with clerical and other assistance, and shall by regulation prescribe the procedures to be followed by each such committee in acting on referrals made under subparagraph (A).

(C) The Secretary shall make public the report and recommendation made by an advisory committee with respect to an application and shall by order, stating the reasons therefor, either affirm the order referred to the advisory committee or reverse such order and, if appropriate, approve or deny approval of the application, reinstate the application's approval, approve the protocol, or place in effect a notice of completion.

(h) Service of orders. Orders of the Secretary under this section shall be served (1) in person by any officer or employee of the department designated by the Secretary, or (2) by mailing the order by registered mail or certified mail addressed to the applicant at his last known address in the records of the Secretary.

(i) Revision

(1) Before December 1, 1995, the Secretary shall by order require manufacturers of devices, which were introduced or delivered for introduction into interstate commerce for commercial distribution before May 28, 1976, and which are subject to revision of classification under paragraph (2), to submit to the Secretary a summary of and citation to any information known or otherwise available to the manufacturer respecting such devices, including adverse safety or effectiveness information which has not been submitted under section 519. The Secretary may require the manufacturer to submit the adverse safety or effectiveness data for which a summary and citation were submitted, if such data are available to the manufacturer.

(2) After the issuance of an order under paragraph (1) but before December 1, 1995, the Secretary shall publish a regulation in the Federal Register for each device—

(A) which the Secretary has classified as a class III device, and

(B) for which no final regulation has been promulgated under section 515(b) [subsec. (b) of this section], revising the classification of the device so that the device is classified into class I or class II, unless the regulation requires the device to remain in class III. In determining whether to revise the classification of a device or to require a device to remain in class III, the Secretary shall apply the criteria set forth in section 513(a). Before the publication of a regulation requiring a device to remain in class III or revising its classification, the Secretary shall publish a proposed regulation respecting the classification of a device under this paragraph and provide reasonable opportunity for the submission of comments on any such regulation. No regulation requiring a device to remain in class III or revising its classification may take effect before the expiration of 90 days from the date of its publication in the Federal Register as a proposed regulation.

(3) The Secretary shall, as promptly as is reasonably achievable, but not later than 12 months after the effective date of the regulation requiring a device to remain in class III, establish a schedule for the promulgation of a section 515(b) [subsec. (b) of this section] regulation for each device which is subject to the regulation requiring the device to remain in class III.

SEC. 515A. [21 USC §360e-1] Pediatric Uses of Devices

Note: This section was added in February 2008.

(a) New devices.

(1) In general. A person that submits to the Secretary an application under section 520(m) [21 USC § 360j(m)], or an application (or supplement to an application) or a product development protocol under section 515 [21 USC § 360e], shall include in the application or protocol the information described in paragraph (2).

(2) Required information. The application or protocol described in paragraph (1) shall include, with respect to the device for which approval is sought and if readily available--

(A) a description of any pediatric subpopulations that suffer from the disease or condition that the device is intended to treat, diagnose, or cure; and

(B) the number of affected pediatric patients.

(3) Annual report. Not later than 18 months after the date of the enactment of this section [enacted Sept. 27, 2007], and annually thereafter, the Secretary shall submit to the Committee on Health, Education, Labor, and Pensions of the Senate and the Committee on Energy and Commerce of the House of Representatives a report that includes--

(A) the number of devices approved in the year preceding the year in which the report is submitted, for which there is a pediatric subpopulation that suffers from the disease or condition that the device is intended to treat, diagnose, or cure;

(B) the number of devices approved in the year preceding the year in which the report is submitted, labeled for use in pediatric patients;

(C) the number of pediatric devices approved in the year preceding the year in which the report is submitted, exempted from a fee pursuant to section 738(a)(2)(B)(v) [21 USC § 379j(a)(2)(B)(v)]; and

(D) the review time for each device described in subparagraphs (A), (B), and (C).

(b) Determination of pediatric effectiveness based on similar course of disease or condition or similar effect of device on adults.

(1) In general. If the course of the disease or condition and the effects of the device are sufficiently similar in adults and pediatric patients, the Secretary may conclude that adult data may be used to support a determination of a reasonable assurance of effectiveness in pediatric populations, as appropriate.

(2) Extrapolation between subpopulations. A study may not be needed in each pediatric subpopulation if data from one subpopulation can be extrapolated to another subpopulation.

(c) Pediatric subpopulation. For purposes of this section, the term "***pediatric subpopulation***" has the meaning given the term in section 520(m)(6)(E)(ii) [21 USC § 360j(m)(6)(E)(ii)].

SEC. 516. [21 USC §360f] Banned Devices; General Rule

(a) General Rule. Whenever the Secretary finds, on the basis of all available data and information, that—

(1) a device intended for human use presents substantial deception or an unreasonable and substantial risk of illness or injury; and

(2) in the case of substantial deception or an unreasonable and substantial risk of illness or injury which the Secretary determined could be corrected or eliminated by labeling or change in labeling and with respect to which the Secretary provided written notice to the manufacturer specifying the deception or risk of illness or injury, the labeling or change in labeling to correct the deception or eliminate or reduce such risk, and the period within which such labeling or change in labeling was to be done, such labeling or change in labeling was not done within such period;

he may initiate a proceeding to promulgate a regulation to make such device a banned device.

(b) Special Effective Date. The Secretary may declare a proposed regulation under subsection (a) to be effective upon its publication in the Federal Register and until the effective date of any final action taken respecting such regulation if (1) he determines, on the basis of all available data and information, that the deception or risk of illness or injury associated with the use of the device which is subject to the regulation presents an unreasonable, direct, and substantial danger to the health of individuals, and (2) before the date of the publication of such regulation, the Secretary notifies the manufacturer of such device that such regulation is to be made so effective. If the Secretary makes a proposed regulation so effective, he shall, as expeditiously as possible, give interested persons prompt notice of his action under this subsection, provide reasonable opportunity for an informal hearing on the proposed regulation, and either affirm, modify, or revoke such proposed regulation.

SEC. 517. [21 USC §360g] Judicial Review; Application of Section

(a) Application of Section. Not later than thirty days after—

(1) the promulgation of a regulation under section 513 classifying a device in class I or changing the classification of a device to class I or an order under subsection (f)(2) of such section reclassifying a device or denying a petition for reclassification of a device,

(2) the promulgation of a regulation under section 514 establishing, amending, or revoking a performance standard for a device,

(3) the issuance of an order under section 514(b)(2) or 515 (b)(2)(B) denying a request for reclassification of a device,

(4) the promulgation of a regulation under paragraph (3) of section 515(b) requiring a device to have an approval of a premarket application, a regulation under paragraph (4) of that section amending or revoking a regulation under paragraph (3), or an order pursuant to section 515(g)(1) or 515(g)(2)(C),

(5) the promulgation of a regulation under section 516 (other than a proposed regulation made effective under subsection (b) of such section upon the regulation's publication) making a device a banned device,

(6) the issuance of an order under section 520(f)(2),

(7) an order under section 520(g)(4) disapproving an application for an exemption of a device for investigational use or an order under section 520(g)(5) withdrawing such an exemption for a device,

(8) an order pursuant to section 513(i), or

(9) a regulation under section 515(i)(2) or 520(l)(5)(B),

any person adversely affected by such regulation or order may file a petition with the United States Court of Appeals for the District of Columbia or for the circuit wherein such person resides or has his principal place of business for Judicial review of such regulation or order. A copy of the petition shall be transmitted by the clerk of the court to the Secretary or other officer designated by him for that purpose. The Secretary shall file in the court the record of the proceedings on which the Secretary based his regulation or order as provided in section 2112 of title 28, United States Code. For purposes of this section, the term "record" means all notices and other matter published in the Federal Register with respect to the regulation or order reviewed, all information submitted to the Secretary with respect to such regulation or order, proceedings of any panel or advisory committee with respect to such regulation or order, any hearing held with respect to such regulation or order, and any other information identified by the Secretary, in the administrative proceeding held with respect to such regulation or order, as being relevant to such regulation or order.

(b) Additional Data, Views, and Arguments. If the petitioner applies to the court for leave to adduce additional data, views, or arguments respecting the regulation or order being reviewed and shows to the satisfaction of the court that such additional data, views, or arguments are material and that there were reasonable grounds for the petitioner's failure to adduce such data, views, or arguments in the proceedings before the Secretary, the court may order the Secretary to provide additional opportunity for the oral presentation of data, views, or arguments and for written submissions. The Secretary may modify his findings, or make new findings by reason of the additional data, views, or arguments so taken and shall file with the court such modified or new findings, and his recommendation, if any, for the modification or setting aside of the regulation or order being reviewed, with the return of such additional data, views, or arguments.

(c) Standard for Review. Upon the filing of the petition under subsection (a) of this section for judicial review of a regulation or order, the court shall have jurisdiction to review the regulation or order in accordance with chapter 7 of title 5, United States Code, and to grant appropriate relief, including interim relief, as provided in such chapter. A regulation described in paragraph (2) or (5) of subsection (a) and an order issued after the review provided by section 515(g) shall not be affirmed if it is found to be unsupported by substantial evidence on the record taken as a whole.

(d) Finality of Judgments, The judgment of the court affirming or setting aside, in whole or in part, any regulation or order shall be final, subject to review by the Supreme Court of the United States upon certiorari or certification, as provided in section 1254 of title 28 of the United States Code.

(e) Other Remedies. The remedies provided for in this section shall be in addition to and not in lieu of any other remedies provided by law.

(f) Statement of Reasons. To facilitate judicial review under this section or under any other provision of law of a regulation or order issued under section 513, 514, 515, 516, 518, 519, 520, or 521 each such regulation or order shall contain a statement of the reasons for its issuance and the basis, in the record of the proceedings held in connection with its issuance, for its issuance.

SEC. 518. [21 USC §360h] Notification and Other Remedies; Notification

(a) Notification. If the Secretary determines that—

(1) a device intended for human use which is introduced or delivered for introduction into interstate commerce for commercial distribution presents an unreasonable risk of substantial harm to the public health, and

(2) notification under this subsection is necessary to eliminate the unreasonable risk of such harm and no more practicable means is available under the provisions of this Act (other than this section) to eliminate such risk,

the Secretary may issue such order as may be necessary to assure that adequate notification is provided in an appropriate form, by the persons and means best suited under the circumstances involved, to all health professionals who prescribe or use the device and to any other person (including manufacturers, importers, distributors, retailers, and device users) who should properly receive such notification in order to eliminate such risk. An order under this subsection shall require that the individuals subject to the risk with respect to which the order is to be issued be included in the persons to be notified of the risk unless the Secretary determines that notice to such individuals would present a greater danger to the health of such individuals than no such notification. If the Secretary makes such a determination with respect to such individuals, the order shall require that the health professionals who prescribe or use the device provide for the notification of the individuals whom the health professionals treated with the device of the risk presented by the device and of any action which may be taken by or on behalf of such individuals to eliminate or reduce such risk. Before issuing an order under this subsection, the Secretary shall consult with the persons who are to give notice under the order.

(b) Repair, Replacement, or Refund

(1)(A) If, after affording opportunity for an informal hearing, the Secretary determines that—

(i) a device intended for human use which is introduced or delivered for introduction into interstate commerce for commercial distribution presents an unreasonable risk of substantial harm to the public health.

(ii) there are reasonable grounds to believe that the device was not properly designed or manufactured with reference to the state of the art as it existed at the time of its design or manufacture,

(iii) there are reasonable grounds to believe that the unreasonable risk was not caused by failure of a person other than a manufacturer, importer, distributor, or retailer of the device to exercise due care in the installation, maintenance, repair, or use of the device, and

(iv) the notification authorized by subsection (a) would not by itself be sufficient to eliminate the unreasonable risk and action described in paragraph (2) of this subsection is necessary to eliminate such risk,

the Secretary may order the manufacturer, importer, or any distributor of such device, or any combination of such persons, to submit to him within a reasonable time a plan for taking one or more of the actions described in paragraph (2). An order issued under the preceding sentence which is directed to more than one person shall specify which person may decide which action shall be taken under such plan and the person specified shall be the person who the Secretary determines bears the principal, ultimate financial responsibility for action taken under the plan unless the Secretary cannot determine who bears such responsibility or the Secretary determines that the protection of the public health requires that such decision be made by a person (including a device user or health professional) other than the person he determines bears such responsibility.

(B) The Secretary shall approve a plan submitted pursuant to an order issued under subparagraph (A) unless he determines (after affording opportunity for an informal hearing) that the action or actions to be taken under the plan or the manner in which such action or actions are to be taken under the plan will not assure that the unreasonable risk with respect to which such order was issued will be eliminated. If the Secretary disapproves a plan, he shall order a revised plan to be submitted to him within a reasonable time. If the Secretary determines (after affording opportunity for an informal hearing) that the revised plan is unsatisfactory or if no revised plan or no initial plan has been submitted to the Secretary within the prescribed time, the Secretary shall (i) prescribe a plan to be carried out by the person or persons to whom the order issued under subparagraph (A) was directed, or (ii) after affording an opportunity for an informal hearing, by order prescribe a plan to be carried out by a person who is a manufacturer, importer, distributor, or retailer of the device with respect to which the order was issued but to whom the order under subparagraph (A) was not directed.

(2) The actions which may be taken under a plan submitted under an order issued under paragraph (1) are as follows:

(A) To repair the device so that it does not present the unreasonable risk of substantial harm with respect to which the order under paragraph (1) was issued.

(B) To replace the device with a like or equivalent device which is in conformity with all applicable requirements of this Act.

(C) To refund the purchase price of the device (less a reasonable allowance for use if such device has been in the possession of the device user for one year or more—

(i) at the time of notification ordered under subsection (a), or

(ii) at the time the device user receives actual notice of the unreasonable risk with respect to which the order was issued under paragraph (1), whichever first occurs).

(3) No charge shall be made to any person (other than a manufacturer, importer, distributor or retailer) for availing himself of any remedy, described in paragraph (2) and provided under an order issued under paragraph (1), and the person subject to the order shall reimburse each person (other than a manufacturer, importer, distributor, or retailer) who is entitled to such a remedy for any reasonable and foreseeable expenses actually incurred by such person in availing himself of such remedy.

(c) Reimbursement. An order issued under subsection (b) with respect to a device may require any person who is a manufacturer, importer, distributor, or retailer of the device to reimburse any other person who is a manufacturer, importer, distributor, or retailer of such device for such other person's expenses actually incurred in connection with carrying out the order if the Secretary determines such reimbursement is required for the protection of the public health. Any such requirement shall not affect any rights or obligations under any contract to which the person receiving reimbursement or the person making such reimbursement is a party.

(d) Effect on Other Liability. Compliance with an order issued under this section shall not relieve any person from liability under Federal or State law. In awarding damages for economic loss in an action brought for the enforcement of any such liability, the value to the plaintiff in such action of any remedy provided him under such order shall be taken into account.

(e) Recall Authority

(1) If the Secretary finds that there is a reasonable probability that a device intended for human use would cause serious, adverse health consequences or death, the Secretary shall issue an order requiring the appropriate person (including the manufacturers, importers, distributors, or retailers of the device)—

(A) to immediately cease distribution of such device, and

(B) to immediately notify health professionals and device user facilities of the order and to instruct such professionals and facilities to cease use of such device.

The order shall provide the person subject to the order with an opportunity for an informal hearing, to be held not later than 10 days after the date of the issuance of the order, on the actions required by the order and on whether the order should be amended to require a recall of such device. If, after providing an opportunity for such a hearing, the Secretary determines that inadequate grounds exist to support the actions required by the order, the Secretary shall vacate the order.

(2)(A) If, after providing an opportunity for an informal hearing under paragraph (1), the Secretary determines that the order should be amended to include a recall of the device with respect to which the order was issued, the Secretary shall, except as provided in subparagraphs (B) and (C), amend the order to require a recall. The Secretary shall specify a timetable in which the device recall will occur and shall require periodic reports to the Secretary describing the progress of the recall.

(B) An amended order under subparagraph (A)—

(i) shall—

(I) not include recall of a device from individuals, and

(II) not include recall of a device from device user facilities if the Secretary determines that the risk of recalling such device from the facilities presents a greater health risk than the health risk of not recalling the device from use, and

(ii) shall provide for notice to individuals subject to the risks associated with the use of such device.

In providing the notice required by clause (ii), the Secretary may use the assistance of health professionals who prescribed or used such a device for individuals. If a significant number of such individuals cannot be identified, the Secretary shall notify such individuals pursuant to section 705(b).

(3) The remedy provided by this subsection shall be in addition to remedies provided by subsections (a), (b), and (c).

SEC. 519. [21 USC §360i] Records and Reports on Devices; General Rule

Note: revisions were posted to this section in February 2008.

(a) General rule. Every person who is a manufacturer or importer of a device intended for human use shall establish and maintain such records, make such reports, and provide such information, as the Secretary may by regulation reasonably require to assure that such device is not adulterated or misbranded and to otherwise assure its safety and effectiveness. Regulations prescribed under the preceding sentence—

(1) shall require a device manufacturer or importer to report to the Secretary whenever the manufacturer or importer receives or otherwise becomes aware of information that reasonably suggests that one of its marketed devices—

(A) may have caused or contributed to a death or serious injury, or

(B) has malfunctioned and that such device or a similar device marketed by the manufacturer or importer would be likely to cause or contribute to a death or serious injury if the malfunction were to recur, which report under this subparagraph--

(i) shall be submitted in accordance with part 803 of title 21, Code of Federal Regulations (or successor regulations), unless the Secretary grants an exemption or variance from, or an alternative to, a requirement under such regulations pursuant to section 803.19 of such part, if the device involved is—

(I) a class III device;

(II) a class II device that is permanently implantable, is life supporting, or is life sustaining; or

(III) a type of device which the Secretary has, by notice published in the Federal Register or letter to the person who is the manufacturer or importer of the device, indicated should be subject to such part 803 in order to protect the public health;

(ii) shall, if the device is not subject to clause (i), be submitted in accordance with criteria established by the Secretary for reports made pursuant to this clause, which criteria shall require the reports to be in summary form and made on a quarterly basis; or

(iii) shall, if the device is imported into the United States and for which part 803 of title 21, Code of Federal Regulations (or successor regulations) requires an importer to submit a report to the manufacturer, be submitted by the importer to the manufacturer in accordance with part 803 of title 21, Code of Federal Regulations (or successor regulations)

(2) shall define the term "***serious injury***" to mean an injury that—

(A) is life threatening,

(B) results in permanent impairment of a body function or permanent damage to a body structure, or

(C) necessitates medical or surgical intervention to preclude permanent impairment of a body function or permanent damage to a body structure;

(3) shall require reporting of other significant adverse device experiences as determined by the Secretary to be necessary to be reported;

(4) shall not impose requirements unduly burdensome to a device manufacturer or importer taking into account his cost of complying with such requirements and the need for the protection of the public health and the implementation of this Act;

(5) which prescribe the procedure for making requests for reports or information shall require that each request made under such regulations for submission of a report or information to the Secretary state the reason or purpose for such request and identify to the fullest extent practicable such report or information;

(6) which require submission of a report or information to the Secretary shall state the reason or purpose for the submission of such report or information and identify to the fullest extent practicable such report or information;

(7) may not require that the identity of any patient be disclosed in records, reports, or information required under this subsection unless required for the medical welfare of an individual, to determine the safety or effectiveness of a device, or to verify a record, report, or information submitted under this Act; and

(8) may not require a manufacturer or importer of a class I device to—

(A) maintain for such a device records respecting information not in the possession of the manufacturer or importer, or

(B) to submit for such a device to the Secretary any report or information—

(i) not in the possession of the manufacturer or importer, or

(ii) on a periodic basis,

unless such report or information is necessary to determine if the device should be reclassified or if the device is adulterated or misbranded. and [43]

In prescribing such regulations, the Secretary shall have due regard for the professional ethics of the medical profession and the interests of patients. The prohibitions of paragraph (7) of this subsection continue to apply to records, reports, and information concerning any individual who has been a patient, irrespective of whether or when he ceases to be a patient. The Secretary shall by regulation require distributors to keep records and make such records available to

[43] So in law. See section 213(a)(1)(D)(ii) of Public Law 105–115 (111 Stat. 2347). That section struck former paragraph (9), and amended paragraph (8) "by striking the semicolon at the end and inserting a period", rather than by striking "; and"; and inserting a period.

the Secretary upon request. Paragraphs (4) and (8) apply to distributors to the same extent and in the same manner as such paragraphs apply to manufacturers and importers.

(b) User reports

(1)(A) Whenever a device user facility receives or otherwise becomes aware of information that reasonably suggests that a device has or may have caused or contributed to the death of a patient of the facility, the facility shall, as soon as practicable but not later than 10 working days after becoming aware of the information, report the information to the Secretary and, if the identity of the manufacturer is known, to the manufacturer of the device. In the case of deaths, the Secretary may by regulation prescribe a shorter period for the reporting of such information.

(B) Whenever a device user facility receives or otherwise becomes aware of—

(i) information that reasonably suggests that a device has or may have caused or contributed to the serious illness of, or serious injury to, a patient of the facility, or

(ii) other significant adverse device experiences as determined by the Secretary by regulation to be necessary to be reported,

the facility shall, as soon as practicable but not later than 10 working days after becoming aware of the information, report the information to the manufacturer of the device or to the Secretary if the identity of the manufacturer is not known.

(C) Each device user facility shall submit to the Secretary on an annual basis a summary of the reports made under subparagraphs (A) and (B). Such summary shall be submitted on January 1 of each year. The summary shall be in such form and contain such information from such reports as the Secretary may require and shall include—

(i) sufficient information to identify the facility which made the reports for which the summary is submitted,

(ii) in the case of any product which was the subject of a report, the product name, serial number, and model number,

(iii) the name and the address of the manufacturer of such device, and

(iv) a brief description of the event reported to the manufacturer.

(D) For purposes of subparagraphs (A), (B), and (C), a device user facility shall be treated as having received or otherwise become aware of information with respect to a device of that facility when medical personnel who are employed by or otherwise formally affiliated with the facility receive or otherwise become aware of information with respect to that device in the course of their duties.

(2) The Secretary may not disclose the identity of a device user facility which makes a report under paragraph (1) except in connection with—

(A) an action brought to enforce section 301(q), or

(B) a communication to a manufacturer of a device which is the subject of a report under paragraph (1).

This paragraph does not prohibit the Secretary from disclosing the identity of a device user facility making a report under paragraph (1) or any information in such a report to employees of the Department of Health and Human Services, to the Department of Justice, or to the duly authorized committees and subcommittees of the Congress.

(3) No report made under paragraph (1) by—

(A) a device user facility,

(B) an individual who is employed by or otherwise formally affiliated with such a facility, or

(C) a physician who is not required to make such a report,

shall be admissible into evidence or otherwise used in any civil action involving private parties unless the facility, individual, or physician who made the report had knowledge of the falsity of the information contained in the report.

(4) A report made under paragraph (1) does not affect any obligation of a manufacturer who receives the report to file a report as required under subsection (a).

(5) With respect to device user facilities:

(A) The Secretary shall by regulation plan and implement a program under which the Secretary limits user reporting under paragraphs (1) through (4) to a subset of user facilities that constitutes a representative profile of user reports for device deaths and serious illnesses or serious injuries.

(B) During the period of planning the program under subparagraph (A), paragraphs (1) through (4) continue to apply.

(C) During the period in which the Secretary is providing for a transition to the full implementation of the program, paragraphs (1) through (4) apply except to the extent that the Secretary determines otherwise.

(D) On and after the date on which the program is fully implemented, paragraphs (1) through (4) do not apply to a user facility unless the facility is included in the subset referred to in subparagraph (A).

(E) Not later than 2 years after the date of the enactment of the Food and Drug Administration Modernization Act ofof 1997 [enacted Nov. 21, 1997], the Secretary shall submit to the Committee on Commerce of the House of Representatives, and to the Committee on Labor and Human Resources of the Senate, a report describing the plan developed by the Secretary under subparagraph (A) and the progress that has been made toward the implementation of the plan.

(6) For purposes of this subsection:

(A) The term "device user facility" means a hospital, ambulatory surgical facility, nursing home, or outpatient treatment facility which is not a physician's office. The Secretary may by regulation include an outpatient diagnostic facility which is not a physician's office in such term.

(B) The terms "serious illness" and "serious injury" mean illness or injury, respectively, that—

(i) is life threatening,

(ii) results in permanent impairment of a body function or permanent damage to a body structure, or

(iii) necessitates medical or surgical intervention to preclude permanent impairment of a body function or permanent damage to a body structure.cture, or

(c) Persons exempt. Subsection (a) shall not apply to—

(1) any practitioner who is licensed by law to prescribe or administer devices intended for use in humans and who manufactures or imports devices solely for use in the course of his professional practice;

(2) any person who manufactures or imports devices intended for use in humans solely for such person's use in research or teaching and not for sale (including any person who uses a device under an exemption granted under section 520(g)); and

(3) any other class of persons as the Secretary may by regulation exempt from subsection (a) upon a finding that compliance with the requirements of such subsection by such class with respect to a device is not necessary to (A) assure that a device is not adulterated or misbranded or (B) otherwise to assure its safety and effectiveness.

(d) [Repealed by Pub. L. 105–115, November 21, 1997.]

(e) Device tracking

(1) The Secretary may by order require a manufacturer to adopt a method of tracking a class II or class III device--

(A) the failure of which would be reasonably likely to have serious adverse health consequences; or

(B) which is—

(i) intended to be implanted in the human body for more than one year, or

(ii) a life sustaining or life supporting device used outside a device user facility.

(2) Any patient receiving a device subject to tracking under paragraph (1) may refuse to release, or refuse permission to release, the patient's name, address, social security number, or other identifying information for the purpose of tracking.

(f) Unique device identification system. The Secretary shall promulgate regulations establishing a unique device identification system for medical devices requiring the label of devices to bear a unique identifier, unless the Secretary requires an alternative placement or provides an exception for a particular device or type of device. The unique identifier shall adequately identify the device through distribution and use, and may include information on the lot or serial number.

(g) Reports of removals and corrections.

(1) Except as provided in paragraph (2), the Secretary shall by regulation require a manufacturer or importer of a device to report promptly to the Secretary any correction or removal of a device undertaken by such manufacturer or importer if the removal or correction was undertaken—

(A) to reduce a risk to health posed by the device, or

(B) to remedy a violation of this Act caused by the device which may present a risk to health.

A manufacturer or importer of a device who undertakes a correction or removal of a device which is not required to be reported under this paragraph shall keep a record of such correction or removal.

(2) No report of the corrective action or removal of a device may be required under paragraph (1) if a report of the corrective action or removal is required and has been submitted under subsection (a).

(3) For purposes of paragraphs (1) and (2), the terms "***correction***" and "***removal***" do not include routine servicing.

SEC. 520. [21 USC §360j] General Provisions Respecting Control of Devices Intended for Human Use; General Rule

Note: revisions were posted to this section in September 2007 and February 2008.

(a) General rule. Any requirement authorized by or under section 501, 502, 510, or 519 applicable to a device intended for human use shall apply to such device until the applicability of the requirement to the device has been changed by action taken under section 513, 514, or 515 or under subsection (g) of this section, and any requirement established by or under section 501, 502, 510, or 519 which is inconsistent with a requirement imposed on such device under section 514 or 515 or under subsection (g) of this section shall not apply to such device.

(b) Custom devices. Sections 514 and 515 do not apply to any device which, in order to comply with the order of an individual physician or dentist (or any other specially qualified person designated under regulations promulgated by the Secretary after an opportunity for an oral hearing) necessarily deviates from an otherwise applicable performance standard or requirement prescribed by or under section 515 if

(1) the device is not generally available in finished form for purchase or for dispensing upon prescription and is not offered through labeling or advertising by the manufacturer, importer, or distributor thereof for commercial distribution, and

(2) such device

(A)(i) is intended for use by an individual patient named in such order of such physician or dentist (or other specially qualified person so designated) and is to be made in a specific form for such patient, or

(ii) is intended to meet the special needs of such physician or dentist (or other specially qualified person so designated) in the course of the professional practice of such physician or dentist (or other specially qualified person so designated), and

(B) is not generally available to or generally used by other physicians or dentists (or other specially qualified persons so designated).

(c) Trade secrets. Any information reported to or otherwise obtained by the Secretary or his representative under section 513, 514, 515, 516, 518, 519, or 704 or under subsection (f) or (g) of this section which is exempt from disclosure pursuant to subsection (a) of section 552 of title 5, United States Code, by reason of subsection (b)(4) of such section shall be considered confidential and shall not be disclosed and may not be used by the Secretary as the basis for the reclassification of a device from class III to class II or class I or as the basis for the establishment or amendment of a performance standard under section 514 for a device reclassified from class III to class II, except (1) in accordance with subsection (h), and (2) that such information may be disclosed to other officers or employees concerned with carrying out this Act or when relevant in any proceeding under this Act (other than section 513 or 514 thereof).

(d) Notices and findings. Each notice of proposed rulemaking under section 513, 514, 515, 516, 518, or 519, or under this section, any other notice which is published in the Federal Register with respect to any other action taken under any such section and which states the reasons for such action, and each publication of findings required to be made in connection with rulemaking under any such section shall set forth

(1) the manner in which interested persons may examine data and other information on which the notice or findings is based, and

(2) the period within which interested persons may present their comments on the notice or findings (including the need therefor) orally or in writing, which period shall be at least sixty days but may not exceed ninety days unless the time is extended by the Secretary by a notice published in the Federal Register stating good cause therefor.

(e) Restricted devices.

(1) The Secretary may by regulation require that a device be restricted to sale, distribution, or use

(A) only upon the written or oral authorization of a practitioner licensed by law to administer or use such device, or

(B) upon such other conditions as the Secretary may prescribe in such regulation,

if, because of its potentiality for harmful effect or the collateral measures necessary to its use, the Secretary determines that there cannot otherwise be reasonable assurance of its safety and effectiveness. No condition prescribed under subparagraph (B) may restrict the use of a device to persons with specific training or experience in its use or to persons for use in certain facilities unless the Secretary determines that such a restriction is required for the safe and effective use of the device. No such condition may exclude a person from using a device solely because the person does not have the training or experience to make him eligible for certification by a certifying board recognized by the American Board of Medical Specialties or has not been certified by such a Board. A device subject to a regulation under this subsection is a restricted device.

(2) The label of a restricted device shall bear such appropriate statements of the restrictions required by a regulation under paragraph (1) as the Secretary may in such regulation prescribe.

(f) Good manufacturing practice requirements.

(1)(A) The Secretary may, in accordance with subparagraph (B), prescribe regulations requiring that the methods used in, and the facilities and controls used for, the manufacture, pre-production design validation (including a process to assess the performance of a device but not including an evaluation of the safety or effectiveness of a device), packing, storage, and installation of a device conform to current good manufacturing practice, as prescribed in such regulations, to assure that the device will be safe and effective and otherwise in compliance with this Act.

(B) Before the Secretary may promulgate any regulation under subparagraph (A) he shall

(i) afford the advisory committee established under paragraph (3) an opportunity to submit recommendations to him with respect to the regulation proposed to be promulgated;

(ii) afford opportunity for an oral hearing; and

(iii) ensure that such regulation conforms, to the extent practicable, with internationally recognized standards defining quality systems, or parts of the standards, for medical devices.

The Secretary shall provide the advisory committee a reasonable time to make its recommendation with respect to proposed regulations under subparagraph (A).

(2)(A) Any person subject to any requirement prescribed by regulations under paragraph (1) may petition the Secretary for an exemption or variance from such requirement. Such a petition shall be submitted to the Secretary in such form and manner as he shall prescribe and shall—

(i) in the case of a petition for an exemption from a requirement, set forth the basis for the petitioner's determination that compliance with the requirement is not required to assure that the device will be safe and effective and otherwise in compliance with this Act,

(ii) in the case of a petition for a variance from a requirement, set forth the methods proposed to be used in, and the facilities and controls proposed to be used for, the manufacture, packing, storage, and installation of the device in lieu of the methods, facilities, and controls prescribed by the requirement, and

(iii) contain such other information as the Secretary shall prescribe.

(B) The Secretary may refer to the advisory committee established under paragraph (3) any petition submitted under subparagraph (A). The advisory committee shall report its recommendations to the Secretary with respect to a petition referred to it within sixty days of the date of the petition's referral. Within sixty days after

(i) the date the petition was submitted to the Secretary under subparagraph (A), or

(ii) if the petition was referred to an advisory committee, the expiration of the sixty-day period beginning on the date the petition was referred to the advisory committee,

whichever occurs later, the Secretary shall by order either deny the petition or approve it.

(C) The Secretary may approve

(i) a petition for an exemption for a device from a requirement if he determines that compliance with such requirement is not required to assure that the device will be safe and effective and otherwise in compliance with this Act, and

(ii) a petition for a variance for a device from a requirement if he determines that the methods to be used in, and the facilities and controls to be used for, the manufacture, packing, storage, and installation of the device in lieu of the methods, controls, and facilities prescribed by the requirement are sufficient to assure that the device will be safe and effective and otherwise in compliance with this Act.

An order of the Secretary approving a petition for a variance shall prescribe such conditions respecting the methods used in, and the facilities and controls used for, the manufacture, packing, storage, and installation of the device to be granted the variance under the petition as may be necessary to assure that the device will be safe and effective and otherwise in compliance with this Act.

(D) After the issuance of an order under subparagraph (B) respecting a petition, the petitioner shall have an opportunity for an informal hearing on such order.

(3) The Secretary shall establish an advisory committee for the purpose of advising and making recommendations to him with respect to regulations proposed to be promulgated under paragraph (1)(A) and the approval or disapproval of petitions submitted under paragraph (2). The advisory committee shall be composed of nine members as follows:

(A) Three of the members shall be appointed from persons who are officers or employees of any State or local government or of the Federal Government.

(B) Two of the members shall be appointed from persons who are representative of interests of the device manufacturing industry; two of the members shall be appointed from persons who are representative of the interests of physicians and other health professionals; and two of the members shall be representative of the interests of the general public.

Members of the advisory committee who are not officers or employees of the United States, while attending conferences or meetings of the committee or otherwise engaged in its business, shall be entitled to receive compensation at rates to be fixed by the Secretary, which rates may not exceed the daily equivalent of the rate in effect for grade GS-18 of the General Schedule [44], for each day (including travel time) they are so engaged; and while so serving away from their homes or regular places of business each member may be allowed travel expenses, including per diem in lieu of subsistence, as authorized by section 5703 of title 5 of the United States Code for persons in the Government service employed intermittently. The Secretary shall designate one of the members of the advisory committee to serve as its chairman. The Secretary shall furnish the advisory committee with clerical and other assistance. Section 14 of the Federal Advisory Committee Act [5 USC Appx. § 14] shall not apply with respect to the duration of the advisory committee established under this paragraph.

(g) Exemption for devices for investigational use.

(1) It is the purpose of this subsection to encourage, to the extent consistent with the protection of the public health and safety and with ethical standards, the discovery and development of useful devices intended for human use and to that end to maintain optimum freedom for scientific investigators in their pursuit of that purpose.

(2)(A) The Secretary shall, within the one hundred and twenty day period beginning on the date of the enactment of this section [enacted May 28, 1976], by regulation prescribe procedures and conditions under which devices intended for human use may upon application be granted an exemption from the requirements of section 502, 510, 514, 515, 516, 519, or 721 or subsection (e) or (f) of this section or from any combination of such requirements to permit the investigational use of such devices by experts qualified by scientific training and experience to investigate the safety and effectiveness of such devices.

(B) The conditions prescribed pursuant to subparagraph (A) shall include the following:

(i) A requirement that an application be submitted to the Secretary before an exemption may be granted and that the application be submitted in such form and manner as the Secretary shall specify.

(ii) A requirement that the person applying for an exemption for a device assure the establishment and maintenance of such records, and the making of such reports to the Secretary of data obtained as a result of the investigational use of the device during the

[44] The General Schedule under section 5332 of title 5, United States Code, no longer includes the grade GS-18. The grades are GS-1 through GS-15.

Chapter V

exemption, as the Secretary determines will enable him to assure compliance with such conditions, review the progress of the investigation, and evaluate the safety and effectiveness of the device.

(iii) Such other requirements as the Secretary may determine to be necessary for the protection of the public health and safety.

(C) Procedures and conditions prescribed pursuant to subparagraph (A) for an exemption may appropriately vary depending on (i) the scope and duration of clinical testing to be conducted under such exemption, (ii) the number of human subjects that are to be involved in such testing, (iii) the need to permit changes to be made in the device subject to the exemption during testing conducted in accordance with a clinical testing plan required under paragraph (3)(A), and (iv) whether the clinical testing of such device is for the purpose of developing data to obtain approval for the commercial distribution of such device.

(3) Procedures and conditions prescribed pursuant to paragraph (2)(A) shall require, as a condition to the exemption of any device to be the subject of testing involving human subjects, that the person applying for the exemption

(A) submit a plan for any proposed clinical testing of the device and a report of prior investigations of the device (including, where appropriate, tests on animals) adequate to justify the proposed clinical testing

(i) to the local institutional review committee which has been established in accordance with regulations of the Secretary to supervise clinical testing of devices in the facilities where the proposed clinical testing is to be conducted, or

(ii) to the Secretary, if

(I) no such committee exists, or

(II) the Secretary finds that the process of review by such committee is inadequate (whether or not the plan for such testing has been approved by such committee),

for review for adequacy to justify the commencement of such testing; and, unless the plan and report are submitted to the Secretary, submit to the Secretary a summary of the plan and a report of prior investigations of the device (including, where appropriate, tests on animals);

(B) promptly notify the Secretary (under such circumstances and in such manner as the Secretary prescribes) of approval by a local institutional review committee of any clinical testing plan submitted to it in accordance with subparagraph (A);

(C) in the case of a device to be distributed to investigators for testing, obtain signed agreements from each of such investigators that any testing of the device involving human subjects will be under such investigator's supervision and in accordance with subparagraph (D) and submit such agreements to the Secretary; and

(D) assure that informed consent will be obtained from each human subject (or his representative) of proposed clinical testing involving such device, except where subject to such conditions as the Secretary may prescribe, the investigator conducting or supervising the proposed clinical testing of the device determines in writing that there exists a life threatening situation involving the human subject of such testing which necessitates the use of such device and it is not feasible to obtain informed consent from the subject and there is not sufficient time to obtain such consent from his representative.

The determination required by subparagraph (D) shall be concurred in by a licensed physician who is not involved in the testing of the human subject with respect to which such determination is made unless immediate use of the device is required to save the life of the human subject of such testing and there is not sufficient time to obtain such concurrence.

(4)(A) An application, submitted in accordance with the procedures prescribed by regulations under paragraph (2), for an exemption for a device (other than an exemption from section 516) shall be deemed approved on the thirtieth day after the submission of the application to the Secretary unless on or before such day the Secretary by order disapproves the application and notifies the applicant of the disapproval of the application.

(B) The Secretary may disapprove an application only if he finds that the investigation with respect to which the application is submitted does not conform to procedures and conditions prescribed under regulations under paragraph (2). Such a notification shall contain the order of disapproval and a complete statement of the reasons for the Secretary's disapproval of the application and afford the applicant opportunity for an informal hearing on the disapproval order.

(5) The Secretary may by order withdraw an exemption granted under this subsection for a device if the Secretary determines that the conditions applicable to the device under this subsection for such exemption are not met. Such an order may be issued only after opportunity for an informal hearing, except that such an order may be issued before the provision of an opportunity for an informal hearing if the Secretary determines that the continuation of testing under the exemption with respect to which the order is to be issued will result in an unreasonable risk to the public health.

(6)(A) Not later than 1 year after the date of the enactment of the Food and Drug Administration Modernization Act of 1997 [enacted Nov. 21, 1997], the Secretary shall by regulation establish, with respect to a device for which an exemption under this subsection is in effect, procedures and conditions that, without requiring an additional approval of an application for an exemption or the approval of a supplement to such an application, permit

(i) developmental changes in the device (including manufacturing changes) that do not constitute a significant change in design or in basic principles of operation and that are made in response to information gathered during the course of an investigation; and

(ii) changes or modifications to clinical protocols that do not affect

(I) the validity of data or information resulting from the completion of an approved protocol, or the relationship of likely patient risk to benefit relied upon to approve a protocol;

(II) the scientific soundness of an investigational plan submitted under paragraph (3)(A); or

(III) the rights, safety, or welfare of the human subjects involved in the investigation.

(B) Regulations under subparagraph (A) shall provide that a change or modification described in such subparagraph may be made if

(i) the sponsor of the investigation determines, on the basis of credible information (as defined by the Secretary) that the applicable conditions under subparagraph (A) are met; and

(ii) the sponsor submits to the Secretary, not later than 5 days after making the change or modification, a notice of the change or modification.

(7)(A) In the case of a person intending to investigate the safety or effectiveness of a class III device or any implantable device, the Secretary shall ensure that the person has an opportunity, prior to submitting an application to the Secretary or to an institutional review committee, to submit to the Secretary, for review, an investigational plan (including a clinical protocol). If the applicant submits a written request for a meeting with the Secretary regarding such review, the Secretary shall, not later than 30 days after receiving the request, meet with the applicant for the purpose of reaching agreement regarding the investigational plan (including a clinical protocol). The written request shall include a detailed description of the device, a detailed description of the proposed conditions of use of the device, a proposed plan (including a clinical protocol) for determining whether there is a reasonable assurance of effectiveness, and, if available, information regarding the expected performance from the device.

(B) Any agreement regarding the parameters of an investigational plan (including a clinical protocol) that is reached between the Secretary and a sponsor or applicant shall be reduced to writing and made part of the administrative record by the Secretary. Any such agreement shall not be changed, except

(i) with the written agreement of the sponsor or applicant; or

(ii) pursuant to a decision, made in accordance with subparagraph (C) by the director of the office in which the device involved is reviewed, that a substantial scientific issue essential to determining the safety or effectiveness of the device involved has been identified.

(C) A decision under subparagraph (B)(ii) by the director shall be in writing, and may be made only after the Secretary has provided to the sponsor or applicant an opportunity for a meeting at which the director and the sponsor or applicant are present and at which the director documents the scientific issue involved.

(h) Release of information respecting safety and effectiveness.

(1) The Secretary shall promulgate regulations under which a detailed summary of information respecting the safety and effectiveness of a device which information was submitted to the Secretary and which was the basis for

(A) an order under section 515(d)(1)(A) approving an application for premarket approval for the device or denying approval of such an application or an order under section 515(e) withdrawing approval of such an application for the device,

(B) an order under section 515(f)(6)(A) revoking an approved protocol for the device, an order under section 515(f)(6)(B) declaring a protocol for the device completed or not completed, or an order under section 515(f)(7) revoking the approval of the device, or

(C) an order approving an application under subsection (g) for an exemption for the device from section 516 or an order disapproving, or withdrawing approval of, an application for an exemption under such subsection for the device,

shall be made available to the public upon issuance of the order. Summaries of information made available pursuant to this paragraph respecting a device shall include information respecting any adverse effects on health of the device.

(2) The Secretary shall promulgate regulations under which each advisory committee established under section 515(g)(2)(B) shall make available to the public a detailed summary of information respecting the safety and effectiveness of a device which information was submitted to the advisory committee and which was the basis for its recommendation to the Secretary made pursuant to section 515(g)(2)(A). A summary of information upon which such a recommendation is based shall be made available pursuant to this paragraph only after the issuance of the order with respect to which the

recommendation was made and each summary shall include information respecting any adverse effect on health of the device subject to such order.

(3) Except as provided in paragraph (4), any information respecting a device which is made available pursuant to paragraph (1) or (2) of this subsection (A) may not be used to establish the safety or effectiveness of another device for purposes of this Act by any person other than the person who submitted the information so made available, and (B) shall be made available subject to subsection (c) of this section.

(4)(A) Any information contained in an application for premarket approval filed with the Secretary pursuant to section 515(c) (including information from clinical and preclinical tests or studies that demonstrate the safety and effectiveness of a device, but excluding descriptions of methods of manufacture and product composition and other trade secrets) shall be available, 6 years after the application has been approved by the Secretary, for use by the Secretary in

(i) approving another device;

(ii) determining whether a product development protocol has been completed, under section 515 for another device;

(iii) establishing a performance standard or special control under this Act; or

(iv) classifying or reclassifying another device under section 513 and subsection (l)(2).

(B) The publicly available detailed summaries of information respecting the safety and effectiveness of devices required by paragraph (1)(A) shall be available for use by the Secretary as the evidentiary basis for the agency actions described in subparagraph (A).

(i) Proceedings of advisory panels and committees. Each panel under section 513 and each advisory committee established under section 514(b)(5)(B) or 515(g) or under subsection (f) of this section shall make and maintain a transcript of any proceeding of the panel or committee. Each such panel and committee shall delete from any transcript made pursuant to this subsection information which under subsection (c) of this section is to be considered confidential.

(j) Traceability. Except as provided in section 519(e), no regulation under this Act may impose on a type or class of device requirements for the traceability of such type or class of device unless such requirements are necessary to assure the protection of the public health.

(k) Research and development. The Secretary may enter into contracts for research, testing, and demonstrations respecting devices and may obtain devices for research, testing, and demonstration purposes without regard to sections 3648 and 3709 of the Revised Statutes (31 USC 529, 41 USC 5) [45].

(l) Transitional provisions for devices considered as new drugs.

(1) Any device intended for human use

(A) for which on the date of enactment of the Medical Device Amendments of 1976 [enacted May 28, 1976][46] (hereinafter in this subsection referred to as the "enactment date") an approval of an application submitted under section 505(b) was in effect;

(B) for which such an application was filed on or before the enactment date [enacted May 28, 1976] and with respect to which application no order of approval or refusing to approve had been issued on such date under subsection (c) or (d) of such section;

(C) for which on the enactment date [enacted May 28, 1976] an exemption under subsection (i) of such section was in effect;

(D) which is within a type of device described in subparagraph (A), (B), or (C) and is substantially equivalent to another device within that type;

(E) which the Secretary in a notice published in the Federal Register before the enactment date [enacted May 28, 1976] has declared to be a new drug subject to section 505; or

(F) with respect to which on the enactment date [enacted May 28, 1976] an action is pending in a United States court under section 302, 303, or 304 for an alleged violation of a provision of section 301 which enforces a requirement of section 505 or for an alleged violation of section 505(a),

is classified in class III unless the Secretary in response to a petition submitted under paragraph (2) has classified such device in class I or II.

(2) The Secretary may initiate the reclassification of a device classified into class III under paragraph (1) of this subsection or the manufacturer or importer of a device classified under paragraph (1) may petition the Secretary (in such form and manner as he shall prescribe) for the issuance of an order classifying the device in class I or class II. Within thirty days of the filing of such a petition, the Secretary shall notify the petitioner of any deficiencies in the petition which prevent the Secretary from making a decision on the petition. Except as provided in paragraph (3)(D)(ii), within one hundred and eighty days after the filing of a petition under this paragraph, the Secretary shall, after consultation with the appropriate panel under section 513, by

Chapter V

[45] Section 3648 of the Revised Statutes has been superseded by subsections (a) and (b) of section 3324 of title 31, United States Code. See Public Law 97–258.

[46] Public Law 94–295, enacted May 28, 1976.

order either deny the petition or order the classification, in accordance with the criteria prescribed by section 513(a)(1)(A) or 513(a)(1)(B), of the device in class I or class II.

(3)(A) In the case of a device which is described in paragraph (1)(A) and which is in class III—

(i) such device shall on the enactment date [enacted May 28, 1976] be considered a device with an approved application under section 515, and

(ii) the requirements applicable to such device before the enactment date [enacted May 28, 1976] under section 505 shall continue to apply to such device until changed by the Secretary as authorized by this Act.

(B) In the case of a device which is described in paragraph (1)(B) and which is in class III, an application for such device shall be considered as having been filed under section 515 on the enactment date [enacted May 28, 1976]. The period in which the Secretary shall act on such application in accordance with section 515(d)(1) shall be one hundred and eighty days from the enactment date [enacted May 28, 1976] (or such greater period as the Secretary and the applicant may agree upon after the Secretary has made the finding required by section 515(d)(1)(B)(i)) less the number of days in the period beginning on the date an application for such device was filed under section 505 and ending on the enactment date [enacted May 28, 1976]. After the expiration of such period such device is required, unless exempt under subsection (g), to have in effect an approved application under section 515.

(C) A device which is described in paragraph (1)(C) and which is in class III shall be considered a new drug until the expiration of the ninety-day period beginning on the date of the promulgation of regulations under subsection (g) of this section. After the expiration of such period such device is required, unless exempt under subsection (g), to have in effect an approved application under section 515.

(D)(i) Except as provided in clauses (ii) and (iii), a device which is described in subparagraph (D), (E), or (F) of paragraph (1) and which is in class III is required, unless exempt under subsection (g) of this section, to have on and after sixty days after the enactment date [enacted May 28, 1976] in effect an approved application under section 515.

(ii) If—

(I) a petition is filed under paragraph (2) for a device described in subparagraph (D), (E), or (F) of paragraph (1), or

(II) an application for premarket approval is filed under section 515 for such a device, within the sixty-day period beginning on the enactment date [enacted May 28, 1976] (or within such greater period as the Secretary, after making the finding required under section 515(d)(1)(B), and the petitioner or applicant may agree upon), the Secretary shall act on such petition or application in accordance with paragraph (2) or section 515 except that the period within which the Secretary must act on the petition or application shall be within the one hundred and twenty-day period beginning on the date the petition or application is filed. If such a petition or application is filed within such sixty-day (or greater) period, clause (i) of this subparagraph shall not apply to such device before the expiration of such one hundred and twenty day period, or if such petition is denied or such application is denied approval, before the date of such denial, whichever occurs first.

(iii) In the case of a device which is described in subparagraph (E) of paragraph (1), which the Secretary in a notice published in the Federal Register after March 31, 1976, declared to be a new drug subject to section 505, and which is in class III—

(I) the device shall, after eighteen months after the enactment date, have in effect an approved application under section 515 unless exempt under subsection (g) of this section, and

(II) the Secretary may, during the period beginning one hundred and eighty days after the enactment date [enacted May 28, 1976] and ending eighteen months after such date, restrict the use of the device to investigational use by experts qualified by scientific training and experience to investigate the safety and effectiveness of such device, and to investigational use in accordance with the requirements applicable under regulations under subsection (g) of this section to investigational use of devices granted an exemption under such subsection.

If the requirements under subsection (g) of this section are made applicable to the investigational use of such a device, they shall be made applicable in such a manner that the device shall be made reasonably available to physicians meeting appropriate qualifications prescribed by the Secretary.

(4) [Deleted] [Repealed by Pub. L. 105–115, November 21, 1997.]

(5)(A) Before December 1, 1991, the Secretary shall by order require manufacturers of devices described in paragraph (1), which are subject to revision of classification under subparagraph (B), to submit to the Secretary a summary of and citation to any information known or otherwise available to the manufacturers respecting the devices, including adverse safety or effectiveness information which has not been submitted under section 519. The Secretary may require a manufacturer to submit the adverse safety or effectiveness data for which a summary and citation were submitted, if such data are available to the manufacturer.

(B) Except as provided in subparagraph (C), after the issuance of an order under subparagraph (A) but before December 1, 1992, the Secretary shall publish a regulation in the Federal Register for each device which is classified in class III under paragraph (1) revising the classification of the device so that the device is classified into class I or class II, unless the regulation requires the device to remain in class III. In determining whether to revise the classification of a device or to require a device to remain in class III, the Secretary shall apply the criteria set forth in section 513(a). Before the publication of a regulation requiring a device to remain in class III or revising its classification, the Secretary shall publish a proposed regulation respecting the classification of a device under this subparagraph and provide an opportunity for the submission of comments on any such regulation. No regulation under this subparagraph requiring a device to remain in class III or revising its classification may take effect before the expiration of 90 days from the date of the publication in the Federal Register of the proposed regulation.

(C) The Secretary may by notice published in the Federal Register extend the period prescribed by subparagraph (B) for a device for an additional period not to exceed 1 year.

(m) Humanitarian device exemption.

(1) To the extent consistent with the protection of the public health and safety and with ethical standards, it is the purpose of this subsection to encourage the discovery and use of devices intended to benefit patients in the treatment and diagnosis of diseases or conditions that affect fewer than 4,000 individuals in the United States.

(2) The Secretary may grant a request for an exemption from the effectiveness requirements of sections 514 and 515 for a device for which the Secretary finds that—

(A) the device is designed to treat or diagnose a disease or condition that affects fewer than 4,000 individuals in the United States,

(B) the device would not be available to a person with a disease or condition referred to in subparagraph (A) unless the Secretary grants such an exemption and there is no comparable device, other than under this exemption, available to treat or diagnose such disease or condition, and

(C) the device will not expose patients to an unreasonable or significant risk of illness or injury and the probable benefit to health from the use of the device outweighs the risk of injury or illness from its use, taking into account the probable risks and benefits of currently available devices or alternative forms of treatment.

The request shall be in the form of an application submitted to the Secretary. Not later than 75 days after the date of the receipt of the application, the Secretary shall issue an order approving or denying the application and such application shall include the certification required under section 402(j)(5)(B) of the Public Health Service Act [42 USC § 282(j)(5)(B)] (which shall not be considered an element of such application).

(3) Except as provided in paragraph (6), no person granted an exemption under paragraph (2) with respect to a device may sell the device for an amount that exceeds the costs of research and development, fabrication, and distribution of the device.

(4) Devices granted an exemption under paragraph (2) may only be used—

(A) in facilities that have established, in accordance with regulations of the Secretary, a local institutional review committee to supervise clinical testing of devices in the facilities, and

(B) if, before the use of a device, an institutional review committee approves the use in the treatment or diagnosis of a disease or condition referred to in paragraph (2)(A), unless a physician determines in an emergency situation that approval from a local institutional review committee can not be obtained in time to prevent serious harm or death to a patient.

In a case described in subparagraph (B) in which a physician uses a device without an approval from an institutional review committee, the physician shall, after the use of the device, notify the chairperson of the local institutional review committee of such use. Such notification shall include the identification of the patient involved, the date on which the device was used, and the reason for the use.

(5) The Secretary may require a person granted an exemption under paragraph (2) to demonstrate continued compliance with the requirements of this subsection if the Secretary believes such demonstration to be necessary to protect the public health, if the Secretary has reason to believe that the requirements of paragraph (6) are no longer met, or if the Secretary has reason to believe that the criteria for the exemption are no longer met. If the person granted an exemption under paragraph (2) fails to demonstrate continued compliance with the requirements of this subsection, the Secretary may suspend or withdraw the exemption from the effectiveness requirements of sections 514 and 515 for a humanitarian device only after providing notice and an opportunity for an informal hearing.

(6)(A) Except as provided in subparagraph (D), the prohibition in paragraph (3) shall not apply with respect to a person granted an exemption under paragraph (2) if each of the following conditions apply:

(i) (I) The device with respect to which the exemption is granted is intended for the treatment or diagnosis of a disease or condition that occurs in pediatric patients or in a pediatric subpopulation, and such device is labeled for use in pediatric patients or in a pediatric subpopulation in which the disease or condition occurs.

(II) The device was not previously approved under this subsection for the pediatric patients or the pediatric subpopulation described in subclause (I) prior to the date of the enactment of the Pediatric Medical Device Safety and Improvement Act of 2007 [enacted Sept. 27, 2007].

(ii) During any calendar year, the number of such devices distributed during that year does not exceed the annual distribution number specified by the Secretary when the Secretary grants such exemption. The annual distribution number shall be based on the number of individuals affected by the disease or condition that such device is intended to treat, diagnose, or cure, and of that number, the number of individuals likely to use the device, and the number of devices reasonably necessary to treat such individuals. In no case shall the annual distribution number exceed the number identified in paragraph (2)(A).

(iii) Such person immediately notifies the Secretary if the number of such devices distributed during any calendar year exceeds the annual distribution number referred to in clause (ii).

(iv) The request for such exemption is submitted on or before October 1, 2012.

(B) The Secretary may inspect the records relating to the number of devices distributed during any calendar year of a person granted an exemption under paragraph (2) for which the prohibition in paragraph (3) does not apply.

(C) A person may petition the Secretary to modify the annual distribution number specified by the Secretary under subparagraph (A)(ii) with respect to a device if additional information on the number of individuals affected by the disease or condition arises, and the Secretary may modify such number but in no case shall the annual distribution number exceed the number identified in paragraph (2)(A).

(D) If a person notifies the Secretary, or the Secretary determines through an inspection under subparagraph (B), that the number of devices distributed during any calendar year exceeds the annual distribution number, as required under subparagraph (A)(iii), and modified under subparagraph (C), if applicable, then the prohibition in paragraph (3) shall apply with respect to such person for such device for any sales of such device after such notification.

(E)(i) In this subsection, the term "***pediatric patients***" means patients who are 21 years of age or younger at the time of the diagnosis or treatment.

(ii) In this subsection, the term "***pediatric subpopulation***" means 1 of the following populations:

(I) Neonates.

(II) Infants.

(III) Children.

(IV) Adolescents.

(7) The Secretary shall refer any report of an adverse event regarding a device for which the prohibition under paragraph (3) does not apply pursuant to paragraph (6)(A) that the Secretary receives to the Office of Pediatric Therapeutics, established under section 6 of the Best Pharmaceuticals for Children Act [21 USC § 393a] (Public Law 107-109). In considering the report, the Director of the Office of Pediatric Therapeutics, in consultation with experts in the Center for Devices and Radiological Health, shall provide for periodic review of the report by the Pediatric Advisory Committee, including obtaining any recommendations of such committee regarding whether the Secretary should take action under this Act in response to the report.

(8) The Secretary, acting through the Office of Pediatric Therapeutics and the Center for Devices and Radiological Health, shall provide for an annual review by the Pediatric Advisory Committee of all devices described in paragraph (6) to ensure that the exemption under paragraph (2) remains appropriate for the pediatric populations for which it is granted.

(n) Regulation of contact lens as devices.

(1) All contact lenses shall be deemed to be devices under section 201(h).

(2) Paragraph (1) shall not be construed as bearing on or being relevant to the question of whether any product other than a contact lens is a device as defined by section 201(h) or a drug as defined by section 201(g).

SEC. 521. [21 USC §360k] State and Local Requirements Respecting Devices; General Rule

(a) General Rule. Except as provided in subsection (b), no State or political subdivision of a State may establish or continue in effect with respect to a device intended for human use any requirement—

(1) which is different from, or in addition to, any requirement applicable under this Act to the device, and

(2) which relates to the safety or effectiveness of the device or to any other matter included in a requirement applicable to the device under this Act.

(b) Exempt Requirements. Upon application of a State or a political subdivision thereof, the Secretary may, by regulation promulgated after notice and opportunity for an oral hearing, exempt from subsection (a), under such conditions as may be prescribed in such regulation, a requirement of such State or political subdivision applicable to a device intended for human use if—

(1) the requirement is more stringent than a requirement under this Act which would be applicable to the device if an exemption were not in effect under this subsection; or

(2) the requirement—

(A) is required by compelling local conditions, and

(B) compliance with the requirement would not cause the device to be in violation of any applicable requirement under this Act.

SEC. 522. [21 USC §360l] Postmarket Surveillance

(a) [47] IN GENERAL.—The Secretary may by order require a manufacturer to conduct postmarket surveillance for any device of the manufacturer which is a class II or class III device the failure of which would be reasonably likely to have serious adverse health consequences or which is intended to be—

(1) implanted in the human body for more than one year, or

(2) a life sustaining or life supporting device used outside a device user facility.

(b) SURVEILLANCE APPROVAL.—Each manufacturer required to conduct a surveillance of a device shall, within 30 days of receiving an order from the Secretary prescribing that the manufacturer is required under this section to

[47] Section 212 of Public Law 107–250 (116 Stat. 1614), as amended by section 2(d)(3)(C) of Public Law 108–214 (118 Stat. 577), provides for a study whose purpose is determining whether the system under the Federal Food, Drug, and Cosmetic Act for the postmarket surveillance of medical devices provides adequate safeguards regarding the use of devices in pediatric populations. The study is required to be submitted not later than four years after the date of the enactment of Public Law 107–250, which was enacted October 26, 2002.

conduct such surveillance, submit, for the approval of the Secretary, a plan for the required surveillance. The Secretary, within 60 days of the receipt of such plan, shall determine if the person designated to conduct the surveillance has appropriate qualifications and experience to undertake such surveillance and if the plan will result in the collection of useful data that can reveal unforeseen adverse events or other information necessary to protect the public health. The Secretary, in consultation with the manufacturer, may by order require a prospective surveillance period of up to 36 months. Any determination by the Secretary that a longer period is necessary shall be made by mutual agreement between the Secretary and the manufacturer or, if no agreement can be reached, after the completion of a dispute resolution process as described in section 562.

SEC. 523. [21 USC §360m] Accredited Persons

Note: revisions were posted to this section in February 2008.

(a) In general.

(1) Review and classification of devices. Not later than 1 year after the date of the enactment of the Food and Drug Administration Modernization Act of 1997 [enacted Nov. 21, 1997], the Secretary shall, subject to paragraph (3), accredit persons for the purpose of reviewing reports submitted under section 510(k) and making recommendations to the Secretary regarding the initial classification of devices under section 513(f)(1).

(2) Requirements regarding review.

(A) In general. In making a recommendation to the Secretary under paragraph (1), an accredited person shall notify the Secretary in writing of the reasons for the recommendation.

(B) Time period for review. Not later than 30 days after the date on which the Secretary is notified under subparagraph (A) by an accredited person with respect to a recommendation of an initial classification of a device, the Secretary shall make a determination with respect to the initial classification.

(C) Special rule. The Secretary may change the initial classification under section 513(f)(1) that is recommended under paragraph (1) by an accredited person, and in such case shall provide to such person, and the person who submitted the report under section 510(k) for the device, a statement explaining in detail the reasons for the change.

(3) Certain devices.

(A) In general. An accredited person may not be used to perform a review of—

(i) a class III device;

(ii) a class II device which is intended to be permanently implantable or life sustaining or life supporting; or

(iii) a class II device which requires clinical data in the report submitted under section 510(k) for the device, except that the number of class II devices to which the Secretary applies this clause for a year, less the number of such reports to which clauses (i) and (ii) apply, may not exceed 6 percent of the number that is equal to the total number of reports submitted to the Secretary under such section for such year less the number of such reports to which such clauses apply for such year.

(B) Adjustment. In determining for a year the ratio described in subparagraph (A)(iii), the Secretary shall not include in the numerator class III devices that the Secretary reclassified into class II, and the Secretary shall include in the denominator class II devices for which reports under section 510(k) were not required to be submitted by reason of the operation of section 510(m).

(b) Accreditation.

(1) Programs. The Secretary shall provide for such accreditation through programs administered by the Food and Drug Administration, other government agencies, or by other qualified non government organizations.

(2) Accreditation.

(A) In general. Not later than 180 days after the date of the enactment of the Food and Drug Administration Modernization Act of 1997 [enacted Nov. 21, 1997], the Secretary shall establish and publish in the Federal Register criteria to accredit or deny accreditation to persons who request to perform the duties specified in subsection (a). The Secretary shall respond to a request for accreditation within 60 days of the receipt of the request. The accreditation of such person shall specify the particular activities under subsection (a) for which such person is accredited.

(B) Withdrawal of accreditation. The Secretary may suspend or withdraw accreditation of any person accredited under this paragraph, after providing notice and an opportunity for an informal hearing, when such person is substantially not in compliance with the requirements of this section or poses a threat to public health or fails to act in a manner that is consistent with the purposes of this section.

(C) Performance auditing. To ensure that persons accredited under this section will continue to meet the standards of accreditation, the Secretary shall—

(i) make onsite visits on a periodic basis to each accredited person to audit the performance of such person; and

(ii) take such additional measures as the Secretary determines to be appropriate.

(D) Annual report. The Secretary shall include in the annual report required under section 903(g) the names of all accredited persons and the particular activities under subsection (a) for which each such person is accredited and the name of each accredited person whose accreditation has been withdrawn during the year.

(3) Qualifications. An accredited person shall, at a minimum, meet the following requirements:

(A) Such person may not be an employee of the Federal Government.

(B) Such person shall be an independent organization which is not owned or controlled by a manufacturer, supplier, or vendor of devices and which has no organizational, material, or financial affiliation with such a manufacturer, supplier, or vendor.

(C) Such person shall be a legally constituted entity permitted to conduct the activities for which it seeks accreditation.

(D) Such person shall not engage in the design, manufacture, promotion, or sale of devices.

(E) The operations of such person shall be in accordance with generally accepted professional and ethical business practices and shall agree in writing that as a minimum it will—

(i) certify that reported information accurately reflects data reviewed;

(ii) limit work to that for which competence and capacity are available;

(iii) treat information received, records, reports, and recommendations as proprietary information;

(iv) promptly respond and attempt to resolve complaints regarding its activities for which it is accredited; and

(v) protect against the use, in carrying out subsection (a) with respect to a device, of any officer or employee of the person who has a financial conflict of interest regarding the device, and annually make available to the public disclosures of the extent to which the person, and the officers and employees of the person, have maintained compliance with requirements under this clause relating to financial conflicts of interest.

(4) Selection of accredited persons. The Secretary shall provide each person who chooses to use an accredited person to receive a section 510(k) report a panel of at least two or more accredited persons from which the regulated person may select one for a specific regulatory function.

(5) Compensation of accredited persons. Compensation for an accredited person shall be determined by agreement between the accredited person and the person who engages the services of the accredited person, and shall be paid by the person who engages such services.

(c) Duration. The authority provided by this section terminates October 1, 2012.

(d) Report. Not later than January 10, 2007, the Secretary shall conduct a study based on the experience under the program under this section and submit to the Committee on Energy and Commerce of the House of Representatives, and the Committee on Health, Education, Labor, and Pensions of the Senate, a report describing the findings of the study. The objectives of the study shall include determining--

(1) the number of devices reviewed under this section;

(2) the number of devices reviewed under this section that were ultimately cleared by the Secretary;

(3) the number of devices reviewed under this section that were ultimately not cleared by the Secretary;

(4) the average time period for a review under this section (including the time it takes for the Secretary to review a recommendation of an accredited person under subsection (a) and determine the initial device classification);

(5) the average time period identified in paragraph (4) compared to the average time period for review of devices solely by the Secretary pursuant to section 510(k);

(6) if there is a difference in the average time period under paragraph (4) and the average time period under paragraph (5), the reasons for such difference;

(7) whether the quality of reviews under this section for devices for which no guidance has been issued is qualitatively inferior to reviews by the Secretary for devices for which no guidance has been issued;

(8) whether the quality of reviews under this section of devices for which no guidance has been issued is qualitatively inferior to reviews under this section of devices for which guidance has been issued;

(9) whether this section has in any way jeopardized or improved the public health;

(10) any impact of this section on resources available to the Secretary to review reports under section 510(k); and

(11) any suggestions for continuation, modification (including contraction or expansion of device eligibility), or termination of this section that the Secretary determines to be appropriate.

Subchapter B — Drugs for Rare Diseases and Conditions

SEC. 524. [21 USC §360n] Priority Review to Encourage Treatments for Tropical Diseases

Note: This section was added in May 2008.

(a) Definitions. In this section:

(1) Priority review. The term "***priority review***", with respect to a human drug application as defined in section 735(1) [21 USC § 379g(l)], means review and action by the Secretary on such application not later than 6 months after receipt by the Secretary of such application, as described in the Manual of Policies and Procedures of the Food and Drug Administration and goals identified in the letters described in section 101(c) of the Food and Drug Administration Amendments Act of 2007 [21 USC § 379g note].

(2) Priority review voucher. The term "***priority review voucher***" means a voucher issued by the Secretary to the sponsor of a tropical disease product application that entitles the holder of such voucher to priority review of a single human drug application submitted under section 505(b)(1) [21 USC § 355(b)(1)] or section 351 of the Public Health Service Act [42 USC § 262] after the date of approval of the tropical disease product application.

(3) Tropical disease. The term "***tropical disease***" means any of the following:

(A) Tuberculosis.

(B) Malaria.

(C) Blinding trachoma.

(D) Buruli Ulcer.

(E) Cholera.

(F) Dengue/dengue haemorrhagic fever.

(G) Dracunculiasis (guinea-worm disease).

(H) Fascioliasis.

(I) Human African trypanosomiasis.

(J) Leishmaniasis.

(K) Leprosy.

(L) Lymphatic filariasis.

(M) Onchocerciasis.

(N) Schistosomiasis.

(O) Soil transmitted helmithiasis.

(P) Yaws.

(Q) Any other infectious disease for which there is no significant market in developed nations and that disproportionately affects poor and marginalized populations, designated by regulation by the Secretary.

(4) Tropical disease product application. The term "***tropical disease product application***" means an application that--

(A) is a human drug application as defined in section 735(1) [21 USC § 379g(1)]--

(i) for prevention or treatment of a tropical disease; and

(ii) the Secretary deems eligible for priority review;

(B) is approved after the date of the enactment of the Food and Drug Administration Amendments Act of 2007 [enacted Sept. 27, 2007], by the Secretary for use in the prevention, detection, or treatment of a tropical disease; and

(C) is for a human drug, no active ingredient (including any ester or salt of the active ingredient) of which has been approved in any other application under section 505(b)(1) [21 USC § 355(b)(1)] or section 351 of the Public Health Service Act [42 USC § 262].

(b) Priority review voucher.

(1) In general. The Secretary shall award a priority review voucher to the sponsor of a tropical disease product application upon approval by the Secretary of such tropical disease product application.

(2) Transferability. The sponsor of a tropical disease product that receives a priority review voucher under this section may transfer (including by sale) the entitlement to such voucher to a sponsor of a human drug for which an application under section 505(b)(1) [21 USC § 355(b)(1)] or section 351 of the Public Health Service Act [42 USC § 262] will be submitted after the date of the approval of the tropical disease product application.

(3) Limitation.

(A) No award for prior approved application. A sponsor of a tropical disease product may not receive a priority review voucher under this section if the tropical disease product application was submitted to the Secretary prior to the date of the enactment of this section.

(B) One-year waiting period. The Secretary shall issue a priority review voucher to the sponsor of a tropical disease product no earlier than the date that is 1 year after the date of the enactment of the Food and Drug Administration Amendments Act of 2007 [enacted Sept. 27, 2007].

(4) Notification. The sponsor of a human drug application shall notify the Secretary not later than 365 days prior to submission of the human drug application that is the subject of a priority review voucher of an intent to submit the human drug application, including the date on which the sponsor intends to submit the application. Such notification shall be a legally binding commitment to pay for the user fee to be assessed in accordance with this section.

(c) Priority review user fee.

(1) In general. The Secretary shall establish a user fee program under which a sponsor of a human drug application that is the subject of a priority review voucher shall pay to the Secretary a fee determined under paragraph (2). Such fee shall be in addition to any fee required to be submitted by the sponsor under chapter VII [21 USC §§ 371 et seq.].

(2) Fee amount. The amount of the priority review user fee shall be determined each fiscal year by the Secretary and based on the average cost incurred by the agency in the review of a human drug application subject to priority review in the previous fiscal year.

(3) Annual fee setting. The Secretary shall establish, before the beginning of each fiscal year beginning after September 30, 2007, for that fiscal year, the amount of the priority review user fee.

(4) Payment.

(A) In general. The priority review user fee required by this subsection shall be due upon the submission of a human drug application under section 505(b)(1) [21 USC § 355(b)(1)] or section 351 of the Public Health Services Act [42 USC § 262] for which the priority review voucher is used.

(B) Complete application. An application described under subparagraph (A) for which the sponsor requests the use of a priority review voucher shall be considered incomplete if the fee required by this subsection and all other applicable user fees are not paid in accordance with the Secretary's procedures for paying such fees.

(C) No waivers, exemptions, reductions, or refunds. The Secretary may not grant a waiver, exemption, reduction, or refund of any fees due and payable under this section.

(5) Offsetting collections. Fees collected pursuant to this subsection for any fiscal year--

(A) shall be deposited and credited as offsetting collections to the account providing appropriations to the Food and Drug Administration; and

(B) shall not be collected for any fiscal year except to the extent provided in advance in appropriation Acts.

SEC. 525. [21 USC §360aa] Recommendations for Investigations of Drugs for Rare Diseases or Conditions

(a) [48] The sponsor of a drug for a disease or condition which is rare in the States may request the Secretary to provide written recommendations for the nonclinical and clinical investigations which must be conducted with the drug before—

(1) it may be approved for such disease or condition under section 505, or

(2) if the drug is a biological product, it may be licensed for such disease or condition under section 351 of the Public Health Service Act.

If the Secretary has reason to believe that a drug for which a request is made under this section is a drug for a disease or condition which is rare in the States, the Secretary shall provide the person making the request written recommendations for the nonclinical and clinical investigations which the Secretary believes, on the basis of information available to the Secretary at the time of the request under this section, would be necessary for approval of such drug for such disease or condition under section 505 or licensing of such drug for such disease or condition under section 351 of the Public Health Service Act.

(b) The Secretary shall by regulation promulgate procedures for the implementation of subsection (a).

SEC. 526. [21 USC §360bb] Designation of Drugs for Rare Disesases or Conditions

(a)(1) The manufacturer or the sponsor of a drug may request the Secretary to designate the drug as a drug for a rare disease or condition. A request for designation of a drug shall be made before the submission of an application under section 505(b) for the drug, or the submission of an application for licensing of the drug under section 351 of the Public Health Service Act. If the Secretary finds that a drug for which a request is submitted under this subsection is being or will be investigated for a rare disease or condition and—

(A) if an application for such drug is approved under section 505, or

(B) if a license for such drug is issued under section 351of the Public Health Service Act, the approval, certification, or license would be for use for such disease or condition, the Secretary shall designate the drug as a drug

[48] Section 5 of the Orphan Drug Act (21 U.S.C. 360ee) (Public Law 97–414), which is included in the appendix, establishes a program to make grants and enter into contracts regarding the development of drugs for rare diseases and conditions. Authorizations of appropriations for that program are currently provided through fiscal year 2006. See section 3 of Public Law 107–281 (116 Stat. 1993).

for such disease or condition. A request for a designation of a drug under this subsection shall contain the consent of the applicant to notice being given by the Secretary under subsection (b) respecting the designation of the drug.

(2) For purposes of paragraph (1), the term "rare disease or condition" means any disease or condition which (A) affects less than 200,000 persons in the United States, or (B) affects more than 200,000 in the United States and for which there is no reasonable expectation that the cost of developing and making available in the United States a drug for such disease or condition will be recovered from sales in the United States of such drug. Determinations under the preceding sentence with respect to any drug shall be made on the basis of the facts and circumstances as of the date the request for designation of the drug under this subsection is made.

(b) A designation of a drug under subsection (a) shall be subject to the condition that—

(1) if an application was approved for the drug under section 505(b) or a license was issued for the drug under section 351 of the Public Health Service Act, the manufacturer of the drug will notify the Secretary of any discontinuance of the production of the drug at least one year before discontinuance, and

(2) if an application has not been approved for the drug under section 505(b) or a license has not been issued for the drug under section 351 of the Public Health Service Act and if preclinical investigations or investigations under section 505(i) are being conducted with the drug, the manufacturer or sponsor of the drug will notify the Secretary of any decision to discontinue active pursuit of approval of an application under section 505(b) or approval of a license under section 351 of the Public Health Service Act.

(c) Notice respecting the designation of a drug under subsection (a) shall be made available to the public.

(d) The Secretary shall by regulation promulgate procedures for the implementation of subsection (a).

SEC. 526. [21 USC §360bb] Designation of Drugs for Rare Diseases or Conditions

(a)(1) The manufacturer or the sponsor of a drug may request the Secretary to designate the drug as a drug for a rare disease or condition. A request for designation of a drug shall be made before the submission of an application under section 505(b) for the drug, or the submission of an application for licensing of the drug under section 351 of the Public Health Service Act. If the Secretary finds that a drug for which a request is submitted under this subsection is being or will be investigated for a rare disease or condition and—

(A) if an application for such drug is approved under section 505, or

(B) if a license for such drug is issued under section 351of the Public Health Service Act, the approval, certification, or license would be for use for such disease or condition, the Secretary shall designate the drug as a drug for such disease or condition. A request for a designation of a drug under this subsection shall contain the consent of the applicant to notice being given by the Secretary under subsection (b) respecting the designation of the drug.

(2) For purposes of paragraph (1), the term "rare disease or condition" means any disease or condition which (A) affects less than 200,000 persons in the United States, or (B) affects more than 200,000 in the United States and for which there is no reasonable expectation that the cost of developing and making available in the United States a drug for such disease or condition will be recovered from sales in the United States of such drug. Determinations under the preceding sentence with respect to any drug shall be made on the basis of the facts and circumstances as of the date the request for designation of the drug under this subsection is made.

(b) A designation of a drug under subsection (a) shall be subject to the condition that—

(1) if an application was approved for the drug under section 505(b) or a license was issued for the drug under section 351 of the Public Health Service Act, the manufacturer of the drug will notify the Secretary of any discontinuance of the production of the drug at least one year before discontinuance, and

(2) if an application has not been approved for the drug under section 505(b) or a license has not been issued for the drug under section 351 of the Public Health Service Act and if preclinical investigations or investigations under section 505(i) are being conducted with the drug, the manufacturer or sponsor of the drug will notify the Secretary of any decision to discontinue active pursuit of approval of an application under section 505(b) or approval of a license under section 351 of the Public Health Service Act.

(c) Notice respecting the designation of a drug under subsection (a) shall be made available to the public.

(d) The Secretary shall by regulation promulgate procedures for the implementation of subsection (a).

SEC. 527. [21 USC §360cc] Protection for Drugs for Rare Diseases or Conditions

(a) Except as provided in subsection (b), if the Secretary—

(1) approves an application filed pursuant to section 505, or

(2) issues a license under section 351 of the Public Health Service Act for a drug designated under section 526 for a rare disease or condition, the Secretary may not approve another application under section 505 or issue another license under section 351 of the Public Health Service Act for such drug for such disease or condition for a person who is not the holder of such approved application, of or of such license until the expiration of seven years from the date of the approval of the approved application, or the issuance of the license. Section 505(c)(2) does not apply to the refusal to approve an application under the preceding sentence.

(b) If an application filed pursuant to section 505 is approved for a drug designated under section 526 for a rare disease or condition or if a license is issued under section 351 of the Public Health Service Act for such a drug, the Secretary may, during the seven year period beginning on the date of the application approval or of the issuance of the license, approve another application under section 505 or issue a license under section 351 of the Public Health Service Act, for such drug for such disease or condition for a person who is not the holder of such approved application or of such license if—

(1) the Secretary finds, after providing the holder notice and opportunity for the submission of views, that in such period the holder of the approved application or of the license cannot assure the availability of sufficient quantities of the drug to meet the needs of persons with the disease or condition for which the drug was designated; or

(2) such holder provides the Secretary in writing the consent of such holder for the approval of other applications or the issuance of other licenses before the expiration of such seven year period.

SEC. 528. [21 USC §360dd] Open Protocols for Investigations of Drugs for Rare Diseases or Conditions

If a drug is designated under section 526 as a drug for a rare disease or condition and if notice of a claimed exemption under section 505(i) or regulations issued thereunder is filed for such drug, the Secretary shall encourage the sponsor of such drug to design protocols for clinical investigations of the drug which may be conducted under the exemption to permit the addition to the investigations of persons with the disease or condition who need the drug to treat the disease or condition and who cannot be satisfactorily treated by available alternative drugs.

Subchapter C — Electronic Product Radiation Control

SEC. 531. [21 USC §360hh] Definitions

As used in this subchapter—

(1) the term "***electronic product radiation***" means—

(A) any ionizing or non-ionizing electromagnetic or particulate radiation, or

(B) any sonic, infrasonic, or ultrasonic wave, which is emitted from an electronic product as the result of the operation of an electronic circuit in such product;

(2) the term "***electronic product***" means (A) any manufactured or assembled product which, when in operation, (i) contains or acts as part of an electronic circuit and (ii) emits (or in the absence of effective shielding or other controls would emit) electronic product radiation, or (B) any manufactured or assembled article which is intended for use as a component, part, or accessory of a product described in clause (A) and which when in operation emits (or in the absence of effective shielding or other controls would emit) such radiation;

(3) the term "***manufacturer***" means any person engaged in the business of manufacturing, assembling, or importing of electronic products;

(4) the term "***commerce***" means (A) commerce between any place in any State and any place outside thereof; and (B) commerce wholly within the District of Columbia; and

(5) the term "***State***" includes the District of Columbia, the Commonwealth of Puerto Rico, the Northern Mariana Islands, the Virgin Islands, Guam, and American Samoa.

SEC. 532. [21 USC §360ii] Electronic Product Radiation Control Program

(a) The Secretary shall establish and carry out an electronic product radiation control program designed to protect the public health and safety from electronic product radiation. As a part of such program, he shall—

(1) pursuant to section 534, develop and administer performance standards for electronic products;

(2) plan, conduct, coordinate, and support research, development, training, and operational activities to minimize the emissions of and the exposure of people to, unnecessary electronic product radiation;

(3) maintain liaison with and receive information from other Federal and State departments and agencies with related interests, professional organizations, industry, industry and labor associations, and other organizations on present and future potential electronic product radiation;

(4) study and evaluate emissions of, and conditions of exposure to, electronic product radiation and intense magnetic fields;

(5) develop, test, and evaluate the effectiveness of procedures and techniques for minimizing exposure to electronic product radiation; and

(6) consult and maintain liaison with the Secretary of Commerce, the Secretary of Defense, the Secretary of Labor, the Atomic Energy Commission, and other appropriate Federal departments and agencies on (A) techniques, equipment, and programs for testing and evaluating electronic product radiation, and (B) the development of performance standards pursuant to section 534 to control such radiation emissions.

(b) In carrying out the purposes of subsection (a), the Secretary is authorized to—

(1)(A) collect and make available, through publications and other appropriate means, the results of, and other information concerning, research and studies relating to the nature and extent of the hazards and control of electronic product radiation; and (B) make such recommendations relating to such hazards and control as he considers appropriate;

(2) make grants to public and private agencies, organizations, and institutions, and to individuals for the purposes stated in paragraphs (2), (4), and (5) of subsection (a) of this section;

(3) contract with public or private agencies, institutions, and organizations, and with individuals, without regard to section 3324 of title 31, United States Code, and section 3709 of the Revised Statutes of the United States (41 U.S.C. 5); and

(4) procure (by negotiation or otherwise) electronic products for research and testing purposes, and sell or otherwise dispose of such products.

(c)(1) Each recipient of assistance under this subchapter pursuant to grants or contracts entered into under other than competitive bidding procedures shall keep such records as the Secretary shall prescribe, including records which fully disclose the amount and disposition by such recipient of the proceeds of such assistance, the total cost of the project or undertaking in connection with which such assistance is given or used, and the amount of that portion of the cost of the project or undertaking supplied by other sources, and such other records as will facilitate an effective audit.

(2) The Secretary and the Comptroller General of the United States, or any of their duly authorized representatives, shall have access for the purpose of audit and examination to any books, documents, papers, and records of the recipient that are pertinent to the grants or contracts entered into under this subchapter under other than competitive bidding procedures.

SEC. 533. [21 USC §360jj] Studies by the Secretary

(a) The Secretary shall conduct the following studies, and shall make a report or reports of the results of such studies to the Congress on or before January 1, 1970, and from time to time thereafter as he may find necessary, together with such recommendations for legislation as he may deem appropriate:

(1) A study of present State and Federal control of health hazards from electronic product radiation and other types of ionizing radiation, which study shall include, but not be limited to—

(A) control of health hazards from radioactive materials other than materials regulated under the Atomic Energy Act of 1954;

(B) any gaps and inconsistencies in present controls;

(C) the need for controlling the sale of certain used electronic products, particularly antiquated X-ray equipment, without upgrading such products to meet the standards for new products or separate standards for used products;

(D) measures to assure consistent and effective control of the aforementioned health hazards;

(E) measures to strengthen radiological health programs of State governments; and

(F) the feasibility of authorizing the Secretary to enter into arrangements with individual States or groups of States to define their respective functions and responsibilities for the control of electronic product radiation and other ionizing radiation;

(2) A study to determine the necessity for the development of standards for the use of nonmedical electronic products for commercial and industrial purposes; and

(3) A study of the development of practicable procedures for the detection and measurement of electronic product radiation which may be emitted from electronic products manufactured or imported prior to the effective date of any applicable standard established pursuant to this subchapter.

(b) In carrying out these studies, the Secretary shall invite the participation of other Federal departments and agencies having related responsibilities and interests, State governments—particularly those of States which regulate radioactive materials under section 274 of the Atomic Energy Act of 1954, as amended, and interested professional, labor, and industrial organizations. Upon request from congressional committees interested in these studies, the Secretary shall keep these committees currently informed as to the progress of the studies and shall permit the committees to send observers to meetings of the study groups.

(c) The Secretary or his designee shall organize the studies and the participation of the invited participants as he deems best. Any dissent from the findings and recommendations of the Secretary shall be included in the report if so requested by the dissenter.

SEC. 534. [21 USC §360kk] Performance Standards for Electronic Products

(a)(1) The Secretary shall by regulation prescribe performance standards for electronic products to control the emission of electronic product radiation from such products if he determines that such standards are necessary for the protection of the public health and safety. Such standards may include provisions for the testing of such products and the measurement of their electronic product radiation emissions, may require the attachment of warning signs and labels, and may require the provision of instructions for the installation, operation, and use of such products. Such standards may be prescribed from time to time whenever such determinations are made, but the first of such standards shall be prescribed prior to January 1, 1970. In the development of such standards, the Secretary shall consult with Federal and State departments and agencies having related responsibilities or interests and with appropriate professional organizations and interested persons, including representatives of industries and labor organizations which would be affected by such standards, and shall give consideration to—

(A) the latest available scientific and medical data in the field of electronic product radiation;

(B) the standards currently recommended by (i) other Federal agencies having responsibilities relating to the control and measurement of electronic product radiation, and (ii) public or private groups having an expertise in the field of electronic product radiation;

(C) the reasonableness and technical feasibility of such standards as applied to a particular electronic product;

(D) the adaptability of such standards to the need for uniformity and reliability of testing and measuring procedures and equipment; and

(E) in the case of a component, or accessory described in paragraph (2)(B) of section 531, the performance of such article in the manufactured or assembled product for which it is designed.

(2) The Secretary may prescribe different and individual performance standards, to the extent appropriate and feasible, for different electronic products so as to recognize their different operating characteristics and uses.

(3) The performance standards prescribed under this section shall not apply to any electronic product which is intended solely for export if (A) such product and the outside of any shipping container used in the export of such product are labeled or tagged to show that such product is intended for export, and (B) such product meets all the applicable requirements of the country to which such product is intended for export.

(4) The Secretary may by regulation amend or revoke any performance standard prescribed under this section.

(5) The Secretary may exempt from the provisions of this section any electronic product intended for use by departments or agencies of the United States provided such department or agency has prescribed procurement specifications governing emissions of electronic product radiation and provided further that such product is of a type used solely or predominantly by departments or agencies of the United States.

(b) The provisions of subchapter II of chapter 5 of title 5 of the United States Code (relating to the administrative procedure for rulemaking), and of chapter 7 of such title (relating to judicial review), shall apply with respect to any regulation prescribing, amending, or revoking any standard prescribed under this section.

(c) Each regulation prescribing, amending, or revoking a standard shall specify the date on which it shall take effect which, in the case of any regulation prescribing, or amending any standard, may not be sooner than one year or not later than two years after the date on which such regulation is issued, unless the Secretary finds, for good cause shown, that an earlier or later effective date is in the public interest and publishes in the Federal Register his reason for such finding, in which case such earlier or later date shall apply.

(d)(1) In a case of actual controversy as to the validity of any regulation issued under this section prescribing, amending, or revoking a performance standard, any person who will be adversely affected by such regulation when it is effective may at any time prior to the sixtieth day after such regulation is issued file a petition with the United States court of appeals for the circuit wherein such person resides or has his principal place of business, for a judicial review of such regulation. A copy of the petition shall be forthwith transmitted by the clerk of the court to the Secretary or other officer designated by him for that purpose. The Secretary thereupon shall file in the court the record of the proceedings on which the Secretary based the regulation, as provided in section 2112 of title 28 of the United States Code.

(2) If the petitioner applies to the court for leave to adduce additional evidence, and shows to the satisfaction of the court that such additional evidence is material and that there were reasonable grounds for the failure to adduce such evidence in the proceeding before the Secretary, the court may order such additional evidence (and evidence in rebuttal thereof) to be taken before the Secretary, and to be adduced upon the hearing, in such manner and upon such terms and conditions as to the court may seem proper. The Secretary may modify his findings, or make new findings, by reason of the additional evidence so taken, and he shall file such modified or new findings, and his recommendations, if any, for the modification or setting aside of his original regulation, with the return of such additional evidence.

(3) Upon the filing of the petition referred to in paragraph (1) of this subsection, the court shall have jurisdiction to review the regulation in accordance with

chapter 7 of title 5 of the United States Code and to grant appropriate relief as provided in such chapter.

(4) The judgment of the court affirming or setting aside, in whole or in part, any such regulation of the Secretary shall be final, subject to review by the Supreme Court of the United States upon certiorari or certification as provided in section 1254 of title 28 of the United States Code.

(5) Any action instituted under this subsection shall survive, notwithstanding any change in the person occupying the office of Secretary or any vacancy in such office.

(6) The remedies provided for in this subsection shall be in addition to and not in substitution for any other remedies provided by law.

(e) A certified copy of the transcript of the record and administrative proceedings under this section shall be furnished by the Secretary to any interested party at his request, and payment of the costs thereof, and shall be admissible in any criminal, exclusion of imports, or other proceeding arising under or in respect of this subchapter, irrespective of whether proceedings with respect to the regulation have previously been initiated or become final under this section.

(f)(1)(A) The Secretary shall establish a Technical Electronic Product Radiation Safety Standards Committee (hereafter in this subchapter referred to as the Committee") which he shall consult before prescribing any standard under this section. The Committee shall be appointed by the Secretary, after consultation with public and private agencies concerned with the technical aspect of electronic product radiation safety, and shall be composed of fifteen members each of whom shall be technically qualified by training and experience in one or more fields of science or engineering applicable to electronic product radiation safety, as follows:

(i) Five members shall be selected from governmental agencies, including State and Federal Governments;

(ii) Five members shall be selected from the affected industries after consultation with industry representatives; and

(iii) Five members shall be selected from the general public, of which at least one shall be a representative of organized labor.

(B) The Committee may propose electronic product radiation safety standards to the Secretary for his consideration. All proceedings of the Committee shall be recorded and the record of each such proceeding shall be available for public inspection.

(2) Payments to members of the Committee who are not officers or employees of the United States pursuant to subsection (c) of section 208 of the Public Health Service Act shall not render members of the Committee officers or employees of the United States for any purpose.

(g) The Secretary shall review and evaluate on a continuing basis testing programs carried out by industry to assure the adequacy of safeguards against hazardous electronic product radiation and to assure that electronic products comply with standards prescribed under this section.

(h) Every manufacturer of an electronic product to which is applicable a standard in effect under this section shall furnish to the distributor or dealer at the time of delivery of such product, in the form of a label or tag permanently affixed to such product or in such manner as approved by the Secretary, the certification that such product conforms to all applicable standards under this section. Such certification shall be based upon a test, in accordance with such standard, of the individual article to which it is attached or upon a testing program which is in accord with good manufacturing practice and which has not been disapproved by the Secretary (in such manner as he shall prescribe by regulation) on the grounds that it does not assure the adequacy of safeguards against hazardous electronic product radiation or that it does not assure that electronic products comply with the standards prescribed under this section.

SEC. 535. [21 USC §360ll] Notification of Defects in, and Repair or Replacement of, Electronic Products

(a)(1) Every manufacturer of electronic products, who discovers that an electronic product produced, assembled, or imported by him has a defect which relates to the safety of use of such product by reason of the emission of electronic product radiation, or that an electronic product produced, assembled, or imported by him on or after the effective date of an applicable standard prescribed pursuant to section 534 fails to comply with such standard, shall immediately notify the Secretary of such defect or failure to comply if such product has left the place of manufacture and shall (except as authorized by paragraph (2)) with reasonable promptness furnish notification of such defect or failure to the persons (where known to the manufacturer) specified in subsection (b) of this section.

(2) If, in the opinion of such manufacturer, the defect or failure to comply is not such as to create a significant risk of injury, including genetic injury, to any person, he may, at the time of giving notice to the Secretary of such defect or failure to comply, apply to the Secretary for an exemption from the requirement of notice to the persons specified in subsection (b). If such application states reasonable grounds for such exemption, the Secretary shall afford such manufacturer an opportunity to present his views and evidence in support of the application, the burden of proof being on the manufacturer. If, after such presentation, the Secretary is satisfied that such defect or failure to comply is not such as to create a significant risk of injury, including genetic injury, to any person, he shall exempt such manufacturer from the requirement of notice to the persons specified in subsection (b) of this section and from the requirements of repair or replacement imposed by subsection (f) of this section.

(b) The notification (other than to the Secretary) required by paragraph (1) of subsection (a) of this section shall be accomplished—

 (1) by certified mail to the first purchaser of such product for purposes other than resale, and to any subsequent transferee of such product; and

 (2) by certified mail or other more expeditious means to the dealers or distributors of such manufacturer to whom such product was delivered.

(c) The notifications required by paragraph (1) of subsection (a) of this section shall contain a clear description of such defect or failure to comply with an applicable standard, an evaluation of the hazard reasonably related to such defect or failure to comply, and a statement of the measures to be taken to repair such defect. In the case of a notification to a person referred to in subsection (b) of this section, the notification shall also advise the person of his rights under subsection (f) of this section.

(d) Every manufacturer of electronic products shall furnish to the Secretary a true or representative copy of all notices, bulletins, and other communications to the dealers or distributors of such manufacturer or to purchasers (or subsequent transferees) of electronic products of such manufacturer regarding any such defect in such product or any such failure to comply with a standard applicable to such product. The Secretary shall disclose to the public so much of the information contained in such notice or other information obtained under section 537 as he deems will assist in carrying out the purposes of this subchapter, but he shall not disclose any information which contains or relates to a trade secret or other matter referred to in section 1905 of title 18 of the United States Code unless he determines that it is necessary to carry out the purposes of this subchapter.

(e) If through testing, inspection, investigation, or research carried out pursuant to this subchapter, or examination of reports submitted pursuant to section 537, or otherwise, the Secretary determines that any electronic product—

 (1) does not comply with an applicable standard prescribed pursuant to section 534; or

 (2) contains a defect which relates to the safety of use of such product by reason of the emission of electronic product radiation;

he shall immediately notify the manufacturer of such product of such defect or failure to comply. The notice shall contain the findings of the Secretary and shall include all information upon which the findings are based. The Secretary shall afford such manufacturer an opportunity to present his views and evidence in support thereof, to establish that there is no failure of compliance or that the alleged defect does not exist or does not relate to safety of use of the product by reason of the emission of such radiation hazard. If after such presentation by the manufacturer the Secretary determines that such product does not comply with an applicable standard prescribed pursuant to section 534, or that it contains a defect which relates to the safety of use of such product by reason of the emission of electronic product radiation, the Secretary shall direct the manufacturer to furnish the notification specified in subsection (c) of this section to the persons specified in paragraphs (1) and (2) of subsection (b) of this section (where known to the manufacturer), unless the manufacturer has applied for an exemption from the requirement of such notification on the ground specified in paragraph (2) of subsection (a) and the Secretary is satisfied that such noncompliance or defect is not such as to create a significant risk of injury, including genetic injury, to any person.

(f) If any electronic product is found under subsection (a) or (e) to fail to comply with an applicable standard prescribed under this subchapter or to have a defect which relates to the safety of use of such product, and the notification specified in subsection (c) is required to be furnished on account of such failure or defect, the manufacturer of such product shall (1) without charge, bring such product into conformity with such standard or remedy such defect and provide reimbursement for any expenses for transportation of such product incurred in connection with having such product brought into conformity or having such defect remedied, (2) replace such product with a like or equivalent product which complies with each applicable standard prescribed under this subchapter and which has no defect relating to the safety of its use, or (3) make a refund of the cost of such product. The manufacturer shall take the action required by this subsection in such manner, and with respect to such persons, as the Secretary by regulations shall prescribe.

(g) This section shall not apply to any electronic product that was manufactured before the date of the enactment of this subchapter[49].

SEC. 536. [21 USC §360mm] Imports

(a) Any electronic product offered for importation into the United States which fails to comply with an applicable standard prescribed under this subchapter, or to which is not affixed a certification in the form of a label or tag in conformity with section 534(h) shall be refused admission into the United States. The Secretary of the Treasury shall deliver to the Secretary of Health and Human Services, upon the latter's request, samples of electronic products which are being imported or offered for import into the United States, giving notice thereof to the owner or consignee, who may have a hearing before the Secretary of Health and Human Services. If it appears from an examination of such samples or otherwise that any electronic product fails to comply with applicable standards prescribed pursuant

[49] This subchapter was enacted by Public Law 90–602, which was enacted October 18, 1968. (The subchapter was originally enacted as part of the Public Health Service Act, and was transferred to this Act by section 19 of Public Law 101–629.)

to section 534, then, unless subsection (b) of this section applies and is complied with, (1) such electronic product shall be refused admission, and (2) the Secretary of the Treasury shall cause the destruction of such electronic product unless such article is exported, under regulations prescribed by the Secretary of the Treasury, within 90 days after the date of notice of refusal of admission or within such additional time as may be permitted by such regulations.

(b) If it appears to the Secretary of Health and Human Services that any electronic product refused admission pursuant to subsection (a) of this section can be brought into compliance with applicable standards prescribed pursuant to section 534, final determination as to admission of such electronic product may be deferred upon filing of timely written application by the owner or consignee and the execution by him of a good and sufficient bond providing for the payment of such liquidated damages in the event of default as the Secretary of Health and Human Services may by regulation prescribe. If such application is filed and such bond is executed the Secretary of Health and Human Services may, in accordance with rules prescribed by him, permit the applicant to perform such operations with respect to such electronic product as may be specified in the notice of permission.

(c) All expenses (including travel, per diem or subsistence, and salaries of officers or employees of the United States) in connection with the destruction provided for in subsection (a) of this section and the supervision of operations provided for in subsection (b) of this section, and all expenses in connection with the storage, cartage, or labor with respect to any electronic product refused admission pursuant to subsection (a) of this section, shall be paid by the owner or consignee, and, in event of default, shall constitute a lien against any future importations made by such owner or consignee.

(d) It shall be the duty of every manufacturer offering an electronic product for importation into the United States to designate in writing an agent upon whom service of all administrative and judicial processes, notices, orders, decisions, and requirements may be made for and on behalf of said manufacturer, and to file such designation with the Secretary, which designation may from time to time be changed by like writing, similarly filed. Service of all administrative and judicial processes, notices, orders, decisions, and requirements may be made upon said manufacturer by service upon such designated agent at his office or usual place of residence with like effect as if made personally upon said manufacturer, and in default of such designation of such agent, service of process, notice, order, requirement, or decision in any proceeding before the Secretary or in any judicial proceeding for enforcement of this subchapter or any standards prescribed pursuant to this subchapter may be made by posting such process, notice, order, requirement, or decision in the Office of the Secretary or in a place designated by him by regulation.

SEC. 537. [21 USC §360nn] Inspection and Reports

(a) If the Secretary finds for good cause that the methods, tests, or programs related to electronic product radiation safety in a particular factory, warehouse, or establishment in which electronic products are manufactured or held, may not be adequate or reliable, officers or employees duly designated by the Secretary, upon presenting appropriate credentials and a written notice to the owner, operator, or agent in charge, are thereafter authorized (1) to enter, at reasonable times, any area in such factory, warehouse, or establishment in which the manufacturer's tests (or testing programs) required by section 534(h) are carried out, and (2) to inspect, at reasonable times and within reasonable limits and in a reasonable manner, the facilities and procedures within such area which are related to electronic product radiation safety. Each such inspection shall be commenced and completed with reasonable promptness. In addition to other grounds upon which good cause may be found for purposes of this subsection, good cause will be considered to exist in any case where the manufacturer has introduced into commerce any electronic product which does not comply with an applicable standard prescribed under this subchapter and with respect to which no exemption from the notification requirements has been granted by the Secretary under section 535(a)(2) or 535(e).

(b) Every manufacturer of electronic products shall establish and maintain such records (including testing records), make such reports, and provide such information, as the Secretary may reasonably require to enable him to determine whether such manufacturer has acted or is acting in compliance with this subchapter and standards prescribed pursuant to this subchapter and shall, upon request of an officer or employee duly designated by the Secretary, permit such officer or employee to inspect appropriate books, papers, records, and documents relevant to determining whether such manufacturer has acted or is acting in compliance with standards prescribed pursuant to this subchapter.

(c) Every manufacturer of electronic products shall provide to the Secretary such performance data and other technical data related to safety as may be required to carry out the purposes of this subchapter. The Secretary is authorized to require the manufacturer to give such notification of such performance and technical data at the time of original purchase to the ultimate purchaser of the electronic product, as he determines necessary to carry out the purposes of this subchapter after consulting with the affected industry.

(d) Accident and investigation reports made under this subchapter by any officer, employee, or agent of the Secretary shall be available for use in any civil, criminal, or other judicial proceeding arising out of such accident. Any such officer, employee, or agent may be required to testify in such proceedings as to the fact developed in such investigations. Any such report shall be made available to the public in a manner which need not identify individuals. All reports on research projects, demonstration projects, and other related activities shall be public information.

(e) The Secretary or his representative shall not disclose any information reported to or otherwise obtained by him, pursuant to subsection (a) or (b) of this section, which concerns any information which contains or relates to a trade secret or other matter referred to in section 1905 of title 18 of the United States Code, except that such information may be disclosed to other officers or employees of the Department and of other agencies concerned with carrying out this subchapter or when relevant in any proceeding under this subchapter. Nothing in this section shall authorize the withholding of information by the Secretary, or by any officers or employees under his control, from the duly authorized committees of the Congress.

(f) The Secretary may by regulation (1) require dealers and distributors of electronic products, to which there are applicable standards prescribed under this subchapter and the retail prices of which is not less than $50, to furnish manufacturers of such products such information as may be necessary to identify and locate, for purposes of section 535, the first purchasers of such products for purposes other than resale, and (2) require manufacturers to preserve such information. Any regulation establishing a requirement pursuant to clause (1) of the preceding sentence shall (A) authorize such dealers and distributors to elect, in lieu of immediately furnishing such information to the manufacturer, to hold and preserve such information until advised by the manufacturer or Secretary that such information is needed by the manufacturer for purposes of section 535, and (B) provide that the dealer or distributor shall, upon making such election, give prompt notice of such election (together with information identifying the notifier and the product) to the manufacturer and shall, when advised by the manufacturer or Secretary, of the need therefor for the purposes of section 535, immediately furnish the manufacturer with the required information. If a dealer or distributor discontinues the dealing in or distribution of electronic products, he shall turn the information over to the manufacturer. Any manufacturer receiving information pursuant to this subsection concerning first purchasers of products for purposes other than resale shall treat it as confidential and may use it only if necessary for the purpose of notifying persons pursuant to section 535(a).

SEC. 538. [21 USC §360oo] Prohibited Acts

(a) It shall be unlawful—

(1) for any manufacturer to introduce, or to deliver for introduction, into commerce, or to import into the United States, any electronic product which does not comply with an applicable standard prescribed pursuant to section 534;

(2) for any person to fail to furnish any notification or other material or information required by section 535 or 537; or to fail to comply with the requirements of section 535(f);

(3) for any person to fail or to refuse to establish or maintain records required by this subchapter or to permit access by the Secretary or any of his duly authorized representatives to, or the copying of, such records, or to permit entry or inspection, as required by or pursuant to section 537;

(4) for any person to fail or to refuse to make any report required pursuant to section 537(b) or to furnish or preserve any information required pursuant to section 537(f); or

(5) for any person (A) to fail to issue a certification as required by section 534(h), or (B) to issue such a certification when such certification is not based upon a test or testing program meeting the requirements of section 534(h) or when the issuer, in the exercise of due care, would have reason to know that such certification is false or misleading in a material respect.

(b) The Secretary may exempt any electronic product, or class thereof, from all or part of subsection (a), upon such conditions as he may find necessary to protect the public health or welfare, for the purpose of research, investigations, studies, demonstrations, or training, or for reasons of national security.

SEC. 539. [21 USC §360pp] Enforcement

(a) The district courts of the United States shall have jurisdiction, for cause shown, to restrain violations of section 538 and to restrain dealers and distributors of electronic products from selling or otherwise disposing of electronic products which do not conform to an applicable standard prescribed pursuant to section 534 except when such products are disposed of by returning them to the distributor or manufacturer from whom they were obtained. The district courts of the United States shall also have jurisdiction in accordance with section 1355 of title 28 of the United States Code to enforce the provisions of subsection (b) of this section.

(b)(1) Any person who violates section 538 shall be subject to a civil penalty of not more than $1,000. For purposes of this subsection, any such violation shall with respect to each electronic product involved, or with respect to each act or omission made unlawful by section 538, constitute a separate violation, except that the maximum civil penalty imposed on any person under this subsection for any related series of violations shall not exceed $300,000.

(2) Any such civil penalty may on application be remitted or mitigated by the Secretary. In determining the amount of such penalty, or whether it should be remitted or mitigated and in what amount, the appropriateness of such penalty to the size of the business of the person charged and the gravity of the violation shall be considered. The amount of such penalty, when finally determined, may be deducted from any sums owing by the United States to the person charged.

(c) Actions under subsections (a) and (b) of this section may be brought in the district court of the United States for the district wherein any act or omission or transaction constituting the violation occurred, or in such court for the district where the defendant is found or transacts business, and process in such cases may be served in any other district of which the defendant is an inhabitant or wherever the defendant may be found.

(d) Nothing in this subchapter shall be construed as requiring the Secretary to report for the institution of proceedings minor violations of this subchapter whenever he believes that the public interest will be adequately served by a suitable written notice or warning.

(e) Except as provided in the first sentence of section 542, compliance with this subchapter or any regulations issued thereunder shall not relieve any person from liability at common law or under statutory law.

(f) The remedies provided for in this subchapter shall be in addition to and not in substitution for any other remedies provided by law.

[Sec. 540 repealed by P.L. 105–362, § 601(a)(2)(A).]

SEC. 541. [21 USC §360rr] Federal-State Cooperation

[50] The Secretary is authorized (1) to accept from State and local authorities engaged in activities related to health or safety or consumer protection, on a reimbursable basis or otherwise, any assistance in the administration and enforcement of this subchapter which he may request and which they may be able and willing to provide and, if so agreed, may pay in advance or otherwise for the reasonable cost of such assistance, and (2) he may, for the purpose of conducting examinations, investigations, and inspections, commission any officer or employee of any such authority as an officer of the Department.

SEC. 542. [21 USC §360ss] Effect on State Standards

Whenever any standard prescribed pursuant to section 534 with respect to an aspect of performance of an electronic product is in effect, no State or political subdivision of a State shall have any authority either to establish, or to continue in effect, any standard which is applicable to the same aspect of performance of such product and which is not identical to the Federal standard. Nothing in this subchapter shall be construed to prevent the Federal Government or the government of any State or political subdivision thereof from establishing a requirement with respect to emission of radiation from electronic products procured for its own use if such requirement imposes a more restrictive standard than that required to comply with the otherwise applicable Federal standard.

[50] Section 540 was repealed by section 601(a)(2)(A) of Public Law 105–362 (112 Stat. 3285).

Subchapter D — Dissemination of Treatment Information[51]

SEC. 551. [21 USC §360aaa] Requirements for Dissemination of Treatment Information on Drugs or Devices

(a) IN GENERAL.—Notwithstanding sections 301(d), 502(f), and 505, and section 351 of the Public Health Service Act (42 U.S.C. 262), a manufacturer may disseminate to—

(1) a health care practitioner;

(2) a pharmacy benefit manager;

(3) a health insurance issuer;

(4) a group health plan; or

(5) a Federal or State governmental agency;

written information concerning the safety, effectiveness, or benefit of a use not described in the approved labeling of a drug or device if the manufacturer meets the requirements of subsection (b).

(b) SPECIFIC REQUIREMENTS.—A manufacturer may disseminate information under subsection (a) on a new use only if—

(1)(A) in the case of a drug, there is in effect for the drug an application filed under subsection (b) or (j) of section 505 or a biologics license issued under section 351 of the Public Health Service Act; or

(B) in the case of a device, the device is being commercially distributed in accordance with a regulation under subsection (d) or (e) of section 513, an order under subsection (f) of such section, or the approval of an application under section 515;

(2) the information meets the requirements of section 552;

---

[51] This subchapter was added by section 401(a) of P.L. 105–115. Subsections (d) and (e) of such section provides the following:

(d) EFFECTIVE DATE.—The amendments made by this section shall take effect 1 year after the date of enactment of this Act, or upon the Secretary's issuance of final regulations pursuant to subsection (c), whichever is sooner.

(e) SUNSET.—The amendments made by this section cease to be effective September 30, 2006, or 7 years after the date on which the Secretary promulgates the regulations described in subsection (c), whichever is later.

(3) the information to be disseminated is not derived from clinical research conducted by another manufacturer or if it was derived from research conducted by another manufacturer, the manufacturer disseminating the information has the permission of such other manufacturer to make the dissemination;

(4) the manufacturer has, 60 days before such dissemination, submitted to the Secretary—

(A) a copy of the information to be disseminated; and

(B) any clinical trial information the manufacturer has

relating to the safety or effectiveness of the new use, any reports of clinical experience pertinent to the safety of the new use, and a summary of such information;

(5) the manufacturer has complied with the requirements of section 554 (relating to a supplemental application for such use);

(6) the manufacturer includes along with the information to be disseminated under this subsection—

(A) a prominently displayed statement that discloses—

(i) that the information concerns a use of a drug or device that has not been approved or cleared by the Food and Drug Administration;

(ii) if applicable, that the information is being disseminated at the expense of the manufacturer;

(iii) if applicable, the name of any authors of the information who are employees of, consultants to, or have received compensation from, the manufacturer, or who have a significant financial interest in the manufacturer;

(iv) the official labeling for the drug or device and all updates with respect to the labeling;

(v) if applicable, a statement that there are products or treatments that have been approved or cleared for the use that is the subject of the information being disseminated pursuant to subsection (a)(1); and

(vi) the identification of any person that has provided funding for the conduct of a study relating to the new use of a drug or device for which such information is being disseminated; and

(B) a bibliography of other articles from a scientific reference publication or scientific or medical journal that have been previously published about the use of the drug or device covered by the information disseminated (unless the information already includes such bibliography).

(c) ADDITIONAL INFORMATION.—If the Secretary determines, after providing notice of such determination and an opportunity for a meeting with respect to such determination, that the information submitted by a manufacturer under subsection (b)(3)(B), with respect to the use of a drug or device for which the manufacturer intends to disseminate information, fails to provide data, analyses, or other written matter that is objective and balanced, the Secretary may require the manufacturer to disseminate—

(1) additional objective and scientifically sound information that pertains to the safety or effectiveness of the use and is necessary to provide objectivity and balance, including any information that the manufacturer has submitted to the Secretary or, where appropriate, a summary of such information or any other information that the Secretary has authority to make available to the public; and

(2) an objective statement of the Secretary, based on data or other scientifically sound information available to the Secretary, that bears on the safety or effectiveness of the new use of the drug or device.

SEC. 552. [21 USC §360aaa–1] Information Authorized To Be Disseminated

(a) AUTHORIZED INFORMATION.—A manufacturer may disseminate information under section 551 on a new use only if the information—

(1) is in the form of an unabridged—

(A) reprint or copy of an article, peer-reviewed by experts qualified by scientific training or experience to evaluate the safety or effectiveness of the drug or device involved, which was published in a scientific or medical journal (as defined in section 556(5)), which is about a clinical investigation with respect to the drug or device, and which would be considered to be scientifically sound by such experts; or

(B) reference publication, described in subsection (b), that includes information about a clinical investigation with respect to the drug or device that would be considered to be scientifically sound by experts qualified by scientific training or experience to evaluate the safety or effectiveness of the drug or device that is the subject of such a clinical investigation; and

(2) is not false or misleading and would not pose a significant risk to the public health.

(b) REFERENCE PUBLICATION.—A reference publication referred to in subsection (a)(1)(B) is a publication that—

(1) has not been written, edited, excerpted, or published specifically for, or at the request of, a manufacturer of a drug or device;

(2) has not been edited or significantly influenced by such a manufacturer;

(3) is not solely distributed through such a manufacturer but is generally available in bookstores or other distribution channels where medical textbooks are sold;

(4) does not focus on any particular drug or device of a manufacturer that disseminates information under section 551and does not have a primary focus on new uses of drugs or devices that are marketed or under investigation by a manufacturer supporting the dissemination of information; and

(5) presents materials that are not false or misleading.

SEC. 553. [21 USC §360aaa–2] Establishment of List of Articles and Publications Disseminated and List of Providers That Received Articles and Reference Publications

(a) IN GENERAL.—A manufacturer may disseminate information under section 551 on a new use only if the manufacturer prepares and submits to the Secretary biannually—

(1) a list containing the titles of the articles and reference publications relating to the new use of drugs or devices that were disseminated by the manufacturer to a person described in section 551(a) for the 6-month period preceding the date on which the manufacturer submits the list to the Secretary; and

(2) a list that identifies the categories of providers (as described in section 551(a)) that received the articles and reference publications for the 6-month period described in paragraph (1).

(b) RECORDS.—A manufacturer that disseminates information under section 551 shall keep records that may be used by the manufacturer when, pursuant to section 555, such manufacturer is required to take corrective action and shall be made available to the Secretary, upon request, for purposes of ensuring or taking corrective action pursuant to such section. Such records, at the Secretary's discretion, may identify the recipient of information provided pursuant to section 551 or the categories of such recipients.

Chapter V

SEC. 554. [21 USC §360aaa–3] Requirement Regarding Submission of Supplemental Application for New Use; Exemption From Requirement

(a) IN GENERAL.—A manufacturer may disseminate information under section 551 on a new use only if—

(1)(A) the manufacturer has submitted to the Secretary a supplemental application for such use; or

(B) the manufacturer meets the condition described in subsection (b) or (c) (relating to a certification that the manufacturer will submit such an application); or

(2) there is in effect for the manufacturer an exemption under subsection (d) from the requirement of paragraph (1).

(b) CERTIFICATION ON SUPPLEMENTAL APPLICATION; CONDITION IN CASE OF COMPLETED STUDIES.—For purposes of subsection (a)(1)(B), a manufacturer may disseminate information on a new use if the manufacturer has submitted to the Secretary an application containing a certification that—

(1) the studies needed for the submission of a supplemental application for the new use have been completed; and

(2) the supplemental application will be submitted to the Secretary not later than 6 months after the date of the initial dissemination of information under section 551.

(c) CERTIFICATION ON SUPPLEMENTAL APPLICATION; CONDITION IN CASE OF PLANNED STUDIES.—

(1) IN GENERAL.—For purposes of subsection (a)(1)(B), a manufacturer may disseminate information on a new use if—

(A) the manufacturer has submitted to the Secretary an application containing—

(i) a proposed protocol and schedule for conducting the studies needed for the submission of a supplemental application for the new use; and

(ii) a certification that the supplemental application will be submitted to the Secretary not later than 36 months after the date of the initial dissemination of information under section 551 (or, as applicable, not later than such date as the Secretary may specify pursuant to an extension under paragraph (3)); and

(B) the Secretary has determined that the proposed protocol is adequate and that the schedule for completing such studies is reasonable.

(2) PROGRESS REPORTS ON STUDIES.—A manufacturer that submits to the Secretary an application under paragraph (1) shall submit to the Secretary periodic reports describing the status of the studies involved.

(3) EXTENSION OF TIME REGARDING PLANNED STUDIES.—The period of 36 months authorized in paragraph (1)(A)(ii) for the completion of studies may be extended by the Secretary if—

(A) the Secretary determines that the studies needed to submit such an application cannot be completed and submitted within 36 months; or

(B) the manufacturer involved submits to the Secretary a written request for the extension and the Secretary determines that the manufacturer has acted with due diligence to conduct the studies in a timely manner, except that an extension under this subparagraph may not be provided for more than 24 additional months.

(d) EXEMPTION FROM REQUIREMENT OF SUPPLEMENTAL APPLICATION.—

(1) IN GENERAL.—For purposes of subsection (a)(2), a manufacturer may disseminate information on a new use if—

(A) the manufacturer has submitted to the Secretary an application for an exemption from meeting the requirement of subsection (a)(1); and

(B)(i) the Secretary has approved the application in accordance with paragraph (2); or

(ii) the application is deemed under paragraph (3)(A) to have been approved (unless such approval is terminated pursuant to paragraph (3)(B)).

(2) CONDITIONS FOR APPROVAL.—The Secretary may approve an application under paragraph (1) for an exemption if the Secretary makes a determination described in subparagraph (A) or (B), as follows:

(A) The Secretary makes a determination that, for reasons defined by the Secretary, it would be economically prohibitive with respect to such drug or device for the manufacturer to incur the costs necessary for the submission of a supplemental application. In making such determination, the Secretary shall consider (in addition to any other considerations the Secretary finds appropriate)—

(i) the lack of the availability under law of any period during which the manufacturer would have exclusive marketing rights with respect to the new use involved; and

(ii) the size of the population expected to benefit from approval of the supplemental application.

(B) The Secretary makes a determination that, for reasons defined by the Secretary, it would be unethical to conduct the studies necessary for the supplemental application. In making such determination, the Secretary shall consider (in addition to any other considerations the Secretary finds appropriate) whether the new use involved is the standard of medical care for a health condition.

(3) TIME FOR CONSIDERATION OF APPLICATION; DEEMED APPROVAL.—

(A) IN GENERAL.—The Secretary shall approve or deny an application under paragraph (1) for an exemption not later than 60 days after the receipt of the application. If the Secretary does not comply with the preceding sentence, the application is deemed to be approved.

(B) TERMINATION OF DEEMED APPROVAL.—If pursuant to a deemed approval under subparagraph (A) a manufacturer disseminates written information under section 551 on a new use, the Secretary may at any time terminate such approval and under section 555(b)(3) order the manufacturer to cease disseminating the information.

(e) REQUIREMENTS REGARDING APPLICATIONS.—Applications under this section shall be submitted in the form and manner prescribed by the Secretary.

SEC. 555. [21 USC §360aaa–4] Corrective Actions; Cessation of Dissemination

(a) POSTDISSEMINATION DATA REGARDING SAFETY AND EFFECTIVENESS.—

(1) CORRECTIVE ACTIONS.—With respect to data received by the Secretary after the dissemination of information under section 551 by a manufacturer has begun (whether received pursuant to paragraph (2) or otherwise), if the Secretary determines that the data indicate that the new use involved may not be effective or may present a significant risk to public health, the Secretary shall, after consultation with the manufacturer, take such action regarding the dissemination of the information as the Secretary determines to be appropriate for the protection of the public health, which may include ordering that the manufacturer cease the dissemination of the information.

(2) RESPONSIBILITIES OF MANUFACTURERS TO SUBMIT DATA.—After a manufacturer disseminates information under section 551, the manufacturer shall submit to the Secretary a notification of any additional knowledge of the manufacturer on clinical research or other data that relate to the safety or effectiveness of the new use involved. If the manufacturer is in possession of the data, the notification shall include the data. The Secretary shall by regulation establish the scope of the responsibilities of manufacturers under this paragraph, including such limits on the responsibilities as the Secretary determines to be appropriate.

(b) CESSATION OF DISSEMINATION.—

(1) FAILURE OF MANUFACTURER TO COMPLY WITH REQUIREMENTS.— The Secretary may order a manufacturer to cease the dissemination of information pursuant to section 551 if the Secretary

determines that the information being disseminated does not comply with the requirements established in this subchapter. Such an order may be issued only after the Secretary has provided notice to the manufacturer of the intent of the Secretary to issue the order and (unless paragraph (2)(B) applies) has provided an opportunity for a meeting with respect to such intent. If the failure of the manufacturer constitutes a minor violation of this subchapter, the Secretary shall delay issuing the order and provide to the manufacturer an opportunity to correct the violation.

(2) SUPPLEMENTAL APPLICATIONS.—The Secretary may order a manufacturer to cease the dissemination of information pursuant to section 551 if—

(A) in the case of a manufacturer that has submitted a supplemental application for a new use pursuant to section 554(a)(1), the Secretary determines that the supplemental application does not contain adequate information for approval of the new use for which the application was submitted;

(B) in the case of a manufacturer that has submitted a certification under section 554(b), the manufacturer has not, within the 6-month period involved, submitted the supplemental application referred to in the certification; or

(C) in the case of a manufacturer that has submitted a certification under section 554(c) but has not yet submitted the supplemental application referred to in the certification, the Secretary determines, after an informal hearing, that the manufacturer is not acting with due diligence to complete the studies involved.

(3) TERMINATION OF DEEMED APPROVAL OF EXEMPTION REGARDING SUPPLEMENTAL APPLICATIONS.—If under section 554(d)(3) the Secretary terminates a deemed approval of an exemption, the Secretary may order the manufacturer involved to cease disseminating the information. A manufacturer shall comply with an order under the preceding sentence not later than 60 days after the receipt of the order.

(c) CORRECTIVE ACTIONS BY MANUFACTURERS.—

(1) IN GENERAL.—In any case in which under this section the Secretary orders a manufacturer to cease disseminating information, the Secretary may order the manufacturer to take action to correct the information that has been disseminated, except as provided in paragraph (2).

(2) TERMINATION OF DEEMED APPROVAL OF EXEMPTION REGARDING SUPPLEMENTAL APPLICATIONS.—In the case of an order under subsection (b)(3) to cease disseminating information, the Secretary may not order the manufacturer involved to take action to correct the information that has been disseminated unless the Secretary determines

that the new use described in the information would pose a significant risk to the public health.

SEC. 556. [21 USC §360aaa–5] Definitions

For purposes of this subchapter:

(1) The term "***health care practitioner***" means a physician, or other individual who is a provider of health care, who is licensed under the law of a State to prescribe drugs or devices.

(2) The terms "***health insurance issuer***" and "group health plan" have the meaning given such terms under section 2791 of the Public Health Service Act.

(3) The term "***manufacturer***" means a person who manufactures a drug or device, or who is licensed by such person to distribute or market the drug or device.

(4) The term "***new use***"—

(A) with respect to a drug, means a use that is not included in the labeling of the approved drug; and

(B) with respect to a device, means a use that is not included in the labeling for the approved or cleared device.

(5) The term "***scientific or medical journal***" means a scientific or medical publication—

(A) that is published by an organization—

(i) that has an editorial board;

(ii) that utilizes experts, who have demonstrated expertise in the subject of an article under review by the organization and who are independent of the organization, to review and objectively select, reject, or provide comments about proposed articles; and

(iii) that has a publicly stated policy, to which the organization adheres, of full disclosure of any conflict of interest or biases for all authors or contributors involved with the journal or organization;

(B) whose articles are peer-reviewed and published in accordance with the regular peer-review procedures of the organization;

(C) that is generally recognized to be of national scope and reputation;

(D) that is indexed in the Index Medicus of the National Library of Medicine of the National Institutes of Health; and

(E) that is not in the form of a special supplement that has been funded in whole or in part by one or more manufacturers.

SEC. 557. [21 USC §360aaa–6] Rules of Construction

(a) UNSOLICITED REQUEST.—Nothing in section 551 shall be construed as prohibiting a manufacturer from disseminating information in response to an unsolicited request from a health care practitioner.

(b) DISSEMINATION OF INFORMATION ON DRUGS OR DEVICES NOT EVIDENCE OF INTENDED USE.—Notwithstanding subsection (a), (f), or (o) of section 502, or any other provision of law, the dissemination of information relating to a new use of a drug or device, in accordance with section 551, shall not be construed by the Secretary as evidence of a new intended use of the drug or device that is different from the intended use of the drug or device set forth in the official labeling of the drug or device. Such dissemination shall not be considered by the Secretary as labeling, adulteration, or misbranding of the drug or device.

(c) PATENT PROTECTION.—Nothing in section 551 shall affect patent rights in any manner.

(d) AUTHORIZATION FOR DISSEMINATION OF ARTICLES AND FEES FOR REPRINTS OF ARTICLES.—Nothing in section 551 shall be construed as prohibiting an entity that publishes a scientific journal (as defined in section 556(5)) from requiring authorization from the entity to disseminate an article published by such entity or charging fees for the purchase of reprints of published articles from such entity.

Subchapter E — General Provisions Relating To Drugs And Devices

SEC. 561. [21 USC §360bbb] Expanded Access to Unapproved Therapies and Diagnostics

Note: revisions were posted to this section in May 2008.

(a) Emergency situations. The Secretary may, under appropriate conditions determined by the Secretary, authorize the shipment of investigational drugs or investigational devices for the diagnosis, monitoring, or treatment of a serious disease or condition in emergency situations.

(b) Individual patient access to investigational products intended for serious diseases. Any person, acting through a physician licensed in accordance with State law, may request from a manufacturer or distributor, and any manufacturer or distributor may, after complying with the provisions of this subsection, provide to such physician an investigational drug or investigational device for the diagnosis, monitoring, or treatment of a serious disease or condition if--

(1) the licensed physician determines that the person has no comparable or satisfactory alternative therapy available to diagnose, monitor, or treat the disease or condition involved, and that the probable risk to the person from the investigational drug or investigational device is not greater than the probable risk from the disease or condition;

(2) the Secretary determines that there is sufficient evidence of safety and effectiveness to support the use of the investigational drug or investigational device in the case described in paragraph (1);

(3) the Secretary determines that provision of the investigational drug or investigational device will not interfere with the initiation, conduct, or completion of clinical investigations to support marketing approval; and

(4) the sponsor, or clinical investigator, of the investigational drug or investigational device submits to the Secretary a clinical protocol consistent with the provisions of section 505(i) or 520(g), including any regulations promulgated under section 505(i) or 520(g), describing the use of the investigational drug or investigational device in a single patient or a small group of patients.

(c) Treatment investigational new drug applications and treatment investigational device exemptions. Upon submission by a sponsor or a physician of a protocol intended to provide widespread access to an investigational drug or investigational device for eligible patients (referred to in this subsection as an "expanded access protocol"), the Secretary shall permit such investigational drug or investigational device to be made available for expanded access under a treatment investigational new drug application or treatment investigational device exemption if the Secretary determines that--

(1) under the treatment investigational new drug application or treatment investigational device exemption, the investigational drug or investigational device is intended for use in the diagnosis, monitoring, or treatment of a serious or immediately life-threatening disease or condition;

(2) there is no comparable or satisfactory alternative therapy available to diagnose, monitor, or treat that stage of disease or condition in the population of patients to which the investigational drug or investigational device is intended to be administered;

(3)(A) the investigational drug or investigational device is under investigation in a controlled clinical trial for the use described in paragraph (1) under an investigational drug application in effect under section 505(i) or investigational device exemption in effect under section 520(g); or

(B) all clinical trials necessary for approval of that use of the investigational drug or investigational device have been completed;

(4) the sponsor of the controlled clinical trials is actively pursuing marketing approval of the investigational drug or investigational device for the use described in paragraph (1) with due diligence;

(5) in the case of an investigational drug or investigational device described in paragraph (3)(A), the provision of the investigational drug or investigational device will not interfere with the enrollment of patients in ongoing clinical investigations under section 505(i) or 520(g);

(6) in the case of serious diseases, there is sufficient evidence of safety and effectiveness to support the use described in paragraph (1); and

(7) in the case of immediately life-threatening diseases, the available scientific evidence, taken as a whole, provides a reasonable basis to conclude that the investigational drug or investigational device may be effective for its intended use and would not expose patients to an unreasonable and significant risk of illness or injury.

A protocol submitted under this subsection shall be subject to the provisions of section 505(i) or 520(g), including regulations promulgated under section 505(i) or 520(g). The Secretary may inform national, State, and local medical associations and societies, voluntary health associations, and other appropriate persons about the availability of an investigational drug or investigational device under expanded access protocols submitted under this subsection. The information provided by the Secretary, in accordance with the preceding sentence, shall be the same type of information that is required by section 402(j)(3) of the Public Health Service Act.

(d) Termination. The Secretary may, at any time, with respect to a sponsor, physician, manufacturer, or distributor described in this section, terminate expanded access provided under this section for an investigational drug or investigational device if the requirements under this section are no longer met.

(e) Definitions. In this section, the terms "***investigational drug***", "***investigational device***", "***treatment investigational new drug application***", and "***treatment investigational device exemption***" shall have the meanings given the terms in regulations prescribed by the Secretary.

SEC. 562. [21 USC §360bbb–1] Dispute Resolution

If, regarding an obligation concerning drugs or devices under this Act or section 351 of the Public Health Service Act, there is a scientific controversy between the Secretary and a person who is a sponsor, applicant, or manufacturer and no specific provision of the Act involved, including a regulation promulgated under such Act, provides a right of review of the matter in controversy, the Secretary shall, by regulation, establish a procedure under which such sponsor, applicant, or manufacturer may request a review of such controversy, including a review by an appropriate scientific advisory panel described in section 505(n) or an advisory committee described in section 515(g)(2)(B). Any such review shall take place in a timely manner. The Secretary shall promulgate such regulations within 1 year after the date of the enactment of the Food and Drug Administration Modernization Act of 1997.

SEC. 563. [21 USC §360bbb–2] Classification of Products

(a) REQUEST. A person who submits an application or submission (including a petition, notification, and any other similar form of request) under this Act for a product, may submit a request to the Secretary respecting the classification of the product as a drug, biological product, device, or a combination product subject to section 503(g) or respecting the component of the Food and Drug Administration that will regulate the product. In submitting the request, the person shall recommend a classification for the product, or a component to regulate the product, as appropriate.

(b) STATEMENT. Not later than 60 days after the receipt of the request described in subsection (a), the Secretary shall determine the classification of the product under subsection (a), or the component of the Food and Drug Administration that will regulate the product, and shall provide to the person a written statement that identifies such classification or such component, and the reasons for such determination. The Secretary may not modify such statement except with the written consent of the person, or for public health reasons based on scientific evidence.

(c) INACTION OF SECRETARY. If the Secretary does not provide the statement within the 60-day period described in subsection (b), the recommendation made by the person under subsection (a) shall be considered to be a final determination by the Secretary of such classification of the product, or the component of the Food and Drug Administration that will regulate the product, as applicable, and may not be modified by the Secretary except with the written consent of the person, or for public health reasons based on scientific evidence.

SEC. 564. [21 USC §360bbb–3] Authorization fo Medical Products for Use in Emergencies

(a) In General. (1) Emergency uses. Notwithstanding sections 505, 510(k), and 515 of this Act and section 351 of the Public Health Service Act, and subject to the provisions of this section, the Secretary may authorize the introduction into interstate commerce, during the effective period of a declaration under subsection (b), of a drug, device, or biological product intended for use in an actual or potential emergency (referred to in this section as an "emergency use").

(2) Approval status of product. An authorization under paragraph (1) may authorize an emergency use of a product that

(A) is not approved, licensed, or cleared for commercial distribution under a provision of law referred to in such paragraph (referred to in this section as an "unapproved product"); or

(B) is approved, licensed, or cleared under such a provision, but which use is not under such provision an approved, licensed, or cleared use of the product (referred to in this section as an "unapproved use of an approved product").

(3) Relation to other uses. An emergency use authorized under paragraph (1) for a product is in addition to any other use that is authorized for the product under a provision of law referred to in such paragraph.

(4) Definitions. For purposes of this section:

(A) The term "***biological product***" has the meaning given such term in section 351 of the Public Health Service Act.

(B) The term "***emergency use***" has the meaning indicated for such term in paragraph (1).

(C) The term "***product***" means a drug, device, or biological product.

(D) The term "***unapproved product***" has the meaning indicated for such term in paragraph (2)(A).

(E) The term "***unapproved use of an approved product***" has the meaning indicated for such term in paragraph (2)(B).

(b) DECLARATION OF EMERGENCY.

(1) IN GENERAL. The Secretary may declare an emergency justifying the authorization under this subsection for a product on the basis of

(A) a determination by the Secretary of Homeland Security that there is a domestic emergency, or a significant potential for a domestic emergency, involving a heightened risk of attack with a specified biological, chemical, radiological, or nuclear agent or agents;

(B) a determination by the Secretary of Defense that there is a military emergency, or a significant potential for a military emergency, involving a heightened risk to United States military forces of attack with a specified biological, chemical, radiological, or nuclear agent or agents; or

(C) a determination by the Secretary of a public health emergency under section 319 of the Public Health Service Act that affects, or has a significant potential to affect, national security, and that involves a specified biological, chemical, radiological, or nuclear agent or agents, or a specified disease or condition that may be attributable to such agent or agents.

(2) Termination of declaration.

(A) In general. A declaration under this subsection shall terminate upon the earlier of

(i) a determination by the Secretary, in consultation with the Secretary of Defense, that the circumstances described in paragraph (1) have ceased to exist; or

(ii) the expiration of the one-year period beginning on the date on which the declaration is made.

(B) Renewal. Notwithstanding subparagraph (A), the Secretary may renew a declaration under this subsection, and this paragraph shall apply to any such renewal.

(C) Disposition of product. If an authorization under this section with respect to an unapproved product ceases to be effective as a result of a termination under subparagraph (A) of this paragraph, the Secretary shall consult with the manufacturer of such product with respect to the appropriate disposition of the product.

(3) Advance notice of termination. The Secretary shall provide advance notice that a declaration under this subsection will be terminated. The period of advance notice shall be a period reasonably determined to provide

(A) in the case of an unapproved product, a sufficient period for disposition of the product, including the return of such product (except such quantities of product as are necessary to provide for continued use consistent with subsection (f)(2)) to the manufacturer (in the case of a manufacturer that chooses to have such product returned); and

(B) in the case of an unapproved use of an approved product, a sufficient period for the disposition of any labeling, or any information under subsection (e)(2)(B)(ii), as the case may be, that was provided with respect to the emergency use involved.

(4) Publication. The Secretary shall promptly publish in the Federal Register each declaration, determination, advance notice of termination, and renewal under this subsection.

(c) Criteria for Issuance of Authorization. The Secretary may issue an authorization under this section with respect to the emergency use of a product only if, after consultation with the Director of the National Institutes of Health and the Director of the Centers for Disease Control and Prevention (to the extent feasible and appropriate given the circumstances of the emergency involved), the Secretary concludes

(1) that an agent specified in a declaration under subsection (b) can cause a serious or life-threatening disease or condition;

(2) that, based on the totality of scientific evidence available to the Secretary, including data from adequate and well-controlled clinical trials, if available, it is reasonable to believe that

(A) the product may be effective in diagnosing, treating, or preventing

(i) such disease or condition; or

(ii) a serious or life-threatening disease or condition caused by a product authorized under this section, approved or cleared under this Act, or licensed under section 351 of the Public Health Service Act, for diagnosing, treating, or preventing such a disease or condition caused by such an agent; and

(B) the known and potential benefits of the product, when used to diagnose, prevent, or treat such disease or condition, outweigh the known and potential risks of the product;

(3) that there is no adequate, approved, and available alternative to the product for diagnosing, preventing, or treating such disease or condition; and

(4) that such other criteria as the Secretary may by regulation prescribe are satisfied.

(d) Scope of Authorization. An authorization of a product under this section shall state (1) each disease or condition that the product may be used to diagnose, prevent, or treat within the scope of the authorization;

(2) the Secretary's conclusions, made under subsection (c)(2)(B), that the known and potential benefits of the product, when used to diagnose, prevent, or treat such disease or condition, outweigh the known and potential risks of the product; and

(3) the Secretary's conclusions, made under subsection (c), concerning the safety and potential effectiveness of the product in diagnosing, preventing, or treating such diseases or conditions, including an assessment of the available scientific evidence.

(e) Conditions of Authorization.

(1) Unapproved product.

(A) Required conditions. With respect to the emergency use of an unapproved product, the Secretary, to the extent practicable given the circumstances of the emergency, shall, for a person who carries out any activity for which the authorization is issued, establish such conditions on an authorization under this section as the Secretary finds necessary or appropriate to protect the public health, including the following:

(i) Appropriate conditions designed to ensure that health care professionals administering the product are informed

(I) that the Secretary has authorized the emergency use of the product;

(II) of the significant known and potential benefits and risks of the emergency use of the product, and of the extent to which such benefits and risks are unknown; and

(III) of the alternatives to the product that are available, and of their benefits and risks.

(ii) Appropriate conditions designed to ensure that individuals to whom the product is administered are informed

(I) that the Secretary has authorized the emergency use of the product;

(II) of the significant known and potential benefits and risks of such use, and of the extent to which such benefits and risks are unknown; and

(III) of the option to accept or refuse administration of the product, of the consequences, if any, of refusing administration of the product, and of the alternatives to the product that are available and of their benefits and risks.

(iii) Appropriate conditions for the monitoring and reporting of adverse events associated with the emergency use of the product.

(iv) For manufacturers of the product, appropriate conditions concerning recordkeeping and reporting, including records access by the Secretary, with respect to the emergency use of the product.

(B) Authority for additional conditions. With respect to the emergency use of an unapproved product, the Secretary may, for a person who carries out any activity for which the authorization is issued, establish such conditions on an authorization under this section as the Secretary finds necessary or appropriate to protect the public health, including the following:

(i) Appropriate conditions on which entities may distribute the product with respect to the emergency use of the product (including limitation to distribution by government entities), and on how distribution is to be performed.

(ii) Appropriate conditions on who may administer the product with respect to the emergency use of the product, and on the categories of individuals to whom, and the circumstances under which, the product may be administered with respect to such use.

(iii) Appropriate conditions with respect to the collection and analysis of information, during the period when the authorization is in effect, concerning the safety and effectiveness of the product with respect to the emergency use of such product.

(iv) For persons other than manufacturers of the product, appropriate conditions concerning recordkeeping and reporting, including records access by the Secretary, with respect to the emergency use of the product.

(2) Unapproved use. With respect to the emergency use of a product that is an unapproved use of an approved product:

(A) For a manufacturer of the product who carries out any activity for which the authorization is issued, the Secretary shall, to the extent practicable given the circumstances of the emergency, establish conditions described in clauses (i) and (ii) of paragraph (1)(A), and may establish conditions described in clauses (iii) and (iv) of such paragraph.

(B)(i) If the authorization under this section regarding the emergency use authorizes a change in the labeling of the product, but the manufacturer of the product chooses not to make such change, such authorization may not authorize distributors of the product or any other person to alter or obscure the labeling provided by the manufacturer.

(ii) In the circumstances described in clause (i), for a person who does not manufacture the product and who chooses to act under this clause, an authorization under this section regarding the emergency use shall, to the extent practicable given the circumstances of the emergency, authorize such person to provide appropriate information with respect to such product in addition to the labeling provided by the manufacturer, subject to compliance with clause (i). While the authorization under this section is effective, such additional information shall not be considered labeling for purposes of section 502.

(C) The Secretary may establish with respect to the distribution and administration of the product for the unapproved use conditions no more restrictive than those established by the Secretary with respect to the distribution and administration of the product for the approved use.

(3) Good manufacturing practice. With respect to the emergency use of a product for which an authorization under this section is issued (whether an unapproved product or an unapproved use of an approved product), the Secretary may waive or limit, to the extent appropriate given the circumstances of the emergency, requirements regarding current good manufacturing practice otherwise applicable to the manufacture, processing, packing, or holding of products subject to regulation under this Act, including such requirements established under section 501.

(4) Advertising. The Secretary may establish conditions on advertisements and other promotional descriptive printed matter that relate to the emergency use of a product for which an authorization under this section is issued (whether an unapproved product or an unapproved use of an approved product), including, as appropriate

(A) with respect to drugs and biological products, requirements applicable to prescription drugs pursuant to section 502(n); or

(B) with respect to devices, requirements applicable to restricted devices pursuant to section 502(r).

(f) Duration of Authorization.

(1) In general. Except as provided in paragraph (2), an authorization under this section shall be effective until the earlier of the termination of the declaration under subsection (b) or a revocation under subsection (g).

(2) Continued use after end of effective period. Notwithstanding the termination of the declaration under subsection (b) or a revocation under subsection (g), an authorization shall continue to be effective to provide for continued use of an unapproved product with respect to a patient to whom it was administered during the period described by paragraph (1), to the extent found necessary by such patient's attending physician.

(g) Revocation of Authorization.

(1) Review. The Secretary shall periodically review the circumstances and the appropriateness of an authorization under this section.

(2) Revocation. The Secretary may revoke an authorization under this section if the criteria under subsection (c) for issuance of such authorization are no longer met or other circumstances make such revocation appropriate to protect the public health or safety.

(h) Publication; Confidential Information.

(1) Publication. The Secretary shall promptly publish in the Federal Register a notice of each authorization, and each termination or revocation of an authorization under this section, and an explanation of the reasons therefore (which may include a summary of data or information that has been submitted to the Secretary in an application under section 505(i) or section 520(g), even if such summary may indirectly reveal the existence of such application).

(2) Confidential information. Nothing in this section alters or amends section 1905 of title 18, United States Code, or section 552(b)(4) of title 5 of such Code.

(i) Actions Committed to Agency Discretion. Actions under the authority of this section by the Secretary or by the Secretary of Defense are committed to agency discretion.

(j) Rules of Construction. The following applies with respect to this section:

(1) Nothing in this section impairs the authority of the President as Commander in Chief of the Armed Forces of the United States under article II, section 2 of the United States Constitution.

(2) Nothing in this section impairs the authority of the Secretary of Defense with respect to the Department of Defense, including the armed forces, under other provisions of Federal law.

(3) Nothing in this section (including any exercise of authority by a manufacturer under subsection (e)(2)) impairs the authority of the United States to use or manage quantities of a product that are owned or controlled by the United States (including quantities in the stockpile maintained under section 319F-2 of the Public Health Service Act).

(k) Relation to Other Provisions. If a product is the subject of an authorization under this section, the use of such product within the scope of the authorization shall not be considered to constitute a clinical investigation for purposes of section 505(i), section 520(g), or any other provision of this Act or section 351 of the Public Health Service Act.

(l) Option to Carry Out Authorized Activities. Nothing in this section provides the Secretary any authority to require any person to carry out any activity that becomes lawful pursuant to an authorization under this section, and no person is required to inform the Secretary that the person will not be carrying out such activity, except that a manufacturer of a sole-source unapproved product authorized for emergency use shall report to the Secretary within a reasonable period of time after the issuance by the Secretary of such authorization if such manufacturer does not intend to carry out any activity under the authorization. This section only has legal effect on a person who carries out an activity for which an authorization under this section is issued. This section does not modify or affect activities carried out pursuant to other provisions of this Act or section 351 of the Public Health Service Act. Nothing in this subsection may be construed as restricting the Secretary from imposing conditions on persons who carry out any activity pursuant to an authorization under this section.

SEC. 565. [21 USC §360bbb–4] Technical Assistance

Note: revisions were posted to this section in September 2007.

The Secretary, in consultation with the Commissioner of Food and Drugs, shall establish within the Food and Drug Administration a team of experts on manufacturing and regulatory activities (including compliance with current Good Manufacturing Practice) to provide both off-site and on-site technical assistance to the manufacturers of qualified countermeasures (as defined in section 319F-1 of the Public Health Service Act [42 USC § 247d-6a]), security countermeasures (as defined in section 319F-2 of such Act [42 USC § 247d-6b]), or vaccines, at the request of such a manufacturer and at the discretion of the Secretary, if the Secretary determines that a shortage or potential shortage may occur in the United States in the supply of such vaccines or countermeasures and that the provision of such assistance would be beneficial in helping alleviate or avert such shortage.

SEC. 566. [21 USC §360bbb–5] Critical Path Public-Private Partnerships

Note: This section was added in February 2008.

(a) Establishment. The Secretary, acting through the Commissioner of Food and Drugs, may enter into collaborative agreements, to be known as Critical Path Public-Private Partnerships, with one or more eligible entities to implement the Critical Path Initiative of the Food and Drug Administration by developing innovative, collaborative projects in research, education, and outreach for the purpose of fostering medical product innovation, enabling the acceleration of medical product development, manufacturing, and translational therapeutics, and enhancing medical product safety.

(b) Eligible entity. In this section, the term "eligible entity" means an entity that meets each of the following:

(1) The entity is--

(A) an institution of higher education (as such term is defined in section 101 of the Higher Education Act of 1965 [20 USC § 1001]) or a consortium of such institutions; or

(B) an organization described in section 501(c)(3) of the Internal Revenue Code of 1986 [26 USC § 501(c)(3)] and exempt from tax under section 501(a) of such Code [26 USC § 501(a)].

(2) The entity has experienced personnel and clinical and other technical expertise in the biomedical sciences, which may include graduate training programs in areas relevant to priorities of the Critical Path Initiative.

(3) The entity demonstrates to the Secretary's satisfaction that the entity is capable of--

(A) developing and critically evaluating tools, methods, and processes--

(i) to increase efficiency, predictability, and productivity of medical product development; and

(ii) to more accurately identify the benefits and risks of new and existing medical products;

(B) establishing partnerships, consortia, and collaborations with health care practitioners and other providers of health care goods or services; pharmacists; pharmacy benefit managers and purchasers; health maintenance organizations and other managed health care organizations; health care insurers; government agencies; patients and consumers; manufacturers of prescription drugs, biological products, diagnostic technologies, and devices; and academic scientists; and

(C) securing funding for the projects of a Critical Path Public-Private Partnership from Federal and nonfederal governmental sources, foundations, and private individuals.

(c) Funding. The Secretary may not enter into a collaborative agreement under subsection (a) unless the eligible entity involved provides an assurance that the entity will not accept funding for a Critical Path Public-Private Partnership project from any organization that manufactures or distributes products regulated by the Food and Drug Administration unless the entity provides assurances in its agreement with the Food and Drug Administration that the results of the Critical Path Public-Private Partnership project will not be influenced by any source of funding.

(d) Annual report. Not later than 18 months after the date of the enactment of this section [enacted Sept. 27, 2007], and annually thereafter, the Secretary, in collaboration with the parties to each Critical Path Public-Private Partnership, shall submit a report to the Committee on Health, Education, Labor, and Pensions of the Senate and the Committee on Energy and Commerce of the House of Representatives--

(1) reviewing the operations and activities of the Partnerships in the previous year; and

(2) addressing such other issues relating to this section as the Secretary determines to be appropriate.

(e) Definition. In this section, the term "medical product" includes a drug, a biological product as defined in section 351 of the Public Health Service Act [42 USC § 262], a device, and any combination of such products.

(f) Authorization of appropriations. To carry out this section, there are authorized to be appropriated $ 5,000,000 for fiscal year 2008 and such sums as may be necessary for each of fiscal years 2009 through 2012.

SEC. 567. [21 USC §360bbb–6] Risk communication

Note: This section was added in February 2008.

(a) Advisory Committee on Risk Communication.

(1) In general. The Secretary shall establish an advisory committee to be known as the "Advisory Committee on Risk Communication" (referred to in this section as the "Committee").

(2) Duties of Committee. The Committee shall advise the Commissioner on methods to effectively communicate risks associated with the products regulated by the Food and Drug Administration.

(3) Members. The Secretary shall ensure that the Committee is composed of experts on risk communication, experts on the risks described in subsection (b), and representatives of patient, consumer, and health professional organizations.

(4) Permanence of Committee. Section 14 of the Federal Advisory Committee Act [5 USC Appx] shall not apply to the Committee established under this subsection.

(b) Partnerships for risk communication.

(1) In general. The Secretary shall partner with professional medical societies, medical schools, academic medical centers, and other stakeholders to develop robust and multi-faceted systems for communication to health care providers about emerging postmarket drug risks.

(2) Partnerships. The systems developed under paragraph (1) shall--

(A) account for the diversity among physicians in terms of practice, willingness to adopt technology, and medical specialty; and

(B) include the use of existing communication channels, including electronic communications, in place at the Food and Drug Administration.

Subchapter F — New Animal Drugs for Minor Use and Minor Species

SEC. 571. [21 USC §360ccc] Conditional Approval of New Animal Drugs for Minor Use and Minor Species

(a)(1) [52] Except as provided in paragraph (3) of this section, any person may file with the Secretary an application for conditional approval of a new animal drug intended for a minor use or a minor species. Such an application may not be a supplement to an application approved under section 512. Such application must

[52] This subchapter, consisting of sections 571 through 573, was added by section 102(b)(4) of Public Law 108–282. Section 102(b)(6) of the Public Law concerns regulations to implement sections 571 through 573 and is included in the appendix to this compiliation under the heading "Section 102(b)(6) of Minor Use and Minor Species Animal Health Act of 2004".

comply in all respects with the provisions of section 512 of this Act except sections 512(a)(4), 512(b)(2), 512(c)(1), 512(c)(2), 512(c)(3), 512(d)(1), 512(e), 512(h), and 512(n) unless otherwise stated in this section, and any additional provisions of this section. New animal drugs are subject to application of the same safety standards that would be applied to such drugs under section 512(d) (including, for antimicrobial new animal drugs, with respect to antimicrobial resistance).

(2) The applicant shall submit to the Secretary as part of an application for the conditional approval of a new animal drug—

(A) all information necessary to meet the requirements of section 512(b)(1) except section 512(b)(1)(A);

(B) full reports of investigations which have been made to show whether or not such drug is safe under section 512(d) (including, for an antimicrobial new animal drug, with respect to antimicrobial resistance) and there is a reasonable expectation of effectiveness for use;

(C) data for establishing a conditional dose;

(D) projections of expected need and the justification for that expectation based on the best information available;

(E) information regarding the quantity of drug expected to be distributed on an annual basis to meet the expected need; and

(F) a commitment that the applicant will conduct additional investigations to meet the requirements for the full demonstration of effectiveness under section 512(d)(1)(E) within 5 years.

(3) A person may not file an application under paragraph (1) if—

(A) the application seeks conditional approval of a new animal drug that is contained in, or is a product of, a transgenic animal.

(B) the person has previously filed an application for conditional approval under paragraph (1) for the same drug in the same dosage form for the same intended use whether or not subsequently conditionally approved by the Secretary under subsection (b), or

(C) the person obtained the application, or data or other information contained therein, directly or indirectly from the person who filed for conditional approval under paragraph (1) for the same drug in the same dosage form for the same intended use whether or not subsequently conditionally approved by the Secretary under subsection (b).

(b) Within 180 days after the filing of an application pursuant to subsection (a), or such additional period as may be agreed upon by the Secretary and the applicant, the Secretary shall either—

(1) issue an order, effective for one year, conditionally approving the application if the Secretary finds that none of the grounds for denying conditional approval, specified in subsection (c) of this section applies and publish a Federal Register notice of the conditional approval, or

(2) give the applicant notice of an opportunity for an informal hearing on the question whether such application can be conditionally approved.

(c) If the Secretary finds, after giving the applicant notice and an opportunity for an informal hearing, that—

(1) any of the provisions of section 512(d)(1) (A) through (D) or (F) through (I) are applicable;

(2) the information submitted to the Secretary as part of the application and any other information before the Secretary with respect to such drug, is insufficient to show that there is a reasonable expectation that the drug will have the effect it purports or is represented to have under the conditions of use prescribed, recommended, or suggested in the proposed labeling thereof; or

(3) another person has received approval under section 512 for the same drug in the same dosage form for the same intended use, and that person is able to assure the availability of sufficient quantities of the drug to meet the needs for which the drug is intended;

the Secretary shall issue an order refusing to conditionally approve the application. If, after such notice and opportunity for an informal hearing, the Secretary finds that paragraphs (1) through (3) do not apply, the Secretary shall issue an order conditionally approving the application effective for one year and publish a Federal Register notice of the conditional approval. Any order issued under this subsection refusing to conditionally approve an application shall state the findings upon which it is based.

(d) A conditional approval under this section is effective for a 1-year period and is thereafter renewable by the Secretary annually for up to 4 additional 1-year terms. A conditional approval shall be in effect for no more than 5 years from the date of approval under subsection (b)(1) or (c) of this section unless extended as provided for in subsection (h) of this section. The following shall also apply:

(1) No later than 90 days from the end of the 1-year period for which the original or renewed conditional approval is effective, the applicant may submit a request to renew a conditional approval for an additional 1-year term.

(2) A conditional approval shall be deemed renewed at the end of the 1-year period, or at the end of a 90-day extension that the Secretary may, at the Secretary's discretion, grant by letter in order to complete review of the

renewal request, unless the Secretary determines before the expiration of the 1-year period or the 90-day extension that—

(A) the applicant failed to submit a timely renewal request;

(B) the request fails to contain sufficient information to show that—

(i) the applicant is making sufficient progress toward meeting approval requirements under section 512(d)(1)(E), and is likely to be able to fulfill those requirements and obtain an approval under section 512 before the expiration of the 5-year maximum term of the conditional approval;

(ii) the quantity of the drug that has been distributed is consistent with the conditionally approved intended use and conditions of use, unless there is adequate explanation that ensures that the drug is only used for its intended purpose; or

(iii) the same drug in the same dosage form for the same intended use has not received approval under section 512, or if such a drug has been approved, that the holder of the approved application is unable to assure the availability of sufficient quantities of the drug to meet the needs for which the drug is intended; or

(C) any of the provisions of section 512(e)(1) (A) through (B) or (D) through (F) are applicable.

(3) If the Secretary determines before the end of the 1-year period or the 90-day extension, if granted, that a conditional approval should not be renewed, the Secretary shall issue an order refusing to renew the conditional approval, and such conditional approval shall be deemed withdrawn and no longer in effect. The Secretary shall thereafter provide an opportunity for an informal hearing to the applicant on the issue whether the conditional approval shall be reinstated.

(e)(1) The Secretary shall issue an order withdrawing conditional approval of an application filed pursuant to subsection (a) if the Secretary finds that another person has received approval under section 512 for the same drug in the same dosage form for the same intended use and that person is able to assure the availability of sufficient quantities of the drug to meet the needs for which the drug is intended.

(2) The Secretary shall, after due notice and opportunity for an informal hearing to the applicant, issue an order withdrawing conditional approval of an application filed pursuant to subsection (a) if the Secretary finds that—

(A) any of the provisions of section 512(e)(1) (A) through (B) or (D) through (F) are applicable; or

(B) on the basis of new information before the Secretary with respect to such drug, evaluated together with the evidence available to the Secretary when the application was conditionally approved, that there is not a reasonable expectation that such drug will have the effect it purports or is represented to have under the conditions of use prescribed, recommended, or suggested in the labeling thereof.

(3) The Secretary may also, after due notice and opportunity for an informal hearing to the applicant, issue an order withdrawing conditional approval of an application filed pursuant to subsection (a) if the Secretary finds that any of the provisions of section 512(e)(2) are applicable.

(f)(1) The label and labeling of a new animal drug with a conditional approval under this section shall—

(A) bear the statement, "conditionally approved by FDA pending a full demonstration of effectiveness under application number"; and

(B) contain such other information as prescribed by the Secretary.

(2) An intended use that is the subject of a conditional approval under this section shall not be included in the same product label with any intended use approved under section 512.

(g) A conditionally approved new animal drug application may not be amended or supplemented to add indications for use.

(h) 180 days prior to the termination date established under subsection (d) of this section, an applicant shall have submitted all the information necessary to support a complete new animal drug application in accordance with section 512(b)(1) or the conditional approval issued under this section is no longer in effect. Following review of this information, the Secretary shall either—

(1) issue an order approving the application under section 512(c) if the Secretary finds that none of the grounds for denying approval specified in section 512(d)(1) applies, or

(2) give the applicant an opportunity for a hearing before the Secretary under section 512(d) on the question whether such application can be approved.

Upon issuance of an order approving the application, product labeling and administrative records of approval shall be modified accordingly. If the Secretary has not issued an order under section 512(c) approving such application prior to the termination date established under subsection (d) of this section, the conditional approval issued under this section is no longer in effect unless the Secretary grants an extension of an additional 180-day period so that the Secretary can complete review of the application. The decision to grant an extension is committed to the discretion of the Secretary and not subject to judicial review.

(i) The decision of the Secretary under subsection (c), (d), or (e) of this section refusing or withdrawing conditional approval of an application shall constitute final agency action subject to judicial review.

(j) In this section and section 572, the term "transgenic animal" means an animal whose genome contains a nucleotide sequence that has been intentionally modified in vitro, and the progeny of such an animal; Provided that the term "transgenic animal" does not include an animal of which the nucleotide sequence of the genome has been modified solely by selective breeding.

SEC. 572. [21 USC §360ccc–1] Index of Legally Marketed Unapproved New Animal Drugs for Minor Species

(a)(1) [53] The Secretary shall establish an index limited to—

(A) new animal drugs intended for use in a minor species for which there is a reasonable certainty that the animal or edible products from the animal will not be consumed by humans or food-producing animals; and

(B) new animal drugs intended for use only in a hatchery, tank, pond, or other similar contained man-made structure in an early, non-food life stage of a food-producing minor species, where safety for humans is demonstrated in accordance with the standard of section 512(d) (including, for an antimicrobial new animal drug, with respect to antimicrobial resistance).

(2) The index shall not include a new animal drug that is contained in or a product of a transgenic animal.

(b) Any person intending to file a request under this section shall be entitled to one or more conferences to discuss the requirements for indexing a new animal drug.

(c)(1) Any person may submit a request to the Secretary for a determination whether a new animal drug may be eligible for inclusion in the index. Such a request shall include—

(A) information regarding the need for the new animal drug, the species for which the new animal drug is intended, the proposed intended use and conditions of use, and anticipated annual distribution;

(B) information to support the conclusion that the proposed use meets the conditions of subparagraph (A) or (B) of subsection (a)(1) of this section;

(C) information regarding the components and composition of the new animal drug;

Chapter V

[53] See footnote for section 571.

(D) a description of the methods used in, and the facilities and controls used for, the manufacture, processing, and packing of such new animal drug;

(E) an environmental assessment that meets the requirements of the National Environmental Policy Act of 1969, as amended, and as defined in 21 CFR Part 25, as it appears on the date of enactment of this provision [54] and amended thereafter or information to support a categorical exclusion from the requirement to prepare an environmental assessment;

(F) information sufficient to support the conclusion that the proposed use of the new animal drug is safe under section 512(d) with respect to individuals exposed to the new animal drug through its manufacture or use; and

(G) such other information as the Secretary may deem necessary to make this eligibility determination.

(2) Within 90 days after the submission of a request for a determination of eligibility for indexing based on subsection (a)(1)(A) of this section, or 180 days for a request submitted based on subsection (a)(1)(B) of this section, the Secretary shall grant or deny the request, and notify the person who requested such determination of the Secretary's decision. The Secretary shall grant the request if the Secretary finds that—

(A) the same drug in the same dosage form for the same intended use is not approved or conditionally approved;

(B) the proposed use of the drug meets the conditions of subparagraph (A) or (B) of subsection (a)(1), as appropriate;

(C) the person requesting the determination has established appropriate specifications for the manufacture and control of the new animal drug and has demonstrated an understanding of the requirements of current good manufacturing practices;

(D) the new animal drug will not significantly affect the human environment; and

(E) the new animal drug is safe with respect to individuals exposed to the new animal drug through its manufacture or use.

If the Secretary denies the request, the Secretary shall thereafter provide due notice and an opportunity for an informal conference. A decision of the Secretary to deny an eligibility request following an informal conference shall constitute final agency action subject to judicial review.

[54] Provision was added by section 102(b)(4) of Public Law 108–282, which was enacted August 2, 2004.

(d)(1) With respect to a new animal drug for which the Secretary has made a determination of eligibility under subsection (c), the person who made such a request may ask that the Secretary add the new animal drug to the index established under subsection (a). The request for addition to the index shall include—

(A) a copy of the Secretary's determination of eligibility issued under subsection (c);

(B) a written report that meets the requirements in subsection (d)(2) of this section;

(C) a proposed index entry;

(D) facsimile labeling;

(E) anticipated annual distribution of the new animal drug;

(F) a written commitment to manufacture the new animal drug and animal feeds bearing or containing such new animal drug according to current good manufacturing practices;

(G) a written commitment to label, distribute, and promote the new animal drug only in accordance with the index entry;

(H) upon specific request of the Secretary, information submitted to the expert panel described in paragraph (3); and

(I) any additional requirements that the Secretary may prescribe by general regulation or specific order.

(2) The report required in paragraph (1) shall—

(A) be authored by a qualified expert panel;

(B) include an evaluation of all available target animal safety and effectiveness information, including anecdotal information;

(C) state the expert panel's opinion regarding whether the benefits of using the new animal drug for the proposed use in a minor species outweigh its risks to the target animal, taking into account the harm being caused by the absence of an approved or conditionally approved new animal drug for the minor species in question;

(D) include information from which labeling can be written; and

(E) include a recommendation regarding whether the new animal drug should be limited to use under the professional supervision of a licensed veterinarian.

(3) A qualified expert panel, as used in this section, is a panel that—

(A) is composed of experts qualified by scientific training and experience to evaluate the target animal safety and effectiveness of the new animal drug under consideration;

(B) operates external to FDA [55]; and

(C) is not subject to the Federal Advisory Committee Act, 5 U.S.C. App. 2.

The Secretary shall define the criteria for selection of a qualified expert panel and the procedures for the operation of the panel by regulation.

(4) Within 180 days after the receipt of a request for listing a new animal drug in the index, the Secretary shall grant or deny the request. The Secretary shall grant the request if the request for indexing continues to meet the eligibility criteria in subsection (a) and the Secretary finds, on the basis of the report of the qualified expert panel and other information available to the Secretary, that the benefits of using the new animal drug for the proposed use in a minor species outweigh its risks to the target animal, taking into account the harm caused by the absence of an approved or conditionally-approved new animal drug for the minor species in question. If the Secretary denies the request, the Secretary shall thereafter provide due notice and the opportunity for an informal conference. The decision of the Secretary following an informal conference shall constitute final agency action subject to judicial review.

(e)(1) The index established under subsection (a) shall include the following information for each listed drug—

(A) the name and address of the person who holds the index listing;

(B) the name of the drug and the intended use and conditions of use for which it is being indexed;

(C) product labeling; and

(D) conditions and any limitations that the Secretary deems necessary regarding use of the drug.

(2) The Secretary shall publish the index, and revise it periodically.

(3) The Secretary may establish by regulation a process for reporting changes in the conditions of manufacturing or labeling of indexed products.

(f)(1) If the Secretary finds, after due notice to the person who requested the index listing and an opportunity for an informal conference, that—

(A) the expert panel failed to meet the requirements as set forth by the Secretary by regulation;

---

[55] So in law. See section 102(b)(4) of Public Law 108-282. Probably should be "the Food and

(B) on the basis of new information before the Secretary, evaluated together with the evidence available to the Secretary when the new animal drug was listed in the index, the benefits of using the new animal drug for the indexed use do not outweigh its risks to the target animal;

(C) the conditions of subsection (c)(2) of this section are no longer satisfied;

(D) the manufacture of the new animal drug is not in accordance with current good manufacturing practices;

(E) the labeling, distribution, or promotion of the new animal drug is not in accordance with the index entry;

(F) the conditions and limitations of use associated with the index listing have not been followed; or

(G) the request for indexing contains any untrue statement of material fact,

the Secretary shall remove the new animal drug from the index. The decision of the Secretary following an informal conference shall constitute final agency action subject to judicial review.

(2) If the Secretary finds that there is a reasonable probability that the use of the drug would present a risk to the health of humans or other animals, the Secretary may—

(A) suspend the listing of such drug immediately;

(B) give the person listed in the index prompt notice of the Secretary's action; and

(C) afford that person the opportunity for an informal conference.

The decision of the Secretary following an informal conference shall constitute final agency action subject to judicial review.

(g) For purposes of indexing new animal drugs under this section, to the extent consistent with the public health, the Secretary shall promulgate regulations for exempting from the operation of section 512 minor species new animal drugs and animal feeds bearing or containing new animal drugs intended solely for investigational use by experts qualified by scientific training and experience to investigate the safety and effectiveness of minor species animal drugs. Such regulations may, at the discretion of the Secretary, among other conditions relating to the protection of the public health, provide for conditioning such exemption upon the establishment and maintenance of such records, and the making of such reports to the Secretary, by the manufacturer or the sponsor of the investigation of such article, of data (including but not limited to analytical reports by investigators) obtained as a result of such investigational use of such article, as the Secretary finds will enable the Secretary to evaluate the safety and effectiveness of such article in the event of the filing of a request for an index listing pursuant to this section.

(h) The labeling of a new animal drug that is the subject of an index listing shall state, prominently and conspicuously—

(1) "NOT APPROVED BY FDA.—Legally marketed as an FDA indexed product. Extra-label use is prohibited.";

(2) except in the case of new animal drugs indexed for use in an early life stage of a food-producing animal, "This product is not to be used in animals intended for use as food for humans or other animals."; and

(3) such other information as may be prescribed by the Secretary in the index listing.

(i)(1) In the case of any new animal drug for which an index listing pursuant to subsection (a) is in effect, the person who has an index listing shall establish and maintain such records, and make such reports to the Secretary, of data relating to experience, and other data or information, received or otherwise obtained by such person with respect to such drug, or with respect to animal feeds bearing or containing such drug, as the Secretary may by general regulation, or by order with respect to such listing, prescribe on the basis of a finding that such records and reports are necessary in order to enable the Secretary to determine, or facilitate a determination, whether there is or may be ground for invoking subsection (f). Such regulation or order shall provide, where the Secretary deems it to be appropriate, for the examination, upon request, by the persons to whom such regulation or order is applicable, of similar information received or otherwise obtained by the Secretary.

(2) Every person required under this subsection to maintain records, and every person in charge or custody thereof, shall, upon request of an officer or employee designated by the Secretary, permit such officer or employee at all reasonable times to have access to and copy and verify such records.

(j)(1) Safety and effectiveness data and information which has been submitted in support of a request for a new animal drug to be indexed under this section and which has not been previously disclosed to the public shall be made available to the public, upon request, unless extraordinary circumstances are shown—

(A) if no work is being or will be undertaken to have the drug indexed in accordance with the request,

(B) if the Secretary has determined that such drug cannot be indexed and all legal appeals have been exhausted,

(C) if the indexing of such drug is terminated and all legal appeals have been exhausted, or

(D) if the Secretary has determined that such drug is not a new animal drug.

(2) Any request for data and information pursuant to paragraph (1) shall include a verified statement by the person making the request that any data or information received under such paragraph shall not be disclosed by such person to any other person—

(A) for the purpose of, or as part of a plan, scheme, or device for, obtaining the right to make, use, or market, or making, using, or marketing, outside the United States, the drug identified in the request for indexing; and

(B) without obtaining from any person to whom the data and information are disclosed an identical verified statement, a copy of which is to be provided by such person to the Secretary, which meets the requirements of this paragraph.

SEC. 573. [21 USC §360ccc–2] Designated New Animal Drugs for Minor Use or Minor Species

(a) [56] DESIGNATION.—

(1) The manufacturer or the sponsor of a new animal drug for a minor use or use in a minor species may request that the Secretary declare that drug a "designated new animal drug". A request for designation of a new animal drug shall be made before the submission of an application under section 512(b) or section 571 for the new animal drug.

(2) The Secretary may declare a new animal drug a "***designated new animal drug***" if—

(A) it is intended for a minor use or use in a minor species; and

(B) the same drug in the same dosage form for the same intended use is not approved under section 512 or 571 or designated under this section at the time the request is made.

(3) Regarding the termination of a designation—

(A) the sponsor of a new animal drug shall notify the Secretary of any decision to discontinue active pursuit of approval under section 512 or 571 of an application for a designated new animal drug. The Secretary shall terminate the designation upon such notification;

(B) the Secretary may also terminate designation if the Secretary independently determines that the sponsor is not actively pursuing approval under section 512 or 571 with due diligence;

Chapter V

[56] See footnote for section 571.

(C) the sponsor of an approved designated new animal drug shall notify the Secretary of any discontinuance of the manufacture of such new animal drug at least one year before discontinuance. The Secretary shall terminate the designation upon such notification; and

(D) the designation shall terminate upon the expiration of any applicable exclusivity period under subsection (c).

(4) Notice respecting the designation or termination of designation of a new animal drug shall be made available to the public.

(b) GRANTS AND CONTRACTS FOR DEVELOPMENT OF DESIGNATED NEW ANIMAL DRUGS.—

(1) The Secretary may make grants to and enter into contracts with public and private entities and individuals to assist in defraying the costs of qualified safety and effectiveness testing expenses and manufacturing expenses incurred in connection with the development of designated new animal drugs.

(2) For purposes of paragraph (1) of this section—

(A) The term '***qualified safety and effectiveness testing***' means testing—

(i) which occurs after the date such new animal drug is designated under this section and before the date on which an application with respect to such drug is submitted under section 512; and

(ii) which is carried out under an investigational exemption under section 512(j).

(B) The term "***manufacturing expenses***" means expenses incurred in developing processes and procedures associated with manufacture of the designated new animal drug which occur after the new animal drug is designated under this section and before the date on which an application with respect to such new animal drug is submitted under section 512 or 571.

(c) EXCLUSIVITY FOR DESIGNATED NEW ANIMAL DRUGS.—

(1) Except as provided in subsection (c)(2), if the Secretary approves or conditionally approves an application for a designated new animal drug, the Secretary may not approve or conditionally approve another application submitted for such new animal drug with the same intended use as the designated new animal drug for another applicant before the expiration of seven years from the date of approval or conditional approval of the application.

(2) If an application filed pursuant to section 512 or section 571 is approved for a designated new animal drug, the Secretary may, during the 7-year exclusivity

period beginning on the date of the application approval or conditional approval, approve or conditionally approve another application under section 512 or section 571 for such drug for such minor use or minor species for another applicant if—

(A) the Secretary finds, after providing the holder of such an approved application notice and opportunity for the submission of views, that in the granted exclusivity period the holder of the approved application cannot assure the availability of sufficient quantities of the drug to meet the needs for which the drug was designated; or

(B) such holder provides written consent to the Secretary for the approval or conditional approval of other applications before the expiration of such exclusivity period.

FD&C Act Chapter VI: Cosmetics

Sections in Chapter VI

- SEC. 601. [21 USC §361] Adulterated Cosmetics
- SEC. 602. [21 USC §362] Misbranded Cosmetics
- SEC. 603. [21 USC §363] Regulations Making Exemptions

SEC. 601. [21 USC §361] Adulterated Cosmetics

A cosmetic shall be deemed to be adulterated— [1]

(a) If it bears or contains any poisonous or deleterious substance which may render it injurious to users under the conditions of use prescribed in the labeling thereof, or, under such conditions of use as are customary or usual, except that this provision shall not apply to coal-tar hair dye, the label of which bears the following legend conspicuously displayed thereon: "Caution—This product contains ingredients which may cause skin irritation on certain individuals and a preliminary test according to accompanying directions should first be made. This product must not be used for dyeing the eyelashes or eyebrows; to do so may cause blindness.", and the labeling of which bears adequate directions for such preliminary testing. For the purposes of this paragraph and paragraph (e) the term "hair dye" shall not include eyelash dyes or eyebrow dyes.

(b) If it consists in whole or in part of any filthy, putrid, or decomposed substance.

(c) If it has been prepared, packed, or held under insanitary conditions whereby it may have become contaminated with filth, or whereby it may have been rendered injurious to health.

(d) If its container is composed, in whole or in part, of any poisonous or deleterious substance which may render the contents injurious to health.

(e) If it is not a hair dye and it is, or it bears or contains, a color additive which is unsafe within the meaning of section 721(a).

---

[1] See footnote for section 403(h)(3) regarding the stylistic use of a list consisting of "(a)", "(b)", etc.

SEC. 602. [21 USC §362] Misbranded Cosmetics

A cosmetic shall be deemed to be misbranded—

(a) If its labeling is false or misleading in any particular.

(b) If in package form unless it bears a label containing (1) the name and place of business of the manufacturer, packer, or distributor; and (2) an accurate statement of the quantity of the contents in terms of weight, measure, or numerical count: Provided, That under clause (2) of this paragraph reasonable variations shall be permitted, and exemptions as to small packages shall be established, by regulations prescribed by the Secretary.

(c) If any word, statement, or other information required by or under authority of this Act to appear on the label or labeling is not prominently placed thereon with such conspicuousness (as compared with other words, statements, designs, or devices in the labeling) and in such terms as to render it likely to be read and understood by the ordinary individual under customary conditions of purchase and use.

(d) If its container is so made, formed, or filled as to be misleading.

(e) If it is a color additive, unless its packaging and labeling are in conformity with such packaging and labeling requirements, applicable to such color additive, as may be contained in regulations issued under section 721. This paragraph shall not apply to packages of color additives which, with respect to their use for cosmetics, are marketed and intended for use only in or on hair dyes (as defined in the last sentence of section 601(a)).

(f) If its packaging or labeling is in violation of an applicable regulation issued pursuant to section 3 or 4 of the Poison Prevention Packaging Act of 1970.

SEC. 603. [21 USC §363] Regulations Making Exemptions

The Secretary shall promulgate regulations exempting from any labeling requirement of this Act cosmetics which are, in accordance with the practice of the trade, to be processed, labeled, or repacked in substantial quantities at establishments other than those where originally processed or packed, on condition that such cosmetics are not adulterated or misbranded under the provisions of this Act upon removal from such processing, labeling, or repacking establishment.

FD&C Act Chapter VII: General Authority

Sections in Chapter VII

Subchapter A — General Administrative Provisions

- SEC. 701. [21 USC §371] Regulations and Hearings
- SEC. 702. [21 USC §372] Examinations and Investigations
- SEC. 703. [21 USC §373] Records of Interstate Shipment
- SEC. 704. [21 USC §374] Factory Inspection
- SEC. 705. [21 USC §375] Publicity
- SEC. 706. [21 USC §376] Seafood Inspection
- SEC. 707. [21 USC §378] Advertising of Certain Foods
- SEC. 708. [21 USC §379] Confidential Information
- SEC. 709. [21 USC §379a] Presumption
- SEC. 710. [21 USC §379b] Consolidated Administrative and Laboratory Facility
- SEC. 711. [21 USC §379d] Automation of Food and Drug Administration
- SEC. 712. [21 USC §379d-1] Conflicts of Interest
- SEC. 713. [21 USC §379d-2] Policy on the Review and Clearance of Scientific Articles Published by FDA Employees

Subchapter B — Colors

- SEC. 721. [21 USC §379e] Listing and Certification of Color Additives for Foods, Drugs, and Cosmetics

Subchapter C — Fees

- SEC. 731. [21 USC 379f] Recovery and Retention of Fees for Freedom of Information Requests
- SEC. 735. [21 USC §379g] Definitions

- SEC. 736. [21 USC §379h] Authority to Assess and Use Drug Fees
- SEC. 736A. [21 USC §379h–1] Fees Relating to Advisory Review of Prescription-Drug Television Advertising
- SEC. 736B. [21 USC §379h–2] Reauthorization; Reporting Requirements
- SEC. 737. [21 USC §379i] Definitions
- SEC. 738. [21 USC §379j] Authority to Assess and Use Device Fees
- SEC. 738A. [21 USC §379j–1] Reauthorization; Reporting Requirements
- SEC. 739. [21 USC §379j–11] Definitions
- SEC. 740. [21 USC §379j–12] Authority to Assess and Use Animal Drug Fees.

Subchapter D — Information and Education

- SEC. 741. [21 USC §379k] Information System
- SEC. 742. [21 USC §379l] Education

Subchapter E — Environmental Impact Review

- SEC. 746. [21 USC §379o] Environmental Impact

Subchapter F — National Uniformity for Nonprescription Drugs and Preemption for Labeling or Packaging of Cosmetics

- SEC. 751. [21 USC §379r] National Uniformity for Nonprescription Drugs
- SEC. 752. [21 USC §379s] Preemption for Labeling or Packaging of Cosmetics

Subchapter G — Safety Reports

- SEC. 756. [21 USC §379v] Safety Report Disclaimers
- SEC. 760. [21 USC §379aa] Serious Adverse Event Reporting for Nonprescription Drugs
- SEC. 761. [21 USC §379aa–1] Serious Adverse Event Reporting for Dietary Supplements

Subchapter I — Reagan-Udall Foundation for the Food and Drug Administration

- SEC. 770. [21 USC §379dd] Establishment and Functions of the Foundation
- SEC. 771. [21 USC §379dd–1] Location of Foundation

- SEC. 772. [21 USC §379dd–2] Activities of the Food and Drug Administration

Subchapter A — General Administrative Provisions

SEC. 701. [21 USC §371] Regulations and Hearings

(a) The authority to promulgate regulations for the efficient enforcement of this Act, except as otherwise provided in this section, is hereby vested in the Secretary.

(b) The Secretary of the Treasury and the Secretary of Health and Human Services shall jointly prescribe regulations for the efficient enforcement of the provisions of section 801, except as otherwise provided therein. Such regulations shall be promulgated in such manner and take effect at such time, after due notice, as the Secretary of Health and Human Services shall determine.

(c) Hearings authorized or required by this Act shall be conducted by the Secretary or such officer or employee as he may designate for the purpose.

(d) The definitions and standards of identity promulgated in accordance with the provisions of this Act shall be effective for the purposes of the enforcement of this Act, notwithstanding such definitions and standards as may be contained in other laws of the United States and regulations promulgated thereunder.

(e)(1) Any action for the issuance, amendment, or repeal of any regulation under section 403(j), 404(a), 406, 501(b), or 502 (d) or (h) of this Act, and any action for the amendment or repeal of any definition and standard of identity under section 401 of this Act for any dairy product (including products regulated under parts 131, 133 and 135 of title 21, Code of Federal Regulations) or maple sirup (regulated under section 168.140 of title 21, Code of Federal Regulations) [1] shall be begun by a proposal made (A) by the Secretary on his own initiative, or (B) by petition of any interested persons, showing reasonable grounds therefor, filed with the Secretary. The Secretary shall publish such proposal and shall afford all interested persons an opportunity to present their views thereon, orally or in writing. As soon as practicable thereafter, the Secretary shall by order act upon such proposal and shall make such order public. Except as provided in paragraph (2), the order shall become effective at such time as may be specified therein, but not prior to the day following the last day on which objections may be filed under such paragraph.

(2) On or before the thirtieth day after the date on which an order entered under paragraph (1) is made public, any person who will be adversely affected by

[1] The probable intent of the Congress is that the reference to maple sirup be struck. Section 3(b) of Public Law 103–396 attempted to amend subsection (e)(1) by striking "or maple syrup (regulated under section 168.140 of title 21, Code of Federal Regulations).". The amendment cannot be executed because the amendatory instructions referred to "maple syrup" rather than "maple sirup".

such order if placed in effect may file objections thereto with the Secretary, specifying with particularity the provisions of the order deemed objectionable, stating the grounds therefor, and requesting a public hearing upon such objections. Until final action upon such objections is taken by the Secretary under paragraph (3), the filing of such objections shall operate to stay the effectiveness of those provisions of the order to which the objections are made. As soon as practicable after the time for filing objections has expired the Secretary shall publish a notice in the Federal Register specifying those parts of the order which have been stayed by the filing of objections and, if no objections have been filed, stating that fact.

(3) As soon as practicable after such request for a public hearing, the Secretary, after due notice, shall hold such a public hearing for the purpose of receiving evidence relevant and material to the issues raised by such objections. At the hearing, any interested person may be heard in person or by representative. As soon as practicable after completion of the hearing, the Secretary shall by order act upon such objections and make such order public. Such order shall be based only on substantial evidence of record at such hearing and shall set forth, as part of the order, detailed findings of fact on which the order is based. The Secretary shall specify in the order the date on which it shall take effect, except that it shall not be made to take effect prior to the ninetieth day after its publication unless the Secretary finds that emergency conditions exist necessitating an earlier effective date, in which event the Secretary shall specify in the order his findings as to such conditions.

(f)(1) In a case of actual controversy as to the validity of any order under subsection (e), any person who will be adversely affected by such order if placed in effect may at any time prior to the ninetieth day after such order is issued file a petition with the Circuit Court of Appeals of the United States for the circuit wherein such person resides or has his principal place of business, for a judicial review of such order. A copy of the petition shall be forthwith transmitted by the clerk of the court to the Secretary or other officer designated by him for that purpose. The Secretary thereupon shall file in the court the record of the proceedings on which the Secretary based his order, as provided in section 2112 of title 28, United States Code.

(2) If the petitioner applies to the court for leave to adduce additional evidence, and shows to the satisfaction of the court that such additional evidence is material and that there were reasonable grounds for the failure to adduce such evidence in the proceeding before the Secretary the court may order such additional evidence (and evidence in rebuttal thereof) to be taken before the Secretary, and to be adduced upon the hearing, in such manner and upon such terms and conditions as to the court may seem proper. The Secretary may modify his findings as to the facts, or make new findings, by reason of the additional evidence, so taken, and he shall file such modified or new

findings, and his recommendation, if any, for the modification or setting aside of his original order, with the return of such additional evidence.

(3) Upon the filing of the petition referred to in paragraph (1) of this subsection, the court shall have jurisdiction to affirm the order, or to set it aside in whole or in part, temporarily or permanently. If the order of the Secretary refuses to issue, amend, or repeal a regulation and such order is not in accordance with law the court shall by its judgment order the Secretary to take action with respect to such regulation, in accordance with law. The findings of the Secretary as to the facts, if supported by substantial evidence, shall be conclusive.

(4) The judgment of the court affirming or setting aside, in whole or in part, any such order of the Secretary shall be final, subject to review by the Supreme Court of the United States upon certiorari or certification as provided in section 1254 of title 28, United States Code.

(5) Any action instituted under this subsection shall survive notwithstanding any change in the person occupying the office of Secretary or any vacancy in such office.

(6) The remedies provided for in this subsection shall be in addition to and not in substitution for any other remedies provided by law.

(g) A certified copy of the transcript of the record and proceedings under subsection (e) shall be furnished by the Secretary to any interested party at his request, and payment of the costs thereof, and shall be admissible in any criminal libel for condemnation, exclusion of imports, or other proceeding arising under or in respect of this Act, irrespective of whether proceedings with respect to the order have previously been instituted or become final under subsection (f).

(h)(1)(A) The Secretary shall develop guidance documents with public participation and ensure that information identifying the existence of such documents and the documents themselves are made available to the public both in written form and, as feasible, through electronic means. Such documents shall not create or confer any rights for or on any person, although they present the views of the Secretary on matters under the jurisdiction of the Food and Drug Administration.

(B) Although guidance documents shall not be binding on the Secretary, the Secretary shall ensure that employees of the Food and Drug Administration do not deviate from such guidances without appropriate justification and supervisory concurrence. The Secretary shall provide training to employees in how to develop and use guidance documents and shall monitor the development and issuance of such documents.

(C) For guidance documents that set forth initial interpretations of a statute or regulation, changes in interpretation or policy that are of more than a minor nature, complex scientific issues, or highly controversial issues, the

Secretary shall ensure public participation prior to implementation of guidance documents, unless the Secretary determines that such prior public participation is not feasible or appropriate. In such cases, the Secretary shall provide for public comment upon implementation and take such comment into account.

(D) For guidance documents that set forth existing practices or minor changes in policy, the Secretary shall provide for public comment upon implementation.

(2) In developing guidance documents, the Secretary shall ensure uniform nomenclature for such documents and uniform internal procedures for approval of such documents. The Secretary shall ensure that guidance documents and revisions of such documents are properly dated and indicate the nonbinding nature of the documents. The Secretary shall periodically review all guidance documents and, where appropriate, revise such documents.

(3) The Secretary, acting through the Commissioner, shall maintain electronically and update and publish periodically in the Federal Register a list of guidance documents. All such documents shall be made available to the public.

(4) The Secretary shall ensure that an effective appeals mechanism is in place to address complaints that the Food and Drug Administration is not developing and using guidance documents in accordance with this subsection.

(5) Not later than July 1, 2000, the Secretary after evaluating the effectiveness of the Good Guidance Practices document, published in the Federal Register at 62 Fed. Reg. 8961, shall promulgate a regulation consistent with this subsection specifying the policies and procedures of the Food and Drug Administration for the development, issuance, and use of guidance documents.

SEC. 702. [21 USC §372] Examinations and Investigations

(a)(1) The Secretary is authorized to conduct examinations and investigations for the purposes of this Act through officers and employees of the Department or through any health, food, or drug officer or employee of any State, Territory, or political subdivision thereof, duly commissioned by the Secretary as an officer of the Department.

(2)(A) In addition to the authority established in paragraph (1), the Secretary, pursuant to a memorandum of understanding between the Secretary and the head of another Federal department or agency, is authorized to conduct examinations and investigations for the purposes of this Act through the officers and employees of such other department or agency, subject to subparagraph (B). Such a memorandum shall include provisions to ensure adequate training of such officers and employees to conduct the examinations and investigations. The memorandum of understanding shall contain provisions regarding reimbursement. Such provisions may, at the sole discretion of the head of the other department or agency, require reimbursement, in whole or in part, from the Secretary for the examinations or investigations performed under this section by the officers or employees of the other department or agency.

(B) A memorandum of understanding under subparagraph (A) between the Secretary and another Federal department or agency is effective only in the case of examinations or inspections at facilities or other locations that are jointly regulated by the Secretary and such department or agency.

(C) For any fiscal year in which the Secretary and the head of another Federal department or agency carries out one or more examinations or inspections under a memorandum of understanding under subparagraph (A), the Secretary and the head of such department or agency shall with respect to their respective departments or agencies submit to the committees of jurisdiction (authorizing and appropriating) in the House of Representatives and the Senate a report that provides, for such year--

(i) the number of officers or employees that carried out one or more programs, projects, or activities under such memorandum;

(ii) the number of additional articles that were inspected or examined as a result of such memorandum; and

(iii) the number of additional examinations or investigations that were carried out pursuant to such memorandum.

(3) In the case of food packed in the Commonwealth of Puerto Rico or a Territory the Secretary shall attempt to make inspection of such food at the first point of entry within the United States, when in his opinion and with due regard to the enforcement of all the provisions of this Act, the facilities at his disposal will permit of such inspection.

(4) For the purposes of this subsection the term " United States" means the States and the District of Columbia.

(b) Where a sample of a food, drug, or cosmetic is collected for analysis under this Act the Secretary shall, upon request, provide a part of such official sample for examination or analysis by any person named on the label of the article, or the owner thereof, or his attorney or agent; except that the Secretary is authorized, by regulations, to make such reasonable exceptions from, and impose such reasonable terms and conditions relating to, the operation of this subsection as he finds necessary for the proper administration of the provisions of this Act.

(c) For purposes of enforcement of this Act, records of any department or independent establishment in the executive branch of the Government shall be open to inspection by any official of the Department duly authorized by the Secretary to make such inspection.

(d) The Secretary is authorized and directed, upon request from the Under Secretary of Commerce for Intellectual Property and Director of the United States Patent and Trademark Office, to furnish full and complete information with respect to such questions relating to drugs as the Director may submit concerning any patent application. The Secretary is further authorized, upon receipt of any such request, to conduct or cause to be conducted, such research as may be required.

(e) Any officer or employee of the Department designated by the Secretary to conduct examinations, investigations, or inspections under this Act relating to counterfeit drugs may, when so authorized by the Secretary—

(1) carry firearms;

(2) execute and serve search warrants and arrest warrants;

(3) execute seizure by process issued pursuant to libel under section 304;

(4) make arrests without warrant for offenses under this Act with respect to such drugs if the offense is committed in his presence or, in the case of a felony, if he has probable cause to believe that the person so arrested has committed, or is committing, such offense; and

(5) make, prior to the institution of libel proceedings under section 304(a)(2), seizures of drugs or containers or of equipment, punches, dies, plates, stones, labeling, or other things, if they are, or he has reasonable grounds to believe that they are, subject to seizure and condemnation under such section 304(a)(2). In the event of seizure pursuant to this paragraph (5) [2], libel proceedings under section 304(a)(2) shall be instituted promptly and the property seized be placed under the jurisdiction of the court.

SEC. 703. [21 USC §373] Records of Interstate Shipment

Note: revisions were posted to this section in May 2008.

(a) In general.For the purpose of enforcing the provisions of this Act, carriers engaged in interstate commerce, and persons receiving food, drugs, devices, or cosmetics in interstate commerce or holding such articles so received, shall, upon the request of an officer or employee duly designated by the Secretary, permit such officer or employee, at reasonable times, to have access to and to copy all records showing the movement in interstate commerce of any food, drug, device, or cosmetic, or the holding thereof during or after such movement, and the quantity, shipper, and consignee thereof; and it shall be unlawful for any such carrier or person to fail to permit such access to and copying of any such record

[2] So in law. Probably should be "this paragraph".

so requested when such request is accompanied by a statement in writing specifying the nature or kind of food, drug, device, or cosmetic to which such request relates, except that evidence obtained under this section, or any evidence which is directly or indirectly derived from such evidence, shall not be used in a criminal prosecution of the person from whom obtained, and except that carriers shall not be subject to the other provisions of this Act by reason of their receipt, carriage, holding, or delivery of food, drugs, devices, or cosmetics in the usual course of business as carriers except as provided in subsection (b).

(b) Food transportation records. A shipper, carrier by motor vehicle or rail vehicle, receiver, or other person subject to section 416 shall, on request of an officer or employee designated by the Secretary, permit the officer or employee, at reasonable times, to have access to and to copy all records that the Secretary requires to be kept under section 416(c)(1)(E).

SEC. 704. [21 USC §374] Factory Inspection

Note: revisions were posted to this section in February 2008.

(a) Right of agents to enter; scope of inspection; notice; promptness; exclusions.

(1) For purposes of enforcement of this Act, officers or employees duly designated by the Secretary, upon presenting appropriate credentials and a written notice to the owner, operator, or agent in charge, are authorized (A) to enter, at reasonable times, any factory, warehouse, or establishment in which food, drugs, devices, or cosmetics are manufactured, processed, packed, or held, for introduction into interstate commerce or after such introduction, or to enter any vehicle being used to transport or hold such food, drugs, devices, or cosmetics in interstate commerce; and (B) to inspect, at reasonable times and within reasonable limits and in a reasonable manner, such factory, warehouse, establishment, or vehicle and all pertinent equipment, finished and unfinished materials, containers, and labeling therein. In the case of any person (excluding farms and restaurants) who manufactures, processes, packs, transports, distributes, holds, or imports foods, the inspection shall extend to all records and other information described in section 414 when the Secretary has a reasonable belief that an article of food is adulterated and presents a threat of serious adverse health consequences or death to humans or animals, subject to the limitations established in section 414(d). In the case of any factory, warehouse, establishment, or consulting laboratory in which prescription drugs, nonprescription drugs intended for human use, or restricted devices are manufactured, processed, packed, or held, the inspection shall extend to all things therein (including records, files, papers, processes, controls, and facilities) bearing on whether prescription drugs, nonprescription drugs intended for human use, or restricted devices which are adulterated or misbranded within the meaning of this Act, or which may not be

Chapter VII

manufactured, introduced into interstate commerce, or sold, or offered for sale by reason of any provision of this Act, have been or are being manufactured, processed, packed, transported, or held in any such place, or otherwise bearing on violation of this Act. No inspection authorized by the preceding sentence or by paragraph (3) shall extend to financial data, sales data other than shipment data, pricing data, personnel data (other than data as to qualifications of technical and professional personnel performing functions subject to this Act), and research data (other than data relating to new drugs, antibiotic drugs, and devices and subject to reporting and inspection under regulations lawfully issued pursuant to section 505(i) or (k) [3] section 519, or 520(g), and data relating to other drugs or devices which in the case of a new drug would be subject to reporting or inspection under lawful regulations issued pursuant to section 505(j)). A separate notice shall be given for each such inspection, but a notice shall not be required for each entry made during the period covered by the inspection. Each such inspection shall be commenced and completed with reasonable promptness.

(2) The provisions of the third sentence of paragraph (1) shall not apply to—

(A) pharmacies which maintain establishments in conformance with any applicable local laws regulating the practice of pharmacy and medicine and which are regularly engaged in dispensing prescription drugs or devices, upon prescriptions of practitioners licensed to administer such drugs or devices to patients under the care of such practitioners in the course of their professional practice, and which do not, either through a subsidiary or otherwise, manufacture, prepare, propagate, compound, or process drugs or devices for sale other than in the regular course of their business of dispensing or selling drugs or devices at retail;

(B) practitioners licensed by law to prescribe or administer drugs, or prescribe or use devices, as the case may be, and who manufacture, prepare, propagate, compound, or process drugs, or manufacture or process devices solely for use in the course of their professional practice;

(C) persons who manufacture, prepare, propagate, compound, or process drugs or manufacture or process devices solely for use in research, teaching, or chemical analysis and not for sale;

(D) such other classes of persons as the Secretary may by regulation exempt from the application of this section upon a finding that inspection as applied to such classes of persons in accordance with this section is not necessary for the protection of the public health.

(3) An officer or employee making an inspection under paragraph (1) for purposes of enforcing the requirements of section 412 applicable to infant

[3] So in law. A comma probably should appear after "section 505(i) or (k)". See the amendment made by section 125(b)(2)(L) of Public Law 105–115 (111 Stat. 2326).

formulas shall be permitted, at all reasonable times, to have access to and to copy and verify any records—

(A) bearing on whether the infant formula manufactured or held in the facility inspected meets the requirements of section 412, or

(B) required to be maintained under section 412.

(b) Written report to owner; copy to Secretary. Upon completion of any such inspection of a factory, warehouse, consulting laboratory, or other establishment, and prior to leaving the premises, the officer or employee making the inspection shall give to the owner, operator, or agent in charge a report in writing setting forth any conditions or practices observed by him which, in his judgment, indicate that any food, drug, device, or cosmetic in such establishment (1) consists in whole or in part of any filthy, putrid, or decomposed substance, or (2) has been prepared, packed, or held under insanitary conditions whereby it may have become contaminated with filth, or whereby it may have been rendered injurious to health. A copy of such report shall be sent promptly to the Secretary.

(c) Receipt for samples taken. If the officer or employee making any such inspection of a factory, warehouse, or other establishment has obtained any sample in the course of the inspection, upon completion of the inspection and prior to leaving the premises he shall give to the owner, operator, or agent in charge a receipt describing the samples obtained.

(d) Analysis of samples furnished owner. Whenever in the course of any such inspection of a factory or other establishment where food is manufactured, processed, or packed, the officer or employee making the inspection obtains a sample of any such food, and an analysis is made of such sample for the purpose of ascertaining whether such food consists in whole or in part of any filthy, putrid, or decomposed substance, or is otherwise unfit for food, a copy of the results of such analysis shall be furnished promptly to the owner, operator, or agent in charge.

(e) Accessibility of records. Every person required under section 519 or 520(g) to maintain records and every person who is in charge or custody of such records shall, upon request of an officer or employee designated by the Secretary, permit such officer or employee at all reasonable times to have access to, and to copy and verify, such records.

(f) Recordkeeping.

(1) An accredited person described in paragraph (3) shall maintain records documenting the training qualifications of the person and the employees of the person, the procedures used by the person for handling confidential information, the compensation arrangements made by the person, and the procedures used by the person to identify and avoid conflicts of interest.

Upon the request of an officer or employee designated by the Secretary, the person shall permit the officer or employee, at all reasonable times, to have access to, to copy, and to verify, the records.

(2) Within 15 days after the receipt of a written request from the Secretary to an accredited person described in paragraph (3) for copies of records described in paragraph (1), the person shall produce the copies of the records at the place designated by the Secretary.

(3) For purposes of paragraphs (1) and (2), an accredited person described in this paragraph is a person who—

(A) is accredited under subsection (g); or

(B) is accredited under section 523.

(g) Inspections by accredited persons

(1) The Secretary shall, subject to the provisions of this subsection, accredit persons for the purpose of conducting inspections of establishments that manufacture, prepare, propagate, compound, or process class II or class III devices, which inspections are required under section 510(h) or are inspections of such establishments required to register under section 510(i). The owner or operator of such an establishment that is eligible under paragraph (6) may, from the list published under paragraph (4), select an accredited person to conduct such inspections.

(2) The Secretary shall publish in the Federal Register criteria to accredit or deny accreditation to persons who request to perform the duties specified in paragraph (1). Thereafter, the Secretary shall inform those requesting accreditation, within 60 days after the receipt of such request, whether the request for accreditation is adequate for review, and the Secretary shall promptly act on the request for accreditation. Any resulting accreditation shall state that such person is accredited to conduct inspections at device establishments identified in paragraph (1). The accreditation of such person shall specify the particular activities under this subsection for which such person is accredited.

(3) An accredited person shall, at a minimum, meet the following requirements:

(A) Such person may not be an employee of the Federal Government.

(B) Such person shall be an independent organization which is not owned or controlled by a manufacturer, supplier, or vendor of articles regulated under this Act and which has no organizational, material, or financial affiliation (including a consultative affiliation) with such a manufacturer, supplier, or vendor.

(C) Such person shall be a legally constituted entity permitted to conduct the activities for which it seeks accreditation.

(D) Such person shall not engage in the design, manufacture, promotion, or sale of articles regulated under this Act.

(E) The operations of such person shall be in accordance with generally accepted professional and ethical business practices, and such person shall agree in writing that at a minimum the person will--

(i) certify that reported information accurately reflects data reviewed, inspection observations made, other matters that relate to or may influence compliance with this Act, and recommendations made during an inspection or at an inspection's closing meeting;

(ii) limit work to that for which competence and capacity are available;

(iii) treat information received, records, reports, and recommendations as confidential commercial or financial information or trade secret information, except such information may be made available to the Secretary;

(iv) promptly respond and attempt to resolve complaints regarding its activities for which it is accredited; and

(v) protect against the use, in carrying out paragraph (1), of any officer or employee of the accredited person who has a financial conflict of interest regarding any product regulated under this Act, and annually make available to the public disclosures of the extent to which the accredited person, and the officers and employees of the person, have maintained compliance with requirements under this clause relating to financial conflicts of interest.

(F) Such person shall notify the Secretary of any withdrawal, suspension, restriction, or expiration of certificate of conformance with the quality systems standard referred to in paragraph (7) for any device establishment that such person inspects under this subsection not later than 30 days after such withdrawal, suspension, restriction, or expiration.

(G) Such person may conduct audits to establish conformance with the quality systems standard referred to in paragraph (7).

(4) The Secretary shall publish on the Internet site of the Food and Drug Administration a list of persons who are accredited under paragraph (2). Such list shall be updated to ensure that the identity of each accredited person, and the particular activities for which the person is accredited, is known to the public. The updating of such list shall be no later than one month after the accreditation of a person under this subsection or the suspension or withdrawal of accreditation, or the modification of the particular activities for which the person is accredited.

(5)(A) To ensure that persons accredited under this subsection continue to meet the standards of accreditation, the Secretary shall (i) audit the performance of such persons on a periodic basis through the review of inspection reports and inspections by persons designated by the Secretary to evaluate the compliance status of a device establishment and the performance of accredited persons, and (ii) take such additional measures as the Secretary determines to be appropriate.

(B) The Secretary may withdraw accreditation of any person accredited under paragraph (2), after providing notice and an opportunity for an informal hearing, when such person is substantially not in compliance with the standards of accreditation, poses a threat to public health, fails to act in a manner that is consistent with the purposes of this subsection, or where the Secretary determines that there is a financial conflict of interest in the relationship between the accredited person and the owner or operator of a device establishment that the accredited person has inspected under this subsection. The Secretary may suspend the accreditation of such person during the pendency of the process under the preceding sentence.

(6)(A) Subject to subparagraphs (B) and (C), a device establishment is eligible for inspection by persons accredited under paragraph (2) if the following conditions are met:

(i) The Secretary classified the results of the most recent inspection of the establishment described in paragraph (1) as "no action indicated" or "voluntary action indicated".

(ii) With respect to inspections of the establishment to be conducted by an accredited person, the owner or operator of the establishment submits to the Secretary a notice that--

(I) provides the date of the last inspection of the establishment by the Secretary and the classification of that inspection;

(II) states the intention of the owner or operator to use an accredited person to conduct inspections of the establishment ;

(III) identifies the particular accredited person the owner or operator intends to select to conduct such inspections; and

(IV) includes a certification that, with respect to the devices that are manufactured, prepared, propagated, compounded, or processed in the establishment--

(aa) at least 1 of such devices is marketed in the United States; and

(bb) at least 1 of such devices is marketed, or is intended to be marketed, in 1 or more foreign countries, 1 of which countries certifies, accredits, or otherwise recognizes the person accredited under paragraph (2) and identified under subclause (III) as a person authorized to conduct inspections of device establishments.

(B)(i) Except with respect to the requirement of subparagraph (A)(i), a device establishment is deemed to have clearance to participate in the program and to use the accredited person identified in the notice under subparagraph (A)(ii) for inspections of the establishment unless the Secretary, not later than 30 days after receiving such notice, issues a response that--

(I) denies clearance to participate as provided under subparagraph (C); or

(II) makes a request under clause (ii).

(ii) The Secretary may request from the owner or operator of a device establishment in response to the notice under subparagraph (A)(ii) with respect to the establishment, or from the particular accredited person identified in such notice--

(I) compliance data for the establishment in accordance with clause (iii)(I); or

(II) information concerning the relationship between the owner or operator of the establishment and the accredited person identified in such notice in accordance with clause (iii)(II).The owner or operator of the establishment, or such accredited person, as the case may be, shall respond to such a request not later than 60 days after receiving such request.

(iii)(I) The compliance data to be submitted by the owner or operator of a device establishment in response to a request under clause (ii) (I) are data describing whether the quality controls of the establishment have been sufficient for ensuring consistent compliance with current good manufacturing practice within the meaning of section 501(h) and with other applicable provisions of this Act. Such data shall include complete reports of inspectional findings regarding good manufacturing practice or other quality control audits that, during the preceding 2-year period, were conducted at the establishment by persons other than the owner or operator of the establishment, together with all other compliance data the Secretary deems necessary. Data under the preceding sentence shall demonstrate to the Secretary whether the establishment has facilitated consistent compliance by promptly correcting any compliance problems identified in such inspections.

(II) A request to an accredited person under clause (ii)(II) may not seek any information that is not required to be maintained by such person in records under subsection (f)(1).

(iv) A device establishment is deemed to have clearance to participate in the program and to use the accredited person identified in the notice under subparagraph (A)(ii) for inspections of the establishment unless the Secretary, not later than 60 days after receiving the information requested under clause (ii), issues a response that denies clearance to participate as provided under subparagraph (C).

(C)(i) The Secretary may deny clearance to a device establishment if the Secretary has evidence that the certification under subparagraph (A)(ii)(IV) is untrue and the Secretary provides to the owner or operator of the establishment a statement summarizing such evidence.

(ii) The Secretary may deny clearance to a device establishment if the Secretary determines that the establishment has failed to demonstrate consistent compliance for purposes of subparagraph (B)(iii)(I) and the Secretary provides to the owner or operator of the establishment a statement of the reasons for such determination.

(iii)(I) The Secretary may reject the selection of the accredited person identified in the notice under subparagraph (A)(ii) if the Secretary provides to the owner or operator of the establishment a statement of the reasons for such rejection. Reasons for the rejection may include that the establishment or the accredited person, as the case may be, has failed to fully respond to the request, or that the Secretary has concerns regarding the relationship between the establishment and such accredited person.

(II) If the Secretary rejects the selection of an accredited person by the owner or operator of a device establishment, the owner or operator may make an additional selection of an accredited person by submitting to the Secretary a notice that identifies the additional selection. Clauses (i) and (ii) of subparagraph (B), and subclause (I) of this clause, apply to the selection of an accredited person through a notice under the preceding sentence in the same manner and to the same extent as such provisions apply to a selection of an accredited person through a notice under subparagraph (A)(ii).

(iv) In the case of a device establishment that is denied clearance under clause (i) or (ii) or with respect to which the selection of the accredited person is rejected under clause (iii), the Secretary shall designate a person to review the statement of reasons, or statement summarizing such evidence, as the case may be, of the Secretary under such clause if, during the 30-day period beginning on the date on which the owner or operator of the establishment receives such statement, the owner or operator requests the review. The review shall commence not later than 30 days after the owner or operator requests the review, unless the Secretary and the owner or operator otherwise agree.

(7)(A) Persons accredited under paragraph (2) to conduct inspections shall record in writing their inspection observations and shall present the observations to the device establishment's designated representative and describe each observation. Additionally, such accredited person shall prepare an inspection report in a form and manner designated by the Secretary to conduct inspections, taking into consideration the goals of international harmonization of quality systems standards. Any official classification of the inspection shall be determined by the Secretary.

(B) At a minimum, an inspection report under subparagraph (A) shall identify the persons responsible for good manufacturing practice compliance at the inspected device establishment, the dates of the inspection, the scope of the inspection, and shall describe in detail each observation identified by the accredited person, identify other matters that relate to or may influence compliance with this Act, and describe any recommendations during the inspection or at the inspection's closing meeting.

(C) An inspection report under subparagraph (A) shall be sent to the Secretary and to the designated representative of the inspected device establishment at the same time, but under no circumstances later than three weeks after the last day of the inspection. The report to the Secretary shall be accompanied by all written inspection observations previously provided to the designated representative of the establishment.

(D) Any statement or representation made by an employee or agent of a device establishment to a person accredited under paragraph (2) to conduct inspections shall be subject to section 1001 of title 18, United States Code.

(E) If at any time during an inspection by an accredited person the accredited person discovers a condition that could cause or contribute to an unreasonable risk to the public health, the accredited person shall immediately notify the Secretary of the identification of the device establishment subject to inspection and such condition.

(F) For the purpose of setting risk-based inspectional priorities, the Secretary shall accept voluntary submissions of reports of audits assessing conformance with appropriate quality systems standards set by the International Organization for Standardization (ISO) and identified by the Secretary in public notice. If the owner or operator of an establishment elects to submit audit reports under this subparagraph, the owner or operator shall submit all such audit reports with respect to the establishment during the preceding 2-year periods.

(8) Compensation for an accredited person shall be determined by agreement between the accredited person and the person who engages the services of the accredited person, and shall be paid by the person who engages such services.

(9) Nothing in this subsection affects the authority of the Secretary to inspect any device establishment pursuant to this Act.

(10)(A) For fiscal year 2005 and each subsequent fiscal year, no device establishment may be inspected during the fiscal year involved by a person accredited under paragraph (2) if—

(i) of the amounts appropriated for salaries and expenses of the Food and Drug Administration for the preceding fiscal year (referred to in this subparagraph as the "first prior fiscal year"), the amount obligated by the Secretary for inspections of device establishments by the Secretary was less than the adjusted base amount applicable to such first prior fiscal year; and

(ii) of the amounts appropriated for salaries and expenses of the Food and Drug Administration for the fiscal year preceding the first prior fiscal year (referred to in this subparagraph as the "second prior fiscal year"), the amount obligated by the Secretary for inspections of device establishments by the Secretary was less than the adjusted base amount applicable to such second prior fiscal year.

(B)(i) Subject to clause (ii), the Comptroller General of the United States shall determine the amount that was obligated by the Secretary for fiscal year 2002 for compliance activities of the Food and Drug Administration with respect to devices (referred to in this subparagraph as the "compliance budget"), and of such amount, the amount that was obligated for inspections by the Secretary of device establishments (referred to in this subparagraph as the "inspection budget").

(ii) For purposes of determinations under clause (i), the Comptroller General shall not include in the compliance budget or the inspection budget any amounts obligated for inspections of device establishments conducted as part of the process of reviewing applications under section 515.

(iii) Not later than March 31, 2003 , the Comptroller General shall complete the determinations required in this subparagraph and submit to the Secretary and the Congress a report describing the findings made through such determinations.

(C) For purposes of this paragraph:

(i) The term "***base amount***" means the inspection budget determined under subparagraph (B) for fiscal year 2002.

(ii) The term "***adjusted base amount***", in the case of applicability to fiscal year 2003, means an amount equal to the base amount increased by 5 percent.

(iii) The term "***adjusted base amount***", with respect to applicability to fiscal year 2004 or any subsequent fiscal year, means the adjusted based amount 5 applicable to the preceding year increased by 5 percent.

(11) The authority provided by this subsection terminates on October 1, 2012 .

(12) No later than four years after the enactment of this subsection [enacted Oct. 26, 2002] the Comptroller General shall report to the Committee on Energy and Commerce of the House of Representatives and the Committee on Health, Education, Labor and Pensions of the Senate—

(A) the number of inspections conducted by accredited persons pursuant to this subsection and the number of inspections conducted by Federal employees pursuant to section 510(h) and of device establishments required to register under section 510(i);

(B) the number of persons who sought accreditation under this subsection, as well as the number of persons who were accredited under this subsection;

(C) the reasons why persons who sought accreditation, but were denied accreditation, were denied;

(D) the number of audits conducted by the Secretary of accredited persons, the quality of inspections conducted by accredited persons, whether accredited persons are meeting their obligations under this Act, and whether the number of audits conducted is sufficient to permit these assessments;

(E) whether this subsection is achieving the goal of ensuring more information about device establishment compliance is being presented to the Secretary, and whether that information is of a quality consistent with information obtained by the Secretary pursuant to inspections conducted by Federal employees;

(F) whether this subsection is advancing efforts to allow device establishments to rely upon third-party inspections for purposes of compliance with the laws of foreign governments; and

(G) whether the Congress should continue, modify, or terminate the program under this subsection.

(13) The Secretary shall include in the annual report required under section 903(g) the names of all accredited persons and the particular activities under this subsection for which each such person is accredited and the name of each accredited person whose accreditation has been withdrawn during the year.

(14) Notwithstanding any provision of this subsection, this subsection does not have any legal effect on any agreement described in section 803(b) between the Secretary and a foreign country.

SEC. 705. [21 USC §375] Publicity

(a) The Secretary shall cause to be published from time to time reports summarizing all judgments, decrees, and court orders which have been rendered under this Act, including the nature of the charge and the disposition thereof.

(b) The Secretary may also cause to be disseminated information regarding food, drugs, devices, or cosmetics in situations involving, in the opinion of the Secretary, imminent danger to health, or gross deception of the consumer. Nothing in this section shall be construed to prohibit the Secretary from collecting, reporting, and illustrating the results of the investigations of the Department.

SEC. 706. [21 USC §376] Seafood Inspection

The Secretary, upon application of any packer of any seafood for shipment or sale within the jurisdiction of this Act, may, at his discretion, designate inspectors to examine and inspect such food and the production, packing, and labeling thereof. If on such examination and inspection compliance is found with the provisions of this Act and regulations promulgated thereunder, the applicant shall be authorized or required to mark the food as provided by regulation to show such compliance. Services under this section shall be rendered only upon payment by the applicant of fees fixed by regulation in such amounts as may be necessary to provide, equip, and maintain an adequate and efficient inspection service. Receipts from such fees shall be covered into the Treasury and shall be available to the Secretary for expenditures incurred in carrying out the purposes of this section, including expenditures for salaries of additional inspectors when necessary to supplement the number of inspectors for whose salaries Congress has appropriated. The Secretary is hereby authorized to promulgate regulations governing the sanitary and other conditions under which the service herein provided shall be granted and maintained and for otherwise carrying out the purposes of this section. Any person who forges, counterfeits, simulates, or falsely represents, or without proper authority uses any mark, stamp, tag, label, or other identification devices authorized or required by the provisions of this section or regulations thereunder, shall be guilty of a misdemeanor, and shall on conviction thereof be subject to imprisonment for not more than one year or a fine of not less than $1,000 nor more than $5,000 or both such imprisonment and fine.

SEC. 707. [21 USC §378] Advertising of Certain Foods

(a)(1) Except as provided in subsection (c), before the Secretary may initiate any action under chapter III—

(A) with respect to any food which the Secretary determines is misbranded under section 403(a)(2) because of its advertising, or

(B) with respect to a food's advertising which the Secretary determines causes the food to be so misbranded,

the Secretary shall, in accordance with paragraph (2), notify in writing the Federal Trade Commission of the action the Secretary proposes to take respecting such food or advertising.

(2) The notice required by paragraph (1) shall—

(A) contain (i) a description of the action the Secretary proposes to take and of the advertising which the Secretary has determined causes a food to be misbranded, (ii) a statement of the reasons for the Secretary's determination that such advertising has caused such food to be misbranded, and

(B) be accompanied by the records, documents, and other written materials which the Secretary determines supports his determination that such food is misbranded because of such advertising.

(b)(1) If the Secretary notifies the Federal Trade Commission under subsection (a) of action proposed to be taken under chapter III with respect to a food or food advertising and the Commission notifies the Secretary in writing, within the 30-day period beginning on the date of the receipt of such notice, that—

(A) it has initiated under the Federal Trade Commission Act an investigation of such advertising to determine if it is prohibited by such Act or any order or rule under such Act,

(B) it has commenced (or intends to commence) a civil action under section 5, 13, or 19 with respect to such advertising or the Attorney General has commenced (or intends to commence) a civil action under section 5 with respect to such advertising,

(C) it has issued and served (or intends to issue and serve) a complaint under section 5(b) of such Act respecting such advertising, or

(D) pursuant to section 16(b) of such Act it has made a certification to the Attorney General respecting such advertising, the Secretary may not, except as provided by paragraph (2), initiate the action described in the Secretary's notice to the Federal Trade Commission.

(2) If, before the expiration of the 60-day period beginning on the date the Secretary receives a notice described in paragraph (1) from the Federal Trade Commission in response to a notice of the Secretary under subsection (a)—

(A) the Commission or the Attorney General does not commence a civil action described in subparagraph (B) of paragraph (1) of this subsection respecting the advertising described in the Secretary's notice,

(B) the Commission does not issue and serve a complaint described in subparagraph (C) of such paragraph respecting such advertising, or

(C) the Commission does not (as described in subparagraph (D) of such paragraph) make a certification to the Attorney General respecting such advertising, or, if the Commission does make such a certification to the Attorney General respecting such advertising, the Attorney General, before the expiration of such period, does not cause appropriate criminal proceedings to be brought against such advertising,

the Secretary may, after the expiration of such period, initiate the action described in the notice to the Commission pursuant to subsection (a). The Commission shall promptly notify the Secretary of the commencement by the Commission of such a civil action, the issuance and service by it of such a complaint, or the causing by the Attorney General of criminal proceedings to be brought against such advertising.

(c) The requirements of subsections (a) and (b) do not apply with respect to action under chapter III with respect to any food or food advertising if the Secretary determines that such action is required to eliminate an imminent hazard to health.

(d) For the purpose of avoiding unnecessary duplication, the Secretary shall coordinate any action taken under chapter III because of advertising which the Secretary determines causes a food to be misbranded with any action of the Federal Trade Commission under the Federal Trade Commission Act with respect to such advertising.

SEC. 708. [21 USC §379] Confidential Information

The Secretary may provide any information which is exempt from disclosure pursuant to subsection (a) of section 552 of title 5, United States Code, by reason of subsection (b)(4) of such section to a person other than an officer or employee of the Department if the Secretary determines such other person requires the information in connection with an activity which is undertaken under contract with the Secretary, which relates to the administration of this Act, and with respect to which the Secretary (or an officer or employee of the Department) is not prohibited from using such information. The Secretary shall require as a condition to the provision of information under this section that the person receiving it take such security precautions respecting the information as the Secretary may by regulation prescribe.

SEC. 709. [21 USC §379a] Presumption

In any action to enforce the requirements of this Act respecting a device, food, drug, or cosmetic the connection with interstate commerce required for jurisdiction in such action shall be presumed to exist.

SEC. 710. [21 USC §379b] Consolidated Administrative and Laboratory Facility

(a) AUTHORITY.—The Secretary, in consultation with the Administrator of the General Services Administration, shall enter into contracts for the design, construction, and operation of a consolidated Food and Drug Administration administrative and laboratory facility.

(b) AWARDING OF CONTRACT.—The Secretary shall solicit contract proposals under subsection (a) from interested parties. In awarding contracts under such subsection, the Secretary shall review such proposals and give priority to those alternatives that are the most cost effective for the Federal Government and that allow for the use of donated land, federally owned property, or lease-purchase arrangements. A contract under this subsection shall not be entered into unless such contract results in a net cost savings to the Federal Government over the duration of the contract, as compared to the Government purchase price including borrowing by the Secretary of the Treasury.

(c) DONATIONS.—In carrying out this section, the Secretary shall have the power, in connection with real property, buildings, and facilities, to accept on behalf of the Food and Drug Administration gifts or donations of services or property, real or personal, as the Secretary determines to be necessary.

(d) AUTHORIZATION OF APPROPRIATIONS.—There are authorized to be appropriated to carry out this section $100,000,000 for fiscal year 1991, and such sums as may be necessary for each of the subsequent fiscal years, to remain available until expended.

SEC. 711. [21 USC §379d] Automation of Food and Drug Administration

(a) IN GENERAL.—The Secretary, acting through the Commissioner of Food and Drugs, shall automate appropriate activities of the Food and Drug Administration to ensure timely review of activities regulated under this Act.

(b) AUTHORIZATION OF APPROPRIATIONS.—There are authorized to be appropriated each fiscal year such sums as are necessary to carry out this section.

SEC. 712. [21 USC §379d-1] Conflicts of Interest

Note: This section was added in May 2008.

(a) Definitions. For purposes of this section:

(1) Advisory committee. The term "***advisory committee***" means an advisory committee under the Federal Advisory Committee Act [5 USC Appx] that provides advice or recommendations to the Secretary regarding activities of the Food and Drug Administration.

(2) Financial interest. The term "***financial interest***" means a financial interest under section 208(a) of title 18, United States Code.

(b) Appointments to advisory committees.

(1) Recruitment

(A) In general. The Secretary shall--

(i) develop and implement strategies on effective outreach to potential members of advisory committees at universities, colleges, other academic research centers, professional and medical societies, and patient and consumer groups;

(ii) seek input from professional medical and scientific societies to determine the most effective informational and recruitment activities; and

(iii) take into account the advisory committees with the greatest number of vacancies.

(B) Recruitment activities. The recruitment activities under subparagraph (A) may include--

(i) advertising the process for becoming an advisory committee member at medical and scientific society conferences;

(ii) making widely available, including by using existing electronic communications channels, the contact information for the Food and Drug Administration point of contact regarding advisory committee nominations; and

(iii) developing a method through which an entity receiving funding from the National Institutes of Health, the Agency for Healthcare Research and Quality, the Centers for Disease Control and Prevention, or the Veterans Health Administration can identify a person who the Food and Drug Administration can contact regarding the nomination of individuals to serve on advisory committees.

(2) Evaluation and criteria. When considering a term appointment to an advisory committee, the Secretary shall review the expertise of the individual and the financial disclosure report filed by the individual pursuant to the Ethics in Government Act of 1978 [5 USC Appx] for each individual under

consideration for the appointment, so as to reduce the likelihood that an appointed individual will later require a written determination as referred to in section 208(b)(1) of title 18, United States Code, a written certification as referred to in section 208(b)(3) of title 18, United States Code, or a waiver as referred to in subsection (c)(2) of this section for service on the committee at a meeting of the committee.

(c) Disclosures; prohibitions on participation; waivers.

(1) Disclosure of financial interest. Prior to a meeting of an advisory committee regarding a "particular matter" (as that term is used in section 208 of title 18, United States Code), each member of the committee who is a full-time Government employee or special Government employee shall disclose to the Secretary financial interests in accordance with subsection (b) of such section 208.

(2) Prohibitions and waivers on participation.

(A) In general. Except as provided under subparagraph (B), a member of an advisory committee may not participate with respect to a particular matter considered in an advisory committee meeting if such member (or an immediate family member of such member) has a financial interest that could be affected by the advice given to the Secretary with respect to such matter, excluding interests exempted in regulations issued by the Director of the Office of Government Ethics as too remote or inconsequential to affect the integrity of the services of the Government officers or employees to which such regulations apply.

(B) Waiver. If the Secretary determines it necessary to afford the advisory committee essential expertise, the Secretary may grant a waiver of the prohibition in subparagraph (A) to permit a member described in such subparagraph to--

(i) participate as a non-voting member with respect to a particular matter considered in a committee meeting; or

(ii) participate as a voting member with respect to a particular matter considered in a committee meeting.

(C) Limitation on waivers and other exceptions.--

(i) Definition. For purposes of this subparagraph, the term "exception" means each of the following with respect to members of advisory committees:

(I) A waiver under section 505(n)(4) [21 USC § 355(n)(4)] (as in effect on the day before the date of the enactment of the Food and Drug Administration Amendments Act of 2007 [enacted Sept. 27, 2007]).

(II) A written determination under section 208(b) of title 18, United States Code.

(III) A written certification under section 208(b)(3) of such title.

(ii) Determination of total number of members slots and member exceptions during fiscal year 2007. The Secretary shall determine--

(I)(aa) for each meeting held by any advisory committee during fiscal year 2007, the number of members who participated in the meeting; and

(bb) the sum of the respective numbers determined under item (aa) (referred to in this subparagraph as the "total number of 2007 meeting slots"); and

(II)(aa) for each meeting held by any advisory committee during fiscal year 2007, the number of members who received an exception for the meeting; and

(bb) the sum of the respective numbers determined under item (aa) (referred to in this subparagraph as the "total number of 2007 meeting exceptions").

(iii) Determination of percentage regarding exceptions during fiscal year 2007. The Secretary shall determine the percentage constituted by--

(I) the total number of 2007 meeting exceptions; divided by

(II) the total number of 2007 meeting slots.

(iv) Limitation for fiscal years 2008 through 2012. The number of exceptions at the Food and Drug Administration for members of advisory committees for a fiscal year may not exceed the following:

(I) For fiscal year 2008, 95 percent of the percentage determined under clause (iii) (referred to in this clause as the "base percentage").

(II) For fiscal year 2009, 90 percent of the base percentage.

(III) For fiscal year 2010, 85 percent of the base percentage.

(IV) For fiscal year 2011, 80 percent of the base percentage.

(V) For fiscal year 2012, 75 percent of the base percentage.

(v) Allocation of exceptions. The exceptions authorized under clause (iv) for a fiscal year may be allocated within the centers or other organizational units of the Food and Drug Administration as determined appropriate by the Secretary.

(3) Disclosure of waiver. Notwithstanding section 107(a)(2) of the Ethics in Government Act (5 U.S.C. App.), the following shall apply:

(A) 15 or more days in advance. As soon as practicable, but (except as provided in subparagraph (B)) not later than 15 days prior to a meeting of an advisory committee to which a written determination as referred to in section 208(b)(1) of title 18, United States Code, a written certification as referred to in section 208(b)(3) of title 18, United States Code, or a waiver as referred to in paragraph (2)(B) applies, the Secretary shall disclose (other than information exempted from disclosure under section 552 of title 5, United States Code, and section 552a of title 5, United States Code (popularly known as the Freedom of Information Act and the Privacy Act of 1974, respectively)) on the Internet Web site of the Food and Drug Administration--

(i) the type, nature, and magnitude of the financial interests of the advisory committee member to which such determination, certification, or waiver applies; and

(ii) the reasons of the Secretary for such determination, certification, or waiver.

(B) Less than 30 days in advance. In the case of a financial interest that becomes known to the Secretary less than 30 days prior to a meeting of an advisory committee to which a written determination as referred to in section 208(b)(1) of title 18, United States Code, a written certification as referred to in section 208(b)(3) of title 18, United States Code, or a waiver as referred to in paragraph (2)(B) applies, the Secretary shall disclose (other than information exempted from disclosure under section 552 of title 5, United States Code, and section 552a of title 5, United States Code) on the Internet Web site of the Food and Drug Administration, the information described in clauses (i) and (ii) of subparagraph (A) as soon as practicable after the Secretary makes such determination, certification, or waiver, but in no case later than the date of such meeting.

(d) Public record. The Secretary shall ensure that the public record and transcript of each meeting of an advisory committee includes the disclosure required under subsection (c)(3) (other than information exempted from disclosure under section 552 of title 5, United States Code, and section 552a of title 5, United States Code).

(e) Annual report. Not later than February 1 of each year, the Secretary shall submit to the Committee on Appropriations and the Committee on Health, Education, Labor, and Pensions of the Senate, and the Committee on Appropriations and the Committee on Energy and Commerce of the House of Representatives a report that describes--

(1) with respect to the fiscal year that ended on September 30 of the previous year, the number of vacancies on each advisory committee, the number of

nominees received for each committee, and the number of such nominees willing to serve;

(2) with respect to such year, the aggregate number of disclosures required under subsection (c)(3) for each meeting of each advisory committee and the percentage of individuals to whom such disclosures did not apply who served on such committee for each such meeting;

(3) with respect to such year, the number of times the disclosures required under subsection (c)(3) occurred under subparagraph (B) of such subsection; and

(4) how the Secretary plans to reduce the number of vacancies reported under paragraph (1) during the fiscal year following such year, and mechanisms to encourage the nomination of individuals for service on an advisory committee, including those who are classified by the Food and Drug Administration as academicians or practitioners.

(f) Periodic review of guidance. Not less than once every 5 years, the Secretary shall review guidance of the Food and Drug Administration regarding conflict of interest waiver determinations with respect to advisory committees and update such guidance as necessary.

SEC. 713. [21 USC §379d-2] Policy on the Review and Clearance of Scientific Articles Published by FDA Employees

Note: This section was added in May 2008.

(a) Definition. In this section, the term "***article***" means a paper, poster, abstract, book, book chapter, or other published writing.

(b) Policies. The Secretary, through the Commissioner of Food and Drugs, shall establish and make publicly available clear written policies to implement this section and govern the timely submission, review, clearance, and disclaimer requirements for articles.

(c) Timing of submission for review. If an officer or employee, including a Staff Fellow and a contractor who performs staff work, of the Food and Drug Administration is directed by the policies established under subsection (b) to submit an article to the supervisor of such officer or employee, or to some other official of the Food and Drug Administration, for review and clearance before such officer or employee may seek to publish or present such an article at a conference, such officer or employee shall submit such article for such review and clearance not less than 30 days before submitting the article for publication or presentation.

(d) Timing for review and clearance. The supervisor or other reviewing official shall review such article and provide written clearance, or written clearance on the condition of specified changes being made, to such officer or employee not later than 30 days after such officer or employee submitted such article for review.

(e) Non-timely review. If, 31 days after such submission under subsection (c), the supervisor or other reviewing official has not cleared or has not reviewed such article and provided written clearance, such officer or employee may consider such article not to have been cleared and may submit the article for publication or presentation with an appropriate disclaimer as specified in the policies established under subsection (b).

(f) Effect. Nothing in this section shall be construed as affecting any restrictions on such publication or presentation provided by other provisions of law.

Subchapter B — Colors

SEC. 721. [21 USC §379e] Listing and Certification of Color Additives for Foods, Drugs, and Cosmetics

When Color Additives Deemed Unsafe

(a) [4] A color additive shall, with respect to any particular use (for which it is being used or intended to be used or is represented as suitable) in or on food or drugs or devices or cosmetics be deemed unsafe for the purposes of the application of section 402(c), section 501(a)(4), or section 601(e), as the case may be unless—

(1)(A) there is in effect, and such additive and such use are in conformity with, a regulation issued under subsection (b) of this section listing such additive for such use, including any provision of such regulation prescribing the conditions under which such additive may be safely used, and (B) such additive either (i) is from a batch certified, in accordance with regulations issued pursuant to subsection (c), for such use, or (ii) has, with respect to such use, been exempted by the Secretary from the requirement of certification; or

(2) such additive and such use thereof conform to the terms of an exemption which is in effect pursuant to subsection (f) of this section.

While there are in effect regulations under subsections (b) and (c) of this section relating to a color additive or an exemption pursuant to subsection (f) with respect to such additive, an article shall not, by reason of bearing or containing such additive in all respects in accordance with such regulations or such exemption, be considered adulterated within the meaning of clause (1) of section 402(a) if such article is a food, or within the meaning of section 601(a) if such article is a cosmetic other than a hair dye (as defined in the last sentence of section 601(a)). A

Chapter VII

[4] See the revolving fund provision in the appendix.

color additive for use in or on a device shall be subject to this section only if the color additive comes in direct contact with the body of man or other animals for a significant period of time. The Secretary may by regulation designate the uses of color additives in or on devices which are subject to this section.

Listing of Colors

(b)(1) The Secretary shall, by regulation, provide for separately listing color additives for use in or on food, color additives for use in or on drugs or devices, and color additives for use in or on cosmetics, if and to the extent that such additives are suitable and safe for any such use when employed in accordance with such regulations.

(2)(A) Such regulations may list any color additive for use generally in or on food, or in or on drugs or devices, or in or on cosmetics, if the Secretary finds that such additive is suitable and may safely be employed for such general use.

(B) If the data before the Secretary do not establish that the additive satisfies the requirements for listing such additive on the applicable list pursuant to subparagraph (A) of this paragraph, or if the proposal is for listing such additive for a more limited use or uses, such regulations may list such additive only for any more limited use or uses for which it is suitable and may safely be employed.

(3) Such regulations shall, to the extent deemed necessary by the Secretary to assure the safety of the use or uses for which a particular color additive is listed, prescribe the conditions under which such additive may be safely employed for such use or uses (including, but not limited to, specifications, hereafter in this section referred to as tolerance limitations, as to the maximum quantity or quantities which may be used or permitted to remain in or on the article or articles in or on which it is used; specifications as to the manner in which such additive may be added to or used in or on such article or articles; and directions or other labeling or packaging requirements for such additive).

(4) The Secretary shall not list a color additive under this section for a proposed use unless the data before him establish that such use, under the conditions of use specified in the regulations, will be safe: Provided, however, That a color additive shall be deemed to be suitable and safe for the purpose of listing under this subsection for use generally in or on food, while there is in effect a published finding of the Secretary declaring such substance exempt from the term "food additive" because of its being generally recognized by qualified experts as safe for its intended use, as provided in section 201(s).

(5)(A) In determining, for the purposes of this section, whether a proposed use of a color additive is safe, the Secretary shall consider, among other relevant factors—

(i) the probable consumption of, or other relevant exposure from, the additive and of any substance formed in or on food, drugs or devices, or cosmetics because of the use of the additive;

(ii) the cumulative effect, if any, of such additive in the diet of man or animals, taking into account the same or any chemically or pharmacologically related substance or substances in such diet;

(iii) safety factors which, in the opinion of experts qualified by scientific training and experience to evaluate the safety of color additives for the use or uses for which the additive is proposed to be listed, are generally recognized as appropriate for the use of animal experimentation data; and

(iv) the availability of any needed practicable methods of analysis for determining the identity and quantity of (I) the pure dye and all intermediates and other impurities contained in such color additive, (II) such additive in or on any article of food, drug or devices, or cosmetic, and (III) any substance formed in or on such article because of the use of such additive.

(B) A color additive (i) shall be deemed unsafe, and shall not be listed, for any use which will or may result in ingestion of all or part of such additive, if the additive is found by the Secretary to induce cancer when ingested by man or animal, or if it is found by the Secretary, after tests which are appropriate for the evaluation of the safety of additives for use in food, to induce cancer in man or animal, and (ii) shall be deemed unsafe, and shall not be listed, for any use which will not result in ingestion of any part of such additive, if, after tests which are appropriate for the evaluation of the safety of additives for such use, or after other relevant exposure of man or animal to such additive, it is found by the Secretary to induce cancer in man or animal: Provided, That clause (i) of this subparagraph (B) shall not apply with respect to the use of a color additive as an ingredient of feed for animals which are raised for food production, if the Secretary finds that, under the conditions of use and feeding specified in proposed labeling and reasonably certain to be followed in practice, such additive will not adversely affect the animals for which such feed is intended, and that no residue of the additive will be found (by methods of examination prescribed or approved by the Secretary by regulations, which regulations shall not be subject to subsection (d)) in any edible portion of such animals after slaughter or in any food yielded by or derived from the living animal.

(C)(i) In any proceeding for the issuance, amendment, or repeal of a regulation listing a color additive, whether commenced by a proposal of the Secretary on his own initiative or by a proposal contained in a petition, the petitioner, or any other person who will be adversely affected by such proposal or by the Secretary's order issued in accordance with paragraph (1) of section 701(e) if placed in effect, may request, within the time specified in this subparagraph, that the petition or order thereon, or the Secretary's proposal, be referred to an advisory committee for a report and recommendations with respect to any matter arising under subparagraph (B) of this paragraph, which is involved in such proposal or order and which requires the exercise of scientific judgment. Upon such request, or if the Secretary within such time deems such a referral necessary, the Secretary shall forthwith appoint an advisory committee under subparagraph (D) of this paragraph and shall refer to it, together with all the data before him, such matter arising under subparagraph (B) for study thereof and for a report and recommendations on such matter. A person who has filed a petition or who has requested the referral of a matter to an advisory committee pursuant to this subparagraph (C) [5], as well as representatives of the Department, shall have the right to consult with such advisory committee in connection with the matter referred to it. The request for referral under this subparagraph, or the Secretary's referral on his own initiative, may be made at any time before, or within thirty days after, publication of an order of the Secretary acting upon the petition or proposal.

(ii) Within sixty days after the date of such referral, or within an additional thirty days if the committee deems such additional time necessary, the committee shall, after independent study of the data furnished to it by the Secretary and other data before it, certify to the Secretary a report and recommendations, together with all underlying data and a statement of the reasons or basis for the recommendations. A copy of the foregoing shall be promptly supplied by the Secretary to any person who has filed a petition, or who has requested such referral to the advisory committee. Within thirty days after such certification, and after giving due consideration to all data then before him, including such report, recommendation, underlying data, and statement, and to any prior order issued by him in connection with such matter, the Secretary shall by order confirm or modify any order therefore issued or, if no such prior order has been issued, shall by order act upon the petition or other proposal.

(iii) Where—

(I) by reason of subparagraph (B) of this paragraph, the Secretary has initiated a proposal to remove from listing a color additive previously listed pursuant to this section; and

(II) a request has been made for referral of such proposal to an advisory committee; the Secretary may not act by order on such proposal until the advisory committee has made a report and

[5] So in law. Probably should be "this subparagraph".

recommendations to him under clause (ii) of this subparagraph and he has considered such recommendations, unless the Secretary finds that emergency conditions exist necessitating the issuance of an order notwithstanding this clause.

(D) The advisory committee referred to in subparagraph (C) of this paragraph shall be composed of experts selected by the National Academy of Sciences, qualified in the subject matter referred to the committee and of adequately diversified professional background, except that in the event of the inability or refusal of the National Academy of Sciences to act, the Secretary shall select the members of the committee. The size of the committee shall be determined by the Secretary. Members of any advisory committee established under this Act, while attending conferences or meetings of their committees or otherwise serving at the request of the Secretary, shall be entitled to receive compensation at rates to be fixed by the Secretary but at rates not exceeding the daily equivalent of the rate specified at the time of such service for grade GS–18 of the General Schedule [6], including travel time; and while away from their homes or regular places of business they may be allowed travel expenses, including per diem in lieu of subsistence, as authorized by section 5703 of title 5 of the United States Code for persons in the Government service employed intermittently. The members shall not be subject to any other provisions of law regarding the appointment and compensation of employees of the United States. The Secretary shall furnish the committee with adequate clerical and other assistance, and shall by rules and regulations prescribe the procedure to be followed by the committee.

(6) The Secretary shall not list a color additive under this subsection for a proposed use if the data before him show that such proposed use would promote deception of the consumer in violation of this Act or would otherwise result in misbranding or adulteration within the meaning of this Act.

(7) If, in the judgment of the Secretary, a tolerance limitation is required in order to assure that a proposed use of a color additive will be safe, the Secretary—

(A) shall not list the additive for such use if he finds that the data before him do not establish that such additive, if used within a safe tolerance limitation, would achieve the intended physical or other technical effect; and

(B) shall not fix such tolerance limitation at a level higher than he finds to be reasonably required to accomplish the intended physical or other technical effect.

[6] The General Schedule under section 5332 of title 5, United States Code, no longer includes the grade GS-18. The grades are GS-1 through GS-15.

(8) If, having regard to the aggregate quantity of color additive likely to be consumed in the diet or to be applied to the human body, the Secretary finds that the data before him fail to show that it would be safe and otherwise permissible to list a color additive (or pharmacologically related color additives) of all uses proposed therefor and at the levels of concentration proposed, the Secretary shall, in determining for which use or uses such additive (or such related additives) shall be or remain listed, or how the aggregate allowable safe tolerance for such additive or additives shall be allocated by him among the uses under consideration, take into account, among other relevant factors (and subject to the paramount criterion of safety), (A) the relative marketability of the articles involved as affected by the proposed uses of the color additive (or of such related additives) in or on such articles, and the relative dependence of the industries concerned on such uses; (B) the relative aggregate amounts of such color additive which he estimates would be consumed in the diet or applied to the human body by reason of the various uses and levels of concentration proposed; and (C) the availability, if any, of other color additives suitable and safe for one or more of the uses proposed.

Certification of Colors

(c) The Secretary shall further, by regulation, provide (1) for the certification, with safe diluents or without diluents, of batches of color additives listed pursuant to subsection (b) and conforming to the requirements for such additives established by regulations under such subsection and this subsection, and (2) for exemption from the requirement of certification in the case of any such additive, or any listing or use thereof, for which he finds such requirement not to be necessary in the interest of the protection of the public health: Provided, That, with respect to any use in or on food for which a listed color additive is deemed to be safe by reason of the proviso to paragraph (4) of subsection (b), the requirement of certification shall be deemed not to be necessary in the interest of public health protection.

Procedure for Issuance, Amendment, or Repeal of Regulations

(d) The provisions of section 701 (e), (f), and (g) of this Act shall, subject to the provisions of subparagraph (C) of subsection (b)(5) of this section, apply to and in all respects govern proceedings for the issuance, amendment, or repeal of regulations under subsection (b) or (c) of this section (including judicial review of the Secretary's action in such proceedings) and the admissibility of transcripts of the record of such proceedings in other proceedings, except that—

(1) if the proceeding is commenced by the filing of a petition, notice of the proposal made by the petition shall be published in general terms by the Secretary within thirty days after such filing, and the Secretary's order (required by paragraph (1) of section 701(e)) acting upon such proposal shall,

in the absence of prior referral (or request for referral) to an advisory committee, be issued within ninety days after the date of such filing, except that the Secretary may (prior to such ninetieth day) by written notice to the petitioner, extend such ninety-day period to such time (not more than one hundred and eighty days after the date of filing of the petition) as the Secretary deems necessary to enable him to study and investigate the petition;

(2) any report, recommendations, underlying data, and reasons certified to the Secretary by an advisory committee appointed pursuant to subparagraph (D) of subsection (b)(5) of this section, shall be made a part of the record of any hearing if relevant and material, subject to the provisions of section 7(c) of the Administrative Procedure Act (5 U.S.C., sec. 1006(c)) [7]. The advisory committee shall designate a member to appear and testify at any such hearing with respect to the report and recommendations of such committee upon request of the Secretary, the petitioner, or the officer conducting the hearing, but this shall not preclude any other member of the advisory committee from appearing and testifying at such hearing;

(3) the Secretary's order after public hearing (acting upon objections filed to an order made prior to hearings) shall be subject to the requirements of section 409(f)(2); and

(4) the scope of judicial review of such order shall be in accordance with the fourth sentence of paragraph (2), and with the provisions of paragraph (3), of section 409(g).

Fees

(e) The admitting to listing and certification of color additives, in accordance with regulations prescribed under this Act, shall be performed only upon payment of such fees, which shall be specified in such regulations, as may be necessary to provide, maintain, and equip an adequate service for such purposes.

Exemptions

(f) The Secretary shall by regulations (issued without regard to subsection (d)) provide for exempting from the requirements of this section any color additive or any specific type of use thereof, and any article of food, drug or device, or cosmetic bearing or containing such additive, intended solely for investigational use by qualified experts when in his opinion such exemption is consistent with the public health.

NOTE.—Section 201 of the Labor-Federal Security Appropriation Act, 1944 (21 U.S.C. 377), provides that the Secretary in carrying into effect this Act "is authorized to cooperate with associations and scientific societies in the revision of the United States

Chapter VII

[7] Section 7(c) of the Administrative Procedure Act has been superseded by section 556(d) of title 5, United States Code. See Public Law 89-554.

Pharmacopeia and in the development of methods of analysis and mechanical and physical tests necessary to carry out the work of the Food and Drug Administration.

Subchapter C — Fees

SEC. 731. [21 USC 379f] Recovery and Retention of Fees for Freedom of Information Requests

(a) IN GENERAL. The Secretary, acting through the Commissioner of Food and Drugs, may

(1) set and charge fees, in accordance with section 552(a)(4)(A) of title 5, United States Code, to recover all reasonable costs incurred in processing requests made under section 552 of title 5, United States Code, for records obtained or created under this Act or any other Federal law for which responsibility for administration has been delegated to the Commissioner by the Secretary;

(2) retain all fees charged for such requests; and

(3) establish an accounting system and procedures to control receipts and expenditures of fees received under this section.

(b) USE OF FEES. The Secretary and the Commissioner of Food and Drugs shall not use fees received under this section for any purpose other than funding the processing of requests described in subsection (a)(1). Such fees shall not be used to reduce the amount of funds made to carry out other provisions of this Act.

(c) WAIVER OF FEES. Nothing in this section shall supersede the right of a requester to obtain a waiver of fees pursuant to section 552(a)(4)(A) of title 5, United States Code.

SEC. 735. [21 USC §379g] Definitions

Note: revisions were posted to this section in May 2008.

[8] For purposes of this part:

(1) The term "***human drug application***" means an application for--

(A) approval of a new drug submitted under section 505(b), or

---

[8] Sections 503 and 504 of Public Law 107–188 (116 Stat. 688, 689) amended sections 735 and 736, respectively. Section 509 of such Public Law provides as follows:

SEC. 509. SUNSET CLAUSE.
The amendments made by sections 503 and 504 cease to be effective October 1, 2007, and section 505 ceases to be effective 120 days after such date.

(B) licensure of a biological product under section 351 of the Public Health Service Act.

(C) [Redesignated]

Such term does not include a supplement to such an application, does not include an application with respect to whole blood or a blood component for transfusion, does not include an application with respect to a bovine blood product for topical application licensed before September 1, 1992, an allergenic extract product, or an in vitro diagnostic biologic product licensed under section 351 of the Public Health Service Act, does not include an application with respect to a large volume parenteral drug product approved before September 1, 1992, does not include an application for a licensure of a biological product for further manufacturing use only, and does not include an application or supplement submitted by a State or Federal Government entity for a drug that is not distributed commercially. Such term does include an application for licensure, as described in subparagraph (B), of a large volume biological product intended for single dose injection for intravenous use or infusion.

(2) The term "***supplement***" means a request to the Secretary to approve a change in a human drug application which has been approved.

(3) The term "***prescription drug product***" means a specific strength or potency of a drug in final dosage form--

(A) for which a human drug application has been approved,

(B) which may be dispensed only under prescription pursuant to section 503(b) , and

(C) which is on the list of products described in section 505(j)(7)(A) (not including the discontinued section of such list) or is on a list created and maintained by the Secretary of products approved under human drug applications under section 351 of the Public Health Service Act (not including the discontinued section of such list).

Such term does not include whole blood or a blood component for transfusion, does not include a bovine blood product for topical application licensed before September 1, 1992, an allergenic extract product, or an in vitro diagnostic biologic product licensed under section 351 of the Public Health Service Act. Such term does not include a biological product that is licensed for further manufacturing use only, and does not include a drug that is not distributed commercially and is the subject of an application or supplement submitted by a State or Federal Government entity. Such term does include a large volume biological product intended for single dose injection for intravenous use or infusion.

(4) The term "***final dosage form***" means, with respect to a prescription drug product, a finished dosage form which is approved for administration to a

patient without substantial further manufacturing (such as capsules, tablets, or lyophilized products before reconstitution).

(5) The term "***prescription drug establishment***" means a foreign or domestic place of business which is at one general physical location consisting of one or more buildings all of which are within five miles of each other and at which one or more prescription drug products are manufactured in final dosage form. For purposes of this paragraph, the term "manufactured" does not include packaging.

(6) The term "***process for the review of human drug applications***" means the following activities of the Secretary with respect to the review of human drug applications and supplements:

(A) The activities necessary for the review of human drug applications and supplements.

(B) The issuance of action letters which approve human drug applications or which set forth in detail the specific deficiencies in such applications and, where appropriate, the actions necessary to place such applications in condition for approval.

(C) The inspection of prescription drug establishments and other facilities undertaken as part of the Secretary's review of pending human drug applications and supplements.

(D) Activities necessary for the review of applications for licensure of establishments subject to section 351 of the Public Health Service Act and for the release of lots of biologics under such section.

(E) Monitoring of research conducted in connection with the review of human drug applications.

(F) Postmarket safety activities with respect to drugs approved under human drug applications or supplements, including the following activities:

(i) Collecting, developing, and reviewing safety information on approved drugs, including adverse event reports.

(ii) Developing and using improved adverse-event data-collection systems, including information technology systems.

(iii) Developing and using improved analytical tools to assess potential safety problems, including access to external data bases

(iv) Implementing and enforcing section 505(o) [21 USC § 355(o)] (relating to postapproval studies and clinical trials and labeling changes) and section 505(p) [21 USC § 355(p)] (relating to risk evaluation and mitigation strategies).

(v) Carrying out section 505(k)(5) [21 USC § 355(k)(5)] (relating to adverse event reports and postmarket safety activities).

(7) The term "***costs of resources allocated for the process for the review of human drug applications***" means the expenses incurred in connection with the process for the review of human drug applications for

(A) officers and employees of the Food and Drug Administration, contractors of the Food and Drug Administration, advisory committees, and costs related to such officers, employees, and committees and to contracts with such contractors,

(B) management of information, and the acquisition, maintenance, and repair of computer resources,

(C) leasing, maintenance, renovation, and repair of facilities and acquisition, maintenance, and repair of fixtures, furniture, scientific equipment, and other necessary materials and supplies, and

(D) collecting fees under section 736 and accounting for resources allocated for the review of human drug applications and supplements.

(8) The term "***adjustment factor***" applicable to a fiscal year is the Consumer Price Index for all urban consumers (all items; United States city average) for October of the preceding fiscal year divided by such Index for October 1996.

(9) The term "***person***" includes an affiliate thereof.

(10) The term "***active***", with respect to a commercial investigational new drug application, means such an application to which information was submitted during the relevant period.

(11) The term "***affiliate***" means a business entity that has a relationship with a second business entity if, directly or indirectly--

(A) one business entity controls, or has the power to control, the other business entity; or

(B) a third party controls, or has power to control, both of the business entities.

SEC. 736. [21 USC §379h] Authority to Assess and Use Drug Fees

Note: revisions were posted to this section in May 2008.

(a) [9] Types of fees. Beginning in fiscal year 2008, the Secretary shall assess and collect fees in accordance with this section as follows:

(1) Human drug application and supplement fee.

[9] See footnote for the beginning of section 735.

Chapter VII

(A) In general. Each person that submits, on or after September 1, 1992, a human drug application or a supplement shall be subject to a fee as follows:

(i) A fee established under subsection (c)(5) for a human drug application for which clinical data (other than bioavailability or bioequivalence studies) with respect to safety or effectiveness are required for approval.

(ii) A fee established under subsection (c)(5) for a human drug application for which clinical data with respect to safety or effectiveness are not required or a supplement for which clinical data (other than bioavailability or bioequivalence studies) with respect to safety or effectiveness are required. Such fee shall be half of the amount of the fee established under clause (i).

(B) Payment. The fee required by subparagraph (A) shall be due upon submission of the application or supplement.

(C) Exception for previously filed application or supplement. If a human drug application or supplement was submitted by a person that paid the fee for such application or supplement, was accepted for filing, and was not approved or was withdrawn (without a waiver), the submission of a human drug application or a supplement for the same product by the same person (or the person's licensee, assignee, or successor) shall not be subject to a fee under subparagraph (A).

(D) Refund of fee if application refused for filing or withdrawn before filing. The Secretary shall refund 75 percent of the fee paid under subparagraph (B) for any application or supplement which is refused for filingor withdrawn without a waiver before filing.

(E) Fees for applications previously refused for filing or withdrawn before filing. A human drug application or supplement that was submitted but was refused for filing, or was withdrawn before being accepted or refused for filing, shall be subject to the full fee under subparagraph (A) upon being resubmitted or filed over protest, unless the fee is waived or reduced under subsection (d).

(F) Exception for designated orphan drug or indication. . A human drug application for a prescription drug product that has been designated as a drug for a rare disease or condition pursuant to section 526 shall not be subject to a fee under subparagraph (A), unless the human drug application includes an indication for other than a rare disease or condition. A supplement proposing to include a new indication for a rare disease or condition in a human drug application shall not be subject to a fee under subparagraph (A), if the drug has been designated pursuant to section 526 as a drug for a rare disease or condition with regard to the indication proposed in such supplement.

(G) Refund of fee if application withdrawn. If an application or supplement is withdrawn after the application or supplement was filed, the Secretary may refund the fee or a portion of the fee if no substantial work was performed on the application or supplement after the application or supplement was filed. The Secretary shall have the sole discretion to refund a fee or a portion of the fee under this subparagraph. A determination by the Secretary concerning a refund under this paragraph shall not be reviewable.

(2) Prescription drug establishment fee.

(A) In general. Except as provided in subparagraphs (B) and (C), each person that--

(i) is named as the applicant in a human drug application; and

(ii) after September 1, 1992, had pending before the Secretary a human drug application or supplement,

shall be assessed an annual fee established under subsection (c)(5) for each prescription drug establishment listed in its approved human drug application as an establishment that manufactures the prescription drug product named in the application. The annual establishment fee shall be assessed in each fiscal year in which the prescription drug product named in the application is assessed a fee under paragraph (3) unless the prescription drug establishment listed in the application does not engage in the manufacture of the prescription drug product during the fiscal year. The establishment fee shall be payable on or before October 1 of each year. Each such establishment shall be assessed only one fee per establishment, notwithstanding the number of prescription drug products manufactured at the establishment. In the event an establishment is listed in a human drug application by more than one applicant, the establishment fee for the fiscal year shall be divided equally and assessed among the applicants whose prescription drug products are manufactured by the establishment during the fiscal year and assessed product fees under paragraph (3).

(B) Exception. If, during the fiscal year, an applicant initiates or causes to be initiated the manufacture of a prescription drug product at an establishment listed in its human drug application

(i) that did not manufacture the product in the previous fiscal year; and

(ii) for which the full establishment fee has been assessed in the fiscal year at a time before manufacture of the prescription drug product was begun; the applicant will not be assessed a share of the establishment fee for the fiscal year in which the manufacture of the product began.

(C) Special rules for positron emission tomography drugs.

(i) In general. Except as provided in clause (ii), each person who is named as the applicant in an approved human drug application for a positron emission tomography drug shall be subject under subparagraph (A) to one-sixth of an annual establishment fee with respect to each such establishment identified in the application as producing positron emission tomography drugs under the approved application.

(ii) Exception from annual establishment fee. Each person who is named as the applicant in an application described in clause (i) shall not be assessed an annual establishment fee for a fiscal year if the person certifies to the Secretary, at a time specified by the Secretary and using procedures specified by the Secretary, that--

(I) the person is a not-for-profit medical center that has only 1 establishment for the production of positron emission tomography drugs; and

(II) at least 95 percent of the total number of doses of each positron emission tomography drug produced by such establishment during such fiscal year will be used within the medical center.

(iii) Definition. For purposes of this subparagraph, the term "positron emission tomography drug" has the meaning given to the term "compounded positron emission tomography drug" in section 201(ii)], except that paragraph (1)(B) of such section shall not apply.

(3) Prescription drug product fee.

(A) In general. Except as provided in subparagraph (B), each person who is named as the applicant in a human drug application, and who, after September 1, 1992, had pending before the Secretary a human drug application or supplement, shall pay for each such prescription drug product the annual fee established under subsection (c)(5). Such fee shall be payable on or before October 1 of each year. Such fee shall be paid only once for each product for a fiscal year in which the fee is payable.

(B) Exception. A prescription drug product shall not be assessed a fee under subparagraph (A) if such product is identified on the list compiled under section 505(j)(7)(A) with a potency described in terms of per 100 mL, or if such product is the same product as another product approved under an application filed under section 505(b) or 505(j), under an abbreviated application filed under section 507 [10] (as in effect on the day before the date of enactment of the Food and Drug Administration Modernization Act of 1997 [enacted Nov. 21, 1997]), or under an abbreviated new drug application pursuant to regulations in effect prior to the implementation

[10] Section 507 was repealed by section 125(b)(1) of Public Law 105–115 (111 Stat. 2325).

of the Drug Price Competition and Patent Term Restoration Act of 1984.

(b) Fee revenue amounts.

(1) In general. For each of the fiscal years 2008 through 2012, fees under subsection (a) shall, except as provided in subsections (c), (d), (f), and (g), shall be established to generate a total revenue amount under such subsection that is equal to the sum of--

(A) $ 392,783,000; and

(B) an amount equal to the modified workload adjustment factor for fiscal year 2007 (as determined under paragraph (3)).

(2) Types of fees. Of the total revenue amount determined for a fiscal year under paragraph (1)--

(A) one-third shall be derived from fees under subsection (a)(1) (relating to human drug applications and supplements);

(B) one-third shall be derived from fees under subsection (a)(2) (relating to prescription drug establishments); and

(C) one-third shall be derived from fees under subsection (a)(3) (relating to prescription drug products).

(3) Modified workload adjustment factor for fiscal year 2007. For purposes of paragraph (1)(B), the Secretary shall determine the modified workload adjustment factor by determining the dollar amount that results from applying the methodology that was in effect under subsection (c)(2) for fiscal year 2007 to the amount $ 354,893,000, except that, with respect to the portion of such determination that is based on the change in the total number of commercial investigational new drug applications, the Secretary shall count the number of such applications that were active during the most recent 12-month period for which data on such submissions is available.

(4) Additional fee revenues for drug safety.

(A) In general. For each of the fiscal years 2008 through 2012, paragraph (1)(A) shall be applied by substituting the amount determined under subparagraph (B) for "$ 392,783,000".

(B) Amount determined. For each of the fiscal years 2008 through 2012, the amount determined under this subparagraph is the sum of--

(i) $ 392,783,000; plus

(ii)(I) for fiscal year 2008, $ 25,000,000;

(II) for fiscal year 2009, $ 35,000,000;

(III) for fiscal year 2010, $ 45,000,000;

(IV) for fiscal year 2011, $ 55,000,000; and

(V) for fiscal year 2012, $ 65,000,000.

(c) Adjustments.

(1) Inflation adjustment. For fiscal year 2009 and subsequent fiscal years, the revenues established in subsection (b) shall be adjusted by the Secretary by notice, published in the Federal Register, for a fiscal year to reflect the greater of--

(A) the total percentage change that occurred in the Consumer Price Index for all urban consumers (all items; U.S. city average) for the 12 month period ending June 30 preceding the fiscal year for which fees are being established, or

(B) the total percentage change for the previous fiscal year in basic pay under the General Schedule in accordance with section 5332 of title 5, United States Code [5 USC § 5332], as adjusted by any locality-based comparability payment pursuant to section 5304 of such title [5 USC § 5304] for Federal employees stationed in the District of Columbia, or

(C) the average annual change in the cost, per full-time equivalent position of the Food and Drug Administration, of all personnel compensation and benefits paid with respect to such positions for the first 5 years of the preceding 6 fiscal years.

The adjustment made each fiscal year by this subsection will be added on a compounded basis to the sum of all adjustments made each fiscal year after for fiscal year 2008 under this subsection.

(2) Workload adjustment. For fiscal year 2009 and subsequent fiscal years, after the fee revenues established in subsection (b) are adjusted for a fiscal year for inflation in accordance with paragraph (1), the fee revenues shall be adjusted further for such fiscal year to reflect changes in the workload of the Secretary for the process for the review of human drug applications. With respect to such adjustment:

(A) The adjustment shall be determined by the Secretary based on a weighted average of the change in the total number of human drug applications, (adjusted for changes in review activities, as described in the notice that the Secretary is required to publish in the Federal Register under this subparagraph), efficacy supplements, and manufacturing supplements submitted to the Secretary. The Secretary shall publish in the Federal Register the fee revenues and fees resulting from the adjustment and the supporting methodologies and the change in the total number of active commercial investigational new drug applications (adjusted for changes in review activities, as so described) during the most recent 12-month period for which data on such submissions is available.

(B) Under no circumstances shall the adjustment result in fee revenues for a fiscal year that are less than the fee revenues for the fiscal year established in subsection (b), as adjusted for inflation under paragraph (1). Any adjustment for changes in review activities made in setting fees and revenue amounts for fiscal year 2009 may not result in the total workload adjustment being more than 2 percentage points higher than it would have been in the absence of the adjustment for changes in review activities.

(C) The Secretary shall contract with an independent accounting firm to study the adjustment for changes in review activities applied in setting fees and revenue amounts for fiscal year 2009 and to make recommendations, if warranted, for future changes in the methodology for calculating the adjustment. After review of the recommendations, the Secretary shall, if warranted, make appropriate changes to the methodology, and the changes shall be effective for each of the fiscal years 2010 through 2012. The Secretary shall not make any adjustment for changes in review activities for any fiscal year after 2009 unless such study has been completed.

(3) Rent and rent-related cost adjustment. For fiscal year 2010 and each subsequent fiscal year, the Secretary shall, before making adjustments under paragraphs (1) and (2), decrease the fee revenue amount established in subsection (b) if actual costs paid for rent and rent-related expenses for the preceding fiscal year are less than estimates made for such year in fiscal year 2006. Any reduction made under this paragraph shall not exceed the amount by which such costs fall below the estimates made in fiscal year 2006 for such fiscal year, and shall not exceed $ 11,721,000 for any fiscal year.

(4) Final year adjustment.

(A) Increase in fees. For fiscal year 2012, the Secretary may, in addition to adjustments under this paragraph and paragraphs (1), (2), and (3), further increase the fee revenues and fees established in subsection (b) if such an adjustment is necessary to provide for not more than 3 months of operating reserves of carryover user fees for the process for the review of human drug applications for the first 3 months of fiscal year 2013. If such an adjustment is necessary, the rationale for the amount of the increase shall be contained in the annual notice establishing fee revenues and fees for fiscal year 2012. If the Secretary has carryover balances for such process in excess of 3 months of such operating reserves, the adjustment under this subparagraph shall not be made.

(B) Decrease in fees.

(i) In general. For fiscal year 2012, the Secretary may, in addition to adjustments under this paragraph and paragraphs (1), (2), and (3),

Chapter VII

decrease the fee revenues and fees established in subsection (b) by the amount determined in clause (ii), if, for fiscal year 2009 or 2010--

(I) the amount of the total appropriations for the Food and Drug Administration for such fiscal year (excluding the amount of fees appropriated for such fiscal year) exceeds the amount of the total appropriations for the Food and Drug Administration for fiscal year 2008 (excluding the amount of fees appropriated for such fiscal year), adjusted as provided under paragraph (1); and

(II) the amount of the total appropriations expended for the process for the review of human drug applications at the Food and Drug Administration for such fiscal year (excluding the amount of fees appropriated for such fiscal year) exceeds the amount of appropriations expended for the process for the review of human drug applications at the Food and Drug Administration for fiscal year 2008 (excluding the amount of fees appropriated for such fiscal year), adjusted as provided under paragraph (1).

(ii) Amount of decrease. The amount determined in this clause is the lesser of--

(I) the amount equal to the sum of the amounts that, for each of fiscal years 2009 and 2010, is the lesser of--

(aa) the excess amount described in clause (i)(II) for such fiscal year; or

(bb) the amount specified in subsection (b)(4)(B)(ii) for such fiscal year; or

(II) $ 65,000,000.

(iii) Limitations.

(I) Fiscal year condition. In making the determination under clause (ii), an amount described in subclause (I) of such clause for fiscal year 2009 or 2010 shall be taken into account only if subclauses (I) and (II) of clause (i) apply to such fiscal year.

(II) Relation to subparagraph (A). The Secretary shall limit any decrease under this paragraph if such a limitation is necessary to provide for the 3 months of operating reserves described in subparagraph (A).

(5) Annual fee setting. The Secretary shall, 60 days before the start of each fiscal year that begins after September 30, 2007, establish, for the next fiscal year, application, product, and establishment fees under subsection (a), based on

the revenue amounts established under subsection (b) and the adjustments provided under this subsection.

(6) Limit. The total amount of fees charged, as adjusted under this subsection, for a fiscal year may not exceed the total costs for such fiscal year for the resources allocated for the process for the review of human drug applications.

(d) Fee waiver or reduction.

(1) In general. The Secretary shall grant to a person who is named as the applicant in a human drug application a waiver from or a reduction of one or more fees assessed to that person under subsection (a) where the Secretary finds that--

(A) such waiver or reduction is necessary to protect the public health,

(B) the assessment of the fee would present a significant barrier to innovation because of limited resources available to such person or other circumstances,

(C) the fees to be paid by such person will exceed the anticipated present and future costs incurred by the Secretary in conducting the process for the review of human drug applications for such person, or

(D) the applicant involved is a small business submitting its first human drug application to the Secretary for review.

(2) Considerations. In determining whether to grant a waiver or reduction of a fee under paragraph (1), the Secretary shall consider only the circumstances and assets of the applicant involved and any affiliate of the applicant.

(3) Use of standard costs. In making the finding in paragraph (1)(C), the Secretary may use standard costs.

(4) Rules relating to small businesses.

(A) Definition. In paragraph (1)(D), the term "small business" means an entity that has fewer than 500 employees, including employees of affiliates, and that does not have a drug product that has been approved under a human drug application and introduced or delivered for introduction into interstate commerce.

(B) Waiver of application fee. The Secretary shall waive under paragraph (1)(D) the application fee for the first human drug application that a small business or its affiliate submits to the Secretary for review. After a small business or its affiliate is granted such a waiver, the small business or its affiliate shall pay--

(i) application fees for all subsequent human drug applications submitted to the Secretary for review in the same manner as an entity that does not qualify as a small business; and

(ii) all supplement fees for all supplements to human drug applications submitted to the Secretary for review in the same manner as an entity that does not qualify as a small business.

(e) Effect of failure to pay fees. A human drug application or supplement submitted by a person subject to fees under subsection (a) shall be considered incomplete and shall not be accepted for filing by the Secretary until all fees owed by such person have been paid.

(f) Limitations.

(1) In general. Fees under subsection (a) shall be refunded for a fiscal year beginning after fiscal year 1997 unless appropriations for salaries and expenses of the Food and Drug Administration for such fiscal year (excluding the amount of fees appropriated for such fiscal year) are equal to or greater than the amount of appropriations for the salaries and expenses of the Food and Drug Administration for the fiscal year 1997 (excluding the amount of fees appropriated for such fiscal year) multiplied by the adjustment factor applicable to the fiscal year involved.

(2) Authority. If the Secretary does not assess fees under subsection (a) during any portion of a fiscal year because of paragraph (1) and if at a later date in such fiscal year the Secretary may assess such fees, the Secretary may assess and collect such fees, without any modification in the rate, for human drug applications and supplements, prescription drug establishments, and prescription drug products at any time in such fiscal year notwithstanding the provisions of subsection (a) relating to the date fees are to be paid.

(g) Crediting and availability of fees.

(1) In general. Fees authorized under subsection (a) shall be collected and available for obligation only to the extent and in the amount provided in advance in appropriations Acts. Such fees are authorized to remain available until expended. Such sums as may be necessary may be transferred from the Food and Drug Administration salaries and expenses appropriation account without fiscal year limitation to such appropriation account for salaries and expenses with such fiscal year limitation. The sums transferred shall be available solely for the process for the review of human drug applications.

(2) Collections and appropriation acts.

(A) In general. The fees authorized by this section--

(i) shall be retained in each fiscal year in an amount not to exceed the amount specified in appropriation Acts, or otherwise made available for obligation, for such fiscal year, and

(ii) shall only be collected and available to defray increases in the costs of the resources allocated for the process for the review of human drug applications (including increases in such costs for an additional number of fulltime equivalent positions in the Department of Health and Human Services to be engaged in such process) over such costs, excluding costs paid from fees collected under this section, for fiscal year 1997 multiplied by the adjustment factor.

(B) Compliance. The Secretary shall be considered to have met the requirements of subparagraph (A)(ii) in any fiscal year if the costs funded by appropriations and allocated for the process for the review of human drug applications

(i) are not more than 3 percent below the level specified in subparagraph (A)(ii); or

(ii)(I) are more than 3 percent below the level specified in subparagraph (A)(ii), and fees assessed for the fiscal year following the subsequent fiscal year are decreased by the amount in excess of 3 percent by which such costs fell below the level specified in such subparagraph; and

(II) such costs are not more than 5 percent below the level specified in such subparagraph.

(3) Authorization of appropriations. For each of the fiscal years 2008 through 2012, there is authorized to be appropriated for fees under this section an amount equal to the total revenue amount determined under subsection (b) for the fiscal year, as adjusted or otherwise affected under subsection (c) and paragraph (4) of this subsection.

(4) Offset. If the sum of the cumulative amount of fees collected under this section for the fiscal years 2008 through 2010 and the amount of fees estimated to be collected under this section for fiscal year 2011 exceeds the cumulative amount appropriated under paragraph (3) for the fiscal years 2008 through 2011, the excess shall be credited to the appropriation account of the Food and Drug Administration as provided in paragraph (1), and shall be subtracted from the amount of fees that would otherwise be authorized to be collected under this section pursuant to appropriation Acts for fiscal year 2012.

(h) Collection of unpaid fees. In any case where the Secretary does not receive payment of a fee assessed under subsection (a) within 30 days after it is due, such fee shall be treated as a claim of the United States Government subject to subchapter II of chapter 37 of title 31, United States Code [31 USC §§ 3711 et seq.]

(i) Written requests for waivers, reductions, and refunds. To qualify for consideration for a waiver or reduction under subsection (d), or for a refund of any fee collected in accordance with subsection (a), a person shall submit to the Secretary a written request for such waiver, reduction, or refund not later than 180 days after such fee is due.

(j) Construction. This section may not be construed to require that the number of full-time equivalent positions in the Department of Health and Human Services, for officers, employers, and advisory committees not engaged in the process of the review of human drug applications, be reduced to offset the number of officers, employees, and advisory committees so engaged.

(k) Orphan drugs.

(1) Exemption. A drug designated under section 526 [21 USC § 360bb] for a rare disease or condition and approved under section 505 [21 USC § 355] or under section 351 of the Public Health Service Act [42 USC § 262] shall be exempt from product and establishment fees under this section, if the drug meets all of the following conditions:

(A) The drug meets the public health requirements contained in this Act [21 USC §§ 301 et seq.] as such requirements are applied to requests for waivers for product and establishment fees.

(B) The drug is owned or licensed and is marketed by a company that had less than $ 50,000,000 in gross worldwide revenue during the previous year.

(2) Evidence of qualification. An exemption under paragraph (1) applies with respect to a drug only if the applicant involved submits a certification that its gross annual revenues did not exceed $ 50,000,000 for the preceding 12 months before the exemption was requested.

SEC. 736A. [21 USC §379h–1] Fees Relating to Advisory Review of Prescription-Drug Television Advertising

Note: This section was added in May 2008.

(a) Types of direct-to-consumer television advertisement review fees. Beginning in fiscal year 2008, the Secretary shall assess and collect fees in accordance with this section as follows:

(1) Advisory review fee.

(A) In general. With respect to a proposed direct-to-consumer television advertisement (referred to in this section as a "DTC advertisement"), each person that on or after October 1, 2007, submits such an advertisement for advisory review by the Secretary prior to its initial public dissemination shall, except as provided in subparagraph (B), be subject to a fee established under subsection (c)(3).

(B) Exception for required submissions. A DTC advertisement that is required to be submitted to the Secretary prior to initial public dissemination is not subject to a fee under subparagraph (A) unless the sponsor designates the submission as a submission for advisory review.

(C) Notice to Secretary of number of advertisements. Not later than June 1 of each fiscal year, the Secretary shall publish a notice in the Federal Register requesting any person to notify the Secretary within 30 days of the number of DTC advertisements the person intends to submit for advisory review in the next fiscal year. Notwithstanding the preceding sentence, for fiscal year 2008, the Secretary shall publish such a notice in the Federal Register not later than 30 days after the date of the enactment of the Food and Drug Administration Amendments Act of 2007 [enacted Sept. 27, 2007].

(D) Payment.

(i) In general. The fee required by subparagraph (A) (referred to in this section as "an advisory review fee") shall be due not later than October 1 of the fiscal year in which the DTC advertisement involved is intended to be submitted for advisory review, subject to subparagraph (F)(i). Notwithstanding the preceding sentence, the advisory review fee for any DTC advertisement that is intended to be submitted for advisory review during fiscal year 2008 shall be due not later than 120 days after the date of the enactment of the Food and Drug Administration Amendments of 2007 [enacted Sept. 27, 2007] or an earlier date as specified by the Secretary.

(ii) Effect of submission. Notification of the Secretary under subparagraph (C) of the number of DTC advertisements a person intends to submit for advisory review is a legally binding commitment by that person to pay the annual advisory review fee for that number of submissions on or before October 1 of the fiscal year in which the advertisement is intended to be submitted. Notwithstanding the preceding sentence, the commitment shall be a legally binding commitment by that person to pay the annual advisory review fee for that number of submissions for fiscal year 2008 by the date specified in clause (i).

(iii) Notice regarding carryover submissions. In making a notification under subparagraph (C), the person involved shall in addition notify the Secretary if under subparagraph (F)(i) the person intends to submit a DTC advertisement for which the advisory review fee has already been paid. If the person does not so notify the Secretary, each DTC advertisement submitted by the person for advisory review in the fiscal year involved shall be subject to the advisory review fee.

(E) Modification of advisory review fee.

(i) Late payment. If a person has submitted a notification under subparagraph (C) with respect to a fiscal year and has not paid all advisory review fees due under subparagraph (D) not later than November 1 of such fiscal year (or, in the case of such a notification submitted with respect to fiscal year 2008, not later than 150 days after the date of the enactment of the Food and Drug Administration Amendments Act of 2007 [enacted Sept. 27, 2007] or an earlier date specified by the Secretary), the fees shall be regarded as late and an increase in the amount of fees applies in accordance with this clause, notwithstanding any other provision of this section. For such person, all advisory review fees for such fiscal year shall be due and payable 20 days before any direct-to-consumer advertisement is submitted to the Secretary for advisory review, and each such fee shall be equal to 150 percent of the fee that otherwise would have applied pursuant to subsection (c)(3).

(ii) Exceeding identified number of submissions. If a person submits a number of DTC advertisements for advisory review in a fiscal year that exceeds the number identified by the person under subparagraph (C), an increase in the amount of fees applies under this clause for each submission in excess of such number, notwithstanding any other provision of this section. For each such DTC advertisement, the advisory review fee shall be due and payable 20 days before the advertisement is submitted to the Secretary, and the fee shall be equal to 150 percent of the fee that otherwise would have applied pursuant to subsection (c)(3).

(F) Limits.

(i) Submissions. For each advisory review fee paid by a person for a fiscal year, the person is entitled to acceptance for advisory review by the Secretary of one DTC advertisement and acceptance of one resubmission for advisory review of the same advertisement. The advertisement shall be submitted for review in the fiscal year for which the fee was assessed, except that a person may carry over not more than one paid advisory review submission to the next fiscal year. Resubmissions may be submitted without regard to the fiscal year of the initial advisory review submission.

(ii) No refunds. Except as provided by subsections (d)(4) and (f), fees paid under this section shall not be refunded.

(iii) No waivers, exemptions, or reductions. The Secretary shall not grant a waiver, exemption, or reduction of any fees due or payable under this section.

(iv) Right to advisory review not transferable. The right to an advisory review under this paragraph is not transferable, except to a successor in interest.

(2) Operating reserve fee.

(A) In general. Each person that on or after October 1, 2007, is assessed an advisory review fee under paragraph (1) shall be subject to fee established under subsection (d)(2) (referred to in this section as an "operating reserve fee") for the first fiscal year in which an advisory review fee is assessed to such person. The person is not subject to an operating reserve fee for any other fiscal year.

(B) Payment. Except as provided in subparagraph (C), the operating reserve fee shall be due no later than--

(i) October 1 of the first fiscal year in which the person is required to pay an advisory review fee under paragraph (1); or

(ii) for fiscal year 2008, 120 days after the date of the enactment of the Food and Drug Administration Amendments Act of 2007 [enacted Sept. 27, 2007] or an earlier date specified by the Secretary.

(C) Late notice of submission. If, in the first fiscal year of a person's participation in the program under this section, that person submits any DTC advertisements for advisory review that are in excess of the number identified by that person in response to the Federal Register notice described in subsection (a)(1)(C), that person shall pay an operating reserve fee for each of those advisory reviews equal to the advisory review fee for each submission established under paragraph (1)(E)(ii). Fees required by this subparagraph shall be in addition to any fees required by subparagraph (A). Fees under this subparagraph shall be due 20 days before any DTC advertisement is submitted by such person to the Secretary for advisory review.

(D) Late payment.

(i) In general. Notwithstanding subparagraph (B), and subject to clause (ii), an operating reserve fee shall be regarded as late if the person required to pay the fee has not paid the complete operating reserve fee by--

(I) for fiscal year 2008, 150 days after the date of the enactment of the Food and Drug Administration Amendments Act of 2007 [enacted Sept. 27, 2007] or an earlier date specified by the Secretary; or

(II) in any subsequent year, November 1.

(ii) Complete payment. The complete operating reserve fee shall be due and payable 20 days before any DTC advertisement is submitted by such person to the Secretary for advisory review.

(iii) Amount. Notwithstanding any other provision of this section, an operating reserve fee that is regarded as late under this subparagraph shall be equal to 150 percent of the operating reserve fee that otherwise would have applied pursuant to subsection (d).

(b) Advisory review fee revenue amounts. Fees under subsection (a)(1) shall be established to generate revenue amounts of $ 6,250,000 for each of fiscal years 2008 through 2012, as adjusted pursuant to subsections (c) and (g)(4).

(c) Adjustments.

(1) Inflation adjustment. Beginning with fiscal year 2009, the revenues established in subsection (b) shall be adjusted by the Secretary by notice, published in the Federal Register, for a fiscal year to reflect the greater of--

(A) the total percentage change that occurred in the Consumer Price Index for all urban consumers (all items; U.S. city average), for the 12-month period ending June 30 preceding the fiscal year for which fees are being established;

(B) the total percentage change for the previous fiscal year in basic pay under the General Schedule in accordance with section 5332 of title 5, United States Code [5 USC § 5332], as adjusted by any locality-based comparability payment pursuant to section 5304 of such title [5 USC § 5304] for Federal employees stationed in the District of Columbia; or

(C) the average annual change in the cost, per full-time equivalent position of the Food and Drug Administration, of all personnel compensation and benefits paid with respect to such positions for the first 5 fiscal years of the previous 6 fiscal years.

The adjustment made each fiscal year by this subsection shall be added on a compounded basis to the sum of all adjustments made each fiscal year after fiscal year 2008 under this subsection.

(2) Workload adjustment. Beginning with fiscal year 2009, after the fee revenues established in subsection (b) are adjusted for a fiscal year for inflation in accordance with paragraph (1), the fee revenues shall be adjusted further for

such fiscal year to reflect changes in the workload of the Secretary with respect to the submission of DTC advertisements for advisory review prior to initial dissemination. With respect to such adjustment:

(A) The adjustment shall be determined by the Secretary based upon the number of DTC advertisements identified pursuant to subsection (a)(1)(C) for the upcoming fiscal year, excluding allowable previously paid carry over submissions. The adjustment shall be determined by multiplying the number of such advertisements projected for that fiscal year that exceeds 150 by $ 27,600 (adjusted each year beginning with fiscal year 2009 for inflation in accordance with paragraph (1)). The Secretary shall publish in the Federal Register the fee revenues and fees resulting from the adjustment and the supporting methodologies.

(B) Under no circumstances shall the adjustment result in fee revenues for a fiscal year that are less than the fee revenues established for the prior fiscal year.

(3) Annual fee setting for advisory review.

(A) In general. Not later than August 1 of each fiscal year (or, with respect to fiscal year 2008, not later than 90 days after the date of the enactment of the Food and Drug Administration Amendments Act of 2007 [enacted Sept. 27, 2007]), the Secretary shall establish for the next fiscal year the DTC advertisement advisory review fee under subsection (a)(1), based on the revenue amounts established under subsection (b), the adjustments provided under paragraphs (1) and (2), and the number of DTC advertisements identified pursuant to subsection (a)(1)(C), excluding allowable previously-paid carry over submissions. The annual advisory review fee shall be established by dividing the fee revenue for a fiscal year (as adjusted pursuant to this subsection) by the number of DTC advertisements so identified, excluding allowable previously-paid carry over submissions under subsection (a)(1)(F)(i).

(B) Fiscal year 2008 fee limit. Notwithstanding subsection (b) and the adjustments pursuant to this subsection, the fee established under subparagraph (A) for fiscal year 2008 may not be more than $ 83,000 per submission for advisory review.

(C) Annual fee limit. Notwithstanding subsection (b) and the adjustments pursuant to this subsection, the fee established under subparagraph (A) for a fiscal year after fiscal year 2008 may not be more than 50 percent more than the fee established for the prior fiscal year.

(D) Limit. The total amount of fees obligated for a fiscal year may not exceed the total costs for such fiscal year for the resources allocated for the process for the advisory review of prescription drug advertising.

(d) Operating reserves.

(1) In general. The Secretary shall establish in the Food and Drug Administration salaries and expenses appropriation account without fiscal year limitation a Direct-to-Consumer Advisory Review Operating Reserve, of at least $ 6,250,000 in fiscal year 2008, to continue the program under this section in the event the fees collected in any subsequent fiscal year pursuant to subsection (a)(1) do not generate the fee revenue amount established for that fiscal year.

(2) Fee setting. The Secretary shall establish the operating reserve fee under subsection (a)(2)(A) for each person required to pay the fee by multiplying the number of DTC advertisements identified by that person pursuant to subsection (a)(1)(C) by the advisory review fee established pursuant to subsection (c)(3) for that fiscal year, except that in no case shall the operating reserve fee assessed be less than the operating reserve fee assessed if the person had first participated in the program under this section in fiscal year 2008.

(3) Use of operating reserve. The Secretary may use funds from the reserves only to the extent necessary in any fiscal year to make up the difference between the fee revenue amount established for that fiscal year under subsections (b) and (c) and the amount of fees actually collected for that fiscal year pursuant to subsection (a)(1), or to pay costs of ending the program under this section if it is terminated pursuant to subsection (f) or not reauthorized beyond fiscal year 2012.

(4) Refund of operating reserves. Within 120 days after the end of fiscal year 2012, or if the program under this section ends early pursuant to subsection (f), the Secretary, after setting aside sufficient operating reserve amounts to terminate the program under this section, shall refund all amounts remaining in the operating reserve on a pro rata basis to each person that paid an operating reserve fee assessment. In no event shall the refund to any person exceed the total amount of operating reserve fees paid by such person pursuant to subsection (a)(2).

(e) Effect of failure to pay fees. Notwithstanding any other requirement, a submission for advisory review of a DTC advertisement submitted by a person subject to fees under subsection (a) shall be considered incomplete and shall not be accepted for review by the Secretary until all fees owed by such person under this section have been paid.

(f) Effect of inadequate funding of program.

(1) Initial funding. If on November 1, 2007, or 120 days after the date of the enactment of the Food and Drug Administration Amendments Act of 2007 [enacted Sept. 27, 2007], whichever is later, the Secretary has not received at least $ 11,250,000 in advisory review fees and operating reserve fees

combined, the program under this section shall not commence and all collected fees shall be refunded.

(2) Later fiscal years. Beginning in fiscal year 2009, if, on November 1 of the fiscal year, the combination of the operating reserves, annual fee revenues from that fiscal year, and unobligated fee revenues from prior fiscal years falls below $ 9,000,000, adjusted for inflation (as described in subsection (c)(1)), the program under this section shall terminate, and the Secretary shall notify all participants, retain any money from the unused advisory review fees and the operating reserves needed to terminate the program, and refund the remainder of the unused fees and operating reserves. To the extent required to terminate the program, the Secretary shall first use unobligated advisory review fee revenues from prior fiscal years, then the operating reserves, and finally, unused advisory review fees from the relevant fiscal year.

(g) Crediting and availability of fees.

(1) In general. Fees authorized under subsection (a) shall be collected and available for obligation only to the extent and in the amount provided in advance in appropriations Acts. Such fees are authorized to remain available until expended. Such sums as may be necessary may be transferred from the Food and Drug Administration salaries and expenses appropriation account without fiscal year limitation to such appropriation account for salaries and expenses with such fiscal year limitation. The sums transferred shall be available solely for the process for the advisory review of prescription drug advertising.

(2) Collections and appropriation acts.

(A) In general. The fees authorized by this section--

(i) shall be retained in each fiscal year in an amount not to exceed the amount specified in appropriation Acts, or otherwise made available for obligation for such fiscal year; and

(ii) shall be available for obligation only if the amounts appropriated as budget authority for such fiscal year are sufficient to support a number of full-time equivalent review employees that is not fewer than the number of such employees supported in fiscal year 2007.

(B) Review employees. For purposes of subparagraph (A)(ii), the term "full-time equivalent review employees" means the total combined number of full-time equivalent employees in--

(i) the Center for Drug Evaluation and Research, Division of Drug Marketing, Advertising, and Communications, Food and Drug Administration; and

(ii) the Center for Biologics Evaluation and Research, Advertising and Promotional Labeling Branch, Food and Drug Administration.

(3) Authorization of appropriations. For each of the fiscal years 2008 through 2012, there is authorized to be appropriated for fees under this section an amount equal to the total revenue amount determined under subsection (b) for the fiscal year, as adjusted pursuant to subsection (c) and paragraph (4) of this subsection, plus amounts collected for the reserve fund under subsection (d).

(4) Offset. Any amount of fees collected for a fiscal year under this section that exceeds the amount of fees specified in appropriation Acts for such fiscal year shall be credited to the appropriation account of the Food and Drug Administration as provided in paragraph (1), and shall be subtracted from the amount of fees that would otherwise be collected under this section pursuant to appropriation Acts for a subsequent fiscal year.

(h) Definitions. For purposes of this section:

(1) The term "***advisory review***" means reviewing and providing advisory comments on DTC advertisements regarding compliance of a proposed advertisement with the requirements of this Act [21 USC §§ 301 et seq.] prior to its initial public dissemination.

(2) The term "***advisory review fee***" has the meaning indicated for such term in subsection (a)(1)(D).

(3) The term "***carry over submission***" means a submission for an advisory review for which a fee was paid in one fiscal year that is submitted for review in the following fiscal year.

(4) The term "***direct-to-consumer television advertisement***" means an advertisement for a prescription drug product (as defined in section 735(3) [21 USC § 379g(3)]) intended to be displayed on any television channel for less than 3 minutes.

(5) The term "***DTC advertisement***" has the meaning indicated for such term in subsection (a)(1)(A).

(6) The term "***operating reserve fee***" has the meaning indicated for such term in subsection (a)(2)(A).

(7) The term "***person***" includes an individual, partnership, corporation, and association, and any affiliate thereof or successor in interest.

(8) The term "***process for the advisory review of prescription drug advertising***" means the activities necessary to review and provide advisory comments on DTC advertisements prior to public dissemination and, to the extent the Secretary has additional staff resources available under the program under this section that are not necessary for the advisory review of DTC advertisements, the activities necessary to review and provide advisory comments on other proposed advertisements and promotional material prior to public dissemination.

(9) The term "***resources allocated for the process for the advisory review of prescription drug advertising***" means the expenses incurred in connection with the process for the advisory review of prescription drug advertising for--

(A) officers and employees of the Food and Drug Administration, contractors of the Food and Drug Administration, advisory committees, and costs related to such officers, employees, and committees, and to contracts with such contractors;

(B) management of information, and the acquisition, maintenance, and repair of computer resources;

(C) leasing, maintenance, renovation, and repair of facilities and acquisition, maintenance, and repair of fixtures, furniture, scientific equipment, and other necessary materials and supplies;

(D) collection of fees under this section and accounting for resources allocated for the advisory review of prescription drug advertising; and

(E) terminating the program under this section pursuant to subsection (f)(2) if that becomes necessary.

(10) The term "***resubmission***" means a subsequent submission for advisory review of a direct-to-consumer television advertisement that has been revised in response to the Secretary's comments on an original submission. A resubmission may not introduce significant new concepts or creative themes into the television advertisement.

(11) The term "***submission for advisory review***" means an original submission of a direct-to-consumer television advertisement for which the sponsor voluntarily requests advisory comments before the advertisement is publicly disseminated.

SEC. 736B. [21 USC §379h–2] Reauthorization; Reporting Requirements

Note: This section was added in May 2008.

(a) Performance report. Beginning with fiscal year 2008, not later than 120 days after the end of each fiscal year for which fees are collected under this part [21 USC §§ 379g et seq.], the Secretary shall prepare and submit to the Committee on Energy and Commerce of the House of Representatives and the Committee on Health, Education, Labor, and Pensions of the Senate a report concerning the progress of the Food and Drug Administration in achieving the goals identified in the letters described in section 101(c) of the Food and Drug Administration Amendments Act of 2007 [21 USC § 379g note] during such fiscal year and the future plans of the Food and Drug Administration for meeting the goals. The report for a fiscal year shall include information on all previous cohorts for which the Secretary has not given a complete response on all human drug applications and supplements in the cohort.

(b) Fiscal report. Beginning with fiscal year 2008, not later than 120 days after the end of each fiscal year for which fees are collected under this part [21 USC §§ 379g et seq.], the Secretary shall prepare and submit to the Committee on Energy and Commerce of the House of Representatives and the Committee on Health, Education, Labor, and Pensions of the Senate a report on the implementation of the authority for such fees during such fiscal year and the use, by the Food and Drug Administration, of the fees collected for such fiscal year.

(c) Public availability. The Secretary shall make the reports required under subsections (a) and (b) available to the public on the Internet Web site of the Food and Drug Administration.

(d) Reauthorization.

(1) Consultation. In developing recommendations to present to the Congress with respect to the goals, and plans for meeting the goals, for the process for the review of human drug applications for the first 5 fiscal years after fiscal year 2012, and for the reauthorization of this part [21 USC §§ 379g et seq.] for such fiscal years, the Secretary shall consult with--

(A) the Committee on Energy and Commerce of the House of Representatives;

(B) the Committee on Health, Education, Labor, and Pensions of the Senate;

(C) scientific and academic experts;

(D) health care professionals;

(E) representatives of patient and consumer advocacy groups; and

(F) the regulated industry.

(2) Prior public input. Prior to beginning negotiations with the regulated industry on the reauthorization of this part [21 USC §§ 379g et seq.], the Secretary shall--

(A) publish a notice in the Federal Register requesting public input on the reauthorization;

(B) hold a public meeting at which the public may present its views on the reauthorization, including specific suggestions for changes to the goals referred to in subsection (a);

(C) provide a period of 30 days after the public meeting to obtain written comments from the public suggesting changes to this part [21 USC §§ 379g et seq.]; and

(D) publish the comments on the Food and Drug Administration's Internet Web site.

(3) Periodic consultation. Not less frequently than once every month during negotiations with the regulated industry, the Secretary shall hold discussions with representatives of patient and consumer advocacy groups to continue discussions of their views on the reauthorization and their suggestions for changes to this part [21 USC §§ 379g et seq.] as expressed under paragraph (2).

(4) Public review of recommendations. After negotiations with the regulated industry, the Secretary shall--

(A) present the recommendations developed under paragraph (1) to the Congressional committees specified in such paragraph;

(B) publish such recommendations in the Federal Register;

(C) provide for a period of 30 days for the public to provide written comments on such recommendations;

(D) hold a meeting at which the public may present its views on such recommendations; and

(E) after consideration of such public views and comments, revise such recommendations as necessary.

(5) Transmittal of recommendations. Not later than January 15, 2012, the Secretary shall transmit to the Congress the revised recommendations under paragraph (4), a summary of the views and comments received under such paragraph, and any changes made to the recommendations in response to such views and comments.

(6) Minutes of negotiation meetings.

(A) Public availability. Before presenting the recommendations developed under paragraphs (1) through (5) to the Congress, the Secretary shall make publicly available, on the public Web site of the Food and Drug Administration, minutes of all negotiation meetings conducted under this subsection between the Food and Drug Administration and the regulated industry.

(B) Content. The minutes described under subparagraph (A) shall summarize any substantive proposal made by any party to the negotiations as well as significant controversies or differences of opinion during the negotiations and their resolution.

SEC. 737. [21 USC §379i] Definitions

Note: revisions were posted to this section in May 2008.

[11] For purposes of this part:

(1) The term "***premarket application***" means-- (A) an application for approval of a device submitted under section 515(c) or section 351 of the Public Health Service Act [42 USC § 262]; or (B) a product development protocol described in section 515(f). Such term does not include a supplement, a premarket report, or a premarket notification submission.

(2) The term "***premarket report***" means a report submitted under section 515(c)(2).

(3) The term "***premarket notification submission***" means a report submitted under section 510(k).

(4)(A) The term "***supplement***", with respect to a panel-track supplement, a 180-day supplement, a real-time supplement, or an efficacy supplement, means a request to the Secretary to approve a change in a device for which--

(i) an application or report has been approved under section 515(d), or an application has been approved under section 351 of the Public Health Service Act [42 USC § 262]; or

(ii) a notice of completion has become effective under section 515(f).

(B) The term "***panel-track supplement***" means a supplement to an approved premarket application or premarket report under section 515 that requests a significant change in design or performance of the device, or a new indication for use of the device, and for which substantial clinical data are necessary to provide a reasonable assurance of safety and effectiveness.

(C) The term "***180-day supplement***" means a supplement to an approved premarket application or premarket report under section 515 that is not a panel-track supplement and requests a significant change in components, materials, design, specification, software, color additives, or labeling.

(D) The term "***real-time supplement***" means a supplement to an approved premarket application or premarket report under section 515 that requests a minor change to the device, such as a minor change to the

---

[11] Part 3 was added by title I of Public Law 107–250 (116 Stat. 1589). See section 102 of that title. Section 107 of that title provides as follows:

SEC. 107. SUNSET CLAUSE.
The amendments made by this title cease to be effective October 1, 2007, except that section 103 with respect to annual reports ceases to be effective January 31, 2008.

design of the device, software, sterilization, or labeling, and for which the applicant has requested and the agency has granted a meeting or similar forum to jointly review and determine the status of the supplement.

(E) The term "***efficacy supplement***" means a supplement to an approved premarket application under section 351 of the Public Health Service Act [42 USC § 262] that requires substantive clinical data.

(5) The term "***30-day notice***" means a notice under section 515(d)(6) that is limited to a request to make modifications to manufacturing procedures or methods of manufacture affecting the safety and effectiveness of the device.

(6) The term "***request for classification information***" means a request made under section 513(g) for information respecting the class in which a device has been classified or the requirements applicable to a device.

(7) The term "***annual fee***", for periodic reporting concerning a class III device, means the annual fee associated with periodic reports required by a premarket application approval order.

(8) The term "***process for the review of device applications***" means the following activities of the Secretary with respect to the review of premarket applications, premarket reports, supplements, and premarket notification submissions:

(A) The activities necessary for the review of premarket applications, premarket reports, supplements, and premarket notification submissions.

(B) The issuance of action letters that allow the marketing of devices or which set forth in detail the specific deficiencies in such applications, reports, supplements, or submissions and, where appropriate, the actions necessary to place them in condition for approval.

(C) The inspection of manufacturing establishments and other facilities undertaken as part of the Secretary's review of pending premarket applications, premarket reports, and supplements.

(D) Monitoring of research conducted in connection with the review of such applications, reports, supplements, and submissions.

(E) Review of device applications subject to section 351 of the Public Health Service Act [42 USC § 262] for an investigational new drug application under section 505(i) or for an investigational device exemption under section 520(g) and activities conducted in anticipation of the submission of such applications under section 505(i) or 520(g).

(F) The development of guidance, policy documents, or regulations to improve the process for the review of premarket applications, premarket reports, supplements, and premarket notification submissions.

(G) The development of voluntary test methods, consensus standards, or mandatory performance standards under section 514 in connection with the review of such applications, reports, supplements, or submissions and related activities.

(H) The provision of technical assistance to device manufacturers in connection with the submission of such applications, reports, supplements, or submissions.

(I) Any activity undertaken under section 513 or 515(i) in connection with the initial classification or reclassification of a device or under section 515(b) in connection with any requirement for approval of a device.

(J) Evaluation of postmarket studies required as a condition of an approval of a premarket application or premarket report under section 515 or a premarket application under section 351 of the Public Health Service Act.

(K) Compiling, developing, and reviewing information on relevant devices to identify safety and effectiveness issues for devices subject to premarket applications, premarket reports, supplements, or premarket notification submissions.

(9) The term "***costs of resources allocated for the process for the review of device applications***" means the expenses incurred in connection with the process for the review of device applications for--

(A) officers and employees of the Food and Drug Administration, contractors of the Food and Drug Administration, advisory committees, and costs related to such officers, employees, and committees and to contracts with such contractors;

(B) management of information, and the acquisition, maintenance, and repair of computer resources;

(C) leasing, maintenance, renovation, and repair of facilities and acquisition, maintenance, and repair of fixtures, furniture, scientific equipment, and other necessary materials and supplies; and

(D) collecting fees and accounting for resources allocated for the review of premarket applications, premarket reports, supplements, and submissions.

(10) The term "***adjustment factor***" applicable to a fiscal year is the Consumer Price Index for all urban consumers (all items; United States city average) for October of the preceding fiscal year divided by such Index for October 2001.

(11) The term "***person***" includes an affiliate thereof.

(12) The term "***affiliate***" means a business entity that has a relationship with a second business entity (whether domestic or international) if, directly or indirectly--

(A) one business entity controls, or has the power to control, the other business entity; or

(B) a third party controls, or has power to control, both of the business entities.

(13) The term "***establishment subject to a registration fee***" means an establishment that is required to register with the Secretary under section 510 and is one of the following types of establishments:

(A) Manufacturer. An establishment that makes by any means any article that is a device, including an establishment that sterilizes or otherwise makes such article for or on behalf of a specification developer or any other person.

(B) Single-use device reprocessor. An establishment that, within the meaning of section 201(ll)(2)(A) [21 USC § 321(ll)(2)(A)], performs additional processing and manufacturing operations on a single-use device that has previously been used on a patient.

(C) Specification developer. An establishment that develops specifications for a device that is distributed under the establishment's name but which performs no manufacturing, including an establishment that, in addition to developing specifications, also arranges for the manufacturing of devices labeled with another establishment's name by a contract manufacturer.

SEC. 738. [21 USC §379j] Authority to Assess and Use Device Fees

Note: revisions were posted to this section in September 2007.

(a) Types of fees.

(1) In general. Beginning in fiscal year 2008, the Secretary shall assess and collect fees in accordance with this section.

(2) Premarket application, premarket report, supplement, and submission fee, and annual fee for periodic reporting concerning a class III device.

(A) In general. Except as provided in subparagraph (B) and subsections (d) and (e), each person who submits any of the following, on or after October 1, 2002, shall be subject to a fee established under subsection (c)(1) for the fiscal year involved in accordance with the following:

(i) A premarket application.

(ii) For a premarket report, a fee equal to the fee that applies under clause (i).

(iii) For a panel track supplement, a fee equal to 75 percent of the fee that applies under clause (i).

(iv) For a 180-day supplement, a fee equal to 15 percent of the fee that applies under clause (i).

(v) For a real-time supplement, a fee equal to 7 percent of the fee that applies under clause (i).

(vi) a 30-day notice, a fee equal to 1.6 percent of the fee that applies under clause (i).

(vii) For an efficacy supplement, a fee equal to the fee that applies under clause (i).

(viii) For a premarket notification submission, a fee equal to 1.84 percent of the fee that applies under clause (i), subject to any adjustment under subsection (e)(2)(C)(ii).

(ix) For a request for classification information, a fee equal to 1.35 percent of the fee that applies under clause (i).

(x) For periodic reporting concerning a class III device, an annual fee equal to 3.5 percent of the fee that applies under clause (i).

(B) Exceptions.

(i) Humanitarian device exemption. An application under section 520(m) is not subject to any fee under subparagraph (A).

(ii) Further manufacturing use. No fee shall be required under subparagraph (A) for the submission of a premarket application under section 351 of the Public Health Service Act [42 USCS § 262] for a product licensed for further manufacturing use only.

(iii) State or Federal Government sponsors. No fee shall be required under subparagraph (A) for a premarket application, premarket report, supplement, or premarket notification submission submitted by a State or Federal Government entity unless the device involved is to be distributed commercially.

(iv) Premarket notifications by third parties. No fee shall be required under subparagraph (A) for a premarket notification submission reviewed by an accredited person pursuant to section 523.

(v) Pediatric conditions of use.

(I) In general. No fee shall be required under subparagraph (A) for a premarket application, premarket report, or premarket notification submission if the proposed conditions of use for the device involved are solely for a pediatric population. No fee shall be required under such subparagraph for a supplement if the sole purpose of the supplement is to propose conditions of use for a pediatric population.

(II) Subsequent proposal of adult conditions of use. In the case of a person who submits a premarket application or premarket report for which, under subclause (I), a fee under subparagraph (A) is not required, any supplement to such application that proposes conditions of use for any adult population is subject to the fee that applies under such subparagraph for a premarket application.

(C) Payment. The fee required by subparagraph (A) shall be due upon submission of the premarket application, premarket report, supplement, premarket notification submission, 30-day notice, request for classification information, or periodic reporting concerning a class III device. Applicants submitting portions of applications pursuant to section 515(c)(4) shall pay such fees upon submission of the first portion of such applications.

(D) Refunds.

(i) Application refused for filing. The Secretary shall refund 75 percent of the fee paid under subparagraph (A) for any application, report, or supplement that is refused for filing.

(ii) Application withdrawn before filing. The Secretary shall refund 75 percent of the fee paid under subparagraph (A) for any application, report, or supplement that is withdrawn prior to the filing decision of the Secretary.

(iii) Application withdrawn before first action. After receipt of a request for a refund of the fee paid under subparagraph (A) for a premarket application, premarket report, or supplement that is withdrawn after filing but before a first action, the Secretary may return some or all of the fee. The amount of refund, if any, shall be based on the level of effort already expended on the review of such application, report, or supplement. The Secretary shall have sole discretion to refund a fee or portion of the fee under this subparagraph. A determination by the Secretary concerning a refund under this paragraph shall not be reviewable.

(iv) Modular applications withdrawn before first action. The Secretary shall refund 75 percent of the application fee paid for an application submitted under section 515(c)(4) [21 USC § 360e(c)(4)] that is withdrawn before a second portion is submitted and before a first action on the first portion.

(v) Later withdrawn modular applications. If an application submitted under section 515(c)(4) [21 USC § 360e(c)(4)] is withdrawn after a second or subsequent portion is submitted but before any first action, the Secretary may return a portion of the fee. The amount of refund, if any, shall be based on the level of effort already expended on the review of the portions submitted.

(vi) Sole discretion to refund. The Secretary shall have sole discretion to refund a fee or portion of the fee under clause (iii) or (v). A determination by the Secretary concerning a refund under clause (iii) or (v) shall not be reviewable.

(3) Annual establishment registration fee.

(A) In general. Except as provided in subparagraph (B), each establishment subject to a registration fee shall be subject to a fee for each initial or annual registration under section 510 beginning with its registration for fiscal year 2008.

(B) Exception. No fee shall be required under subparagraph (A) for an establishment operated by a State or Federal governmental entity or an Indian tribe (as defined in the Indian Self Determination and Educational Assistance Act), unless a device manufactured by the establishment is to be distributed commercially.

(C) Payment. The fee required under subparagraph (A) shall be due once each fiscal year, upon the initial registration of the establishment or upon the annual registration under section 510.

(b) Fee amounts. Except as provided in subsections (c), (d), (e), and (h) the fees under subsection (a) shall be based on the following fee amounts:

Fee Type	Fiscal Year 2008	Fiscal Year 2009	Fiscal Year 2010	Fiscal Year 2011	Fiscal Year 2012
Premarket Application	$185,000	$200,725	$217,787	$236,298	$256,384
Establishment Registration	$1,706	$1,851	$2,008	$2,179	$2,364

(c) Annual fee setting.

(1) In general. The Secretary shall, 60 days before the start of each fiscal year after September 30, 2002, publish in the Federal Register fees under subsection (a). The fees established for fiscal year 2006 shall be based on a

premarket application fee of $ 259,600, and the fees established for fiscal year 2007 shall be based on a premarket application fee of $ 281,600.

(2) Adjustment.

(A) In general. When setting fees for fiscal year 2010, the Secretary may increase the fee under subsection (a)(3)(A) (applicable to establishments subject to registration) only if the Secretary estimates that the number of establishments submitting fees for fiscal year 2009 is fewer than 12,250. The percentage increase shall be the percentage by which the estimate of establishments submitting fees in fiscal year 2009 is fewer than 12,750, but in no case may the percentage increase be more than 8.5 percent over that specified in subsection (b) for fiscal year 2010. If the Secretary makes any adjustment to the fee under subsection (a)(3)(A) for fiscal year 2010, then such fee for fiscal years 2011 and 2012 shall be adjusted so that such fee for fiscal year 2011 is equal to the adjusted fee for fiscal year 2010 increased by 8.5 percent, and such fee for fiscal year 2012 is equal to the adjusted fee for fiscal year 2011 increased by 8.5 percent.

(B) Publication. For any adjustment made under subparagraph (A), the Secretary shall publish in the Federal Register the Secretary's determination to make the adjustment and the rationale for the determination.

(3) Limit. The total amount of fees charged, as adjusted under this subsection, for a fiscal year may not exceed the total costs for such fiscal year for the resources allocated for the process for the review of device applications.

(4) Supplement.

(A) In general. The Secretary may use unobligated carryover balances from fees collected in previous fiscal years to ensure that sufficient fee revenues are available in that fiscal year, so long as the Secretary maintains unobligated carryover balances of not less than 1 month of operating reserves for the first month of the next fiscal year.

(B) Notice to Congress. Not later than 14 days before the Secretary anticipates the use of funds described in subparagraph (A), the Secretary shall provide notice to the Committee on Health, Education, Labor, and Pensions and the Committee on Appropriations of the Senate and the Committee on Energy and Commerce and the Committee on Appropriations of the House of Representatives.

(d) Small businesses; fee waiver and fee reduction regarding premarket approval fees.

(1) In general. The Secretary shall grant a waiver of the fee required under subsection (a) for one premarket application, or one premarket report, where the Secretary finds that the applicant involved is a small business submitting its first premarket application to the Secretary, or its first premarket report,

respectively, for review. For the purposes of this paragraph, the term "small business" means an entity that reported $ 30,000,000 or less of gross receipts or sales in its most recent Federal income tax return for a taxable year, including such returns of all of its affiliates, partners, and parent firms. In addition, for subsequent premarket applications, premarket reports, and supplements where the Secretary finds that the applicant involved is a small business, the fees specified in clauses (i) through (vi) and clauses (vii), (ix), and (x) of subsection (a)(2)(A) may be paid at a reduced rate in accordance with paragraph (2)(C).

(2) Rules relating to premarket approval fees.

(A) Definition. For purposes of this paragraph, the term "***small business***" means an entity that reported $ 100,000,000 or less of gross receipts or sales in its most recent Federal income tax return for a taxable year, including such returns of all of its affiliates.

(B) Evidence of qualification.

(i) In general. An applicant shall pay the higher fees established by the Secretary each year unless the applicant submits evidence that it qualifies for a waiver of the fee or the lower fee rate.

(ii) Firms submitting tax returns to the United States Internal Revenue Service.The applicant shall support its claim that it meets the definition under subparagraph (A) by submission of a copy of its most recent Federal income tax return for a taxable year, and a copy of such returns of its affiliates, which show an amount of gross sales or receipts that is less than the maximum established in subparagraph (A). The applicant, and each of such affiliates, shall certify that the information provided is a true and accurate copy of the actual tax forms they submitted to the Internal Revenue Service. If no tax forms are submitted for any affiliate, the applicant shall certify that the applicant has no affiliates, partners, or parent firms, respectively.

(iii) Firms not submitting tax returns to the United States Internal Revenue Service. In the case of an applicant that has not previously submitted a Federal income tax return, the applicant and each of its affiliates shall demonstrate that it meets the definition under subparagraph (A) by submission of a signed certification, in such form as the Secretary may direct through a notice published in the Federal Register, that the applicant or affiliate meets the criteria for a small business and a certification, in English, from the national taxing authority of the country in which the applicant or, if applicable, affiliate is headquartered. The certification from such taxing authority shall bear the official seal of such taxing authority and shall provide the applicant's or affiliate's gross receipts or sales for the most recent year in both the local currency of such country and in United States dollars, the exchange rate used in converting such local currency to dollars, and the dates during which these receipts or sales were collected. The applicant shall also submit a statement signed by the head of the applicant's firm or by its chief financial officer that the applicant has submitted certifications for all of its affiliates, or that the applicant has no affiliates.

(C) Reduced fees. Where the Secretary finds that the applicant involved meets the definition under subparagraph (A), the fees established under subsection (c)(1) may be paid at a reduced rate of--

(i) 25 percent of the fee established under such subsection for a premarket application, a premarket report, or a supplement.

(ii) 50 percent of the fee established under such subsection for a 30-day notice or a request for classification information.

(D) Request for fee waiver or reduction. An applicant seeking a fee waiver or reduction under this subsection shall submit supporting information to the Secretary at least 60 days before the fee is required pursuant to subsection (a). The decision of the Secretary regarding whether an entity qualifies for such a waiver or reduction is not reviewable.

(e) Small businesses; fee reduction regarding premarket notification submissions.

(1) In general. For fiscal year 2008 and each subsequent fiscal year, where the Secretary finds that the applicant involved is a small business, the fee specified in subsection (a)(2)(A)(vii) may be paid at a reduced rate in accordance with paragraph (2)(C).

(2) Rules relating to premarket notification submissions.

(A) Definition. For purposes of this subsection, the term "***small business***" means an entity that reported $100,000,000 or less of gross receipts or sales in its most recent Federal income tax return for a taxable year, including such returns of all of its affiliates.

(B) Evidence of qualification.

(i) In general.An applicant shall pay the higher fees established by the Secretary each year unless the applicant submits evidence that it qualifies for the lower fee rate.

(ii) Firms submitting tax returns to the United States Internal Revenue Service.The applicant shall support its claim that it meets the definition under subparagraph (A) by submission of a copy of its most recent Federal income tax return for a taxable year, and a copy of such returns of its affiliates, which show an amount of gross sales or receipts that is less than the maximum established in

Chapter VII

subparagraph (A). The applicant, and each of such affiliates, shall certify that the information provided is a true and accurate copy of the actual tax forms they submitted to the Internal Revenue Service. If no tax forms are submitted for any affiliate, the applicant shall certify that the applicant has no affiliates.

(iii) Firms not submitting tax returns to the United States Internal Revenue Service. In the case of an applicant that has not previously submitted a Federal income tax return, the applicant and each of its affiliates shall demonstrate that it meets the definition under subparagraph (A) by submission of a signed certification, in such form as the Secretary may direct through a notice published in the Federal Register, that the applicant or affiliate meets the criteria for a small business and a certification, in English, from the national taxing authority of the country in which the applicant or, if applicable, affiliate is headquartered. The certification from such taxing authority shall bear the official seal of such taxing authority and shall provide the applicant's or affiliate's gross receipts or sales for the most recent year in both the local currency of such country and in United States dollars, the exchange rate used in converting such local currency to dollars, and the dates during which these receipts or sales were collected. The applicant shall also submit a statement signed by the head of the applicant's firm or by its chief financial officer that the applicant has submitted certifications for all of its affiliates, or that the applicant has no affiliates.

(C) Reduced fees. For fiscal year 2008 and each subsequent fiscal year, where the Secretary finds that the applicant involved meets the definition under subparagraph (A), the fee for a premarket notification submission may be paid at 50 percent of the fee that applies under subsection (a)(2)(A)(viii), and as established under subsection (c)(1).

(D) Request for reduction. An applicant seeking a fee reduction under this subsection shall submit supporting information to the Secretary at least 60 days before the fee is required pursuant to subsection (a). The decision of the Secretary regarding whether an entity qualifies for such a reduction is not reviewable.

(f) Effect of failure to pay fees.

(1) No acceptance of submissions. A premarket application, premarket report, supplement, premarket notification submission, 30-day notice, request for classification information, or periodic reporting concerning a class III device submitted by a person subject to fees under subsections (a)(2) and (a)(3) shall be considered incomplete and shall not be accepted by the Secretary until all fees owed by such person have been paid.

(2) No registration. Registration information submitted under section 510 by an establishment subject to a registration fee shall be considered incomplete and shall not be accepted by the Secretary until the registration fee under subsection (a)(3) owed for the establishment has been paid. Until the fee is paid and the registration is complete, the establishment is deemed to have failed to register in accordance with section 510.

(g) Conditions.

(1) Performance goals; termination of program. With respect to the amount that, under the salaries and expenses account of the Food and Drug Administration, is appropriated for a fiscal year for devices and radiological products , fees may not be assessed under subsection (a) for the fiscal year, and the Secretary is not expected to meet any performance goals identified for the fiscal year, if--

(A) the amount so appropriated for the fiscal year, excluding the amount of fees appropriated for the fiscal year, is more than 1 percent less than $ 205,720,000 multiplied by the adjustment factor applicable to such fiscal year ; or

(B) fees were not assessed under subsection (a) for the previous fiscal year

(2) Authority. If the Secretary does not assess fees under subsection (a) during any portion of a fiscal year because of paragraph (1) and if at a later date in such fiscal year the Secretary may assess such fees, the Secretary may assess and collect such fees, without any modification in the rate for premarket applications, supplements, premarket reports, premarket notification submissions, 30-day notices, requests for classification information, periodic reporting concerning a class III device, and establishment registrations at any time in such fiscal year, notwithstanding the provisions of subsection (a) relating to the date fees are to be paid.

(h) Crediting and availability of fees.

(1) In general. Fees authorized under subsection (a) shall be collected and available for obligation only to the extent and in the amount provided in advance in appropriation Acts. Such fees are authorized to be appropriated to remain available until expended. Such sums as may be necessary may be transferred from the Food and Drug Administration salaries and expenses appropriation account without fiscal year limitation to such appropriation account for salaries and expenses with such fiscal year limitation. The sums transferred shall be available solely for the process for the review of device applications.

(2) Collections and appropriation acts.

(A) In general. The fees authorized by this section--

Chapter VII

(i) shall be retained in each fiscal year in an amount not to exceed the amount specified in appropriation Acts, or otherwise made available for obligation, for such fiscal year, and

(ii) shall only be collected and available to defray increases in the costs of the resources allocated for the process for the review of device applications (including increases in such costs for an additional number of full-time equivalent positions in the Department of Health and Human Services to be engaged in such process) over such costs, excluding costs paid from fees collected under this section, for fiscal year 2002 multiplied by the adjustment factor.

(B) Compliance.

(i) In general. The Secretary shall be considered to have met the requirements of subparagraph (A)(ii) in any fiscal year if the costs funded by appropriations and allocated for the process for the review of device applications--

(I) are not more than 3 percent below the level specified in subparagraph (A)(ii); or

(II)(aa) are more than 3 percent below the level specified in subparagraph (A)(ii), and fees assessed for a subsequent fiscal year are decreased by the amount in excess of 3 percent by which such costs fell below the level specified in such subparagraph; and

(bb) such costs are not more than 5 percent below the level specified in such subparagraph.

(ii) More than 5 percent. To the extent such costs are more than 5 percent below the specified level in subparagraph (A)(ii), fees may not be collected under this section for that fiscal year.

(3) Authorizations of appropriations. There are authorized to be appropriated for fees under this section--

(A) $ 48,431,000 for fiscal year 2008;

(B) $ 52,547,000 for fiscal year 2009;

(C) $ 57,014,000 for fiscal year 2010;

(D) $ 61,860,000 for fiscal year 2011; and

(E) $ 67,118,000 for fiscal year 2012.

(4) Offset. If the cumulative amount of fees collected during fiscal years 2008, 2009, and 2010, added to the amount estimated to be collected for fiscal year 2011, which estimate shall be based upon the amount of fees received by the Secretary through June 30, 2011, exceeds the amount of fees specified in

aggregate in paragraph (3) for these four fiscal years, the aggregate amount in excess shall be credited to the appropriation account of the Food and Drug Administration as provided in paragraph (1), and shall be subtracted from the amount of fees that would otherwise be authorized to be collected under this section pursuant to appropriation Acts for fiscal year 2012.

(i) Collection of unpaid fees. In any case where the Secretary does not receive payment of a fee assessed under subsection (a) within 30 days after it is due, such fee shall be treated as a claim of the United States Government subject to subchapter II of chapter 37 of title 31, United States Code [31 USC §§ 3711 et seq.].

(j) Written requests for refunds. To qualify for consideration for a refund under subsection (a)(2)(D), a person shall submit to the Secretary a written request for such refund not later than 180 days after such fee is due.

(k) Construction. This section may not be construed to require that the number of full-time equivalent positions in the Department of Health and Human Services, for officers, employees, and advisory committees not engaged in the process of the review of device applications, be reduced to offset the number of officers, employees, and advisory committees so engaged.

SEC. 738A. [21 USC §379j–1] Reauthorization; Reporting Requirements

Note: This section was added in May 2008.

(a) Reports.

(1) Performance report. For fiscal years 2008 through 2012, not later than 120 days after the end of each fiscal year during which fees are collected under this part, the Secretary shall prepare and submit to the Committee on Health, Education, Labor, and Pensions of the Senate and the Committee on Energy and Commerce of the House of Representatives, a report concerning the progress of the Food and Drug Administration in achieving the goals identified in the letters described in section 201(c) of the Food and Drug Administration Amendments Act of 2007 during such fiscal year and the future plans of the Food and Drug Administration for meeting the goals. The report for a fiscal year shall include information on all previous cohorts for which the Secretary has not given a complete response on all device premarket applications and reports, supplements, and premarket notifications in the cohort.

(2) Fiscal report. For fiscal years 2008 through 2012, not later than 120 days after the end of each fiscal year during which fees are collected under this part, the Secretary shall prepare and submit to the Committee on Health, Education, Labor, and Pensions of the Senate and the Committee on Energy and Commerce of the House of Representatives, a report on the implementation

of the authority for such fees during such fiscal year and the use, by the Food and Drug Administration, of the fees collected during such fiscal year for which the report is made.

(3) Public availability. The Secretary shall make the reports required under paragraphs (1) and (2) available to the public on the Internet Web site of the Food and Drug Administration.

(b) Reauthorization.

(1) Consultation. In developing recommendations to present to Congress with respect to the goals, and plans for meeting the goals, for the process for the review of device applications for the first 5 fiscal years after fiscal year 2012, and for the reauthorization of this part for such fiscal years, the Secretary shall consult with--

(A) the Committee on Energy and Commerce of the House of Representatives;

(B) the Committee on Health, Education, Labor, and Pensions of the Senate;

(C) scientific and academic experts;

(D) health care professionals;

(E) representatives of patient and consumer advocacy groups; and

(F) the regulated industry.

(2) Prior public input. Prior to beginning negotiations with the regulated industry on the reauthorization of this part [21 USC §§ 379i et seq.], the Secretary shall--

(A) publish a notice in the Federal Register requesting public input on the reauthorization;

(B) hold a public meeting at which the public may present its views on the reauthorization, including specific suggestions for changes to the goals referred to in subsection (a)(1);

(C) provide a period of 30 days after the public meeting to obtain written comments from the public suggesting changes to this part [21 USC §§ 379i et seq.]; and

(D) publish the comments on the Food and Drug Administration's Internet Web site.

(3) Periodic consultation. Not less frequently than once every month during negotiations with the regulated industry, the Secretary shall hold discussions with representatives of patient and consumer advocacy groups to continue discussions of their views on the reauthorization and their suggestions for

changes to this part [21 USC §§ 379i et seq.] as expressed under paragraph (2).

(4) Public review of recommendations. After negotiations with the regulated industry, the Secretary shall--

(A) present the recommendations developed under paragraph (1) to the Congressional committees specified in such paragraph;

(B) publish such recommendations in the Federal Register;

(C) provide for a period of 30 days for the public to provide written comments on such recommendations;

(D) hold a meeting at which the public may present its views on such recommendations; and

(E) after consideration of such public views and comments, revise such recommendations as necessary.

(5) Transmittal of recommendations. Not later than January 15, 2012, the Secretary shall transmit to Congress the revised recommendations under paragraph (4), a summary of the views and comments received under such paragraph, and any changes made to the recommendations in response to such views and comments.

(6) Minutes of negotiation meetings.

(A) Public availability. Before presenting the recommendations developed under paragraphs (1) through (5) to the Congress, the Secretary shall make publicly available, on the public Web site of the Food and Drug Administration, minutes of all negotiation meetings conducted under this subsection between the Food and Drug Administration and the regulated industry.

(B) Content. The minutes described under subparagraph (A) shall summarize any substantive proposal made by any party to the negotiations as well as significant controversies or differences of opinion during the negotiations and their resolution.

SEC. 739. [21 USC §379j–11] Definitions

For purposes of this subchapter:

(1) The term "***animal drug application***" means an application for approval of any new animal drug submitted under section 512(b)(1). Such term does not include either a new animal drug application submitted under section 512(b)(2) or a supplemental animal drug application.

(2) The term "***supplemental animal drug application***" means

(A) a request to the Secretary to approve a change in an animal drug application which has been approved; or

(B) a request to the Secretary to approve a change to an application approved under section 512(c)(2) for which data with respect to safety or effectiveness are required.

(3) The term "***animal drug product***" means each specific strength or potency of a particular active ingredient or ingredients in final dosage form marketed by a particular manufacturer or distributor, which is uniquely identified by the labeler code and product code portions of the national drug code, and for which an animal drug application or a supplemental animal drug application has been approved.

(4) The term "***animal drug establishment***" means a foreign or domestic place of business which is at one general physical location consisting of one or more buildings all of which are within 5 miles of each other, at which one or more animal drug products are manufactured in final dosage form.

(5) The term "***investigational animal drug submission***" means

(A) the filing of a claim for an investigational exemption under section 512(j) for a new animal drug intended to be the subject of an animal drug application or a supplemental animal drug application, or

(B) the submission of information for the purpose of enabling the Secretary to evaluate the safety or effectiveness of an animal drug application or supplemental animal drug application in the event of their filing.

(6) The term "***animal drug sponsor***" means either an applicant named in an animal drug application, except for an approved application for which all subject products have been removed from listing under section 510, or a person who has submitted an investigational animal drug submission that has not been terminated or otherwise rendered inactive by the Secretary.

(7) The term "***final dosage form***" means, with respect to an animal drug product, a finished dosage form which is approved for administration to an animal without substantial further manufacturing. Such term includes animal drug products intended for mixing in animal feeds.

(8) The term "***process for the review of animal drug applications***" means the following activities of the Secretary with respect to the review of animal drug applications, supplemental animal drug applications, and investigational animal drug submissions:

(A) The activities necessary for the review of animal drug applications, supplemental animal drug applications, and investigational animal drug submissions.

(B) The issuance of action letters which approve animal drug applications or supplemental animal drug applications or which set forth in detail the specific deficiencies in animal drug applications, supplemental animal drug applications, or investigational animal drug submissions and, where appropriate, the actions necessary to place such applications, supplements or submissions in condition for approval.

(C) The inspection of animal drug establishments and other facilities undertaken as part of the Secretary's review of pending animal drug applications, supplemental animal drug applications, and investigational animal drug submissions.

(D) Monitoring of research conducted in connection with the review of animal drug applications, supplemental animal drug applications, and investigational animal drug submissions.

(E) The development of regulations and policy related to the review of animal drug applications, supplemental animal drug applications, and investigational animal drug submissions.

(F) Development of standards for products subject to review.

(G) Meetings between the agency and the animal drug sponsor.

(H) Review of advertising and labeling prior to approval of an animal drug application or supplemental animal drug application, but not such activities after an animal drug has been approved.

(9) The term "***costs of resources allocated for the process for the review of animal drug applications***" means the expenses incurred in connection with the process for the review of animal drug applications for

(A) officers and employees of the Food and Drug Administration, contractors of the Food and Drug Administration, advisory committees consulted with respect to the review of specific animal drug applications, supplemental animal drug applications, or investigational animal drug submissions, and costs related to such officers, employees, committees, and contractors, including costs for travel, education, and recruitment and other personnel activities,

(B) management of information, and the acquisition, maintenance, and repair of computer resources,

(C) leasing, maintenance, renovation, and repair of facilities and acquisition, maintenance, and repair of fixtures, furniture, scientific equipment, and other necessary materials and supplies, and

(D) collecting fees under section 740 and accounting for resources allocated for the review of animal drug applications, supplemental animal drug applications, and investigational animal drug submissions.

(10) The term "***adjustment factor***" applicable to a fiscal year refers to the formula set forth in section 735(8) with the base or comparator year being 2003.

(11) The term "***affiliate***" refers to the definition set forth in section 735(9).

SEC. 740. [21 USC §379j–12] Authority to Assess and Use Animal Drug Fees.

(a) TYPES OF FEES. Beginning in fiscal year 2004, the Secretary shall assess and collect fees in accordance with this section as follows:

(1) ANIMAL DRUG APPLICATION AND SUPPLEMENT FEE.

(A) IN GENERAL. Each person that submits, on or after September 1, 2003 , an animal drug application or a supplemental animal drug application shall be subject to a fee as follows:

(i) A fee established in subsection (b) for an animal drug application; and

(ii) A fee established in subsection (b) for a supplemental animal drug application for which safety or effectiveness data are required, in an amount that is equal to 50 percent of the amount of the fee under clause (i).

(B) PAYMENT. The fee required by subparagraph (A) shall be due upon submission of the animal drug application or supplemental animal drug application.

(C) EXCEPTION FOR PREVIOUSLY FILED APPLICATION OR SUPPLEMENT. If an animal drug application or a supplemental animal drug application was submitted by a person that paid the fee for such application or supplement, was accepted for filing, and was not approved or was withdrawn (without a waiver or refund), the submission of an animal drug application or a supplemental animal drug application for the same product by the same person (or the person's licensee, assignee, or successor) shall not be subject to a fee under subparagraph (A).

(D) REFUND OF FEE IF APPLICATION REFUSED FOR FILING. The Secretary shall refund 75 percent of the fee paid under subparagraph (B) for any animal drug application or supplemental animal drug application which is refused for filing.

(E) REFUND OF FEE IF APPLICATION WITHDRAWN. If an animal drug application or a supplemental animal drug application is withdrawn after the application or supplement was filed, the Secretary may refund the fee or portion of the fee paid under subparagraph (B) if no substantial work was performed on the application or supplement after the application or supplement was filed. The Secretary shall have the sole discretion to refund the fee under this paragraph. A determination by the Secretary concerning a refund under this paragraph shall not be reviewable.

(2) ANIMAL DRUG PRODUCT FEE. Each person

(A) who is named as the applicant in an animal drug application or supplemental animal drug application for an animal drug product which has been submitted for listing under section 510, and

(B) who, after September 1, 2003 , had pending before the Secretary an animal drug application or supplemental animal drug application; shall pay for each such animal drug product the annual fee established in subsection (b). Such fee shall be payable for the fiscal year in which the animal drug product is first submitted for listing under section 510, or is submitted for relisting under section 510 if the animal drug product has been withdrawn from listing and relisted. After such fee is paid for that fiscal year, such fee shall be payable on or before January 31 of each year. Such fee shall be paid only once for each animal drug product for a fiscal year in which the fee is payable.

(3) ANIMAL DRUG ESTABLISHMENT FEE. Each person

(A) who owns or operates, directly or through an affiliate, an animal drug establishment, and

(B) who is named as the applicant in an animal drug application or supplemental animal drug application for an animal drug product which has been submitted for listing under section 510, and

(C) who, after September 1, 2003, had pending before the Secretary an animal drug application or supplemental animal drug application, shall be assessed an annual fee established in subsection (b) for each animal drug establishment listed in its approved animal drug application as an establishment that manufactures the animal drug product named in the application. The annual establishment fee shall be assessed in each fiscal year in which the animal drug product named in the application is assessed a fee under paragraph (2) unless the animal drug establishment listed in the application does not engage in the manufacture of the animal drug product during the fiscal year. The fee shall be paid on or before January 31 of each year. The establishment shall be assessed only one fee per fiscal year under this section: Provided, however, That where a single establishment manufactures both animal drug products and prescription drug products, as defined in section 735(3), such establishment shall be assessed both the animal drug establishment fee and the prescription drug establishment fee, as set forth in section 736(a)(2), within a single fiscal year.

(4) ANIMAL DRUG SPONSOR FEE. Each person

(A) who meets the definition of an animal drug sponsor within a fiscal year; and

(B) who, after September 1, 2003 , had pending before the Secretary an animal drug application, a supplemental animal drug application, or an investigational animal drug submission, shall be assessed an annual fee established under subsection (b). The fee shall be paid on or before January 31 of each year. Each animal drug sponsor shall pay only one such fee each fiscal year.

(b) FEE AMOUNTS. Except as provided in subsection (a)(1) and subsections (c), (d), (f), and (g), the fees required under subsection (a) shall be established to generate fee revenue amounts as follows:

(1) TOTAL FEE REVENUES FOR APPLICATION AND SUPPLEMENT FEES. The total fee revenues to be collected in animal drug application fees under subsection (a)(1)(A)(i) and supplemental animal drug application fees under subsection (a)(1)(A)(ii) shall be $1,250,000 in fiscal year 2004, $2,000,000 in fiscal year 2005, and $2,500,000 in fiscal years 2006, 2007, and 2008.

(2) TOTAL FEE REVENUES FOR PRODUCT FEES. The total fee revenues to be collected in product fees under subsection (a)(2) shall be $1,250,000 in fiscal year 2004, $2,000,000 in fiscal year 2005, and $2,500,000 in fiscal years 2006, 2007, and 2008. PUBL130

(3) TOTAL FEE REVENUES FOR ESTABLISHMENT FEES. The total fee revenues to be collected in establishment fees under subsection (a)(3) shall be $1,250,000 in fiscal year 2004, $2,000,000 in fiscal year 2005, and $2,500,000 in fiscal years 2006, 2007, and 2008.

(4) TOTAL FEE REVENUES FOR SPONSOR FEES. The total fee revenues to be collected in sponsor fees under subsection(a)(4) shall be $1,250,000 in fiscal year 2004, $2,000,000 in fiscal year 2005, and $2,500,000 in fiscal years 2006, 2007, and 2008.

(c) ADJUSTMENTS.

(1) INFLATION ADJUSTMENT. The revenues established in subsection (b) shall be adjusted by the Secretary by notice, published in the Federal Register, for a fiscal year to reflect the greater of

(A) the total percentage change that occurred in the Consumer Price Index for all urban consumers (all items; United States city average) for the 12-month period ending June 30 preceding the fiscal year for which fees are being established; or

(B) the total percentage change for the previous fiscal year in basic pay under the General Schedule in accordance with section 5332 of title 5, United States Code, as adjusted by any locality-based comparability payment pursuant to section 5304 of such title for Federal employees stationed in the District of Columbia. The adjustment made each fiscal year by this subsection will be added on a compounded basis to the sum of all adjustments made each fiscal year after fiscal year 2004 under this subsection.

(2) WORKLOAD ADJUSTMENT. After the fee revenues are adjusted for inflation in accordance with paragraph (1), the fee revenues shall be further adjusted each fiscal year after fiscal year 2004 to reflect changes in review workload. With respect to such adjustment:

(A) This adjustment shall be determined by the Secretary based on a weighted average of the change in the total number of animal drug applications, supplemental animal drug applications for which data with respect to safety or effectiveness are required, manufacturing supplemental animal drug applications, investigational animal drug study submissions, and investigational animal drug protocol submissions submitted to the Secretary. The Secretary shall publish in the Federal Register the fees resulting from this adjustment and the supporting methodologies.

(B) Under no circumstances shall this workload adjustment result in fee revenues for a fiscal year that are less than the fee revenues for that fiscal year established in subsection (b), as adjusted for inflation under paragraph (1).

(3) FINAL YEAR ADJUSTMENT. For fiscal year 2008, the Secretary may further increase the fees to provide for up to 3 months of operating reserves of carryover user fees for the process for the review of animal drug applications for the first 3 months of fiscal year 2009. If the Food and Drug Administration has carryover balances for the process for the review of animal drug applications in excess of 3 months of such operating reserves, then this adjustment will not be made. If this adjustment is necessary, then the rationale for the amount of the increase shall be contained in the annual notice setting fees for fiscal year 2008.

(4) ANNUAL FEE SETTING. The Secretary shall establish, 60 days before the start of each fiscal year beginning after September 30, 2003, for that fiscal year, animal drug application fees, supplemental animal drug application fees, animal drug sponsor fees, animal drug establishment fees, and animal drug product fees based on the revenue amounts established under subsection (b) and the adjustments provided under this subsection.

(5) LIMIT. The total amount of fees charged, as adjusted under this subsection, for a fiscal year may not exceed the total costs for such fiscal year for the resources allocated for the process for the review of animal drug applications.

(d) FEE WAIVER OR REDUCTION.

(1) IN GENERAL. The Secretary shall grant a waiver from or a reduction of 1 or more fees assessed under subsection (a) where the Secretary finds that

(A) the assessment of the fee would present a significant barrier to innovation because of limited resources available to such person or other circumstances,

(B) the fees to be paid by such person will exceed the anticipated present and future costs incurred by the Secretary in conducting the process for the review of animal drug applications for such person,

(C) the animal drug application or supplemental animal drug application is intended solely to provide for use of the animal drug in

(i) a Type B medicated feed (as defined in section 558.3(b)(3) of title 21, Code of Federal Regulations (or any successor regulation)) intended for use in the manufacture of Type C free-choice medicated feeds, or

(ii) a Type C free-choice medicated feed (as defined in section 558.3(b)(4) of title 21, Code of Federal Regulations (or any successor regulation)),

(D) the animal drug application or supplemental animal drug application is intended solely to provide for a minor use or minor species indication, or

(E) the sponsor involved is a small business submitting its first animal drug application to the Secretary for review.

(2) USE OF STANDARD COSTS. In making the finding in paragraph (1)(B), the Secretary may use standard costs.

(3) RULES FOR SMALL BUSINESSES.

(A) DEFINITION. In paragraph (1)(E), the term 'small business' means an entity that has fewer than 500 employees, including employees of affiliates.

(B) WAIVER OF APPLICATION FEE. The Secretary shall waive under paragraph (1)(E) the application fee for the first animal drug application that a small business or its affiliate submits to the Secretary for review. After a small business or its affiliate is granted such a waiver, the small business or its affiliate shall pay application fees for all subsequent animal drug applications and supplemental animal drug applications for which safety or effectiveness data are required in the same manner as an entity that does not qualify as a small business.

(C) CERTIFICATION. The Secretary shall require any person who applies for a waiver under paragraph (1)(E) to certify their qualification for the waiver. The Secretary shall periodically publish in the Federal Register a list of persons making such certifications.

(e) EFFECT OF FAILURE TO PAY FEES. An animal drug application or supplemental animal drug application submitted by a person subject to fees under subsection (a) shall be considered incomplete and shall not be accepted for filing by the Secretary until all fees owed by such person have been paid. An investigational animal drug submission under section 739(5)(B) that is submitted by a person subject to fees under subsection (a) shall be considered incomplete and shall not be accepted for review by the Secretary until all fees owed by such person have been paid. The Secretary may discontinue review of any animal drug application, supplemental animal drug application or investigational animal drug submission from a person if such person has not submitted for payment all fees owed under this section by 30 days after the date upon which they are due.

(f) ASSESSMENT OF FEES.

(1) LIMITATION. Fees may not be assessed under subsection (a) for a fiscal year beginning after fiscal year 2003unless appropriations for salaries and expenses of the Food and Drug Administration for such fiscal year (excluding the amount of fees appropriated for such fiscal year) are equal to or greater than the amount of appropriations for the salaries and expenses of the Food and Drug Administration for the fiscal year 2003 (excluding the amount of fees appropriated for such fiscal year) multiplied by the adjustment factor applicable to the fiscal year involved.

(2) AUTHORITY. If the Secretary does not assess fees under subsection (a) during any portion of a fiscal year because of paragraph (1) and if at a later date in such fiscal year the Secretary may assess such fees, the Secretary may assess and collect such fees, without any modification in the rate, for animal drug applications, supplemental animal drug applications, investigational animal drug submissions, animal drug sponsors, animal drug establishments and animal drug products at any time in such fiscal year notwithstanding the provisions of subsection (a) relating to the date fees are to be paid.

(g) CREDITING AND AVAILABILITY OF FEES.

(1) IN GENERAL. Fees authorized under subsection (a) shall be collected and available for obligation only to the extent and in the amount provided in advance in appropriations Acts. Such fees are authorized to be appropriated to remain available until expended. Such sums as may be necessary may be transferred from the Food and Drug Administration salaries and expenses

appropriation account without fiscal year limitation to such appropriation account for salary and expenses with such fiscal year limitation. The sums transferred shall be available solely for the process for the review of animal drug applications.

(2) COLLECTIONS AND APPROPRIATION ACTS.

(A) IN GENERAL. The fees authorized by this section

(i) shall be retained in each fiscal year in an amount not to exceed the amount specified in appropriation Acts, or otherwise made available for obligation for such fiscal year, and

(ii) shall only be collected and available to defray increases in the costs of the resources allocated for the process for the review of animal drug applications (including increases in such costs for an additional number of full-time equivalent positions in the Department of Health and Human Services to be engaged in such process) over such costs, excluding costs paid from fees collected under this section, for fiscal year 2003 multiplied by the adjustment factor.

(B) COMPLIANCE. The Secretary shall be considered to have met the requirements of subparagraph (A)(ii) in any fiscal year if the costs funded by appropriations and allocated for the process for the review of animal drug applications

(i) are not more than 3 percent below the level specified in subparagraph (A)(ii); or

(ii)(I) are more than 3 percent below the level specified in subparagraph (A)(ii), and fees assessed for the fiscal year following the subsequent fiscal year are decreased by the amount in excess of 3 percent by which such costs fell below the level specified in subparagraph (A)(ii); and

(II) such costs are not more than 5 percent below the level specified in subparagraph (A)(ii).

(3) AUTHORIZATION OF APPROPRIATIONS. There are authorized to be appropriated for fees under this section

(A) $5,000,000 for fiscal year 2004;

(B) $8,000,000 for fiscal year 2005;

(C) $10,000,000 for fiscal year 2006;

(D) $10,000,000 for fiscal year 2007; and

(E) $10,000,000 for fiscal year 2008; as adjusted to reflect adjustments in the total fee revenues made under this section and changes in the total amounts collected by animal drug application fees, supplemental animal drug application fees, animal drug sponsor fees, animal drug establishment fees, and animal drug product fees.

(4) OFFSET. Any amount of fees collected for a fiscal year under this section that exceeds the amount of fees specified in appropriations Acts for such fiscal year shall be credited to the appropriation account of the Food and Drug Administration as provided in paragraph (1), and shall be subtracted from the amount of fees that would otherwise be authorized to be collected under this section pursuant to appropriation Acts for a subsequent fiscal year.

(h) COLLECTION OF UNPAID FEES. In any case where the Secretary does not receive payment of a fee assessed under subsection (a) within 30 days after it is due, such fee shall be treated as a claim of the United States Government subject to subchapter II of chapter 37 of title 31, United States Code.

(i) WRITTEN REQUESTS FOR WAIVERS, REDUCTIONS, AND REFUNDS. To qualify for consideration for a waiver or reduction under subsection (d), or for a refund of any fee collected in accordance with subsection (a), a person shall submit to the Secretary a written request for such waiver, reduction, or refund not later than 180 days after such fee is due.

(j) CONSTRUCTION. This section may not be construed to require that the number of full-time equivalent positions in the Department of Health and Human Services, for officers, employees, and advisory committees not engaged in the process of the review of animal drug applications, be reduced to offset the number of officers, employees, and advisory committees so engaged.

(k) ABBREVIATED NEW ANIMAL DRUG APPLICATIONS. The Secretary shall

(1) to the extent practicable, segregate the review of abbreviated new animal drug applications from the process for the review of animal drug applications, and

(2) adopt other administrative procedures to ensure that review times of abbreviated new animal drug applications do not increase from their current level due to activities under the user fee program.

Subchapter D — Information and Education

SEC. 741. [21 USC §379k] Information System

The Secretary shall establish and maintain an information system to track the status and progress of each application or submission (including a petition, notification, or other similar form of request) submitted to the Food and Drug Administration requesting agency action.

SEC. 742. [21 USC §379l] Education

Note: revisions were posted to this section in June 2008.

(a) In general. The Secretary shall conduct training and education programs for the employees of the Food and Drug Administration relating to the regulatory responsibilities and policies established by this Act, including programs for—

(1) scientific training;

(2) training to improve the skill of officers and employees authorized to conduct inspections under section 704;

(3) training to achieve product specialization in such inspections; and

(4) training in administrative process and procedure and integrity issues.

(b) Intramural fellowships and other training programs. The Secretary, acting through the Commissioner, may, through fellowships and other training programs, conduct and support intramural research training for predoctoral and postdoctoral scientists and physicians. Any such fellowships and training programs under this section or under section 770(d)(2)(A)(ix) may include provision by such scientists and physicians of services on a voluntary and uncompensated basis, as the Secretary determines appropriate. Such scientists and physicians shall be subject to all legal and ethical requirements otherwise applicable to officers or employees of the Department of Health and Human Services.

Subchapter E — Environmental Impact Review

SEC. 746. [21 USC §379o] Environmental Impact

Notwithstanding any other provision of law, an environmental impact statement prepared in accordance with the regulations published in part 25 of title 21, Code of Federal Regulations (as in effect on August 31, 1997) in connection with an action carried out under (or a recommendation or report relating to) this Act, shall be considered to meet the requirements for a detailed statement under section 102(2)(C) of the National Environmental Policy Act of 1969 (42 U.S.C. 4332(2)(C)).

Subchapter F — National Uniformity for Nonprescription Drugs and Preemption for Labeling or Packaging of Cosmetics

SEC. 751. [21 USC §379r] National Uniformity for Nonprescription Drugs

(a) IN GENERAL.—Except as provided in subsection (b), (c)(1), (d), (e), or (f), no State or political subdivision of a State may establish or continue in effect any requirement—

(1) that relates to the regulation of a drug that is not subject to the requirements of section 503(b)(1) or 503(f)(1)(A); and

(2) that is different from or in addition to, or that is otherwise not identical with, a requirement under this Act, the Poison Prevention Packaging Act of 1970 (15 U.S.C. 1471 et seq.), or the Fair Packaging and Labeling Act (15 U.S.C. 1451 et seq.).

(b) EXEMPTION.—

(1) IN GENERAL.—Upon application of a State or political subdivision thereof, the Secretary may by regulation, after notice and opportunity for written and oral presentation of views, exempt from subsection (a), under such conditions as may be prescribed in such regulation, a State or political subdivision requirement that—

(A) protects an important public interest that would otherwise be unprotected, including the health and safety of children;

(B) would not cause any drug to be in violation of any applicable requirement or prohibition under Federal law; and

(C) would not unduly burden interstate commerce.

(2) TIMELY ACTION.—The Secretary shall make a decision on the exemption of a State or political subdivision requirement under paragraph (1) not later than 120 days after receiving the application of the State or political subdivision under paragraph(1).

(c) SCOPE.—

(1) IN GENERAL.—This section shall not apply to—

(A) any State or political subdivision requirement that relates to the practice of pharmacy; or

(B) any State or political subdivision requirement that a drug be dispensed only upon the prescription of a practitioner licensed by law to administer such drug.

(2) SAFETY OR EFFECTIVENESS.—For purposes of subsection (a), a requirement that relates to the regulation of a drug shall be deemed to include any requirement relating to public information or any other form of public communication relating to a warning of any kind for a drug.

(d) EXCEPTIONS.—

(1) IN GENERAL.—In the case of a drug described in subsection (a)(1) that is not the subject of an application approved under section 505 or section 507 (as in effect on the day before the date of enactment of the Food and Drug Administration Modernization Act of 1997) or a final regulation promulgated

by the Secretary establishing conditions under which the drug is generally recognized as safe and effective and not misbranded, subsection (a) shall apply only with respect to a requirement of a State or political subdivision of a State that relates to the same subject as, but is different from or in addition to, or that is otherwise not identical with—

(A) a regulation in effect with respect to the drug pursuant to a statute described in subsection (a)(2); or

(B) any other requirement in effect with respect to the drug pursuant to an amendment to such a statute made on or after the date of enactment of the Food and Drug Administration Modernization Act of 1997.

(2) STATE INITIATIVES.—This section shall not apply to a State requirement adopted by a State public initiative or referendum enacted prior to September 1, 1997 .

(e) NO EFFECT ON PRODUCT LIABILITY LAW.—Nothing in this section shall be construed to modify or otherwise affect any action or the liability of any person under the product liability law of any State.

(f) STATE ENFORCEMENT AUTHORITY.—Nothing in this section shall prevent a State or political subdivision thereof from enforcing, under any relevant civil or other enforcement authority, a requirement that is identical to a requirement of this Act.

SEC. 752. [21 USC §379s] Preemption for Labeling or Packaging of Cosmetics

(a) IN GENERAL.—Except as provided in subsection (b), (d), or (e), no State or political subdivision of a State may establish or continue in effect any requirement for labeling or packaging of a cosmetic that is different from or in addition to, or that is otherwise not identical with, a requirement specifically applicable to a particular cosmetic or class of cosmetics under this Act, the Poison Prevention Packaging Act of 1970 (15 U.S.C. 1471 et seq.), or the Fair Packaging and Labeling Act (15 U.S.C. 1451 et seq.).

(b) EXEMPTION.—Upon application of a State or political subdivision thereof, the Secretary may by regulation, after notice and opportunity for written and oral presentation of views, exempt from subsection (a), under such conditions as may be prescribed in such regulation, a State or political subdivision requirement for labeling or packaging that—

(1) protects an important public interest that would otherwise be unprotected;

(2) would not cause a cosmetic to be in violation of any applicable requirement or prohibition under Federal law; and

(3) would not unduly burden interstate commerce.

(c) SCOPE.—For purposes of subsection (a), a reference to a State requirement that relates to the packaging or labeling of a cosmetic means any specific requirement relating to the same aspect of such cosmetic as a requirement specifically applicable to that particular cosmetic or class of cosmetics under this Act for packaging or labeling, including any State requirement relating to public information or any other form of public communication.

(d) NO EFFECT ON PRODUCT LIABILITY LAW.—Nothing in this section shall be construed to modify or otherwise affect any action or the liability of any person under the product liability law of any State.

(e) STATE INITIATIVE.—This section shall not apply to a State requirement adopted by a State public initiative or referendum enacted prior to September 1, 1997.

Subchapter G — Safety Reports

SEC. 756. [21 USC §379v] Safety Report Disclaimers

With respect to any entity that submits or is required to submit a safety report or other information in connection with the safety of a product (including a product that is a food, drug, device, dietary supplement, or cosmetic) under this Act (and any release by the Secretary of that report or information), such report or information shall not be construed to reflect necessarily a conclusion by the entity or the Secretary that the report or information constitutes an admission that the product involved malfunctioned, caused or contributed to an adverse experience, or otherwise caused or contributed to a death, serious injury, or serious illness. Such an entity need not admit, and may deny, that the report or information submitted by the entity constitutes an admission that the product involved malfunctioned, caused or contributed to an adverse experience, or caused or contributed to a death, serious injury, or serious illness.

SEC. 760. [21 USC §379aa] Serious Adverse Event Reporting for Nonprescription Drugs

Note: revisions were posted to this section in September 2007.

Serious adverse event reporting for nonprescription drugs [Caution: This section is effective 1 year after enactment, pursuant to § 2(e)(1) of Act Dec. 22, 2006, P.L. 109-462]

(a) Definitions. In this section:

(1) Adverse event. The term "***adverse event***" means any health-related event associated with the use of a nonprescription drug that is adverse, including--

(A) an event occurring from an overdose of the drug, whether accidental or intentional;

(B) an event occurring from abuse of the drug;

(C) an event occurring from withdrawal from the drug; and

(D) any failure of expected pharmacological action of the drug.

(2) Nonprescription drug. The term "***nonprescription drug***" means a drug that is--

(A) not subject to section 503(b) [21 USC § 353(b)]; and

(B) not subject to approval in an application submitted under section 505 [21 USC § 355].

(3) Serious adverse event. The term "***serious adverse event***" is an adverse event that--

(A) results in--

(i) death;

(ii) a life-threatening experience;

(iii) inpatient hospitalization;

(iv) a persistent or significant disability or incapacity; or

(v) a congenital anomaly or birth defect; or

(B) requires, based on reasonable medical judgment, a medical or surgical intervention to prevent an outcome described under subparagraph (A).

(4) Serious adverse event report. The term "***serious adverse event report***" means a report that is required to be submitted to the Secretary under subsection (b).

(b) Reporting requirement.

(1) In general. The manufacturer, packer, or distributor whose name (pursuant to section 502(b)(1) [21 USC § 352(b)(1)]) appears on the label of a nonprescription drug marketed in the United States (referred to in this section as the "responsible person") shall submit to the Secretary any report received of a serious adverse event associated with such drug when used in the United States, accompanied by a copy of the label on or within the retail package of such drug.

(2) Retailer. A retailer whose name appears on the label described in paragraph (1) as a distributor may, by agreement, authorize the manufacturer or packer of the nonprescription drug to submit the required reports for such drugs to the Secretary so long as the retailer directs to the manufacturer or packer all adverse events associated with such drug that are reported to the retailer

through the address or telephone number described in section 502(x) [21 USC § 352(x)].

(c) Submission of reports.

(1) Timing of reports. The responsible person shall submit to the Secretary a serious adverse event report no later than 15 business days after the report is received through the address or phone number described in section 502(x) [21 USC § 352(x)].

(2) New medical information. The responsible person shall submit to the Secretary any new medical information, related to a submitted serious adverse event report that is received by the responsible person within 1 year of the initial report, no later than 15 business days after the new information is received by the responsible person.

(3) Consolidation of reports. The Secretary shall develop systems to ensure that duplicate reports of, and new medical information related to, a serious adverse event shall be consolidated into a single report.

(4) Exemption. The Secretary, after providing notice and an opportunity for comment from interested parties, may establish an exemption to the requirements under paragraphs (1) and (2) if the Secretary determines that such exemption would have no adverse effect on public health.

(d) Contents of reports. Each serious adverse event report under this section shall be submitted to the Secretary using the MedWatch form, which may be modified by the Secretary for nonprescription drugs, and may be accompanied by additional information.

(e) Maintenance and inspection of records.

(1) Maintenance. The responsible person shall maintain records related to each report of an adverse event received by the responsible person for a period of 6 years.

(2) Records inspection.

(A) In general. The responsible person shall permit an authorized person to have access to records required to be maintained under this section, during an inspection pursuant to section 704 [21 USC § 374].

(B) Authorized person. For purposes of this paragraph, the term "authorized person" means an officer or employee of the Department of Health and Human Services who has--

(i) appropriate credentials, as determined by the Secretary; and

(ii) been duly designated by the Secretary to have access to the records required under this section.

(f) Protected information. A serious adverse event report submitted to the Secretary under this section, including any new medical information submitted under subsection (c)(2), or an adverse event report voluntarily submitted to the Secretary shall be considered to be--

(1) a safety report under section 756 [21 USC § 379v] and may be accompanied by a statement, which shall be a part of any report that is released for public disclosure, that denies that the report or the records constitute an admission that the product involved caused or contributed to the adverse event; and

(2) a record about an individual under section 552a of title 5, United States Code [5 USC § 552a] (commonly referred to as the "Privacy Act of 1974") and a medical or similar file the disclosure of which would constitute a violation of section 552 of such title 5 [5 USC § 552] (commonly referred to as the "Freedom of Information Act"), and shall not be publicly disclosed unless all personally identifiable information is redacted.

(g) Rule of construction. The submission of any adverse event report in compliance with this section shall not be construed as an admission that the nonprescription drug involved caused or contributed to the adverse event.

(h) Preemption.

(1) In general. No State or local government shall establish or continue in effect any law, regulation, order, or other requirement, related to a mandatory system for adverse event reports for nonprescription drugs, that is different from, in addition to, or otherwise not identical to, this section.

(2) Effect of section.

(A) In general. Nothing in this section shall affect the authority of the Secretary to provide adverse event reports and information to any health, food, or drug officer or employee of any State, territory, or political subdivision of a State or territory, under a memorandum of understanding between the Secretary and such State, territory, or political subdivision.

(B) Personally-identifiable information. Notwithstanding any other provision of law, personally-identifiable information in adverse event reports provided by the Secretary to any health, food, or drug officer or employee of any State, territory, or political subdivision of a State or territory, shall not--

(i) be made publicly available pursuant to any State or other law requiring disclosure of information or records; or

(ii) otherwise be disclosed or distributed to any party without the written consent of the Secretary and the person submitting such information to the Secretary.

(C) Use of safety reports. Nothing in this section shall permit a State, territory, or political subdivision of a State or territory, to use any safety report received from the Secretary in a manner inconsistent with subsection (g) or section 756 [21 USC § 379v].

(i) Authorization of appropriations. There are authorized to be appropriated to carry out this section such sums as may be necessary.

SEC. 761. [21 USC §379aa–1] Serious Adverse Event Reporting for Dietary Supplements

Note: revisions were posted to this section in September 2007.

[Caution: This section is effective 1 year after enactment, pursuant to § 3(d)(1) of Act Dec. 22, 2006, P.L. 109-462]

(a) Definitions. In this section:

(1) Adverse event. The term "***adverse event***" means any health-related event associated with the use of a dietary supplement that is adverse.

(2) Serious adverse event. The term "***serious adverse event***" is an adverse event that--

(A) results in--

(i) death;

(ii) a life-threatening experience;

(iii) inpatient hospitalization;

(iv) a persistent or significant disability or incapacity; or

(v) a congenital anomaly or birth defect; or

(B) requires, based on reasonable medical judgment, a medical or surgical intervention to prevent an outcome described under subparagraph (A).

(3) Serious adverse event report. The term "***serious adverse event report***" means a report that is required to be submitted to the Secretary under subsection (b).

(b) Reporting requirement.

(1) In general. The manufacturer, packer, or distributor of a dietary supplement whose name (pursuant to section 403(e)(1) [21 USC § 343(e)(1)]) appears on the label of a dietary supplement marketed in the United States (referred to in this section as the "responsible person") shall submit to the Secretary any report received of a serious adverse event associated with such dietary supplement when used in the United States, accompanied by a copy of the label on or within the retail packaging of such dietary supplement.

(2) Retailer. A retailer whose name appears on the label described in paragraph (1) as a distributor may, by agreement, authorize the manufacturer or packer of the dietary supplement to submit the required reports for such dietary supplements to the Secretary so long as the retailer directs to the manufacturer or packer all adverse events associated with such dietary supplement that are reported to the retailer through the address or telephone number described in section 403(y) [21 USC § 343(y)].

(c) Submission of reports.

(1) Timing of reports. The responsible person shall submit to the Secretary a serious adverse event report no later than 15 business days after the report is received through the address or phone number described in section 403(y) [21 USC § 343(y)].

(2) New medical information. The responsible person shall submit to the Secretary any new medical information, related to a submitted serious adverse event report that is received by the responsible person within 1 year of the initial report, no later than 15 business days after the new information is received by the responsible person.

(3) Consolidation of reports. The Secretary shall develop systems to ensure that duplicate reports of, and new medical information related to, a serious adverse event shall be consolidated into a single report.

(4) Exemption. The Secretary, after providing notice and an opportunity for comment from interested parties, may establish an exemption to the requirements under paragraphs (1) and (2) if the Secretary determines that such exemption would have no adverse effect on public health.

(d) Contents of reports. Each serious adverse event report under this section shall be submitted to the Secretary using the MedWatch form, which may be modified by the Secretary for dietary supplements, and may be accompanied by additional information.

(e) Maintenance and inspection of records.

(1) Maintenance. The responsible person shall maintain records related to each report of an adverse event received by the responsible person for a period of 6 years.

(2) Records inspection.

(A) In general. The responsible person shall permit an authorized person to have access to records required to be maintained under this section during an inspection pursuant to section 704 [21 USC § 374].

(B) Authorized person. For purposes of this paragraph, the term "authorized person" means an officer or employee of the Department of Health and Human Services, who has—

(i) appropriate credentials, as determined by the Secretary; and

(ii) been duly designated by the Secretary to have access to the records required under this section.

(f) Protected information. A serious adverse event report submitted to the Secretary under this section, including any new medical information submitted under subsection (c)(2), or an adverse event report voluntarily submitted to the Secretary shall be considered to be--

(1) a safety report under section 756 [21 USC § 379v] and may be accompanied by a statement, which shall be a part of any report that is released for public disclosure, that denies that the report or the records constitute an admission that the product involved caused or contributed to the adverse event; and

(2) a record about an individual under section 552a of title 5, United States Code [5 USC § 552a] (commonly referred to as the "Privacy Act of 1974") and a medical or similar file the disclosure of which would constitute a violation of section 552 of such title 5 [5 USC § 552] (commonly referred to as the "Freedom of Information Act"), and shall not be publicly disclosed unless all personally identifiable information is redacted.

(g) Rule of construction. The submission of any adverse event report in compliance with this section shall not be construed as an admission that the dietary supplement involved caused or contributed to the adverse event.

(h) Preemption.

(1) In general. No State or local government shall establish or continue in effect any law, regulation, order, or other requirement, related to a mandatory system for adverse event reports for dietary supplements, that is different from, in addition to, or otherwise not identical to, this section.

(2) Effect of section.

(A) In general. Nothing in this section shall affect the authority of the Secretary to provide adverse event reports and information to any health, food, or drug officer or employee of any State, territory, or political subdivision of a State or territory, under a memorandum of understanding between the Secretary and such State, territory, or political subdivision.

(B) Personally-identifiable information. Notwithstanding any other provision of law, personally-identifiable information in adverse event reports provided by the Secretary to any health, food, or drug officer or employee of any State, territory, or political subdivision of a State or territory, shall not--

(i) be made publicly available pursuant to any State or other law requiring disclosure of information or records; or

(ii) otherwise be disclosed or distributed to any party without the written consent of the Secretary and the person submitting such information to the Secretary.

(C) Use of safety reports. Nothing in this section shall permit a State, territory, or political subdivision of a State or territory, to use any safety report received from the Secretary in a manner inconsistent with subsection (g) or section 756 [21 USC § 379v].

(i) Authorization of appropriations. There are authorized to be appropriated to carry out this section such sums as may be necessary.

Subchapter I — Reagan-Udall Foundation for the Food and Drug Administration

SEC. 770. [21 USC §379dd] Establishment and Functions of the Foundation

(a) In general. A nonprofit corporation to be known as the Reagan-Udall Foundation for the Food and Drug Administration (referred to in this subchapter as the "Foundation") shall be established in accordance with this section. The Foundation shall be headed by an Executive Director, appointed by the members of the Board of Directors under subsection (e). The Foundation shall not be an agency or instrumentality of the United States Government.

(b) Purpose of Foundation. The purpose of the Foundation is to advance the mission of the Food and Drug Administration to modernize medical, veterinary, food, food ingredient, and cosmetic product development, accelerate innovation, and enhance product safety.

(c) Duties of the Foundation. The Foundation shall--

(1) taking into consideration the Critical Path reports and priorities published by the Food and Drug Administration, identify unmet needs in the development, manufacture, and evaluation of the safety and effectiveness, including postapproval, of devices, including diagnostics, biologics, and drugs, and the safety of food, food ingredients, and cosmetics, and including the incorporation of more sensitive and predictive tools and devices to measure safety;

(2) establish goals and priorities in order to meet the unmet needs identified in paragraph (1);

(3) in consultation with the Secretary, identify existing and proposed Federal intramural and extramural research and development programs relating to the goals and priorities established under paragraph (2), coordinate Foundation activities with such programs, and minimize Foundation duplication of existing efforts;

(4) award grants to, or enter into contracts, memoranda of understanding, or cooperative agreements with, scientists and entities, which may include the Food and Drug Administration, university consortia, public-private partnerships, institutions of higher education, entities described in section 501(c)(3) of the Internal Revenue Code [26 USC § 501(c)(3)] (and exempt from tax under section 501(a) of such Code [26 USC § 501(a)]), and industry, to efficiently and effectively advance the goals and priorities established under paragraph (2);

(5) recruit meeting participants and hold or sponsor (in whole or in part) meetings as appropriate to further the goals and priorities established under paragraph (2);

(6) release and publish information and data and, to the extent practicable, license, distribute, and release material, reagents, and techniques to maximize, promote, and coordinate the availability of such material, reagents, and techniques for use by the Food and Drug Administration, nonprofit organizations, and academic and industrial researchers to further the goals and priorities established under paragraph (2);

(7) ensure that--

(A) action is taken as necessary to obtain patents for inventions developed by the Foundation or with funds from the Foundation;

(B) action is taken as necessary to enable the licensing of inventions developed by the Foundation or with funds from the Foundation; and

(C) executed licenses, memoranda of understanding, material transfer agreements, contracts, and other such instruments, promote, to the maximum extent practicable, the broadest conversion to commercial and noncommercial applications of licensed and patented inventions of the Foundation to further the goals and priorities established under paragraph (2);

(8) provide objective clinical and scientific information to the Food and Drug Administration and, upon request, to other Federal agencies to assist in agency determinations of how to ensure that regulatory policy accommodates scientific advances and meets the agency's public health mission;

(9) conduct annual assessments of the unmet needs identified in paragraph (1); and

(10) carry out such other activities consistent with the purposes of the Foundation as the Board determines appropriate.

(d) Board of Directors.

(1) Establishment.

(A) In general. The Foundation shall have a Board of Directors (referred to in this subchapter [21 USC §§ 379dd et seq.] as the "Board"), which shall be composed of ex officio and appointed members in accordance with this subsection. All appointed members of the Board shall be voting members.

(B) Ex officio members. The ex officio members of the Board shall be the following individuals or their designees:

(i) The Commissioner.

(ii) The Director of the National Institutes of Health.

(iii) The Director of the Centers for Disease Control and Prevention.

(iv) The Director of the Agency for Healthcare Research and Quality.

(C) Appointed members.

(i) In general. The ex officio members of the Board under subparagraph (B) shall, by majority vote, appoint to the Board 14 individuals, of which 9 shall be from a list of candidates to be provided by the National Academy of Sciences and 5 shall be from lists of candidates provided by patient and consumer advocacy groups, professional scientific and medical societies, and industry trade organizations. Of such appointed members--

(I) 4 shall be representatives of the general pharmaceutical, device, food, cosmetic, and biotechnology industries;

(II) 3 shall be representatives of academic research organizations;

(III) 2 shall be representatives of patient or consumer advocacy organizations;

(IV) 1 shall be a representative of health care providers; and

(V) 4 shall be at-large members with expertise or experience relevant to the purpose of the Foundation.

(ii) Requirements.

(I) Expertise. The ex officio members shall ensure the Board membership includes individuals with expertise in areas including the sciences of developing, manufacturing, and evaluating the safety and effectiveness of devices, including diagnostics, biologics, and drugs, and the safety of food, food ingredients, and cosmetics.

(II) Federal employees. No employee of the Federal Government shall be appointed as a member of the Board under this subparagraph or under paragraph (3)(B).

(D) Initial meeting.

(i) In general. Not later than 30 days after the date of the enactment of this subchapter [enacted Sept. 27, 2007], the Secretary shall convene a meeting of the ex officio members of the Board to--

(I) incorporate the Foundation; and

(II) appoint the members of the Board in accordance with subparagraph (C).

(ii) Service of ex officio members. Upon the appointment of the members of the Board under clause (i)(II)--

(I) the terms of service of the Director of the Centers for Disease Control and Prevention and of the Director of the Agency for Healthcare Research and Quality as ex officio members of the Board shall terminate; and

(II) the Commissioner and the Director of the National Institutes of Health shall continue to serve as ex officio members of the Board, but shall be nonvoting members.

(iii) Chair. The ex officio members of the Board under subparagraph (B) shall designate an appointed member of the Board to serve as the Chair of the Board.

(2) Duties of Board. The Board shall--

(A) establish bylaws for the Foundation that--

(i) are published in the Federal Register and available for public comment;

(ii) establish policies for the selection of the officers, employees, agents, and contractors of the Foundation;

(iii) establish policies, including ethical standards, for the acceptance, solicitation, and disposition of donations and grants to the Foundation and for the disposition of the assets of the Foundation, including appropriate limits on the ability of donors to designate, by stipulation or restriction, the use or recipient of donated funds;

(iv) establish policies that would subject all employees, fellows, and trainees of the Foundation to the conflict of interest standards under section 208 of title 18, United States Code;

(v) establish licensing, distribution, and publication policies that support the widest and least restrictive use by the public of information and inventions developed by the Foundation or with Foundation funds to carry out the duties described in paragraphs (6) and (7) of subsection (c), and may include charging cost-based fees for published material produced by the Foundation;

(vi) specify principles for the review of proposals and awarding of grants and contracts that include peer review and that are consistent with those of the Foundation for the National Institutes of Health, to the extent determined practicable and appropriate by the Board;

(vii) specify a cap on administrative expenses for recipients of a grant, contract, or cooperative agreement from the Foundation;

(viii) establish policies for the execution of memoranda of understanding and cooperative agreements between the Foundation and other entities, including the Food and Drug Administration;

(ix) establish policies for funding training fellowships, whether at the Foundation, academic or scientific institutions, or the Food and Drug Administration, for scientists, doctors, and other professionals who are not employees of regulated industry, to foster greater understanding of and expertise in new scientific tools, diagnostics, manufacturing techniques, and potential barriers to translating basic research into clinical and regulatory practice;

(x) specify a process for annual Board review of the operations of the Foundation; and

(xi) establish specific duties of the Executive Director;

(B) prioritize and provide overall direction to the activities of the Foundation;

(C) evaluate the performance of the Executive Director; and

(D) carry out any other necessary activities regarding the functioning of the Foundation.

(3) Terms and vacancies.

(A) Term. The term of office of each member of the Board appointed under paragraph (1)(C) shall be 4 years, except that the terms of offices for the initial appointed members of the Board shall expire on a staggered basis as determined by the ex officio members.

(B) Vacancy. Any vacancy in the membership of the Board--

(i) shall not affect the power of the remaining members to execute the duties of the Board; and

(ii) shall be filled by appointment by the appointed members described in paragraph (1)(C) by majority vote.

(C) Partial term. If a member of the Board does not serve the full term applicable under subparagraph (A), the individual appointed under subparagraph (B) to fill the resulting vacancy shall be appointed for the remainder of the term of the predecessor of the individual.

(D) Serving past term. A member of the Board may continue to serve after the expiration of the term of the member until a successor is appointed.

(4) Compensation. Members of the Board may not receive compensation for service on the Board. Such members may be reimbursed for travel, subsistence, and other necessary expenses incurred in carrying out the duties of the Board, as set forth in the bylaws issued by the Board.

(e) Incorporation. The ex officio members of the Board shall serve as incorporators and shall take whatever actions necessary to incorporate the Foundation.

(f) Nonprofit status. In carrying out subsection (b), the Board shall establish such policies and bylaws under subsection (d), and the Executive Director shall carry out such activities under subsection (g), as may be necessary to ensure that the Foundation maintains status as an organization that--

(1) is described in subsection (c)(3) of section 501 of the Internal Revenue Code of 1986 [26 USCS § 501]; and

(2) is, under subsection (a) of such section, exempt from taxation.

(g) Executive Director.

(1) In general. The Board shall appoint an Executive Director who shall serve at the pleasure of the Board. The Executive Director shall be responsible for the day-to-day operations of the Foundation and shall have such specific duties and responsibilities as the Board shall prescribe.

(2) Compensation. The compensation of the Executive Director shall be fixed by the Board but shall not be greater than the compensation of the Commissioner.

(h) Administrative powers. In carrying out this subchapter [21 USC §§ 379dd et seq.], the Board, acting through the Executive Director, may--

(1) adopt, alter, and use a corporate seal, which shall be judicially noticed;

(2) hire, promote, compensate, and discharge 1 or more officers, employees, and agents, as may be necessary, and define their duties;

(3) prescribe the manner in which--

(A) real or personal property of the Foundation is acquired, held, and transferred;

(B) general operations of the Foundation are to be conducted; and

(C) the privileges granted to the Board by law are exercised and enjoyed;

(4) with the consent of the applicable executive department or independent agency, use the information, services, and facilities of such department or agencies in carrying out this section;

(5) enter into contracts with public and private organizations for the writing, editing, printing, and publishing of books and other material;

(6) hold, administer, invest, and spend any gift, devise, or bequest of real or personal property made to the Foundation under subsection (i);

(7) enter into such other contracts, leases, cooperative agreements, and other transactions as the Board considers appropriate to conduct the activities of the Foundation;

(8) modify or consent to the modification of any contract or agreement to which it is a party or in which it has an interest under this subchapter [21 USC §§ 379dd et seq.];

(9) take such action as may be necessary to obtain patents and licenses for devices and procedures developed by the Foundation and its employees;

(10) sue and be sued in its corporate name, and complain and defend in courts of competent jurisdiction;

(11) appoint other groups of advisors as may be determined necessary to carry out the functions of the Foundation; and

(12) exercise other powers as set forth in this section, and such other incidental powers as are necessary to carry out its powers, duties, and functions in accordance with this subchapter [21 USC §§ 379dd et seq.].

(i) Acceptance of funds from other sources. The Executive Director may solicit and accept on behalf of the Foundation, any funds, gifts, grants, devises, or bequests of real or personal property made to the Foundation, including from private entities, for the purposes of carrying out the duties of the Foundation.

(j) Service of Federal employees. Federal Government employees may serve on committees advisory to the Foundation and otherwise cooperate with and assist the Foundation in carrying out its functions, so long as such employees do not direct or control Foundation activities.

(k) Detail of Government employees; fellowships.

(1) Detail from federal agencies. Federal Government employees may be detailed from Federal agencies with or without reimbursement to those agencies to the Foundation at any time, and such detail shall be without interruption or loss of civil service status or privilege. Each such employee shall abide by the statutory, regulatory, ethical, and procedural standards applicable to the employees of the agency from which such employee is detailed and those of the Foundation.

(2) Voluntary service; acceptance of Federal employees.

(A) Foundation. The Executive Director of the Foundation may accept the services of employees detailed from Federal agencies with or without reimbursement to those agencies.

(B) Food and Drug Administration. The Commissioner may accept the uncompensated services of Foundation fellows or trainees. Such services shall be considered to be undertaking an activity under contract with the Secretary as described in section 708 [21 USCS § 379].

(l) Annual reports.

(1) Reports to Foundation. Any recipient of a grant, contract, fellowship, memorandum of understanding, or cooperative agreement from the Foundation under this section shall submit to the Foundation a report on an annual basis for the duration of such grant, contract, fellowship, memorandum of understanding, or cooperative agreement, that describes the activities carried out under such grant, contract, fellowship, memorandum of understanding, or cooperative agreement.

(2) Report to Congress and the FDA. Beginning with fiscal year 2009, the Executive Director shall submit to Congress and the Commissioner an annual report that--

(A) describes the activities of the Foundation and the progress of the Foundation in furthering the goals and priorities established under subsection (c)(2), including the practical impact of the Foundation on regulated product development;

(B) provides a specific accounting of the source and use of all funds used by the Foundation to carry out such activities; and

(C) provides information on how the results of Foundation activities could be incorporated into the regulatory and product review activities of the Food and Drug Administration.

(m) Separation of funds. The Executive Director shall ensure that the funds received from the Treasury are held in separate accounts from funds received from entities under subsection (i).

(n) Funding. From amounts appropriated to the Food and Drug Administration for each fiscal year, the Commissioner shall transfer not less than $ 500,000 and not more than $ 1,250,000, to the Foundation to carry out subsections (a), (b), and (d) through (m).

SEC. 771. [21 USC §379dd–1] Location of Foundation

The Foundation shall, if practicable, be located not more than 20 miles from the District of Columbia.

SEC. 772. [21 USC §379dd–2] Activities of the Food and Drug Administration

(a) In general. The Commissioner shall receive and assess the report submitted to the Commissioner by the Executive Director of the Foundation under section 770(l)(2).

(b) Report to Congress. Beginning with fiscal year 2009, the Commissioner shall submit to Congress an annual report summarizing the incorporation of the information provided by the Foundation in the report described under section 770(l)(2) and by other recipients of grants, contracts, memoranda of understanding, or cooperative agreements into regulatory and product review activities of the Food and Drug Administration.

(c) Extramural grants. The provisions of this subchapter and section 566 shall have no effect on any grant, contract, memorandum of understanding, or cooperative agreement between the Food and Drug Administration and any other entity entered into before, on, or after the date of the enactment of this subchapter [enacted Sept. 27, 2007].

FD&C Act Chapter VIII: Imports and Exports

Sections in Chapter VIII

SEC. 801. [21 USC §381] Imports and Exports

(a) Imports; list of registered foreign establishments; samples from unregistered foreign establishments; examination and refusal of admission. The Secretary of the Treasury shall deliver to the Secretary of Health and Human Services, upon his request, samples of food, drugs, devices, and cosmetics which are being imported or offered for import into the United States, giving notice thereof to the owner or consignee, who may appear before the Secretary of Health and Human Services and have the right to introduce testimony. The Secretary of Health and Human Services shall furnish to the Secretary of the Treasury a list of establishments registered pursuant to subsection (i) of section 510 [21 USC § 360] and shall request that if any drugs or devices manufactured, prepared, propagated, compounded, or processed in an establishment not so registered are imported or offered for import into the United States, samples of such drugs or devices be delivered to the Secretary of Health and Human Services, with notice of such delivery to the owner or consignee, who may appear before the Secretary of Health and Human Services and have the right to introduce testimony. If it appears from the examination of such samples or otherwise that (1) such article has been manufactured, processed, or packed under insanitary conditions or, in the case of a device, the methods used in, or the facilities or controls used for, the manufacture, packing, storage, or installation of the device do not conform to the requirements of section 520(f) [21 USC § 360j(f)], or (2) such article is forbidden or restricted in sale in the country in which it was produced or from which it was exported, or (3) such article is adulterated, misbranded, or in violation of section 505 [21 USC § 355], or prohibited from introduction or delivery for introduction into interstate commerce under section 301(ll) [21 USC § 331(ll)], then such article shall be refused admission, except as provided in subsection (b) of this section. If such article is subject to a requirement under section 760 or 761 [21 USC §§ 379aa or 379aa-1] and if the Secretary has credible evidence or information indicating that the responsible person (as defined in such section 760 or 761) has not complied with a requirement of such section 760 or 761 with respect to any such article, or has not allowed access to records described in such section 760 or 761, then such article shall be refused admission, except as provided in subsection (b) of this section. The Secretary of the Treasury shall cause the destruction of any such article refused admission unless such article is exported, under regulations prescribed by the Secretary of the Treasury, within ninety days of the date of notice of such refusal or within such additional time as may be permitted pursuant to such regulations. Clause (2) of the third sentence of this paragraph [subsection], shall not be construed to prohibit the admission of narcotic drugs the importation of which is permitted under the Controlled Substances Import and Export Act.

(b) Disposition of refused articles. Pending decision as to the admission of an article being imported or offered for import, the Secretary of the Treasury may authorize delivery of such article to the owner or consignee upon the execution by him of a good and sufficient bond providing for the payment of such liquidated damages in the event of default as may be required pursuant to regulations of the Secretary of the Treasury. If it appears to the Secretary of Health and Human Services that (1) an article included within the provisions of clause (3) of subsection (a) of this section can, by relabeling or other action, be brought into compliance with the Act [21 USC §§ 301 et seq.] or rendered other than a food, drug, device, or cosmetic, or (2) with respect to an article included within the provision of the fourth sentence of subsection (a), the responsible person (as defined in section 760 or 761 [21 USC §§ 379aa or 379aa-1]) can take action that would assure that the responsible person is in compliance with section 760 or 761 [21 USC §§ 379aa or 379aa-1], as the case may be, final determination as to admission of such article may be deferred and, upon filing of timely written application by the owner or consignee and the execution by him of a bond as provided in the preceding provisions of this subsection, the Secretary may, in accordance with regulations, authorize the applicant, or, with respect to clause (2), the responsible person, to perform such relabeling or other action specified in such authorization (including destruction or export of rejected articles or portions thereof, as may be specified in the Secretary's authorization). All such relabeling or other action pursuant to such authorization shall in accordance with regulations be under the supervision of an officer or employee of the Department of Health and Human Services designated by the Secretary, or an officer or employee of the Department of the Treasury designated by the Secretary of the Treasury.

(c) Charges concerning refused articles. All expenses (including travel, per diem or subsistence, and salaries of officers or employees of the United States) in connection with the destruction provided for in subsection (a) of this section and the supervision of the relabeling or other action authorized under the provisions of subsection (b) of this section, the amount of such expenses to be determined in accordance with regulations, and all expenses in connection with the storage, cartage, or labor with respect to any article refused admission under subsection (a) of this section, shall be paid by the owner or consignee and, in default of such payment, shall constitute a lien against any future importations made by such owner or consignee.

(d) Reimportation.

(1) Except as provided in paragraph (2) and section 804 [21 USC § 384], no drug subject to section 503(b) [21 USC § 353(b)] or composed wholly or partly of insulin which is manufactured in a State and exported may be imported into the United States unless the drug is imported by the manufacturer of the drug.

(2) The Secretary may authorize the importation of a drug the importation of which is prohibited by paragraph (1) if the drug is required for emergency medical care.

(3)(A) Subject to subparagraph (B), no component of a drug, no component part or accessory of a device, or other article of device requiring further processing, which is ready or suitable for use for health-related purposes, and no article of a food additive, color additive, or dietary supplement, including a product in bulk form, shall be excluded from importation into the United States under subsection (a) if each of the following conditions is met:

(i) The importer of such article of a drug or device or importer of such article of a food additive, color additive, or dietary supplement submits to the Secretary, at the time of initial importation, a statement in accordance with the following:

(I) Such statement provides that such article is intended to be further processed by the initial owner or consignee, or incorporated by the initial owner or consignee, into a drug, biological product, device, food, food additive, color additive, or dietary supplement that will be exported by the initial owner or consignee from the United States in accordance with subsection (e) or section 802 [21 USC § 382], or with section 351(h) of the Public Health Service Act [42 USC § 262(h)].

(II) The statement identifies the manufacturer of such article and each processor, packer, distributor, or other entity that had possession of the article in the chain of possession of the article from the manufacturer to such importer of the article.

(III) The statement is accompanied by such certificates of analysis as are necessary to identify such article, unless the article is a device or is an article described in paragraph (4).

(ii) At the time of initial importation and before the delivery of such article to the importer or the initial owner or consignee, such owner or consignee executes a good and sufficient bond providing for the payment of such liquidated damages in the event of default as may be required pursuant to regulations of the Secretary of the Treasury.

(iii) Such article is used and exported by the initial owner or consignee in accordance with the intent described under clause (i)(I), except for any portions of the article that are destroyed.

(iv) The initial owner or consignee maintains records on the use or destruction of such article or portions thereof, as the case may be, and submits to the Secretary any such records requested by the Secretary.

(v) Upon request of the Secretary, the initial owner or consignee submits a report that provides an accounting of the exportation or destruction of such article or portions thereof, and the manner in which such owner or consignee complied with the requirements of this subparagraph.

(B) Notwithstanding subparagraph (A), the Secretary may refuse admission to an article that otherwise would be imported into the United States under such subparagraph if the Secretary determines that there is credible evidence or information indicating that such article is not intended to be further processed by the initial owner or consignee, or incorporated by the initial owner or consignee, into a drug, biological product, device, food, food additive, color additive, or dietary supplement that will be exported by the initial owner or consignee from the United States in accordance with subsection (e) or section 802 [21 USC § 382], or with section 351(h) of the Public Health Service Act [42 USC § 262(h)].

(C) This section may not be construed as affecting the responsibility of the Secretary to ensure that articles imported into the United States under authority of subparagraph (A) meet each of the conditions established in such subparagraph for importation.

(4) The importation into the United States of blood, blood components, source plasma, or source leukocytes or of a component, accessory, or part thereof is not permitted pursuant to paragraph (3) unless the importation complies with section 351(a) of the Public Health Service Act [42 USC § 262(a)] or the Secretary permits the importation under appropriate circumstances and conditions, as determined by the Secretary. The importation of tissue or a component or part of tissue is not permitted pursuant to paragraph (3) unless the importation complies with section 361 of the Public Health Service Act [42 USC § 264].

(e) Exports.

(1) A food, drug, device, or cosmetic intended for export shall not be deemed to be adulterated or misbranded under this Act [21 USC §§ 301 et seq.] if it--

(A) accords to the specifications of the foreign purchaser,

(B) is not in conflict with the laws of the country to which it is intended for export,

(C) is labeled on the outside of the shipping package that it is intended for export, and

(D) is not sold or offered for sale in domestic commerce.

(2) Paragraph (1) does not apply to any device--

(A) which does not comply with an applicable requirement of section 514 or 515 [21 USC § 360d or 360e],

(B) which under section 520(g) [21 USC § 360j(g)] is exempt from either such section, or

(C) which is a banned device under section 516 [21 USC § 360f],

unless, in addition to the requirements of paragraph (1), either (i) the Secretary has determined that the exportation of the device is not contrary to public health and safety and has the approval of the country to which it is intended for export or (ii) the device is eligible for export under section 802 [21 USC § 382].

(3) A new animal drug that requires approval under section 512 [21 USC § 360b] shall not be exported pursuant to paragraph (1) if such drug has been banned in the United States.

(4)(A) Any person who exports a drug, animal drug, or device may request that the Secretary--

(i) certify in writing that the exported drug, animal drug, or device meets the requirements of paragraph (1) or section 802 [21 USC § 382(1)]; or

(ii) certify in writing that the drug, animal drug, or device being exported meets the applicable requirements of this Act [21 USC §§ 301 et seq.] upon a showing that the drug or device meets the applicable requirements of this Act [21 USC §§ 301 et seq.].

The Secretary shall issue such a certification within 20 days of the receipt of a request for such certification.

(B) If the Secretary issues a written export certification within the 20 days prescribed by subparagraph (A), a fee for such certification may be charged but shall not exceed $ 175 for each certification. Fees collected for a fiscal year pursuant to this subparagraph shall be credited to the appropriation account for salaries and expenses of the Food and Drug Administration and shall be available in accordance with appropriations Acts until expended without fiscal year limitation. Such fees shall be collected in each fiscal year in an amount equal to the amount specified in appropriations Acts for such fiscal year and shall only be collected and available for the costs of the Food and Drug Administration.

(f) Labeling of exported drugs.

(1) If a drug (other than insulin, an antibiotic drug, an animal drug, or a drug exported under section 802 [21 USC § 382]) being exported in accordance with subsection (e) is being exported to a country that has different or additional labeling requirements or conditions for use and such country requires the drug to be labeled in accordance with those requirements or uses, such drug may be labeled in accordance with such requirements and conditions for use in the country to which such drug is being exported if it also is labeled in accordance with the requirements of this Act [21 USC §§ 301 et seq.].

(2) If, pursuant to paragraph (1), the labeling of an exported drug includes conditions for use that have not been approved under this Act [21 USC §§ 301 et seq.], the labeling must state that such conditions for use have not been approved under this Act [21 USC §§ 301 et seq.]. A drug exported under section 802 [21 USC § 382] is exempt from this section.

(g) Warning notices of importation in violation of 21 USC §§ 301 et seq.

(1) With respect to a prescription drug being imported or offered for import into the United States, the Secretary, in the case of an individual who is not in the business of such importations, may not send a warning notice to the individual unless the following conditions are met:

(A) The notice specifies, as applicable to the importation of the drug, that the Secretary has made a determination that--

(i) importation is in violation of section 801(a) [subsec. (a) of this section] because the drug is or appears to be adulterated, misbranded, or in violation of section 505 [21 USC § 355];

(ii) importation is in violation of section 801(a) [subsec. (a) of this section] because the drug is or appears to be forbidden or restricted in sale in the country in which it was produced or from which it was exported;

(iii) importation is or appears to be in violation of section 801(d)(1) [subsec. (d)(1) of this section]; or

(iv) importation otherwise is or appears to be in violation of Federal law.

(B) The notice does not specify any provision described in subparagraph (A) that is not applicable to the importation of the drug.

(C) The notice states the reasons underlying such determination by the Secretary, including a brief application to the principal facts involved of the provision of law described in subparagraph (A) that is the basis of the determination by the Secretary.

(2) For purposes of this section, the term "warning notice", with respect to the importation of a drug, means a communication from the Secretary (written or otherwise) notifying a person, or clearly suggesting to the person, that importing the drug for personal use is, or appears to be, a violation of this Act [21 USC §§ 301 et seq.].

(h) Protection against adulteration of food.

(1) The Secretary shall give high priority to increasing the number of inspections under this section for the purpose of enabling the Secretary to inspect food offered for import at ports of entry into the United States, with the greatest priority given to inspections to detect the intentional adulteration of food.

(2) The Secretary shall give high priority to making necessary improvements to the information management systems of the Food and Drug Administration that contain information related to foods imported or offered for import into the United States for purposes of improving the ability of the Secretary to allocate resources, detect the intentional adulteration of food, and facilitate the importation of food that is in compliance with this Act [21 USC §§ 301 et seq.].

(3) The Secretary shall improve linkages with other regulatory agencies of the Federal Government that share responsibility for food safety, and shall with respect to such safety improve linkages with the States and Indian tribes (as defined in section 4(e) of the Indian Self-Determination and Education Assistance Act (25 U.S.C. 450b(e))).

(i) Testing for rapid detection of adulteration of food.

(1) For use in inspections of food under this section, the Secretary shall provide for research on the development of tests and sampling methodologies--

(A) whose purpose is to test food in order to rapidly detect the adulteration of the food, with the greatest priority given to detect the intentional adulteration of food; and

(B) whose results offer significant improvements over the available technology in terms of accuracy, timing, or costs.

(2) In providing for research under paragraph (1), the Secretary shall give priority to conducting research on the development of tests that are suitable for inspections of food at ports of entry into the United States.

(3) In providing for research under paragraph (1), the Secretary shall as appropriate coordinate with the Director of the Centers for Disease Control

and Prevention, the Director of the National Institutes of Health, the Administrator of the Environmental Protection Agency, and the Secretary of Agriculture.

(4) The Secretary shall annually submit to the Committee on Energy and Commerce of the House of Representatives, and the Committee on Health, Education, Labor, and Pensions of the Senate, a report describing the progress made in research under paragraph (1), including progress regarding paragraph (2).

(j) Temporary holds at ports of entry.

(1) If an officer or qualified employee of the Food and Drug Administration has credible evidence or information indicating that an article of food presents a threat of serious adverse health consequences or death to humans or animals, and such officer or qualified employee is unable to inspect, examine, or investigate such article upon the article being offered for import at a port of entry into the United States, the officer or qualified employee shall request the Secretary of Treasury to hold the food at the port of entry for a reasonable period of time, not to exceed 24 hours, for the purpose of enabling the Secretary to inspect, examine, or investigate the article as appropriate.

(2) The Secretary shall request the Secretary of Treasury to remove an article held pursuant to paragraph (1) to a secure facility, as appropriate. During the period of time that such article is so held, the article shall not be transferred by any person from the port of entry into the United States for the article, or from the secure facility to which the article has been removed, as the case may be. Subsection (b) does not authorize the delivery of the article pursuant to the execution of a bond while the article is so held.

(3) An officer or qualified employee of the Food and Drug Administration may make a request under paragraph (1) only if the Secretary or an official designated by the Secretary approves the request. An official may not be so designated unless the official is the director of the district under this Act [21 USC §§ 301 et seq.] in which the article involved is located, or is an official senior to such director.

(4) With respect to an article of food for which a request under paragraph (1) is made, the Secretary, promptly after the request is made, shall notify the State in which the port of entry involved is located that the request has been made, and as applicable, that such article is being held under this subsection.

(k) Importation by debarred persons.

(1) If an article of food is being imported or offered for import into the United States, and the importer, owner, or consignee of the article is a person who has been debarred under section 306(b)(3) [21 USC § 335a(b)(3)], such article

shall be held at the port of entry for the article, and may not be delivered to such person. Subsection (b) does not authorize the delivery of the article pursuant to the execution of a bond while the article is so held. The article shall be removed to a secure facility, as appropriate. During the period of time that such article is so held, the article shall not be transferred by any person from the port of entry into the United States for the article, or from the secure facility to which the article has been removed, as the case may be.

(2) An article of food held under paragraph (1) may be delivered to a person who is not a debarred person under section 306(b)(3) [21 USC § 335a(b)(3)] if such person affirmatively establishes, at the expense of the person, that the article complies with the requirements of this Act [21 USC §§ 301 et seq.], as determined by the Secretary.

(l) Failure to register.

[(1)] If an article of food is being imported or offered for import into the United States, and such article is from a foreign facility for which a registration has not been submitted to the Secretary under section 415 [21 USC § 350d], such article shall be held at the port of entry for the article, and may not be delivered to the importer, owner, or consignee of the article, until the foreign facility is so registered. Subsection (b) does not authorize the delivery of the article pursuant to the execution of a bond while the article is so held. The article shall be removed to a secure facility, as appropriate. During the period of time that such article is so held, the article shall not be transferred by any person from the port of entry into the United States for the article, or from the secure facility to which the article has been removed, as the case may be.

(m) Prior notice of imported food shipments.

(1) In the case of an article of food that is being imported or offered for import into the United States, the Secretary, after consultation with the Secretary of the Treasury, shall by regulation require, for the purpose of enabling such article to be inspected at ports of entry into the United States, the submission to the Secretary of a notice providing the identity of each of the following: The article; the manufacturer and shipper of the article; if known within the specified period of time that notice is required to be provided, the grower of the article; the country from which the article originates; the country from which the article is shipped; and the anticipated port of entry for the article. An article of food imported or offered for import without submission of such notice in accordance with the requirements under this paragraph shall be refused admission into the United States. Nothing in this section may be construed as a limitation on the port of entry for an article of food.

(2)(A) Regulations under paragraph (1) shall require that a notice under such paragraph be provided by a specified period of time in advance of the time of the importation of the article of food involved or the offering of the food for import, which period shall be no less than the minimum amount of time necessary for the Secretary to receive, review, and appropriately respond to such notification, but may not exceed five days. In determining the specified period of time required under this subparagraph, the Secretary may consider, but is not limited to consideration of, the effect on commerce of such period of time, the locations of the various ports of entry into the United States, the various modes of transportation, the types of food imported into the United States, and any other such consideration. Nothing in the preceding sentence may be construed as a limitation on the obligation of the Secretary to receive, review, and appropriately respond to any notice under paragraph (1).

(B)(i) If an article of food is being imported or offered for import into the United States and a notice under paragraph (1) is not provided in advance in accordance with the requirements under paragraph (1), such article shall be held at the port of entry for the article, and may not be delivered to the importer, owner, or consignee of the article, until such notice is submitted to the Secretary, and the Secretary examines the notice and determines that the notice is in accordance with the requirements under paragraph (1). Subsection (b) does not authorize the delivery of the article pursuant to the execution of a bond while the article is so held. The article shall be removed to a secure facility, as appropriate. During the period of time that such article is so held, the article shall not be transferred by any person from the port of entry into the United States for the article, or from the secure facility to which the article has been removed, as the case may be.

(ii) In carrying out clause (i) with respect to an article of food, the Secretary shall determine whether there is in the possession of the Secretary any credible evidence or information indicating that such article presents a threat of serious adverse health consequences or death to humans or animals.

(3)(A) This subsection may not be construed as limiting the authority of the Secretary to obtain information under any other provision of this Act [21 USC §§ 301 et seq.].

(B) This subsection may not be construed as authorizing the Secretary to impose any requirements with respect to a food to the extent that it is within the exclusive jurisdiction of the Secretary of Agriculture pursuant to the Federal Meat Inspection Act (21 U.S.C. 601 et seq.), the Poultry Products Inspection Act (21 U.S.C. 451 et seq.), or the Egg Products Inspection Act (21 U.S.C. 1031 et seq.).

(n) Labeling of food refused admission.

(1) If a food has been refused admission under subsection (a), other than such a food that is required to be destroyed, the Secretary may require the owner or consignee of the food to affix to the container of the food a label that clearly

and conspicuously bears the statement: "UNITED STATES: REFUSED ENTRY".

(2) All expenses in connection with affixing a label under paragraph (1) shall be paid by the owner or consignee of the food involved, and in default of such payment, shall constitute a lien against future importations made by such owner or consignee.

(3) A requirement under paragraph (1) remains in effect until the Secretary determines that the food involved has been brought into compliance with this Act [21 USC §§ 301 et seq.].

(o) Registration statement. If an article that is a drug or device is being imported or offered for import into the United States, and the importer, owner, or consignee of such article does not, at the time of offering the article for import, submit to the Secretary a statement that identifies the registration under section 510(i) [21 USC § 360(i)] of each establishment that with respect to such article is required under such section to register with the Secretary, the article may be refused admission. If the article is refused admission for failure to submit such a statement, the article shall be held at the port of entry for the article, and may not be delivered to the importer, owner, or consignee of the article, until such a statement is submitted to the Secretary. Subsection (b) does not authorize the delivery of the article pursuant to the execution of a bond while the article is so held. The article shall be removed to a secure facility, as appropriate. During the period of time that such article is so held, the article shall not be transferred by any person from the port of entry into the United States for the article, or from the secure facility to which the article has been removed, as the case may be.

SEC. 802. [21 USC §382] Exports of Certain Unapproved Products

(a) A drug or device—

(1) which, in the case of a drug —

(A)(i) requires approval by the Secretary under section 505 before such drug may be introduced or delivered for introduction into interstate commerce; or

(ii) requires licensing by the Secretary under section 351 of the Public Health Service Act or by the Secretary of Agriculture under the Act of March 4, 1913 (known as the Virus-Serum Toxin Act) before it may be introduced or delivered for introduction into interstate commerce;

(B) does not have such approval or license; and

(C) is not exempt from such sections or Act; and

(2) which, in the case of a device—

(A) does not comply with an applicable requirement under section 514 or 515;

(B) under section 520(g) is exempt from either such section; or

(C) is a banned device under section 516, is adulterated, misbranded, and in violation of such sections or Act unless the export of the drug or device is, except as provided in subsection (f), authorized under subsection (b), (c), (d), or (e) or section 801(e)(2). If [1] a drug or device described in paragraphs (1) and (2) may be exported under subsection (b) and if an application for such drug or device under section 505 or 515 or section 351 of the Public Health Service Act was disapproved, the Secretary shall notify the appropriate public health official of the country to which such drug will be exported of such disapproval.

(b)(1)(A) A drug or device described in subsection (a) may be exported to any country, if the drug or device complies with the laws of that country and has valid marketing authorization by the appropriate authority—

(i) in Australia, Canada, Israel, Japan, New Zealand, Switzerland, or South Africa; or

(ii) in the European Union or a country in the European Economic Area (the countries in the European Union and the European Free Trade Association) if the drug or device is marketed in that country or the drug or device is authorized for general marketing in the European Economic Area.

(B) The Secretary may designate an additional country to be included in the list of countries described in clauses (i) and (ii) of subparagraph (A) if all of the following requirements are met in such country:

(i) Statutory or regulatory requirements which require the review of drugs and devices for safety and effectiveness by an entity of the government of such country and which authorize the approval of only those drugs and devices which have been determined to be safe and effective by experts employed by or acting on behalf of such entity and qualified by scientific training and experience to evaluate the safety and effectiveness of drugs and devices on the basis of adequate and well-controlled investigations, including clinical investigations, conducted by experts qualified by scientific training and experience to evaluate the safety and effectiveness of drugs and devices.

---

[1] Placement of sentence is so in law. See section 2102(d)(1) of Public Law 104–134 (chapter 1A of title II; 110 Stat. 1321-313, 1321-315). Sentence probably should appear after and below subparagraph (C), with the same indentation as the section designation.

(ii) Statutory or regulatory requirements that the methods used in, and the facilities and controls used for—

(I) the manufacture, processing, and packing of drugs in the country are adequate to preserve their identity, quality, purity, and strength; and

(II) the manufacture, preproduction design validation, packing, storage, and installation of a device are adequate to assure that the device will be safe and effective.

(iii) Statutory or regulatory requirements for the reporting of adverse reactions to drugs and devices and procedures to withdraw approval and remove drugs and devices found not to be safe or effective.

(iv) Statutory or regulatory requirements that the labeling and promotion of drugs and devices must be in accordance with the approval of the drug or device.

(v) The valid marketing authorization system in such country or countries is equivalent to the systems in the countries described in clauses (i) and (ii) of subparagraph (A).

The Secretary shall not delegate the authority granted under this subparagraph.

(C) An appropriate country official, manufacturer, or exporter may request the Secretary to take action under subparagraph (B) to designate an additional country or countries to be added to the list of countries described in clauses (i) and (ii) of subparagraph (A) by submitting documentation to the Secretary in support of such designation. Any person other than a country requesting such designation shall include, along with the request, a letter from the country indicating the desire of such country to be designated.

(2) A drug described in subsection (a) may be directly exported to a country which is not listed in clause (i) or (ii) of paragraph (1)(A) if—

(A) the drug complies with the laws of that country and has valid marketing authorization by the responsible authority in that country; and

(B) the Secretary determines that all of the following requirements are met in that country:

(i) Statutory or regulatory requirements which require the review of drugs for safety and effectiveness by an entity of the government of such country and which authorize the approval of only those drugs which have been determined to be safe and effective by experts employed by or acting on behalf of such entity and qualified by scientific training and experience to evaluate the safety and effectiveness of drugs on the basis of adequate and well-controlled investigations, including clinical investigations, conducted by experts qualified by scientific training and experience to evaluate the safety and effectiveness of drugs.

(ii) Statutory or regulatory requirements that the methods used in, and the facilities and controls used for the manufacture, processing, and packing of drugs in the country are adequate to preserve their identity, quality, purity, and strength.

(iii) Statutory or regulatory requirements for the reporting of adverse reactions to drugs and procedures to withdraw approval and remove drugs found not to be safe or effective.

(iv) Statutory or regulatory requirements that the labeling and promotion of drugs must be in accordance with the approval of the drug.

(3) The exporter of a drug described in subsection (a) which would not meet the conditions for approval under this Act or conditions for approval of a country described in clause (i) or (ii) of paragraph (1)(A) may petition the Secretary for authorization to export such drug to a country which is not described in clause (i) or (ii) of paragraph (1)(A) or which is not described in paragraph (2). The Secretary shall permit such export if—

(A) the person exporting the drug—

(i) certifies that the drug would not meet the conditions for approval under this Act or the conditions for approval of a country described in clause (i) or (ii) of paragraph (1)(A); and

(ii) provides the Secretary with credible scientific evidence, acceptable to the Secretary, that the drug would be safe and effective under the conditions of use in the country to which it is being exported; and

(B) the appropriate health authority in the country to which the drug is being exported—

(i) requests approval of the export of the drug to such country;

(ii) certifies that the health authority understands that the drug is not approved under this Act or in a country described in clause (i) or (ii) of paragraph (1)(A); and

(iii) concurs that the scientific evidence provided pursuant to subparagraph (A) is credible scientific evidence that the drug would be reasonably safe and effective in such country.

The Secretary shall take action on a request for export of a drug under this paragraph within 60 days of receiving such request.

(c) A drug or device intended for investigational use in any country described in clause (i) or (ii) of subsection (b)(1)(A) may be exported in accordance with the laws of that country and shall be exempt from regulation under section 505(i) or 520(g).

(d) A drug or device intended for formulation, filling, packaging, labeling, or further processing in anticipation of market authorization in any country described in clause (i) or (ii) of subsection (b)(1)(A) may be exported for use in accordance with the laws of that country.

(e)(1) A drug or device which is used in the diagnosis, prevention, or treatment of a tropical disease or another disease not of significant prevalence in the United States and which does not otherwise qualify for export under this section shall, upon approval of an application, be permitted to be exported if the Secretary finds that the drug or device will not expose patients in such country to an unreasonable risk of illness or injury and the probable benefit to health from the use of the drug or device (under conditions of use prescribed, recommended, or suggested in the labeling or proposed labeling of the drug or device) outweighs the risk of injury or illness from its use, taking into account the probable risks and benefits of currently available drug or device treatment.

(2) The holder of an approved application for the export of a drug or device under this subsection shall report to the Secretary—

(A) the receipt of any credible information indicating that the drug or device is being or may have been exported from a country for which the Secretary made a finding under paragraph (1)(A) to a country for which the Secretary cannot make such a finding; and

(B) the receipt of any information indicating adverse reactions to such drug.

(3)(A) If the Secretary determines that—

(i) a drug or device for which an application is approved under paragraph (1) does not continue to meet the requirements of such paragraph; or

(ii) the holder of an approved application under paragraph (1) has not made the report required by paragraph (2), the Secretary may, after providing the holder of the application an opportunity for an informal hearing, withdraw the approved application.

(B) If the Secretary determines that the holder of an approved application under paragraph (1) or an importer is exporting a drug or device from the United States to an importer and such importer is exporting the drug or device to a country for which the Secretary cannot make a finding under paragraph (1) and such export presents an imminent hazard, the Secretary shall immediately prohibit the export of the drug or device to such importer, provide the person exporting the drug or device from the

United States prompt notice of the prohibition, and afford such person an opportunity for an expedited hearing.

(f) A drug or device may not be exported under this section—

(1) if the drug or device is not manufactured, processed, packaged, and held in substantial conformity with current good manufacturing practice requirements or does not meet international standards as certified by an international standards organization recognized by the Secretary;

(2) if the drug or device is adulterated under clause (1), (2)(A), or (3) of section 501(a) or subsection (c) or (d) of section 501;

(3) if the requirements of subparagraphs (A) through (D) of section 801(e)(1) have not been met;

(4)(A) if the drug or device is the subject of a notice by the Secretary or the Secretary of Agriculture of a determination that the probability of reimportation of the exported drug or device would present an imminent hazard to the public health and safety of the United States and the only means of limiting the hazard is to prohibit the export of the drug or device; or

(B) if the drug or device presents an imminent hazard to the public health of the country to which the drug or device would be exported;

(5) if the labeling of the drug or device is not—

(A) in accordance with the requirements and conditions for use in—

(i) the country in which the drug or device received valid marketing authorization under subsection (b); and

(ii) the country to which the drug or device would be exported; and

(B) in the language and units of measurement of the country to which the drug or device would be exported or in the language designated by such country; or

(6) if the drug or device is not promoted in accordance with the labeling requirements set forth in paragraph (5).

In making a finding under paragraph (4)(B), (5), or (6) the Secretary shall consult with the appropriate public health official in the affected country.

(g) The exporter of a drug or device exported under subsection (b)(1) shall provide a simple notification to the Secretary identifying the drug or device when the exporter first begins to export such drug or device to any country listed in clause (i) or (ii) of subsection (b)(1)(A). When an exporter of a drug or device first begins to export a drug or device to a country which is not listed in clause (i) or (ii) of subsection (b)(1)A) [2], the exporter shall provide a simple notification to the Secretary identifying the drug or device and the country to which such drug or device is being exported. Any exporter of a drug or device shall maintain records of all drugs or devices exported and the countries to which they were exported.

(h) For purposes of this section—

(1) a reference to the Secretary shall in the case of a biological product which is required to be licensed under the Act of March 4, 1913 (37 Stat. 832–833) (commonly known as the Virus-Serum Toxin Act) be considered to be a reference to the Secretary of Agriculture, and

(2) the term "***drug***" includes drugs for human use as well as biologicals under section 351 of the Public Health Service Act or the Act of March 4, 1913 (37 Stat. 832–833) (commonly known as the Virus-Serum Toxin Act).

(i) Insulin and antibiotic drugs may be exported without regard to the requirements in this section if the insulin and antibiotic drugs meet the requirements of section 801(e)(1).

SEC. 803. [21 USC §383] Office of External Relations

(a) There is established in the Department of Health and Human Services an Office of International Relations.

(b) In carrying out the functions of the office under subsection (a), the Secretary may enter into agreements with foreign countries to facilitate commerce in devices between the United States and such countries consistent with the requirements of this Act. In such agreements, the Secretary shall encourage the mutual recognition of—

(1) good manufacturing practice regulations promulgated under section 520(f), and

(2) other regulations and testing protocols as the Secretary determines to be appropriate.

(c)(1) The Secretary shall support the Office of the United States Trade Representative, in consultation with the Secretary of Commerce, in meetings with representatives of other countries to discuss methods and approaches to reduce the burden of regulation and harmonize regulatory requirements if the Secretary determines that such harmonization continues consumer protections consistent with the purposes of this Act.

[2] So in law. See section 2102(d)(1) of Public Law 104–134 (chapter 1A of title II; 110 Stat.

(2) The Secretary shall support the Office of the United States Trade Representative, in consultation with the Secretary of Commerce, in efforts to move toward the acceptance of mutual recognition agreements relating to the regulation of drugs, biological products, devices, foods, food additives, and color additives, and the regulation of good manufacturing practices, between the European Union and the United States.

(3) The Secretary shall regularly participate in meetings with representatives of other foreign governments to discuss and reach agreement on methods and approaches to harmonize regulatory requirements.

(4) The Secretary shall, not later than 180 days after the date of enactment of the Food and Drug Administration Modernization Act of 1997, make public a plan that establishes a framework for achieving mutual recognition of good manufacturing practices inspections.

(5) Paragraphs (1) through (4) shall not apply with respect to products defined in section 201(ff).

SEC. 804. [21 USC §384] Importation of Prescription Drugs

(a) DEFINITIONS--In this section:

(1) IMPORTER--The term "***importer***" means a pharmacist or wholesaler.

(2) PHARMACIST.--The term "***pharmacist***" means a person licensed by a State to practice pharmacy, including the dispensing and selling of prescription drugs.

(3) PRESCRIPTION DRUG.--The term "***prescription drug***" means a drug subject to section 503(b), other than--

(A) a controlled substance (as defined in section 102 of the Controlled Substances Act (21 U.S.C. 802));

(B) a biological product (as defined in section 351 of the Public Health Service Act (42 U.S.C. 262));

(C) an infused drug (including a peritoneal dialysis solution);

(D) an intravenously injected drug;

(E) a drug that is inhaled during surgery; or

(F) a drug which is a parenteral drug, the importation of which pursuant to subsection (b) is determined by the Secretary to pose a threat to the public health, in which case section 801(d)(1) shall continue to apply.

(4) QUALIFYING LABORATORY.--The term "***qualifying laboratory***" means a laboratory in the United States that has been approved by the Secretary for the purposes of this section.

(5) WHOLESALER.--

(A) IN GENERAL.--The term "***wholesaler***" means a person licensed as a wholesaler or distributor of prescription drugs in the United States under section 503(e)(2)(A).

(B) EXCLUSION.--The term "***wholesaler***" does not include a person authorized to import drugs under section 801(d)(1).

(b) REGULATIONS.--The Secretary, after consultation with the United States Trade Representative and the Commissioner of Customs, shall promulgate regulations permitting pharmacists and wholesalers to import prescription drugs from Canada into the United States .

(c) LIMITATION.--The regulations under subsection (b) shall--

(1) require that safeguards be in place to ensure that each prescription drug imported under the regulations complies with section 505 (including with respect to being safe and effective for the intended use of the prescription drug), with sections 501 and 502, and with other applicable requirements of this Act;

(2) require that an importer of a prescription drug under the regulations comply with subsections (d)(1) and (e); and

(3) contain any additional provisions determined by the Secretary to be appropriate as a safeguard to protect the public health or as a means to facilitate the importation of prescription drugs.

(d) INFORMATION AND RECORDS.--

(1) IN GENERAL. The regulations under subsection (b) shall require an importer of a prescription drug under subsection (b) to submit to the Secretary the following information and documentation:

(A) The name and quantity of the active ingredient of the prescription drug.

(B) A description of the dosage form of the prescription drug.

(C) The date on which the prescription drug is shipped.

(D) The quantity of the prescription drug that is shipped.

(E) The point of origin and destination of the prescription drug.

(F) The price paid by the importer for the prescription drug.

(G) Documentation from the foreign seller specifying--

(i) the original source of the prescription drug; and

(ii) the quantity of each lot of the prescription drug originally received by the seller from that source.

(H) The lot or control number assigned to the prescription drug by the manufacturer of the prescription drug.

(I) The name, address, telephone number, and professional license number (if any) of the importer.

(J)(i) In the case of a prescription drug that is shipped directly from the first foreign recipient of the prescription drug from the manufacturer:

(I) Documentation demonstrating that the prescription drug was received by the recipient from the manufacturer and subsequently shipped by the first foreign recipient to the importer.

(II) Documentation of the quantity of each lot of the prescription drug received by the first foreign recipient demonstrating that the quantity being imported into the United States is not more than the quantity that was received by the first foreign recipient.

(III)(aa) In the case of an initial imported shipment, documentation demonstrating that each batch of the prescription drug in the shipment was statistically sampled and tested for authenticity and degradation.

(bb) In the case of any subsequent shipment, documentation demonstrating that a statistically valid sample of the shipment was tested for authenticity and degradation.

(ii) In the case of a prescription drug that is not shipped directly from the first foreign recipient of the prescription drug from the manufacturer, documentation demonstrating that each batch in each shipment offered for importation into the United States was statistically sampled and tested for authenticity and degradation.

(K) Certification from the importer or manufacturer of the prescription drug that the prescription drug--

(i) is approved for marketing in the United States and is not adulterated or misbranded; and

(ii) meets all labeling requirements under this Act.

(L) Laboratory records, including complete data derived from all tests necessary to ensure that the prescription drug is in compliance with established specifications and standards.

(M) Documentation demonstrating that the testing required by subparagraphs (J) and (L) was conducted at a qualifying laboratory.

(N) Any other information that the Secretary determines is necessary to ensure the protection of the public health.

(2) MAINTENANCE BY THE SECRETARY.--The Secretary shall maintain information and documentation submitted under paragraph (1) for such period of time as the Secretary determines to be necessary.

(e) TESTING.--The regulations under subsection (b) shall require--

(1) that testing described in subparagraphs (J) and (L) of subsection (d)(1) be conducted by the importer or by the manufacturer of the prescription drug at a qualified laboratory;

(2) if the tests are conducted by the importer--

(A) that information needed to--

(i) authenticate the prescription drug being tested; and

(ii) confirm that the labeling of the prescription drug complies with labeling requirements under this Act;

be supplied by the manufacturer of the prescription drug to the pharmacist or wholesaler; and

(B) that the information supplied under subparagraph (A) be kept in strict confidence and used only for purposes of testing or otherwise complying with this Act; and

(3) may include such additional provisions as the Secretary determines to be appropriate to provide for the protection of trade secrets and commercial or financial information that is privileged or confidential.

(f) REGISTRATION OF FOREIGN SELLERS.--Any establishment within Canada engaged in the distribution of a prescription drug that is imported or offered for importation into the United States shall register with the Secretary the name and place of business of the establishment and the name of the United States agent for the establishment.

(g) SUSPENSION OF IMPORTATION.--The Secretary shall require that importations of a specific prescription drug or importations by a specific importer under subsection (b) be immediately suspended on discovery of a pattern of importation of that specific prescription drug or by that specific importer of drugs that are counterfeit or in violation of any requirement under this section, until an investigation is completed and the Secretary determines that the public is adequately protected from counterfeit and violative prescription drugs being imported under subsection (b).

(h) APPROVED LABELING.--The manufacturer of a prescription drug shall provide an importer written authorization for the importer to use, at no cost, the approved labeling for the prescription drug.

(i) CHARITABLE CONTRIBUTIONS.--Notwithstanding any other provision of this section, section 801(d)(1) continues to apply to a prescription drug that is donated or otherwise supplied at no charge by the manufacturer of the drug to a charitable or humanitarian organization (including the United Nations and affiliates) or to a government of a foreign country.

(j) WAIVER AUTHORITY FOR IMPORTATION BY INDIVIDUALS.--

(1) DECLARATIONS.--Congress declares that in the enforcement against individuals of the prohibition of importation of prescription drugs and devices, the Secretary should--

(A) focus enforcement on cases in which the importation by an individual poses a significant threat to public health; and

(B) exercise discretion to permit individuals to make such importations in circumstances in which--

(i) the importation is clearly for personal use; and

(ii) the prescription drug or device imported does not appear to present an unreasonable risk to the individual.

(2) WAIVER AUTHORITY.--

(A) IN GENERAL.--The Secretary may grant to individuals, by regulation or on a case-by-case basis, a waiver of the prohibition of importation of a prescription drug or device or class of prescription drugs or devices, under such conditions as the Secretary determines to be appropriate.

(B) GUIDANCE ON CASE-BY-CASE WAIVERS.--The Secretary shall publish, and update as necessary, guidance that accurately describes circumstances in which the Secretary will consistently grant waivers on a case-by-case basis under subparagraph (A), so that individuals may know with the greatest practicable degree of certainty whether a particular importation for personal use will be permitted.

(3) DRUGS IMPORTED FROM CANADA.--In particular, the Secretary shall by regulation grant individuals a waiver to permit individuals to import into the United States a prescription drug that--

(A) is imported from a licensed pharmacy for personal use by an individual, not for resale, in quantities that do not exceed a 90-day supply;

(B) is accompanied by a copy of a valid prescription;

(C) is imported from Canada, from a seller registered with the Secretary;

(D) is a prescription drug approved by the Secretary under chapter V;

(E) is in the form of a final finished dosage that was manufactured in an establishment registered under section 510; and

(F) is imported under such other conditions as the Secretary determines to be necessary to ensure public safety.

(k) CONSTRUCTION--Nothing in this section limits the authority of the Secretary relating to the importation of prescription drugs, other than with respect to section 801(d)(1) as provided in this section.

(l) EFFECTIVENESS OF SECTION.--

(1) COMMENCEMENT OF PROGRAM.--This section shall become effective only if the Secretary certifies to the Congress that the implementation of this section will--

(A) pose no additional risk to the public's health and safety; and

(B) result in a significant reduction in the cost of covered products to the American consumer.

(2) TERMINATION OF PROGRAM.--

(A) IN GENERAL.--If, after the date that is 1 year after the effective date of the regulations under subsection (b) and before the date that is 18 months after the effective date, the Secretary submits to Congress a certification that, in the opinion of the Secretary, based on substantial evidence obtained after the effective date, the benefits of implementation of this section do not outweigh any detriment of implementation of this section, this section shall cease to be effective as of the date that is 30 days after the date on which the Secretary submits the certification.

(B) PROCEDURE.--The Secretary shall not submit a certification under subparagraph (A) unless, after a hearing on the record under sections 556 and 557 of title 5, United States Code, the Secretary--

(i)(I) determines that it is more likely than not that implementation of this section would result in an increase in the risk to the public health and safety;

(II) identifies specifically, in qualitative and quantitative terms, the nature of the increased risk;

(III) identifies specifically the causes of the increased risk; and

(IV)(aa) considers whether any measures can be taken to avoid, reduce, or mitigate the increased risk; and

(bb) if the Secretary determines that any measures described in item (aa) would require additional statutory authority, submits to Congress a report describing the legislation that would be required;

(ii) identifies specifically, in qualitative and quantitative terms, the benefits that would result from implementation of this section (including the benefit of reductions in the cost of covered products to consumers in the United States, allowing consumers to procure needed medication that consumers might not otherwise be able to procure without foregoing other necessities of life); and

(iii)(I) compares in specific terms the detriment identified under clause (i) with the benefits identified under clause (ii); and

(II) determines that the benefits do not outweigh the detriment.

(m) AUTHORIZATION OF APPROPRIATIONS.--There are authorized to be appropriated such sums as are necessary to carry out this section.

FD&C Act Chapter IX: Miscellaneous

Sections in Chapter IX

SEC. 901. [21 USC §391] Separability Clause

If any provision of this Act is declared unconstitutional, or the applicability thereof to any person or circumstances is held invalid, the constitutionality of the remainder of the Act and the applicability thereof to other persons and circumstances shall not be affected thereby.

SEC. 902. [21 USC §392] Effective Date and Repeals

(a) This Act shall take effect twelve months after the date of its enactment. The Federal Food and Drug Act of June 30, 1906, as amended (U.S.C., 1934 ed., title 21, secs.1–15), shall remain in force until such effective date, and except as otherwise provided in this subsection, is hereby repealed effective upon such date: Provided, That the provisions of section 701 shall become effective on the enactment of this Act, and thereafter the Secretary [of Agriculture] is authorized hereby to (1) conduct hearings and to promulgate regulations which shall become effective on or after the effective date of this Act as the Secretary [of Agriculture] shall direct, and (2) designate prior to the effective date of this Act food having common or usual names and exempt such food from the requirements of clause (2) of section 403(i) for a reasonable time to permit the formulation, promulgation, and effective application of definitions and standards of identity therefor as provided by section 401: Provided further, That sections 502(j), 505, and 601(a), and all other provisions of this Act to the extent that they may relate to the enforcement of such sections, shall take effect on the date of the enactment of this Act, except that in the case of a cosmetic to which the proviso of section 601(a) relates, such cosmetic shall not, prior to the ninetieth day after such date of enactment, be deemed adulterated by reason of the failure of its label to bear the legend prescribed in such proviso: Provided further, That the Act of March 4, 1923 (U.S.C., 1945 ed., title 21, sec. 321a; 32 Stat. 1500, ch. 268), defining butter and providing a standard therefor; the Act of July 24, 1919 (U.S.C., 1946 ed., title 21, sec. 321b; 41 Stat. 271, ch. 26), defining wrapped meats as in package form; and the amendment to the Food and Drug Act, section 10A, approved August 27, 1935 (U.S.C., 1946 ed., title 21, sec. 372a [49 Stat. 871, ch. 739]), shall remain in force and effect and be applicable to the provisions of this Act.

(b) Meats and meat food products shall be exempt from the provisions of this Act to the extent of the application or the extension thereto of the Meat Inspection Act, approved March 4, 1907, as amended (U.S.C., 1946 ed., title 21, secs. 71–96; 34 Stat. 1260 et seq.).

(c) Nothing contained in this Act shall be construed as in any way affecting, modifying, repealing, or superseding the provisions of section 351 of Public Health Service Act (relating to viruses, serums, toxins, and analogous products applicable to man); the virus, serum, toxin, and analogous products provisions, applicable to domestic animals, of the Act of Congress approved March 4, 1913 (37 Stat. 832–833); the Filled Cheese Act of June 6, 1896 (U.S.C., 1946 ed., title 26, ch. 17, secs. 2350–2362); the Filled Milk Act of March 4, 1923 (U.S.C. 1946 ed., title 21, ch. 3, secs. 61–64); or the Import Milk Act of February 15, 1927 (U.S.C., 1946 ed., title 21, ch. 4, secs. 141–149).

SEC. 903. [21 USC §393] Food and Drug Administration

(a) IN GENERAL.—There is established in the Department of Health and Human Services the Food and Drug Administration (hereinafter in this section referred to as the "Administration").

(b) MISSION.—The Administration shall—

(1) promote the public health by promptly and efficiently reviewing clinical research and taking appropriate action on the marketing of regulated products in a timely manner;

(2) with respect to such products, protect the public health by ensuring that—

(A) foods are safe, wholesome, sanitary, and properly labeled;

(B) human and veterinary drugs are safe and effective;

(C) there is reasonable assurance of the safety and effectiveness of devices intended for human use;

(D) cosmetics are safe and properly labeled; and

(E) public health and safety are protected from electronic product radiation;

(3) participate through appropriate processes with representatives of other countries to reduce the burden of regulation, harmonize regulatory requirements, and achieve appropriate reciprocal arrangements; and

(4) as determined to be appropriate by the Secretary, carry out paragraphs (1) through (3) in consultation with experts in science, medicine, and public health, and in cooperation with consumers, users, manufacturers, importers, packers, distributors, and retailers of regulated products.

(c) INTERAGENCY COLLABORATION.—The Secretary shall implement programs and policies that will foster collaboration between the Administration, the National Institutes of Health, and other science-based Federal agencies, to enhance the scientific and technical expertise available to the Secretary in the conduct of the duties of the Secretary with respect to the development, clinical investigation, evaluation, and postmarket monitoring of emerging medical therapies, including complementary therapies, and advances in nutrition and food science.

(d) COMMISSIONER.—

(1) APPOINTMENT.—There shall be in the Administration a Commissioner of Food and Drugs (hereinafter in this section referred to as the "Commissioner") who shall be appointed by the President by and with the advice and consent of the Senate.

(2) GENERAL POWERS.—The Secretary, through the Commissioner, shall be responsible for executing this Act and for—

(A) providing overall direction to the Food and Drug Administration and establishing and implementing general policies respecting the management and operation of programs and activities of the Food and Drug Administration;

(B) coordinating and overseeing the operation of all administrative entities within the Administration;

(C) research relating to foods, drugs, cosmetics, and devices in carrying out this Act;

(D) conducting educational and public information programs relating to the responsibilities of the Food and Drug Administration; and

(E) performing such other functions as the Secretary may prescribe.

(e) TECHNICAL AND SCIENTIFIC REVIEW GROUPS.—The Secretary through the Commissioner of Food and Drugs may, without regard to the provisions of title 5, United States Code, governing appointments in the competitive service and without regard to the provisions of chapter 51 and subchapter III of chapter 53 of such title relating to classification and General Schedule pay rates, establish such technical and scientific review groups as are needed to carry out the functions of the Administration, including functions under the Federal Food, Drug, and Cosmetic Act, and appoint and pay the members of such groups, except that officers and employees of the United States shall not receive additional compensation for service as members of such groups.

(f) AGENCY PLAN FOR STATUTORY COMPLIANCE.—

(1) IN GENERAL.—Not later than 1 year after the date of enactment of the Food and Drug Administration Modernization Act of 1997, the Secretary, after consultation with appropriate scientific and academic experts, health care professionals, representatives of patient and consumer advocacy groups, and the regulated industry, shall develop and publish in the Federal Register a plan bringing the Secretary into compliance with each of the obligations of the Secretary under this Act. The Secretary shall review the plan biannually and shall revise the plan as necessary, in consultation with such persons.

(2) OBJECTIVES OF AGENCY PLAN.—The plan required by paragraph (1) shall establish objectives and mechanisms to achieve such objectives, including objectives related to—

(A) maximizing the availability and clarity of information about the process for review of applications and submissions (including petitions, notifications, and any other similar forms of request) made under this Act;

(B) maximizing the availability and clarity of information for consumers and patients concerning new products;

(C) implementing inspection and postmarket monitoring provisions of this Act;

(D) ensuring access to the scientific and technical expertise needed by the Secretary to meet obligations described in paragraph (1);

(E) establishing mechanisms, by July 1, 1999, for meeting the time periods specified in this Act for the review of all applications and submissions described in subparagraph (A) and submitted after the date of enactment of the Food and Drug Administration Modernization Act of 1997; and

(F) eliminating backlogs in the review of applications and submissions described in subparagraph (A), by January 1, 2000.

(g) ANNUAL REPORT.—The Secretary shall annually prepare and publish in the Federal Register and solicit public comment on a report that—

(1) provides detailed statistical information on the performance of the Secretary under the plan described in subsection (f);

(2) compares such performance of the Secretary with the objectives of the plan and with the statutory obligations of the Secretary; and

(3) identifies any regulatory policy that has a significant negative impact on compliance with any objective of the plan or any statutory obligation and sets forth any proposed revision to any such regulatory policy.

SEC. 904. [21 USC §394] Scientific Review Groups

Without regard to the provisions of title 5, United States Code, governing appointments in the competitive service and without regard to the provisions of chapter 51 and subchapter III of chapter 53 of such title relating to classification and General Schedule pay rates, the Commissioner of Food and Drugs may—

(1) establish such technical and scientific review groups as are needed to carry out the functions of the Food and Drug Administration (including functions prescribed under this Act); and

(2) appoint and pay the members of such groups, except that officers and employees of the United States shall not receive additional compensation for service as members of such groups.

SEC. 905. [21 USC §395] Loan Repayment Program

(a) IN GENERAL.—

(1) AUTHORITY FOR PROGRAM.—Subject to paragraph (2), the Secretary shall carry out a program of entering into contracts with appropriately qualified health professionals under which such health professionals agree to conduct research, as employees of the Food and Drug Administration, in consideration of the Federal Government agreeing to repay, for each year of such service, not more than $20,000 of the principal and interest of the educational loans of such health professionals.

(2) LIMITATION.—The Secretary may not enter into an agreement with a health professional pursuant to paragraph (1) unless such professional—

(A) has a substantial amount of educational loans relative to income; and

(B) agrees to serve as an employee of the Food and Drug Administration for purposes of paragraph (1) for a period of not less than 3 years.

(b) APPLICABILITY OF CERTAIN PROVISIONS.—With respect to the National Health Service Corps Loan Repayment Program established in subpart III of part D of title III of the Public Health Service Act, the provisions of such subpart shall, except as inconsistent with subsection (a) of this section, apply to the program established in such subsection in the same manner and to the same extent as such provisions apply to the National Health Service Corps Loan Repayment Program.

(c) AUTHORIZATION OF APPROPRIATIONS.—For the purpose of carrying out this section, there are authorized to be appropriated such sums as may be necessary for each of the fiscal years 1994 through 1996.

SEC. 906. [21 USC §396] Practice of Medicine

Nothing in this Act shall be construed to limit or interfere with the authority of a health care practitioner to prescribe or administer any legally marketed device to a patient for any condition or disease within a legitimate health care practitioner-patient relationship. This section shall not limit any existing authority of the Secretary to establish and enforce restrictions on the sale or distribution, or in the labeling, of a device that are part of a determination of substantial equivalence, established as a condition of approval, or promulgated through regulations. Further, this section shall not change any existing prohibition on the promotion of unapproved uses of legally marketed devices.

SEC. 907. [21 USC §397] Contracts for Expert Review

(a) IN GENERAL.—

(1) AUTHORITY.—The Secretary may enter into a contract with any organization or any individual (who is not an employee of the Department) with relevant expertise, to review and evaluate, for the purpose of making recommendations to the Secretary on, part or all of any application or submission (including a petition, notification, and any other similar form of request) made under this Act for the approval or classification of an article or made under section 351(a) of the Public Health Service Act (42 U.S.C. 262(a)) with respect to a biological product. Any such contract shall be subject to the requirements of section 708 relating to the confidentiality of information.

(2) INCREASED EFFICIENCY AND EXPERTISE THROUGH CONTRACTS.—The Secretary may use the authority granted in paragraph (1) whenever the Secretary determines that use of a contract described in paragraph (1) will improve the timeliness of the review of an application or submission described in paragraph (1), unless using such authority would reduce the quality, or unduly increase the cost, of such review. The Secretary may use such authority whenever the Secretary determines that use of such a

contract will improve the quality of the review of an application or submission described in paragraph (1), unless using such authority would unduly increase the cost of such review. Such improvement in timeliness or quality may include providing the Secretary increased scientific or technical expertise that is necessary to review or evaluate new therapies and technologies.

(b) REVIEW OF EXPERT REVIEW.—

(1) IN GENERAL.—Subject to paragraph (2), the official of the Food and Drug Administration responsible for any matter for which expert review is used pursuant to subsection (a) shall review the recommendations of the organization or individual who conducted the expert review and shall make a final decision regarding the matter in a timely manner.

(2) LIMITATION.—A final decision by the Secretary on any such application or submission shall be made within the applicable prescribed time period for review of the matter as set forth in this Act or in the Public Health Service Act (42 U.S.C. 201 et seq.).

Chapter IX

SEC. 908. [21 USC §398] Notices to States Regarding Imported Food

(a) IN GENERAL..--If the Secretary has credible evidence or information indicating that a shipment of imported food or portion thereof presents a threat of serious adverse health consequences or death to humans or animals, the Secretary shall provide notice regarding such threat to the States in which the food is held or will be held, and to the States in which the manufacturer, packer, or distributor of the food is located, to the extent that the Secretary has knowledge of which States are so involved. In providing notice to a State, the Secretary shall request the State to take such action as the State considers appropriate, if any, to protect the public health regarding the food involved.

(b) RULE OF CONSTRUCTION.--Subsection (a) may not be construed as limiting the authority of the Secretary with respect to food under any other provision of this Act.

SEC. 909. [21 USC §399] Grants to States for Inspections

(a) IN GENERAL.--The Secretary is authorized to make grants to States, territories, and Indian tribes (as defined in section 4(e) of the Indian Self-Determination and Education Assistance Act (25 U.S.C. 450b(e))) that undertake examinations, inspections, and investigations, and related activities under section 702. The funds provided under such grants shall only be available for the costs of conducting such examinations, inspections, investigations, and related activities.

(b) NOTICES REGARDING ADULTERATED IMPORTED FOOD.--The Secretary may make grants to the States for the purpose of assisting the States with the costs of taking appropriate action to protect the public health in response to notification under section 908, including planning and otherwise preparing to take such action.

(c) AUTHORIZATION OF APPROPRIATIONS.--For the purpose of carrying out this section, there are authorized to be appropriated $10,000,000 for fiscal year 2002, and such sums as may be necessary for each of the fiscal years 2003 through 2006.

SEC. 910. [21 USC 399a] Office of the Chief Scientist

(a) Establishment; appointment. The Secretary shall establish within the Office of the Commissioner an office to be known as the Office of the Chief Scientist. The Secretary shall appoint a Chief Scientist to lead such Office.

(b) Duties of the Office. The Office of the Chief Scientist shall--

- (1) oversee, coordinate, and ensure quality and regulatory focus of the intramural research programs of the Food and Drug Administration;
- (2) track and, to the extent necessary, coordinate intramural research awards made by each center of the Administration or science-based office within the Office of the Commissioner, and ensure that there is no duplication of research efforts supported by the Reagan-Udall Foundation for the Food and Drug Administration;
- (3) develop and advocate for a budget to support intramural research;
- (4) develop a peer review process by which intramural research can be evaluated;
- (5) identify and solicit intramural research proposals from across the Food and Drug Administration through an advisory board composed of employees of the Administration that shall include--
  - (A) representatives of each of the centers and the science-based offices within the Office of the Commissioner; and
  - (B) experts on trial design, epidemiology, demographics, pharmacovigilance, basic science, and public health; and
- (6) develop postmarket safety performance measures that are as measurable and rigorous as the ones already developed for premarket review.

Significant Amendments to the FD&C Act

Since 1980, listed chronologically; date shown is when the Public Law was approved. "Summary" indicates link to a summary of the law; other links are to full text. Provisions of these Public Laws are incorporated into the FD&C Act.

All of the following an be accessed on the FDA website at: http://www.fda.gov/RegulatoryInformation/Legislation/FederalFoodDrugandCosmeticActFDCAct/SignificantAmendmentstotheFDCAct/default.htm.

- Infant Formula Act of 1980 (summary)

  Public Law (PL) 96-359 (Oct. 26, 1980)

- Drug Price Competition and Patent Term Restoration Act of 1984 (summary)

  PL 98-417 (Sept. 24, 1984)

- Generic Animal Drug and Patent Term Restoration Act of 1988 (summary)

  PL 100-670 (Nov. 16, 1988)

- Nutrition Labeling and Education Act of 1990 (summary)

  PL 101-535 (Nov. 8, 1990)

- Safe Medical Devices Act of 1990 (summary)

  PL 101-629 (Nov. 28, 1990)

- Medical Device Amendments of 1992 (summary)

  PL 102-300 (June 16, 1992)

- Prescription Drug User Fee Act (PDUFA) of 1992

  PL 102-571 (Oct. 29, 1992)

- Dietary Supplement Health and Education Act of 1994

  PL 103-417 (Oct. 25, 1994)

- FDA Export Reform and Enhancement Act of 1996

  PL 104-134 (April 26, 1996)

- Food Quality Protection Act of 1996

  PL 104-170 (Aug. 3, 1996)

- Animal Drug Availability Act of 1996

  PL 104-250 (Oct. 9, 1996)
- Best Pharmaceuticals for Children Act

  PL 107-109 (Jan. 4, 2002)
- Pediatric Research Equity Act of 2003

  PL 108-155 (Dec. 3, 2003)
- The Minor Use and Minor Species Animal Health Act of 2004

  PL 108-282 (Aug. 2, 2004)
- Dietary Supplement and Nonprescription Drug Consumer Protection Act

  PL 109-462 (Dec. 22, 2006)
- Food and Drug Administration Amendments Act of 2007

  PL 110-85 (Sept. 27, 2007)
- Family Smoking Prevention and Tobacco Control Act (Public Law 111-31)

  PL 111-31 (June 22, 2009)

Part II

Combined Glossary and Index

Combined Glossary

30-day notice means a notice under section 515(d)(6) that is limited to a request to make modifications to manufacturing procedures or methods of manufacture affecting the safety and effectiveness of the device.

180-day exclusivity period means the 180-day period ending on the day before the date on which an application submitted by an applicant other than a first applicant could become effective under this clause.

180-day supplement means a supplement to an approved premarket application or premarket report under section 515 that is not a panel-track supplement and requests a significant change in components, materials, design, specification, software, color additives, or labeling.

A

Abbreviated drug application means an application submitted under section 505(j) for the approval of a drug that relies on the approved application of another drug with the same active ingredient to establish safety and efficacy, and—

(1) in the case of section 306, includes a supplement to such an application for a different or additional use of the drug but does not include a supplement to such an application for other than a different or additional use of the drug, and

(2) in the case of sections 307 and 308, includes any supplement to such an application.

Active, with respect to a commercial investigational new drug application, means such an application to which information was submitted during the relevant period.

Adjustment factor applicable to a fiscal year is the Consumer Price Index for all urban consumers (all items; United States city average) for October of the preceding fiscal year divided by such Index for October 1996, 2001 or set forth in section 735(8) with the base or comparator year being 2003.

Administrator means the Administrator of the United States Environmental Protection Agency.

Adverse drug experience means any adverse event associated with the use of a drug in humans, whether or not considered drug related, including--

(A) an adverse event occurring in the course of the use of the drug in professional practice;

(B) an adverse event occurring from an overdose of the drug, whether accidental or intentional;

(C) an adverse event occurring from abuse of the drug;

(D) an adverse event occurring from withdrawal of the drug; and

(E) any failure of expected pharmacological action of the drug.

Adverse event means any health-related event associated with the use of a nonprescription drug that is adverse, including--

(A) an event occurring from an overdose of the drug, whether accidental or intentional;

(B) an event occurring from abuse of the drug;

(C) an event occurring from withdrawal from the drug; and

(D) any failure of expected pharmacological action of the drug.

Advisory committee means an advisory committee under the Federal Advisory Committee Act [5 USC Appx] that provides advice or recommendations to the Secretary regarding activities of the Food and Drug Administration.

Advisory review means reviewing and providing advisory comments on DTC advertisements regarding compliance of a proposed advertisement with the requirements of this Act [21 USC §§ 301 et seq.] prior to its initial public dissemination.

Affiliate means a business entity that has a relationship with a second business entity (whether domestic or international) if, directly or indirectly--

(A) one business entity controls, or has the power to control, the other business entity; or

(B) a third party controls, or has power to control, both of the business entities.

Animal drug application means an application for approval of any new animal drug submitted under section 512(b)(1). Such term does not include either a new animal drug application submitted under section 512(b)(2) or a supplemental animal drug application.

Animal drug establishment means a foreign or domestic place of business which is at one general physical location consisting of one or more buildings all of which are within 5 miles of each other, at which one or more animal drug products are manufactured in final dosage form.

Animal drug product means each specific strength or potency of a particular active ingredient or ingredients in final dosage form marketed by a particular manufacturer or distributor, which is uniquely identified by the labeler code and product code portions of the national drug code, and for which an animal drug application or a supplemental animal drug application has been approved.

Animal drug sponsor means either an applicant named in an animal drug application, except for an approved application for which all subject products have been removed from listing under section 510, or a person who has submitted an investigational animal drug submission that has not been terminated or otherwise rendered inactive by the Secretary.

Animal feed, as used in paragraph (w) [(v)] of this section, in section 512, and in provisions of this Act referring to such paragraph or section, means an article which is intended for use for food for animals other than man and which is intended for use as a substantial source of nutrients in the diet of the animal, and is not limited to a mixture intended to be the sole ration of the animal.

Annual fee, for periodic reporting concerning a class III device, means the annual fee associated with periodic reports required by a premarket application approval order.

Antibiotic drug means any drug (except drugs for use in animals other than humans) composed wholly or partly of any kind of penicillin, streptomycin, chlortetracycline, chloramphenicol, bacitracin, or any other drug intended for human use containing any quantity of any chemical substance which is produced by a micro-organism and which has the capacity to inhibit or destroy micro-organisms in dilute solution (including a chemically synthesized equivalent of any such substance) or any derivative thereof.

Application means an application submitted under subsection (b)(2) or (j).

B

Biological product has the meaning given such term in section 351 of the Public Health Service Act.

Bulk vehicle includes a tank truck, hopper truck, rail tank car, hopper car, cargo tank, portable tank, freight container, or hopper bin, and any other vehicle in which food is shipped in bulk, with the food coming into direct contact with the vehicle.

Butter. The Act of March 4, 1923 (21 U.S.C. 321a), defines butter as "the food product usually known as butter, and which is made exclusively from milk or cream, or both, with or without common salt, and with or without additional coloring matter, and containing not less than 80 per centum by weight of milk fat, all tolerances having been allowed for."

C

Carry over submission means a submission for an advisory review for which a fee was paid in one fiscal year that is submitted for review in the following fiscal year.

Color includes black, white, and intermediate grays.

Color additive means a material which—

(A) is a dye, pigment, or other substance made by a process of synthesis or similar artifice, or extracted, isolated, or otherwise derived, with or without intermediate or final change of identity, from a vegetable, animal, mineral, or other source, and

(B) when added or applied to a food, drug, or cosmetic, or to the human body or any part thereof, is capable (alone or through reaction with other substance) of imparting color thereto; except that such term does not include any material which the Secretary, by regulation, determines is used (or intended to be used) solely for a purpose or purposes other than coloring.

Commissioner means the Commissioner of Food and Drugs.

Compounded positron emission tomography drug—

(1) means a drug that—

(A) exhibits spontaneous disintegration of unstable nuclei by the emission of positrons and is used for the purpose of providing dual photon positron emission tomographic diagnostic images; and

(B) has been compounded by or on the order of a practitioner who is licensed by a State to compound or order compounding for a drug described in subparagraph (A), and is compounded in accordance with that State's law, for a patient or for research, teaching, or quality control; and

(2) includes any nonradioactive reagent, reagent kit, ingredient, nuclide generator, accelerator, target material, electronic synthesizer, or other apparatus or computer program to be used in the preparation of such a drug.

Cosmetic means (1) articles intended to be rubbed, poured, sprinkled, or sprayed on, introduced into, or otherwise applied to the human body or any part thereof for cleansing, beautifying, promoting attractiveness, or altering the appearance, and (2) articles intended for use as a component of any such articles; except that such term shall not include soap.

Costs of resources allocated for the process for the review of animal drug applications means the expenses incurred in connection with the process for the review of animal drug applications for

(A) officers and employees of the Food and Drug Administration, contractors of the Food and Drug Administration, advisory committees consulted with respect to the review of specific animal drug applications, supplemental animal drug applications, or investigational animal drug submissions, and costs related to such officers, employees, committees, and contractors, including costs for travel, education, and recruitment and other personnel activities,

(B) management of information, and the acquisition, maintenance, and repair of computer resources,

(C) leasing, maintenance, renovation, and repair of facilities and acquisition, maintenance, and repair of fixtures, furniture, scientific equipment, and other necessary materials and supplies, and

(D) collecting fees under section 740 and accounting for resources allocated for the review of animal drug applications, supplemental animal drug applications, and investigational animal drug submissions.

Costs of resources allocated for the process for the review of device applications means the expenses incurred in connection with the process for the review of device applications for--

(A) officers and employees of the Food and Drug Administration, contractors of the Food and Drug Administration, advisory committees, and costs related to such officers, employees, and committees and to contracts with such contractors;

(B) management of information, and the acquisition, maintenance, and repair of computer resources;

(C) leasing, maintenance, renovation, and repair of facilities and acquisition, maintenance, and repair of fixtures, furniture, scientific equipment, and other necessary materials and supplies; and

(D) collecting fees and accounting for resources allocated for the review of premarket applications, premarket reports, supplements, and submissions.

Costs of resources allocated for the process for the review of human drug applications means the expenses incurred in connection with the process for the review of human drug applications for

(A) officers and employees of the Food and Drug Administration, contractors of the Food and Drug Administration, advisory committees, and costs related to such officers, employees, and committees and to contracts with such contractors,

(B) management of information, and the acquisition, maintenance, and repair of computer resources,

(C) leasing, maintenance, renovation, and repair of facilities and acquisition, maintenance, and repair of fixtures, furniture, scientific equipment, and other necessary materials and supplies, and

(D) collecting fees under section 736 and accounting for resources allocated for the review of human drug applications and supplements.

Counterfeit drug means a drug which, or the container or labeling of which, without authorization, bears the trademark, trade name, or other identifying mark, imprint, or device, or any likeness thereof, of a drug manufacturer, processor, packer, or distributor other than the person or persons who in fact manufactured, processed, packed, or distributed such drug and which thereby falsely purports or is represented to be the product of, or to have been packed or distributed by, such other drug manufacturer, processor, packer, or distributor.

Covered application means--

(1) an application under subsection (b) for a drug that is subject to section 503(b) [21 USC § 353(b)]; and

(2) an application under section 351 of the Public Health Service Act [42 USC § 262].

(3) an application referred to in section 505(p)(1)(A).

Critical reprocessed single-use device means a reprocessed single-use device that is intended to contact normally sterile tissue or body spaces during use.

D

Department means the Department of Health and Human Services.

Device (except when used in paragraph (n) of this section and in sections 301(i), 403(f), 502(c), and 602(c)) means an instrument, apparatus, implement, machine, contrivance, implant, in vitro reagent, or other similar or related article, including any component, part, or accessory, which is--

(1) recognized in the official National Formulary, or the United States Pharmacopeia, or any supplement to them,

(2) intended for use in the diagnosis of disease or other conditions, or in the cure, mitigation, treatment, or prevention of disease, in man or other animals, or

(3) intended to affect the structure or any function of the body of man or other animals, and which does not achieve its primary intended purposes through chemical action within or on the body of man or other animals and which is not dependent upon being metabolized for the achievement of its primary intended purposes.

Dietary supplement means —

(1) a product (other than tobacco) intended to supplement the diet that bears or contains one or more of the following dietary ingredients:

(A) a vitamin;

(B) a mineral;

(C) an herb or other botanical;

(D) an amino acid;

(E) a dietary substance for use by man to supplement the diet by increasing the total dietary intake; or

(F) a concentrate, metabolite, constituent, extract, or combination of any ingredient described in clause (A), (B), (C), (D), or (E);

(2) means a product that—

(A)(i) is intended for ingestion in a form described in section 411(c)(1)(B)(i); or

(ii) complies with section 411(c)(1)(B)(ii);

(B) is not represented for use as a conventional food or as a sole item of a meal or the diet; and

(C) is labeled as a dietary supplement; and

(3) does—

(A) include an article that is approved as a new drug under section 505 or licensed as a biologic under section 351 of the Public Health Service Act (42 U.S.C. 262) and was, prior to such approval, certification, or license, marketed as a dietary supplement or as a food unless the Secretary has issued a regulation, after notice and comment, finding that the article, when used as or in a dietary supplement under the conditions of use and dosages set forth in the labeling for such dietary supplement, is unlawful under section 402(f); and

(B) not include—

(i) an article that is approved as a new drug under section 505, certified as an antibiotic under section 507, or licensed as a biologic under section 351 of the Public Health Service Act (42 U.S.C. 262), or

(ii) an article authorized for investigation as a new drug, antibiotic, or biological for which substantial clinical investigations have been instituted and for which the existence of such investigations has been made public, which was not before such approval, certification, licensing, or authorization marketed as a dietary supplement or as a food unless the Secretary, in the Secretary's discretion, has issued a regulation, after notice and comment, finding that the article would be lawful under this Act.

Except for purposes of section 201(g), a dietary supplement shall be deemed to be a food within the meaning of this Act.

Direct-to-consumer television advertisement means an advertisement for a prescription drug product (as defined in section 735(3) [21 USC § 379g(3)]) intended to be displayed on any television channel for less than 3 minutes.

Drug means (A) articles recognized in the official United States Pharmacopoeia, official Homoeopathic Pharmacopoeia of the United States, or official National Formulary, or any supplement to any of them; and (B) articles intended for use in the diagnosis, cure, mitigation, treatment, or prevention of disease in man or other animals; and (C) articles (other than food) intended to affect the structure or any function of the body of man or other animals; and (D) articles intended for use as a component of any article specified in clause (A), (B), or (C). A food or dietary supplement for which a claim, subject to sections 403(r)(1)(B) and 403(r)(3) or sections 403(r)(1)(B) and 403(r)(5)(D), is made in accordance with the requirements of section 403(r) is not a drug solely because the label or the labeling contains such a claim. A food, dietary ingredient, or dietary supplement for which a truthful and not misleading statement is made in accordance with section 403(r)(6) is not a drug under clause (C) solely because the label or the labeling contains such a statement.

Drug product means a drug subject to regulation under section 505, 512, or 802 of this Act or under section 351 of the Public Health Service Act.

E, F

Efficacy supplement means a supplement to an approved premarket application under section 351 of the Public Health Service Act [42 USC § 262] that requires substantive clinical data.

Electronic product means (A) any manufactured or assembled product which, when in operation, (i) contains or acts as part of an electronic circuit and (ii) emits (or in the absence of effective shielding or other controls would emit) electronic product radiation, or (B) any manufactured or assembled article which is intended for use as a component, part, or accessory of a product described in clause (A) and which when in operation emits (or in the absence of effective shielding or other controls would emit) such radiation;

(1) the term "***manufacturer***" means any person engaged in the business of manufacturing, assembling, or importing of electronic products;

(2) the term "***commerce***" means (A) commerce between any place in any State and any place outside thereof; and (B) commerce wholly within the District of Columbia; and

(3) the term "***State***" includes the District of Columbia, the Commonwealth of Puerto Rico, the Northern Mariana Islands, the Virgin Islands, Guam, and American Samoa.

Electronic product radiation means—

(A) any ionizing or non-ionizing electromagnetic or particulate radiation, or

(B) any sonic, infrasonic, or ultrasonic wave, which is emitted from an electronic product as the result of the operation of an electronic circuit in such product;

Emergency use has the meaning indicated for such term in paragraph (1).

Establishment subject to a registration fee means an establishment that is required to register with the Secretary under section 510 and is one of the following types of establishments:

(A) Manufacturer. An establishment that makes by any means any article that is a device, including an establishment that sterilizes or otherwise makes such article for or on behalf of a specification developer or any other person.

(B) Single-use device reprocessor. An establishment that, within the meaning of section 201(ll)(2)(A) [21 USC § 321(ll)(2)(A)], performs additional processing and manufacturing operations on a single-use device that has previously been used on a patient.

(C) Specification developer. An establishment that develops specifications for a device that is distributed under the establishment's name but which performs no manufacturing, including an establishment that, in addition to developing specifications, also arranges for the manufacturing of devices labeled with another establishment's name by a contract manufacturer.

Final dosage form means, with respect to an animal drug product, a finished dosage form which is approved for administration to an animal without substantial further manufacturing. Such term includes animal drug products intended for mixing in animal feeds.

Financial interest means a financial interest under section 208(a) of title 18, United States Code.

First applicant means an applicant that, on the first day on which a substantially complete application containing a certification described in paragraph (2)(A)(vii)(IV) is submitted for approval of a drug, submits a substantially complete application that contains and lawfully maintains a certification described in paragraph (2)(A)(vii)(IV) for the drug.

Final dosage form means, with respect to a prescription drug product, a finished dosage form which is approved for administration to a patient without substantial further manufacturing (such as capsules, tablets, or lyophilized products before reconstitution).

Food means (1) articles used for food or drink for man or other animals, (2) chewing gum, and (3) articles used for components of any such article.

Food additive means any substance the intended use of which results or may reasonably be expected to result, directly or indirectly, in its becoming a component or otherwise affecting the characteristics of any food (including any substance intended for use in producing, manufacturing, packing, processing, preparing, treating, packaging, transporting, or holding food; and including any source of radiation intended for any such use), if such substance is not generally recognized, among experts qualified by scientific training and experience to evaluate its safety, as having been adequately shown through scientific procedures (or, in the case of a substance used in food prior to January 1, 1958, through either scientific procedures or experience based on common use in food) to be safe under the conditions of its intended use; except that such term does not include—

(1) a pesticide chemical residue in or on a raw agricultural commodity or processed food; or

(2) a pesticide chemical; or

(3) a color additive; or

(4) any substance used in accordance with a sanction or approval granted prior to the enactment of this paragraph pursuant to this Act [enacted Sept. 6, 1958], the Poultry Products Inspection Act (21 U.S.C. 451 and the following) or the Meat Inspection Act of March 4, 1907 (34 Stat. 1260), as amended and extended (21 U.S.C. 71 and the following);

(5) a new animal drug; or

(6) an ingredient described in paragraph (ff) in, or intended for use in, a dietary supplement.

G, H

General controls is a reference to the controls authorized by or under sections 501, 502, 510, 516, 518, 519, and 520.

Health care practitioner means a physician, or other individual who is a provider of health care, who is licensed under the law of a State to prescribe drugs or devices.

Health insurance issuer and "***group health plan***" have the meaning given such terms under section 2791 of the Public Health Service Act.

High managerial agent means (1) —

(A) an officer or director of a corporation or an association,

(B) a partner of a partnership, or

(C) any employee or other agent of a corporation, association, or partnership, having duties such that the conduct of such officer, director, partner, employee, or agent may fairly be assumed to represent the policy of the corporation, association, or partnership, and

(2) includes persons having management responsibility for—

(A) submissions to the Food and Drug Administration regarding the development or approval of any drug product, any drug product,

(B) production, quality assurance, or quality control of any drug product, or

(C) research and development of any drug product.

Human drug application means an application for--

(A) approval of a new drug submitted under section 505(b), or

(B) licensure of a biological product under section 351 of the Public Health Service Act.

(C) [Redesignated]

Such term does not include a supplement to such an application, does not include an application with respect to whole blood or a blood component for transfusion, does not include an application with respect to a bovine blood product for topical application licensed before September 1, 1992, an allergenic extract product, or an in vitro diagnostic biologic product licensed under section 351 of the Public Health Service Act, does not include an application with respect to a large volume parenteral drug product approved before September 1, 1992, does not include an application for a licensure of a biological product for further manufacturing use only, and does not include an application or supplement submitted by a State or Federal Government entity for a drug that is not distributed commercially. Such term does include an application for licensure, as described in subparagraph (B), of a large volume biological product intended for single dose injection for intravenous use or infusion.

I

Immediate container does not include package liners.

Importer means a pharmacist or wholesaler.

Infant formula means a food which purports to be or is represented for special dietary use solely as a food for infants by reason of its simulation of human milk or its suitability as a complete or partial substitute for human milk.

Informal hearing means a hearing which is not subject to section 554, 556, or 557 of title 5 of the United States Code and which provides for the following:

(1) The presiding officer in the hearing shall be designated by the Secretary from officers and employees of the Department who have not participated in any action of the Secretary which is the subject of the hearing and who are not directly responsible to an officer or employee of the Department who has participated in any such action.

(2) Each party to the hearing shall have the right at all times to be advised and accompanied by an attorney.

(3) Before the hearing, each party to the hearing shall be given reasonable notice of the matters to be considered at the hearing, including a comprehensive statement of the basis for the action taken or proposed by the Secretary which is the subject of the hearing and a general summary of the information which will be presented by the Secretary at the hearing in support of such action.

(4) At the hearing the parties to the hearing shall have the right to hear a full and complete statement of the action of the Secretary which is the subject of the

hearing together with the information and reasons supporting such action, to conduct reasonable questioning, and to present any oral or written information relevant to such action.

(5) The presiding officer in such hearing shall prepare a written report of the hearing to which shall be attached all written material presented at the hearing. The participants in the hearing shall be given the opportunity to review and correct or supplement the presiding officer's report of the hearing.

(6) The Secretary may require the hearing to be transcribed. A party to the hearing shall have the right to have the hearing transcribed at his expense. Any transcription of a hearing shall be included in the presiding officer's report of the hearing.

Interstate commerce means (1) commerce between any State or Territory and any place outside thereof, and (2) commerce within the District of Columbia or within any other Territory not organized with a legislative body.

Investigational animal drug submission means

(A) the filing of a claim for an investigational exemption under section 512(j) for a new animal drug intended to be the subject of an animal drug application or a supplemental animal drug application, or

(B) the submission of information for the purpose of enabling the Secretary to evaluate the safety or effectiveness of an animal drug application or supplemental animal drug application in the event of their filing.

J, K, L

Knowingly or "***knew***" means that a person, with respect to information—

(1) has actual knowledge of the information, or

(2) acts in deliberate ignorance or reckless disregard of the truth or falsity of the information.

Label means a display of written, printed, or graphic matter upon the immediate container of any article; and a requirement made by or under authority of this Act that any word, statement, or other information appear on the label shall not be considered to be complied with unless such word, statement, or other information also appears on the outside container or wrapper, if any there be, of the retail package of such article, or is easily legible through the outside container or wrapper.

Labeling means all labels and other written, printed, or graphic matters (1) upon any article or any of its containers or wrappers, or (2) accompanying such article.

M

Major food allergen means any of the following:

(1) Milk, egg, fish (e.g., bass, flounder, or cod), Crustacean shellfish (e.g., crab, lobster, or shrimp), tree nuts (e.g., almonds, pecans, or walnuts), wheat, peanuts, and soybeans.

(2) A food ingredient that contains protein derived from a food specified in paragraph (1), except the following:

(A) Any highly refined oil derived from a food specified in paragraph (1) and any ingredient derived from such highly refined oil.

(B) A food ingredient that is exempt under paragraph (6) or (7) of section 403(w).

Major species means cattle, horses, swine, chickens, turkeys, dogs, and cats, except that the Secretary may add species to this definition by regulation.

Manufacture, preparation, propagation, compounding, or processing shall include repackaging or otherwise changing the container, wrapper, or labeling of any drug package or device package in furtherance of the distribution of the drug or device from the original place of manufacture to the person who makes final delivery or sale to the ultimate consumer or user.

Manufacturer means a person who manufactures a drug or device, or who is licensed by such person to distribute or market the drug or device.

Minor species means animals other than humans that are not major species.

Minor use means the intended use of a drug in a major species for an indication that occurs infrequently and in only a small number of animals or in limited geographical areas and in only a small number of animals annually.

N

Name shall include in the case of a partnership the name of each partner and, in the case of a corporation, the name of each corporate officer and director, and the State of incorporation.

New animal drug means any drug intended for use for animals other than man, including any drug intended for use in animal feed but not including such animal feed—

(1) the composition of which is such that such drug is not generally recognized, among experts qualified by scientific training and experience to evaluate the safety and effectiveness of animal drugs, as safe and effective for use under the conditions prescribed, recommended, or suggested in the labeling thereof; except that such a drug not so recognized shall not be deemed to be a "new animal drug" if at any time prior to June 25, 1938, it was subject to the Food and Drug Act of June 30, 1906, as amended, and if at such time its labeling contained the same representations concerning the conditions of its use; or

(2) the composition of which is such that such drug, as a result of investigations to determine its safety and effectiveness for use under such conditions, has become so recognized but which has not, otherwise than in such investigations, been used to a material extent or for a material time under such conditions.

Provided that any drug intended for minor use or use in a minor species that is not the subject of a final regulation published by the Secretary through notice and comment rulemaking finding that the criteria of paragraphs (1) and (2) have not been met (or that the exception to the criterion in paragraph (1) has been met) is a new animal drug.

New drug means—

(1) Any drug (except a new animal drug or an animal feed bearing or containing a new animal drug) the composition of which is such that such drug is not generally recognized, among experts qualified by scientific training and experience to evaluate the safety and effectiveness of drugs, as safe and effective for use under the condition prescribed, recommended, or suggested in the labeling thereof, except that such a drug not so recognized shall not be deemed to be a "new drug" if at any time prior to the enactment of this Act [enacted June 25, 1938] it was subject to the Food and Drugs Act of June 30, 1906, as amended, and if at such time its labeling contained the same representations concerning the conditions of its use; or

(2) Any drug (except a new animal drug or an animal feed bearing or containing a new animal drug) the composition of which is such that such drug, as a result of investigations to determine its safety and effectiveness for use under such conditions, has become so recognized, but which has not, otherwise than in such investigations, been used to a material extent or for a material time under such conditions.

New safety information, with respect to a drug, means information derived from a clinical trial, an adverse event report, a postapproval study (including a study under section 505(o)(3)), or peer-reviewed biomedical literature; data derived from the postmarket risk identification and analysis system under section 505(k); or other scientific data deemed appropriate by the Secretary about--

(A) a serious risk or an unexpected serious risk associated with use of the drug that the Secretary has become aware of (that may be based on a new analysis of existing information) since the drug was approved, since the risk evaluation and mitigation strategy was required, or since the last assessment of the approved risk evaluation and mitigation strategy for the drug; or

(B) the effectiveness of the approved risk evaluation and mitigation strategy for the drug obtained since the last assessment of such strategy.

New safety information, ***serious risk***, and ***signal of a serious risk*** have the meanings given such terms in section 505-1(b) [21 USC § 355-1(b)].

New use—

(A) with respect to a drug, means a use that is not included in the labeling of the approved drug; and

(B) with respect to a device, means a use that is not included in the labeling for the approved or cleared device.

Nonfat Dry Milk, Milk. The Act of July 2, 1956 (21 U.S.C. 321c), defines nonfat dry milk as "the product resulting from the removal of fat and water from milk, and contains the lactose, milk proteins, and milk minerals in the same relative proportions as in the fresh milk from which made. It contains not over 5 per centum by weight of moisture. The fat content is not over 11⁄2 per centum by weight unless otherwise indicated.", and defines milk to mean sweet milk of cows.

Nonprescription drug means a drug that is--

(A) not subject to section 503(b) [21 USC § 353(b)]; and

(B) not subject to approval in an application submitted under section 505 [21 USC § 355].

O, P

Official compendium means the official United States Pharmacopoeia, official Homoeopathic Pharmacopoeia of the United States, official National Formulary, or any supplement to any of them.

Original device means a new, unused single-use device.

Package. The Act of July 24, 1919 (21 U.S.C. 321b), states "The word 'package' shall include and shall be construed to include wrapped meats inclosed in papers or other materials as prepared by the manufacturers thereof for sale."

Panel-track supplement means a supplement to an approved premarket application or premarket report under section 515 that requests a significant change in design or performance of the device, or a new indication for use of the device, and for which substantial clinical data are necessary to provide a reasonable assurance of safety and effectiveness.

Panel under section 513 is a reference to a panel established or authorized to be used under this section.

Pediatric studies or ***studies*** means at least one clinical investigation (that, at the Secretary's discretion, may include pharmacokinetic studies) in pediatric age groups (including neonates in appropriate cases) in which a drug is anticipated to be used, and, at the discretion of the Secretary, may include preclinical studies.

Person includes an individual, partnership, corporation, and association, and any affiliate thereof or successor in interest.

Pesticide chemical, except as provided in clause (B), means any substance that is a pesticide within the meaning of the Federal Insecticide, Fungicide, and Rodenticide Act, including all active and inert ingredients of such pesticide. Notwithstanding any other provision of law, the term "pesticide" within such meaning includes ethylene oxide and propylene oxide when such substances are applied on food.

(B) In the case of the use, with respect to food, of a substance described in clause (A) to prevent, destroy, repel, or mitigate microorganisms (including bacteria, viruses, fungi, protozoa, algae, and slime), the following applies for purposes of clause (A):

(i) The definition in such clause for the term "pesticide chemical" does not include the substance if the substance is applied for such use on food, or the substance is included for such use in water that comes into contact with the food, in the preparing, packing, or holding of the food for commercial purposes. The substance is not excluded under this subclause from such definition if the substance is ethylene oxide or propylene oxide, and is applied for such use on food. The substance is not so excluded if the substance is applied for such use on a raw agricultural commodity, or the substance is included for such use in water that comes into contact with the commodity, as follows:

(I) The substance is applied in the field.

(II) The substance is applied at a treatment facility where raw agricultural commodities are the only food treated, and the treatment is in a manner that does not change the status of the food as a raw agricultural commodity (including treatment through washing, waxing, fumigating, and packing such commodities in such manner).

(III) The substance is applied during the transportation of such commodity between the field and such a treatment facility.

(ii) The definition in such clause for the term "pesticide chemical" does not include the substance if the substance is a food contact substance as defined in section 409(h)(6), and any of the following circumstances exist: The substance is included for such use in an object that has a food contact surface but is not intended to have an ongoing effect on any portion of the object; the substance is included for such use in an object that has a food contact surface and is intended to have an ongoing effect on a portion of the object but not on the food contact surface; or the substance is included for such use in or is applied for such use on food packaging (without regard to whether the substance is intended to have an ongoing effect on any portion of the packaging). The food contact substance is not excluded under this subclause from such definition if any of the following circumstances exist: The substance is applied for such use on a semipermanent or permanent food contact surface (other than being applied on food packaging); or the substance is included for such use in an object that has a semipermanent or permanent food contact surface (other than being included in food packaging) and the substance is intended to have an ongoing effect on the food contact surface.

With respect to the definition of the term "***pesticide***" that is applicable to the Federal Insecticide, Fungicide, and Rodenticide Act, this clause does not exclude any substance from such definition.

The Administrator may by regulation except a substance from the definition of "pesticide chemical" or "pesticide chemical residue" if—

(A) its occurrence as a residue on or in a raw agricultural commodity or processed food is attributable primarily to natural causes or to human activities not involving the use of any substances for a pesticidal purpose in the production, storage, processing, or transportation of any raw agricultural commodity or processed food; and

(B) the Administrator, after consultation with the Secretary, determines that the substance more appropriately should be regulated under one or more provisions of this Act other than sections 402(a)(2)(B) and 408.

Pesticide chemical residue means a residue in or on raw agricultural commodity or processed food of—

(A) a pesticide chemical; or

(B) any other added substance that is present on or in the commodity or food primarily as a result of the metabolism or other degradation of a pesticide chemical.

The Administrator may by regulation except a substance from the definition of "pesticide chemical" or "pesticide chemical residue" if—

(A) its occurrence as a residue on or in a raw agricultural commodity or processed food is attributable primarily to natural causes or to human activities not involving the use of any substances for a pesticidal purpose in the production, storage, processing, or transportation of any raw agricultural commodity or processed food; and

(B) the Administrator, after consultation with the Secretary, determines that the substance more appropriately should be regulated under one or more provisions of this Act other than sections 402(a)(2)(B) and 408.

Pharmacist means a person licensed by a State to practice pharmacy, including the dispensing and selling of prescription drugs.

Premarket application means-- (A) an application for approval of a device submitted under section 515(c) or section 351 of the Public Health Service Act [42 USC § 262]; or (B) a product development protocol described in section 515(f). Such term does not include a supplement, a premarket report, or a premarket notification submission.

Premarket report means a report submitted under section 515(c)(2).

Premarket notification submission means a report submitted under section 510(k).

Prescription drug means a drug subject to section 503(b), other than--

(A) a controlled substance (as defined in section 102 of the Controlled Substances Act (21 U.S.C. 802));

(B) a biological product (as defined in section 351 of the Public Health Service Act (42 U.S.C. 262));

(C) an infused drug (including a peritoneal dialysis solution);

(D) an intravenously injected drug;

(E) a drug that is inhaled during surgery; or

(F) a drug which is a parenteral drug, the importation of which pursuant to subsection (b) is determined by the Secretary to pose a threat to the public health, in which case section 801(d)(1) shall continue to apply.

Prescription drug establishment means a foreign or domestic place of business which is at one general physical location consisting of one or more buildings all of which are within five miles of each other and at which one or more prescription drug products are manufactured in final dosage form. For purposes of this paragraph, the term "manufactured" does not include packaging.

Prescription drug product means a specific strength or potency of a drug in final dosage form—

(A) for which a human drug application has been approved,

(B) which may be dispensed only under prescription pursuant to section 503(b) , and

(C) which is on the list of products described in section 505(j)(7)(A) (not including the discontinued section of such list) or is on a list created and maintained by the Secretary of products approved under human drug applications under section 351 of the Public Health Service Act (not including the discontinued section of such list).

Priority review, with respect to a human drug application as defined in section 735(1) [21 USC § 379g(l)], means review and action by the Secretary on such application not later than 6 months after receipt by the Secretary of such application, as described in the Manual of Policies and Procedures of the Food and Drug Administration and goals identified in the letters described in section 101(c) of the Food and Drug Administration Amendments Act of 2007 [21 USC § 379g note].

Priority review voucher means a voucher issued by the Secretary to the sponsor of a tropical disease product application that entitles the holder of such voucher to priority review of a single human drug application submitted under section 505(b)(1) [21 USC § 355(b)(1)] or section 351 of the Public Health Service Act [42 USC § 262] after the date of approval of the tropical disease product application.

Process for the advisory review of prescription drug advertising means the activities necessary to review and provide advisory comments on DTC advertisements prior to public dissemination and, to the extent the Secretary has additional staff resources available under the program under this section that are not necessary for the advisory review of DTC advertisements, the activities necessary to review and provide advisory comments on other proposed advertisements and promotional material prior to public dissemination.

Process for the review of animal drug applications means the following activities of the Secretary with respect to the review of animal drug applications, supplemental animal drug applications, and investigational animal drug submissions:

(A) The activities necessary for the review of animal drug applications, supplemental animal drug applications, and investigational animal drug submissions.

(B) The issuance of action letters which approve animal drug applications or supplemental animal drug applications or which set forth in detail the specific deficiencies in animal drug applications, supplemental animal drug applications, or investigational animal drug submissions and, where appropriate, the actions necessary to place such applications, supplements or submissions in condition for approval.

(C) The inspection of animal drug establishments and other facilities undertaken as part of the Secretary's review of pending animal drug applications, supplemental animal drug applications, and investigational animal drug submissions.

(D) Monitoring of research conducted in connection with the review of animal drug applications, supplemental animal drug applications, and investigational animal drug submissions.

(E) The development of regulations and policy related to the review of animal drug applications, supplemental animal drug applications, and investigational animal drug submissions.

(F) Development of standards for products subject to review.

(G) Meetings between the agency and the animal drug sponsor.

(H) Review of advertising and labeling prior to approval of an animal drug application or supplemental animal drug application, but not such activities after an animal drug has been approved.

Process for the review of device applications means the following activities of the Secretary with respect to the review of premarket applications, premarket reports, supplements, and premarket notification submissions:

(A) The activities necessary for the review of premarket applications, premarket reports, supplements, and premarket notification submissions.

(B) The issuance of action letters that allow the marketing of devices or which set forth in detail the specific deficiencies in such applications, reports, supplements, or submissions and, where appropriate, the actions necessary to place them in condition for approval.

(C) The inspection of manufacturing establishments and other facilities undertaken as part of the Secretary's review of pending premarket applications, premarket reports, and supplements.

(D) Monitoring of research conducted in connection with the review of such applications, reports, supplements, and submissions.

(E) Review of device applications subject to section 351 of the Public Health Service Act [42 USC § 262] for an investigational new drug application under section 505(i) or for an investigational device exemption under section 520(g) and activities conducted in anticipation of the submission of such applications under section 505(i) or 520(g).

(F) The development of guidance, policy documents, or regulations to improve the process for the review of premarket applications, premarket reports, supplements, and premarket notification submissions.

(G) The development of voluntary test methods, consensus standards, or mandatory performance standards under section 514 in connection with the review of such applications, reports, supplements, or submissions and related activities.

(H) The provision of technical assistance to device manufacturers in connection with the submission of such applications, reports, supplements, or submissions.

(I) Any activity undertaken under section 513 or 515(i) in connection with the initial classification or reclassification of a device or under section 515(b) in connection with any requirement for approval of a device.

(J) Evaluation of postmarket studies required as a condition of an approval of a premarket application or premarket report under section 515 or a premarket application under section 351 of the Public Health Service Act.

(K) Compiling, developing, and reviewing information on relevant devices to identify safety and effectiveness issues for devices subject to premarket applications, premarket reports, supplements, or premarket notification submissions.

Process for the review of human drug applications means the following activities of the Secretary with respect to the review of human drug applications and supplements:

(A) The activities necessary for the review of human drug applications and supplements.

(B) The issuance of action letters which approve human drug applications or which set forth in detail the specific deficiencies in such applications and, where appropriate, the actions necessary to place such applications in condition for approval.

(C) The inspection of prescription drug establishments and other facilities undertaken as part of the Secretary's review of pending human drug applications and supplements.

(D) Activities necessary for the review of applications for licensure of establishments subject to section 351 of the Public Health Service Act and for the release of lots of biologics under such section.

(E) Monitoring of research conducted in connection with the review of human drug applications.

(F) Postmarket safety activities with respect to drugs approved under human drug applications or supplements, including the following activities:

(i) Collecting, developing, and reviewing safety information on approved drugs, including adverse event reports.

(ii) Developing and using improved adverse-event data-collection systems, including information technology systems.

(iii) Developing and using improved analytical tools to assess potential safety problems, including access to external data bases

(iv) Implementing and enforcing section 505(o) [21 USC § 355(o)] (relating to postapproval studies and clinical trials and labeling changes) and section 505(p) [21 USC § 355(p)] (relating to risk evaluation and mitigation strategies).

(v) Carrying out section 505(k)(5) [21 USC § 355(k)(5)] (relating to adverse event reports and postmarket safety activities).

Processed food means any food other than a raw agricultural commodity and includes any raw agricultural commodity that has been subject to processing, such as canning, cooking, freezing, dehydration, or milling.

Priority supplement means a drug application referred to in section 101(4) of the Food and Drug Administration Modernization Act of 1997 (111 Stat. 2298).

Product means a drug, device, or biological product.

Q, R

Qualifying laboratory means a laboratory in the United States that has been approved by the Secretary for the purposes of this section.

Raw agricultural commodity means any food in its raw or natural state, including all fruits that are washed, colored, or otherwise treated in their unpeeled natural form prior to marketing.

Real-time supplement means a supplement to an approved premarket application or premarket report under section 515 that requests a minor change to the device, such as a minor change to the design of the device, software, sterilization, or labeling, and for which the applicant has requested and the agency has granted a meeting or similar forum to jointly review and determine the status of the supplement.

Reportable food means an article of food (other than infant formula) for which there is a reasonable probability that the use of, or exposure to, such article of food will cause serious adverse health consequences or death to humans or animals.

Reprocessed, with respect to a single-use device, means an original device that has previously been used on a patient and has been subjected to additional processing and manufacturing for the purpose of an additional single use on a patient. The subsequent processing and manufacture of a reprocessed single-use device shall result in a device that is reprocessed within the meaning of this definition.

(B) A single-use device that meets the definition under clause (A) shall be considered a reprocessed device without regard to any description of the device used by the manufacturer of the device or other persons, including a description that uses the term "recycled" rather than the term "reprocessed".

Request for classification information means a request made under section 513(g) for information respecting the class in which a device has been classified or the requirements applicable to a device.

Resources allocated for the process for the advisory review of prescription drug advertising means the expenses incurred in connection with the process for the advisory review of prescription drug advertising for--

(A) officers and employees of the Food and Drug Administration, contractors of the Food and Drug Administration, advisory committees, and costs related to such officers, employees, and committees, and to contracts with such contractors;

(B) management of information, and the acquisition, maintenance, and repair of computer resources;

(C) leasing, maintenance, renovation, and repair of facilities and acquisition, maintenance, and repair of fixtures, furniture, scientific equipment, and other necessary materials and supplies;

(D) collection of fees under this section and accounting for resources allocated for the advisory review of prescription drug advertising; and

(E) terminating the program under this section pursuant to subsection (f)(2) if that becomes necessary.

Responsible party, with respect to an article of food, means a person that submits the registration under section 415(a) [21 USC § 350d(a)] for a food facility that is required to register under section 415(a) [21 USC § 350d(a)], at which such article of food is manufactured, processed, packed, or held.

Responsible person means a person who--

(i) has submitted to the Secretary a covered application that is pending; or

(ii) is the holder of an approved covered application.

Resubmission means a subsequent submission for advisory review of a direct-to-consumer television advertisement that has been revised in response to the Secretary's comments on an original submission. A resubmission may not introduce significant new concepts or creative themes into the television advertisement.

Responsible person means the person submitting a covered application or the holder of the approved such application.

S

Saccharin includes calcium saccharin, sodium saccharin, and ammonium saccharin.

Safe, as used in paragraph (s) of this section and in sections 409, 512, 571, and 721, has reference to the health of man or animal.

Scientific or medical journal means a scientific or medical publication—

(A) that is published by an organization—

(i) that has an editorial board;

(ii) that utilizes experts, who have demonstrated expertise in the subject of an article under review by the organization and who are independent of the organization, to review and objectively select, reject, or provide comments about proposed articles; and

(iii) that has a publicly stated policy, to which the organization adheres, of full disclosure of any conflict of interest or biases for all authors or contributors involved with the journal or organization;

(B) whose articles are peer-reviewed and published in accordance with the regular peer-review procedures of the organization;

(C) that is generally recognized to be of national scope and reputation;

(D) that is indexed in the Index Medicus of the National Library of Medicine of the National Institutes of Health; and

(E) that is not in the form of a special supplement that has been funded in whole or in part by one or more manufacturers.

Secretary means the Secretary of Health and Human Services.

Semi-critical reprocessed single-use device means a reprocessed single-use device that is intended to contact intact mucous membranes and not penetrate normally sterile areas of the body.

Serious adverse event is an adverse event that--

(A) results in--

(i) death;

(ii) a life-threatening experience;

(iii) inpatient hospitalization;

(iv) a persistent or significant disability or incapacity; or

(v) a congenital anomaly or birth defect; or

(B) requires, based on reasonable medical judgment, a medical or surgical intervention to prevent an outcome described under subparagraph (A).

Serious adverse event report means a report that is required to be submitted to the Secretary under Section 760 subsection (b).

Serious adverse drug experience is an adverse drug experience that--

(A) results in--

(i) death;

(ii) an adverse drug experience that places the patient at immediate risk of death from the adverse drug experience as it occurred (not including an adverse drug experience that might have caused death had it occurred in a more severe form);

(iii) inpatient hospitalization or prolongation of existing hospitalization;

(iv) a persistent or significant incapacity or substantial disruption of the ability to conduct normal life functions; or

(v) a congenital anomaly or birth defect; or

(B) based on appropriate medical judgment, may jeopardize the patient and may require a medical or surgical intervention to prevent an outcome described under subparagraph (A).

Serious risk means a risk of a serious adverse drug experience.

Signal of a serious risk means information related to a serious adverse drug experience associated with use of a drug and derived from--

(A) a clinical trial;

(B) adverse event reports;

(C) a postapproval study, including a study under section 505(o)(3);

(D) peer-reviewed biomedical literature;

(E) data derived from the postmarket risk identification and analysis system under section 505(k)(4); or

(F) other scientific data deemed appropriate by the Secretary.

Single-use device means a device that is intended for one use, or on a single patient during a single procedure.

State, except as used in the last sentence of section 702(a), means any State or Territory of the United States, the District of Columbia, and the Commonwealth of Puerto Rico.

Submission for advisory review means an original submission of a direct-to-consumer television advertisement for which the sponsor voluntarily requests advisory comments before the advertisement is publicly disseminated.

Supplement means a request to the Secretary to approve a change in a human drug application which has been approved.

Supplement, with respect to a panel-track supplement, a 180-day supplement, a real-time supplement, or an efficacy supplement, means a request to the Secretary to approve a change in a device for which--

(i) an application or report has been approved under section 515(d), or an application has been approved under section 351 of the Public Health Service Act [42 USC § 262]; or

(ii) a notice of completion has become effective under section 515(f).

Supplemental animal drug application means

(A) a request to the Secretary to approve a change in an animal drug application which has been approved; or

(B) a request to the Secretary to approve a change to an application approved under section 512(c)(2) for which data with respect to safety or effectiveness are required.

T

Tentative approval means notification to an applicant by the Secretary that an application under this subsection meets the requirements of paragraph (2)(A), but cannot receive effective approval because the application does not meet the requirements of this subparagraph, there is a period of exclusivity for the listed drug under subparagraph (F) or section 505A, or there is a 7-year period of exclusivity for the listed drug under section 527.

Territory means any Territory or possession of the United States , including the District of Columbia , and excluding the Commonwealth of Puerto Rico and the Canal Zone.

Transportation means any movement in commerce by motor vehicle or rail vehicle.

Tropical disease means any of the following:

(A) Tuberculosis.

(B) Malaria.

(C) Blinding trachoma.

(D) Buruli Ulcer.

(E) Cholera.

(F) Dengue/dengue haemorrhagic fever.

(G) Dracunculiasis (guinea-worm disease).

(H) Fascioliasis.

(I) Human African trypanosomiasis.

(J) Leishmaniasis.

(K) Leprosy.

(L) Lymphatic filariasis.

(M) Onchocerciasis.

(N) Schistosomiasis.

(O) Soil transmitted helmithiasis.

(P) Yaws.

(Q) Any other infectious disease for which there is no significant market in developed nations and that disproportionately affects poor and marginalized populations, designated by regulation by the Secretary.

Tropical disease product application means an application that--

(A) is a human drug application as defined in section 735(1) [21 USC § 379g(1)]--

(i) for prevention or treatment of a tropical disease; and

(ii) the Secretary deems eligible for priority review;

(B) is approved after the date of the enactment of the Food and Drug Administration Amendments Act of 2007 [enacted Sept. 27, 2007], by the

Secretary for use in the prevention, detection, or treatment of a tropical disease; and

(C) is for a human drug, no active ingredient (including any ester or salt of the active ingredient) of which has been approved in any other application under section 505(b)(1) [21 USC § 355(b)(1)] or section 351 of the Public Health Service Act [42 USC § 262].

U, V

Unexpected serious risk means a serious adverse drug experience that is not listed in the labeling of a drug, or that may be symptomatically and pathophysiologically related to an adverse drug experience identified in the labeling, but differs from such adverse drug experience because of greater severity, specificity, or prevalence.

W, X, Y, Z

Wholesaler. (A) IN GENERAL.--The term "***wholesaler***" means a person licensed as a wholesaler or distributor of prescription drugs in the United States under section 503(e)(2)(A).

(B) EXCLUSION.--The term "***wholesaler***" does not include a person authorized to import drugs under section 801(d)(1).

Index

About the author

Mindy J. Allport-Settle was born in Beckley and raised in Oak Hill, West Virginia. She moved to North Carolina to attend the N.C. School of the Arts for high school and now lives near Raleigh. Following in the footsteps of Gordon Allport, all of her books are built on a foundation of psychology and sociology with a focus on improving some aspect of industry through research and education.

Her career in healthcare began when she was a teenager working as an emergency medical technician. Since then, she has joined the U.S. Navy's advanced hospital corps, worked in organ and human tissue procurement, specialized in ophthalmology, and moved on to serve as a key executive, board member, and consultant for some of the best companies in the pharmaceutical, medical device, and biotechnology industry. She has provided guidance in regulatory compliance, corporate structuring, restructuring and turnarounds, new drug submissions, research and development and product commercialization strategies, and new business development. Her experience and dedication have resulted in international recognition as the developer of the only FDA-recognized and benchmarked quality systems training and development business methodology.

Her education includes a Bachelor's degree from the University of North Carolina, an MBA in Global Management from the University of Phoenix, and completion of the corporate governance course series in audit committees, compensation committees, and board effectiveness at Harvard Business School.

About PharmaLogika

Since 2002, PharmaLogika, Inc has established itself as one of the world's premier consulting firms for Pharmaceutical, Biotech, and Medical Device companies across the globe. In so doing, it has earned the trust of executives in Life Sciences for its integrity, accuracy, and unwavering commitment to independent thought with regard to its products and services as well as those of its customers. Through www.PharmaLogika.com, its involvement in sponsored events, and personal references it has reached millions in print and online. Its mission, to provide flawlessly designed and executed products and services to startups as well as established industry leaders to facilitate their growth from discovery and clinical trial navigation to the commercialization and marketing of their products.

PharmaLogika consults with pharmaceutical, biotech, and medical device quality units to provide third party audits, training, pre approval inspections (PAIs), compliance remediation, and a portfolio of related quality and regulatory affairs products and services. Those products include but are not limited to Quality Assurance Forms, SOP and clinical templates, and the highly successful Integrated Development Training System.

Regulatory action guidance as well as quality systems guidance are delivered as part of its standard products and services. Through the use of highly skilled resources throughout the process, each offering is designed to enact a comprehensive quality systems approach in addressing Quality Assurance (QA) issues. The results insure a close adherence to current Good Manufacturing Practice (cGMP) standards.

PharmaLogika also has a Research and Development OTC line for human consumption that targets alpha 1-antitrypsin deficiency, Fibromyalgia, Restless Legs Syndrome, and Attention Deficit Disorder. A veterinary OTC is currently available that provides canine and feline oral debriding and cleansing agents as well as a stain remover and topical antiseptic. These products combine to provide a strong pipeline of both current and future deliverables.

Other books available

Current Good Manufacturing Practices: Pharmaceutical, Biologics, and Medical Device Regulations and Guidance Documents Concise Reference

Good Manufacturing Practice (GMP) Guidelines: The Rules Governing Medicinal Products in the Eurpean Union, EudraLex Volume 4 Concise Reference

International Conference on Harmonisation (ICH) Quality Guidelines: Pharmaceutical, Biologics, and Medical Device Guidance Documents Concise Reference

FDA Acronyms, Abbreviations and Terminology: Human and Veterinary Regualtory Reference

Course Development 101: Developing Training Programs for Regulated Industries

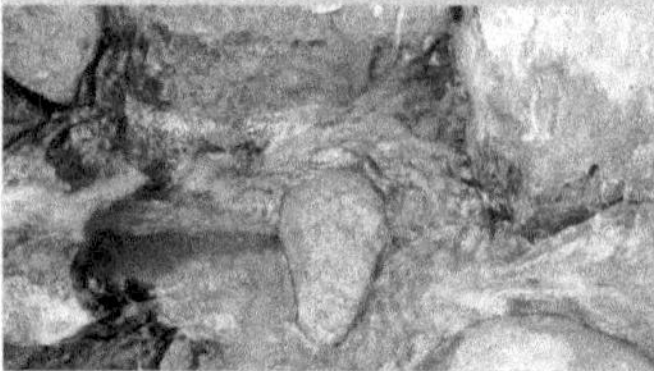

Compliance Remediation for Pharmaceutical Manufacturing: A Project Management Guide for Re-establishing FDA Compliance

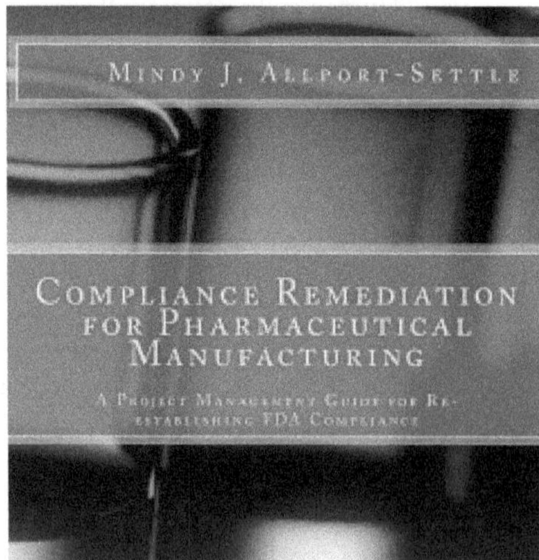

Investigations Operations Manual: FDA Field Inspection and Investigation Policy and Procedure Concise Reference

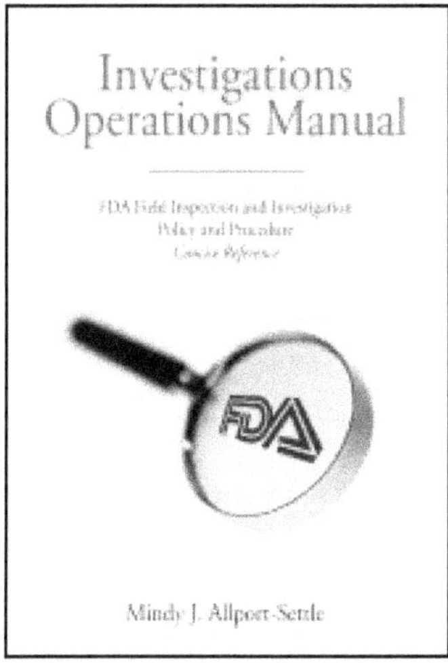

FDA Establishment Inspections: Pharmaceutical, Biotechnology, Medical Device and Food Manufacturing Concise Reference

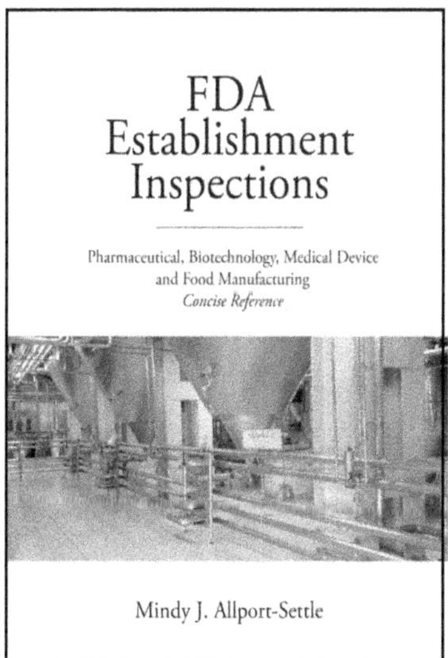

Canadian Good Manufacturing Practices: Pharmaceutical, Biotechnology, and Medical Device Regulations and Guidance Concise Reference

Please visit www.PharmaLogika.com for additional titles and for a list of resellers

or visit your favorite local or internet book seller.

* Companion products and bulk discounts are only available at

www.PharmaLogika.com

www.ingramcontent.com/pod-product-compliance
Lightning Source LLC
Chambersburg PA
CBHW080346220326
41598CB00030B/4616

* 9 7 8 0 9 8 3 0 7 1 9 0 7 *